Eating
&
Drinking

2008
EDITION 8

timeoutnewyork.com

Time Out New York Eating & Drinking 2008
Editors Richard Koss, Jessie Keyt
Copy Editors Lee Magill, Erin Meister
Art Director Marc Whalen
Photo Editors Sarina Finkelstein, Cinzia Reale-Castello
Assistant Photo Editors Beth Levendis, Jodie Love
Researchers Karen Rose, Dan Derouchie
Sales-Marketing Director Lisa Levinson

Time Out New York
Editorial
Editor-in-Chief Brian Farnham
Eat Out Gabriella Gershenson (Editor),
Alex van Buren, Jordana Rothman

Production
Production Director Nestor Cervantes
Associate Production Director Audrey Calle
Associate Production Director, Advertising Tom Oesau
Advertising Production Coordinator Amanda Walters
Production Coordinator Shauna Cagan
Digital Imaging Specialist John Colburn
Digital Imaging Assistant Jay Muhlin
Advertising Designers Stephen de Francesco,
Amanda Walters

Information Technology
Technology Director Jeffrey Vargas
Technology Coordinator Kevin McQueen
Systems Coordinator Michael Fisher

Advertising
Publisher Marisa Guillen Fariña
Advertising Director Melissa Keller
Senior Account Managers Dan Kenefick,
Julia Keefe-Chamberlain
Account Managers John Gregory, Jahan Mantin, Natasha
Marzilli, Rachel Almquist, Abena Adjei, Lauren Weiss, Noelle
Stout, Alana Salvatore
Assistant to the Publisher Nicole Lamoreaux
Assistant to the President Monika Sabian

Marketing
Marketing Director Mike Rucker
Events Manager Leigh Wolinksy
Promotions Designer Ben Killen

Circulation
Group Circulation Director Jennifer Culhane
Associate Circulation Director, Subscriptions Nicola Lathroum
Associate Circulation Director, Newsstands Barbara Parrott
Assistant Circulation Manager Ruby Millien
Circulation Assistant Natila Tongchareon

Finance and Administration
Human Resources Director Kathleen Mora-Kaplan
Associate Human Resources Manager Terri-Ann Rougier
Finance Manager Patty Mauthe

President/Group Publisher Alison Tocci
Chief Financial Officer Daniel P. Reilly
Editorial Director Elizabeth Barr

Digital Business Director Marci Weisler
Digital Content Director Chad Schlegel

Chairman Tony Elliott
Executive Committee William Louis-Dreyfus, Kevin Moore

Printed and bound in the USA
Fry Communications, Inc., Mechanicsburg, PA
ISBN 0-9793984-2-8 and 978-0-9793984-2-1

Contributors

Elizabeth Barr, Alexander Basek, Paula Carino, Maile
Carpenter, Jay Cheshes, Maydelle Fason, Gabriella
Gershenson, Beth Greenfield, Stewart Griffin, Arun
Gupta, Steve Horak, Peter Janssen, Stacey Kalish,
Jessie Keyt, Alexis Korman, Richard Koss, Clare
Lambe, Randall Lane, Kate Lowenstein, Lee Magill,
Caroline McCloskey, Erin Meister, Keith Mulvihill, Anja
Mutic, Patrick Nolan, Leslie Price, Adam Rathe, Josh
Rothkopf, Jordana Rothman, Michael Rucker, Pervaiz
Shallwani, Fabiana Santana, Hank Shteamer, Les
Simpson, AnneLise Sorensen, Alex van Buren, Virginia
Vitzthum and Helen Yun

Cover
Photograph by Kenneth Chen

Street maps
J.S. Graphics

Your light in antioxidant armor.

Introducing
LIGHT POM Tea

Let nothing come between you and your antioxidants – not even calories. Try Light POM Tea. It's light in taste, light in calories, and every sip is packed with powerful antioxidants. Our secret? POM$_x$ – a highly concentrated, all-natural blend of polyphenol antioxidants made from the same California pomegranates as our POM Wonderful 100% Pomegranate Juice. Each glass is lightly sweetened with all-natural ingredients and has just 35 calories per serving. So you can sip lightly and carry big antioxidants.

ONLY 35 CALORIES per serving

Enjoy the tea. Keep the glass. Reap the benefits. | pomtea.com | In produce

feel *diffe*

78-82 Reade st. NY, NY 10007   tel.no. 212.233.7570

breakfast

brunch

lunch

happy hour

dinner

late night lounging

catering & private parties

sit down & takeout

delivery

ent mocca
Restaurant • Lounge
Espresso Bar

www.moccalounge.com   info@moccalounge.com

ASK FOR "青島啤酒" BY NAME.

Contents

PERONI

ITALY

peroniitaly.com

Brewed in Italy and Imported by © 2007 Birra Peroni Internazionale, Eden, NC

The lowdown

How to use this guide

Restaurants are divided alphabetically by cuisine or type of establishment (Chinese, Kosher, Steakhouses). Our three largest sections (American, French and Italian) are each divided into three price categories, based on the average cost of an entrée: $15 and under, $16 to $24, and $25 and over.

Starting on page 269, you'll find subject indexes (such as brunch-noteworthy, outdoor seating), as well as alphabetical and neighborhood indexes. An MTA subway map can be found on page 312, followed by street maps covering Manhattan, Brooklyn and Queens.

★ **Critics' picks**
A red star next to a restaurant's name means we think the place is very good for its cuisine or category, and especially worth checking out.

▲ **Vegetarian-friendly**

☉ **Cheap eats**
This symbol denotes places where the average cost of a main course (or equivalent) is $12 or less. You'll find more than 350 restaurants with this icon in the guide.

▼ **Gay-friendly**
This triangle denotes bars and lounges that are gay-friendly.

Before you set out
Although information was updated right up until this book went to press, some restaurants' hours, chefs and menus may have changed. Please call the restaurant or check timeoutnewyork.com for the latest details.

Addresses
All cross streets are conveniently listed.

Business hours
We include the days and hours that the restaurant is open (though the kitchen may stop taking orders for food earlier than the closing time). Hours may change during summer and holidays.

Cash only
We've noted establishments that only take cash; otherwise, all major credit cards are accepted.

Pricing information
Not everyone orders appetizers, drinks and desserts at each meal, so we've listed the average price of each restaurant's entrées. At places that don't serve meals à la carte or that don't really have main courses, we give an equivalent (e.g., large plain pizza or typical sushi meal).

Other locations
Sister restaurants and branches are listed at the end of reviews. If a place has more than two other locations, they are listed in the alphabetical index.

timeoutnewyork.com

To stay current with all the new places opening throughout the year, be sure to read the Eat Out section in the weekly *Time Out New York* magazine, or visit timeoutnewyork.com. Complete reviews from both the magazine and the *Eating & Drinking* guide can be searched online by many criteria (such as price, neighborhood, critics' picks). If you want the latest news to come to you, sign up online for our free weekly e-mail updates.

Transportation
We list the nearest subway stop for each restaurant. For some places outside Manhattan, transportation information is provided if there is no subway nearby.

2007 Eat Out Awards
Time Out New York magazine bestows awards annually on restaurants and bars of particular note that year. The awards include both Critics' Picks and Readers' Choices. We highlight the entries of winning restaurants and bars by noting their awards in red.

This is how we do it
The establishments that appear in this guide are chosen by *TONY*'s food critics. We visit each one anonymously and pay for our own meals and drinks in order to best evaluate the experience any diner might have when visiting the restaurant or bar.

Our advertisers
The *Time Out New York Eating & Drinking* guide, like the weekly *TONY* magazine, accepts advertising. We would like to stress that our advertisers receive no special favors and have no influence over our editorial content. No establishment in these pages has been included and/or given a favorable review because its owners have advertised in the magazine, online or in this guide. An advertiser may receive a bad review or no review at all.

Of course it tastes better than other beers. We've had over 600 years to get the recipe right. Our esteemed brewery has been producing beer in Leuven since 1366. Which means we've been around a bit longer than most. Mind you, over the years our beer has witnessed the odd change or two. For instance, our customers no longer drink it to ward off the Plague, as they used to in medieval times. However, one thing has stayed the same after all these years. Stella Artois is still painstakingly brewed in a time-honored tradition with the choicest ingredients. Which is why our customers have kept coming back for more, even after 600 years.

Perfection has its price.

Always enjoy responsibly.   www.stellaartois.com

Introduction

Getting a taste of the local color—and flavor.

Dining out is one of New York's truly great passions. Blame the tiny, hard-to-cook-in kitchens that Gothamites contend with or credit their craving for variety and novelty, but restaurants have become indispensable sources of nourishment and pleasure for those who live here.

Visitors avoiding the tourist traps can get a glimpse of New York life in action just by dining out—this applies as much to the neighborhood stalwart as it does to the Next Big Thing (the dining public is composed of as many creatures of habit as it is of slaves to fashion, and the array of restaurants accommodates them all). And, like the city itself, the dining scene is forever changing.

Although by no means new, the local food movement in New York's restaurants has gathered steam in the last year. Eateries that pioneered the farm-forward effort—**Union Square Cafe**, **Savoy**—continue to thrive, and the locavore ethos pervades scores of new spots. Marc Meyer and Vicki Freeman, owners of Greenmarket-friendly eateries **Cookshop** and **Five Points**, revitalized Soho old-timer **Provence** with a southern French iteration of their sustainable cookery. Colin Alevras, the chef-owner behind **The Tasting Room**, moved the ingredient-worshipping spot to a larger space in Nolita. Perhaps the most extreme example of the trend is the revamped **Park Avenue Summer**—the former Park Avenue Café was given a face-lift by hot design firm AvroKO, and an eclectic menu from chef Craig Koketsu (Quality Meats), and the restaurant's interior, menu, waiter's uniforms and even its name will change with the seasons.

Provence and Park Avenue Summer aren't the only joints sporting a new look and, in some cases, a new chef—reopenings have been almost as newsworthy as openings this year. **Le Cirque** traded in its luxe, if stodgy, digs at the New York Palace Hotel for big-top modernity at One Beacon Court in the Bloomberg skyscraper. On a smaller, but no less luxurious scale is chef Terrence Brennan's **Picholine**, a cozy townhouse eatery that acquired new gloss and a winning Mediterranean menu when it opened its doors after a pricey renovation. The **Russian Tea Room**, a 1926 classic, reopened after being shuttered a couple years, its interior faithfully restored to its preclosing, over-the-top glitz. Possibly outdoing all of those high-profile venues was the ultraexclusive **Waverly Inn**, the West Village tavern that became the hardest table to score when Graydon Carter, *Vanity Fair* editor-in-chief, took over with the help of buzz maestros Eric Goode and Sean MacPherson (of the restaurants at the Maritime Hotel). Good luck getting in if you're not a VIP—there's still no phone number (though you can attempt to make a reservation in person); tables for "nobodies" are few and far between.

Somehow, the allure of exclusivity still attracts crowds. The same folks clamoring for a table at the Waverly are fueling demand for several new high-profile restaurants not much easier to get into. Some merit the hype—like **Gordon Ramsay at the London**, which opened in the London Hotel with a perpetually busy reservations line. Others, like **Wakiya**, the new haute Chinese restaurant in Ian Schrager's redesigned Gramercy Park Hotel, which tells diners up front that they can only spend two hours enjoying their costly eats, might just end up rubbing people the wrong way. The no-reservations **Gemma**—the Italian restaurant at the Bowery Hotel from Waverly

Finger-lickin' good Hill Country helped turn NYC into BBQ country.

masterminds Goode and MacPherson—and the latest Keith McNally project, **Morandi**, which has lured the fashionable flocks that worship at his stylish eateries, **Balthazar** and **Pastis**, both demonstrate that sometimes a restaurant's It factor has little to do with the food.

If you're serious about getting your fill, consider barbecue. Last year, steakhouses were the meat troughs of choice—**Quality Meats, Craftsteak, Kobe Club**; every week it seemed a new low-and-slow joint was opening. This year, the porterhouse frenzy was replaced by an appetite for all things 'cue. For Texas style, with its dry rubs, beef ribs and brisket, there's **Hill Country**, a new self-serve spot in Chelsea; or you can savor Georgia-style barbecue at **Georgia's Eastside BBQ** on the Lower East Side. This year, we've devoted an entire chapter to barbecue and provided a handy guide to the thrill of the Korean grill.

And of course you need something to wash all that down with. If last year's hot thing was wine bars, this year has been all about beer. Not only have brew bars—notably the West Village's **Blind Tiger Alehouse**—been opening left and right, but several restaurants have gotten in on the act. The acclaimed **Gramercy Tavern**, for instance, unveiled a vintage beer list. Whatever your drink, you're sure to find it in one of the nearly 100 watering holes covered in our Bars & Lounges section.

In addition to more than 1,300 reviews, we've furnished handy menu glossaries; broken down regional differences within Mexican, Indian and Chinese cuisines; and provided further insight into subjects ranging from tequila to ceviche. Whether you're looking for cheap eats in Chelsea or a king's banquet in Queens, we've got you covered. All you need to do is bring your appetite.
—*Gabriella Gershenson, Eat Out editor*

Ask For A 360 Martini
Eco-Friendly. Vodka360.com Premium Vodka.

100% Recycled Content

4X/5X Four Times Distilled Five Times Filtered

85% RECYCLED GLASS BOTTLE

Paper Processed CHLORINE FREE

100% Post-Consumer Waste

Vodka360.com

360 Vodka Environmental Benefits Statement

Earth Friendly Distilling Co. saved the following resources in the production of 360 Vodka's labeling.

113	Fully Grown Trees
48,371	Gallons of Water
5,409	Lbs of Solid Waste
81	Million BTU of Energy
10,550	Lbs of Greenhouse Gases
9,222	Avg. Driving Miles in U.S. Car

Calculations based on research by Environmental Defense and other members of the Paper Task Force. ©2007 Earth Friendly Distilling Co.

Introducing 360 Vodka

Vodka with a "Green" State of Mind

360 Vodka is crafted from a philosophy of eco-awareness. Quadruple Distilled and Five Times Filtered, it's vodka with an enlightened spirit, it's "The Evolution of Vodka."

 The Evolution of Vodka™
Vodka360.com

Too new to review

These 20 noteworthy newcomers are worth checking out.

Alex Ureña makes Spanish food a bit more casual with **Pamplona**.

If you blink, you might miss a restaurant opening. Maybe several openings. Possibly even the latest culinary trend. It seems as if nothing can stop the onslaught of new eating and drinking establishments in New York— estimated at 25,000 or so when last we checked. Here is a round up of some of the more notable spots that have recently sprung up, or should soon be opening their doors.

RECENTLY OPENED

Allen & Delancey *115 Allen St at Delancey St (no phone yet).* As of press time, Chef Neil Ferguson (Gordon Ramsey at the London) had claimed the reins at this much-awaited American eatery (it was slated to open last year). Expect seasonal eats befitting of the Michelin-trained chef, like slow-roasted Berkshire pork belly, served with pickled pear, creamed parsnip and fenugreek syrup.

Broadway East *171 East Broadway between Jefferson and Rutgers Sts (no phone yet).* Vegetarians and carnivores break bread at this "flexitarian" eatery from veggie vet Peter Berley (Angelica Kitchen) and architect Ron Castellano, who also revived the neighboring Forward Building. The menu is largely plant-based, with meat and fish options all sourced from local purveyors.

Eighty-one *145 W 81st St between Central Park West and Columbus Ave (212-873-8181)* Chef Ed Brown (Sea Grill) will attempt to enliven UWS dining with his eclectic twist on American cuisine. The space, designed by Chris Smith (the man behind

timeoutnewyork.com

Visit us online for information on the latest restaurants, bars and club openings.

stalwarts Nobu and Buddakan in Philly), features a wall of 4,000 wines curated by beverage director Nick Mautone (Gramercy Tavern).

Graffiti *224 E 10th St between First and Second Aves (212-464-7743)* Pastry chef Jehangir Mehta (Aix) takes a savory turn at this wine bar and bistro. Waiters bearing red dots on their foreheads (it's part of the uniform) deliver dishes like cod with coriander and a mushroom-onion confit.

Grayz *13-15 W 54th St (212-262-4600).* Veteran chef Gray Kunz (Lespinasse, Café Gray) aims his knife at the small-plate format. Look for Asian-inflected nibbles like langoustines in a lemongrass and kafir lime rémoulade served on a scorching-hot salt stone—priced to match the extravagant location, a onetime Rockefeller residence.

Forbidden fruit

Fragoli

Liquore
with Whole Wild
Strawberries

Produced and bottled by:
Toschi Vignola srl
Savignano sul Panaro (MO)
Italy
Imported by:
Classic Marketing Co.,
Manhasset, N.Y. 11030
Product of Italy

ALC. 24% BY VOL. - NET CONT. 750 ML - 48 PROOF

TOSCHI

www.fragoli.com

ENJOY RESPONSIBLY
IMPORTED BY: MHW Ltd/Classic Marketing, Manhasset, NY 11030
IMPORTED LIQUEUR, ALCOHOL 24% BY VOL.

Merkato 55 *55–61 Gansevoort St between Greenwich and Washington Sts (no phone yet).* Riding the coattails of his James Beard Award–winning cookbook, *The Soul of a New Cuisine*, Ethiopia-born Marcus Samuelsson (Aquavit) has devised an African menu inflected with Asian, Indian and European elements for this soaring bi-level space in the Meatpacking District.

Pamplona *37 E 28th between Madison Ave and Park Ave South (212-213-2328).* Chef-owner Alex Ureña shuttered his eponymous restaurant to make way for this northern Spanish bistro. Avant-eats will give way to more traditional small plates, like roasted quail served with braised white beans, quail eggs and serrano ham. A beverage program includes seasonal sangrias and *kalimotxo*, a blend of red wine and Coke.

Radegast Hall & Biergarten *113 North 3rd St at Berry St, Williamsburg, Brooklyn (718-963-3973).* This 4,500-square-foot watering hole and restaurant will feature a well-curated selection of beers, including the coriander-spiced Dentergems (a Belgian white beer) and, of course, Pilsner Urquell. Grub includes dishes like quail in porter sauce and rabbit stew. Nods to the melting pot include Spanish chorizo and mussels.

Tailor *525 Broome St between Thompson and Sullivan Sts (no phone yet).* The famously delayed sweet spot that launched a thousand blog posts (*TONY* first reported on Tailor in fall 2006) finally throws open its doors, with former wd-50 pastry chef Sam Mason leading the charge. Expect sweet-meets-savory eats and house-made spirits.

OCTOBER

EvanFord *or* **James Killing** *133 Essex St between Rivington and Stanton Sts (212-228-3100).* Though they're still sorting out the name of this rockabilly restaurant-bar (these two are the final contenders), the brothers Shamlian (Spitzer's Corner) have their priorities straight—the mechanical bull is already installed. Dig into redneck eats like wings and pulled pork, or booze at the brass bar.

Smith's *79 MacDougal St (no phone yet).* From Cindy Smith (Raoul's) and Danny Abrams (the Mermaid Inn, the Red Cat, the Harrison), comes this neighborhood spot in the heart of Greenwich Village, which will serve seasonal, contemporary American cuisine created by chef Pablo Romero (Bouley). Wine director Connor Coffey will offer a list of select New World and eclectic bottles.

NOVEMBER

Adour *12 East 55th Street (no phone yet).* Armed with nine Michelin stars, Alain Ducasse launches Adour in the hope of staging a Gotham comeback. It's an amalgam of high-tech wizardry (an interactive wine bar where tasting notes are projected onto the bar) and classic dining (sole meunière, albeit thoroughly Ducasse-ified) in the St. Regis space that once housed Lespinasse.

Bar Blanc *142 W 10th St (no phone yet).* Presenting the cuisine of César Ramirez (Bouley), Bar Blanc hopes to combine French technique with Italian flavor accents and the highest-quality seasonal products. The restaurant will have a 60-seat dining room and a ten-seat bar, and the decor will be designed by Meyer Davis Studio.

Bar Boulud *1900 Broadway at 64th St (no phone yet).* New York's gustatory darling, Daniel Boulud (Daniel, Café Boulud, DB Bistro Moderne), brings us this French bistro emphasizing artisanal cheeses, charcuterie from France's curing maestro, Gilles Vérot, and a 500-strong wine list from the Rhone and Burgundy regions.

Ivan Kane's Forty Deuce *19 Kenmare St between Bowery and Elizabeth St (no phone yet).* Swarms of besequined pasties will descend on Nolita when this L.A.–born burlesque spot opens shop—thanks in part to the backing of part-owners and rock icons Sting and David Bowie. The faux-seedy bar and restaurant serve a pub-style menu—boobs and burgers, together at last.

Q *308 Bleecker St between Grove St and Seventh Ave South (no phone yet).* This 100-seat Asian-American barbecue restaurant will feature tried-and-true crowd-pleasing dishes by chef Anita Lo (Annisa). The menu will focus on sweet and sticky grilled comfort food for the cosmopolitan palate, but will also offer a raw bar of shellfish and creative sushi to those interested in lighter fare. The restaurant is being designed by Japanese architect Hiromi Tsuruta, who fashioned Jewel Bako and Kyotofu in NYC.

The Smith *55 Third Ave between 10th and 11th Sts (no phone yet).* Glenn Harris and Jeffery Lefcourt (owners of Jane and the Neptune Room) will open this casual, bi-level American brasserie in Manhattan's East Village. Utilizing local products, the Smith will offer a wide selection of familiar bistro dishes.

10 Downing *10 Downing St at Sixth Ave (no phone yet).* 5 Ninth partners Joel Michel and Vincent Seufert bring a new American bistro to Greenwich Village. The market-driven menu will be overseen by chef Scott Bryan (Veritas), and decor will evoke the L.A. School, with artwork from the late '50s to mid '70s.

DECEMBER

Prana *79 Madison Ave (no phone yet).* Husband-and-wife team Payal and Rajiv Sharma will open this eatery with chef Chai Trivedi (Sapa). Chai promises to breathe new life into the familiar Pan-Asian dining scene in NYC, if not the U.S. Around the corner, Prana Market, at 27 E 28th St, will open a bit earlier as an experimental prepared-foods lab for Prana.

Zeppelin *21 W 9th St between Fifth and Sixth Aves (no phone yet).* Cushy banquettes and an early-20th-century moniker indicate the—what else?—speakeasy vibe at this West Village brasserie from chef Keith Harry (Chanterelle) and the team behind Employees Only. Expect Francophile staples like steak with béarnaise sauce and raw-bar selections.

The world is your oyster. Shuck it.

Afghan

See also: *Middle Eastern, Turkish*

Afghan blanket
Warm, savory bites comfort diners at Khyber Pass.

▲**Ariana Afghan Kebab** 787 *Ninth Ave between 52nd and 53rd Sts (212-262-2323). Subway: C, E to 50th St. Daily noon–11pm. Average main course: $13.* The space is small—and the portions are, too—but Ariana's affable waitstaff keeps diners coming back. As the restaurant's name suggests, the savory kebabs (chicken, beef or lamb) are among the main draws here, although nonmeaters will find a sizable list of vegetarian options, including luscious curries with eggplant, pumpkin or potato. Each mildly spiced entrée is offset by a side of brown basmati rice, and salad drizzled with cool, creamy yogurt dressing.

★ ▲**Bamiyan** 358 *Third Ave at 26th St (212-481-3232). Subway: 6 to 28th St. Mon–Thu noon–11pm; Fri, Sat noon–midnight; Sun noon–11pm. Average main course: $15.* This lively space from brothers Ahmed Shah and Sayed Rohani pays homage to the their native Afghan province, where curries, kebabs and yogurt are dietary staples. Window seats feature Bukharan rugs and pillows that surround traditional low-to-the ground tables, while the more intimate main dining room features a sky-blue ceiling. The food is hit-or-miss. Skip the kebabs, which can be dry and overcooked, and stick to more adventuresome fare like the *kadu*, fried pumpkin-filled turnovers paired with a tangy yogurt dip, or a creamy eggplant and lamb curry.

▲**Kabul Kebab House** 42-51 *Main St between Cherry and Franklin Aves, Flushing, Queens (718-461-1919). Subway: 7 to Flushing–Main St. Daily 11am–11pm. Average main course: $12.* This bright, casual place serves Afghan and Persian food, and the brisk takeout trade is primarily for the namesake dish. Dinner can run the geographical gamut: first-rate hummus; tomato-sweetened stews; crisp, delicate sambosas; and *qabeli palaw*, succulent charcoal-grilled meat over spiced, raisin-studded rice.

▲**Khyber Pass** 34 *St. Marks Pl between Second and Third Aves (212-473-0989). Subway: 6 to Astor Pl. Mon–Thu 1pm–1am; Fri, Sat 1pm–2am; Sun 1pm–1am. Average main course: $12.* If you happen to be strolling down cluttered St. Marks Place in search of a spot where you can get loud with your friends, you're in luck. The dining room is timeworn, but there are plenty of comfy pillows to plop down on, and the laid-back staff certainly won't rush you. Seasoning tends to be tame; marinated chicken kebabs may be tender, but lacking in flavor. *Bouranee baunjaun*, thick slices of eggplant over a layer of minty yogurt and coriander, could be the Afghan version of eggplant parmigiana. But look elsewhere for a sweet finish: the *firni*, a rose-water–and–pistachio rice pudding, is an acquired taste.

Read 'em & eat

kadu: fried pumpkin- or squash–filled turnovers, often in a tangy yogurt dip

samsas: puff pastry dumplings filled with meat or vegetables

PHILIP FRIEDMAN

African

See also: *Moroccan*

When in roam
Crowds pass though Nomad for shared plates and pastries.

Pan African

⊙**Kush Café** *17 Putnam Ave between Downing St and Grand Ave, Clinton Hill, Brooklyn (718-230-3471). Subway: C, G to Clinton–Washington Aves. Tue–Fri 4pm–midnight; Sat, Sun noon–midnight. Average price: $11.* Once you find this spot, you'll be glad you ventured outside familiar territory. When the weather is warm, take a seat in the garden with mismatched tables, kitschy umbrellas, a cabanalike nook and groovy music. For a place that blends African and French cuisines, the menu is surprisingly straightforward. The Kush salad, dressed with tangy Dijon, is studded with beets, asparagus and slivers of almonds. Chunks of beef and shrimp in the surf-and-turf brochette are tender, and the grilled chicken breast is loaded with raisins, apricots, toasted nuts and a spicy Cajun rice.

★ **Les Enfants Terribles** *37 Canal St at Ludlow St (212-777-7518). Subway: F to East Broadway. Daily 10am–midnight. Average main course: $15.* A lively hangout, Les Enfants Terribles serves up good food to patrons who enjoy the positive nightlife vibe while lounging in the worn-in brown leather banquettes. From framed wall photos, Picasso looks on at the bohemian hang, which revels in its own artiness, echoed by the suave waitstaff. Although the menu claims French-African influences, the best items come straight from the bistro, like steak frites, dripping with juices and a side of aggressively seasoned fries.

Nomad *78 Second Ave between E 4th and E 5th Sts (212-253-5410). Subway: F, V to Lower East Side–Second Ave; 6 to Astor Pl. Mon–Sat 4pm–midnight; Sun 11am–11pm. Average main course: $15.* Before Nomad opened, Mehenni Zebentout spent months obsessing over the interior, buying North African antiques, and hiring friends to paint a mural and weld Moroccan-style gates over the windows. He also handpicked the chef—Hisham Khiri—who makes great big shareable dishes like the sweet, flaky chicken *briwats* (think egg rolls) and the roasted-eggplant dip. The signature entrée is couscous royale, a deep bowl of stewed, brothy vegetables plated next to a large mound of couscous dotted with three kinds of meat. The waitress admitted to snacking on pastry during her shift, and who could blame her? The baklava, hazelnut halvah and Tunisian sponge cake are completely addictive.

Ethiopian

★▲**Awash** *338 E 6th St between First and Second Aves (212-982-9589). Subway: F, V to Lower East Side–Second Ave; 6 to Astor Pl. Mon–Fri 4–11:30pm; Sat, Sun 4–11:30pm. Average main course: $15.* Awash is ideal for a hot date. Everything is sharable, and everything is finger food—so you can lick your digits and get down and dirty at the table. Even better, you can request to do so at one of the romantic alfresco two-tops at the East Village branch. The catch: Ethiopian food is richly spiced, butter based and, although thoroughly delicious here, not exactly stomach soothing. (The sour, spongy

CINZIA REALE-CASTELLO

injera tends to expand after consumption.) Better to enjoy this joint with friends rather than with dates, and stuff yourselves on smooth shiro, a chickpea puree, and fantastically tender *doro wat*, a slow-simmered spicy chicken stew served with a boiled egg. **Other location** *947 Amsterdam Ave between 106th and 107th Sts (212-961-1416).*

▲**Massawa** *1239 Amsterdam Ave at 121st St (212-663-0505). Subway: 1 to 116th St. Daily 11:30am–11:30pm. Average main course: $16.* Despite the increase in the city's Ethiopian restaurants, their menus tend not to differ greatly, so the prospect of Eritrean as well as Ethiopian dishes seems cause for an extra glass of *tej* (honey wine). Though the waitstaff plays down the contributions of Ethiopia's former coastal province, Massawa features several Eritrean seafood dishes—notably salmon *silsi* (cubes of wine-glazed fish served with *injera*) and several spicy tomato-based shrimp dishes—not usually found on Ethiopian menus. Massawa's *injera* tends to thin to crispness at the edges, yet the Ethiopian staples are consistently good, ensuring a following among local grad students.

▲☉**Meskel** *199 E 3rd St between Aves A & B (212-254-2411). Subay: F to Delancey St. Daily 12:30–11:30pm. Average main course price: $12.* "It is just home cooking," claims the menu, whose modesty is quickly belied by the skillful kitchen. Vegetarian dishes are the strong point at this small, intimate East Village spot, and all seven can be sampled with the combination platter. Among the standouts are the *shiro wat*, ground chickpeas in spicy *berbere*, and *gomen*, a rare dish of shredded collard greens in ginger. The combo is large and the *injera* generous, but it would be a mistake to pass on the cool avocado salad appetizer. Or to order wine without first asking that it be chilled.

★▲**Zoma** *2084 Frederick Douglass Blvd at 113th St (212-662-0620). Subway: B, C to 110th St. Daily 11:30am–10pm. Average main course price: $14.* A truly chic place for eating with your hands, Zoma's sleek, white dining room is lit by candles, a muted chandelier and the fluorescent glow emanating from the backlit bar. The wall art suggests Soho rather than Frederick Douglass Boulevard, and expectations are further jarred by the food. The *azifa* does not come with *injera* but in endive shells that enhance the spicy lentils' dryness, while the *doro wot* blends ginger with *berbere* for a piquant aftertaste. Yet the biggest surprise comes last: The bill for such superior Ethiopian food doesn't break the bank.

Senegalese

☉**Africa Kine** *256 W 116th St between Seventh and Eighth Aves (212-666-9400). Subway: B, C to 116th St–Frederick Douglass Blvd. Daily 11am–1am. Average main course price: $11.* The first—and easily the most elegant—of the eateries to emerge along the Little Senegal stretch of 116th Street, Africa Kine can be found one flight up (a takeout counter is at street level) in a long dining room with exposed brick walls and roomy booths. The four-dish lunch menu features *thu djen*, fish—usually red snapper—swathed in a tasty tomato-based stew, while dinner sees an expanded menu with several French dishes. The char-grilled lamb chops of the signature *dibi* are best paired with a side of plaintains and a glass of homemade ginger.

Dibiterie Cheikh *231 West 116th St between Malcolm X Blvd (Lenox Ave) and Adam Clayton Powell Jr. Blvd (Seventh Ave). (212-663-0717). Subway: B, C to 116th St–Frederick Douglass Blvd . Daily noon–1am. Average main course: $9.* Curiously, this dibiterie doesn't carry its signature *dibi* at lunchtime, instead offering such spicy fare as *yassa* chicken (fish is also available) in a lemon sauce over rice or thiou fish balls in a fiery onion sauce. Come dinner at this small yet airy spot, which plays host to a steady stream of off-duty cab drivers, the *dibi* emerges as juicy cubes of lamb that are a far cry from the chops most Senegalese places cook up. The result is best sampled with sweet plantains, which play well off the onion sauce, though rice and fries are also available.

▲☉**Keur N'Deye** *737 Fulton St between South Elliott Pl and South Portland St, Fort Greene, Brooklyn (718-875-4937). Subway: C to Lafayette Ave, G to Fulton St. Tue–Sun 4–10:30pm. Average main course: $10.* Keur N'Deye (Senegalese for "mother's house") gives good home cooking a gourmet kick without sacrificing charm. Bring a bottle of wine to accompany the nicely dressed salad Keur N'Deye (with asparagus, beets, cashews and palm hearts); stewed okra with couscous; *moules* Keur N'Deye (in red curry and coconut); or the tender, tasty lamb chops. The Senegalese rice pudding is worth saving some room for.

☉**Le Baobab** *120 W 116th St between Adam Clayton Powell Jr. Blvd (Seventh Ave) and Malcolm X Blvd (Lenox Ave) (212-864-4700). Subway: 2, 3 to 116th St. Daily 1pm–3am. Average main course: $11.* With its elegant beige-painted dining room, decorated with burgundy chairs and portraits of African-American politicians, Le Baobab is a stately restaurant that doesn't forget its roots. *Thiebou diene* consists of generous chunks of market-fresh fish stewed in tomato sauce with carrots, eggplant, cabbage and cassava, all spooned over plump, nutty rice. *Soupou kanja*, a savory lamb stew flavored with fish and thickened with okra and palm oil, is both rich and complex. For dessert, *thiakry*, couscous mixed with vanilla-enriched sour cream and fruit, is as comforting as tapioca pudding.

Read 'em & eat

berbere: an Ethiopian seasoning mix of garlic, red pepper, cardamom and other spices

cassava: (also called *manioc* or *yuca*) a long, coarse root that is boiled and pounded to make bread and various other dishes

dibi: sizzling Senegalese lamb chops with onion sauce

injera: a spongy Ethiopian bread that doubles as an eating implement

Beacon of light
Drink in the swank-
boho vibe at
Les Enfants Terribles.

▲☉**Le Grand Dakar** *285 Grand Ave between Clifton Pl and Lafayette Ave , Fort Greene, Brooklyn (718-398-8900). Subway: C, G to Clinton–Washington Aves. Tues–Sun noon–1am. Average main course: $11.* The kitchen at this romantic Senegalese restaurant puts a French twist on the indigenous treasures of Senegal. Beef and shrimp spring rolls come alive with a flamboyant sweet-chili garlic sauce; smoked-oyster rice harks back to the owner's native Casamance region. The ambience evokes a Moroccan harem: pralines-and-cream-colored walls and fertility sculptures. If those don't put you in the mood, the tasty desserts will.

South African

i-Shebeen Madiba *195 DeKalb Ave between Adelphi St and Carlton Ave, Fort Greene, Brooklyn (718-855-9190). Subway: C to Lafayette Ave, G to Clinton–Washington Aves. Mon–Thu, Sun 4pm–midnight; Fri, Sat 4pm–1am. Average main course: $19.* To be New York's first and only anything is impressive, so respect is due this convivial South African spot, inspired by *shebeens* (township dining halls) and named for Nelson Mandela's nickname. Wooden benches and folky art grace the high-ceilinged space; music ranges from Afrobeat to Afropop; the bar pours stiff cocktails; and the menu features curry and stew mainstays as well as offbeat eats like ostrich carpaccio, prawns *piri piri* and the safari platter, featuring cured, salted and dried beef tenderloin. Dinner here is a quintessential Fort Greene experience, though prices are rather steep for a "township" meal.

West African

☉**Ebe Ye Yie** *2364 Jerome Ave between North and 184th Sts, Bronx (718-220-1300). Subway: 4 to 183rd St. Daily 9am–midnight. Average main course: $10.* There's no menu at Ebe Ye Yie. You place your order by pointing through the Plexiglas divider at the steam table's unpredictable offerings of Ghanaian dishes: spicy soups and stews with massive chunks of beef or fish, for about $10. These main courses are accompanied by filling starches like *fufu,* a log made from cooked yams, pounded until they're glutinous and firm; *gari,* a cassava-based couscous; and rice with black-eyed peas. It's customary to eat with your fingers here; a small bottle of liquid soap and a bowl of water are provided at each table. The demure, however, can ask for plastic spoons.

Florence's Restaurant *2099 Frederick Douglass Blvd (Seventh Ave) between 113th and 114th Sts (212-531-0387). Subway: B, C to 116th–Frederick Douglass Blvd. Daily 11:30am–midnight. Average main course: $9.* Whatever your expectations upon reading AFRICAN AMERICAN FOOD on the awning of heavily curtained Florence's, the menu inside this cluttered, one-room restaurant will probably give them a jolt. The fare here is not soul food, but hearty dishes from the Ivory Coast and Ghana. From the former come a variety of fish plates, notably the *poisson braisse,* served with a side of fried plaintains or *attieke.* The Ghanan side of the menu is given over to stews—try the spinach-based version mixed with a choice of meat or fish. In good weather, take your feast to Morningside Park.

▲**Zereoué** *13 E 37th St between Fifth and Madison Aves (212-679-9355). Subway: 7 to Fifth Ave–Bryant Park; 42nd St S, 4, 5, 6, 7 to Grand Central–42nd St. Mon–Fri noon–3:30pm, 5–10:30pm; Sat 5–10:30pm. Average main course price: $21.* Owned by former NFL player Amos Zereoué, this bistro with elegant African art and potted African plants serves up fine French fare (like mussels or steak au poivre) as well as equally stylish dishes from his native Ivory Coast. Stews dominate the latter, among them a hearty *aubergine au poisson* that could use more of the promised eggplant and *kedjenou,* a spicy chicken stew that comes an earthenware pot and can be soaked up in a side of *attineke.* Happy hour draws a chic (for midtown) crowd, who particularly enjoy jazz on Thursdays.

Read 'em & eat

kitfo: an Ethiopian version of steak tartare, prepared with hot chili powder (*mit'mita*), spiced butter and green-chili peppers

shiro: a chickpea puree used in Ethiopian food

thiebou diene: Senegal's national dish; consists of chunks of fish stewed in a tomato sauce with carrots, eggplant, cabbage and cassava over nutty rice

American

See also: *American Creative, American Regional*

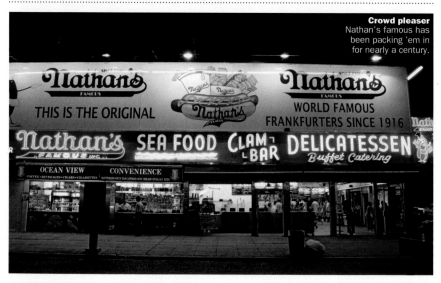

$15 and under

barmarché *14 Spring St at Elizabeth St (212-219-9542). Subway: N, R, W to Prince St; 6 to Spring St. Mon–Wed 11am–midnight; Thu, Fri 11am–2am; Sat 9am–2am; Sun 9am–midnight. Average main course: $15.* The dining room of this bright, white-on-white brasserie sure looks tempting when you walk by: More often than not, passersby can observe lively groups munching on the kitchen's generously portioned bistro hits. The menu is melting-pot American, covering basic dishes from around the world: risotto with pesto, spicy crab soup with mustard Tabasco, salmon tartare with fried plantains and a straight-up juicy burger. The options change seasonally, as do the funky designer drinks—like the Brazilian sangria.

Barney Greengrass *541 Amsterdam Ave between 86th and 87th Sts (212-724-4707). Subway: B, C, 1 to 86th St. Tue–Fri 8:30am–4pm; Sat, Sun 8:30am–5pm. Average main course: $13.* Despite decor that Jewish mothers might call "schmutzy," this legendary deli is a madhouse at breakfast and brunch. Enormous egg platters come with the usual choice of smoked fish (such as sturgeon or Nova Scotia salmon). Prices are high but portions are large—and that goes for the sandwiches, too. Or try the less costly dishes: matzo-ball soup, creamy egg salad or cold pink borscht served in a glass jar.

▲**Bonnie's Grill** *278 Fifth Ave between Garfield Pl and 1st St, Park Slope, Brooklyn (718-369-9527). Subway: M, R to Union St. Mon–Thu noon–11pm; Fri 5pm–midnight; Sat noon–midnight;* Sun 1–10pm. Average sandwich: $9. Unpretentious Bonnie's could easily be overlooked among the ever-changing flash of the Slope's restaurant row. The owner-chef hails from Buffalo, which could explain why the crunchy chicken wings—served mild, medium, hot and hottest—are so good. This may also be one of the only places where you can find authentic "beef on weck," a Buffalo delicacy of sliced roast beef and horseradish served on a kümmelweck roll (a kaiser sprinkled with salt and caraway seeds). Other standouts include crab cakes, a dynamite Black Angus burger and a daily polenta special.

Bruckner Bar & Grill *1 Bruckner Blvd at Third Ave, the Bronx (718-665-2001). Subway: 6 to 138th St. Daily 11:30am –midnight. Average main course: $13.* While the casually hip Bruckner Bar & Grill feels more like it belongs in Williamsburg than at the foot of the Third Avenue Bridge, its immense windows never let you forget this former garage's deserted, noirish environs. The menu is highlighted by the savory ten-ounce burger, served on a toasted English muffin, as well as an appetizer of spicy wings and a variety of salads, while a side lounge dominated by a pool table springs to attention for bimonthly poetry readings. It's a great choice for weekend brunch before a game at Yankee Stadium.

Bubby's *120 Hudson St at North Moore St (212-219-0666). Subway: 1 to Franklin St. Mon–Thu 8am–11pm; Fri 8am–midnight; Sat 9am–4pm, 6pm–midnight; Sun 9am–4pm, 6–10pm. Average main course: $15.* What started in 1990 as a pie company quickly evolved into a steadfast source of reliable food. On weekend mornings, swarms of toddlers and their

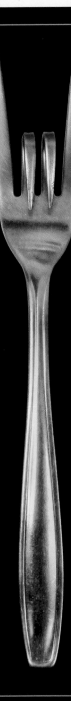

TIMES SQUARE • 1501 BROADWAY
PHONE: 212-343-3355
HARDROCK.COM

frazzled but stylish Tribeca parents descend on the dinerlike interior and outdoor eating areas, where a kid-friendly attitude and no-brunch-reservations policy add up to barely contained chaos. For something calmer, try a weekday dinner of easy favorites: alphabet soup, mac and cheese, and juicy, slow-cooked barbecue ribs. Dessert, of course, is all about pie, like the apple-whiskey with pecan crumble, served in Hummer-size hunks. **Other location** *1 Main St at Water St, Dumbo, Brooklyn (718-222-0666).*

★ ○**Burger Joint** *Le Parker Meridien Hotel, 119 W 56th St between Sixth and Seventh Aves (212-245-5000). Subway: F, N, Q, R, W to 57th St. Daily 11am–11:30pm. Average burger: $5.* Kitsch and chichi mingle at this tiny, hidden spot in the posh Parker Meridien. It's a perfectly re-created burger emporium circa 1972, down to the "wood" paneling, vinyl booths and iconic ingredients, such as Heinz ketchup and Arnold's buns. The burgers are picture-perfect too—juicy and flavorful with the perfect degree of char. Get "the works," with tomato, lettuce, pickle, mayo and red onion. The fries are only fair, but milk shakes are thick and good.

○**Carnegie Deli** *854 Seventh Ave at 55th St (212-757-2245). Subway: B, D, E to Seventh Ave; N, Q, R, W to 57th St. Daily 6:30am–4am. Average sandwich: $12.* If the Carnegie Deli didn't invent schmaltz, it certainly perfected it. All of the gargantuan sandwiches have punny names: Bacon Whoopee (BLT with chicken salad), Carnegie Haul (pastrami, tongue and salami) and Ah, There's the Reuben (a choice of pastrami, corned beef or turkey with sauerkraut under a molten Swiss-cheese dome). A waiter sings the deli's virtues in a corny video loop, and more than 600 celebrity glossies crowd the walls. This sexagenarian legend is a time capsule of the bygone Borscht Belt era, when shtick could make up for cramped quarters, surly waiters and shabby tables—and tourists still eat it up. When you're craving a deli classic, you can't do much better than the Carnegie's obscenely stuffed pastrami and corned-beef sandwiches on rye.

★ ○**Corner Bistro** *331 W 4th St at Jane St (212-242-9502). Subway: A, C, E to 14th St; L to Eighth Ave. Daily 11:30am–4am. Average burger: $6.* The burgers are legendary and the New Yorkers who love them legion. You may have to wait in line for a good hour to get your hands on one (and you will need both hands). Fortunately, several $2.50 drafts are offered, the Yankees are on the tube and a jukebox covers everything from Calexico to Coltrane. The cheeseburger is just $6, but you might as well go for the famed Bistro Burger, a fat patty of broiled beef, cheese and several strips of smoky bacon on a sesame-seed bun for $6.75. Grilled cheese is $3.75 and a plate of crisp shoestring fries runs $2.50, but they're totally beside the point.

○**Crif Dogs** *113 St. Marks Pl between First Ave and Ave A (212-614-2728). Subway: L to First Ave, 6 to Astor Pl. Mon–Fri noon–2am; Fri, Sat noon–4am; Sun noon–midnight. Average hot dog: $3.50.* Relive your high-school stoner days, when you were broke and bored and nothing could satisfy those wicked 2am munchies like a hot dog wrapped in bacon and topped with cheese and a fried egg. Crif's snappy deep-fried or grilled dogs have a cult following among tube-steak aficionados who swarm the joint at all hours for combos like the Spicy Redneck (bacon-wrapped and covered in chili, coleslaw and jalapeños) and the Chihuahua (bacon-wrapped with sour cream and avocado). You'll also get gooey waffle

fries and excellent root-beer floats, and for girls there are Crif-Dog souvenir thong panties, with a giant hot dog on the front that reads "Eat Me."

★ ▲**Diner** *85 Broadway at Berry St, Williamsburg, Brooklyn (718-486-3077). Subway: J, M, Z to Marcy Ave; L to Bedford Ave. Daily 11am–2am. Average main course: $20.* A former greasy spoon in a tricked-out 1920s dining car, Diner was an instant classic when it opened in 1999. Despite its location (off the Bedford Avenue high street in the shadow of the Williamsburg Bridge), this neighborhood icon's popularity has only grown with age. Borough-fabulous locals steam up the windows in winter and smoke up the patios in summer over satisfying eats by former Savoy chef Caroline Fidanza. The number of appetizers (three) and entrées (four) more than doubles when a waitress writes out the daily specials on the white paper tablecloth. Dishes like beefsteak tomato salad, cucumber gazpacho, hanger steak and one-man cherry pies are gastro-diner originals.

Druids *736 Tenth Ave between 50th and 51st Sts (212-307-6410). Subway: C, E to 50th St. Mon–Sat noon–midnight; Sun noon–11pm. Average main course: $15.* Like magic, the ordinary pub facade and grimy neighborhood mask a serene back garden and surprisingly sophisticated menu. Try succulent duck confit or gravlax salad before heading east to make a Broadway show (or hitting any number of Off Broadway theaters in the area). Grilled filet mignon, free-range lamb and baked halibut with sweet mustard sauce are whisked out of the kitchen in record time. If you're just dropping in for a little liquid refreshment (or you're dining solo), belly up to the long mahogany bar.

○**DuMont Burger** *314 Bedford Ave between South 1st and 2nd Sts, Williamsburg, Brooklyn (718-384-6127). Subway: L to Bedford Ave. Daily noon–2am. Average burger: $9.* From the folks who brought you DuMont, this quintessential Williamsburg burgers-and-beer joint could get away with cooking just two things well: burgers, thick and bulging with juice to spare, and fries, browned and pleasantly mealy. Most of the 30 seats in this counter- and communal-table–seating space tend to be occupied by worshipful patty lovers. Surprisingly, the Bibb salad and bacon-studded mac and cheese steal the show.

The Farm on Adderley *2007 Eat Out Award, Critics' Pick: Best reason to ride the Q train 1108 Cortelyou Rd between Stratford and Westminster Rds, Ditmas Park, Brooklyn (718-287-3101). Subway: Q to Cortelyou Rd. Mon 5:30–10:30pm; Tue–Fri 11:30am–2:30pm, 5:30–10:30pm; Sat, Sun 11am–3:30pm, 5:30–10:30pm. Average main course: $15.* Call it back-to-the-land chic: The rustic atmosphere here mixes brick walls, mismatched chairs and a back garden, and lends the restaurant a romantic-getaway vibe (the one-hour subway ride from midtown to the eatery's Ditmas Park location also plays a part). The menu, developed by chef Tom Kearney (Blue Hill), is packed with references to bucolic America: The peas 'n' lettuce salad delivers on its garden-fresh promise, though a barely cooked salmon entrée might be better if it didn't rest on a bed of tough mustard greens. An impressive array of digestifs and spirits, along with the satiny milk-chocolate mousse, ends the meal on a high note.

▲○**Henry Street Ale House** *62 Henry St between Cranberry and Orange Sts, Brooklyn Heights (718-522-4801). Subway: A, C to High St; 2, 3 to*

Constant craving
New Yorkers line up for
Shake Shack burgers.

Average sandwich: $10. This cavernous old dining hall
is a repository of living history. Arrive at 11am on a
Sunday morning, and the line may be out the door. Grab
a ticket and approach the long counter. First, a hot dog.
The weenies here are without peer; crisp-skinned, all-beef
dogs that are worth the $2.75. Then shuffle down and
order your legendarily shareable sandwich. Roast beef
goes quickly (steer clear of the evening remains). The
brisket rates, but don't forsake the horseradish. And the
pastrami? It's simply da best. Everything tastes better
with a glass of the hoppy house lager; if you're on the
wagon, make it a Dr. Brown's. If you haven't been in
awhile, go now: Rumor has it the owner may sell, leaving
Katz's to go the way of Astroland.

▲◉**Life Café Nine 83** *983 Flushing Ave
between Bogart and Central Sts, Bushwick, Brooklyn
(718-386-1133). Subway: L to Morgan Ave. Mon–Thu
11am–midnight; Fri, Sat 11am–1am; Sun 11am–
midnight. Average main course: $11.* The original Life
Café in the East Village has lost the artist vibe that
inspired Jonathan Larson to cite it in Rent, but owner
Kathleen Kirkpatrick has nearly re-created that original
feeling out on the edge of Bushwick. Red-walled and
high-ceilinged, warm and welcoming, Nine 83 is just the
place to settle in for the long haul. Sit at the bar with a
cheap pitcher of beer or grab a table for serious comfort
food, like catfish and Southwestern grilled chicken.
Other location *Life Café, 343 E 10th St at Ave B (212-
477-8791).*

◉**Luscious Food** *59 Fifth Ave between Bergen
St and St. Marks Ave, Park Slope, Brooklyn (718-398-
5800). Subway: B, Q, 2, 3, 4, 5 to Atlantic Ave; D, M,
N, R to Pacific St; 2, 3 to Bergen St. Daily 11am–
8:30pm. Average main course: $9.* Only a seriously
confident restaurant owner would dare to name a place
Luscious. But the expertly prepared comfort food lives
up to the name. Platters of dense, ultracheesy mac and
cheese, savory corn spoonbread and sautéed spinach
studded with lightly browned whole cloves of garlic are
tempting, but you'll also want to scan the list of daily
specials (like better-than-Mom's meat loaf and gravy),
sandwiches (like crisp toasted Cubans) and house salads.
Not enough? Try a caramelly slice of pineapple upside-
down cake.

▲**Marion's Continental Restaurant
& Lounge** *354 Bowery between Great Jones and
E 4th Sts (212-475-7621). Subway: B, D, F, V to
Broadway–Lafayette St; 6 to Bleecker St. Mon–Thu
5:30pm–midnight; Fri, Sat 5:30pm–1am; Sun 5–10pm.
Average main course: $14.* Showbiz folks have been
keeping body and soul together at this old-world hangout
for more than 50 years, tripping down to the Bowery
for well-stocked bouillabaisse *belle-mère,* juicy steak au
poivre, and live cabaret shows on certain nights. The fare
is more refined that you'd expect for a place touting a
fab-'50s decor: Roasted pumpkin gets stuffed into ravioli;
filet mignon gets slathered in a rioja-peppercorn sauce;
and fennel-pepper-crusted tuna comes atop truffled
mashed potatoes. A $19 three-course prix fixe menu
(available 5:30–7pm) includes a glass of wine; enjoy it
while you sit in one of the festive banquettes surrounded
by Pop artwork and hula-girl knickknacks.

★ ◉**Mayrose** *920 Broadway at 21st St (212-533-
3663). Subway: R, W to 23rd St–Broadway, 6 to 23rd St.
Mon–Fri 7am–11pm; Sat 8am–11pm; Sun 8am–4pm.
Average main course: $9.* Mayrose serves "comfortable

*Clark St. Mon–Thu 4–11pm; Sat, Sun noon–midnight.
Average main course: $9.* No, you may not have a
Corona; bottled brews are rare, here. Mix and match
your tapped pint with a burger of your own creation. A
revolving collection of 16 drafts includes brands like Old
Speckled Hen (a rich English ale), Belhaven (Scottish
and creamy) and Staropramen (a light Czech pilsner).
The monstrous burgers are juicy, grilled exactly as
requested and served with your choice of fries (regular
or sweet potato), mashed potatoes, or rice and beans.
You can also get Elvis's favorite: beer-battered kosher
dills. Fried pickles aren't for everyone, but they taste a
lot better with a frothy pint of Humble Patience, a dark
New England ale.

▲◉**Hope & Anchor** *347 Van Brunt St at
Wolcott St, Red Hook, Brooklyn (718-237-0276).
Subway: F, G to Smith–9th Sts. Mon–Fri 11:30am–
10pm; Sat, Sun 9am–10pm. Average main course:
$11.* As a seafaring man comes in to dock, he longs, of
course, for salmon burgers, drag karaoke and nautical
memorabilia. And he'll find them all at Hope & Anchor,
on Red Hook's young restaurant row. Youthful swabbies
might prefer lightly fried calamari with preserved lemons
and hot cherry peppers. Old salts will chortle when they
discover that breakfast is served all day, unless they
prefer to launch into a hearty skirt steak with pasta
squares. Desserts, like a luscious, overstuffed apple pie,
are all house-made.

★ **Katz's Delicatessen** *205 E Houston St
at Ludlow St (212-254-2246). Subway: F, V to Lower
East Side–Second Ave. Mon–Tue 8am–10pm; Wed,
Thu 8am–11pm; Fri, Sat 8am–3am; Sun 8am–10pm.*

Back to the land
Take a trip to the
Farm on Adderley for
country-inspired fare.

TALIA SIMHI

Good fun
Brunch is a family
affair at Bubby's.

food"—but be sure to bring comfortable pants if you plan to have anything more than a muffin from the in-house bakery. The menu seems tailor-made to alleviate hangovers, including blended drinks for hydration and a decent wine list for the hair of the dog. If you have an appetite, hefty omelets are available all day, and Salumeria Biellese supplies the excellent sausages; even the creamy mac and cheese is studded with fortifying bits of ham. A note for the photosensitive: The floor-to-ceiling picture windows look out onto lower Broadway, so bring a pair of sunglasses.

⊖**Nathan's Famous** *1310 Surf Ave at Stillwell Ave, Coney Island, Brooklyn (718-946-2202). Subway: D, F, Q to Coney Island–Stillwell Ave. Mon–Thu 8am–1am; Fri, Sat 8am–2am; Sun 8am–1am. Average hot dog: $2.25.* As much a Coney Island institution as the Cyclone, Nathan's has been serving sizzling, juicy hot dogs with all the fixins since 1916. You can step inside for a burger, sandwich or the fastest-shucked littleneck and cherrystone clams in the kingdom. Or order a dog, a pile of fries and a big, sugary lemonade at one of the sidewalk-counter windows.

⊖**The Northeast Kingdom** *18 Wyckoff Ave at Troutman St, Bushwick, Brooklyn (718-386-3864). Subway: L to Jefferson St. Mon–Wed 5–11pm; Thu, Fri 5–11:30pm; Sat 11am–3pm, 5–11:30pm. Average main course: $11.* The theme inside the 28-seat dining room is one part cabin-in-the-woods (wide-plank wood floors and ceilings, chunky wooden tables) and another part Grandma's living room (flowery vintage wallpaper, fabric-covered wall sconces). Chef Andy

Gilbert has created a short menu focusing on country-style grub. Toast, for example, is smothered with tasty spreads, such as butternut squash baked with brown sugar and cayenne or liver pâté. His organic-chicken potpie is a thick, not-too-creamy stew studded with chunks of tender white meat, peas and carrots and flavored with thyme. Desserts like chocolate pudding and banana cream pie are creamier and fluffier than anything in memory.

⊖**Paloma** *60 Greenpoint Ave between Franklin and West Sts, Greenpoint, Brooklyn (718-349-2400). Subway: G to Greenpoint Ave. Tue–Fri 5–11:30pm; Sat, Sun 11am–4pm, 5–11:30pm. Average main course: $9.* Paloma has quickly edged out the neighborhood competition: The interior is sophisticated (beige banquettes and rotating art shows), and the ingredients are quality (fresh tuna from Tobago, for instance). During the day Monday through Friday, Paloma scales down to an empanada stand, but by dinnertime it's in full restaurant swing, serving crostini with grilled peaches and blue cheese; a pressed sandwich with artichoke, pesto and Parmesan; and a whole grilled brook trout with green-apple coleslaw.

★ ▲⊖**Peanut Butter & Co.** *240 Sullivan St between Bleecker and W 3rd Sts (212-677-3995). Subway: A, C, E, B, D, F, V to W 4th St. Mon–Thu 11am–9pm; Fri, Sat 11am–10pm; Sun 11am–9pm. Average sandwich: $6.* Talk about comfort food: The staff grinds peanuts daily to create pacifiers such as the popular Elvis—the King's infamous favorite of peanut butter, bacon, banana and honey, grilled. The warm cinnamon-raisin-flavored peanut-butter

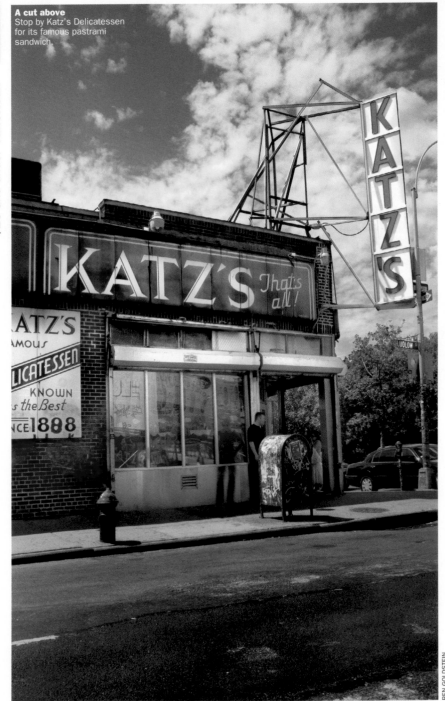

A cut above
Stop by Katz's Delicatessen for its famous pastrami sandwich.

BEN GOLDSTEIN

sandwich with vanilla cream cheese and tart apple slices is good taste and texture rolled into one. Death by Peanut Butter is a landslide of ice cream, Peanut Butter Cap'n Crunch and peanut-butter chips. Goober-free items such as tuna melts and bologna sandwiches also take you back to childhood.

★ ▲☻Philly Slim's Cheesesteaks 789 Ninth Ave between 52nd and 53rd Sts (212-333-3042). Subway: C, E to 50th St. Daily 11am–11pm. Average main course: $6.
Every so often, a Philadelphian decides that New Yorkers have no clue about cheese steaks, and a new sandwich joint is born. Owners John Yih and Steven Kay scoured Philadelphia for six years, tasting hundreds of sandwiches before they designed their definitive version and started selling it in this tin-ceilinged space: thinly sliced top-round beef served on hoagie rolls delivered daily from South Jersey. You can get yours with or without onions and Cheez Whiz. It's a sacrilege, but the partners are selling vegetarian sandwiches, too.

Sarge's Deli 548 Third Ave between 36th and 37th Sts (212-679-0442). Subway: 6 to 33rd St. Daily 24hrs. Average sandwich: $12.
Sarge's is generally believed to be the city's only 24-hour Jewish delicatessen. And it's a really good one, at that. The matzo ball soup is dead-on—a spongy orb submerged in a rich broth (offered, as it should be, with or without noodles), and the sandwiches are as flavorful and enormous as anything at Carnegie or Katz's. The folks at Sarge's are the real thing, from the appropriately gruff-but-friendly waiters to the not-insignificant number of old folks shuffling in. By the time you've finished your meal, you won't be hungry for days.

☻Schnäck 122 Union St at Columbia St, Red Hook, Brooklyn (718-855-2879). Subway: F, G to Carroll St. Daily 11am–1am. Average main course: $5.
A greasy spoon with a sense of humor (just check out the goofily huge hot-dog photo mural), Schnäck has a knack for burgers: You can order up to four small patties stacked on a single bun, with a full array of toppings ("schnäck sauce," spicy onions, chili, kraut, etc.). Buttermilk-soaked onion rings fry up flaky-crisp and are sprinkled with salt-and-parsley seasoning; they'll have you scraping the basket for crumbs. The award-winning beer milk shake tastes just like a regular milk shake except with a nicely bitter, beery aftertaste—and it gives you a buzz.

☻Shake Shack Madison Square Park, 23rd St at Madison Ave (212-889-6600). Subway: 6 to 23rd St. 11am–11pm (open May through October). Average shake: $5.25.
With Shake Shack, Danny Meyer (Union Square Cafe, Gramercy Tavern) takes American fast food to new heights. The zinc-clad, modernist concession stand dispenses superb burgers, hot dogs and shakes to Madison Square Park visitors. Sirloin and brisket are ground daily for excellent beefy patties, and the savory franks are served Chicago-style on poppy seed buns with a "salad" of toppings and a sprinkle of celery salt. Shakes are rich and creamy; there's beer and wine to boot. Expect long lines (and waits).

Stage Deli 834 Seventh Ave between 53rd and 54th Sts (212-245-7850). Subway: B, D to Seventh Ave; C, E to 50th St. Daily 6am–2am. Average sandwich: $15.
Everyone who's anyone—plus John Stamos—is honored with a gargantuan namesake dish at this pricey, touristy deli. Devour the triple-decker Elliott Gould sandwich: turkey, chopped liver, bacon, lettuce and tomato stacked high on fresh rye. The Dolly Parton is composed of twin sandwich rolls (get it?), one with pastrami, the other with corned beef. The stars themselves can be found in Polaroid form on a giant bulletin board near the front door—just past the no-nonsense waiters, sassy waitresses and T-shirt-hawking cashier.

▲☻Toast 3157 Broadway between LaSalle St and Tiemann Pl (212-662-1144). Subway: 1 to 125th St. Mon–Wed 11am–11pm; Thu, Fri 11am–midnight; Sat 10am–midnight; Sun 10am–11pm. Average main course: $10.
Raise a bruschetta to the wonder of Toast, where the pasta with chicken and pesto cream sauce are awesome. The mesquite-smoked barbecued-pork sandwich rules. The skirt-steak appetizer rocks. The raspberry swirl cheesecake kicks ass. In general, Toast is gratifyingly pleasant, and everything is cooked as if you were the only one dining. Rest assured you're not: Toast has caught on with local students and other Upper West Siders. "Where all good things are toasted" is the restaurant's cheerful motto, so let the browning and the brew-downing begin.

☻The Twisted Burger 430 E 14th St between First Ave and Ave A (877-989-4783). Subway: L to First Ave. Mon–Thu 10am–10pm; Fri, Sat 10am–11pm; Sun 10am–10pm. Average burger: $7.
Twisted? More like pleasantly quirky. This East Village burger joint boasts chandeliers, quaint-chic wall art and a wide selection ranging from the traditional (the Bacon Cheese) to the loopy (the Blue Hawaiian, featuring pineapple and blue cheese). The patties are respectable, but the stars of the menu are the decadent chips—thick-sliced fried potatoes, with an optional coating of gooey cheese and bacon bits—and clever "Twisted Drinks" like Sproke (a surprisingly refreshing blend of Sprite and Coke).

Westville East 173 Ave A at 11th St (212-677-2033). Subway: L to First Ave, 6 to Astor Pl. Mon–Fri 11:30am–midnight; Sat, Sun 10am–midnight. Average main course: $12.
An outpost of the superb American eatery, the East Village location has more room than the original—a small bar and a few more tables, plus some banquettes—but the important things haven't changed. The chalkboard menu still advertises market sides—vegetable dishes, like beets with toasted walnuts—that have acquired a cult following. The turkey burger on a toasted Portuguese bun is still juicy and garlicky; and Blue Ribbon–style desserts—like moist carrot layer cake—are as satisfying as ever. The only bummer is the frequent wait. It's worth it. **Other location** Westville, 210 W 10th St at Bleecker St (212-741-7971).

☻Zaitzeff 72 Nassau St at John St (212-571-7272). Subway: A, C to Broadway–Nassau St; J, M, Z, 2, 3, 4, 5 to Fulton St. Mon–Fri 10am–10pm; Sat, Sun 10am–8pm. Average burger: $9.
Juicy burgers are the great social equalizer at this hamburger hut. Stockbrokers, mail-room boys and moneymen from the nearby Federal Reserve mingle at communal tables to chomp quarter-pound kobe and sirloin patties, which are griddle-cooked, topped with fried onions and served on split English muffins. The meat-averse munch veggie burgers, while everyone clamors for salty, hand-cut sweet-potato fries crisped in cast-iron skillets.

Winning combination
Alchemy's organic
ingredients are golden.

American $16 to $24

$16 to $24

Alchemy *56 Fifth Ave between Bergen St and St. Marks Pl, Park Slope, Brooklyn (718-636-4385). Subway: D, M, N, R to Pacific St; B, Q, 2, 3, 4, 5 to Atlantic Ave. Mon–Thu 6–11pm; Fri 6pm–midnight; Sat 11am–4pm, 6–midnight;, Sun 11am–4pm, 6–11pm. Average main course: $18.* Look beyond the well-edited beer list at this Park Slope gastropub, and you'll find a menu loaded with tasty, elevated pub fare. The comfortable, masculine spot (rough-hewn communal tables, exposed filament bulbs) starts off its meals with a small bowl of piping-hot fried chickpeas—a fine complement to a well-pulled pint. As for more-substantial offerings, the Berkshire pork belly is meltingly tender, while an entrée of fish-and-chips is upgraded with flaky skate wing and fingerling potatoes. Don't skip dessert, especially a moist, toffee-sauce–doused pudding spiked with—what else?—Guinness.

▲Applewood *501 11th St at Seventh Ave, Park Slope, Brooklyn (718-768-2044). Subway: F to Seventh Ave. Tue–Sat 5–11pm; Sun 10am–3pm. Average main course: $20.* David and Laura Shea have brought the farm, so to speak: The couple, who met at the Culinary Institute of America and spent a few years in Chicago, returned to New York to open Applewood in Park Slope. The charming eatery has country style and organic produce—two things that make city folk happy. Tables are adorned with bundles of fresh herbs, there's a working fireplace, and many ingredients come from an upstate farm. The menu changes seasonally, but expect rustic dishes like ricotta dumplings with braised pork shoulder, or roasted chicken with chanterelle-sage gravy.

★▲Bistro Ten 18 *1018 Amsterdam Ave at 110th St (212-662-7600). Subway: 1 to 110th St–Cathedral Pkwy. Mon–Fri noon–3pm, 5–11pm; Sat 11am–3pm, 5–11pm; Sun 11am–3pm, 5–10pm. Average main course: $19.* Restaurants in this part of town tend to draw Columbia-affiliated locals. Some of the food at this low-lit American bistro, though, is worthy of a trip. The pan-roasted chicken might not start an uptown stampede, but the accompanying rich, salty mashed potatoes and lavishly buttered spinach elevate the dish from decent to exceptional. The rack of lamb is excellent, and the five meaty little chops, cooked to perfection, get a touch of lively mint-and-cilantro relish. The blackberry crisp à la mode fails as a crisp but excels if regarded as vanilla ice cream sauced with bracingly tart molten fruit.

Brouwers of Stone Street *45 Stone St between Coenties Alley and Hanover Sq (212-785-5400). Subway: 2, 3, 4, 5 to Wall St. Mon–Fri 11am–10pm; Sat, Sun 11:30am–8pm. Average main course: $22.* This American eatery works familiar masculine themes—antique mirrors, auburn leather banquettes—and offers 13 draft beers. Neither the surf-and-turf menu nor the helpful yet amateurish service suggests elegance, but executive chef Michael Sullivan (Le Zinc, Chanterelle) prepares some terrific dishes, such as pan-seared scallops over spinach with a mushroom cream sauce and an especially satisfying strip steak served with potatoes au gratin and asparagus. In warm weather, sit outside in the festive air of Stone Street.

Bryant Park Cafe and Grill *25 W 40th St between Fifth and Sixth Aves (212-840-6500). Subway: B, D, F, V to 42nd St–Bryant Park; 7 to Fifth Ave. Daily 11:30am–3:30pm, 5–10pm. Average main course: $24.*

TALIA SIMHI

This spacious spot, tucked between the library and Bryant Park, features floor-to-ceiling windows that overlook the leafy oasis, and a large-scale Hunt Slonem bird mural that soars high above leaf-print banquettes. The menu balances light and heavy: The salad of sliced Anjou pears, walnuts and blue cheese is a refreshing start. But entrées can be massive. Two thick, well-marbled pork chops come with applesauce and a healthy jumble of fried plantains; wild-mushroom-stuffed chicken breast is paired with garlicky whipped potatoes. After finishing the molten Valrhona chocolate cake, you may well need a walk in the park.

★ ▲**Chestnut** *271 Smith St between DeGraw and Sackett Sts, Carroll Gardens, Brooklyn (718-243-0049). Subway: F, G to Carroll St. Tues–Sat 5:30–11pm; Sun 11:30am–3pm, 5:30–10pm. Average main course: $16.* A big bowl of salty, toasty-brown potato chips sits on the bar in this spare but charming little room. Those stellar house-made chips reveal the soul of the kitchen, one that's long on quality and short on pretense. The seasonal menu is rustic (snappy bread-and-butter pickles as a giveaway table nibble; snacks like caramelized onions and fresh ricotta on toast); but it's also savvy enough to compete on Brooklyn's restaurant row. Moist roasted chicken, scattered with wild mushrooms and strips of lemon peel, has a perfect partner in cushiony polenta, and meaty duck matches deliciously with earthy baked beans and bitter braised celery root.

★ **Cookshop** *156 Tenth Ave at 20th St (212-924-4440). Subway: C, E to 23rd St. Daily noon–midnight. Average main course: $22.* Vicki Freeman and chef-husband–co-owner Marc Meyer have made Cookshop a platform for sustainable ingredients from independent farmers—a place where the dishes are made from vegetables grown with minimal fertilizer and animals that were raised humanely and without growth hormones or antibiotics. True to its mission, Cookshop's ingredients are consistently top-notch—and the menu changes daily. The smoked fillet of bluefish is a terrific starter. A snack of fried spiced hominy is impossible to resist, and while the sautéed brisket—from grass-fed cows—is tender, the sugary barbecue *jus* seems too sweet. Cookshop scores points for getting the homemade ice cream to taste as good as Ben and Jerry's. While organic ingredients alone don't guarantee a great meal, Meyer knows how to let natural flavors speak for themselves.

Cornelia Street Cafe *29 Cornelia St between Bleecker and W 4th Sts (212-989-9319). Subway: A, C, E, B, D, F, V to W 4th St. Mon–Thu 10am–midnight; Fri, Sat 10am–1am; Sun 10am–midnight. Average main course: $14.* This 30-year-old bistro-cum-clubhouse features a miniature basement cabaret devoted to readings and music, along with a genial dining room that opens wide to the sidewalk in summer. The colorful, if dated, menu is consistent with the place's bohemian roots. The eclectic fare ranges from glorified bar food, like a light, gooey flatbread pizza, to more ambitious mains like al dente lobster ravioli surrounded by snow peas or plump, satisfying veal sausage on a mashed potato heap.

Cub Room *131 Sullivan St at Prince St (212-677-4100). Subway: C, E to Spring St. Mon–Sat 11am–2pm, 5–10pm; Sun 11am–2pm, 5–9pm. Average main course: $24.* This swank restaurant and bar, a spirited homage to the inner sanctum at the long-closed Stork Club, offers modern twists on traditional fare. Some dishes are needlessly complex, such as the pan-roasted Atlantic monkfish with braised navy beans, chorizo and roasted vegetables in lobster sauce. On the other hand, the pan-seared duck breast (with black-pepper spaetzle, roasted brussels sprouts and coconut sauce) is superb. On crowded nights, the host may steer you toward the café next door, or point you toward seats in the lounge area. Hold out for the more formal main dining room, whose floor-to-ceiling windows overlook Sullivan Street. **Other location** *Cub Room Café, 131 Prince St at Sullivan St (212-777-0030).*

▲**Deborah** *43 Carmine St between Bedford and Bleecker Sts (212-242-2606). Subway: A, C, E, B, D, F, V to W 4th St. Tue–Sun 11am–11pm. Average main course: $18.* "Small" is actually big in this diminutive spot, beginning with the exposed-brick-walled splinter of a dining room, through the speck of a kitchen and out into the tiniest of gardens. Fortunately, however, that theme doesn't extend to the menu, which offers enormous portions of thoroughly satisfying American fare, including a mammoth macaroni and cheese and an individual "mini" meatloaf big enough to share. Served up quickly and efficiently by an enthusiastically welcoming staff, Deborah is like a taste of home (without the parents).

★ **Dressler** *2007 Eat Out Award, Critics' Pick: Best defense for Billyburg gentrification 149 Broadway between Bedford and Driggs Aves, Williamsburg, Brooklyn (718-384-6343). Subway: J, M, Z to Marcy Ave. Mon–Thu 6–11pm; Fri, Sat 6pm–midnight; Sun 11am–3:30pm, 5:30–10:30pm. Average main course: $22.* The team behind popular Dumont and Dumont Burger recognized that they could launch a fancier spot in a neighborhood that already has a culinary landmark. The short menu bridges two worlds; this is a brasserie with creative American flourishes and an emphasis on seasonal ingredients. Frankly, everything sounds good, but the star behind the fish-and-veggie–heavy appetizers has to be the produce purveyor. The chilled spring pea soup with lobster-meat topping has a powerhouse broth that packs more flavor than any pea has the right to. And the crispy artichoke-and-white-bean salad is alternately crunchy, tender, hot and cold. The seared sea bass is expertly paired with a cream sauce containing a classic cockles-bacon-and-leek combination, while the roasted duck breast comes with sweet, braised duck leg and spicy duck sausage—an onslaught that makes each bite exciting.

Duane Park Cafe *157 Duane St between Hudson St and West Broadway (212-732-5555). Subway: A, C, 1, 2, 3 to Chambers St. Mon–Fri noon–2:30pm, 5:30–10pm; Sat, Sun 5:30–10:30pm. Average main course: $23.* Let the Tribeca celebrities go to Nobu. For 19 years, this understated spot has kept locals returning for chef Seiji Maeda's inventive American dishes. The menu is all over the place and far more sophisticated than at typical cafés. There's organic free-range chicken breast, lamb chops, seared rib-eye steak, and grilled shrimp and calamari with *skordalia* olives. Prices are low for this 'hood; stop by the elegant wood-paneled dining room for a weekday lunch and take advantage of the $24 three-course prix fixe.

▲**DuMont** *432 Union Ave between Devoe St and Metropolitan Ave, Williamsburg, Brooklyn (718-486-7717). Subway: L to Lorimer St, G to Metropolitan Ave. Mon–Thu 11am–3pm, 6–11pm; Fri, Sat 11am–3pm, 6–midnight; Sun 11am–3pm, 6–11pm. Average main course: $16.* DuMont is a warm and welcoming place—a gently worn joint with pressed-tin ceilings, a wooden bar, retro brown-leather booths and plenty of candles. A private den in back

doubles as a bar and holding pen for those who are waiting to dig into comfort food from chefs Cal Elliott and Polo Dobkin, who honed their skills at Gramercy Tavern. The seasonal menu changes regularly, but you might encounter frothy lobster bisque with a dollop of curry butter, or braised duck leg risotto. Luckily, the lardon-laced Dumac & cheese never disappears.

★ **Five Front** *5 Front St between Dock and Old Fulton Sts, Dumbo, Brooklyn (718-625-5559). Subway: A, C to High St; F to York St. Mon, Wed, Fri 5pm–midnight; Sat 11am–4pm, 5pm–midnight; Sun 11am–4pm, 5–11pm. Average main course: $16.* The Brooklyn Bridge towers above Five Front's sprawling back deck, but no noise intrudes as you sip a refreshing cucumber martini. Mussels in a cardamom broth are tender, melting morsels, and the crab cake has just the right crab-to-crust ratio. Garganelli pasta with fava beans, peas and pancetta is a better choice than chewy sliced lamb. The $22 prix fixe, available on Monday, Wednesday and Thursday, combines some of the best dishes from chef Paul Vincino's menu (pick the crème brûlée for dessert).

★ ▲**Five Points** *31 Great Jones St between Bowery and Lafayette St (212-253-5700). Subway B, D, F, V to Broadway–Lafayette St; 6 to Bleecker St. Mon–Fri noon–3pm, 6pm–midnight; Sat, Sun 11:30am–3pm, 6pm–midnight. Average main course: $22.* Every restaurant owner knows that you can't please everyone. Win over the cool kids and you end up alienating the grown-ups; appease the romantics and you lose the scene-seekers. Five Points is a rare exception to the rule, where New Yorkers of all types seem to feel at home. The vaguely country-style dining room bustles nightly the way a great neighborhood

Old school
Feast on classics at Brouwers of Stone Street.

$16 to $24 American

restaurant should. Chef-owner Marc Meyer's ever-changing seasonal menu might include a side dish of roasted corn, a salad of fresh figs, or scallops with deliciously sweet corn chowder. Happy Hour is not to be missed: From 5 to 6pm, martinis are $5, and oysters are just two bucks each.

★ ▲**Freemans** *2 Freeman Alley off Rivington St between Bowery and Chrystie St (212-420-0012). Subway: F, V to Lower East Side–Second Ave. Daily 11am–4pm, 6pm–11:30pm. Average main course: $19.* Lurking at the end of a graffiti-marked alley, Freemans, with its colonial tavern–meets–hunting lodge style, has found a welcome home with retro-loving Lower East Siders. A mounted, snow-white swan stares you down at the entrance, while, further in, garage-sale oil paintings and moose antlers serve as backdrop to a curved zinc bar. The menu recalls a simpler time—think 1950s supper party: devils on horseback (prunes stuffed with Stilton cheese and wrapped in bacon); rum-soaked ribs, the meat falling off the bone with a gentle nudge from the fork; and stiff cocktails that'll get you good and sauced.

▲**Friend of a Farmer** *77 Irving Pl between 18th and 19th Sts (212-477-2188). Subway: L, N, Q, R, W, 4, 5, 6 to 14th St–Union Sq. Mon–Thu 8am–10pm; Fri 8am–11pm; Sat 9:30am–3:30pm, 5–11pm; Sun 9:30am–3:30pm, 5–10pm. Average main course: $16.* That farmer must be raising fowl. No less than seven poultry entrées are on the menu at this comfortable spot, including turkey meat loaf and a chicken breast stuffed Christmas-goose style and served on a slice of lemon bread. On your way to the dining room, take a gander at the pastry case: chocolate-peanut-butter pie, brown Betty, fruit tarts. Daily specials feature fresh fish and pasta dishes like portobello-

mushroom lasagna. Daily breakfast and a popular weekend brunch keep the farmer's hens a-laying.

▲**Giorgio's of Gramercy** *27 E 21st St between Broadway and Park Ave South (212-477-0007). Subway: N, R, W, 6 to 23rd St. Mon–Wed noon–3:30pm, 5:30pm–10:30pm; Thu, Fri noon–3:30pm, 5:30pm–11:30pm; Sat 5–11:30pm; Sun 5–10:30pm. Average main course: $21.* For a restaurant with all the finery of a members-only spot (velvet curtains, hushed lighting and an army of silent, uniformed waitstaff), Giorgio's is one of the more relaxed restaurants in Gramercy Park. Oversized plates of crisp calamari with pecorino black-truffle fondue, airy pasta dishes, and eye-popping desserts like s'mores bread pudding and baked Alaska won't break the bank, while the attentive and eager waiters add to the luxurious feel. Perhaps the reason Giorgio's feels so exclusive is that nobody wants to share their favorite local secret.

▲**Good** *89 Greenwich Ave between Bank and W 12th Sts (212-691-8080). Subway: A, C, E, 1, 2, 3 to 14th St; L to Eighth Ave. Mon 6–11pm; Tue–Thu 8–3pm, 6–11pm; Fri 8–3pm, 6–11:30pm; Sat 11am–3:30pm, 6–11:30pm; Sun 10am–4pm, 6–10pm. Average main course: $17.* Good understates the case at this comfortable West Village spot. With its urbanized-country decor (earthenware pigs, groomed cacti and artfully mottled walls) and amiable service, you sense you're in assured hands before the food hits the table. And when it does come, you may mentally rename the place "great," or even "wonderful." Evoking the latter are two plump chicken sausages and a side of crispy mushroom polenta cake, while a BBQ pulled-pork entrée smacking of a shotgun wedding of sauce to meat approaches the former. A wonderful plate of still-warm orange–sour cream donuts is undermined by a merely passable selection of dipping sauces.

★ ▲**The Grocery** *288 Smith St between Sackett and Union Sts, Carroll Gardens, Brooklyn (718-596-3335). Subway: F, G to Carroll St. Mon–Thu 5:30–10pm; Fri, Sat 5:30–11pm. Average main course: $23.* This sparely decorated eatery never aspired to be more than a terrific neighborhood spot when it opened, but it was lavished with praise and promptly became a Brooklyn destination restaurant. Co-owners Sharon Pachter and Charles Kiely are strict about reservations—forget to confirm and you'll lose your table—but those are the breaks when a hot spot has only 30 seats. Pitfalls aside, expect a wonderful meal, whether you order pan-roasted squid stuffed with black risotto, roasted trout, or artichoke served with lemon-poblano aioli.

★ ▲**The Harrison** *355 Greenwich St at Harrison St (212-274-9310). Subway: 1 to Franklin St. Mon–Thu 5:30–11pm; Fri, Sat 5:30–11:30pm; Sun 5–10pm. Average main course: $24.* Tribeca's reliable brasserie is as welcoming as ever—a warm, wainscoted room is dotted with flickering candles and filled with boisterous conversation. Chef Brian Bistrong (Josephs Citarella) stocks the menu with farm-fresh ingredients—spring peas, rhubarb, artichokes—and delivers the goods in fine form. Duck confit is paired with spiced eggplant and chèvre, and scallop ceviche is tossed with red onions, cucumbers and passion fruit. If you wish to extend your stay, there's a blueberry tart with raspberry ice cream.

HQ *90 Thompson St between Prince and Spring Sts (212-966-2755). Subway: C, E to Spring St. Tue–Thu, Sun 11am–11pm; Fri, Sat 11am–midnight. Average main course: $22.* Terrence Cave, formerly of Metrazur

KRISTY MAY

and Blue Ribbon, plays with top-notch ingredients here: The succulent pork-belly appetizer is served atop smooth applesauce. The duck breast entrée is perfectly plump, juicy and pink. Note that the dishes are entirely seasonal. Autumn perennials like brussels sprouts—both caramelized and steamed al dente—show up in more than one dish. The warm American-bistro decor feels plenty lived-in thanks to the strategic placement of aged mirrors, copper panels, tin ceilings and a chandelier constructed from wineglasses.

Henry's End Restaurant
44 Henry St between Cranberry and Middagh Sts, Brooklyn Heights (718-834-1776). Subway: A, C to High St; 2, 3 to Clark St. Mon–Thu 5:30–10pm; Fri, Sat 5:30–11pm; Sun 5–10pm. Average main course: $21. The name refers to the street, but it could just as well allude to Henry VIII. The autumn and winter wild-game festival should especially satisfy gourmands, who can tear into elk, buffalo and quail; all are prepared with the same sophistication as the meats, poultry and pasta available year-round. Despite the close quarters, the noise level rarely rises above a dull roar. Choosing between the acclaimed wine list and the beer list, which is peppered with choices like Belgium's Chimay Rouge and England's J. W. Lees Harvest Ale, is a challenge. A $22.99 prix fixe (appetizer, entrée and glass of wine) is available early in the evening.

★ ▲**Home** *20 Cornelia St between Bleecker and W 4th Sts (212-243-9579). Subway: A, C, E, B, D, F, V to W 4th St. Mon–Fri 11:30am–4pm, 5–11pm; Sat 10:30am–4:30pm, 5:30–11pm; Sun 10:30am–4:30pm, 5:30–10pm. Average main course: $17.* Open since 1993, the 30-seat boite has a hip, casual ambience—old photos

lining the walls, booths squeezed inside and a cozy back garden—that can hook you before you take your first bite. That would be a shame, though, since locally sourced dishes like the cheese plate with homemade salami and the pan-seared diver scallops are elegant and well thought out. That balance of comfort and class you strive for in your own dwelling can be found at Home.

★ ▲**Jane** *100 W Houston St between La Guardia Pl and Thompson St (212-254-7000). Subway: C, E to Spring St; 1 to Houston St. Mon–Thu 11:30am–11pm; Fri, Sat 11:30am–midnight; Sun 11am–10pm. Average main course: $19.* One visit and you too will have a Jane's addiction. The popular neighborhood spot has warm lighting, plush banquette seating and sunny sidewalk tables; they all match well with the pleasant menu. A flavorful bouquet of baby arugula, blue cheese and pear is sprinkled with dried cranberries and toasted pumpkin seeds; fluffy pillows of ricotta gnocchi sit in a rich pool of white-truffle-Parmesan sauce. At brunch, hollandaise-glossed poached eggs top delicious crab-and-crawfish cakes. You'll be able to save up Soho-shopping cash with the Sunday-night special: Four selected menu items (which can include an excellent garlic-balsamic flatiron steak) are only $12 each.

▲**Josephina** *1900 Broadway between 63rd and 64th Sts (212-799-1000). Subway: 1 to 66th St–Lincoln Ctr. Mon–Fri 11:30am–midnight; Sat 11am–midnight; Sun 11am–11pm. Average main course: $18.* The sedate, upscale edition of owner Louis Lanza's Upper West Side trio (Citrus and Josie's are the others) was styled to attract the Lincoln Center crowd, but the food deserves more than pretheater scrutiny. The menu is

Hitting the spot
HQ satisfies with pork belly and succulent seasonal fare.

TALIA SIMHI

marked by fresh, predominantly organic produce and free-range meats—seared duck, braised lamb shank with white-bean cassoulet—as well as seasonal fish and pasta dishes. The wine list is also very good, and the service is terrific. If you are catching a show, take advantage of the early prix fixe—three courses for $35.95.

Lamb & Jaffy *1073 Manhattan Ave between Dupont and Freeman Sts, Greenpoint, Brooklyn (718-389-3638). Subway: G to Greenpoint Ave. Tue–Thu, 5–10pm; Fri 5–11pm, Sat 10am–3pm, 5–11pm; Sun 10am–3pm, 5–10pm. Average main course: $16.* When this candlelit American bistro with dark French doors arrived in Greenpoint's industrial setting, it offered a welcome alternative to the neighborhood's borscht-dominated eateries. Puff pastry–wrapped Brie is delivered warm, sprinkled with walnuts and a sprightly green-apple vinaigrette, and a yogurt-marinated game hen displays punchy notes of paprika, thyme, rosemary and fennel. In a nod to the Polish community, a kielbasa omelette is on the brunch menu.

Little D Eatery *434 Seventh Ave between 14th and 15th Sts, Park Slope, Brooklyn (718-369-3144). Subway: F to 15th St–Prospect Park. Tue–Fri 6–11pm; Sat 11am–3pm, 6–11pm; Sun 11am–3pm, 6–10pm. Average main course: $16.* This isn't just another small-plates place— you'll also find "big dishes" here too. One of the best is a rabbit leg confit served with lavender sauce and a side of creamy mashed potatoes. Run by husband-and-wife team Colin Wright (in the kitchen) and Mira Friedlaender (in the dining room), the place has a simple decor—unadorned yellow walls, butcher-block tabletops—and a reasonable American menu. For dessert, skip the chocolate cake and try the plate of tangy blue, silky goat and sharp cow's-milk cheeses, served with a fig spread and a baguette—little details that make a difference.

The Morgan Dining Room *225 Madison Ave at 36th St (212-683-2130). Subway: 6 to 33rd St. Tue–Thu noon–2:30pm; Fri noon–2:30pm, 5–8pm; Sat, Sun 11am–2:30pm. Average main course: $22 (museum admission not required).* When you arrive at this restaurant, set in the gorgeously renovated Morgan Library & Museum, an impeccably dressed host seats you in the Morgan family's original dining room—a small, sparely appointed red and white chamber with soaring ceilings. For brunch, try the eggs Benedict with Virginia ham and truffled hollandaise, or the lightly dressed lobster salad of soft butter lettuce tossed with tender claws, juicy grapefruit segments and crunchy slivers of jicama. When the server asks if you'll be having dessert, say yes: The sampler platter offers bites of peach cobbler, panna cotta and other tasty treats.

New Leaf Café *Fort Tryon Park, 1 Margaret Corbin Dr (212-568-5323). Subway: A to 190th St; take elevator to Ft. Washington Ave, then walk into Fort Tryon Park. Tue–Fri noon–3pm, 6–10pm; Sat 9:30–11am, noon–3pm, 6–10pm; Sun 11am–3:30pm, 5:30–9:30pm. Average main course: $23.* Bette Midler's New York Restoration Project, dedicated to the greening and beautification of the city, won the contract to run this restaurant, just inside Fort Tryon Park (and near the Cloisters museum); all profits from the operation go directly to maintaining the park. Whether you enjoy smoked trout and pear salad on the garden patio, or a Bloody Mary with brunch in the dining room of the 1930s stone building, you'll be surrounded by the park's natural beauty, and you'll

be helping to conserve it. The views are more dazzling than the mildly adventurous American food, but this is one case where everybody wins.

Nolita House *47 E Houston St between Mott and Mulberry Sts (212-625-1712). Subway: B, D, F, V to Broadway–Lafayette St; 6 to Bleecker St. Mon–Thu 11:30am–3:30pm, 5–11pm; Fri 11:30am–3:30pm, 5pm–1am; Sat 11:30am–4pm, 5pm–1am; Sun 11:30am–4pm, 5–11pm. Average main course: $16.* Chef Marc Matyas thinks we have a lot to learn about local, seasonal ingredients—so he's turned his restaurant into a classroom. Nolita House makes playful references to a one-room schoolhouse with green chalkboard walls and pegs for your jackets. The menu won't seem like all-new material (it includes pizza and burgers), but diners will learn plenty about artisanal cheeses. The cheese boards are tailored to experience level: beginner (mild, creamy cow, sheep and goat cheeses), intermediate (differently textured cow's-milk cheeses) and adventurous (stinky, earthy and strong). Kinda makes you wish they'd assign some homework.

★ **Norma's** *Le Parker Meridien, 118 W 57th St between Sixth and Seventh Aves (212-708-7460). Subway: F, N, Q, R, W to 57th St. Mon–Fri 6:30am–3pm; Sat, Sun 7am–3pm. Average main course: $17.* As at a casino, you won't find any windows or other indications of the time of day at this brightly lit, modern restaurant—which makes it all the easier to wallow in French toast with Valrhona chocolate sauce at lunchtime. At Norma's, breakfast is the whole affair: Gourmet egg and pancake concoctions are served in impossibly huge portions. Will you go sweet (banana-macadamia-nut flapjacks topped with whipped banana–brown-sugar butter) or savory (a seared-rock-lobster-and-asparagus omelette)? Lean toward simple (warm ham-and-Brie crêpes) or complex (foie gras French toast over wild mushrooms)? It's all as good as it sounds, which makes paying $8 for grapefruit seem almost sane…depending on who's picking up the check.

Philip Marie *569 Hudson St at W 11th St (212-242-6200). Subway: 1 to Christopher St–Sheridan Sq. Tue–Thu noon–11:30pm; Fri noon–1am; Sat 10am–1am; Sun 10am–11:30pm. Average main course: $18.* Chef-owner John Greco III's restaurant may characterize its cuisine as innovative American, but underplaying the place's French heritage misrepresents it. A parsley salad, for example, elevates what is normally an unassuming garnish to star billing. Entrées prove similarly innovative, including the salmon, cooked and served on an oak plank, and molasses-glazed pork chops stuffed with wild mushrooms. The waitstaff is unfailingly courteous. And the private wine cellar for two, in which Greco serves a special five-course meal with wine pairings for $250 per couple, is a great, little-known deal for special occasions.

▲**The Queen's Hideaway** *222 Franklin St between Huron and Green Sts, Greenpoint, Brooklyn (718-383-2355). Subway: G to Greenpoint Ave. Tue–Sat 6–10:30pm; Sun 12:30–5:30pm. Average main course: $16.* Tucked away on a sleepy street in Greenpoint, this funky spot serves great comfort food, and depending on your roots, you might feel right at home. The backyard is decorated with a pink plastic flamingo perched in a pot of jasmine. Not one bite disappoints: Luscious mussels (an occasional special) are served on the half shell with creamed spinach and aioli; the sweet-pea flan, accompanied by roasted carrots and a generous serving of greens, is a refreshing dish on a warm night. Top your meal off with a slice of seasonal fruit pie. The menu changes weekly.

PHILIP FRIEDMAN

Beyond classic
Chestnut pairs roasted
chicken with polenta.

Side dish

Burger kings

*While the Corner Bistro is widely
thought to have the city's reigning
burger, there are many challengers to
the throne. Here, six of our faves:*

BRGR *287 Seventh Ave between 26th and 27th Sts
(212-488-7500). Subway: 1 to 28th St.* This spot adds
gourmet flourishes to the fast-food formula while
offering inventive shakes. Build your own sandwiches,
starting with the type of burger (organic beef, turkey,
veggie), the number of patties, a choice of cheese
(including Gruyère and crumbled goat) and toppings.

J.G. Melon *1291 Third Ave at 74th St (212-1310).
Subway: 6 to 77th St.* Melon's signature burger is served
without any frills: only a few slices of red onion and
pickle and a no-nonsense bun. The patties are extra
juicy, so wolf these babies down quickly, before all
that goodness soaks through the bread.

Paul's *131 Second Avenue between 7th Street and St
Marks Pl (212-529-3033). Subway: 6 to Astor Pl.* East
Villagers like to claim this is the burger to beat: an
eight-ounce, non-nonsense hunk of freshly grilled
ground beef on a squishy white bun that is barely big
enough to keep the loosely bound patty in one place.

PJ Clarks *915 Third Avenue at 55th Street (212-317-
1616). Subway: E, V to Lexington Ave–53rd St.* The
burger at this landmark 19th-century pub is a tasty
six ounces of ground chuck on a simple bun—an
ideal balance of meat and bread that holds together
beautifully. Go ahead, customize it with cheese, bacon,
chili or béarnaise sauce.

Rare Bar & Grill *303 Lexington Avenue between 37th
and 38th Streets (212-481-1999). Subway: 6 to 33rd St.*
Nearly anything you could imagine on your burger is
here, including foie gras, fried eggs, and five dipping
sauces. The Rare classic is eight ounces of freshly
ground Black Angus chuck, served with lettuce,
tomato, Spanish onion and two Guss' half-sour pickles
on a basic sourdough roll.

Stand *24 E 12th St between Fifth Ave and University Pl
(212-488-5900). Subway: L, N, Q, R, W, 4, 5, 6 to 14th
St–Union Sq.* This is a thinking person's comfort-food
spot, complete with floor-to-ceiling windows, table
service and burgers served reverentially on giant white
plates. The patties are hefty
and broiled to requested
doneness, with a cookout-
worthy char, and the
poppy seed buns and
brioche are baked daily.

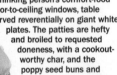

★ **The Red Cat** *227 Tenth Ave between 23rd
and 24th Sts (212-242-1122). Subway: C, E to 23rd St.
Mon–Thu 5–11pm; Fri, Sat 5:30pm–midnight; Sun
4:30–10:30pm. Average main course: $23.* This beloved
Chelsea original features a New Englandish, wainscoted
dining room with red walls, crisp white tablecloths and
plenty of handsome diners. The kitchen gives almost
every dish an intriguing twist: In place of crab cakes, for
instance, are plump rock-shrimp-and-fish cakes served
with a zesty papaya salad and curried citrus crème fraîche.
A wild-mushroom tart is like a big, buttery, earthy cookie
made with Taleggio and served over fragrant truffle-
dressed greens. The Red Cat specializes in all that's hearty:
gargantuan pork chops, Parmesan-covered french fries,
extra-juicy shell steak, and big-time sweets like banana
splits and apple tarts.

★ ▲**Relish** *225 Wythe Ave between Metropolitan Ave
and North 3rd St, Williamsburg, Brooklyn (718-963-4546).
Subway: L to Bedford Ave. Mon–Thu 11am–midnight;
Fri, Sat 11am–1am; Sun 11am–midnight. Average main
course: $18.* You'll find fancy fare in diner digs at this
classic chrome car (the revamped space also houses a plush
back dining room and an 80-seat patio). Start with harpoon
shrimp on stalks of asparagus. Then move on to the
popular lemon-and-thyme roasted half chicken.

Rock Center Café *20 W 50th St between Fifth
and Sixth Aves (212-332-7620). Subway: B, D, F, V to
47–50th Sts–Rockefeller Ctr. Mon–Fri 11:30am–10pm;
Sat 11am–11pm; Sun 11am–10pm. Average main
course: $20.* In wintertime, this restaurant looks out on
one of the city's most romantic spots, the skating rink at
Rockefeller Center. In the summer, the Rink Bar occupies
it—and makes up for the absence of triple axels with $5
drink specials. Given the setting, the food (Italian-inflected
American) is better than it needs to be. The chef even
surprises tourists with an inspired baked crab cake, made
with saffron risotto. Disappointing desserts don't live
up to the view, but you'll still be the envy of gawkers up
above. **Other location** *Rink Bar & Café, 20 W 50th St at
Rockefeller Plaza (212-332-7620).*

★ ▲**Salt** *58 MacDougal St between Houston and
Prince Sts (212-674-4968). Subway: C, E to Spring St;
1 to Houston St. Mon–Thu 11am–3pm, 6–11pm; Fri,
Sat 11am–3pm, 6pm–midnight. Average main course:
$24.* Simplicity is the theme at this bright, white-on-white
restaurant. The kitchen stays focused on raw materials:
Ripe cantaloupe is pureed into a summery soup; bright-
green risotto is studded with asparagus and plump peas;
roasted codfish is moistened with an herbed broth. The
mix-and-match menu allows for a protein plus two sides.
Likewise, desserts come with a twist: A lemon tart features
a buttery, lavender-scented crust and a side of Earl Grey ice
cream. **Other location** *Salt Bar, 29A Clinton St between
Houston and Stanton Sts (212-979-8471).*

★ ▲**Sweetwater Bar & Grill** *105 North 6th St
between Berry St and Wythe Ave, Williamsburg, Brooklyn
(718- 963-0608). Subway: L to Bedford Ave. Mon–Thu
5:30pm–midnight; Fri 5:30pm–2am; Sat 4pm–2am; Sun
noon–5pm, 5:30pm–midnight. Average main course:
$17.* Formality on this side of the Williamsburg Bridge
is about as common as a tucked-in shirt. But in its own,
sepia-toned way, charming Sweetwater manages to
put up a good front. You'll find dark textured wood,
funky tiled floors and soft orange lighting inside and a
leafy back garden outside, making for a quiet retreat.
The bistro menu delivers standards like a heaping pile

KENNETH CHEN

Make history
Sup in the Morgan Dining Room at the fabled Library & Museum.

American $16 to $24

of crisp onion rings, and some gourmet-for-the-'hood offerings like prosciutto-wrapped pork tenderloin served with green apple and potato mash. Pair it with vodka lemonade—by the pitcher.

▲**Taste** *1413 Third Ave at 80th St (212-717-9798). Subway: 6 to 77th St. Mon–Fri 5:30pm–10pm; Sat, Sun 8am–4pm, 5:30–10pm. Cafe 7am–3:30pm. Average main course: $23.* Eli Zabar's five-year-old eatery sits smack dab in the middle of his giant Upper East Side food market. Chef Scott Bieber takes full advantage of his enviable pantry, snatching up all the fresh offerings. You'll love the roasted diver sea scallops and grilled asparagus done up in an egg Dijon vinaigrette. Entrées of grilled Copper River sockeye salmon bask in tasty string beans and walnut salsa, and grilled (Stone Church Farm) chicken is juicy and tender with delectable artichoke caponata. A giant slab of the layered lemon meringue cake and the soothing earth tones of the elegant dining room make it hard to leave.

Vince & Eddie's *70 W 68th St between Central Park West and Columbus Ave (212-721-0068). Subway: 1 to 66th St–Lincoln Ctr. Daily 11am–11pm. Average main course: $22.* Duck decoys establish a preppy theme here, and many of the patrons seem monogrammed, but the kitchen doesn't duck its responsibility to the masses. There's comfort food galore, including rib-eye steak, braised lamb shank, meat loaf, and calamari coated in a feather-light batter. A salad of blanched haricots verts with sweet cubes of beets and tomatoes is excellent. The dark, dense ginger cake, with a scoop of caramel ice cream, is nicely spicy. Relax in the back garden or in front of one of the three fireplaces.

★ ▲**The Waverly Inn** *16 Bank St at Waverly Pl (212-243-7900). Subway: A, C, E, 1, 2, 3 to 14th St; L to Eighth Ave. Mon–Thu 5–10pm; Fri, Sat 5–11pm; Sun 11:30am–3pm, 5–10pm. Average main course: $24.* Eric Goode and Sean MacPherson (both of the Park and Maritime Hotel), along with *Vanity Fair* editor-in-chief Graydon Carter, have breathed new life into this West Village mainstay, which has been open in some form since 1920. The high-profile owners kept the uneven wooden floors, low ceilings and ivy-covered patio, and added a dose of panache—velvet curtains and a mural by *New Yorker* cover artist Edward Sorel. The casual menu consists of bistro bites and comfort-food staples. The city may not need another tuna tartare, but the version here is fantastic. And the best news yet: Half of the dozen or so entrées cost less than $20. Reservations are currently handled only via a private number—good luck getting in.

▲**The Yard** *SoHo Grand Hotel, 310 West Broadway between Canal and Grand Sts (212-965-3000). Subway: A, C, E, 1 to Canal St. Memorial Day–Oct Mon–Thu noon–midnight; Fri, Sat noon–2am; Sun noon–7pm. Average main course: $19.* The SoHo Grand's outdoor restaurant has a menu with a mission: to offer the kinds of food you'd serve in your backyard, if you had one. Cooks fire up the grill for burgers with top-shelf condiments like Cayuga blue cheese, pancetta and radicchio. Try the lobster boil, which includes steamers, mussels and sausages for $39 a person. Desserts are simple and summery: watermelon, fruit pie and ice-cream cones. Check the weather before you go. Just like at home, there's no cookout if it rains. **Other location** *The Gallery SoHo Grand Hotel, 310 West Broadway between Canal and Grand Sts (212-965-3000).*

As seen on TV
Sample *Iron Chef*-
winner Harold
Dieterle's fresh fare
at Perilla.

TALIA SIMHI

$25 and over

Aretsky's Patroon *160 E 46th St between Lexington and Third Aves (212-883-7373). Subway: 42nd St S, 4, 5, 6, 7 to 42nd St–Grand Central. Mon–Fri noon–2:30pm, 5–11pm. Average main course: $35.* Smokers at Patroon (which retains its in-house humidor) may ascend to the roof to puff in midtown bigwig style. Down in the restaurant, the kitchen of Bill Peet (Lutéce, Asia de Cuba, Café des Artistes) dishes out simple steakhouse fare in mover-shaker portions. Of course, as any Volvo driver can attest, conservative does not mean cheap (six cocktail shrimp, $18). The steaks embody the pleasures of the flesh. Even some fish entrées tilt toward the bovine; the halibut "porterhouse" is twice the thickness of a Delmonico beefsteak. Sides, like creamed spinach, are just what you'd expect: heavy and delicious. For dessert, there's the showy tableside preparation of bananas Foster. And with a fine selection of brandies, Patroon offers a number of ways to get lit.

★ **Beacon** *25 W 56th St between Fifth and Sixth Aves (212-332-0500). Subway: F to 57th St. Mon–Thu noon–2:30pm, 5:30–10pm; Fri noon–2:30pm, 5:30–10:30pm; Sat 11:30am–2:30pm, 5:30–10:30pm; Sun 11:30am–2:30pm, 4–8pm. Average main course: $30.* Anyone with a typical New York–size stove will be in awe of the massive wood-burning oven in Beacon's open kitchen. Chef-owner Waldy Malouf grills and roasts nearly everything on his menu, from meaty T-bones to salads. Seasonal specials might include roasted lamb with mint and fava beans. Regular dishes are just as satisfying. Chewy baby octopus and squid with crisp, blackened tentacles rest on a bed of wilted arugula and spinach, surrounded by tender *gigante* beans, mint and grape tomatoes. Woodsy roasted-mushroom ravioli swim in a broth topped with Parmesan. Even the desserts, such as the strawberry shortcake with white-chocolate mousse, are wood-roasted. As befits the he-man cooking techniques, the multilevel dining room is all classy-guy decor: clean lines, wood tones and Frank Lloyd Wright–style stained-glass lamps.

★ **Blue Hill** *75 Washington Pl between Washington Sq West and Sixth Ave (212-539-1776). Subway: A, C, E, B, D, F, V to W 4th St. Mon–Sat 5:30–11pm; Sun 5:30–10pm. Average main course: $28.* More than a mere crusader for sustainability, Dan Barber is also one of the most talented cooks in town. He builds his oft-changing menu around whatever's at its peak on his Westchester farm (home to a sibling restaurant). During fresh pea season, bright green infuses every inch of the menu, from a velvety spring pea soup to *sous-vide* duck breast as soft as sushi fanned over a slivered bed of sugar snap peas. Start to finish, there's a garden on every plate—from buttery ravioli filled with tangy greens to just-picked cherries under a sweet cobbler crust. Once among the most sedate little restaurants in the Village, this cramped subterranean jewel box has become one of the most raucous.

★ ▲**Butter** *415 Lafayette St between Astor Pl and E 4th St (212-253-2828). Subway: 6 to Astor Pl. Mon–Thu 5:30–11pm; Fri, Sat 5:30–11:30pm. Average main course: $29.* The owner collects unique butter plates, which are filled with creamy

French *beurre* and adorn each tabletop. Everything on chef Alexandra Guarnaschelli's menu shines: The seared scallops with foie gras are delectable, as are the grilled halibut with roasted asparagus and a "squashy emulsion," grilled spice-rubbed pork loin and pan-seared tuna. There's an extensive wine list, gorgeous (and delicious) dessert selections, and waiters who make recommendations enthusiastically and knowledgably. Butter up a special client, friend or sweetheart with an extraordinary, imaginative meal.

★ **City Hall** *131 Duane St between Church St and West Broadway (212-227-7777). Subway: A, C, 1, 2, 3 to Chambers St. Tue–Thu 7:30–10:30am, noon–10pm; Fri 7:30–10:30am, noon–11pm; Sat 10am–3pm, 5:30–11pm. Average main course: $28.* One of the grandest restaurant interiors in Tribeca can be found inside this opulent American steakhouse, where black-and-white marble floors help convey a turn-of-the-century classicism (the private room in the basement, with its vaulted arched ceilings, is worth a peek). You may want to start with something from the well-stocked raw bar, which features an impeccable selection of fresh West and East Coast oysters. But meat is what City Hall does best: The chateaubriand for two arrives perfectly marbled, and the aged City Hall Delmonico steak appears with a crispy and charred exterior, which hides wonderfully tender pink meat within. You could go blind looking for a bottle under $50 on the extensive wine list, but the waitstaff will guide you toward what you're looking for—and without the usual stratospheric upsell.

Craft *43 E 19th St between Broadway and Park Ave South (212-780-0880). Subway: N, R, W, 6 to 23rd St. Mon–Thu 5:30–10pm; Fri 5:30–11pm; Sat 5:30–11pm; Sun 5–9pm. Average main course: $36.* Tom Colicchio's restaurant set the trend of eateries "deconstructing" their menus (meaning it's up to you to order your protein, veggies and starch separately), but there's little to recommend this enterprise. The price of a meal mounts with alarming velocity, and the food isn't always worth the cost. Dry medallions of guinea hen plus limp white asparagus and al dente grits with fishy prawns add up to an underwhelming yet pricey meal. Then there's the joyless setting, where patrons sit in near-silence and watch each other chew. Hardly fine dining, no matter how you put it together.

Delmonico's *56 Beaver St at South William St (212-509-1144). Subway: 4, 5 to Wall St. Mon–Fri 11:30am–10pm; Sat 5–10pm. Average main course: $35.* Located in a spectacular, triangle-shaped 1837 building on a corner where three streets meet, Delmonico's has a long, illustrious history. It was the city's first fine-dining institution, and its interior remains the very definition of classic—and clubby. Simple foods are best: The raw-seafood appetizer is pristine, and the Delmonico's cut—a 20-ounce rib-eye monster served on a field of smoky fried onions—will satisfy any appetite. Two classic dishes are said to have been invented here, and they are still served: lobster Newburg (in a superrich brandy cream sauce) and baked Alaska.

Dennis Foy *313 Church St between Lispenard and Walker Sts (212-625-1007). Subway: J, M, Z, N, Q, R, W, 6 to Canal St. Mon–Sat 5:30–11pm.*

Average main course: $28. Artist and restaurateur Dennis Foy (EQ) treats his Tribeca dining room, an oddly compelling fantasyland, like a three-dimensional canvas. Foy adds dashes of color wherever he can—vivid parasol lanterns that resemble large mushrooms, wooden beams painted crazy hues, and his own landscapes and seascapes. His food is equally vivid. Fresh pieces of lump crabmeat and flecks of celery are fused with a small dose of spicy mayonnaise in the delectable crab *tian*; pillowy, lightly seared gnocchi are a playful exercise in texture. It's nice to have the artist in residence.

Devin Tavern *363 Greenwich St between Franklin and Harrison Sts (212-334-7337). Subway: 1 to Franklin St. Mon–Thu noon–3pm, 5:30–11pm; Fri noon–3pm, 5:30pm–midnight; Sat 5:30pm–midnight; Sun 10:30am–3:30pm, 5:30–10pm. Average main course: $28.* This 10,000-square-foot mega-eatery from the steak-lovin' owners of Dylan Prime is a mixed bag: The ambience evokes a strip-mall Applebee's, but the menu is 100 percent Tribeca original. Smart servers, beautiful plating and excellent beverage service add some much-needed elegance. The strongest dish, fittingly for a tavern, is the cheeseburger: grilled pork belly and beef shaped into a Big Mac–like stack of thin patties. The chocolate-covered, waffle-cut potato chips, laced with a trail mix of chocolate *pistoles*, dried fruit and candied nuts, is among the best desserts in the city.

Gin Lane *355 W 14th St at Ninth Ave (212-691-0555). Subway: A, C, E to 14th St; L to Eighth Ave. Mon–Wed 5–11pm; Thu–Sat 5pm–midnight; Sun 5–10pm. Average main course: $27.* Everything about this 4,000-square-foot venue is outsize, bordering on outlandish. Leather club chairs and a bulky clock are hulking presences in the bar area; iron chandeliers and cut-velvet wallpaper suggest an Edward Gorey illustration. The menu proffers upscale steakhouse fare, a raw bar and country-club salads. Entrées are served independent of sides: The soft, fatty slices of porterhouse for two pair well with bitter brussels sprouts. Skip the forgettable desserts and try some of mixologist Dale DeGroff's cocktails instead.

★ **Hearth** *403 E 12th St at First Ave (646-602-1300). Subway: L to First Ave. Tue–Thu 6–10pm; Fri, Sat 6pm–11pm; Sun 6–10pm. Average main course: $27.* The East Village needed a Hearth—an upscale yet relaxed place that wasn't just another surprisingly good ethnic hole-in-the-wall. Skirting the small-plate trend, the hearty fare is big, rich and flavorful. Roasted and braised domestic lamb with lamb sausage, buttercup squash and chanterelle mushrooms is an excellent version of lamb three ways, and roasted sturgeon with prosciutto, sweet potatoes and sage is a novel treatment of this luxurious fish. There is a small hearth in the restaurant, but the real warmth comes from the staff, which takes pains in helping you pick the right dish, and is equally interested in finding out afterward what you thought of it.

Icon *W Court Hotel, 130 E 39th St between Park and Lexington Aves (212-592-8888). Subway: 42nd St S, 4, 5, 6, 7 to 42nd St–Grand Central. Mon–Fri 7–11am, noon–2:30pm, 5:30–10:30pm; Sat 8am–1pm, 5:30–10:30pm; Sun 8am–1pm. Average main course: $25.* Where there's a W hotel, there's also a

scene, but this one doesn't let the glitz outsparkle the food. Snuggle into a cognac-colored velvet banquette surrounded by mirrored walls and relax with an Icontini, a bracing combination of vodka, sour-apple schnapps, apple juice and lime. Chef Brian Wieler (Layla) mixes American classics with Middle Eastern and Asian influences. His appetizer of roasted sea scallops with citrus and hearts of palm is sensational: The scallops are caramelized on the outside, and buttery-soft within. If anything deserves to become an icon, it's the dessert of cinnamon-dusted beignets. Served warm with crème anglaise and chocolate dipping sauces, they're sensuous enough to get you in the mood.

The Lake Club *1150 Clove Rd at Victory Blvd, Staten Island (718-442-3600). Travel: From the Staten Island Ferry, take the S61, S91 or S48 bus to Clove Rd and Victory Blvd. Mon–Thu noon–9pm; Fri noon–10pm; Sat 6–11pm; Sun 11am–2pm. Average main course: $25..* Set in a mansion inside Clove Lakes Park, the Lake Club boasts an elegant dining room overlooking the serene water through floor-to-ceiling windows, as well as an outdoor patio kissing the shore. The contemporary American menu offers specialties like a porterhouse pork chop grilled to perfection, panko-crusted veal and ravioli stuffed with Cajun spiced lobster. For a romantic after dinner treat, rent one of the club's rowboats ($10 an hour) and paddle around the lake.

★ **Lever House** *390 Park Ave between 53rd and 54th Sts (212-888-2700). Subway: E, V to Lexington Ave–53rd St; 6 to 51st St. Mon–Thu 11:45am–2:30pm, 5:30–11pm; Fri 11:45am–2:30pm, 5:30–11:30pm; Sat 5:30–11:30pm. Average main course: $41.* In a beautiful windowless room within the landmarked modernist building, Lever House provides the perfect setting for today's take on the power lunch—or romantic dinner. The decor is simultaneously retro and modern, and this style carries over to the excellent food. Former Union Square Café chef Dan Silverman strikes the perfect balance between classic preparations and his own signature style. Popular items include lobster tempura with tartar sauce and 40-ounce dry-aged côte de boeuf (for two); the Colorado rack of lamb; and the New York State veal chop. The notable wine list includes budget-breaking bottles as well as very fine selections below $50. Fellow Union Square alum Deborah Snyder completes this top-notch dining experience with standouts that include the ultimate in chocolate mint icebox cakes.

One if by Land, Two if by Sea *17 Barrow St between Seventh Ave South and W 4th St (212-228-0822). Subway: 1 to Christopher St–Sheridan Sq. Mon–Thu 5:30–10pm; Fri, Sat 5:15–11:15pm; Sun 11:30am–2pm, 5:30–9:30pm. Three-course prix fixe: $75. Five-course tasting menu: $95.* Many of the dressed-up patrons at this 18th-century former carriage house are celebrating—a birthday, an anniversary or a proposal. Ask for the main floor rather than the cramped mezzanine, and get a better view of the flower arrangements, fireplaces and stained-glass window. Ready to pop the question? Don't be shy: You'll probably have to shout it over the live piano music. Dishes here are expertly executed, despite a few too many fusion-happy details: Sweet crabmeat over gazpacho is a

You can't fight it
City Hall's grand room
has classic appeal.

KENNETH CHEN

Critics' picks

The best...

BBQ
(see Barbecue)
☐ Blue Smoke
☐ Fette Sau
☐ Hill Country
☐ The Smoke Joint

Macaroni and cheese
☐ Dumont
☐ Freemans
☐ Kitchenette Uptown
☐ Westville East

Ice cream sundae
☐ Blue Ribbon Brooklyn
☐ Cookshop
☐ Peter Luger
☐ Shake Shack

Lobster Roll
(see Seafood)
☐ BLT Fish
☐ Ed's Lobster Bar
☐ Mary's Fish Camp
☐ Pearl Oyster Bar

light lead-in to plump pink lamb chops with a ragout of fava and *gigante* beans, or lobster napped with Indian-spiced coconut sauce. Warm chocolate-truffle cake is partnered with surprisingly delicious chipotle ice cream. It'll give you a happily-ever-after glow.

Perilla *9 Jones St between Bleecker and W 4th Sts (212-929-6868). Subway: A, C, E, B, D, F, V to W 4th St; 1 to Christopher St–Sheridan Sq. Mon–Thu 5:30–11pm; Fri, Sat 5:30–11:30pm; Sun 5–10pm. Average main course: $25.* While starstruck diners try to catch a glimpse of Perilla toque and *Top Chef* winner Harold Dieterle, food-minded folk can enjoy a small menu of upscale American standards (duck meatballs, sautéed skate wing) in the comfortable dining room, with handsome wooden tables and fans spinning on a pressed-tin ceiling. Doughnuts with lemon-fennel curd make a fine ending to a polished debut.

★**Perry St.** *176 Perry St at West St (212-352-1900). Subway: A, C, E to 14th St; L to Eighth Ave. Daily noon–3pm, 5:30pm–midnight. Average main course: $31.* Jean-Georges Vongerichten has brought his trademark virtuosity to one of the Richard Meier's gleaming glass towers on the edge of the Village. The sleek, minimalist space fronting Hudson River Park is cast in luminous whites and neutral tones that focus attention where it belongs: on the food. The menu features playful and innovative variations on seasonal favorites (like the savory strawberry gazpacho amuse-bouche or the peekytoe crab salad beautifully presented with edible flowers), though the flavors can border on the subdued, as with the bland red snapper in chili oil. Excellent desserts (try the warm mango upside-down cake) and a decent wine selection round out the experience, though service can be somewhat stiff.

★▲**The River Café** *1 Water St at Old Fulton St, Dumbo, Brooklyn (718-522-5200). Subway: A, C to High St; F to York St. Daily noon–3pm, 5:30–11pm. Three-course prix fixe: $95. Six-course prix fixe: $115.* Many people consider the River Café to be the best restaurant in Brooklyn, and it is probably the most expensive. The romantic waterside eatery, which could easily skate by on its gorgeous views of downtown Manhattan, has spawned a long roster of

great chefs, including Charlie Palmer (Aureole), David Burke (davidburke & donatella) and Rick Moonen (RM, Oceana). Current chef Brad Steelman lives up to his predecessors with two exquisite prix-fixe menus: three courses (you choose) or six courses (he chooses). Stellar dishes include crisp oysters with smoked salmon and caviar, rack of lamb or lobster specials. For dessert, few can resist the chocolate marquise Brooklyn Bridge, shaped like its sparkling namesake.

★**Sidecar** *205 E 55th St at Third Ave (212-317-2044). Subway: E, V to Lexington Ave–53rd St; 6 to 51st St. Mon–Fri noon–3pm, 6–11pm; Sat 6–11pm. Average main course: $27.* The renovation of P.J. Clarke's included an extensive transformation of the upstairs space (formerly a movie-prop warehouse) into a nominally members-only restaurant with its own kitchen. Members swipe their cards; outsiders with reservations are buzzed in. Once inside the sumptuous room, hostesses turn on the flirt for boisterous patrons who look famous but aren't. They order from a clubby menu—shrimp cocktail; refreshingly thin, bacon-dotted New England clam chowder; seared salmon with spinach; and steaks. Revisit once, chat up the staff, and you may be offered a door card.

★**Telepan** *72 W 69th St at Columbus Ave (212-580-4300). Subway: B, C to 72nd St; 1 to 66th St–Lincoln Ctr. Mon, Tue 5–11pm; Wed, Thu 11:30am–2:30pm, 5–11pm; Fri 11:30am–2:30pm, 5pm–midnight; Sat 11am–2:30pm, 5pm–midnight; Sun 11am–2:30pm, 5–10:30pm. Average main course: $31.* Bill Telepan has created a menu that marries local, seasonal ingredients and diner-centric customization—in a sea of European-influenced dishes. He offers three essential columns of food: appetizers, midcourses (including pastas) and entrées. But here, diners can pay $64 for four courses or $74 for five—combining any dishes they like. Telepan's gone out on a limb, mixing high-end ingredients with low-end recipes and vice versa. The results are refreshing. For example, he pairs monkfish with kielbasa, short ribs with borscht dumplings and black truffles with the world's most precious pierogi. And he places a whole coddled egg over scrapple (pork meat loaf), creating an elegant, greaseless version of a culinary joke. Whether highbrow or low, the quality of Telepan's ingredients is exceptional. If you have trouble landing a reservation, dine at the semicircular bar. Telepan's dining rooms feel like a friend's apartment—filled with a bunch of Upper West Side moms and dads—only this friend can cook.

★▲**Tribeca Grill** *375 Greenwich St at Franklin St (212-941-3900). Subway: 1 to Franklin St. Mon–Thu 11:30am–11pm; Fri 11:30am–11:30pm; Sat 5:30–11:30pm; Sun 11:30am–3pm; 5:30–10pm. Average main course: $26.* This former warehouse achieves coziness on a grand scale—an antique wooden bar centers the huge room, and the whimsical paintings of Robert DeNiro Sr. (Jr. being one of the owners) hang on the brick walls. The food tastes more expensive than it is: Seared sea scallops are perfectly carmelized, and the spice-dusted Maine lobster comes bathed in an exquisite vinaigrette of pear, fennel, celery root, vanilla and yogurt. The extensive wine list offers over 70 zinfandels; the servers are knowledgeable and attentive. And the dining experience can be so enjoyable you won't mind not spotting any celebs.

Sky high
Lose yourself in the million-dollar views at Water's Edge.

American $25 and over

★ ▲ **'21' Club** *21 W 52nd St between Fifth and Sixth Aves (212-582-7200). Subway: B, D, F, V to 47–50th Sts–Rockefeller Ctr; E, V to Fifth Ave–53rd St. Mon–Fri noon–2:30pm, 5:30–9pm; Sat 5:30–11pm. Average main course: $42.* After more than 75 years, this clubby sanctum for the powerful remains true to its past while thriving in the present. Chef John Greeley creates contemporary seasonal fare such as crisped black sea bass in champagne sauce. For "21 Classics," Greeley relies on the '21' archives for dishes from the recesses of culinary history; steak Diane, flambéed tableside, was on the restaurant's very first menu. The famous burger is a bargain at $30. Its mix of ground lean meats gets a flavor boost from duck fat. Act like a magnate and sip an after-dinner drink in the front lounge, where original Remingtons line the walls.

Union Square Cafe *21 E 16th St between Fifth Ave and Union Sq West (212-243-4020). Subway: L, N, Q, R, W, 4, 5, 6 to 14th St–Union Sq. Mon–Thu, Sun noon–10pm; Fri, Sat noon–11pm; Sun noon–10pm. Average main course: $30.* The Union Square Cafe's art collection and floor-to-ceiling murals have been here as long as the tuna filet mignon has been on the menu. That '80s throwback, served with a pale green heap of wasabi mashed potatoes, remains hugely popular despite being more dated than a John Hughes movie. Novelty is not what keeps this New York classic packed year after year. Danny Meyer's first New York restaurant—a pioneer in Greenmarket cooking—remains one of the city's most relaxed fine-dining establishments. This past summer, the easy menu, split into classics and seasonal specials, included a bright pancetta-flecked salad of shredded sugar snap peas and a fine flaky filet of wild salmon on a bed of sweet corn.

The Upstairs at '21' *21 W 52nd St between Fifth and Sixth Aves (212-265-1900). Subway: B, D, F, V to 47–50th Sts–Rockefeller Ctr; E, V to Fifth Ave–53rd St. Tues–Sat 5:30–10pm. Average main course: $40, $70 prix fixe.* Climb the stairs at this former speakeasy, and you'll find yourself among full-scale murals of old-time New York. The reasonable prix fixe menu seems to usher you into the ease of the place. The grilled foie gras with corn fritters and honey-poached peaches threatens an early victory, but can be followed by the 21-day dry-aged New York sirloin, which finishes strong. Take your time and savor the atmosphere while you finish your meal with vanilla ice cream profiteroles.

Water's Edge *East River at 44th Dr, Long Island City, Queens (718-482-0033). Travel: E, V to 23rd St–Ely Ave; private shuttle at 34th St Pier on the East River (Mon–Sat starting at 6pm). Mon–Fri noon–3pm, 5:30–11pm; Sat 5:30–11pm. Average main course: $27, prix fixe $62.* Since 1983, this destination restaurant, cinematically perched on the East River, has hosted countless celebratory occasions—and more than a few on-bended-knee proposals. Reserve a window or a deck table well in advance, then hop the free ferry from East 34th Street. Dress nicely; Water's Edge occupies the "fancy" end of upscale. Still, chef Brian Konopka's cuisine is anything but fusty. Try such inventively prepared seafood as roasted cod *grenobloise*, with tomato, saffron and chorizo couscous, or a starter of BBQ Hudson Valley foie gras with toasted cornbread, grilled pineapple and port wine reduction. Linger over dessert, and let requests to the crooning piano player extend the romance.

American Creative

See also: *American, Eclectic*

Staying power
Zoë is a perennial favorite in Soho.

Alias *76 Clinton St at Rivington St (212-505-5011). Subway: J, M, Z to Delancey–Essex Sts. Mon–Thu 6–11pm; Fri 6–11:30pm; Sat 11am–3:30pm, 6–midnight; Sun 10:30am–3:30pm, 6–10pm.. Average main course: $19.* The cheesy neon lights and Vegas-strip signage that colorfully announce Alias's presence on Clinton Street belie the elegant, seasonally inspired culinary arts practiced in the kitchen. Warm charred peaches doused in balsamic vinegar make that ultrasweet fruit wonderfully savory, while crunchy, tender cod fillets lightly coated with cornmeal and perched on a bed of sautéed broccoli rabe turn that humble fish into an airy delicacy. The magic extends to the vibe as well: The modern yet inviting, glass-walled space is home to a regular-studded crowd, and the waitstaff is somehow kind and gracious, even at the apex of Saturday-night fever.

Almond Flower Bistro *96 Bowery between Grand and Hester Sts (212-966-7162). Subway: B, D to Grand St. Daily 11:30am–11pm. Average main course: $21.* This Chinese-owned eatery on the Bowery distances itself from its dim sum–parlor neighbors. With exposed-brick walls and a blond-wood bar, the restaurant is more Lower East Side hipster haven than noodle shop. The dishes, from all over the U.S. and Europe, frequently have East Asian accents. Even the chewy baby back ribs—served with corn on the cob and mac and cheese—evoke Shanghai more than Memphis in their glistening sweetness.

Amalia *204 W 55th St between Seventh Ave and Broadway (212-245-1234). B, D, E to 7th Avenue; A, B, C, D, 1 to 59th St–Columbus Circle. Mon noon–2:30, 5–10pm; Tue–Thu noon–2:30pm, 5–11pm; Fri*

noon–2:30pm, 5pm–midnight; Sat 5pm–midnight; Sun 5–10pm. Average main course price: $29. Black glass chandeliers, silk chinoiserie wallpaper and baroque portraits perfectly balance eclectic and chic at this trendy Midtown restaurant, whose exposed brick walls and dripping candles also manage to create an ambient, romantic setting. Heralded chef Ivy Stark (Dos Caminos, Rosa Mexicano) masterfully prepares American cuisine with a Mediterranean flair, such as succulent beef shortribs and mouthwatering salmon *charmoula*. Down the mosaic tile staircase lies a chic lounge, where a DJ will help you dance off that "worth every calorie" bittersweet chocolate tart.

Arabelle *Plaza Athénée, 37 E 64th St between Madison and Park Aves (212-606-4647). Subway: F to Lexington Ave–63rd St. Mon 6:30–10am; Tue–Sat 6:30–10am, noon–2:30pm, 6–10pm; Sun 11:30am–2:30pm. Average main course: $30.* The domed dining room and its oversize chandeliers here are trussed up with garden trompe l'oeil and pagoda paintings. The food incorporates Asian techniques and flavors (ginger, tempura, bok choy) with seasonal Western ingredients (halibut, microgreens, truffle cream). Rather than subtle, the upshot can be messy, with conflicting tastes lingering on plates too heavily sauced with the likes of cilantro coulis and carrot and ginger reduction. Still, the $64 three-course prix fixe—which includes a larger-than-life Vahlrona soufflé and other desserts—represents excellent value in a sea of expense.

Aspen *30 W 22nd St between Fifth and Sixth Aves (212-645-5040). Subway: F, V, N, R, W to 23rd St. Mon–Wed 6pm–midnight; Thu–Sat 6pm–2am. Average*

A square meal
Goblin Market plates a hearty mix of bistro fare.

small plate: $13. It's no surprise to find taxidermy, roaring fireplaces and wide-plank floors in a place named after a ski town, but Aspen has also been modified for the New York clubgoer. A DJ spins all night long, mounted deer heads are molded out of Lucite, and the place is outfitted with sleek white leather booths. The menu is composed entirely of small plates, and it's fairly safe territory. The signature bison sliders have tons of flavor; succulent baby lamb chops, rubbed with pomegranate juice and rosemary, arrive perfectly pink in the center, perched atop a bed of garlicky wilted greens. The best dish, brook-trout tacos, bundles flaky pan-seared fish, spicy slaw and fresh salsa into two warm tortillas. No ski trip would be complete without booze: Aspen offers several body-warming cocktails, including the Hottentot (Scotch, orange zest, coffee and cloves).

▲**Aureole** *34 E 61st St between Madison and Park Aves (212-319-1660). Subway: F to Lexington Ave–63rd St; N, R, W to Lexington Ave–59th St; 4, 5, 6 to 59th St. Mon–Fri noon–2:30pm, 5:30–11pm; Sat 5–11pm. Three-course prix fixe: $84.* With its cozy townhouse setting and accessible up-market comfort food, Aureole is a restaurant that always seemed tailor-made for visiting parents. While chef Charlie Palmer has moved on to bigger and brighter things—opening splashier restaurants in Las Vegas and California—20 years after it opened, his New York flagship today feels like a late-'80s cliché. Gut-busting yet delicious offerings included an appetizer of cured salmon on a fried potato cake, topped with a huge scoop of crème fraîche. A pyramid-shaped chocolate-hazelnut cake resembles an edible Luxor casino. Daters should request a seat downstairs; the mezzanine lighting far exceeds the recommended wattage for a romantic evening.

★ ▲**Blue Ribbon Brooklyn** *280 Fifth Ave between Garfield Pl and 1st St, Park Slope, Brooklyn (718-840-0404). Subway: M, R to Union St. Mon–Thu 6pm–2am; Fri 6pm–4am; Sat 4pm–4am; Sun 4pm–midnight. Average main course: $23.* With the success of the Soho original, the French-trained brothers Bromberg opened this night-owl draw in Brooklyn, offering up a clever mix of down-home cooking and haute cuisine, all available into the wee hours of the morning. A heaping plate of crispy fried chicken shares the menu with a tender duck club sandwich layered between homemade raisin bread and one of the best cheeseburgers around. The superfresh raw bar boasts fresh oysters, clams, head-on prawns and lobster, while buttery beef marrow with oxtail marmalade is a must- have, especially to cap off a night of wholesome revelry. **Other locations:** *Blue Ribbon, 97 Sullivan St between Prince and Spring Sts (212-274-0404)* ● *Blue Ribbon Bakery, 33 Downing St at Bedford St (212-337-0404).* ● *Blue Ribbon Downing Street Bar, 34 Downing St between Bedford and Varick Sts (212-691-0404).*

Bouley Bakery & Market *130 West Broadway at Duane St (212-608-5829). Subway: A, C, 1, 2, 3 to Chambers St. Bakery: Mon–Thu 7:30am–10pm; Fri–Sun 7:30am–7:30pm. Upstairs: Mon–Thu 5:30–11pm; Fri 5:30–11:30pm; Sat 11am–3pm, 5:30–11:30pm; Sun 11am–4pm. Average sandwich: $9; average main course: $18.* David Bouley's casual tri-level enterprise, across the street from the upscale Bouley, has a handful of identities: A basement houses a small meat and fish counter, a cheese cellar and takeout options, and the street-level patisserie is filled with heavenly loaves, soups and elegant premade sandwiches. The

TALIA SIMHI

real surprises, however, are upstairs, beginning with the six-seat sushi bar. The rest of the upstairs menu—mostly French, with some small Asian twists—is a bargain. It's an everyman's Bouley: a 35-seat, no-reservations bistro. The halibut with sweet corn and shiitake mushrooms in a lemon-thyme sauce is a steal at $15, and every dish could pass muster at Bouley proper at twice the price.

★**Café at Country** *Carlton Hotel, 90 Madison Ave at 29th St (212-889-7100). Subway: 6 to 28th St. Daily 7am–11pm. Average main course: $23.* The David Rockwell–designed, übermasculine Café at Country, with its auburn leather chairs, dark wood accents and wrap-around zinc bar, feels at once clubby and grandiose. This is that rare hotel restaurant that attracts as many locals as visitors, and the playful, creative American food merits the crowds. The salty, cool foie gras terrine is shiny and waxy, like a stick of meat butter. Gimmicky touches, like the jelly jar that holds the zesty, chunky beef tartare, do nothing to detract from the dish itself. The service is superlative: smooth, professional, knowledgeable.

Café Condesa *183 W 10th St between Seventh Ave South and W 4th St (212-352-0050). Subway: 1 to Christopher St. Mon–Fri 8am–4pm, 6–11pm; Sat 8am–11pm; Sun 8:30am–11pm. Average main course: $14.* It took remarkable vision to turn a cell-phone store the size of a closet into an adorable neighborhood restaurant. The spot seems twice as big as it really is, thanks to the intelligent use of exposed brick and sultry lighting. The owners—three partners who worked at nearby French Roast—have developed an ambitious, Latin-inflected dinner menu. Chef Luis Mota (Jefferson) is clearly not afraid of butter and spices: The handmade crab ravioli, a great starter, is swimming in both. The priciest dish on the menu, the rack of lamb topped with chimichurri, comes with mashed potatoes so luscious they might as well be butter—and it costs just $18.25.

Core One Nine One *191 Orchard St between Houston and Stanton Sts (212-228-9888). Subway: F, V to Lower East Side–Second Ave. Tue–Fri 5–11pm; Sat 11am–11pm; Sun noon–11pm. Average small plate: $8.* In this sprawling space you'll find a small-bites menu with mass appeal, created by chef Stephan Boissel (La Côte Basque, Gilt): miniburgers for simple tastes, arctic char with apple gnocchi, or scallops with sherry-hazelnut vinaigrette for the adventurous. Chorizo-stuffed olives are hot from the fryer, while a salad of root vegetables and chestnuts, and slivers of spiced duck breast both stand out. Dishes, priced around $9 each, can be small even for small plates—come for snacks and you'll leave happy.

★**Country** *Carlton Hotel, 90 Madison Ave at 29th St (212-889-7100). Subway: 6 to 28th St. Tue–Sat 5:30–11pm. Prix fixe: $105.* Aside from offering some typical rustic ingredients, Geoffrey Zakarian's Country is about as provincial as a ride on the 7 train. Designer David Rockwell has restored the original beaux-arts style, uncovering architectural gems such as a tiled floor and a Tiffany-style, green-and-white glass dome. An informal café and bar is located in a subterranean space; the serious cooking takes place upstairs, under executive chef Doug Psaltis. You'll be offered four or five options for each round of the four-course, $105 prix-fixe menu. Starters include a foie gras terrine with accompaniments like caramelized oranges and fennel jam. A more cosmopolitan dish is the dazzling shellfish velouté, smokier and brinier than bisque. The veal entreé is full of

delicious bite-size morsels, including dried sweetbreads (sautéed until crispy), veal cheeks and veal breast (in cream gravy). Country might have the best bargain wine list in a high-end joint in New York. It's no wonder this place has become a tough reservation to score; city slickers seem to enjoy this Country living.

▲**Craftbar** *900 Broadway between 19th and 20th Sts (212-461-4300). Subway: N, R, W to 23rd St. Mon–Wed noon–10pm; Thu–Fri noon–11pm; Sat 10am–11pm; Sun 10am–10pm. Average main course: $20.* At celebrity chef Tom Colicchio's culinary blockbuster, Craft, food lovers compose their own dishes from basic menu categories. At Colicchio's less formal Craftbar, the concept and the mood are not so rigid. After 5pm, and on weekends, this Flatiron hot spot crackles with high-spirited get-togethers. Duck is prepared in a sumptuous confit, salmon is truffled, smoked pork loin is blanketed with fatback bacon. Pair foie gras with figs, octopus with chorizo, skate with tomato conserves and sweetbreads with vanilla beans. Desserts are nowhere as rich as the main courses, but the far-ranging wine list suggests elegant, semisweet quaffs to close a memorable meal.

★ **davidburke & donatella** *133 E 61st St between Park and Lexington Aves (212-813-2121). Subway: N, R, W to Lexington Ave–59th St; 4, 5, 6 to 59th St. Mon–Sat, noon–3pm, 5–11pm; Sun 11am–3pm, 4:30–10pm. Average main course: $36.* Both of the restaurant's namesakes are distracted by other projects, but the bi-level townhouse-style dining rooms still pack in the semi-famous and wanna-bes for over-the-top, caloric excellence. Decadence rules—nearly half the offerings employ lobster—as do gimmicks: One winning combination mixes lobster chunks with sea urchin, covered in a "BLT" sauce of dried tomatoes, bacon shards and lettuce emulsion. Even the simple dishes run heavy: Burke deep-sears salt and pepper into a halibut "T-bone" cut doused with lobster bordelaise, or the restaurant's signature stunt, a two-foot tree of cheesecake lollipops. Easy to ridicule if, like so much here, it weren't so good. The three-course, prix-fixe lunch is a bargain at $24.

▲**Eleven Madison Park** *2007 Eat Out Award, Critics' Pick: Best changing of the guard 11 Madison Ave at 24th St (212-889-0905). Subway: N, R, W, 6 to 23rd St. Mon–Thu 11:30am–2pm, 5:30–10pm; Fri, Sat 11:30am–2pm, 5:30–10:30pm; Sun 11:30am–2pm, 5:30–10pm. Three-course tasting menu: $82.* Chef Daniel Humm has replaced the rustic New American menu at Danny Meyer's vast Art Deco jewel with one that's more refined and far-reaching. His lofty intentions are clear from the first bites: Creative hors d'oeuvres include a truffle-scented goat-cheese galette and a cornet of sweetbreads, which set the tone for the rest of the meal. Diners can choose between a three-course, four-course ($96) or 11-course gourmand ($145) menu. At the end of the meal, the chef attaches a signed thank-you note to the little take-home cake; he wants you to leave with his name (and food) on your lips.

The Four Seasons Restaurant *99 E 52nd St between Park and Lexington Aves (212-754-9494). Subway: E, V to Lexington Ave–53rd St; 6 to 51st St. Mon–Fri noon–2:30pm, 5–9:30pm; Sat 5–11pm. Average main course: $46.* For almost half a century, New York's grande dame of special-occasion restaurants has held court on 52nd Street. Though the Grill Room's famously high-rolling power lunch is the institution's true

Rocky Mountain high
Retreat to Aspen's
city-chic lodge of a
restaurant.

CINZIA REALE-CASTELLO

raison'être, dinner in the Pool Room—a palatial dining arena centered on a bubbling marble pool—certainly has its charms. Signature dishes like the crisp-skinned duck, carved tableside, and delicate quenelles of Maryland crab haven't lost their luster, but the song and dance of starched-white waiters spouting canned New York–isms can make even the most hardened Manhattanite feel like a tourist. Freebies, like great hives of bubblegum-pink cotton candy, soften the economic blow.

★**Goblin Market** *2007 Eat Out Award, Critics'*
Pick: Best reason to look past a name 199 Prince St at
Sullivan St 212-375-8275). Subway: C, E to Spring St; N,
R to Prince St. Mon–Wed 5:30–11pm; Thu, Fri 5:30pm–
1am; Sat 11am–3pm, 5:30pm–1am; Sun 11am–3pm,
5:30–11pm. Average main course: $22. Prince Street is dotted with cookie-cutter Euro bistros, but those in the know have been packing this intimate spot since it opened in 2006. The brick walls, French doors and chandelier fashioned from a butcher's scale make a tasteful setting for the stunning seasonal menu. Take the exceptional chicken potpie: The flaky pastry layers taste like strudel, and the sea-salt-heavy filling is a silky stew of chicken and veggies. Goblin Market is a lovely spot for brunch or a weekday dinner, but weekend crowds can be deafening.

★ **Gotham Bar and Grill** *12 E 12th St*
between Fifth Ave and University Pl (212-620-4020).
Subway: L, N, Q, R, W, 4, 5, 6 to 14th St–Union Sq.
Mon–Thu noon–2:15pm, 5:30–10pm; Fri noon–2:15pm,
5:30–11pm; Sat 5–11pm; Sun 5–10pm. Average main
course: $36. Chef-owner Alfred Portale made his name with towering New American constructions, and though the menu doesn't push any boundaries, the execution is

impressive—as is the restaurant's soaring, masculine space. A beet and mango salad with fennel, red onions and feta sounds like any other upscale beet salad. But the beautifully simple dish—deep red and vibrant orange cubes with ribbons of shaved vegetables on a narrow, rectangular plate—has a presentation as sharp as its crystalline flavors. Juicy fried soft-shell crabs with morels, fresh peas, ramps and couscous is a thoroughly satisfying, borderline architectural tangle of bodies and legs.

★ ▲**Gramercy Tavern** *2007 Eat Out Award,*
Readers' Choice: New chef of the year. 42 E 20th St
between Broadway and Park Ave South (212-477-0777).
Subway: N, R, W, 6 to 23rd St. Mon–Thu noon–2pm,
5:30–10pm; Fri noon–2pm, 5:30–11pm; Sat 5:30–
11pm; Sun 5:30–10pm. Three-course prix fixe: $82. The handoff from founding chef Tom Colicchio to Michael Anthony (Blue Hill at Stone Barns) carries the rarity of a papal succession, yet the farmhouse-style setting, with its decorative brambles, pinecones and intoxicating smell from the wood-burning oven, is still here. Colicchio and his hearty, meat-heavy fare are not, however, and it's delicate constructions of vegetables and fish that now dominate. This shift is apparent as soon as the first course (of the main dining room's mandated $76 three-course prix fixe) is rolled out: The broccoli soup is a light broth poured over dried shiitakes, airy sweetbreads and a runny quail egg.

◉**Jimmy's No. 43** *43 E 7 St between Second and*
Third Aves (212-982-3006). Subway: F, V to Lower East
Side–Second Ave; 6 to Astor Pl. Daily 5pm–midnight.
Average main course: $11. You could easily miss this worthy subterranean spot if it weren't for the sign

Side dish

Dinner and a show

Get more bang for your dining buck with tableside entertainment.

Le Souk

Despite having extraordinarily varied and excellent eats at your proverbial doorstep, sometimes you want a little something extra with your dining experience. Visit pan-Asian eatery **Lucky Cheng's** *(24 First Ave between Houston and E 2nd Sts, 212-995-5500)*, where the ultratheatrical drag servers offer comedic cabaret performances nightly—the fun keeps going after dinner with a raucous, audience-participation karaoke session. If gender-bending isn't your thing, swinging of a different sort is what you'll get at French bistro **Seppi's** *(123 W 56th St between Sixth and Seventh Aves, 212-708-7444)* on Mondays, Wednesdays, Thursdays and Saturdays, when saxist and composer Rick Bogart takes the stage with his jazz trio for an evening of New Orleans–style classics. At the cozily dark but capacious North African **Le Souk** *(47 Ave B between 3rd and 4th Sts, 212-777-5454)* an almost nightly one-woman belly-dancing show accompanies your meal of meze, tagine and couscous. More intimate is Spanish tapas bar **Xunta** *(174 First Ave between 10th and 11th Sts, 212-614-0620)* you'll be treated to a pair of flamenco dancers accompanied by live guitar while you savor such authentic Iberian plates as grilled sardines and octopus with paprika. For an eclectic array of music (anything from folk singer-songwriters to a harp quartet) in an old-world setting, stop by charming West Village piano bar–cum–bistro **Caffè Vivaldi** *(32 Jones St between Bleecker and W 4th Sts, 212-691-7538)*, whose combo of fireplace and excellent desserts is especially alluring when the air gets chilly. If you prefer that your chef does the entertaining, pay a visit to Staten Island or Bay Ridge's **Arirang Hibachi Steakhouse and Sushi Bar** *(8812-14 Fourth Ave, Bay Ridge, Brooklyn; 718-238-9880 and 23A Nelson Ave, Staten Island; 718-966-9600)* for the choreographed knife-play of a scarily deft hibachi chef while he artfully turns slabs of meat (steak, lobster, shrimp and the like) and veggies into a custom, flaming-hot meal at your table. And if you'd rather orchestrate your own sideshow, stop by cheese-lovers' mecca **Artisanal** *(2 Park Ave South at 32nd St, 212-725-8585)* for one of four types of fondue and indulge in a '70s dinner-party throwback that not only tastes divine, but it's just plain gooey fun.

painted on a doorway over an inconspicuous set of stairs. Descend them and you'll encounter burnt-yellow walls displaying taxidermy, mismatched wood tables and medieval-style arched passageways that lead to different rooms. Live jazz wafts in from the small stage around the corner (Jimmy's is also a music venue). Beer is a star here, with 14 quality selections on tap (23 in the bottle), many of which also make it into the slow-food dishes filled with organic ingredients. A hearty beef stew, for example, is made with Victory IPA, and mussels are steamed in Belgian *gueuze* lambic.

★ **The Mercer Kitchen** *The Mercer, 99 Prince St at Mercer St (212-966-5454). Subway: R, W to Prince St. Mon–Thu 7am–midnight; Fri, Sat 7am–1am; Sun 7am–11pm. Average main course: $24.* The Kitchen leans toward the simple end of the range that Jean-Georges Vongerichten laid out in his book *Simple to Spectacular: How to Take One Basic Recipe to Four Levels of Sophistication.* The flavors of organic vegetables and meats are revealed without fuss. A tuna spring roll with soybean puree is light and satisfying. Crisp thin-crust pizzas are creatively presented with raw tuna and wasabi, or black truffle and fontina. Entrées—all exquisitely prepared—include roasted chicken and aged-sirloin steak with frites. Valrhona-chocolate cake with vanilla ice cream is a classic finish. The sleek underground space draws both Soho sophisticates and savvy hotel guests.

The Modern *9 W 53rd St between Fifth and Sixth Aves (212-333-1220). Subway: E, V to Fifth Ave–53rd St. Mon–Thu 11:30am–10:30pm; Fri, Sat 11:30am–11pm; Sun 11:30am–9:30pm. Three-course prix fixe: $74. Six-course tasting menu: $95..* Good looks aren't everything, but they're serious business here, where tables overlook MoMA's sculpture garden and diners carve their meat with Porsche steak knives. The prix-fixe menus are as carefully curated as any museum show, from a vibrant opening bite of asparagus tart to a bright green pistachio macaroon petit-four. While servers attend to every detail, Alsatian chef Gabriel Kreuther sends out dish after gorgeous dish: an immaculate cube of warm watermelon topped with tomato confit, or a rosy duck breast carved tableside. Other than a few disjointed dishes (a golden potato "gateau" holds a clunky mix of sweetbread chunks and rock shrimp), the menu is inspired and tasty. Get an early reservation so you can look out at the garden while the sun's still out. **Other location** *Bar Room at the Modern, 9 W 53rd St between Fifth and Sixth Aves (212-333-1220).*

★ **Ouest** *2315 Broadway at 84th St (212-580-8700). Subway: 1 to 86th St. Daily 5–11pm. Average main course: $27.* The cuisine at Ouest hits every note every night of the week, but you won't forget that you are on the Upper West Side. Diners tend to look like moms, dads and grandparents—a fine thing, unless you want to impress a downtown date. The friendly servers are all pros; the kitchen is open to the dining room; tables and chairs are immensely comfortable, and the round red booths are reminiscent of Tilt-A-Whirls. Tom Valenti adds some marvelously unexpected twists. Sautéed baby calamari in a spicy tomato *soppressata* sauce delivers the promised heat. Potato gnocchi shares a bowl with hen-of-the-woods mushrooms, artichoke and prosciutto. Valenti is famous for his way with a hunk of meat, and that holds true whether he's preparing his signature roasted pork tenderloin, pan-roasted rabbit or tender lamb shank.

LANE JOHNSON

KENNETH CHEN

Eye opening
Discover imaginative,
decadent combinations at
davidburke & donatella.

★Park Avenue Summer (Autumn...)

100 E 63rd St between Park and Lexington Aves (212-644-1900). Subway: F to Lexington Ave–63rd St. Mon–Thu 11:30am–11pm; Fri 11:30am–11:30pm; Sat 5:30–11:30pm; Sun, 11am–10pm. Average main course: $34. . Manager Michael Stillman, chef Craig Koketsu and design firm AvroKO have conceived an ode to the legendary Four Seasons, except that the design, the uniforms and the very name (yes, it will be Park Avenue Autumn, Winter and Spring, too) will rotate along with the menu. "Summer" means sunny wall panels and ample clusters of flowers to go with the warm weather foods. Appetizers showcase produce (baby beet salad, corn soup) and seafood (peekytoe crab salad, fluke sashimi), often mixing both with winning results. Koketsu (who helped launch Quality Meats) nails the steak, but even more head-turning is a seared John Dory fillet, the fish's clean taste brought to life by an audaciously rich combo of truffles (both slices and oil) and egg (poached with a fried brioche crust). Pastry chef Richard Leach, a James Beard Award winner, dazzles with a sweet corn panna cotta, complemented by roasted peaches and adorned Corn Pops. His very adult signature, moist chocolate cake and whipped mascarpone, suggests that Leach is as serious about sophistication as he is about play.

★ Prune

54 E 1st St between First and Second Aves (212-677-6221). Subway: F, V to Lower East Side–Second Ave. Mon–Thu 11:30am–3pm, 6–11pm; Fri 11:30am–3pm, 6pm–midnight; Sat 10am–3:30pm, 6pm–midnight; Sun 10am–3:30pm, 5–10pm. Average main course: $24. Tiny, well-lit Prune is still as popular as it was the day it opened. Gabrielle Hamilton's French mother developed this fearless chef's palate early on: Expect creative dishes like Manila clams with hominy and smoked paprika butter, and roasted suckling pig with pickled tomatoes, black-eyed-pea salad and chipotle mayo. This is the area's go-to brunch spot, so beware: The wait for a table can stretch over an hour.

Quaint

2007 Eat Out Award, Readers' Choice: Best new Queens restaurant. 46-10 Skillman Ave between 46th and 47th Sts, Sunnyside, Queens (917-779-9220). Subway: 7 to 46th St. Mon 5–10pm; Wed–Sat 5–11pm; Sun 5–10pm. Average main course: $16. It's appropriate that Quaint is located in Sunnyside—and down the block from a restaurant called Bliss. Thankfully, the decor isn't as precious as the name. The rather masculine interior features dark-wood booths, and plank floors salvaged from a Massachusetts barn. The menu focuses on seasonal, rustic New American dishes with quirky touches—hanger steak comes with coffee sauce and chopped peanuts, herb-braised mussels stew in a coconut broth. A petite back garden and friendly service make the place seem all the more...quaint.

▲Saul Restaurant

140 Smith St between Bergen and Dean Sts, Boerum Hill, Brooklyn (718-935-9844). Subway: F, G to Bergen St. Mon–Wed 5:30–10pm; Thu–Sat 5:30–10:30pm; Sun–Wed 5:30–10pm. Average main course: $26. Manhattan culinary pilgrims and dressed-down locals break bread in the butter-yellow dining room of this unpretentious, but excellent Smith Street bastion. The draw? Le Bernardin alum Saul Bolton's solid, seasonally inspired New American fare. Thanks to seamless service, a top-notch wine list and such first-rate dishes as a starter of warm salad with chanterelle mushrooms, farro and a poached egg; Maine diver scallops; and a miniature baked Alaska, you might never set your fork down anywhere else.

Savoy

70 Prince St at Crosby St (212-219-8570). Subway: N, R, W to Prince St. Mon–Thu 11:30am–10:30pm; Fri, Sat 11:30am–11:30pm; Sun 11:30am–10:30pm. Average main course: $28. One of the pioneering restaurants in the local foods movement, this paean to all that is seasonal has maintained its charm—and culinary edge—since it opened in 1990. The airy yet intimate downstairs dining room, with its honey-colored wooden tables and creamy walls, is a mellow space that allows diners to focus on the food. The knowledgeable and relaxed waitstaff is happy to reveal the contents of the restaurant's changing seasonal dishes. Carnivores will savor the enormous portion of luscious duck breast, which comes nice and rare, and is crusted over with salt for a satisfying crunch.

★ ▲Stone Park Cafe

324 Fifth Ave at 3rd St, Park Slope, Brooklyn (718-369-0082). Subway: F to Fourth Ave–9th St; M, R to Union St. Mon–Thu 5:30–10pm; Fri 5:30–11pm; Sat 10:30am–3pm, 5:30–11pm; Sun 10:30am–3pm, 5:30–9pm. Average main course: $24. Chef Josh Grinker's spirited menu is described by some as "contemporary" American, but he achieves his intensely rich flavors through the use of old-school ingredients. A thick pork chop is bumped up a notch with the addition of pork belly gravy; a mini hamburger benefits from silken short ribs; and oily bluefish translates well when prepped as pan-seared cakes. From appetizers to desserts, Grinker sends out food that may not be flashy, but sure is delicious. A lively staff, a wine list with genuine bargains and creative, fairly priced cocktails round out this first-rate neighborhood dining experience.

★ ▲The Tasting Room

264 Elizabeth St between Houston and Prince Sts (212-358-7831). Subway: N, R, W to Prince St. Tue–Thu 5:30–10:30pm; Fri 5:30–11pm; Sat 11am–3pm, 5:30–11pm; Sun 11am–3pm, 5:30–10:30pm. Average main course: $34. Chef-owner Colin Alevras changes the menu daily, marrying unusual combinations of top-quality, market-driven ingredients. A chilled pear soup is buttressed by fennel and black pepper, and a pork rib chop has the consistency of prime rib and comes with porcini mushrooms so rich they could pass for foie gras. The vast wine list is dominated by unusual regional American offerings; a dozen or so are offered by the glass.

Tocqueville

1 E 15th St between Fifth Ave and Union Sq West (212-647-1515). Subway: L, N, Q, R, W, 4, 5, 6 to 14th St–Union Sq. Mon–Sat 11:45am–2pm, 5:30–10:30pm; Sun 5:30–10pm. Average main course: $27. Just entering this elegant French-American off Union Square is a pleasure—the draped fabrics, warm hues and airiness of the soaring ceilings create a singularly inviting space. Husband-and-wife team Marco Moreira and Jo-Ann Makovitzky serve luxurious, expertly executed dishes that are well worth the price. Signature fare like the California sea urchin with angel hair carbonara appetizer and the spiced honey-glazed Peking duck main are at once aesthetically pleasing and delicious. Equally fabulous are the desserts, notably the strawberry granite and the goat cheesecake parfait. An impressive selection of European and American wines rounds out an unforgettable dining experience.

★ ▲Town

Chambers Hotel, 15 W 56th St between Fifth and Sixth Aves (212-582-4445). Subway: E, V to Fifth Ave–53rd St; N, R, W to Fifth Ave–59th St. Mon–Fri 7–10:30am, noon–2:30pm, 5:30–10:30pm;

Magically delicious
Wunderkind Wylie Dufresne whips up the unimaginable at wd-50.

KRISTY MAY

Fruit or vegetable? Sample all that's seasonal at the Tasting Room.

Sat 7–10:30am, 5:30–10:30pm; Sun 7–10:30am, 11am–2:30pm, 5:30–9pm. *Average main course: $30. Five-course tasting menu: $95.* A hot, sexy restaurant can easily become last year's news—especially when it gets a popular new sibling (Country). Town, however, has been gracefully transformed from It Spot into a timeless classic. The dining room is at once cavernous and warm: Soaring ceilings mimic those of a concert hall, while plush banquettes, soft lighting and muted acoustics bring the space back to earth. Geoffrey Zakarian's kitchen plays with similar contradictions, sending out hyperstyled, borderline fussy dishes, but surprisingly, the best ones are also the simplest: a phenomenal Flintstones-sized venison chop; a simple slice of rosy roasted lamb; and a sweet, buttery lemon square.

★ **Veritas** *43 E 20th St between Broadway and Park Ave South (212-353-3700). Subway: N, R, W, 6 to 23rd St. Mon–Sat 5:30–10:30pm; Sun 5–10pm. Three-course prix fixe: $76.* This wine-focused restaurant won't win any awards for innovative decor or cuisine. The owners left the slim, sultry dining room largely unadorned, relying on mood lighting and a few strategically placed colored-vase accents to enliven the room, while the ambitions of chef Scott Bryan (Le Bernardin, Lespinasse) never upstage the wine. The restaurant's impressive cellar, chronicled in a textbook-thick list, can be daunting. The vast majority of the bottles crack the $80 mark with a few—like a 1945 Petrus listed at $20,000—much pricier than that. The sommelier, however, will gladly steer you toward something more reasonable to go with your seared foie gras with pineapple marmalade, or the barbecued squab with tender pink flesh and sweet, blistered skin.

★ **wd-50** *50 Clinton St between Rivington and Stanton Sts (212-477-2900). Subway: F to Delancey St; J, M, Z to Delancey–Essex Sts. Mon–Sat 6–11:30pm; Sun 6–10pm. Average main course: $29; tasting menu $115.* Obviously, Wylie Dufresne's parents never scolded him for playing with his food. The culinary genius's spirit of fun and innovation can be found in riffs on the humble (his air-puffed pizza pebbles are the ultimate combo) to the exalted (a creamy ribbon of foie gras slips down the throat with barely a twitch of the jaw). And for those who might balk at sweetbreads and lamb belly, wd's are the perfect introduction—the former is a tender nougat of flavor enshrined in a delicate crust, while the latter comes as crisp "bacon" alongside sweet/tart cherried cucumbers. Although the 12-course tasting menu could be pared to the advertised nine (you might get blasé by the time the too-cute peanut-butter-and-jelly balls arrive), you'll be grateful Dufresne's caprices were indulged.

▲**Zoë** *90 Prince St between Broadway and Mercer St (212-966-6722). Subway: N, R, W to Prince St. Mon noon–3pm; Tue–Thu noon–3pm, 6–10:30pm; Fri noon–3pm, 5:30–11pm; Sat 11:30am–3:30pm, 5:30–11pm; Sun 11:30am–3:30pm, 5:30–10pm. Average main course: $21.* Like little else in Soho, this eatery has been in the same location since 1992. That staying power comes from a seriousness about wine, a stellar staff and an unpretentious vibe. Diners can observe the chefs in the open kitchen or stay up front, have a drink and watch shoppers come and go. Locals love the scallop-and-pumpkin chowder, the layered spinach salad with cheese and lemon-pistachio dressing, and the seared scallops on cauliflower risotto.

American Regional

See also: *Barbecue, Caribbean, Latin American, Mexican*

Just like home
You'll be well
looked after at
Mama's Food Shop.

▲**Adobe Blues** *63 Lafayette Ave at Fillmore St, Staten Island (718-720-2583). Travel: From the Staten Island Ferry, take the S44 bus to Fillmore St. Mon–Thu, 11:30am–11pm; Fri, Sat 11:30am–1am; Sun 11:30am–11pm. Average main course: $14.* Travel from the southwest (of Manhattan) to this Southwestern haven with a Santa Fe look: faux-adobe walls, terra-cotta sconces and a kiva fireplace. It's the perfect backdrop for New Mexican–inspired food such as soft corn tacos, steamed tamales and deep-fried minitacos filled with piquant ground chicken. The house favorite is beer-soaked "drunken shrimp" on top of rice flecked with herbs, onions, bacon, jalapeño and garlic. You should also take a nip from one of the 62 tequilas that fuel the lively bar scene.

★ **Amy Ruth's** *113 W 116th St between Malcolm X Blvd (Lenox Ave) and Adam Clayton Powell Jr. Blvd (Seventh Ave) (212-280-8779). Subway: 2, 3 to 116th St. Mon–Thu 7:30am–11pm; Fri, Sat 24hrs; Sun 7:30am–11pm. Average main course: $13.* Amy Ruth's serves some of the city's finest Southern cooking. Fried chicken is nearly perfect—its crunchy, peppery coating holds up even when dipped in fresh honey (reportedly harvested from the restaurant's rooftop apiary) or paired with waffles and drenched in maple syrup. Mac and cheese has just the right balance of gooey and crispy. Most dishes are named for prominent African-Americans, and the dining room acts as an unofficial home base for uptown's elected officials.

Bar Americain *152 W 52nd St between Sixth and Seventh Aves (212-265-9700). Subway: N, R, W to 49th St; 1 to 50th St. Mon 11:45am–2:30pm, 5pm–10pm; Tue–Thu 11:45am–2:30pm, 5pm–* *11pm; Fri 11:45am–2:30pm, 5pm–11:30pm; Sat 11:30am–2:30pm, 5pm–11pm; Sun 11:30am–2:30pm, 5pm–10pm. Average main course: $28.* Food Network behemoth Bobby Flay's American brasserie hits the old showman stride here. Though the menu often speaks to the tastes of the tourists who pack the Rockwell-designed space, the kitchen does turn out the occasional gem. The bustling room, complete with deep banquettes and vaulted ceilings hung with massive orange lamps, is a fitting stage for the raw bar's theatric dispatches, like sweet lobster meat given a vibrant jolt from avocado and sprigs of fresh chervil, and crabmeat that dallies with cubes of just-cut mango. Follow the kitchen's lead and focus on the steaks: Caked in a spicy rub and seared to perfection, the meats make a fine foil to kicked-up sides like a cauliflower and goat cheese gratin.

▲●**Birdies** *149 First Ave between 9th and 10th Sts (212-529-2512). Subway: L to First Ave; 6 to Astor Pl. Daily 11:30am–11pm. Average main course: $6.* Named after the owner's grandma (Birdie watches over the place from black-and-white photos lining one wall), this quaint soul-food spot offers myriad preparations of organic, antibiotic-free chicken, including crunchy fried and spicy-sweet barbecue-jerk, both moist and succulent under well-seasoned crusts. Don't dismiss the full roster of "veggie chick'n" alternatives like veggie nuggets, which have an oddly compelling texture that's a cross between string cheese and fowl. Even a hardened carnivore may find them surprisingly craveable.

●**Charles' Southern Style Kitchen** *2837-2841 Frederick Douglass Blvd (Eighth Ave) between 151st and 152nd Sts (212-926-4313). Subway:*

KRISTY MAY

Heavyweight champ
Gorge on Mac and cheese and Coca-Cola cake at Chat 'n' Chew.

B, D to 155th St. Daily 8am–1am. Average main course: $8. Prix-fixe buffet: $13. Charles Gabriel grew up cooking for 19 siblings in North Carolina, so he knows from Southern cooking. His Harlem kitchen launches a multilateral assault on the arteries, offering breakfast, fried seafood, takeout fare and an eat-in buffet. He whips up four specials a day—a hit parade of soulful grub, like panfried chicken, barbecued ribs, meaty oxtails, flash-fried whiting, and pork chops smothered in peppery brown gravy. Raise the white flag when you're full. **Other location:** *308 Lenox Ave between 125th and 126th Sts (212-722-7727).*

★ **Chat 'n' Chew** *10 E 16th St between Fifth Ave and Union Sq West (212-243-1616). Subway: L, N, Q, R, W, 4, 5, 6 to 14th St–Union Sq. Mon–Fri 11am–midnight; Sat 10am–midnight; Sun 10am–11pm. Average main course: $12.* Unsubtle cuisine, served in an Americana-heavy dining room plastered with college flags and Route 66 signs, appeals to our baser instincts (fat, sugar, must…have…more). Supersize portions of Uncle Red's Addiction (honey-dipped fried chicken) and the best-selling macaroni and cheese (covered in a savory, crisp crust) arrive steaming hot. Who needs the free soda refills when you can have Coca-Cola cake—chocolate cake baked with Coke in place of water—for dessert? Diners are encouraged to linger—but that may just mean they can't get up from their seats.

★ ▲**Cowgirl** *519 Hudson St at W 10th St (212-633-1133). Subway: 1 to Christopher St–Sheridan Sq. Mon–Thu 11am–11pm; Fri 11am–midnight; Sat 10am–midnight; Sun 10am–11pm. Average main course: $15.* This neighborhood fave continues to be

one of those rare spots that successfully appeals to both adults and children. Unwind with a pitcher of potent margaritas amidst the kitschy '50s-era ranch decor. The whimsical setting, along with a small old-time candy shop and plenty of crayons, is enough to keep kids from having meltdowns, so the whole crowd remains buoyant while waiting for rib-sticking fare such as quesadillas, pulled pork sandwiches, chicken fried steak, and gooey mac and cheese. Finish your meal with traditional pie à la mode, or order a nightcap and settle into a cozy nook in the rustic back room.

⊕**Dirty Bird to Go** *204 W 14th St between Seventh and Eighth Aves (212-620-4836). Subway: A, C, E, 1, 2, 3 to 14th St; L to Eighth Ave. Daily 11am–10pm. Average meal: $8.* Fried chicken isn't health food, but the fowl at the six-seat Dirty Bird To-Go is as close as it comes. Their free-range, hormone-free cluckers are brined, dipped in buttermilk, double-battered and fried for an extra crunch. It makes for an exceptionally juicy bird, if one lacking a sinful fattiness. Sides, including a ho-hum mac and cheese, are an afterthought, so double up instead with a fantastic rotisserie chicken. Coated in a crackling, piquant skin, it's quickly dispatched into halves or quarters by the speedy staff for delivery.

Great Jones Café *54 Great Jones St between Bowery and Lafayette St (212-674-9304). Subway: B, D, F, V to Broadway–Lafayette St; 6 to Bleecker St. Mon 5pm–midnight; Tue–Thu, noon–4pm, 5pm–midnight; Fri noon–4pm, 5pm–1am; Sat 11:30am–4pm, 5pm–1am; Sun 11:30am–4pm, 5pm–midnight. Average main course: $14.* A changing daily roster of New

CINZIA REALE-CASTELLO

Orleans faves and other Southern staples has kept New Yorkers coming here for more than two decades. The space is small and unassuming (just a wee bar, a few wooden tables and a modest chalkboard menu on the wall), and selections are likely to include the usual, along with a chili special and perhaps more-ambitious entrées, such as pan-seared mahi-mahi with tomato relish. During crayfish season (roughly spring to midsummer), stop by to sample a spicy bayou-style boil.

▲Jacques-Imo's
366 Columbus Ave at 77th St (212-799-0150). Subway: 1 to 79th St. Mon–Thu 5–10pm; Fri, Sat 11:30am–11pm; Sun 11:30am–10pm. Average main course: $20. The decor is slightly cheesy—plastic alligators on the wall, Cajun bric-a-brac. However, there's serious cooking going on here; proprietor Jacques Leonardi studied under the legendary Paul Prudhomme. Once your party is seated (it can be a while), make sure someone picks the perfectly crisp fried chicken. The blackened redfish topped with crab-chili hollandaise and the Carpetbagger's Steak (a filet mignon stuffed with oysters, blue cheese and onions) are winners too. The Southern hospitality extends right up to Leonardi, who often makes his dining-room rounds wearing a chef's coat and loud Bermuda shorts.

★ ▲◎Mama's Food Shop
200 E 3rd St between Aves A and B (212-777-4425). Subway: F, V to Lower East Side–Second Ave. Mon–Sat 11am–10pm. Average main course: $10. Your mama wouldn't let you go hungry, and neither will Mama's. Indulge in rib-sticking basics, like fried or grilled chicken, hearty meat loaf and chunky mashed potatoes. Vegetarians can pig out on fresh corn salad, steamed baby bok choy, and 15 or so other meat-free sides. The cozy space is as down-home as the eats: Diners sit at Formica tables and gaze at portraits of other people's moms.

▲Mara's Homemade
342 E 6th St between First and Second Aves (212-598-1110). Subway: F, V to Lower East Side–Second Ave; L to First Ave; 6 to Astor Pl. Mon, Wed, Thu 5–10:30pm; Fri 5–11:30pm; Sat 4–11:30pm; Sun 4–10:30pm. Average main course: $19. Light Southern food might seem an oxymoron, but not at Mara's Homemade. The tiny, brightly hued East Village eatery, whose walls are covered with photos of New Orleans' musicians, serves a seafood-oriented menu of Cajun specialties and barbecue. Owner Mara Levi and her husband David are here nightly waiting tables; food is prepared carefully to order and takes time to arrive. An artichoke, boiled in a seriously hot spice mixture, arrives with a side of creamy rémoulade. A delicate fillet of catfish, fried till crisp, comes with a side of smoky mashed potatoes. Everything pairs well with one of the seven Abita beers offered, and a slice of moist red velvet cake is a fitting send-off note.

◎Margie's Red Rose
275 W 144th St between Adam Clayton Powell Jr. Blvd (Seventh Ave) and Frederick Douglass Blvd (Eighth Ave) (212-491-3665). Subway: A, C, B, D to 145th St. Mon–Sat 6am–7:30pm; Sun 6am–4pm. Average main course: $8. Your heart will soon belong to Margie's fried chicken. The key to a tasty bird lies not in a secret blend of spices, but in the consistency of the batter; it should be a thin, dark, crunchy layer that clings tenaciously to the meat. Margie, a sweet South Carolinian who's been a restaurateur for more than three decades, knows her batter. Her subtle, addictive coating will have the most refined diner gnawing

bits of brittle crust off the drumsticks. Portions are generous, so show up hungry.

▲Melba's
300 W 114th St at Frederick Douglass Blvd (Eighth Ave) (212-864-7777). Subway: B, C to 116th St. Tue–Sat 5pm–10:30pm; Sun 10am–3pm, 5–11pm. Average main course: $14. Owner Melba Wilson—an original partner at Virgil's Real BBQ—personally works this Harlem dining room. Exposed-brick walls and chandeliers create a warm backdrop for some fine eats: The house specialty, wine-braised short ribs, is so tender that calling it meat seems like false advertising. Order the dish with a cheddar-cheese-topped grits cake or a side of garlicky sautéed spinach. You can also turn to the classics, like chicken and waffles, which are better (and more expensive) than almost anywhere else in the neighborhood.

▲Mesa Grill
102 Fifth Ave between 15th and 16th Sts (212-807-7400). Subway: L, N, Q, R, W, 4, 5, 6 to 14th St–Union Sq. Mon–Thu noon–2:30pm, 5:30–10:30pm; Fri noon–2:30pm, 5:30–11pm; Sat 11:30am–2:30pm, 5–11pm; Sun 11:30am–3pm, 5:30–10:30pm. Average main course: $30. Jacked-up Southwestern dishes routinely appear on menus around the city, but the party started here when chef Bobby Flay opened this soaring dining room in 1991, before he became a Food Network celeb. Bold flavors still rule: The signature blue-corn pancake stuffed with shredded barbecued duck is a tasty beginning, as are the grilled mahi-mahi tacos with smoked tomato salsa, avocado relish and charred pineapple hot sauce. Entrées include a spice-rubbed sirloin served with Mesa Grill's secret steak sauce and a double-baked potato with horseradish, green onions and crème fraîche.

Jonesing for grub
Regulars pack Great Jones Café for Southern-style fixin's.

KRISTY MAY

Chuck wagon
Rib-stickers like pulled pork and pie à la mode are a Cowgirl must.

and pies come fall; and of course there is always a chocolate option.

NoNO Kitchen *293 Seventh Ave between 7th and 8th Sts, Park Slope, Brooklyn (718-369-8348). Subway: F to Seventh Ave. Mon–Wed noon–10pm; Thu noon–11pm; Fri noon–midnight; Sat 10am–midnight; Sun 10am–10pm. Average main course: $20.* Chef Gregory Tatis (K-Paul's Louisiana Kitchen) has packed the menu at this Park Slope Cajun joint with regional classics (four types of po' boy, three gumbos, crawfish étouffée) and a few inventive reinterpretations (like jambalaya wontons). The one-room space steers clear of N'awlins party clichés, but keeps the mood festive with a jazz soundtrack and lazily spinning fans. A bowl of duck gumbo can be overly salty, while a hot, generously seasoned blackened catfish fillet is juicy and tender. And spicy, hearty jambalaya is so aggressive, it might make your nose drip.

Rack & Soul *2818 Broadway at 109th St (212-222-4800). Subway: 1 to 110th St–Cathedral Pkwy. Mon–Thu 11am–10pm; Fri, Sat 11am–11:30pm; Sun 11am–9:30pm. Average main course: $15.* When Charles Gabriel decided to open an offshoot of Charles' Southern Style Kitchen, fried-chicken fans took notice. Gabriel's crisp, meaty bird is often ranked among New York's best, with reason; you'll lick every morsel off your fingers. The Rack half of the name refers to sweet, sticky, glistening baby back ribs. And if those don't satisfy, a slew of sides—like smoky collard greens and gooey mac and cheese—will. A drinks list featuring rieslings and Austrian beers suggests that this soul food eatery is onto something—these are great beverages to pair with a fried chicken dinner.

★ **Miss Maude's Spoonbread Too**
547 Malcolm X Blvd (Lenox Ave) between 137th and 138th Sts (212-690-3100). Subway: 2, 3 to 135th St. Mon–Thu noon–9:30pm; Fri, Sat noon–10:30pm; Sun 11am–9:30pm. Average main course: $15. Norma Jean Darden knows that sometimes nothing will do but real home cookin'. The offshoot of Darden's original Morningside Heights restaurant doesn't have tour buses parked out front like the more famous Sylvia's, but it should because the food is better. Everything is made from scratch. Get a load of fall-off-the-bone short ribs, flaky cornmeal-crusted catfish or thick-cut pork chops smothered in creamy gravy, and dig into sides like smoky collard greens. On weekends the brunch menu includes nap-inducing favorites like pecan waffles, fried fish and biscuits. If the sight of coconut and chocolate layer cakes oozing with icing doesn't set your mouth watering, you need glasses. **Other location:** *Miss Mamie's Spoonbread Too, 366 W 110th St between Manhattan and Columbus Aves (212-865-6744).*

Ninth Street Market *337 E 9th St between First and Second Aves (212-473-0242). Subway: L to First Ave, 6 to Astor Pl. Tue–Thu 5:30–11pm; Fri–Sun 10am–3:30pm, 5:30–11pm. Average main course: $16.* Fresh flowers, throw pillows and a fireplace make Ninth Street Market ideal for a romantic evening. The menu features Southern-inspired, American comfort food like chicken fried steak and vegetable potpie. The pecan-encrusted catfish is served with a dollop of bourbon maple syrup—rather unconventional for fish fry, but purists can opt for a traditional battered and fried preparation. Seasonal ingredients are used for dessert—that means berry tarts in the summer

The Shark Bar Restaurant *307 Amsterdam Ave between 74th and 75th Sts (212-874-8500). Subway: 1, 2, 3 to 72nd St. Mon–Wed 5–10:30pm; Thu 5pm–midnight; Fri, Sat 5pm–1am; Sun 11:30am–3pm, 4–10:30pm. Average main course: $19.* Soul food at this city-slick, romantically lit Upper West Side spot is as good as any you'll find further uptown. A platter for two is packed with expertly prepared fried catfish strips, crab cakes, barbecued grilled shrimp, Harlem black jack and jerk wings. Not enough? The honey-dipped Southern fried chicken and barbeque rib combo will shut you up for a while. The Cajun-style entrée shrimp étouffee is seasoned just right: plenty of heat without the buzz-killing burn. Choose from a stellar lineup of sides served in heaping mounds: The black-eyed peas and collard greens are smoky and satisfying.

⊙**Stan's Place** *411 Atlantic Ave between Bond and Nevins Sts, Boerum Hill, Brooklyn (718-596-3110). Subway: A, C, G to Hoyt–Schermerhorn. Mon–Thu 11am–10pm; Fri 11am–11pm; Sat 10am–11pm; Sun 10am–9pm. Average main course: $14.* In true New Orleans style, patrons walking through the door of Stan's Place will be greeted with a blast of frigid air and a dose of Southern hospitality. The owner may even hover over your shoulder and guide you through the classic Creole menu, steering you toward po' boys—crisp French bread stuffed with fried catfish or pulled pork—or bowls of chicken and sausage or seafood gumbo. The Big Easy brunch is a relaxing affair at which you can load up on large platters (Bananas Foster pancakes), or do the morning Café Du Monde–style with beignets (three for $4) and chicory café au lait.

Argentine

See also: *Brazilian, Latin American, Peruvian, Steakhouses*

Steak out
Settle in for a juicy filet mignon and polenta fries at Chimichurri Grill.

★ ▲**Azul Bistro** *152 Stanton St at Suffolk St (646-602-2004). Subway: F to Delancey St; J, M, Z to Delancey–Essex Sts. Mon–Thu 6pm–midnight; Fri, Sat 6pm–1am; Sun 6pm–midnight. Average main course: $23.* Order a workhorse Malbec, sniff the leather-bound menu and you're ready to tackle an iron platter of sizzling meat at this LES outpost. Prime yourself with exquisitely flaky empanadas nestling a hearty beef and olive filling. Skip the bland sirloin and concentrate on an earthy skirt steak, red as a plum inside. You may not be in Buenos Aires, but you can perch at the dinky bar, slather the Uruguayan beef with a fine chimichurri and watch a televised Argentine *futbol* match along with transfixed waiters in this low-lit brick-and-wood bistro.

Boca Junior Argentine Steakhouse

81-08 Queens Blvd at 51st Ave, Elmhurst, Queens (718-429-2077). Subway: R to Grand Ave–Newtown. Mon–Fri 11am–11pm; Sat, Sun noon–11pm. Average main course: $15. To most Argentines, the only thing better than a big, juicy steak is a big, juicy steak consumed while watching soccer. They can convene for the latter at the spacious Boca Junior Argentine Steakhouse. The name comes from the world-renowned soccer team, and the theme comes through in the decor: The blue-and-yellow dining room (team colors) is covered with soccer memorabilia, and owner Walter Coni has installed four plasma TVs for watching games. The menu is all about meat: filet mignon, short ribs topped with chimichurri sauce, and a sizzling mixed grill.

Buenos Aires *513 E 6th St between Aves A and B (212-228-2775). Subway: F, V to Lower East Side–Second Ave; 6 to Astor Pl. Daily noon–midnight.*

Average main course: $14. It's no fun scanning a wine list in search of an affordable bottle. At Buenos Aires, a bustling, bright Argentine spot, there isn't a bottle that isn't reasonably priced. The list, packed with Malbecs for around $25, delivers maximum flavor for your buck. So does the menu. Fat, succulent steaks; plump, snappy sausages; juicy, lemony chicken fresh off the grill—this is a carnivore's playground, where meat may come with a side of meat (a jumbo slab of skirt steak is paired with blood sausage!). If you must get your greens, load up on the vibrant, shamelessly garlicky chimichurri sauce (a lovely chartreuse, thanks to the parsley); there's a bottle on every table, and you should slather it on everything but dessert. Your breath will reek for days, but that's a small price to pay for a tasty meal, decent service and a bill that won't break the bank.

Chimichurri Grill *606 Ninth Ave between 43rd and 44th Sts (212-586-8655). Subway: A, C, E to 42nd St–Port Authority. Mon–Fri noon–11:30pm; Sat noon–midnight; Sun noon–10:30pm. Average main course: $25.* Curiously, to savor the slabs of grilled carnal joy at Chimichurri Grill, you don't actually need to splash them with the namesake South American condiment at this Argentine steakery. Sequestered from the noisy bustle of Ninth Avenue and swaddled in a dark-wooded decor with oil paintings of bandolion players and bullfighters, this relaxing nook is a carnivore's delight. The chicken and fish alternatives to gaucho-style steak are top-notch, but don't deny yourself the filet mignon, plated with a medium-tangy Cabrales cheese sauce and flanked by four creamy polenta fries.

KENNETH CHEN

Enlightened one
Industria Argentina offers a modern spin on the classic steakhouse.

fries and a sauceboat of garlic-and-parsley chimichurri, and you've got a perfect meal.

Industria Argentina *329 Greenwich St between Duane and Jay Sts (212-965-8560). Subway: 1 to Franklin St. Mon–Sat noon–5pm, 6pm–midnight; Sun noon–6pm. Average main course: $22.* In both decor and spirit, Industria Argentina may be New York's most thoroughly modern Argentine steakhouse. The presentation begins with a miniature, flaky empanada delivered as an amuse-bouche—it's more artful than it sounds. The tuna *tiradito*, often a rustic raw fish jumble at other places, is a delicate appetizer that layers frothy avocado puree atop silky tuna slices. Whisper-thin, oven-dried tomato slivers are added to a ramekin of oozing smoked provolone, making for another stellar starter. For the main event, the kitchen hews more closely to the classic steakhouse formula, serving flame-licked steaks with piquant chimichurri. Check out the *parrillada*, a mixed grill for two, featuring a platter of lamb chops, sausages, hanger steak and short ribs.

La Fusta *80-32 Baxter Ave between Ketcham and Layton Sts, Elmhurst, Queens (718-429-8222). Subway: G, R, V to Elmhurst Ave; 7 to 82nd St–Jackson Hts. Mon–Thu 11:30am–10:30pm; Fri, Sat 11:30am–11:30pm; Sun 11:30am–10:30pm. Average main course: $17.* Patriarch "El Tata," his gracious son Gaspar and a complement of cousins, nephews and longtime waiters run La Fusta, which means "riding whip." Savory house-made empanadas and a tangy watercress and avocado salad are ace appetizers, but the main attraction is flavorful, perfectly flamed beef. Go for lusciously marbled *entraña* or the sky-high *parrilladas*, a mixed grill of meats, sausages, sweetbreads and liver-stuffed tripe. A bottle of Malbec adds gusto to your gaucho getaway.

★ **Novecento** *343 West Broadway between Broome and Grand Sts (212-925-4706). Subway: A, C, E, 1 to Canal St. Mon–Thu noon–midnight; Fri, Sat noon–1am; Sun noon–midnight. Average main course: $20.* Those in a rush would be wise to avoid this charming Argentine spot, where Soho shoppers and foreign-language-speaking tourists come to relax over reliable bistro standards. Some of the better basics here include a nice, thick, juicy filet mignon and plump steamed mussels in a buttery garlic-and-white-wine sauce. After finishing a reasonably priced bottle of red, a steak and an order of the wet chocolate cake (molten on the inside)—with vanilla ice cream and strawberries—you'll be ready to lounge here all night.

Estancia 460 *460 Greenwich St between Desbrosses and Watts Sts (212-431-5093). Subway: A, C, E, 1 to Canal St. Daily 10:30am–10pm. Average main course: $26.* This breezy spot, whitewashed from bar to ceiling and serenaded by a sultry Latin soundtrack, features a hearty menu diverse enough to attract a repeat-business neighborhood crowd. The selection runs the gamut from pizza and pasta to salmon and steak. An individually portioned pizza *bianco*, featuring extra-thin blistered crust, a few splashes of pesto, and a blend of four cheeses, makes a fine solo meal at the bar. The kitchen, though, is in finest form when searing meats on the grill. Gorgeously charred, thick, grassy, strip steak from Uruguay is accompanied by piquant chimichurri and a generous heap of crisp *papas fritas*. The mixed-grill *parillada*, featuring grill-marked short ribs, spicy sausage and chicken, is ample enough for a party of two.

★ **Hacienda de Argentina** *339 E 75th St between First and Second Aves (212-472-5300). Subway: 6 to 77th St. Daily 5pm–midnight. Average main course: $28.* Latin American–goth decor—votive-illuminated brick walls and wrought-iron candelabras—adds to the red-blooded fun at this Argentine steakhouse. Though a few dishes nod to the chicken-fish-vegetarian crowd, Hacienda is really built for hard-core carnivores. Whet your appetite with grilled starters like earthy *morcilla* (blood sausage) or sweetbreads. Then stake out your steak: Choose from Argentine-style (grass-fed) or American-style (grain-fed) beef. Stateside eaters tend to find the latter more flavorful. The juicy *entraña*, or skirt steak, is a deliciously marbled Buenos Aires favorite. Add a bottle of Argentine Malbec, a side of garlic-strewn

Read 'em & eat

chimichurri: a pestolike mixture of oil, garlic, onion and herbs (typically basil and parsley)

dulce de leche: (literally "milk candy") a caramelized dessert

entraña: skirt steak

milanesa: a thin, breaded slice of beef, chicken or veal

parrillada: an entrée of grilled meats

Asian

See also: *Chinese, Japanese, Korean, Thai, Vietnamese*

Small wonder
Tuna tartar in wonton cones is a star attraction at Satsko.

CINZIA REALE-CASTELLO

Pan Asian

★ ▲**Aja** *1066 First Ave at 58th St (212-888-8008). Subway: N, R, W to Lexington Ave–59th St; 4, 5, 6 to 59th St. Mon–Thu 5pm–midnight; Fri, Sat 5pm–1 am; Sun 5pm–midnight. Average main course: $20.* Surrounded by glittering stone walls and exposed beams and watched by an eight-foot-tall Buddha, well-dressed eaters chat away at this sceney Pan-Asian spot. Servers are in a rush to get you out the door and the prices are steep, but the plates are bountiful and the sushi here is so creamy and fresh it melts in your mouth. The Peking duck, large enough to feed a table of four, is a mound of crisp skin and moist meat with a side of warm moo shu pancakes and a salty-tangy sauce for DIY-style eating. Avoid the grocery-freezer quality desserts and cap the meal with a fancy cocktail.

▲**Asia de Cuba** *Morgans Hotel, 237 Madison Ave between 37th and 38th Sts (212-726-7755). Subway: N, R, F, W, Q to 34th St. Mon–Wed noon–3pm, 5:30pm–11pm; Thu, Fri noon–3pm, 5:30pm–midnight; Sat 5:30pm–midnight. Average main course: $36.* Cuban cooking finds its Zen at Asia de Cuba. The menu is a careful combination of Asian inflections and Cuban flavor, a concept most successful in seafood dishes like the calamari salad with banana, cashews and orange sesame dressing. Beef dumplings are steamed with coconut rice for island flavor, while traditional Cuban entrées like roast pork nod to the East with their pairing with bok choy. The Philippe Starck–designed bi-level restaurant, a sea of white with subtle hints of amber and orange, features a balcony-like lounge and dining area overlooking a giant communal table downstairs.

Asiakan *710 Amsterdam Ave between 94th and 95th Sts (212-280-8878). Subway: 1, 2, 3 to 96th St. Mon–Thu noon–11pm; Fri, Sat noon–midnight; Sun noon–11pm. Average main course: $17.* It's not related to Buddakan—the Meatpacking District behemoth—but this addition to the Upper West Side does have a sprawling Pan-Asian menu, a trendy downstairs lounge and its own Buddha statue. Forgo the mushy miso black cod for the octopus ceviche—mixed cucumber, cherry tomatoes, cilantro, mango and chopped meat in a tasty lime-soy sauce. On the sushi list, "Salmon, Salmon Caviar Love" is rich, raw salmon with earthy shiitake mushrooms, buttery avocado and fragrant mango, all topped with salmon roe. At $100 for two, a meal here is a splurge, but still cheaper than one at Buddakan.

★ **Asiate** *Mandarin Oriental Hotel in the Time Warner Center, 80 Columbus Circle at 60th St (212-805-8881). Subway: A, C, B, D, 1 to 59th St–Columbus Circle. Mon–Fri 7–10:30am, noon–2pm, 5:30–10pm; Sat 8–11am, 11am–2pm, 5:30–11pm; Sun 8–11am, 11:30am–2:30pm, 6–8:30pm. Prix-fixe dinner: $65. Tasting menu: $85.* The first treat is the view—sweeping vistas down Central Park South and over the park itself—the second is the food, a prix-fixe menu of dressed-up, French-accented Asian fare. Chef Noriyuki Sugie tantalizes monied tourists and expense-accounters with an amuse-bouche of Caesar salad...soup. Bright green liquefied lettuce is layered over tapiocalike couscous, topped with bacon foam.

We've captured 2 cultures, 4 stars, and thousands of hearts.

Each unforgettable dish has a personality of its own.
Stop by, we'll introduce you.

Safran
french vietnamese cooking

88 seventh ave. btw 15th & 16th st | 212 929 1778
mon-thu 11:30am-11:30pm | fri-sat 12noon-2:00am | sun 12noon-11:30pm

Pressed suckling pig arrives as two squares of fatty meat, its cheek made into a foie gras–rich confit and its feet fried into a croquette. Lobster en cocotte in a shellfish-citrus broth is a lot like the best tom yum gung you've ever had.

Bamboo 52 *344 W 52nd St between Eighth and Ninth Aves (212-315-2777). Subway: C, E to 50th St. Mon–Sat noon–4am, Sun 4pm–4am. Average main course: $20.* Advertised as a sushi restaurant (with a bamboo garden, no less), this Hell's Kitchen eatery feels more like a bar with an extended raw fish menu: There's loungy seating—patrons nestle on low banquettes and nibble off knee-high tables—a DJ and a thriving drinking scene. The fun (if slightly immature) spirit prevails on the menu. Don't be surprised to see ingredients like buffalo chicken in the specialty rolls, though the naughtily delicious spicy sushi sandwich— a triangle of seasoned rice layered with spicy tuna, avocado, eel and American cheese—is preferable.

★ ▲**Bluechili** *251 W 51st St between Broadway and Eighth Ave (212-246-3330). Subway: C, E, 1 to 50th St. Mon–Thu noon–11:30pm; Fri, Sat noon–midnight; Sun noon–10pm. Average main course: $20.* This swank subterranean lounge goes deeper than the standard-issue Asian and Italian restaurants clustered on this block. The bar and sushi bar, tricked out in white Lucite, are backlit with changing colored lights, making your plate suddenly turn into a dinner of a different color. Snack on smoked oysters with lemongrass or spicy-sour lobster soup. You can also fill up on duck in yellow curry or a seasonal special of soft-shell crabs covered in basil sauce with sun-dried tomatoes and roasted garlic cloves. For a pretheater dinner with a side of cool, Bluechili is just the ticket.

▲☺**Chai Home Kitchen** *124 North 6th St between Bedford Ave and Berry St, Williamsburg, Brooklyn (718-599-5889). Subway: L to Bedford Ave. Mon 4pm–midnight; Tue–Sun noon–midnight. Average main course: $8.* Apart from its water-lily pool, Chai's decor is simple. And the prices are rock-bottom: Plump, crunchy peanut dumplings are $1 apiece, and most curry, noodle and meat dishes cost less than $10. Chef Suwat "Noi" Hoengmo flavors his Thai recipes with subtle twists: The khao pad lychee is a toss of light, fluffy fried rice with fleshy bits of the eponymous fruit; chicken bathes in an unusual floral-perfumed yellow-curry sauce. Lean, smoky slices of barbecued beef are a stellar choice, particularly when accompanied by the green-papaya salad. **Other location** *930 Eighth Ave at 55th St (212-707-8778).*

▲☺**Dumpling Man** *100 St Marks Pl between First Ave and Ave A (212-505-2121). Subway: L to First Ave; F, V to Lower East Side–Second Ave. Mon–Thu 11am–11pm; Fri, Sat 11am–midnight; Sun 11am–11pm. Average dumpling order: $7.* The Dumpling Man is the perfect boyfriend. He's honest: Every one of his mouthwatering hot pockets is made by hand in full view of hungry diners. He's never boring: Each order of dumplings comes seared or steamed, with four different fillings, such as a classic pork, chive and scallion or a mix of tofu, seitan, shiitake mushrooms and bok choy. He can mix it up: The Marco Polo dumplings are bathed in an Italian-style tomato-basil-Parmesan sauce. And finally, he's sweet: After such delectable savory snacks, he proffers a hard-to-find Japanese dessert of shaved ice, condensed milk and red beans with green-tea ice cream.

Regional influence Je'Bon Noodle House draws flavors from all across Asia.

The only catch: You'll have to share him. Line up early, because he might not have enough to go around as the night wears on.

Fatty Crab *643 Hudson St between Gansevoort and Horatio St (212-352-3590). Subway: A, C, E to 14th St; L to Eighth Ave. Thu–Sat noon–4am; Sun noon–midnight. Average main course: $14.* Chef Zak Pelaccio named this 30-seat restaurant after his favorite joint in Kuala Lumpur. Unlike his other Meatpacking District restaurant, 5 Ninth, there's not much visual impact here, but the food is dazzling. Dishes come out haphazardly, as the open kitchen finishes each one, and they are meant to be served family-style. The result is a tongue-frazzling delight. Pelaccio's "fatty duck" is brined, steamed and fried, and then dusted with sugar and salt. His Dungeness crab is steamed and then bathed in a chili-based syrup that tastes like a deliciously aggressive oyster sauce, and the watermelon pickle and crispy pork is divine.

Forbidden City *212 Ave A between 13th and 14th Sts (212-598-0500). Subway: L to First Ave; N, Q, R, W, 4, 5, 6 to 14th St–Union Sq. Tue–Sun 6pm–4am. Average main course: $12.* It isn't really Chinese. It's Japanese with a Sinophile bent. And it's not really a restaurant. It's more of a late-serving dim sum bar, with a hefty emphasis on sakes and fancy cocktails. Dishes like shark-fin dumplings and wasabi baby octopus come in take-a-bite-and-pass-it-on portions, and the salt-and-pepper squid—a steaming mound of it—turns into a perfect beer snack for four. Visiting DJs, scenesters and a steady projection of anime and surf movies help fill the

Flavor pouch
Dumpling Man proffers scrumptious pillows of flavor.

downtime between visits from the sweet, cheery servers. Sesame balls are a weekend-only treat, but the green-tea crème brûlée is good six nights a week.

Fusia *972 Second Ave between 51st and 52nd Sts (212-421-2294). Subway: E, V to Lexington Ave–53rd St; 6 to 51 St. Daily 11am–11pm. Average main course: $13.* As the name might imply, this tiny, sparsely decorated restaurant serves a mix of cuisines: Japanese, Chinese and Thai. It's hard to go wrong when ordering here—everything comes out of the kitchen fresh and impeccably plated. Start with one or two creative rolls, like the Crazy Tuna (black pepper tuna and avocado) or the Golden Angel (yellowtail tuna and salmon with bonito flakes), then move on to one of the delicately flavored entrées such as tender, flaky Chilean sea bass or crispy rock shrimp tempura nuggets sprinkled with roe and tossed in a creamy and spicy sauce. Desserts, including a deep-fried banana spring roll and a chocolate-fondue plate, are equally delectable.

★**Geisha** *33 E 61st St between Madison and Park Aves (212-813-1112). Subway: N, R, W to Fifth Ave–59th St; 4, 5, 6 to 59th St. Mon–Fri noon–3:30pm, 5:30–11pm; Sat 5:30–11pm. Average main course: $27.* A flashy crowd jockeys for seating in the posh downstairs lounge and upstairs dining room—both impeccably designed by David Rockwell. The menu, crafted by Eric Ripert (Le Bernardin), includes tons of fresh sushi, as well as starters like grilled shrimp "lollipops" (shrimp, ginger and scallions on sugarcane skewers) with a sesame oil, sweet soy sauce, white vinegar and chili dipping sauce. The result: some of the best Japanese-fusion cuisine in New York.

⊙**Je'Bon Noodle House** *15 St. Mark's Pl between Second and Third Aves (212-388-1313). Subway: R, W to 8th St–NYU; 6 to Astor Pl. Mon–Wed noon–11pm; Thu, Fri noon–midnight; Sat 12:30pm–midnight; Sun 12:30pm–11pm. Average main course: $10.* The menu at this superb noodle house features dishes—along with detailed explanations of their origins—from all over Asia. "Silver needles" are a satisfying $10 plate of panfried noodles with a confetti of shredded pork, chicken, baby shrimp, bean sprouts, egg, and slivers of carrot and onion. One more dollar gets you a seemingly bottomless bowl of tum yum soup, the spicy broth stocked with seafood, noodles and assorted vegetables. The space inspires sensory overload—blue bulbs fill the bathrooms, orange lights illuminate a brick wall—but it's a small price to pay for inexpensive food this good.

★ ⊙**Kelley and Ping East Village** *325 Bowery at Second St (212-475-8600). Subway: 6 to Bleecker St.. Mon–Fri 11:30am–5pm, 5:30–11pm; Sat, Sun 5:30–11pm. Average main course: $12.* Brad Kelley's pan-Asian eatery specializes in East and Southeast Asian cuisines. The spare dining room is soothing; the space has a beige tin ceiling, maroon flooring and dim lighting from bare, antique-style lightbulbs. Start with greaseless Vietnamese vegetarian spring rolls (packed with a savory mélange of shiitake mushrooms, carrots and cabbage) or Chinese-style salt-and-pepper shrimp dusted with flour and fried in their shells until golden. For entrées, a Thai-inspired boneless duck breast suffused with soy, ginger and tamarind has crunchy skin and succulent meat. Desserts include warm, crispy dumplings filled with minced mango and pineapple.**Other location**

Kelley and Ping 127 Greene St between Houston and Prince Sts (212-228-1212).

King 5 Noodle House *39-07 Prince St between Roosevelt and 39th Aves, #1G, Flushing, Queens (718-888-1268). Subway: 7 to Flushing–Main St. Daily 10am–midnight. Average main course: $6.*
Here's something you don't have often: Taiwanese breakfast. Served from 10am until 2pm every day, Taipei-style small plates mix sweet and savory offerings such as crisp foot-long crullers meant to be dunked in steaming soybean milk, and scallion pancakes filled with beef and hoisin sauce. The sparse dining room's red-and-yellow decor may remind you of McDonald's, but that's where the similarities end. Late risers, don't despair: Red-pepper–spiked soup noodles and braised beef, served in the evening, are equally satisfying.

⊖Koca Lounge *76 Orchard St between Broome and Grand Sts (212-477-9977). Subway: F to Delancey St; J, M, Z to Delancey–Essex Sts. Mon–Thu 5–11pm; Fri, Sat 5pm–midnight; Sun 5–11pm. Average main course: $14.* Tasty Southeast Asian fare, a swank, candlelit darkwood interior, and a spare, homey garden make for a winning addition to the bar- and trend-heavy hood. The chance to cook your own *shaburi* (hot pot)—pick from four different broths and add in your choice of fresh seafood or meat at the table—is Koca's forte. However, should the weather be too hot for *shabu-shabu*, sharable small plates like fried sea scallops with curry aioli, salt-and-pepper prawns and crisp veggie dumplings are a midsummer night's treat and pair perfectly with the house *nama* (raw, unfiltered) sake.

★ ▲⊖Kuma Inn *113 Ludlow St between Delancey and Rivington Sts (212-353-8866). Subway: F to Delancey St; J, M, Z to Delancey–Essex Sts. Tue–Sun 6pm–midnight. Average small plate: $8.* A hidden second-floor location, gracious service and chef King Phojanakong's pan-Asian small plates make this tiny dinner-only spot a true find. Phojanakong channels his culinary pedigree (Bouley and Boulud) and heritage (his mother is Filipino and his father is Thai) into such elegantly presented dishes as an omelet studded with plump Washington Bay oysters, thumb-sized, non-greasy spring rolls and bite-sized hunks of seared ahi tuna luxuriating in a spicy miso vinaigrette. Desserts like subtly piquant chocolate-chili ice cream and a twist on key lime pie with Asian citrus fruit *kalamansi* might inspire you to keep Kuma Inn secret.

★ ▲⊖Lovely Day *196 Elizabeth St between Prince and Spring Sts (212-925-3310). Subway: J, M, Z to Bowery; 6 to Spring St. Daily noon–11pm. Average main course: $10.* Cash-strapped twentysomethings (and their admirers) pack this inexpensive Nolita eatery to gossip and dine on Thai-inspired curries and noodle dishes. Everything is laid-back here—the decor features simple red booths and floral wallpaper, and the service is amiably slow. If you're looking for a little heat, try the ginger-fried chicken topped with spicy aioli. For some sweetness, consider the crispy banana rolls served with vanilla ice cream, honey and sesame.

▲O.G. *507 E 6th St between Aves A and B (212-477-4649). Subway: F, V to Lower East Side–Second Ave. Mon–Thu 6–11:30pm; Fri, Sat 6pm–12:30am; Sun 6–11:30pm. Average main course: $16.* This pioneering eatery introduced East Villagers to refined Asian cuisine, and it continues to offer traditional

dishes in a stylish yet attitude-free setting. The cozy space, filled with handkerchief-size café tables and soft candlelight, is equally suitable for a serious date or a casual dinner. The flavorful chicken with five spices and plum barbecue sauce was just right, and the deftly prepared Thai beef salad, coconut soup and pan-browned dumplings were all winners. While Asian cuisine does not usually conjure images of tasty desserts, the oozy chocolate soufflé is an exception.

▲Rain *100 W 82nd St between Columbus and Amsterdam Aves (212-501-0776). Subway: B, C to 81st St–Museum of Natural History. Mon–Thu 6–11pm; Fri 6pm–midnight; Sat 5pm–midnight; Sun 5–10pm. Average main course: $19.* It's no wonder Rain's cavernous space is teeming with families, tourists and first dates: The UWS East Asian stalwart coddles its clientele from start to finish with attentive if slightly brisk service and polished American-hybrid fare (read: nothing too exotic). Entrées such as halibut with a passion-fruit glaze and a special of soy-brushed tuna with taro-root puree don't disappoint—or break any culinary ground. Still, Rain's swank tiki-bar-ish décor, well-chosen wines and exceptional desserts like fried coconut ice cream could well have you joining the crowds coming back for more.

▲⊖Republic *37 Union Sq West between 16th and 17th Sts (212-627-7168). Subway: L, N, Q, R, W, 4, 5, 6 to 14th St–Union Sq. Mon–Wed 11:30am–10:30pm; Thu–Sat 11:30am–11:30pm; Sun 11:30am–10:30pm. Average main course: $8.* After 14 years, this Pan-Asian hot spot, off Union Square, is still packing 'em in to its sleek, blond, communal tables. The key to its success is the consistently satisfying bowls of noodles like spicy coconut, Vietnamese vegetable and pad thai for cheap. Speedy service keeps the waiting-for-a-table times short and the long roomy bar is a nice place to enjoy the din of this bustling New York staple.

▲⊖Rickshaw Dumpling Bar *61 W 23rd St between Fifth and Sixth Aves (212-924-9220). Subway: F, V, N, R, W to 23rd St. Mon–Sat 11:30am–9:30pm; Sun 11:30am–8:30pm. Average dumpling order (6 dumplings): $5.* Kenny Lao's concept for a new dumpling bar was a winner in a business-plan contest at NYU's Stern School of Business, so he's put it to the test at Rickshaw Dumpling Bar. Annisa chef Anita Lo developed the menu, which includes six different dumplings, each inspired by an Asian cuisine and matched with its own dipping sauce: classic Chinese pork and chive with a soy vinegar, for instance, or Thai chicken with peanut satay. If you want a full meal, pair your dumplings with a big bowl of noodle soup, then top it all off with a green-tea milk shake or a dessert dumpling of molten chocolate in a mochi wrapper.

Room 18 *18 Spring St between Elizabeth and Mott Sts (212-219-2592). Subway: N, R, W to Prince St; 6 to Spring St. Mon–Thu noon–midnight; Fri, Sat noon–1:30am; Sun noon–midnight. Average main course: $15.* Blurring the line between bar and restaurant, Room 18 provides large, Ultrasuede-covered cubes as seats, encouraging diners to lounge lazily while perusing the menu. Dishes meander into Spanish and Asian territory: miso scallops with guacamole and tortilla chips, chorizo wontons with shiitake mushrooms. Though the place is designed for evening escapades (and is open late on weekends), inexpensive lunch options make it a fine Nolita shopper's stop. Need a hangover

cure? Try the salty-sweet fried rice with chunks of pineapple and minced sausage, or the roasted duck in a warm tortilla wrap.

Satsko 245 Eldridge St between Houston and Stanton Sts (212-358-7773). Subway: F, V to Lower East Side–Second Ave. Tue–Thu 5pm–2am; Fri, Sat 5pm–4am; Sun 5pm–2am. Average main course: $15. It may just look like another Asian-tinged Lower East Side spot, with red hanging lamps, bamboo embellishments and chinois-upholstery, and you may think you've had all of these pan-Asian menu items before. Stay for dinner and you'll be pleasantly surprised. The signature starter of tuna tartar in fried wonton cones is a light-hearted, one-bite snack. Fried calamari, with a spicy mayo dipping sauce, are greaseless and crisp, and diagonally sliced towers of nori-crusted ahi tuna, with fleshy sweet potatoes and crunchy baby bok choy, impress even the most jaded palates.

Tigerland 85 Ave A between 5th and 6th Sts (212-477-9887). Subway: F, V to Lower East Side–Second Ave; 6 to Astor Pl. Mon–Thu 5:30–11pm; Fri, Sat 5:30–11pm. Average main course: $16. Brother-sister team Judy and Jimmy Tu recognized that while the 'hood was filled with Pan-Asian menus—maybe too many of them—there wasn't any place offering organic ingredients prepared by a chef with a fine-dining pedigree. Mr. Tu, an alum of Eleven Madison Park, Nicole's and Citarella, has assembled a small collection of recipes from his eclectic background (his Chinese parents were born in Vietnam but raised their kids in Thailand). No sprawling menus. No endless variations on classics. Instead: an odd but consistently flavorful assortment of not-so-obvious Asian dishes: Thai shrimp cakes; Berkshire ribs braised in coconut juice; tamarind, ginger and homemade lime sodas.

★ ▲☉**Wild Ginger** 51 Grove St between Seventh Ave South and Bleecker St (212-367-7200). Subway: 1 to Christopher St–Sheridan Sq. Mon–Fri 11am–11:30pm; Sat, Sun 11:30am–11:30pm. Average main course: $9. You'll be wild about Ginger's range: wonton soup, Indian pancakes and Indonesian-style fried rice along with the expected curries and noodles. The main dishes—categorized as "land," "sea" and "sky"—are impressive, considering that most are priced well under 15 bucks. Pleasingly crisp deep-fried bass is served whole and upright as though it were about to swim off its jade-colored plate. Pork chops marinated

Read 'em & eat

goreng: fried rice, flavored with chilies, garlic, cumin, coriander, egg, chicken and shrimp

mee: noodles

rendang: a dry curry whose meat is cooked in coconut milk

roti canai: a fried and unleavened bread often dipped in curry

sambal: condiment made with chili peppers, salt and sugar

in lemongrass, though slightly on the salty side, are perfectly grilled. Warm, rich coconut rice is brightened with slices of sweet-tart mango.

Burmese

★ ▲☉**Mingala Burmese** 1393B Second Ave between 72nd and 73rd Sts (212-744-8008). Subway: 6 to 68th St–Hunter College. Mon–Thu 11:30am–11pm; Fri, Sat 11:30am–midnight; Sun 11:30am–11pm. Average main course: $10. In a narrow dining room adorned with hand-painted murals of pagodas, Cafe Mingala adeptly serves sumptuous portions of Burmese food, which is influenced by Indian, Chinese and Thai cuisine. Golden fried triangles of delicate pastry filled with curried potatoes make great starters, as does the mango salad, with fresh and pickled slivers of the fruit. Chewy, oversize dumplings, called phet-htoke, burst with pork and shrimp in a basil sauce, while crispy thousand-layer bread steeped in sweet coconut milk makes a compelling dessert. **Other location** Village Mingala 21–23 E 7th St between Second and Third Aves (212-529-3656).

▲☉**Village Mingala** 21–23 E 7th St between Second and Third Aves (212-529-3656). Subway: R, W to 8th St–NYU, 6 to Astor Pl. Mon–Thu 11:30am–11pm; Fri, Sat 11:30am–midnight; Sun 11:30am–11pm. Average main course: $8. Burma's cuisine reflects the flavors of its neighbors—China, India and Thailand—and the epic menu here covers some serious territory. A cheat sheet will help you find the stars in the lineup, like refreshing (and addictive) young ginger salad, a riot of crisp roasted ginger, toasted lentils, sesame seeds, peanuts, crowned with delicate fried onions. It's a perfect opener for more mellow main courses. Among the best: mohinga ("Festival Noodle Fish Broth" on the menu), a stewlike combination of minced fish, vermicelli noodles, lemongrass, black pepper and chopped hard-boiled eggs. The chicken curry is another hit: tender chunks of chicken swaddled in a pleasant sauce spiced with onions, ginger, cilantro and turmeric. **Other location** Mingala Burmese, 1393B Second Ave between 72nd and 73rd Sts (212-744-8008).

Filipino

▲**Cendrillon** 45 Mercer St between Broome and Grand Sts (212-343-9012). Subway: J, M, Z, N, Q, R, W, 6 to Canal St. Tue–Sun 11am–11pm. Average main course: $21. This lofty spot with wooden tables and swooping curtains seems like nothing out of the ordinary, but the subtle Filipino dishes are more exotic than much Asian fare. Strips of air-dried beef marinated in kalamansi, garlic and soy lie atop a bed of greens like crackling bacon. Crisp pork spring rolls are enlivened by a tangy carrot-mango sauce and chicken adobo is a massive juicy breast and leg braised in sour-rice-vinegar and soy. For dessert, steer toward the housemade ice creams, like banana-rum-macadamia-praline (yes, that's all one flavor).

☉**Krystal's Cafe** 171 First Ave between 10th and 11th Sts (212-614-8080). Subway: L to First Ave; 6 to Astor Pl. Mon, Wed, Thu 7:30am–midnight; Tue 7:30am–10pm; Fri, Sat 7:30am–3am; Sun 7:30am–midnight. Average main course: $8. Marinate a pork skewer in a little sugar, garlic and soy sauce,

Orange crush
You'll be smitten
with Bamboo 52's
raw-fish menu.

Asian

KENNETH CHEN

and it's transformed into *inihaw*, a mighty Filipino kebab that can outmuscle even Korean *bulgogi* and Chinese sparribs. Along with that addictive pork (also available as part of a $5.95 lunch buffet), Krystal's specializes in pastries, such as gigantic *ensaimadas* (sweet rolls), *puto* (rice muffins) and hot, yeasty *pan de sal* (salt bread) rolls. Finish with rich, eggy leche flan. The dining room is strictly bare-bones, but the real party's on your plate. **Other location** *69-02 Roosevelt Ave at 69th St, Woodside, Queens, Woodside, Queens (718-426-8676).*

Indonesian

▲◉**Borobudur** *128 E 4th St between First and Second Aves (212-614-9079). Subway: F, V to Lower East Side–Second Ave. Daily 11am–11pm. Average main course: $9.* You have to figure that a country made up of 18,000 islands and home to more than 200 ethnicities is going to cook some interesting food. You can practically eat your way through Southeast Asia at this family-run restaurant. The kitchen won't subject you to authentically fiery spices—which is all the better, as you'll want to be able to taste the richly seasoned dishes: soft fried pancakes with a mild chicken curry; piles of steamed bean curd dressed with sweet peanut sauce; bits of lamb in a chili-spiked coconut broth and "fried salty fish," which tastes like a fishy potato chip.

Java *455 Seventh Ave at 16th St, Park Slope, Brooklyn (718-832-4583). Subway: F to 15th St–Prospect Park. Mon, Tue 5–11pm; Wed, Thu 2–11pm; Fri, Sat 2pm–midnight; Sun 2–11pm. Average main course: $12.* Set in what looks like a railroad apartment, this family-run find is known for its *rijsttafel*, a 12-dish sampler (including soup and dessert) priced at just $36 for two people. Other must-orders: flavorful chicken soup with potato balls and fried onions; *rendang*, beef spiced with chili and cooked in coconut milk; *satay madura*, chicken satay with tamarind and lime leaves. Batik squares serve as napkins, and the background music is Indonesian folk-drumming.

★ ▲◉**New Indonesia & Malaysia Restaurant** *18 Doyers St between Bowery and Pell St (212-267-0088). Subway: J, M, Z, N, Q, R, W, 6 to Canal St. Tue–Sun 8am–10pm. Average main course: $10.* Doyers Street was one of the first streets in New York to be inhabited by Asian immigrants, and the prices at this downstairs gem are still stuck in the past. Prepare for vivid flavors in dishes like curried crab with transparent noodles: A clay pot is filled with four red cracked-in-half crustaceans in a thick broth of coconut milk, red curry, red chili and lemongrass. Indonesian fried chicken is bathed in dark, thick, sweet soy sauce. Another regional favorite, *mee rebus*, combines crunchy crackers, egg noodles, cucumber, bean sprouts and egg in a thick, intense sweet-and-sour sauce. Even the Tsingtao beer is cheap, at $2.50.

Malaysian

◉**New Malaysia Restaurant** *Chinatown Arcade #28, 46–48 Bowery between Bayard and Canal Sts (212-964-0284). Subway: B, D to Grand St; J, M, Z, N, Q, R, W, 6 to Canal St. Daily 10:30am–11pm. Average main course: $10.* The menu at New Malaysia Restaurant resembles those found in many Indian,

Thai, Chinese and other Asian eateries—and with good reason: Malaysian cuisine comes from an amalgam of those cultures. So you'll have your pick of chicken curry, pad thai, beef satay, sweet-and-sour pork and kung pao squid, along with specific Malaysian specialties like *roti canai*—a flat, fluffy tortilla-meets-matzo appetizer served with chicken curry. The location of the restaurant might be the most exotic thing about it: in a minimall just off Bowery. There's certainly a sense that you've found a locals-only eatery.

Sanur *18 Doyers St between Bowery and Pell St (212-267-0088). Subway: J, M, N, Q, R, W, Z, 6 to Canal St. Tue–Sun 8am–10pm. Average main course: $6.95.* Located on a serpentine Chinatown backstreet, this subterranean, sparsely decorated restaurant boasts an expansive menu full of Indonesian and Malaysian treats. Start with *roti canai*, a paper-thin pancake with a curried dipping sauce, or greaseless, crispy fried squid. The strength here is the seafood: The succulent hard-shell crabs are slathered in a Malaysian-Chinese sauce infused with ginger. The shaved-ice desserts are refreshing—as are the low prices.

◉**Sentosa Malaysian Cuisine** *39-07 Prince St between Roosevelt and 39th Aves, unit 1F, Flushing, Queens (718-886-6331). Subway: 7 to Flushing–Main St. Mon–Thu 11am–11pm; Fri, Sat 11am–11:30pm; Sun 11am–11pm. Average main course: $11.* Like many New Yorkers, Sentosa made a successful rent-reducing move out of Manhattan. Its spacious new digs feature teak walls, black-lacquered tables and college boy–waiters sporting New York Dolls shags. You'll find fried rice and sparribs on the menu, along with Javanese and Sumatran dishes. Seafood entrées are a specialty; "sizzling seafood" tosses squid, scallops and shrimp in a delectably sweet garlic-tinged sauce.

Tibetan

▲**Café Himalaya** *78 E 1st St, , (212-358-0160). F, V to Lower East Side–Second Ave. Tue–Sat noon–11pm; Sun noon–10pm. Average main course price: $8.* Despite its industrial, bare-bones decor (white walls, bright lights, linoleum floor) and insufficient staffing, Café Himalaya's exotic fare—yes, even for New York—makes it worth a visit if only for the purpose of breaking one's culinary habits. Plump, round *tsel momo* (vegetable dumplings) are fresh and light as an appetizer, while dense, earthy chili shrimp and cinnamony "Himalayan-style" chicken curry are rich and warming, as befits the inhabitants living on the majestic Rooftop of the World. Pair either one with the excellent whole-wheat paratha, which just about outshines every other dish.

▲◉**Tsampa** *212 E 9th St between Second and Third Aves (212-614-3226). Subway: L to Third Ave; 6 to Astor Pl. Daily 5–11:30pm. Average main course: $10.* Dining at this serene spot is like checking into a Buddhist retreat. The homeland *momo* (dumplings) are a must: Choose from steamed or fried wheat noodles, then select one of three fillings (chicken with vegetables, shiitake mushrooms with vegetables, or baby potato and scallions). Skip entrées with curries or sauces, like the *sherpa khala*; there's often too much oil. The customary end note: roasted, finely ground barley whipped with creamy yogurt and honey, sprinkled with dried cranberries.

Australian

Eastern outback
The Lower East Side meets Aussie fare at Bondi Road.

Bondi Road *153 Rivington St between Clinton and Suffolk Sts (212-253-5311). Subway: F to Delancey St; J, M, Z to Delancey–Essex Sts. Mon 6–10pm; Tue–Sat 6pm–midnight; Sun 6–10pm. Average main course: $15.* Photos of Sydney's Bondi Beach,. a projection screen playing movies of wave riders and a fishcentric menu make the surfer theme obvious at this breezy Aussie nook. The cheerful service is just as refreshing as the bar's Bloody Mary oyster shooters, fueled with pepper-infused vodka. Despite their homey appeal, crisply fried fillet of barramundi, addictive French fries and *pavlova*, a featherlight meringue topped with passion fruit, are all elegantly presented—a welcome counterpoint to the casualness of it all.

Eight Mile Creek *2007 Eat Out Award, Readers' Choice: Best Australian 240 Mulberry St between Prince and Spring Sts (212-431-4635). Subway: N, R, W to Prince St; 6 to Spring St. Mon–Fri 5pm–midnight; Sat, Sun 11am–midnight. Average main course: $18.* The kangaroo steaks are as thick as the waiters' Aussie accents, but Eight Mile Creek is no mere showroom for Down Under kitsch. Bacon and Worcestershire sauce give the already tangy seasonal Tasmanian oysters an extra jolt. The crisp barramundi fillet is light and flavorful, as is the lemon-myrtle roasted chicken. The treats continue with desserts such as sticky date pudding and an intriguing plate of Aussie cheeses.

The Sunburnt Cow *137 Ave C between 8th and 9th Sts (212-529-0005). Subway: L to First Ave. Mon–Fri 6pm–midnight; Sat, Sun noon–midnight. Average main course: $18.* The Cow puts together plates loaded with inventive comfort food from Down Under.

Peppery kangaroo sausage on buttery smashed potatoes and caramelized onions puts an Aussie twist on bangers and mash. Other nods to Australia include emu burgers, barramundi and fish-and-chips battered with Coopers beer. The laid-back staff is eager to ply visitors with Moo Juice, potent, fruity cocktails served in baby bottles. Ripper, mate.

Tuck Shop *68 E 1st St between First and Second Aves (212-979-5200). Subway: F, V to Lower East Side–Second Ave. Mon–Wed 8am–midnight; Thu 8am–2am; Fri, Sat 8am–5am; Sun noon–10pm. Average pie: $5.* The pies at Tuck Shop, an unpretentious café, are filled with minced beef, chicken or tofu and make an excellent midday snack or meat lovers can add a sausage roll, a light pastry shell filled with pork and sage. The grub is cheap enough that you can top off any meal with the requisite dessert—sticky date pudding or lamington, a tasty jam-filled sponge cake rolled in chocolate and sprinkled with coconut. **Other location** *250 W 49th St between Broadway and Eighth Ave (212-757-8481).*

Wombat *613 Grand St between Leonard and Lorimer Sts, Williamsburg, Brooklyn (718-218-7077). Subway: L to Lorimer St, G to Metropolitan Ave. Daily 11am–2am. Average main course: $18.* This no-frills space, with its stark metal tables and black walls, looks less like a restaurant than a bar. Chef Joe Pounds' (Sweetwater, Pacifico) food transcends the surroundings, including an appetizer of rare, soy-cured venison medallions and crispy buckwheat fritters. The chicken Wellington "Floater" is a delectable piece of white meat poached in olive oil, topped with *duxelles* (butter-sautéed minced mushrooms, shallots and herbs) and wrapped in flaky puff pastry, floating in green-pea broth.

Austrian

See also: *German*

Blaue Gans *139 Duane St between Church St and West Broadway (212-571-8880). Subway: A, C, 1, 2, 3 to Chambers St. Daily 11am–midnight. Average main course: $22.* Kurt Gutenbrunner draws from his Austrian roots at this Tribeca restaurant, located inside the former Le Zinc space. The restaurateur hasn't done much in the way of decoration—he has kept the large posters from the previous tenant and added oversize mirrors—and instead focused on the food. For starters, choose from savory sausages like *weisswurst* (pork and veal sausage served with a soft pretzel). The Wiener schnitzel, the traditional German breaded and fried pork cutlet, is superb. You may be too stuffed afterward to finish the *kaiserschmarrn,* a cinnamon-dusted crumbled pancake with apple compote.

★ **Café Sabarsky** *Neue Galerie New York, 1048 Fifth Ave at 86th St (212-288-0665). Subway: 4, 5, 6 to 86th St. Mon, Wed 9am–6pm; Thu–Sun 9am–9pm. Average main course: $16.* Come for the culture, stay for the *schlag?* Well, actually, it's the other way around: Many of the well-heeled, gray-haired patrons stop by the elegant Neue Galerie specifically to visit this Viennese restaurant (operated by Wallsé chef Kurt Gutenbrunner). Who wouldn't prefer fresh, frothy pea soup with mint to the tortured nudes of Egon Schiele? But the real works of art are the desserts—apple strudel swaddled in fabulous flaky pastry, cherry-bedecked Black Forest cake—and cream-topped coffee, strong enough to propel you upstairs to tour the Neue Galerie's small but exquisite collection of German and Austrian art.

▲◔**Café Steinhof** *422 Seventh Ave at 14th St, Park Slope, Brooklyn (718-369-7776). Subway: F to Seventh Ave. Mon 5–11pm; Tue–Thu 11am–4pm, 5–11pm; Fri, Sat 11am–4pm, 5pm–midnight; Sun 11am–4pm. Average main course: $10.* On a summer evening when the windows are wide open, this breezy brick-walled space feels extra-European, as locals sit around the bar guzzling tall beers and sipping elderflower prosecco. The kitchen churns out simple but hearty Austrian comfort food, and there's no better time to indulge than Monday nights, when the menu is devoted to just two entrées: Six bucks buys you a heaping bowl of goulash with tender chunks of beef, or, for non–meat eaters, breaded and fried trout filet. (As if a real vegetarian dish could possibly be an option!) On any other night of the week, be sure to try the thin Wiener schnitzel paired with tangy pickled cucumbers.

▲**Danube** *30 Hudson St at Duane St (212-791-3771). Subway: A, C, 1, 2, 3 to Chambers St. Mon–Sat 5–11:30pm. Average main course: $30.* David Bouley's Austrian eatery recalls a Klimt canvas—walls are a moody blue, the banquettes plum suede and reproductions of the artist's work abound. If only the experience were as inspiring. A starter of beets with horseradish *fromage blanc* can be an unappetizing terrine of stiff white mousse layered with beet slices trapped in a gelée. A rack of lamb is cooked to perfect rareness, but the halibut entrée can be woefully dry. True, the desserts

are good (especially the warm apricot strudel), but not good enough to excuse the overall disappointment of the dining experience.

Thomas Beisl *25 Lafayette Ave at Ashland Pl, Fort Greene, Brooklyn (718-222-5800). Subway: B, Q, 2, 3, 4, 5 to Atlantic Ave; D, M, N, R to Pacific St. Mon 3:30pm–midnight; Tue–Fri 12:30pm–midnight; Sat, Sun 10:30am–midnight. Average main course: $16.* Beisl is Austrian slang for "pub," making this place a step down on the formality scale for Thomas Ferlesch, who was a star chef at the posh Vienna '79 when he was 23. The comfortable, wainscoted restaurant serves Viennese classics along with traditional bistro food. Goulash made with fall-apart-tender beef cheeks is served with rich, raggedy spaetzle that soak up every drop of sauce. The sauerbraten comes with nearly candied, cinnamon-spiked red cabbage, which draws out the meat's flavor. For dessert, have the almond- and hazelnut-filled *linzertorte,* said by Austrian expats to be better than anything you can find in Vienna (or Linz, for that matter). Reserve ahead; the entire BAM audience seems to march across the street for dinner every night. In warm weather, the garden patio helps accommodate everyone.

★ **Wallsé** *344 W 11th St at Washington St (212-352-2300). Subway: 1 to Christopher St–Sheridan Sq. Mon–Fri 5:30–11:30pm; Sat, Sun 11:30am–3pm, 5:30–11:30pm. Average main course: $30.* Kurt Gutenbrunner wrings maximum flavor from first-rate ingredients in his elegantly stark West Village restaurant, turning the native Austrian's Viennese specialties—like thin, crumb-coated Wiener schnitzel or tender white asparagus buoyed by sherry foam—into contemporary masterpieces. Other exemplary dishes include a vivid spring-pea soup, thyme-roasted red snapper with Reisling sauerkraut and black truffle sauce, and mandarin-glazed duck. The staff ably suggests fine flavor marriages from the selection of Austrian wines. Finish with the renowned apple strudel. Art from the personal collection of painter-epicure—and Wallsé regular—Julian Schnabel hangs on the white walls.

Read 'em & eat

mit schlag: topped with whipped cream

schnitzel: breaded and panfried cutlet of veal or pork

spaetzle: dumpling or noodle dish made from eggs, flour, water or milk, salt and occasionally nutmeg

strudel: pastry made of thin layers with sweet or savory fillings

Barbecue

See also: *American Regional*

Bar BQ *689 Sixth Ave at 20th St, Park Slope, Brooklyn (718-499-4872). Subway: F to Seventh Ave; M, R to Prospect Ave. Mon–Fri 3–11pm; Sat noon–11pm. Average main course: $13.* The 'cue here is prepared in the tradional eastern North Carolina way: pulled pork from the whole pig (ideally cooked 15–18 hours over wood), with a strict no-tomato policy—just tangy, peppery vinegar sauce. The flavorful, freshly pulled pig meat is served in sandwiches or in paper containers, presented with a squirt bottle of sharp eastern-NC vinegar sauce.

★ **Blue Smoke** *2007 Eat Out Award, Readers' Choice: Best barbecue* *116 E 27th St between Park Ave South and Lexington Ave (212-447-7733). Subway: 6 to 28th St. Mon 11:30am–10pm; Tue–Thu 11:30am–11pm; Fri, Sat 11:30am–1am; Sun 11:30am–10pm. Average main course: $24.* St. Louis native Danny Meyer's barbecue joint tops the short list of Manhattan's best 'cue contenders. Chef Kenny Callaghan knows his wet sauces and dry rubs: The menu includes traditional St. Louis spareribs, Texas salt-and-pepper beef ribs, Memphis baby backs and Kansas City spareribs. The atmosphere is sports-heavy and includes a prominent bourbon bar and galvanized-metal buckets for your bones.

Bone Lick Park *75 Greenwich Ave between Seventh Ave South and Bank St (212-647-9600). Subway: 1, 2, 3 to 14th St. Daily 11:30am–11pm. Average main course: $14.* Sure, it sounds like a Dirk Diggler movie, but telling friends you're eating at Bone Lick Park is well worth the sniggers. The decor is rightly downplayed, except for a three-foot-high scarlet neon Coca-Cola sign behind the bar. This place is all about the 'cue, slow-cooked out back in a wood-burning pit. The scent of hickory, apple and cherry wood emanates from the terrific baby back ribs, which are sticky and supple beneath a shroud of peppery sauce. And the Carolina pulled-pork sandwich delivers smoky flavor with less mess. The corn bread needs an upgrade (it's hard and dry), but side-plate salvation is found in the semisweet baked beans and some of the crunchiest onion rings in town.

ⓒ **Daisy May's** *623 Eleventh Ave at 46th St (212-977-1500). Subway: A, C, E to 42nd St–Port Authority. Mon 11am–9pm, Tue–Fri 11am–10pm, Sat noon–10pm, Sun noon–9pm. Average main course: $8.* Former Daniel chef Adam Perry Lang's menu stretches from the hills of Tennessee (beer-can chicken) to the Midwest (Kansas City sweet ribs) and back again. Carolina pulled pork, Memphis-style 'cue—the range is troublesome if you have strong feelings about where real barbecue comes from (that'd be eastern North Carolina). Nevertheless, the man has a smoker, and it's cranking out tender, flavorful meat, along with bacony beans and chili-spiked creamed corn.

PHILIP FRIEDMAN

Dinosaur Bar-B-Que *646 W 131st St between Broadway and Riverside Dr (212-694-1777). Subway: 1 to 125th St. Tue–Thu 11:30am–11pm; Fri, Sat 11:30am–midnight; Sun noon–10pm. Average main course: $15.* Barbecue always tastes best in a place that's gritty and worn-in. The first Manhattan branch of this honky-tonk saloon, located in an old West Harlem meatpacking warehouse, comes close to authentic with weathered gas-station signage and 19th-century barbershop mirrors. The enormous menu opens with fried-green tomatoes, chicken wings and beer-boiled shrimp, but barbecue lovers will go straight for the beef brisket, ribs and pulled pork—all of which get a dry rub, up to 18 hours of smoking over hickory, apple and cherry woods, and a slather of secret sauce.

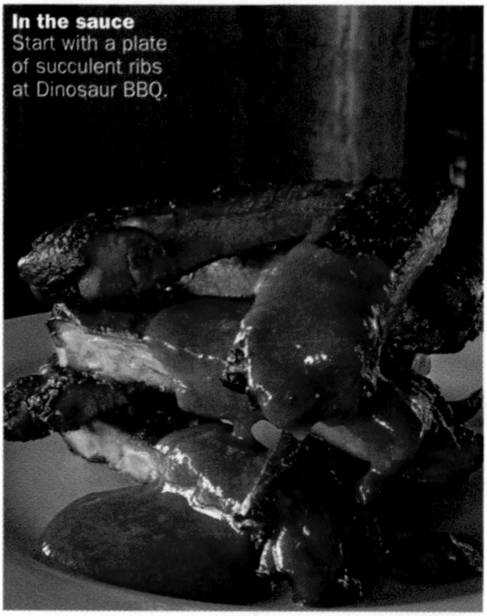

In the sauce
Start with a plate of succulent ribs at Dinosaur BBQ.

Fette Sau *354 Metropolitan Ave between Havemeyer and Roebling Sts, Williamsburg, Brooklyn (718-963-3404). Subway: L to Lorimer St; G to Metropolitan Ave. Mon–Thu 5pm–2am; Fri, Sat 5pm–4am; Sun 5pm–2am. Average main course: $15.* With a name that's German for "fat pig," this hipster barbecue draw goes straight for your inner glutton. Joe Carroll and Kim Barbour (Spuyten Duyvil) have refurbished a former auto body shop, and the driveway and cement floors are now packed with picnic tables. A self-service 'cue station features glistening cuts of beef, lamb and pork (there is no chicken here) by the pound. Stick to staples like tender baby back ribs with a hint of smoke and a light rub of espresso and brown sugar, and the less orthodox pastrami. The sides and desserts, unfortunately, leave something to be desired, but the bar makes up for it with an encyclopedic bourbon menu and ten tap beers available in gallon-size jugs.

Georgia's Eastside BBQ *192 Orchard St between Houston and Stanton Sts (212-253-6280).*

Subway: F, V to Lower East Side–Second Ave. Tue–Sat noon–11pm, Sun 3–10pm. Average main course: $13 Short-lived Café Trotsky has given way to yet another barbecue place. This one comes from Alan Natkiel (the General Store), who's put together a tiny space with ramshackle charm (mismatched wooden chairs, a counter made from salvaged wood) and meats that represent the namesake state's melting-pot 'cue philosophy. Look for dry-rubbed pork and chicken slathered in Natkiel's own spicy-sweet sauce.

Hill Country *30 W 26th St between Broadway and Sixth Ave (212-255-4544). Subway: N, R, W to 28th St. Mon–Thu 11:30am–11pm; Fri, Sat 11:30am–midnight; Sun 11:30am–11pm. Average pound of meat: $18.* The guys behind Hill Country are about as Texan as Bloomberg in a Stetson, but Queens-native Robbie Richter's cooking is an authentic, world-class take on the restaurant's namesake region, including sausage imported from Lockhart, Texas, barbecue stalwart Kreuz market and two options for brisket: Go for the "moist" (read: fatty) one—its luscious finish can last ten seconds on your tongue. Beef shoulder emerges from the smoker in 20-pound slabs, and show-stealing tips-on pork ribs are hefty, with just enough fat to imbue proper flavor. The excellent sides carry twists: Penne is baked with Gruyère, cheddar and fontina; deviled eggs have a hint of chipotle; while desserts, like jelly-filled cupcakes with peanut butter frosting, live out some kind of *Leave It to Beaver fantasy.* June Cleaver would probably not approve of the two dozen tequilas and bourbons, but they work especially well in this basement tavern with Texas cred.

R.U.B. *208 W 23rd St between Seventh and Eighth Aves (212-524-4300). Subway: C, E to 23rd St. Mon–Thu 11:30–11pm; Fri, Sat 11:30–midnight; Sun 11:30–10pm. Average main course: $16.* The name stands for "Righteous Urban Barbecue," and that's not all that's cocky about this 'cue joint. RUB takes no reservations and doesn't apologize for it—or for the paper plates and paper towels they call dishes and napkins. The message: Our barbecue is so good, nothing else matters. Paul Kirk, a seven-time world barbecue champion, is the man behind the mission, and while the grub ain't flawless by Kansas City Barbecue Society standards, less discerning eaters will find much to praise. Ribs are lean and tender, and the details are just right: Wonder Bread comes with each platter, and the slew of ever-important side dishes includes delicious baked beans studded with bits of brisket.

Sawa *617 Ninth Ave between 43rd and 44th Sts (212-757-0305). Subway: A, C, E to 42nd St–Port Authority. Mon–Fri 11am–10pm; Sat noon–10pm. Average main course: $15.* Nothing inside Sawa suggests barbecue. The squeaky-clean, white tile walls and bamboo kitchen door at this takeout spot look more like something out of a Japanese restaurant. And gas-fired ovens don't scream "low and slow." But owner Takashi Sawa, a Japanese-born meat maven, is serious about his barbecue. He's developed his own top-secret seasoning blend—a recipe that combines more than 20 spices—and serves traditional dishes like St. Louis ribs, BBQ chicken and Brunswick stew. His most unusual item: a country-style pork rib dish in which the meat is cut diagonally across the grain.

The Smoke Joint *2007 Eat Out Award, Critics' Pick: Best south-of-the-Mason-Dixon shout-out 87 South Elliott Pl between Fulton St and Lafayette Ave, Fort Greene, Brooklyn (718-797-1011). Subway: C to Lafayette Ave; G to Fulton St; B, M, Q, R to DeKalb Ave. Mon–Thu noon–10pm; Fri, Sat noon–11pm; Sun noon–10pm. Average main course: $15.* What sets this Fort Greene spot apart is its claim to offering "real New York barbecue." But partners Craig Samuel (City Hall) and Ben Grossman (Picholine, La Grenouille) don't really stray far from the four basic 'cue groups: ribs, chicken, brisket and pork. "Brooklyn wings" have plenty of smoky flavor, and the lean, slightly singed baby back ribs taste of hickory, mesquite and maple woods. The house sauces are especially addictive: Piquant "joint smoke" is cooked for six hours, and the vinegary "holla-peña" is made with sambal spice. The space sports a honky-tonk look, with a bright-orange paint job and enclosed porch.

Spanky's BBQ *127 W 43rd St between Broadway and Sixth Ave (212-302-9507). Subway: B, D, F, V to 42nd St– Bryant Park; 7 to Fifth Ave. Mon–Sat 11:30am–11:30pm, Sun 12:30pm–8pm. Average main course: $16.* It's tough to make barbecue in this town—and it's even tougher to do so a block away from Virgil's, one of the first restaurants in the city to serve passable 'cue. Like Virgil's, Spanky's is huge and raucous, if not quite as crowded as its competitor. Although the smoker (and cords of wood, stacked to the ceiling) are a focal point of the restaurant, the smoky flavor isn't evident in all the dishes. One definite winner is the St. Louis cut ribs (leaner than spareribs but fattier than baby backs), napped with a terrific spicy-sweet sauce. And the shredded pulled pork is moist and nicely vinegary. Sides, too, live up to the promise of a bona fide house of barbecue: corn bread stocked with kernels of corn and flecks of chive, and smooth, creamy cheese grits. Service is friendly, if somewhat spacey.

⊙**Texas Smokehouse BBQ and Bourbon Bar** *637 Second Ave between 34th and 35th Sts (212-679-0868). Subway: 6 to 23rd St. Mon–Sat noon–midnight; Sun noon–10pm. Average main course: $12.* Judging by the long lines at the 2007 barbecue fest in Madison Square Park, New Yorkers are desperate for more 'cue. Just a few blocks north of Blue Smoke, chef-owner John Lewis—who honed his skills in pits throughout Texas and Louisiana—brings the flavors of those regions, plus Kansas City and the Carolinas, to the table. To make his Texas-style beef ribs and brisket, Lewis dry-rubs meat with spices, then slow-cooks the stuff in the smoker, before finishing it on a grill. There's no need for sauce—unless you're talking about small-batch bourbon or beer.

★ **Virgil's Real BBQ** *152 W 44th St between Sixth Ave and Broadway (212-921-9494). Subway: B, D, F, V to 42nd St–Bryant Park; 7 to Fifth Ave. Mon 9am–11pm; Tue–Sat 9am–midnight; Sun 9am–11pm. Average main course: $18.* Even the most skeptical Southerners vouch for the barbecue here; Virgil's has some of the tastiest brisket, ribs and pulled pork north of the Mason-Dixon, all smoked over hickory, oak and fruitwoods. Portions are Texas-size, and your knife and fork are folded in a hand towel, not a white cloth napkin, in case things get messy at the trough. Cram in a slice of sweet-potato pie or a bowl of banana pudding and you'll be more than ready to put yourself out to pasture—in this case, nearby Times Square.

Belgian

See also: *French*

B. Café *240 E 75th St between Second and Third Aves (212-249-3300). Subway: 6 to 77th St. Mon–Fri 5–11pm, Sat 11:30am–11pm, Sun 11:30am–10pm. Average main course: $20.* A Belgian eatery can pretty much be judged by the quality of its beer, mussels and fries. This subterranean space makes the grade in all three. The menu focuses on classics, and so should you. A perfect meal consists of delicious Grimbergen brown ale served in a distinctive Chimay goblet, delectable Malay mussels (sweet and small) in a coconut-and-curry–scented broth, and meaty golden fries with chili aioli, mayonnaise and ketchup for dipping. The casual space—with its globe-shaped sconces and vaguely medieval plaster wall with coat-of-arms moldings—encourages lingering.

★ **Café de Bruxelles** *118 Greenwich Ave at 13th St (212-206-1830). Subway: A, C, E to 14th St; L to Eighth Ave. Mon–Thu noon–11:30pm; Fri, Sat noon–midnight; Sun noon–10:30pm. Average main course: $19.* In 1982, "Belgian restaurant" sounded like a joke. But the sophisticated menu, attentive service, impressive beer selection and unsurpassed *moules* here blazed a new trail. If you're dizzied by the selection, try the simplest mussels, *moules marinière*, steamed in a broth of onion, garlic and white wine (the frites, served on the side, are perfectly crisped). Other appealing choices include calf liver sautéed with bacon, rabbit with prunes, and veal sweetbreads with salsify. Finish with lemon tart or chocolate cake, or another of the 20 Belgian beers.

◐**F&B** *269 W 23rd St between Seventh and Eighth Aves (646-486-4441). Subway: C, E to 23rd St. Mon 11:30am–10pm; Tue–Fri 11:30am–11pm; Sat 11am–11pm; Sun 11:30am–10pm. Average main course: $7.* If you can get past the American-fast-food-chain look of the place (brushed-steel tables and chairs, picture menus above the register, a brigade of condiments), there is plenty of *güdt* food to be had here. You'll find frites and *beignets* on the menu (the F and B of this Eurocentric minichain), and the food is much more healthful than the decor suggests: The more than two dozen varieties of hot dogs are steamed and the faultlessly crisp, golden pommes frites (choose from regular or sweet potato) are cooked in trans-fat–free sunflower oil and paired with zesty dipping sauces like garlic aioli and sweet Thai chili. **Other location** *150 E 52nd St between Lexington and Third Aves (212-421-8600).*

Markt *676 Sixth Ave at 21st St (212-727-3314). Subway: C, E to 23st St. Mon–Fri 8am–midnight; Sat, Sun 10am–midnight. Average main course: $21.* Priced out of the Meatpacking District, this popular Belgian bar and restaurant moved north to Chelsea, re-creating the look and feel of the original in a smaller space. The high prices and mediocre food haven't kept the crowds at bay. The frites are limp and pale, and the pots of oversize mussels envelop the restaurant in a surprisingly unappetizing aroma. At least the beer—a fine selection of Belgian brews—arrives nicely chilled and in the appropriate logo-stamped glass.

Potato bed Tuck into the beef cheek *carbonnade* at Resto.

Petite Abeille *134 West Broadway between Duane and Thomas Sts (212-791-1360). Subway: A, C, 1, 2, 3 to Chambers St. Mon–Fri 7:30am–11pm; Sat, Sun 9am–11pm. Average main course: $16. Authentic* is not synonymous with *serious*. Check out the drawings of Tintin at this charming minichain that draws its name from another Continental cartoon favorite, the Little Bee. Locals keep coming back for fresh mussels (all you can eat for $15.95 on Wednesdays) and the three-course prix fixe ($18.95), offered weekdays from 5 to 7pm. Try the *vol-au-vent*, a chicken stew covered with a puff-pastry lid, or the croque-monsieur, made with cheddar cheese and red onion. At brunch, golden waffles topped with strawberries are authentic, serious fun. **Other locations** *466 Hudson St between Barrow and Grove Sts (212-741-6479)* ● *44 W 17th St between Fifth and Sixth Aves (212-604-9350)* ● *401 E 20th St at First Ave (212-727-1505).*

Resto *111 E 29th St between Park and Lexington Aves (212-685-5585). Subway: 6 to 28th St. Mon–Fri 4pm–1am; Sat 10:30am–1am; Sun 10:30am–10:30pm. Average main course: $19.* Belgian cuisine had its New York moment a few years back, but this pubby new restaurant signals a revival. The bare-bones dining room features a pressed-tin ceiling and a long bar where patrons sip from custom-logoed glassware, designed to accommodate specific artisanal brews. Chef Ryan Skeen (5 Ninth, Café Boulud) offers shareable plates that showcase an eclectic range of Belgian flavors. From the Dutch comes a tidy bowl of meatballs, and from the French, a cast-iron crock of *carbonnade*—tender caramelized beef cheeks slow-cooked in dark beer.

JEFF GURWIN

Brazilian

See also: *Argentine, Latin American, Peruvian, Portuguese*

Side show
Carne Vale offers more than great meat.

★**Buzina Pop** *1022A Lexington Ave at 73rd St (212-879-6190). Subway: 6 to 68th St. Daily 11am–11pm. Average main course: $26.* You never quite forget you're in an Upper East Side townhouse—the price of the caipirinhas won't let you. The menu adopts a markedly haute sensibility, using Brazilian ingredients to inspired effect. Thus, the tuna tartare appetizer arrives with foie gras in a piquant *cachaça*-molasses reduction, while hearts of palm garnish a delightful yellowtail ceviche. Salmon steak is complemented by a crisp *mandioquinha* (a root vegetable). As bossa nova struggles to dislodge technopop on the soundtrack, you may doubt how Brazilian Buzina Pop truly is, but when the Carmen Miranda—a caramelized banana tart dripping in syrup—arrives, you won't care.

Carne Vale *46 Ave B between 3rd and 4th Sts (212-777-4686). Subway: F, V to Lower East Side–Second Ave. Mon–Fri 5pm–midnight; Sat, Sun 11am–midnight. Prix fixe churrascaria: $35.* There's no telling when the ladies with the big headdresses and skimpy outfits will come out and strut their stuff—that's part of the charm (or shock) of this East Village Brazilian steakhouse. The big open space features large tables on the left, a long bar on the right and a runway-style stretch in the center. The food is exactly like that at other all-you-can-eat extravaganzas: There's a small salad bar with an assortment of pastas, veggies, cheeses and sliced meats, and an endless procession of chicken, lamb, steak and sausage. At $35, it may be the least expensive feeding frenzy you'll ever have.

★**Casa** *72 Bedford St at Commerce St (212-366-9410). Subway: 1 to Christopher St–Sheridan Sq. Mon–Sat 6pm–midnight. Average main course: $18.* Sure, you'll find *feijoada* and several trusty steak platters, but Casa is one of the few Brazilian restaurants in Manhattan to venture successfully into the regional cuisines of Bahia and Minas Gerais. A youthful crowd of Villagers dotted with expats fills the narrow, white-walled single room to sample the cheese bread and appetizers like the lime-infused *lula frita* (calamari). Entrées explore the entire country, but it's the Bahian stews cooked in palm oil—like the sultry *moqueca de frutos do mar* (seafood) and *xinxim de galinha* (chicken)—that underscore just how far you are from 46th Street's "Little Brazil."

▲◉**Churrascaria Girassol** *33-18 28th Ave between 33rd and 34th Sts, Astoria, Queens (718-545-8250). Subway: N, W to 30th Ave. Daily noon–11pm. Average main course: $12.* The area's growing Brazilian

Read 'em & eat

farofa: seasoned, fried yuca flour

feijoada: a traditional black-bean stew with pork, beef and sausage

moqueca: seafood stew

pão de queijo: cheese-stuffed bread balls

rodizio: an all-you-can-eat restaurant with an emphasis on skewered meat

TALIA SIMHI

community frequents this lunch counter and dining room. All-you-can-eat barbecued meats are limited to a few cuts, so order a Bohemia beer and sample the ample, long-simmered stews: tender, tomato-bathed "house-style" chicken or the massive *moqueca de peixe*—tilefish fillets in a coconut broth. *Feijoada* lovers may be disappointed; the black-bean base can be garlicky (in a good way), but the meat can be almost inedibly fatty. Creamy passion-fruit mousse or *doce de leite com coco* are as sweet as Sugarloaf.

★Delicia Brazil *322 W 11th St at Hudson St (212-242-2002). Subway: 1 to Christopher St–Sheridan Sq. Daily 6–11pm. Average main course: $16 ($29 all-you-can-eat prix fixe).* Brazilian nostalgia gets the dorm-room treatment at this subterranean spot, with exposed bulbs and walls covered with colorful beach towels, frayed posters and incongruous trinkets. With caipirinhas lacking bite and the waitstaff lacking luster, it's no small relief that the food is a success: appetizers of spicy *linguiça frita* (fried sausage) and puffy cheese rolls complement each other wonderfully; the *feijoada* comes in a pot that helps retain its garlicky piquancy; and the cilantro-inflected *muqueca de peixe ou camarao* teems with shrimp and swordfish. Grab a sidewalk table if weather—and service—permits.

Green Field Churrascaria *108-01 Northern Blvd at 108th St, Corona, Queens (718-672-5202). Subway: 7 to 111th St. Mon–Thu 11am–1am; Fri, Sat 11am–midnight; Sun 11am–11pm. All you can eat: $27.* Warning: Diners consuming all they can at this Queens *rodizio* are going to be treated to frequent waiter choruses of "Feliz Aniversário" (the windowed area at the front of the 500-seat meat emporium is quieter). The appetizer bar sags under tropical soups, a colorful display of exotic salads and *brasileiro* specialties like garlic-speckled chicken and *farofa*, fried yuca flour. The main event is a parade of skewered proteins: sirloin, rib eye, roast beef, pork, duck, rabbit, fennel-seeded sausage and chicken. Moist suckling pig and planked salmon make the rounds on carts, and you'll want seconds of juicy skirt steak and bacon-wrapped turkey.

★☺Malagueta *25-35 36th Ave at 28th St, Astoria, Queens (718-937-4821). Subway: N, W to 36th Ave. Tue–Thu 5–10pm; Fri 5–11pm; Sat 1–11pm; Sun 1–10pm. Average main course: $13.* Seductive little Brazilian eateries don't normally slip in under the cheapie wire. This Queens find is not only affordable, it's also a lively, fun spot, bustling with young Cariocas and Paulistas in low-slung jeans. Named for an Amazonian chili pepper, the place is, in a word, hot. Perfectly spiced appetizers include shrimp-topped pea fritters, and *linguiça* sausage served with yuca fries and delectable cilantro mayo. Hearty entrées follow, like *moqueca de camarao*, coconut-enriched shrimp and rice. Regulars come on Saturday for live samba and first-rate *feijoada*.

Porção Churrascaria *360 Park Ave South at 26th St (212-252-7080). Subway: 6 to 28th St. Mon–Thu noon–4pm, 5–11pm; Fri noon–midnight; Sat 2pm–midnight; Sun 1–10pm. Prix-fixe dinner: $50.90.* The fun at this Brazilian steakhouse begins when the drink cart rolls by. Snag a caipirinha, take all you want from the salad bar, and when you're ready, flip the chip that sits by your fork from red to green. Spit-wielding servers come flying out of the kitchen, proudly explaining what's so special about their skewers. The best meats? Sirloin and filet mignon. The meal comes to a close when the dessert cart rolls up. You'll like the green grapes covered in sweet condensed milk—if only because you probably can manage little more than fruit after this feast.

Sabor Tropical *36-18 30th Ave, Astoria, Queens (718-777-8506). Subway: N, W to 30th Ave. Mon–Thu, noon–10pm; Fri, Sat noon–11pm; Sun noon–10pm. $15.* In converting an Astoria diner into a Brazilian restaurant, the owners of Sabor Tropical did little more than slap on colorful murals of Rio's fabled beaches, but it's the food that draws the hood's growing expat community. Centered on Carioca and Paulista staples, the menu's divided into fish, shrimp, meat and poultry (read chicken) dishes. Standouts include the *fraldinha com palmito* (succulent skirt steak topped with tender palm hearts) and the *camarão com catupir* (baked shrimp drenched in tangy Catupiry cheese). *Feijoada* fanatics note: That dish is only available as a Saturday house special.

SUGARCANE *243 Park Ave South between 19th and 20th Sts (212-475-9377). Subway: 6 to 23rd St. Mon–Wed 4:30pm–1am; Thu–Sat 4:30pm–2am; Sun 4:30–midnight. Average small plate: $11.* Behind a low canopy of brushed-metal palm leaves, glowing red light illuminates this tunnellike space, which is essentially the lounge for next-door Sushi Samba (which shares the kitchen). In addition to the terrific rolls, fresh and complex ceviches work well with the extensive sake list. One superstar: wide, tender strips of yellowtail with slivers of tomato, mango, hot pepper and mint, dressed in a zingy lemongrass vinaigrette. Make sure someone orders the tea sugar-drops at dessert; the doughnutlike fritters, dusted in brown sugar and cinnamon, hide molten bittersweet chocolate. A gorgeous back room with sliding doors is available for private parties.

Precision cut
Porção Churrascaria has just what you want.

Brazilian

British/Irish

Bread winner
The burgers at Donovan's Pub are among the city's best.

▲◐**Atlantic Chip Shop** *129 Atlantic Ave between Clinton and Henry Sts, Cobble Hill, Brooklyn (718-855-7775). Subway: 2, 3, 4, 5 to Borough Hall. Mon–Thu noon–11pm; Fri noon–2am; Sat 11am–2am; Sun 11am–11pm. Average main course: $9.* Brooklynites know that a deep-fried Twinkie is much more than the sum of its parts. This English-Irish pub and restaurant, set in a 100-year-old building with tin ceilings, serves the same fish-and-chips, bangers and mash and other U.K. staples made famous at the original. Boozers will be happy to find 16 draught beers, bitters and ales, and various Scotches, bourbons and whiskeys. **Other location** *Chip Shop, 383 Fifth Ave at 6th St, Park Slope, Brooklyn (718-832-7701).*

◐**Ceol** *191 Smith St at Warren St, Carroll Gardens, Brooklyn (347-643-9911). Subway: F, G to Bergen St. Mon–Thu 5pm–2am, Fri 5pm–4am, Sat 11am–4am, Sun 11am–2am. Average main course: $12.* Just past this Irish pub's impressive (and well-peopled) mahogany bar, you'll find its homey dining room, replete with fireplace. But you may not find many diners here, which is a shame, since the dishes served are far tastier than typical pub grub. An appetizer of Irish spring rolls, stuffed with corned beef and cabbage offers a refreshing twist on the staple. The fish-and-chips entrée is blessedly, deliciously greasy, yet retains its crispiness even after cooling down. Post-meal, join the lively crowd at the bar and ask one of the Irish bartenders to pull you a proper Guinness.

◐**Donovan's Pub** *57-24 Roosevelt Ave at 58th St, Woodside, Queens (718-429-9339). Subway: 7 to Woodside–61st St. Mon–Thu 11am–11pm; Fri–Sat 11am–1am; Sun 11am–11pm. Average main course: $12.* You can order perfectly decent renditions of baked clams or buffalo wings in this dark, *Goodfellas*-esque Irish bar, only steps away from the overhead 7 line. But the real draw is NYC's finest burger (still): swimming in salty juices, peeking out of a soft bun, and hardly requiring condiments or cheese of any kind, only several napkins. It's a mantle of pride the pub wears lightly, with servers only asking the desired level of doneness (don't go higher than medium-rare) and the option of a slice of raw onion. From such humble beginnings: genius.

◐**St. Dymphna's** *118 St Marks Pl between Ave A and First Ave (212-254-6636). Subway: L to First Ave; 6 to Astor Pl. Daily 11am–4am. Average main course: $12.* It's hard to miss the cuisine theme at a candlelit pub that serves fish-and-chips in an Irish beer batter, fettucine with Irish smoked salmon, soup with a side of Irish brown bread and Baileys Irish Cream cheesecake. The rest of the menu balances standard pub grub—like beef-and-Guinness casserole, steak sandwiches and shepherd's pie—with gastropub twists, such as chili aioli and handmade garden burgers. Service hiccups are quickly forgotten when a waitress with a warm smile arrives with dessert, served with your choice of whipped cream, ice cream or custard.

Spike Hill *184 Bedford Ave between North 6th and 7th Sts, Williamsburg, Brooklyn (718-218-9737). Subway: L to Bedford Ave. Mon–Thu noon–2am; Fri noon–4am; Sat 11am–4am; Sun 11am–2am. Average main course: $13.* The effects of too many beers can always be tempered with a gut-busting meal—and you can put this theory to test at this laid-back Irish pub, where the pints are free-flowing and the grub is hard-core. The Irish Fry Up: black-and-white pudding (made with pork-blood sausage and pork), back rashers (strips of bacon cut from the back of the pig), house-made baked beans, home fries, Guinness bread, grilled tomatoes and, in case you didn't get enough meat, Irish sausage. The fish-and-chips is a bundle of fries and cumin coleslaw with extracrisp, *panko*-crusted black cod. If you need some greens, those are going to be spiked too: The mixed-green salad comes with Guinness croutons.

◐**Tea & Sympathy** *108–110 Greenwich Ave between 12th and 13th Sts (212-989-9735). Subway: 1, 2, 3 to 14th St. Mon–Fri 11:30am–10:30pm; Sat 9:30am–10:30pm; Sun 9:30am–10pm. Average main course: $12.* You'll get excellent tea at this tiny, tightly packed British emporium, but the waitresses are usually saucy rather than sympathetic. The menu is food for homesick Brits: shepherd's pie, bangers and mash, Cornish pasties, and a Sunday dinner of roast beef and Yorkshire pudding. Of course, you must try the classic afternoon tea, a $20 spread that includes a fresh pot, finger sandwiches, cakes and scones with clotted cream and jam.

KRISTY MAY

Cafés and diners

See also: *American, French, Italian*

Instant gratification
Pick up just-made chocolate at Jacques Torres.

★ ▲**Alice's Tea Cup** *102 W 73rd St at Columbus Ave (212-799-3006). Subway: B, C, 1, 2, 3 to 72nd St. Daily 8am–8pm. Average sandwich: $10.* Wander into this sequestered basement and you'll be transported to a story land inspired by Lewis Carroll. First, pass through the quirky gift-boutique-cum-bakeshop, where you can browse Wonderland–themed knickknacks along with dense, delicious scones and muffins. Proceed farther in (not easy on weekends) and you'll discover a sweet room serving big brunch plates (sandwiches, salads, eggs) and the full teatime monty ($25). It's a fairy tale indeed, except for the service, which can be slow. **Other locations** ● *Alice's Tea Cup Chapter II 156 E 64th Street between Third and Lexington Aves (212-486-9200)* ● *220 E 81st St between Second and Third Aves (212-734-4832).*

◉**Almondine** *85 Water St between Main and Dock Sts, Dumbo, Brooklyn (718-797-5026). Subway: A, C to High St. Mon–Thu 7am–7pm; Fri 7am–9pm; Sat 7am–7pm; Sun 10am–6pm. Average pastry: $3.* Jacques Torres expanded a weekend Dumbo phenomenon into a weeklong gold mine. French pastries, once sold only on Saturday mornings at his Water Street chocolate shop, are the main event across the street. In addition to Gallic staples like croissants, brioches and tarts, Almondine serves American-inspired sweets like cheesecake, strawberry shortcake and chocolate blackout cake with peanut butter.

Arium *31 Little West 12th St between Ninth Ave and Washington St (212-463-8630). Subway: A, C, E to 14th St. Tue–Sat 12–9pm; Sun 11am–6pm; tea service Tue–Sun 3–6pm. Average main course: $14; prix-fixe tea ($14–$42).* The fanciful aesthetics of this salon/gallery/café primes you for a beautifully presented but ultimately fussy

meal in which appearances sometimes upstage execution. Lunch is a mostly organic selection of New American items like Asian Smoked Trout Salad, heavy on the greens, or a beef brisket sandwich, whose promises of pickled cabbage and cherry marmalade prove moot, buried as they are by the oversauced brisket. Instead, come for afternoon tea to sample delicacies from Richard Guier (former pastry chef at Ixta, Vox, Lot 61), such as scones with lemon curd and clotted cream; cucumber sandwiches and goat-cheese tarts; and white and dark chocolate biscotti accompanied by one of the 90 teas. Brewed rarities include a black tea from the oldest organic garden in India and China's White Peony, picked two days of the year only.

◉**Big Booty Bread Co** *216 W 23rd St between Seventh and Eighth Aves (212-414-3056). Subway: C, E, 1 to 23rd St. 8am–9pm. Average bun: $1.75.* This Latin-influenced bakery sells heaven in a bun—something called a "booty bun," to be exact. It's hard to resist this signature offering: brioche-like sweet bread filled with a choice of dulce de leche, Nutella or guava. A savory version subs a cheese filling, though we prefer its sturdier cousin: the cheese rock, a dense, fist-size ball made with yuca flour. Heartier offerings include beef and chicken empanadas, and delicious little corn cakes that look like flattened arepas. If you want something more familiar, grilled sandwiches—known as "booty-press specials"—include two sweet fillings (your choice of guava jelly or bananas and fluff) hot-pressed between thick slices of homemade bread.

◉**Big Daddy's Diner** *239 Park Ave South between 19th and 20th Sts (212-477-1500). Subway: 6 to 23rd St. Mon–Wed 7am–midnight; Thu 7am–2am; Fri,*

Sat 24 hours; Sun 7am–midnight. Average main course: $11. The beauty of dining in a diner is that you usually don't have to wait for a table, and your grub typically arrives within moments of ordering it. Big Daddy's has all the requisites of a hokey greasy spoon—a bright neon sign; faux-retro Formica tables and comfy booths—but it hasn't quite figured out the pacing in the kitchen: We had to wait 35 minutes for a BLT and poached eggs. It's a good thing substance trumps service. Blue-plate specials are the best way to go: You'll find yourself elbow-deep in heaps of crisp fries, fat grilled sandwiches and pancakes so big they hang over the side of the plate (breakfast is available anytime). Plus, Big Daddy serves some of the best fried chicken in the five boroughs. It's all delicious stuff, but it may not be worth the wait.

Bourgeois Pig 122 E 7th St between First Ave and Ave A+ west location) (212-475-2246). Subway: F, V to Lower East Side–Second Ave; 6 to Astor Pl. Mon–Fri 7am–midnight; Sat, Sun 9am–midnight. Average fondue: $18. There's nothing bourgeois about the industrial metal steps down to this Greenwich Village wine-and-fondue spot. But inside, ornate mirrors and antique chairs give the tiny red-lit space a decidedly decadent feel. Trendy locals snack on tasty bruschette or bubbling cheese fondue—the raclette is extremely good—served with heaps of assorted breads, crudités and fresh fruit for dipping. The brief wine list is well chosen and prices are halved during the daily happy hour (4–7pm) and all night on Mondays and Tuesdays. At those prices, it's easy to make a pig of yourself. **Other location** The Bourgeois Pig West, 124 MacDougal St between W 3rd and Bleecker Sts (212-254-0575).

Burke in the Box, Burke Bar Café 1150 E 59th St between Lexington and Third Aves (212-705-3800). Subway: N, R, W to Lexington Ave–59th St; 4, 5, 6 to 59th St. Daily 9am–8:30pm. Average main course (takeout): $12. Average main course (café): $19. Chanel No. 5 or Smoked Bacon bottled flavor spray? Such are the options at Bloomie's now that chef David Burke runs two eateries in the midtown department store. Adventurous shoppers can try them both: At Burke in the Box, the celebrity chef is serving inventive takeout grub like chicken dumplings with coffee barbecue sauce, sexed-up chicken salad with apples, raisins and tarragon and French fries with truffle oil and asiago. At Burke Bar Café, the more elegant spot, he offers breakfast, lunch and a prix-fixe menu in the evenings.

★ **Caffe Falai** 2007 Eat Out Award, Critics' Pick: Best jack-of-all-trades 265 Lafayette St between Prince and Spring Sts (917-338-6207). Subway: B, D, F, V to Broadway–Lafayette St; N, R to Prince St; 6 to Bleecker St. Mon–Thu 7am–10:30pm; Fri 7am–11pm; Sat 8am–11pm; Sun 8am–10:30pm. Average main course: $12. Iacopo Falai's third downtown outpost melds this former pastry chef's diverse skills: The place is at once a restaurant, a bakery, a café and a panini shop. Daytime idlers linger over well-executed cappuccinos, flaky house-baked croissants, and, at lunchtime, crusty panini oozing with fillings like fontina and speck. From the tiny open kitchen come heartier offerings (at half the price the chef charges at Falai), like charred baby-octopus nuggets tossed onto slices of roasted potato, or potato tortelli with sweet bolognese. Artful desserts, including a citrus-and-strawberry bombe, are plucked from the display case up front. **Other locations** Falai, 68 Clinton St between Rivington and Stanton Sts (212-253-1960) • Falai Panetteria, 79 Clinton St at Rivington St (212-777-8956).

○**Cha-An Tea Room** 230 East 9th St between Second and Third Aves (212-228-8030). Subway: L to Third Ave; N, R to 8th St–NYU; 6 to Astor Place. Mon–Thu 2–11pm; Fri, Sat noon–midnight; Sun noon–10pm. Prix-fixe tea: $15. You have to climb a flight of stairs and peek behind a curtain to find this tranquil teahouse, which offers a succession of deftly crafted plates accompanied by a thoughtful list of teas and sake. Each night features two special "sets" that take you from an amuse-bouche like creamy soy-milk quiche through a selection of tiny bites (pickled eggplant, marinated lotus root) to entrées such as tea-smoked salmon with sliced radish, Dijon mustard and tarragon. It's a great escape from the East Village crowds.

○**Cheyenne Diner** 411 Ninth Ave at 33rd St (212-465-8750). Subway: A, C, E to 34th St–Penn Station. Daily 24hrs. Average main course: $9. Slouched behind the General Post Office and around the corner from the Midtown South police station, the Cheyenne diner is within stun-gun distance of mobs of hungry public servants. The diner food (bison burgers, club sandwiches, omelettes, etc.) may be unremarkable, but it doesn't make anyone skip their lunch hour. Established in 1922, the Cheyenne is the quintessential diner—Naugahyde booths, counter seating, pies behind glass, syrup pumps, fast service and, most important, grease. It's been featured in countless films and advertisements, making it only appropriate that head shots of showbiz luminaries such as Fred "Rerun" Berry and some guy named Hugh Grant hang above the register.

★ **ChikaLicious** 203 E 10th St between First and Second Aves (212-995-9511). Subway: L to Third Ave; 6 to Astor Pl. Wed–Fri 3–5pm, 7–10:45pm; Sat, Sun 3–10:45pm.. Dessert prix fixe: $12. Pastry Chef Chika Tillman, the chick with a whisk, gives diners a voyeuristic thrill as she preps, pipes and plates her desserts in expert fashion. A multicourse "meal" may include an amuse-bouche such as coconut sorbet in a little pool of chocolate-infused tea gelée. The main course might be a warm chocolate tart with pink-peppercorn ice cream, a mocha-and-hazelnut trifle or a delicious fromage blanc cheesecake. It all ends with darling petit fours.

○**Chocolate Haven** 350 Hudson St at King St (212-414-2462). Subway: 1 to Houston St. Mon–Sat 9am–7pm; Sun 10am–6pm. Average chocolate: $1. Legendary chocolatier Jacques Torres's most irresistible creation yet is this 8,000-square-foot factory that serves as the Manhattan hub for the pastry chef's chocolate empire. The space features a cocoa-pod–shaped café overlooking the candy-making facilities, so visitors can sip hot chocolate and watch as cocoa beans are transformed into chocolate bars. A terra-cotta statue of the Aztec cocoa god, Quetzalcoatl, greets customers as they enter. Chances are, you'll be praying to the deity for mercy when you overdo it yet again.

○**The Chocolate Room** 86 Fifth Avenue between St. Mark's Ave and Warren St, Park Slope, Brooklyn (718-783-2900). Subway: B, Q to Seventh Ave; 2, 3 to Bergen St. Tue–Thu noon–11pm; Fri, Sat noon–midnight; Sun noon–11pm. Average dessert: $7. This dessert café and chocolate shop is the perfect place to park your rear (and maybe inadvertently expand it): The relentlessly chocolatey desserts, such as a truly sublime brownie piled high with generous scoops of house-made mint chocolate-chip ice cream and smothered in bittersweet hot fudge (whipped cream and a teetering cherry on top), change with the season. Dip into chocolate

Cash and carry
Burke in the Box prepares inventive eats to go.

Cafés and diners

fondue, sip hot chocolate, or just pound some truffles if you desire. A glass of wine will make you forget whatever damage you've done.

★ ▲**City Bakery** *3 W 18th St between Fifth and Sixth Aves (212-366-1414). Subway: L, N, Q, R, W, 4, 5, 6 to 14th St–Union Sq. Mon–Fri 7:30am–7pm; Sat 7:30am–6pm; Sun 9am–5pm. Salad bar: $12 per pound.* Pastry genius Maury Rubin's loft-size City Bakery is jammed with Chelsea shoppers loading up on unusual salad-bar choices (grilled pineapple with ancho chili, bean sprouts with smoked tofu, excellent salmon salad). There's also a small selection of soups, pizzas and hot dishes. But to heck with all that: The thick, incredibly rich hot chocolate with fat house-made marshmallows is heaven in a cup (replaced by fruit-infused lemonade in the summer), and the moist "melted" chocolate-chip cookies are better than a marked-down pair of Prada pumps.

★ ▲**Clinton Street Baking Company & Restaurant** *4 Clinton St between Houston and Stanton Sts (646-602-6263). Subway: F to Delancey St; J, M, Z to Delancey–Essex Sts. Mon–Fri 8am–4pm, 6pm–11pm; Sat 10am–4pm, 6–11pm; Sun 10am–4pm. Average main course: $13.* The warm buttermilk biscuits and fluffy plate-size pancakes at this pioneering little eatery are reason enough to face the brunchtime crowds. If you want to avoid the onslaught, the homey LES spot is just as reliable at lunch and dinner, when locals drop in for fish tacos and a daily $10 beer-and-burger special from 6 to 8pm: eight ounces of Black Angus topped with Swiss cheese and caramelized onions, served with a Brooklyn Lager. Luckily, the blueberry pancakes are on the menu day and night.

◉**Cocoa Bar** *228 Seventh Ave between 3rd and 4th Sts, Park Slope, Brooklyn (718-499-4080). Subway: F to Seventh Ave. Mon–Wed 8am–midnight; Thu–Sat 8am–2am; Sun 8am–midnight. Average dessert: $6.* Husband-and-wife team Liat Cohen and Yaniv Reeis have turned their three favorite things—chocolate, coffee and wine—into a lifestyle at this luxe Park Slope café. You can drop in for early-morning coffee drinks and chocolaty breakfast treats (like chocolate-chip challah); at night, the place becomes a bar offering 40 wines paired with decadent chocolate desserts or rich Belgian confections. You can sample new flavors at occasional chocolate and wine tastings or get yourself hooked on the signature drink: a "chocolatte" (espresso, steamed milk and pure melted chocolate). Assuming you're not too stimulated to focus, you can log on to free Wi-Fi, too. **Other location** *21 Clinton St between Houston and Stanton Sts (212-677-7417).*

▲**Coffee Shop** *29 Union Sq West at 16th St (212-243-7969). Subway: L, N, Q, R, W, 4, 5, 6 to 14th St–Union Sq. Mon 7am–2am; Tue–Sat 7am–6am; Sun 7am–2am. Average main course: $11.* Its heyday is past, but crowds still flock to this converted diner, perhaps because its sidewalk seating still makes for good people-watching and caipirinha sipping. The tropical drinks are refreshing and there's still evidence of a gaudy past: The retro glass-and-metal facade, neon sign and ludicrously superfluous velvet rope reflect the joint's early-'90s glory. The menu boasts Brazilian flavah, but a few dishes prove to be less interesting than described (grilled salmon, for example, comes drenched in mango puree). Sounder alternatives are the paella, rib-eye steak, raw-bar selections and numerous salads. Just imagine how many models have planted their Brazilian-waxed bottoms in your seat.

◉**Dizzy's** *511 9th St at Eighth Ave, Park Slope, Brooklyn (718-499-1966). Subway: F to Seventh Ave. Mon–Fri 7am–10pm; Sat, Sun 9am–4pm, 6–10pm. Average main course: $11.* This self-proclaimed "finer diner," all red vinyl and chrome, is a Slope fave. Carry-you-back dinners include bacon-wrapped meat loaf and Rice Krispies–topped mac and cheese. Weekend brunch brings fabulous indulgences such as cream-cheese flapjacks and chocolate-stuffed French toast, along with the usual breakfast mainstays.

◉**Egg** *135A North 5th St at Bedford St, Williamsburg, Brooklyn (718-302-5151). Subway: L to Bedford Ave. Mon–Fri 7am–noon; Sat, Sun 8am–noon. Average main course: $6.* This Southern-accented breakfast-only abode has no parallel. Mismatched chairs sit in front of paper-covered tables. The waitresses play old-time folk music on the sound system and serve a cheap meal that may include eggs Rothko (a slice of brioche with a hole in the middle that accommodates a sunny-side-up egg, all of which is covered with sharp cheddar) and a terrific country-ham-biscuit sandwich. If you must have dessert at breakfast, finish with caramelized grapefruit and mint.

Empire Diner *210 Tenth Ave at 22nd St (212-243-2736). Subway: C, E to 23rd St. Daily 24hrs. Average main course: $13.* It's 3am—do you know where your middle-of-the-night grub is? This Fodero-style diner is a longtime Chelsea fave. It looks like a classic— gleaming stainless-steel walls and rotating stools—but few other hash houses have candlelight, sidewalk café tables and a pianist playing dinner music. Fewer still

CINZIA REALE-CASTELLO

attempt dishes such as sesame noodles with chicken, and linguine with smoked salmon, watercress and garlic. The more standard platters are terrific—like a juicy blue-cheese steak burger—and desserts live up to diner standards, especially a thick, chocolate pudding.

⊖**Financier Patisserie** 62 Stone St between Hanover Sq and Mill Lane (212-344-5600). Subway: 2, 3 to Wall Street. Mon–Fri 7am–9pm, Sat 9am–5:30pm. Average sandwich: $7.
Tucked down a cobblestone street, this sweet gem with lemon mousse-colored walls offers tasty café fare to office workers, tourists and locals seeking a pleasant alternative to the Financial District's ubiquitous pubs and delis. Savory items, including hot pressed sandwiches (try the croque-monsiuer), fresh salads, tarts and quiches are all delicious. But the pastries are where Financier excels, including classic Éclairs, Opera cake, St. Honoré, Paris Brest—and miniature financiers, which are complementary with each coffee. **Other locations** 35 Cedar St at William St (212-952-3838) ● 3-4 World Financial Center (212-786-3220).

▲**Gold St** 2 Gold St between Maiden Ln and Platt St (212-747-0797). Subway: A, C to Broadway–Nassau; 4, 5 to Fulton St. Daily 24 hrs. Average main course: $14.
The neon-lit spot, with Formica tabletops in French's-mustard yellow, is the latest from father-son team Harry and Peter Poulakakos (Harry's Café & Steak, Ulysses). The eatery does brisk business at lunch, but caters its dinner service to the area's crush of new residents. In the spirit of convenience, Gold St strives to offer whatever it is you're craving. There are kobe sliders made with American Wagyu, Momofuku-style pork buns and even a full sushi bar with pristine raw fish. Though service can be slow, even poor, but if you live upstairs or around the corner, this place could easily become your daily canteen.

⊖**Hinsch's Confectionery** 8518 Fifth Ave between 85th and 86th Sts, Bay Ridge, Brooklyn (718-748-2854). Subway: R to 86th St. Mon–Sat 8am–7:30pm; Sun 10am–5pm. Average main course: $8.
Hinsch's is an almost perfectly preserved piece of old Brooklyn, right down to the candy-filled windows shaded by a retractable green-canvas awning. This soda fountain–luncheonette still makes its own ice cream and chocolates. In addition to old-time fountain favorites, there's some serious griddle action: Denver omelettes, burgers and carved-to-order sandwiches. Although the pancakes stop flapping at 11am, the waffle iron never grows cold. And the shelves are well stocked with freshly made, giant chocolate Santas and Easter bunnies.

★ ⊖**Jacques Torres** 66 Water St at Main St, Dumbo, Brooklyn (718-875-9772). Subway: F to York St. Mon–Wed 9am–7pm; Thu 9am–8pm; Fri, Sat 9am–7pm; Sun 10am–6pm. Average chocolate: $1.
The only thing that beats a decadent piece of chocolate is one that comes fresh off the conveyor belt. Indulge in choc-master Jacques Torres's otherworldly delights at his shop and chocolate factory in Dumbo. If you'd rather sip your chocolate than munch on it, indulge in the famously suave, rich hot chocolate.

Junior's Restaurant 386 Flatbush Ave at DeKalb Ave, Downtown, Brooklyn (718-852-5257). Subway: M, N, Q, R to DeKalb Ave. Mon–Thu 6:30am–midnight; Fri, Sat 6:30am–1am; Sun 6:30am–midnight. Average main course: $12.
Brooklyn may be filling up with flashy eateries, but Junior's is still the lord of Flatbush. Its neon sign has illuminated this corner of DeKalb Avenue since 1950. The institution remains the same, for better or worse. For better: Customers are greeted with bowls of vinegary coleslaw, pickles and beets, and trays of caraway-studded onion rolls—all gratis. Deli sandwiches are pure Jackie Gleason: comically oversized and irresistible. At breakfast you can get what may be the city's best corned-beef hash, and servers are eager to please. For worse: Some dishes fell short, like an unnaturally yellow, overly salty matzo-ball soup. But you know what to order for dessert—Junior's made its name on cheesecake, prepared nine different ways. Get a whole one to go from the adjacent bakery. **Other locations** Junior's Restaurant/Bakery, Grand Central Terminal, Lower Concourse near track 36, 42nd St at Park Ave (212-692-9800; 212-983-5257) ● 1515 Broadway at 44th St (212-302-2000).

★ ▲⊖**Kyotofu** 2007 Eat Out Award, Critics' Pick: Best soy-based sugar rush 705 Ninth Ave between 48th and 49th Sts (212-974-6012). Subway: A, C, E to 42nd St–Port Authority. Tue, Wed, Thu noon–12:30am; Fri, Sat noon–1:30am; Sun noon–12:30am. Average dessert: $9.
Dining at this Japanese, dessert-driven eatery can be surreal. Ritsuko Yamaguchi (Daniel) combines French technique with Japanese ingredients, swapping out milk and cream for a preponderance of tofu in dishes like a large shot glass filled with black sugar syrup and silky tofu—the perfect eggless crème caramel. A miniature sampler features tofu cheesecake and tofu rice pudding (both luscious and creamy), and a fine molten chestnut-chocolate cake. If you're looking for more than a sugary fix, you can cobble together a full-blown meal from the selection of appetizer-like bites: fresh, creamy tofu with

Cover me
The Tea Box is a zen den in midtown.

Design sweet
Ritsuko Yamaguchi
creates Japanese
treats using French
technique at Kyotofu.

JEFF GURWIN

sweet and salty dipping sauces; nutty black edamame; gently spiced miniature rice balls and fluffy chicken-and-tofu meatballs. If they don't fully sate your hunger, the cube of peach *yokan* (red bean-paste jelly) that comes with the bill should finish the job.

▲**Lady Mendl's** *The Inn at Irving Place, 56 Irving Pl between 17th and 18th Sts (212-533-4466). Subway: L, N, Q, R, W, 4, 5, 6 to 14th St–Union Sq. Wed–Fri 3, 5pm seatings; Sat, Sun 2, 4:30pm seatings. Prix fixe: $35.* Inspired by Elsie de Wolfe, famed socialite and former neighbor of 56 Irving Place, the rooms of this brownstone (an inn since 1994) are decorated in parlor pinks, soft greens and florals, with antiques tucked into every corner. The fancy five-course tea service begins with a mixed-greens salad, followed by a sampling of tea sandwiches (standard cucumber as well as salmon with cream cheese, and goat cheese with sun-dried tomato). Then come the scones with raspberry preserves and clotted cream, cookies, cakes and dainty petit fours. It's all accompanied by a pot of tea, naturally, or you can opt for a demurely rebellious concoction (gin, grapefruit juice and Cointreau) called the Pink Lady.

◒**Lexington Candy Shop** *1226 Lexington Ave at 83rd St (212-288-0057). Subway: 4, 5, 6 to 86th St. Mon–Sat 7am–7pm; Sun 9am–6pm. Average main course: $9.* You won't find much candy for sale at Lexington Candy Shop. Instead, you'll find a wonderfully preserved retro diner, its long counter lined with chatty locals on their lunch hours, digging into gigantic chocolate malteds or peanut butter–and–bacon sandwiches. They even make lime rickeys. The shop was founded in 1925 and has appeared in numerous commercials, as well as the 1975 Robert Redford movie *Three Days of the Condor.*

★ **Little Giant** *85 Orchard St at Broome St (212-226-5047). Subway: F to Delancey St; J, M, Z to Delancey–Essex Sts. Mon–Thu 11am–3pm, 6–11pm; Fri 11am–3pm, 6pm–midnight; Sat 11am–4pm, 6pm–midnight; Sun 11am–4pm, 6–10pm. Average main course: $20.* If kids ran the restaurant business, we might have a few more endearing eateries like Little Giant. This is a place where milk shakes get as much attention as main courses, and where you can fill up on pickles before your meal, then decide to eat nothing but cheese. Feel free to tuck your feet under your legs at the cushioned banquettes (all the blond-wood furniture was constructed, Lego-style, by an owner's brother) while you contemplate how much pork you can handle in one night. Mac and cheese with applewood-smoked bacon? Sure. "Swine of the week"? Definitely. For dessert, warm, freshly baked cookies come with a glass of liqueur-spiked milk.

Marquet Pâtisserie *15 E 12th St between Fifth Ave and University Pl (212-229-9313). Subway: L, N, Q, R, W, 4, 5, 6 to 14th St–Union Sq. Mon 7:30am–6pm; Tue–Sat 7:30am–10pm; Sun 9am–4pm. Average main course: $18.* Perfect slices of house-made country bread appear at your table between courses, proving that a rustic-looking patisserie can have a sophisticated kitchen. A heaping helping of steamed mussels is accompanied by a creamy citrus sauce for dunking. The rack of lamb, with a surprisingly sweet side of grilled autumn squash, comes au jus. The extensive pastry selection will tempt you, but zero in on the bread pudding with bananas flambé.

★ ◒**Mudspot** *307 E 9th St between First and Second Aves (212-288-9074). Subway: L to First Ave; 6 to Astor Pl. Mon–Fri 7:30am–midnight; Sat, Sun 8am–midnight. Average small plate: $6.* Nina and Greg Northrop started selling coffee out of mobile Mud Trucks a few years ago because they were low on cash. After their truck became a runaway success, they opened the stationary Mudspot. In addition to joe, you'll find a free-form menu of panini and tapas, as well as a selection of beer and wine.

◒**Mule Café and Wine Bar** *67 Fourth Ave between Bergen St and St. Marks Pl, Park Slope, Brooklyn (718-766-8510). Subway: M, R to Union St; 2, 3 to Bergen St. Daily 7am–7pm. Average coffee: $1.50.* Park Slope has plenty of coffeehouses, but no notable caffeine pit stops on auto-garage row—the rapidly gentrifying Fourth Avenue. Hil Sherman found a video store on the strip that had been closed for 15 years and reinvented it as Mule Café and Wine Bar, a bright, rustic refuge. Handsomely lacquered floors lead to a backyard with a boat-size picnic table big enough for 20. In addition to java, he's serving croissants from Soho patisserie Ceci-Cela and muffins made at Park Slope's Two Little Red Hens bakery. Oil lubes remain across the street.

P*ong *150 W 10th St at Waverly Pl (212-929-0898). Subway: A, C, E, B, D, F, V to W 4th St. Tue–Thu 5:30pm–midnight; Fri, Sat 11am–4pm, 5:30pm–1am; Sun 11am–4pm, 5:30pm–11pm. Average dessert: $15; Ten-course tasting menu: $59.* Unlike dessert-only spots that stick to all things sugary, pastry whiz Pichet Ong (Spice Market, 66) brings a sweet worldview to savory eats at his tiny, mod perch. Expect flavor-straddling specialties like *burrata* cheese with paddlefish caviar and lemon olive oil—that same ingredient finds its way into the olive-oil pound-cake finale, served with strawberries and *miso* ice cream.

▲◒**Palacinka** *28 Grand St between Sixth Ave and Thompson St (212-625-0362). Subway: A, C, E, 1 to Canal St. Daily 10:30am–midnight. Average crêpe: $8.* During the day, this downtown café is filled with gorgeous natural light; in the evening, Palacinka, which is Slavic for *crêpe,* gets an intimate glow from candlelight reflecting off the pressed-tin ceiling and tiny metal tables. The thin flapjacks—made with buckwheat flour for savory fillings and white flour for sweet—come in combinations both classic (spinach and garlic) and novel (tiger shrimp, black-bean paste and basil crème fraîche). Large sandwiches, like the tarragon chicken panino with goat cheese and red peppers, and a savory brunch menu are tasty enough to lure diners past the pancakes.

▲◒**Panino'teca 275** *275 Smith St between DeGraw and Sackett Sts, Carroll Gardens, Brooklyn (718-237-2728). Subway: F, G to Carroll St. Tue, Wed 5:30pm–11pm; Thu 5:30pm–2am; Fri 5:30pm–4am; Sat 11am–4pm, 5:30pm–4am; Sun 11am–4pm, 5:30pm–11pm. Average main course: $9.* The well-made, toasty pressed sandwiches prepared here remain consistently pleasing and come in a long list of inventive combinations: Green apples give Genoa salami and soft Gorgonzola a lively zing; red peppers with olive paste and Asiago cheese layer perfectly on hot white Pullman bread. The pretty garden—deep and lush, set off by a bright-red wood fence—adds seating for 70 diners.

◒**Picnic Market and Cafe** *2665 Broadway between 101st and 102nd Sts (212-222-8222). Subway: 1 to 103 St. Daily 8:30am–11:30pm. Average main course: $20.* Gallic-inspired goodies are sold "to go" for alfresco enjoyment or can be savored tableside in the sunny café. Chef Jean-Luc Kieffer and wife Jennifer Rau keep recipes simple and flavors bright, such as a calamari salad with daikon, cucumber and sesame oil. Extensive charcuterie, cheese and fish plates are heartier options, and dinner entrées include coq au vin, steak au poivre, frites and a succulent pan-seared duck breast imbued with orange and star anise.

★ ▲**Podunk** *231 E 5th St between Second and Third Aves (212-677-7722). Subway: F to Lower East Side–Second Ave; 6 to Astor Pl. Tue–Sun 11am–9pm. Average pastry: $4..* Step through the creaky screened door and out of Manhattan. In her round granny glasses and bandana, Elspeth, the Minnesotan owner, brings a mellow rural vibe to her knickknacked tea shop. She offers more than 85 types of tea (try spicy ginger-verbena or iced strawberry-hibiscus); and 22 "informal tea meals" featuring freshly baked vanilla cupcakes, lemon-ginger cookies and cranberry-pecan scones. While away the afternoon in an Adirondack chair or gather a dozen of your best friends for a private tea party.

⊘**Prime Burger** *5 E 51st St between Madison and Fifth Aves (212-759-4729). Subway: E, V to Fifth Ave–53rd St. Mon–Fri 6am–7pm; Sat 6am–5pm. Average main course: $7.* If shopping at nearby Saks has sapped your savings, behold Prime Burger, the venerable coffeeshop with a 1960s wood-paneled interior, swing-tray seats and $4.25 burgers. The plump quarter-pound patty is flame broiled and served on a toasted sesame-seed bun, and the fries are long blond beauties. Don't exercise moderation here; make sure there's room in your belly for a slice of one of Eddie Adams's homemade pies. The 86-year-old pastry whiz has been whipping up flaky delights (apple, cherry, sweet potato, peach and more) on site for nearly 60 years.

⊘**Sammy's Donut Shop** *453–461 Sixth Ave at 11th St (212-924-6688). Subway: F, V to 14th St; L to Sixth Ave. Daily 11am–11:30pm. Average donut: 70¢.* Chinese food and donuts don't necessarily make sense together, but as we all learned from *Green Eggs and Ham*, that's no reason to rule out the combo. Sammy's Chinese Noodle Shop on Sixth Avenue has a next-door sibling, Sammy's Donut Shop, where a fresh selection of fried beauties shows up every morning: powdered-sugar–dusted and raspberry-filled, Boston cream, toasted-coconut–covered—all best consumed with a cup of dark Dallis Brothers coffee. The quasi–health-conscious might prefer lightly glazed whole-wheat donuts with a cup of hand-bagged tisanes (herbal tea), Tiger Spice chai or *coco loco*, a sweet infusion of vanilla, chocolate and rooibos tea.

⊘**Sullivan Diner** *169 Sullivan St at W Houston St (212-228-6091). Subway: 1 to Houston St. Mon–Thu 8am–11pm; Fri 8am–midnight; Sat 9am–midnight; Sun 9am–11pm. Average main course: $8.* The Sullivan Diner has retro-sleek decor, and the menu carries dishes from the Netherlands (the place was formerly called NL and has kept the Dutch pancakes intact). The space is filled with bright-orange banquettes, and for the most part, the food doesn't tread any foreign territory—you'll find matzo-ball soup, mac and cheese—but it's all good, and prices are ridiculously low for the neighborhood. The best meal is breakfast, served until 4pm daily.

▲**The Tea Box at Takashimaya** *693 Fifth Ave between 54th and 55th Sts (212-350-0180). Subway: E, V to Fifth Ave– 53rd St. Mon–Sat 11:30am–5:30pm. Bento box: $18.* Sleek banquettes and brushed-steel walls create an oasis for power shoppers and lunching ladies.

One starter consists of three shot glasses, each filled with a colorful soup. Most patrons prefer the daily bento special, which may feature seared ginger-soy scallops with stewed eggplant or chicken tempura with curried cauliflower and tea-infused sticky rice. Come for afternoon tea (Monday through Saturday from 3 to 5:30pm) and pair a pot of one of 40 varieties with the confection of your choice.

⊘**Tom's Restaurant** *782 Washington Ave at Sterling Pl, Prospect Heights, Brooklyn (718-636-9738). Subway: 2, 3 to Grand Army Plaza. Mon–Sat 6am–4pm. Average main course: $8.* Giving early birds something to chirp about, this old fashioned diner serves breakfast and lunch, plus egg creams that are a Brooklyn institution. In its kitsch-heavy digs—faux-flower garlands, '50s-style signs, a stained-glass window strewn with Christmas lights—morning-people fuel up on light-as-a-feather lemon-ricotta pancakes with cinnamon butter, deep-fried crab cakes and eggs Benedict. Don't let the brunch lines, which frequently spill out the door, put you off: The staff hands out orange wedges and chocolate-chip cookies to buck up waiting customers.

▲⊘**Vesuvio Bakery** *160 Prince St between West Broadway and Thompson St (212-925-8248). Subway: C, E to Spring St. Mon–Thu 7am–10pm; Fri–Sun 7am– 11pm. Average sandwich: $8.* Since 1920, this tiny storefront has offered freshly baked Italian breads, created from the generations-old recipes of the Dapolito family. Footsore Soho shoppers and local worker bees stop for breakfast specialties like Neapolitan eggs (fried and tucked into a slice of Italian bread), salads, made-to-order sandwiches and house-made desserts. The signature Vesuvio panino includes a generous helping of Italian charcuterie layered with mozzarella, tomato and olive spread, all neatly encased between two dense slices of surprisingly tender, buttery bread.

★⊘▲**'wichcraft** *397 Greenwich St at Beach St (212-780-0577). Subway: 1 to Franklin St. Mon–Thu 7am–8:30pm; Fri 7am–6pm; Sat, Sun 8:30am–6pm. Average sandwich: $8.* The panini craze has not yet passed; witness long lines of lunchers at Tom Colicchio's sophisticated sammicheria. Breakfast sandwiches (available all day) play it straight, as does the corned beef with Swiss cheese and mustard-seed sauce. But you can catch a heady whiff of Craft and Craftbar in the sandwich of marinated white anchovies, soft-cooked egg, roasted onion and frisée on country bread. End with a peanut-butter cream'wich. **Other locations** *60 E 8th St at Broadway (212-780-0577)* ● *269 Eleventh Ave between 27th and 28th Sts (212-780-0577)* ● *Equinox 69 Prince St at Crosby St (212-780-0577)* ● *555 Fifth Ave at 46th St* ● *11 E 20th St between Fifth Ave and Broadway (212-780-0577)* ● *1 Park Ave at 33rd St (212-780-0577).*

⊘**William Greenberg Jr. Desserts** *1100 Madison Ave between 82nd and 83rd Sts (212-744-0304). Subway: 6 to 77th St. Mon–Fri 8am–6:30pm; Sat 8am–6pm; Sun 10am–4pm. Average dessert: $3.* Legend has it that William Greenberg Jr. started his first family bakery in 1946 with money he'd won playing cards. Over the years, several of his uptown shops came and went and this is the latest iteration, still serving all of the man's signature kosher cookies, cakes and brownies. Dive into favorites like *schnecken*, shortbread linzer tarts filled with raspberry preserves, apple strudel, black-and-white cookies and cinnamon *babka* (coffee cake covered with streusel crumbs).

Caribbean

See also: *American Regional, Latin American*

Good times
Belly up to the
100-foot bar and dive
into seafood *piaya*
at Sofrito.

Caribbean

The Blue Mahoe *243 E 14th St between Second and Third Aves (212-358-0012). Subway: L to Third Ave; N, Q, R, W, 4, 5, 6 to 14th St–Union Sq. Mon–Sat 11am–11pm; Sun 11:30am–4pm. Average main course: $20.* The forest-green decor of the former Bambou has been transformed into one of soothing beige and breezy royal blue, a tropical romantic effect enhanced by the overhead ceiling fans, palm trees and candlelight. The Caribbean fusion menu remains unchanged: crisp calamari are served with a Creole *rémoulade* that suggests Russian dressing; a mango-ginger vinaigrette tops a saffron-infused crab cake, and the superb jerk chicken has molasses undertones and a mild Scotch-bonnet-pepper finish.

Cafe con Leche *726 Amsterdam Ave between 95th and 96th Sts (212-678-7000). Subway: 1, 2, 3 to 96th St. Mon–Wed 10am–11pm; Thu–Sat 10am–11pm; Sun 10am–11pm. Average main course: $12.* Be sure to roll your *r*s when you order. One authentic feature here is the language barrier you'll experience with the vivacious waitstaff. It's forgotten instantly when free garlic bread and two divine dipping sauces appear. The menu covers all the bases: crusted chicken or beef empanadas; rice with chicken, shrimp and Spanish sausage; and such vegetarian offerings as assorted vegetables in coconut or mango sauce. In these vibrant surroundings, a couple of the lethally strong fruit-flavored margaritas will turn dinner into a fiesta. **Other location** *424 Amsterdam Ave between 80th and 81st Sts (212-595-7000).*

★ **Calle Ocho** *446 Columbus Ave between 81st and 82nd Sts (212-873-5025). Subway: B, C to 81st St–Museum of Natural History. Mon–Thu 6–11pm; Fri 6pm–midnight; Sat 5pm–midnight; Sun 11:30am–3pm, 5–10pm. Average main course: $25.* Locals sardine themselves into this vibrant joint with Cuban-themed collages to enjoy inventive pan-Latin food as well as excellent homemade sangrias. The harried waitstaff delivers a starter round of velvety goat-cheese empanadas and rum-glazed shrimp without much more than a stressed smile, but the mouth-watering appetizers soon make up for the coldness. A pumpkin seed–encrusted mahi-mahi has the sultriness of a Havana summer night, while thin sheets of rosy, tender tuna *tiradito* are dressed with roasted pineapple, avocado and jalapeños. Coconut sorbet in a luscious chocolate shell, and peanut butter–drenched cheesecake are the best part of an already *buena noche*; don't worry—you won't hear your conscience over the peppy salsa music anyway.

Hispaniola *839 W 181st St at Cabrini Blvd (212-740-5222). Subway: A to 181st St. Daily 11am–midnight. Average main course: $21.* A leading light in northern Manhattan's upscale Nuevo Latino movement, Hispaniola offers beautifully plated fusions of Caribbean and Asian cuisines in a lovely setting overlooking the George Washington Bridge. While a surprisingly light steamed snapper proves a delicious union with caramelized plaintains, some things are better left unfused: An (overcooked) duck breast on a mound of shrimp fried rice suffers from the accompanying foie gras terrine. Simple starters like pillowy stuffed empanadas are also more successful than their fussier counterparts (a chicken and guava tortilla wrap is a confusing blend of colors, tastes

TALIA SIMHI

and textures). But there's nothing confusing about the gracious service and perfectly sweet mango cheesecake.

⊖Orchid Caribbean/Soul Cuisine 675
Ninth Ave between 46th and 47th Sts (212-582-9742). Subway: C, E to 50th St. Tue–Thu 11:30am–11pm; Fri, Sat 11:30am–midnight; Sun noon–midnight. Average main course: $10. This earnest little Hell's Kitchen spot is a classic mom-and-pop eatery: Married cochefs Mel (a local boy) and Trinidad-raised Anesha met while working at Macy's nearly 20 years ago and realized their restaurant dreams meshed. His family's soul-food recipes and her island dishes are popular for takeout, but dining in the restaurant is also a treat. Festive with twinkling little lights, palm trees and orchids, the place feels more like a beachfront shack than a Ninth Avenue storefront. Jerk preparations are filled with pungent brown spices, and the slow-cooked curries, ribs, oxtail and roasted chicken are crowd-pleasers. Mel's supreme potato salad, made with secret seasonings, is so good he won't even share the recipe with the missus.

Ricardo Steakhouse 2145 Second Ave between
110th and 111th Sts (212-289-5895). Subway: 6 to 110th St. Mon–Wed 4–11pm; Thu–Sat 4pm–midnight; Sun 4–11pm. Average main course: $28. Most steakhouses cluster in midtown, catering to businessmen with corporate accounts. This meat lover's mecca is set in Spanish Harlem, and is designed to appeal to locals. The food is hearty and the setting evokes the casual counter-style design of *cuchifrito* restaurants. Appetizers stick to the traditional steakhouse agenda: oysters, clams, shrimp and salad. But entrées and sides show Latin flavors, as in a house-special platter (grilled skirt steak and pork chop served with rice and beans and ripe sweet plantains) and rotisserie pork with an apple-raisin relish.

▲⊖Sisters Caribbean Cuisine 47 E 124th St
between Madison and Park Aves (212-410-3000). Subway: 4, 5, 6 to 125th St. Daily 11am–9pm. Average main course: $9. Consider this a one-stop culinary tour of the Caribbean, with a taste of the American South thrown in for good measure: Chicken is curried, jerked or caramelized into a state of deliciousness, and there are enough sides to make the counterperson impatient as you try to pick just two. Among the best are crisp-on-the-outside mac and cheese, hearty collard greens, and rice and peas with a strong dose of coconut. The bright dining room is the nicest spot on a rather desolate block—arrive early, because dishes start selling out as the afternoon becomes the evening.

▲Sugarcane 238 Flatbush Ave at Bergen St, Park
Slope, Brooklyn (718-230-3954). Subway: B, Q to Seventh Ave; 2, 3 to Bergen St. Tue–Thu 5:30pm–midnight; Fri, Sat 5:30pm–2am; Sun 3–11pm. Average main course: $15. You'll find a lively scene at stylish Sugarcane. The stainless-steel bar glints in the wall mirrors, and a bamboo floor the color of sand makes the space feel larger than it is. Settle into a booth prettified by tall vases of banana leaves and prepare to seriously stuff yourself with Pan-Caribbean menu items like plantain-crusted red snapper and tangy guava-glazed ribs. Two sides (choose from pigeon peas, fried plantains, callaloo and creamed kale, among others) come with every main course.

Cuban

Café Fuego 9 St. Marks Pl between Second and
Third Aves (212-677-7300). Subway: 6 to Astor Pl. Mon–Thu 8am–1am; Fri, Sat 8am–2am; Sun 8am–1am.

Average main course: $13. One need only look at how a few classic dishes are prepared to see if a Cuban restaurant is any good. The roasted pork is a succulent heap of shredded meat with an intense garlic aroma, which is exactly how it's served at this subterranean East Village spot. Chef Eduardo Bover knows when to up the visual flair: Al dente grilled calamari is tossed with a colorful relish of crisp carrots, peppers and corn—a refreshing start to the meal and a serious bargain at $5.95. And while the non-Cuban decor—leather banquettes, red brick walls and black candelabras—doesn't do much to channel Havana, the addictive churros served with dulce du leche thankfully do.

★ ⊖Cafe Habana 17 Prince St at Elizabeth St
(212-625-2001). Subway: N, R, W to Prince St; 6 to Spring St. Daily 9am–midnight. Average main course: $10. The fashionable people milling around Nolita at all hours don't look like they eat, but they do—here. They storm this chrome corner fixture for the sexy scene and the addictive grilled corn: golden ears doused in fresh mayo, char-grilled, and generously sprinkled with chili powder and grated *cotija* cheese. Staples include a Cuban sandwich of roasted pork, ham, melted Swiss and sliced pickles; crisp beer-battered catfish with spicy mayo; and marinated skirt steak with rice and beans. For dessert, try the *cajeta* (that's caramel) flan. Locals love the takeout annex next door, where you can get that corn-on-a-stick to go. **Other location** *Cafe Habana to Go, 229 Elizabeth St between Houston and Prince Sts (212-625-2002).*

Cuba 222 Thompson St between Bleecker and W 4th
Sts (212-420-7878). Subway: A, C, E, B, D, F, V to W 4th St. Mon–Wed noon–11pm; Thu–Sat noon–midnight; Sun noon–11pm. Average main course $15. Cuba lives up to its namesake with exuberant salsa, charming waiters and a guy rolling cigars in the window on weekends. David Martinez, former chef at Havana's celebrated Hotel Nacional, has created a menu that's full-on tropical: snapper *en guayabera de platano* ("a Cuban shirt of crusty plantains") and halibut *al estilo* Hemingway. On a warm summer evening, with people and music spilling out through the sidewalk greenery, the place is transporting.

⊖Havana New York 27 W 38th St between Fifth
and Sixth Aves (212-944-0990). Subway: B, D, F, V, N, Q, R, W to 34th St–Herald Sq. Mon–Fri 11am–9:30pm. Average main course: $12. Don't be fooled by the fancy digs. The dark Spanish ceramic floors are shiny, and the huge paintings of pre-Castro tropics look great on the exposed-brick walls. But this is pretty much a Cuban lunch counter dressed in its Sunday best: From the *ropa vieja* and the smoky red beans to the never-changing daily specials listed in both Spanish and English, the only distinction is that here you actually have a little room to stretch out and relax. Trust the specials—Thursday's is *vaca frita*, which is not "fried cow" (as your high-school Spanish might suggest), but rather tender chunks of beef marinated in citrus sauce.

▲Little Havana 30 Cornelia St between Bleecker
and W 4th Sts (212-255-2212). Subway: A, C, E, B, D, F, V to W 4th St. Tue–Sun 2:30–11pm. Average main course: $17. In a space as narrow as a pressed cubano, Lydia Sharpe's passion for Cuban cooking shines. The most cursory knowledge of the cuisine on your part will melt her mercantile exterior—if you want her to get downright motherly, order the *moros y cristianos*. The black beans cooked in white rice have fragrant cinnamon and smoky pork nuances, adding sparkle to entrées such as a plump fillet of roasted salmon, pork medallions with a slightly sour *tomatillo* sauce, and

savory, olive-studded *picadillo*. The place may be small, but the flavors are huge.

Dominican

★809 Sangria Bar and Grill *2007 Eat Out Award, Critics' Pick: Best bite uptown—way uptown 112 Dyckman St between Nagle and Sherman Aves (212-304-3800). Subway: 1 to Dyckman St. Mon–Fri 11am–midnight; Sat, Sun 11am–1am. Average main course: $20.* As the name suggests, this is sangria heaven, and you'd be silly to order any other beverage. But the food's the real star: This notable spot is the best thing to happen to Nuevo Latino cuisine in some time. Consulting chef Ricardo Cardona's reinterpretations of classic dishes include marinated pork-filled empanadas, *arepas* jazzed up with a pork topping, and a whole shelled lobster, roasted and stuffed with a truffled taro-root mash. Come ready to party: Music blares in the dining rooms, and a hidden speakeasy-like bar is packed with locals dressed to the nines.

▲◉El Castillo de Jagua *113 Rivington St between Essex and Ludlow Sts (212-982-6412). Subway: F to Delancey St; J, M, Z to Delancey–Essex Sts. Mon–Thu 8am–midnight; Fri, Sat 8am–1am; Sun 8am–midnight. Average main course: $8.* Leaving any Dominican restaurant hungry is almost impossible, as every dish seems designed to stuff you full. *Mofongo*, a dense mash of garlicky green plantains and fried pork (meant for dipping in tomato broth), is the champion gut-plugger, though *sancocho* vies for the title by welcoming potatoes and plantains to an already-starchy stew. The hot Cuban sandwich here is uncharacteristically light, featuring crisp

Side show
The *Trio de Arepas* is as good as the signature drink at 809 Sangria Bar and Grill.

bread, pickles, runny mayo and pork-on-pork action: ham and fabulous *pernil* (roasted pork). Better yet, just try a serving of roasted pork by itself. It takes over the plate and comes capped with a shard of crackling skin, and a heap of rice and kidney beans on the side.

It's a Dominican Thing *144 W 19th St between Sixth and Seventh Aves (212-924-3344). Subway: 1 to 18th St. Tue–Thu noon–3:30pm, 5:30–10pm; Fri, Sat noon–3:30pm, 5:30pm–midnight; Sun noon–3:30pm, 5:30–10pm. Average main course: $16.* At this candlelit, brick-walled 26-seater, stylish types dig into chef Eva Martinez's hearty Dominican home cooking. Conch, *cassava* and plantains are spotlighted in soups, stews and lopsided fritters. A mixed-appetizer platter presents various *pastelitos* (meat turnovers) and croquettes, among them an especially delicious one made with codfish. Regulars crave Martinez's shrimp with coconut-tomato sauce, served in a casserole dish. Her marvelous panfried snapper, "Boca Chica" (named for the beach town where fresh-caught fish are traditionally flash-fried), is indeed a Dominican thing.

Sabrosura *1200 Castle Hill Ave at Gleason Ave, Bronx (718-597-1344). Subway: 6 to Castle Hill Ave. Mon–Thu 11:30am–10pm; Fri, Sat 11:30am–10:30pm; Sun 11:30am–10pm. Average main course: $13.* According to one linguist, *sabrosura* "means more than its English translation of 'flavor'; there is a hint of picante in the term." There's also a hint of it in the food of Nelson Ng, who learned to cook in Santo Domingo's Chinatown and opened this eclectic restaurant in the Bronx in 1982. Locals have been packing in under the candy-colored hanging lights ever since. You can get *mofongo* (a mash of fried plantains, garlic, and either shellfish or chicken), mojito-spiced charbroiled chicken, and excellent bone-in sweet-and-sour pork chops. Ng doesn't limit himself to Chino-Latino; he also serves American-style seafood dishes, simply because he likes them.

Haitian

Kombit Bar & Restaurant *279 Flatbush Ave between Prospect Pl and St. Marks Ave, Prospect Heights, Brooklyn (718-399-2000). Subway: B, Q to Seventh Ave; 2, 3 to Bergen St. Daily noon–10pm. Average main course: $14.* Few NYC restaurants are devoted solely to this Caribbean nation's specialties, but Kombit, on the border of two Brooklyn neighborhoods, has the country covered. The menu features typical dishes such as *lambi* (tenderized conch in a stew of carrots and tomatoes), *riz djon djon* (wild rice mixed with black mushrooms) and *poulet en sauce* (baked chicken in a tangy tomato gravy). Kombit is owned and operated by three expat sisters—Denise, Pascale and Maryse—who've made sure that the atmosphere is just as down-home as the cooking.

Jamaican

▲Maroons *244 W 16th St between Seventh and Eighth Aves (212-206-8640). Subway: A, C, E, 1, 2, 3 to 14th St; L to Eighth Ave. Mon 5pm–midnight; Tue–Sun 11:30am–3:30pm, 5pm–midnight. Average main course: $18.* It would be wonderful to be marooned in Maroons, cast adrift in its three tin-ceilinged dining rooms full of pretty people, colorful drinks and scattered rose petals. The dishes could perk up any desert island: smoky Jamaican pepper-pot soup, its potent broth thick with collard greens and chunks of turkey; or juicy fried green tomatoes jazzed

Cuban outpost
Regulars dig the grilled
corn at Cafe Habana
and Habana To Go.

KRISTY MAY

up with slices of mango. And one could happily feast on the fried chicken, with its crunchy, spectacularly seasoned skin and moist meat, for a lifetime. If you had to grab just one dish with which to be washed ashore, make it Mama's Sunday layer cake.

▲**Mo-Bay** *17 W 125th St between Fifth Ave and Malcolm X Blvd (Lenox Ave) (212-876-9300). Subway: 2, 3 to 125th St. Mon–Wed noon–10pm; Thu, Fri noon–11pm; Sat 1–11pm; Sun 1–10pm. Average main course: $12.* Charming Mo-Bay prides itself on re-creating Jamaican hospitality. Caribbean beats propel diners through appetizers like codfish cakes with curry-pineapple dip and killer jerk chicken. The highlights on the menu are corn bread (garnished with a coconut-pineapple-cream sauce) and catfish—or if you're not hungry, have a seat at the thin bar that puts drinkers right across from each other and try one of MoBay's concoctions. The Harlem Mojito is made with cognac, while the Triple Threat mixes three 150-proof rums in a pint glass ($18)—this libation is lethal.

Negril Village *70 W 3rd St between La Guardia Pl and Thompson St (212-477-2804). Subway: A, C, E, B, D, F, V to W 4th St. Tue–Thu noon–11:30pm; Fri, Sat noon–2am; Sun noon–11:30pm. Average main course: $18.* Everyone gets a warm island welcome at this offshoot of Chelsea's original Negril. A sophisticated crowd buzzes in the red-and-ivory main dining room dotted with potted palms and lush flowers. Live steel-drum trios and reggae bands and an extensive rum list are all here to help you unwind. Appetizers and desserts win higher marks than entrées, so fill up on bites like spicy vegetable patties or giant coconut-crusted shrimp before calling it a night with creamy mango cheesecake or ginger crème brûlée. **Other locations** *Negril, 362 W 23rd St between Eighth and Ninth Aves (212-807-6411)* ● *Caribbean Spice, 402 W 44th St between Ninth and Tenth Aves (212-765-1737).*

☺**Vernon's New Jerk House** *987 E 233rd St at Paulding Ave, Bronx (718-655-8348). Subway: 2, 5 to 233rd St. Mon–Sat 8am–midnight; Sun 8am–8pm.*

Read 'em & eat

breadfruit: a softball-size, green-skinned fruit with sweet, creamy flesh the texture of bread

conch: a shellfish whose meat is added raw to salads or cooked and served in soup or as fritters

jerk: a mixture of chili and other hot spices used to marinate chicken or pork

mofongo: mashed plantains mixed with meat, cheese or vegetables

picadillo: ground meat with tomato, garlic and onion

ropa vieja: a dish made with chunks of shredded beef

sancocho: a stew that can be chicken- or fish-based, or made from a combination of chicken, beef and pork

Average main course: $10. New is a relative term: This north Bronx restaurant has served the same justly famous jerk dishes for more than 20 years. The chicken, lively with allspice, nutmeg and Scotch bonnet, chopped and served with sweet plantains and veggies, is plenty spicy but won't make you gasp for breath. Vernon's jerk pork is a skin-on, fat-in flavor bomb. Save the fried fish and masterfully subtle curried chicken or goat for your second trip, but grab the rum cake and sweet-potato pudding, as these favorites may run out. At the little bar, a friendly local crowd sips Hennessy or Jamaican rum from plastic cups.

Puerto Rican

☺**Cabo Rojo** *254 Tenth Ave between 24th and 25th Sts (212-929-9752). Subway: C, E to 23rd St. Mon–Fri 6am–7pm; Sat 7am–7pm. Average main course: $8.* This peasant-food haven has been dishing out hearty, delicious food for more than 40 years. Less a restaurant than a lunch counter, Cabo Rojo serves straightforward Puerto Rican fare like *sancocho* (a hearty soup) and *pollo asado* (roasted chicken). Daily specials sometimes run out before dinnertime, so come earlier in the day and join the policemen, Hispanic locals from the (old) neighborhood and, yes, arty types.

Camaradas el Barrio Bar & Restaurant

2241 First Ave at 115th St (212-348-2703). Subway: 6 to 116th St. Mon–Wed 3pm–midnight; Thu–Sat 3pm–4am; Sun 3pm–midnight. Average main course: $7. Owners Raúl Rivera and Orlando Plaza celebrate their working-class Puerto Rican heritage at this beer-and-wine bar in Spanish Harlem. Exposed brick, a vintage sewing machine, and wooden benches and tables evoke proletariat chic. Rich Puerto Rican snacks like *alcapurrias* (meat-filled fritters), *pastelillos* (meat turnovers), and yuca *croquetas* with chorizo and cheese are well suited to their downsized, tapas-style portions. Mainstream tastes will appreciate the hummus, chicken wings (rechristened *alitas*), Barrio burgers and charred steak infused with spicy garlic.

☺**La Fonda Boricua** *169 E 106th St between Lexington and Third Aves (212-410-7292). Subway: 6 to 103rd St. Mon–Wed 11am–10pm; Thu 11am–11pm; Fri–Sun 11am–10pm. Average main course: $9.* This working-class diner cranks out all sorts of filling Puerto Rican dishes, and almost every one comes with piles of rice and beans, plus bread. There's no menu (and no telling what's going to be offered on any given day), but no matter: Maybe you'll end up with a plate of pulled roasted pork—crisp and slightly smoky—tossed with onions and peppers and served with lime wedges. Or maybe a thin steak topped with onions. Many of the Spanish-speaking diners are regulars who know exactly what they want, so just tell the server you'll have what they're having.

Sofrito *400 E 57th St between First Ave and Sutton Pl (212-754-5999). Subway: N, R, W to Lexington Ave– 59th St; 4, 5, 6 to 59th St. Daily 5pm–2am. Average main course: $15.* Uptown restaurateur and nightclub impresario Jimmy Rodriguez is behind this humble eatery. Located in the old, somewhat updated Jimmy's Downtown—now with graffiti murals and earth-toned walls—Sofrito boasts one of the city's longest bars, at 100 feet. But that's where the excesses end. The menu is dominated by accessible comfort food; $12 versions of pork chops and arroz con pollo—Puerto Rico's greatest hits. But the *ropa vieja* distinguishes itself with a salty glaze that paints every crevice of the stewed meat.

Chinese

See also: *Asian*

Delicate flower
Chinatown Brasserie
specializes in pretty
little things.

CINZIA REALE-CASTELLO

★**Buddakan** *2007 Eat Out Award, Readers'
Choice: Best new Asian restaurant; Best new out-of-town
restaurateur, Stephen Starr 75 Ninth Ave between 15th
and 16th Sts (212-989-6699). Subway: A, C, E to 14th St;
L to Eighth Ave. Mon 5:30–11pm; Tue, Wed 5:30pm–
midnight; Thu–Sat 5:30pm–1am; Sun 5:30–11pm.
Average main course: $25.* This stunning, 16,000-square-
foot theme park of a space from Philly-based restaurateur
Stephen Starr has become a food-fan favorite. After
entering, you pass a bustling front bar, a birdcage filled
with taxidermy, and European tapestries, all leading to a
grand staircase that descends into a soaring, golden-hued
main room with a 35-foot ceiling and a long communal
table. The food—yes, there's food here, too—sounds
fancier than it is. Chinese standards are gussied up (e.g.,
dumplings filled with edamame paste in shallot broth),
while noodle and rice dishes—reasonably priced between
$8 and $13—offer great bang for your buck. The kaffir
lime tart with steamed *yuzu* soufflé is a fragrant ending.

▲**Chance** *223 Smith St at Butler St, Carroll
Gardens, Brooklyn (718-242-1515). Subway: F, G to
Bergen St. Mon–Thu noon–11pm; Fri, Sat noon–
midnight; Sun noon–11pm. Average main course: $16.*
Chance seems to have been driven by design: First,
come up with a snappy name (China+France=Chance).
Then, overhaul a bodega and turn it into an angular
open space that stands out on Smith Street's overloaded
restaurant row. Fill it with comely, black-clad waitstaff.
Oh, and serve some food. Instead of Sino-Gallic fusion, the
menu sticks with a separate-but-equal concept, serving
well-executed, artfully composed plates of rack of lamb
or scallops in *xo* sauce. Peking duck is crisp and moist in
all the right places, its wrappers and condiments neatly

compartmentalized. Best of all is a ramekin of piping-hot,
made-to-order chocolate soufflé.

Chinatown Brasserie *380 Lafayette St at
Great Jones St (212-533-7000). Subway: B, D, F, V to
Broadway–Lafayette St; 6 to Bleecker St. Mon–Wed
11am–3:30pm, 5–11:30pm; Thu, Fri 11:30am–3:30pm,
5pm–midnight; Sat 11am–3:30pm, 5pm–midnight; Sun
11am–3:30pm, 5–10pm. Average main course: $25.*
This Sinocentric mega-eatery offers pretty but pricey
Eastern exoticism in the former Time Café space: Dark
brocade curtains, wooden room dividers and red-and-
yellow silk lanterns greet you upstairs, while a downstairs
lounge (formerly the music venue Fez) shoots for tiki
cool. Eats are by the book: orange beef, pork lo mein and
General Tso's chicken. What you're paying for is quality
ingredients—you can taste the pungently sour pork, for
example, in the dried string beans with pork. Among
the dim sum options, shrimp-and-snow-pea dumplings
practically snap with freshness.

★ ▲**Chinese Mirch** *120 Lexington Ave at 28th
St (212 532 3663). Subway: 6 to 28th St. Mon–Thu
noon–3pm, 5:30–10:30pm; Fri noon–3pm, 5:30–11pm;
Sat 12:30–3:30pm, 5:30–11pm; Sun 12:30–3:30pm,
5:30–10pm. Average main course: $12.* Although few
cuisines remain unfused in New York, Indo-Chinese is still
an unusual marriage (it has long been popular in India).
True to its name (*mirch* means "spicy" in Hindi), Chinese
Mirch does heat best. A mountain of crunchy deep-fried
okra is fiery, with a salty, tangy seasoning (try to eat just
20). Seafood and lamb selections provide the most inspired
examples of border crossing: Sliced morsels of Szechuan
lamb are twice-cooked for a crisp outer layer; they're

Refreshing choice
Ginger focuses on
healthful, organic fare.

TALIA SIMHI

deliciously tender and lightly coated with a garlicky Chinese brown sauce. The date-pancake dessert—four thin triangles filled with a sweet date paste and topped with a dollop of ice cream—makes you want to bless this union.

▲◉Congee Village 100 Allen St between
Broome and Delancey Sts (212-941-1818). Subway: F to Delancey St; J, M, Z to Delancey–Essex Sts. Mon–Thu 10:30am–12:30am; Fri, Sat 10:30am–2am; Sun 10:30am–12:30am. Average main course: $12. If you've never indulged in the starchy comfort of congee, this is a good place to be initiated. The rice porridge, cooked to a bubbling in a clay pot over a slow fire, is best early in the day; pick a chunky version, such as the treasure-laden seafood or sliced fish. Razor clams in black-bean sauce are pulled out of the wok at precisely the moment of maximum tenderness. Crabs are impeccably fresh, as is the well-seasoned whole fish served over glistening Chinese broccoli. Service is brisk, but on a typical night, it's easy to see why: The line winds out the door.

★ ▲◉Dumpling House 118 Eldridge St between
Broome and Grand Sts (212-625-8008). Subway: F to Delancey St; J, M, Z to Delancey–Essex Sts. Daily 7:30am–9:30pm. Average main course (8 dumplings): $2. As diminutive as its namesake nibbles, this pot-sticker pit stop with just a few seats serves five chive-and-pork dumplings, fried or steamed, for a buck. If you want them vegetarian, you'll have to splurge and spend $2, but then you get eight of the tasty morsels. Fifty cents buys a sesame pancake the size of a pizza wedge. Even on rainy nights, a motley throng of Lower East Siders and Chinatown moms overflows onto the street, congregating below the cupola-shaped awning to order from the street-side window.

◉Excellent Pork Chop House 3 Doyers St
off Bowery at Chatham Sq (212-791-7007). Subway: B, D to Grand St; J, M, Z, N, Q, R, W, 6 to Canal St. Mon, Wed–Sun 10am–9pm. Average pork chop: $2. All kinds of Chinese restaurants flourish in Flushing, but this is one of the few spots in Manhattan where you'll find classic street fare and soul food from Taiwan. Excellent Pork Chop House does its name proud by serving several tasty plates of pig, including pork chops on rice, on noodles, in soup and so on. The photo album of a menu allows you to point to what you want. The brightly lit room filled with big, round cafeteria tables isn't really a place for lingering, but if you do, try a unique and delicious Taiwanese dessert: Three bucks buys your choice of three ingredients—tapioca pearls, taro, red kidney beans, black jelly, toasted peanuts, plum, pineapple chunks, sweet corn or condensed milk—over shaved ice

▲Fuleen Seafood 11 Division St between
Confucius Pl and East Broadway (212-941-6888). Subway: F to East Broadway. Daily 11:30am–3:30am. Average main course: $15. Always inquire about the specials. You might find yourself with a steaming basket of shrimp just plucked from their pool, a briny soup studded with scallops, a meltingly tender whole fish with ginger and scallions, or a chili-flecked Dungeness crab. Onshore, the kitchen is equally adept: Garlic-tossed baby bok choy is superb, and a deep-fried whole chicken with sticky-rice stuffing will draw covetous glances—and copycat orders (but they'll have to come back for it; two-day's advance notice is required). Fuleen doles out $5 lunch specials to long lines of food-savvy downtown professionals; late at night, there's a reversal, and you'll see downtown-savvy food professionals.

Gala Manor 37-02 Main St at 37th Ave, Flushing,
Queens (718-888-9293). Subway: 7 to Flushing–Main St. Daily 11am–midnight. Average dim sum: $3. Brave the crowds of brunching extended families at this palatial Flushing banquet hall for uniquely fresh dim sum, memorable enough to offset the madhouse atmosphere. Speaking Cantonese is not a requirement (so long as you watch the hostess crossing off her seating chart); just point to the trundling, steaming carts of addictive pork dumplings, vegetable pancakes, fried shrimp and eggplant morsels. Unless you come with a large party, expect to be seated with others—never a bad thing with dim sum (there's more to share).

▲Ginger 1400 Fifth Ave at 116th St (212-423-
1111). Subway: 2, 3,to 116th St–Lenox Ave; 6 to 116th St–Lexington Ave. Mon–Thu 5:30–10:30pm; Fri, Sat 5:30–11:30pm; Sun 5:30–10:30pm. Average main course: $12. On an unassuming Harlem corner stands this unexpected Chinese restaurant with a simple decor of red lanterns and bamboo-beamed ceilings. What's special here, though, is that Ginger successfully champions healthful, organic fare: No deep frying, no salt. Instead, dishes are infused with flavor through sauces and spices. The grilled Angus beef spareribs, for example, are coated in a thick dark sauce that betrays hints of hoisin, smoke and chocolate. The entrées are enormous—two can easily share—and won't leave much room for dessert, which is far more posh than any fortune cookies. Then again, ginger-infused crème brûlée isn't exactly a Chinese staple.

◉Golden Unicorn 18 East Broadway between
Catherine and Market Sts (212-941-0911). Subway: F to East Broadway. Daily 10am–11pm. Average dim sum: $3. Dim sum novices should visit this Chinatown spot, where carts bear English labels so you'll know what you're getting. The hostess shouting into a walkie-talkie in the lobby will herd the crowd into an elevator and assign patrons to a floor. Spring rolls, shumai and shrimp dumplings are familiar and satisfying. Arrive before 11am on weekends to beat the crowds.

▲◉Grand Sichuan 125 Canal St between Bowery
and Chrystie St (212-625-9212). Subway: B, D to Grand St; J, M, Z to Canal St. Daily 11:30am–11pm. Average

Read 'em & eat

bao: a sweet, steamed bun, typically filled with pork

congee: a watery, rice-based porridge often accompanied by chicken, bamboo shoots or fish

General Tso's chicken: a sweet and spicy deep-fried Hunanese dish usually served with broccoli

hoisin: (also known as Peking sauce) a thick, piquant-sweet dark-brown sauce of garlic, soybeans, chilies and spices, served as a condiment or as an ingredient in dishes

lychee: (also litchi), a small, juicy, sweet fruit

Side dish

Land of plenty

Explore the myriad cuisines of mainland China.

Chinese food is so familiar to Americans that few have trouble negotiating a menu. But there's still a lack of knowledge when it comes to the subtle (and not so subtle) differences between the regional cuisines of the mainland.

The Chinese food most Americans grow up on is **Cantonese**, largely due to the significant Cantonese population here. The focus is on the integrity of its ingredients—this southeastern region's raw materials are some of China's best. Cantonese restaurants are more partial to using quick-cooking techniques, like stir-frying, deep-frying and steaming, and the dishes are typically lighter on seasoning. Fresh fish is also common in this coastal province. Some typical Cantonese dishes are shark fin soup, fish balls and fried rice. If these are familiar from your dim sum jaunts, it's because the small-bite meals originated in Canton's teahouses.

Unlike Cantonese food, which tends to be on the blander side, **Shanghai** dishes are often aggressively seasoned and richly sauced—sugar is also liberally used in savory dishes. The cuisine of the eastern, coastal municipality of China is a bit of a melting pot, borrowing and improving on dishes from surrounding provinces. Dishes associated with Shanghai include soup dumplings and sweet and sour pork.

If you like spice, go for **Szechuan**. The climate of the southwestern province is known for its heat.

So is its food. The Szechuan peppercorn punches up many dishes, as does a supporting cast of flavors like sesame oil and fermented bean curd paste. Like Cantonese, Szechuan dishes are often stir- or deep-fried, though braising is also common. Among the more popular Szechuan eats are kung pao chicken, dandan noodles and tea-smoked duck.

Rivaling Szechuan cuisine for spiciness is the **Hunan** province, whose hot, humid climate fosters a culture of spicy eating. Hunan's dishes are typically oilier, darker and more pungent than their Szechuan counterparts (sweet-and-sour sauces are standard in Hunanese fare). Typical dishes include sizzling rice soup, orange beef and General Tso's chicken—actually invented in NYC by a Hunanese restaurateur and virtually unknown in China.

main course: $11. Grand Sichuan's comprehensive menu comes with an annotated booklet describing the history and cooking process for each of the 100-plus dishes. Szechuan cuisine is based on heat, so prepare for a meal that is not only mouthwatering but eyewatering as well. The *dandan* rice-noodle starter, loaded with dried peppercorns and minced pork, will open your sinuses. Waiters routinely caution those who order the memorable braised beef in chili sauce—it's an inferno on a plate. Panfried *au zhao* chicken offers equally addictive flavor with less heat. Experiment, because gems abound on the menu, and you have nothing to lose but your fear of fire.

▲◉**Jing Fong** *20 Elizabeth St between Bayard and Canal St (212-964-5256). Subway: J, M, Z, N, Q, R, W, 6 to Canal St. Daily 9:30am–11pm. Average main course: $15.* For some, Jing Fong might be intimidating: It's marked by giant escalators, a vast dining room and walkie-talkie–toting waiters marshalling diners. But it has remarkable dim sum. The shrimp *shumai* with glass noodles is exceptional, as is the ground pork and shrimp wrapped in a big black mushroom. The freshness and originality of its most mundane offerings keep people coming back for more

▲**Lili's Noodle Shop & Grill** *1500 Third Ave between 84th and 85th Sts (212-639-1313). Subway: 4, 5, 6 to 86th St. Daily 11am–11pm. Average main course: $15.* Sleek looks, glamorous cocktails and a cute, turbocharged waitstaff set Lili's apart from the rest of the noodle-shop bunch. You can chow down on big bowls of noodles here, but what really beckon are oversize platters of seafood, like grilled-shrimp kebabs with Lili's "special sauce," or Cantonese-style lobster cooked with scallions and ginger. The delicious Lion's Head—a plate of enormous beef meatballs served on a bed of sweet bok choy—will provide you with a week's worth of tasty leftovers. **Other locations** *102 North End Ave between Murray and Vesey Sts (212-786-1300)* ● *Lili's 57, 200 W 57th St between Sixth and Seventh Aves (212-586-5333).*

New Bo Ky Restaurant *80 Bayard St between Mott and Mulberry Sts (212-406-2292). Subway: B, D to Grand St; J, M, Z, N, Q, R, W, 6 to Canal St. Daily 9am–10pm. Average main course: $5.* Don't be intimated by the lack of English spoken at this king of Chinatown noodleries, sure to rock both the seasoned palate and anyone confident enough to choose by pointing at the picture-menu. Broths zing with flavor and the dozens of toppings will have your buds humming, especially a *teochew* chili paste (just say "Number 47") served on flat noodles with a slice of lemon. The peach-tiled decor is merely functional, but the taste-to-cost ratio is ridiculously slanted in your favor.

★ ◉**New York Noodle Town** *28 Bowery at Bayard St (212-349-0923). Subway: J, M, Z, N, Q, R, W, 6 to Canal St. Daily 9am–4am. Average main course: $10.* Over the years, New York Noodle Town has proven that it can deliver on the promise of its name. Choose from panfried selections (boiled angel-hair noodles that are lightly fried for a crunchy-soft texture) or softer preparations (served floating in flavorful chicken broth); they can be ordered with roasted pork, duck, chicken or ribs. Suckling pig is also a treat, but the supply usually runs out by 8pm. In a signature combination, Chinese flowering chives are sautéed with duck, scallops, fish or squid. The chives lose their pungency and sweeten in the flash of heat, making them a great accompaniment to delicate fowl or seafood.

⊖Noodle Bar *26 Carmine St at Bleecker St (212-524-6800). Subway: A, C, E, B, D, F, V to W 4th St. Mon–Sat 11:30am–11pm; Sun 11:30am–10pm. Average main course: $11.* At this aptly named casual Asian spot, chef Meng Cheong fries pork dumplings over a furious flame just feet from the 14-seat bar (there are only three tables in the tiny, brightly lit restaurant). The best dishes, not surprisingly, showcase noodles. The pastas steeped in broth stand out in particular: One pairs tender duck with Chinese broccoli and delicate egg noodles in a complex soup made from chicken and duck bones. But the menu doesn't start and end with starches: The appetizers, such as sticky sesame wings and fried squid with a wasabi aioli dipping sauce, are generous. Desserts are limited to a choice of five-spiced cheesecake, ginger-lemongrass crème brûlée or cool almond *dofu*, a panna cotta–like mixture of cream, gelatin and almond flavor.

Ollie's Noodle Shop & Grille *1991 Broadway between 67th and 68th Sts (212-595-8181). Subway: 1 to 66th St–Lincoln Ctr. Mon–Thu 11:30am–midnight; Fri, Sat 11:30am–1am; Sun 11:30am–midnight. Average main course: $9.* Office lunchers, college students and deal seekers crowd into Ollie's for lightning-fast service and big, cheap, slurp-worthy bowls. Perfectly warming on a frigid day, Mandarin noodle soups are packed with fish, meat and vegetables and come in five different variations. (The indecisive can opt for the Little Bit of Everything soup.)

▲Peking Duck House *28 Mott St between Mosco and Pell Sts (212-227-1810). Subway: J, M, Z, N, Q, R, W, 6 to Canal St. Mon–Thu 11:30am–10:30pm; Fri, Sat 11:30am–11:30pm; Sun 11:30am–10:30pm. Average main course: $15.* Your waiter parades the roasted duck past your party before placing it on the center show table. A chef brandishes his knives dramatically, then slices the aromatic, crisp-skinned, succulent meat with great flair. Folks at other tables drool with envy. (Don't they know that this establishment doesn't require you to order the specialty in advance? Pity.) Select the "three-way," and your duck will yield the main course (complete with pancakes and plum sauce for rolling up the goods), a vegetable stir-fry with leftover bits of meat and a cabbage soup made with the remaining bone. Yes, the menu lists many dishes besides Peking duck, but reading it will only delay the inevitable.

▲⊖Phoenix Garden *242 E 40th St between Second and Third Aves (212-983-6666). Subway: 42nd St S, 4, 5, 6, 7 to 42nd St–Grand Central. Daily noon–9:45pm. Average main course: $10.* Here's proof that you don't have to go to Chinatown to get the good stuff. Crunchy jellyfish, sautéed minced squab and abalone with Asian vegetables—all free of cloying, cornstarch-thickened sauces—are hardly ever found north of Grand Street. Everything tastes incredible, especially dumplings stuffed with chives and crisp sea bass with shredded pork and black mushrooms. Don't overlook casseroles like the robust eggplant with minced pork and ham. "It's just like home cooking!" exclaimed one Chinese woman during her meal.

★ ▲Shanghai Pavilion *1378 Third Ave between 78th and 79th Sts (212-585-3388). Subway: 6 to 77th St. Daily 11:30am–10:30pm. Average main course: $15.* Don't be startled by a lack of chopsticks: This restaurant is elegant and for serious gourmands.

KENNETH CHEN

Roll call
At Buddakan, Chinese
standards are offered in a
temple-like setting.

CINZIA REALE-CASTELLO

Try Lion's Head—meatballs in a thick, savory sauce. Innovative twists include the delicious smoky black-bean sauce that's served with the seasonal soft-shell crabs. The crowning jewel is, surprisingly, a dessert: "fried soup," or panfried cakes of water-chestnut starch sprinkled with black-sesame-seed powder and sugar. Crisp on the outside and custardlike on the inside, the dish is subtly sweet, nutty and utterly delicious. Creativity such as this deserves the fancy setting.

★ **Shun Lee Palace** *155 E 55th St between Lexington and Third Aves (212-371-8844). Subway: E, V to Lexington Ave–53rd St; 6 to 51st St. Mon–Sat noon–11:30pm; Sun noon–11pm. Average main course: $28.* This luxe restaurant has been wowing midtown diners since the '70s. Whether you prefer Cantonese, Shanghai or Szechuan food, you'll find it done in style. The menu offers no fewer than five duck entrées and a slew of nontraditional items, such as "Lily in the Woods" (Chinese cabbage hearts simmered in broth and served with black wood mushrooms). Waiters theatrically assemble your table's centerpiece—vegetables skillfully carved into animal shapes. The menagerie heralds the arrival of the fancy food: moist shredded duck or "Neptune's Net," a potato nest bursting with scallops, shrimp, lobster and sea bass. The experience doesn't come cheap, but for top-notch regional cuisine served graciously beside a taro dove, there is no other choice. **Other locations** *Shun Lee Café, 43 W 65th St between Central Park West and Columbus Ave (212-769-3888)* ●*Shun Lee West, 43 W 65th St between Central Park West and Columbus Ave (212-595-8895).*

▲⊙**Spicy & Tasty** *39-07 Prince St between Roosevelt and 39th Aves, Flushing, Queens (718-359-1601). Subway: 7 to Flushing–Main St. Daily 11am–11pm. Average main course: $12.95.* Any serious trip to Flushing for a taste of its local Chinatown's volcanically spicy Szechuan food begins—and maybe even ends—here. Revered by its crowd of in-the-know regulars and giddy experimenters from other boroughs, this brightly lit box serves plates of peppercorn-laden pork and lamb swimming in chili sauce, sure to set even the most seasoned palate aflame. First, stock up on the cold bar's offerings—zesty sesame noodles, crunchy chopped cucumbers, delicately smooth tofu—you'll need the relief. Then, order specials and brace yourself. Service is speedy and mercifully attentive to water requests.

▲**Tse Yang** *34 E 51st St between Madison and Park Aves (212-688-5447). Subway: E, V to Fifth Ave–53rd St; 6 to 51st St. Daily noon–3pm, 6–11pm. Average main course: $27.* An effusive reception, an entryway lined with intricate wood carvings and stained glass, a menu written in French (and English) with detailed descriptions of duck, veal and frog-leg dishes: This is expense-account heaven *au chinois.* Your accounting department won't let you charge late-night pay-per-view movies to your hotel room, but who's going to notice a bowl of Borneo swallow's nest or shark's fin soup (which is supposedly aphrodisiacal) on your tab? The elaborately executed food is top-shelf, but you'll be glad you brought your corporate card—the $26 lunch special is about as cheap as it gets (unless you're just having white rice, a steal at $1.50).

Wakiya *Gramercy Park Hotel, 2 Lexington Ave at 21st St (212-995-1330). Subway: 6 to 23rd St. Mon–Sat 5:45–11:15pm; Sun 5:45–10:15pm. Average small plate $15.* It's no surprise that Wakiya is tough

Birds of a feather
Inevitably, diners at the Peking Duck House go for the roasted meat.

to get into: The cuisine is brought to you by Nobu Matsuhisa, who oversees the venture, and his Chinese-food equivalent, chef Yuji Wakiya, and it's located Ian Schrager's redesigned Gramercy Park Hotel. And the food lives up to expectations. Delicate flavors, sweeping variety and small plates turn every meal into a tasting menu. A subtle ginger-scallion chicken is poached, the poultry a blank canvas for candylike slivers of ginger, a few vibrant basil leaves and chilis. Wakiya reverses the very idea of egg fried rice, stuffing the rice into a wonderfully soft omelette, drizzled with briny XO sauce. Spicy, crunchy "golden sand"—panko bread crumbs and toasted garlic—spread over soft-shell crabs give the juicy crustaceans an addictive, savory crunch. The desserts are exceptional. A Vietnamese coffee affogato is brewed at the table, dripping espresso onto condensed-milk ice cream and coffee crunch. Showier still is the excellent lemon-infused mango pudding, plated atop a three-spouted teapot spewing dry-ice vapor. The drawback? The restaurant's nose-in-the-air policies and outrageous pricing, threaten to undermine its culinary achievements.

⊙**Yi Mei Gourmet Food Inc.** *51 Division St between Catherine and Market Sts (212-925-1921). Subway: B, D to Grand St; F to East Broadway. Daily 7am–9pm. Four-choices special: $3.* "Four choices," says the woman at the counter, leaving patrons to scan two dozen trays piled with sautéed crab pieces, salmon heads and some less familiar Fujianese dishes. The options change daily and might include crunchy shell-on shrimp slathered with salty paste, or deliciously chewy beef tripe. Garlic-bombed Chinese greens and strips of seaweed resemble (and sort of taste like) spinach fettuccine.

Eastern European

See also: *Russian*

Night and day
24-hour Veselka dishes out hearty Ukrainian grub around the clock.

⊙Bulgara *37-10 11th St at 37th Ave, Long Island City, Queens (718-392-5373). Subway: F to 21 St–Queensbridge. Thu noon–11pm; Fri, Sat noon–2am; Sun noon–11pm. Average main course price: $11.* Take a dance hall out of Sofia, plop it onto a deserted industrial stretch of Long Island City and you get this Bulgarian restaurant, draped in red curtains and faux-rustic art. Grilled meats and feta-heavy salads are served Friday nights with live music, starring female singers who wail Bulgarian pop songs accompanied by synthesizer or a prerecorded soundtrack. The meat platter features pork or chicken—from *kufte* (pork patties) and *shashlik* (pork skewers) to chicken shish kebabs. Popular with ex-pat groups, the spot is great for a night of kitschy fun.

⊙Cevabdzinica Sarajevo *37-18 34th Ave at 38th St, Astoria, Queens (718-752-9528). Subway: G, R, V to Steinway St. Daily 10am–10pm. Average main course: $8.* Vegetarians beware: meat steals the show here. Tables are filled with non-English-speaking regulars scarfing down *cevapcici*—little logs of ground beef shaped like sausage links, stuffed inside *somun*, thick slabs of bread. The best way to partake in the carnivore's fest here is the mixed platter. Designed for two, it brims with *cevapcici*, juicy chicken kebabs and, for diners who dare to eat like locals, veal kidneys and hearts too.

⊙Djerdan Burek *221 W 38th St between Seventh and Eighth Aves (212-921-1183). Subway: N, Q, R, W, 42nd St S, 1, 2, 3, 7 to 42nd St–Times Sq. Mon–Fri 11am–10pm; Sat, Sun noon–10pm. Average main course: $10.* Under varying names, *bureks* can

be found in many cuisines, but the spinach, cheese and meat ones at this Balkan luncheonette are special. They look like oversize wheels of Brie when they're pulled out of the oven, before being sliced into pizzalike wedges. They're at once flaky and chewy, light yet substantial. After a tangy yogurt drink, move on to delicious stuffed cabbage or tomato-based veal stew. **Other locations** *2301 65th St at 23rd Ave, Midwood, Brooklyn (718-336-9880)* ● *34-04A 31st Ave at 34th St, Astoria, Queens (718-721-2694).*

⊙Istria Sport Club *28-09 Astoria Blvd between 28th and 29th Sts , Astoria, Queens (718-728-3181). Subway: N, W to Astoria Blvd. Mon, Wed, Thu 3–10pm; Fri–Sun 1–10pm. Average main course: $10.* Since 1959, the Istria Sport club has been serving Istrian cuisine, a mix of Northern Italian and Eastern European comfort food at ridiculously low prices. The regulars, a mix of the old neighborhood boys and Italian couples, don't need menus. First-timers will be guided by a waiter, who might lead you to *njoki*, plump little potato dumplings sauced with light gravy and chunks of veal, or golden-brown chicken *paiarda*, pounded thin and served with a potato-and–Swiss-chard mash.

⊙Kasia's Restaurant *146 Bedford Ave at North 9th St, Williamsburg, Brooklyn (718-387-8780). Subway: L to Bedford Ave. Mon–Fri 7am–9pm (open weekends in winter). Average main course price: $10.* To have survived the hipification of Billyburg's Bedford Ave is no small feat, so this physically bland, diner-style eatery must be doing something right. That something is serving up cheap large portions of filling Polish eats like stuffed cabbage, beef goulash, kielbasa,

IMOGEN BROWN

and pierogi, as well as American favorites including sandwiches—from hero to club—and all-day breakfast items. Local Poles and neighborhood kids converge on this place, open on weekdays only. For a morning kick, get a freshly squeezed juice with health-conscious ingredients like kale, celery and ginger.

⊙Old Bridge (Stari Most) 28-52 42nd St
between 30th and 28th Aves, Astoria, Queens (718-932-7683). Subway: N, W to 30 Ave. Daily 10am–10pm. Average main course $11. Everyone in Astoria's Bosnian expat community has their favorite spot for scarfing down *çevapi*, minced beef sausages typically served with a flatbread and two spreads—cheesy *kajmak* and slightly spicy red-peppery *ajvar*. Most swear by those at Stari Most, named after the landmark Mostar Bridge, whose stone arch replica graces the interior. On a sunny day, enjoy your *çevapi*—or an alternative like sweetbreads or thin burger-like *pljeskavica*—on a sidewalk table, rounding out the meat feast with the super-sweet *hurmaçica* pastry and potent Bosnian coffee.

⊙Romanian Garden 46-04 Skillman Ave at
46th St, Sunnyside, Queens (718-786-7894). Subway: 7 to 46th St. Mon–Sat noon–midnight, Sun noon–11pm. Average main course: $10. It's very easy to embrace any cuisine that wraps pork sausage in smoky pork, and here the dish comes in a red-wine–spiked sauce next to mashed potatoes. Fake flowers wound around latticework successfully re-create the feeling of a real garden—but only after you've been drugged with a seductive version of polenta (*mamaliga cu brinza si smintina*), to which Italians only wish they could lay claim: Shreds of salty feta cover the cornmeal mush; five scoops of sour cream provide a cool counterpoint.

Sammy's Roumanian Steak House
157 Chrystie St between Delancey and Rivington Sts (212-673-0330). Subway: B, D to Grand St; F, V to Lower East Side–Second Ave; J, M, Z to Bowery. Mon–Thu 4–10pm; Fri, Sat 4–11pm; Sun 3–9:30pm. Average main course: $25. Walk into this LES basement old-timer on a crowded evening and you may think you've stumbled into a bar mitzvah—Yiddish sing-alongs and impromptu dancing are ignited by the live synthesizer and further fuelled by the frozen vodka. But you don't have to join the horah to have a

Read 'em & eat

bigos: Polish stew made with assorted meat, tomatoes, onions and cabbage

borscht: (also *borsch*) Polish or Russian beet soup; it can contain meat or other vegetables, and is served hot or cold

burek: (also *borek* or *boureka*) savory pastries made from phyllo or yufka dough, filled with cheese (often feta), minced meat, potatoes or other vegetables

cevapcici: ground Yugoslavian meat patties made from beef, veal, pork or lamb

kasha: a sticky, nutty roasted buckwheat

blast. Instead, focus on the true-and-tried Jewish dishes featuring meat in all its guises—from chicken livers and garlicky *karnatzlack* sausage patties to enormous Romanian tenderloins. The decor of this low-ceilinged spot with photo-plastered walls may be outdated, but the prices aren't.

⊙Teresa's 80 Montague St between Hicks St and
Montague Terr, Brooklyn Heights (718-797-3996). Subway: M, R to Court St; 2, 3 to Clark St. Daily 7am–11pm. Average main course: $10. This Polish diner, with blond wood and blonder servers, pumps out gargantuan old-world fare at old-world prices. The kitchen excels at anything combined with sour cream or applesauce, like garlicky, discus-sized potato pancakes and pillowy pierogi. Breakfasts—larded with kielbasa, *kasha* and *babka* (yeast cake) whenever possible—are so substantial you'll want to thresh some wheat afterwards. Staples like burgers and sandwiches are passable, but stay Slavic and you'll be rewarded with the good stuff, like crisp cucumber salad spiked with dill and cream.

⊙Ukrainian East Village 140 Second Ave
between 8th and 9th Sts (212-614-3283). 6 to Astor Pl; F, V to Lower East Side–Second Ave; R, W to 8th St–NYU. Daily noon–11pm. Average main course: $9. Escape the throngs that swarm nearby Veselka and head to this East Village alternative located inside the Ukrainian National Home. Served in a rustic room with an all-wood decor and no natural light, the hit-and-miss fare is of an Eastern European variety with an accent on Ukrainian staples. Meat rules the menu—veal, beef, pork, lamb, chicken… you name it; the seafood dishes are a mere afterthought. Expect anything from Wiener schnitzel to *letcho* Hungarian goulash and Ukrainian borscht. All entrées come with a starchy side and a salad.

▲⊙Veselka 144 Second Ave at 9th St (212-228-
9682). Subway: L to Third Ave; 6 to Astor Pl. Daily 24hrs. Average main course: $11. When you need food to soak up the mess of drinks you've consumed in the East Village, Veselka is a dream come true: a relatively inexpensive Eastern European restaurant with plenty of seats and loads of options, open 24 hours a day. Hearty appetites can get a platter of classic Ukrainian grub: goulash, kielbasa, beef Stroganoff or *bigos* stew. If you just want a nosh, try the sweet stuff: They've got many pies, cakes, egg creams and milk shakes—plus Ukrainian poppy seed cake and *kutya* (traditional Ukrainian pudding made with berries, raisins, walnuts, poppy seeds and honey).

Zlata Praha 28-48 31st St between Newtown
and 30th Aves, Astoria, Queens (718-721-6422). Subway: N, W to 30th Ave. Tue–Sun noon–11pm. Average main course: $12. Zlata Praha—"golden Prague"—is a Central European haven in central Astoria, and you're the tourist: Very little English is spoken, and the walls are decorated with traditional folk costumes, old currency and pictures of Prague. Zlata Praha's rustic, filling chow references many Eastern European nations—there's a Hungarian salami and goulash and "Slovak-style" pierogi—but the Czech platter for two is one of the best deals going: smoked pork, flavorful pork loin and half a crisp roasted duck. Three types of cabbage and doughy "bread dumplings"—steamed sourdough slices—guarantee a satisfied stomach.

Eclectic

See also: *American Creative, Asian, French*

Outer dimension
Gilt was designed for gastronomic explorers.

★ **August** *359 Bleecker St between Charles and W 10th Sts (212-929-4774). Subway: 1 to Christopher St–Sheridan Sq. Mon–Thu noon–3:30, 5:30–11pm; Fri noon–3:30, 5:30–midnight; Sat 11am–3:30pm, 5:30–midnight; Sun 11am–3:30pm, 5:30–10pm. Average main course: $22.* The tiny, rustic space, with its cork ceiling and antique-yellow stucco walls, is a little piece of the countryside in the West Village, where seasonal fare is consistently excellent. Fava beans tossed with fresh mint on sheep's-milk-cheese–smothered peasant bread is a taste of spring, and the codfish brandade is as fluffy as cotton candy. The braised rabbit with pea puree and carrots falls off the bone, and a chubby, whole trout, baked in the wood-burning oven and stuffed with morels, ramps and scallions, is crisp, chewy and packed with earthy flavor.

Bamn! *37 St. Marks Pl at Second Ave (888-400-2266). Subway: 6 to Astor Pl. Mon–Thu 11:30am–1am; Fri, Sat 11:30am–3am; Sun 11:30am–1am. Average main course: $2.* Serial noshers flock to this cheery pink-and-white revival of the '50s Automat, which—despite its name—shares no affiliation with TV chef Emeril Lagasse. An army of silver coin-operated doors dispenses immediate gratification via a bevy of delectable, freshly prepared American, Middle Eastern and Pan-Asian snacks such as still-warm (heated bases keep hot fare toasty) pork buns, freshly fried cauliflower-filled samosas and Nutella-slathered waffles. Don't worry about bringing your piggybank: Two machines dispense silver dollars and quarters, plus there's an ATM.

★ ▲**Blue Ribbon Bakery** *33 Downing St at Bedford St (212-337-0404). Subway: A, C, E, B, D, F, V to W 4th St; 1 to Houston St. Mon–Thu noon–midnight; Fri noon–2am; Sat 11:30am–2am; Sun 11:30am–* midnight. *Average main course: $25.* The 150-year-old oven downstairs produces beautiful, crusty breads, but the real magnet at this window-walled, congenially noisy spot is the lengthy something-for-everyone menu. Cross-cultural nibbles, soups, sandwiches and entrées (including lots of bistro basics like leeks in mustard vinaigrette and marrow bones in red wine sauce) are all expertly prepared. The wine list offers somewhat expensive selections by the small, medium or large glass. Big groups can request one of the semiprivate alcoves downstairs. **Other locations** *Blue Ribbon, 97 Sullivan St between Prince and Spring Sts (212-274-0404)* ● *Blue Ribbon Brooklyn, 280 Fifth Ave between Garfield Pl and 1st St, Park Slope, Brooklyn (718-840-0404)* ● *Blue Ribbon Downing Street Bar, 34 Downing St between Bedford and Varick Sts (212-691-0404).*

★ ▲**Crave** *570 Henry St between Carroll and Summit Sts, Carroll Gardens, Brooklyn (718-643-0361). Subway: F, G to Carroll St. Tue–Thu 6–10:30pm; Fri, Sat 6–11pm; Sun 11am–4pm, 5–10pm. Average main course: $21.* This unassuming storefront (also a catering service) channels two undercurrents in the stream of Carroll Garden's evolution: While the sophisticated New American menu appeals to discerning Smith Street carpetbaggers, the no-frills decor and chummy service provide a welcoming atmosphere for longtime residents and families. Adventurous dishes mesh sweet comfort with spicy surprise—the chocolate chili cake demands your mouth's full attention, and the allspice-laced rice that accompanies the goat-cheese-stuffed pork loin boasts a chewy berry compote. Even straight-up traditional fare, like the penne with sausage and fennel, or crab cake appetizer, tastes delicate and somehow novel.

JEFF GURWIN

E.U. (European Union) 235 E 4th St between Aves A and B (212-254-2900). Subway: F, V to Lower East Side–Second Ave. Mon–Thu 11am–4pm, 6pm–midnight; Fri, Sat 11am–4pm, 6pm–1am; Sun 11am–4pm, 6pm–midnight. Average main course: $20. With Akhtar Nawab (Craftbar) at the helm, this gastropub's finally rid of its beleaguered past. Butcher-paper menus do extra duty as place mats and bread-basket lining, tables are spaced tightly, and the music is cranked to an intolerable volume. Nawab has added American touches like hamburgers and chicken potpie to the menu, along with a few twists: Foie gras terrine comes lathered with foamy lemon curd, while Berkshire pork medallions are paired with peppercorn-studded sauerkraut. Desserts are less surprising—steer clear of the middling toffee pudding.

Employees Only 510 Hudson St between Christopher and W 10th Sts (212-242-3021). Subway: 1 to Christopher St–Sheridan Sq. Mon–Fri 6pm–4am; Sat, Sun 11am–4am. Average main course: $25. Don't let the psychic palm reader in the window scare you away. She's part of the high-concept decor at Employees Only, a restaurant in the West Village inspired by the speakeasies of yore. Peek behind the purple curtain in the foyer and you'll see mahogany walls, a working fireplace, a shiny tin ceiling and a collection of vintage cocktail books and bottles—inspiration for co-owner Jason Kosmas's innovative drinks. Chef Jeremy Spector has conceived a "rustic European" menu that features a Serbian charcuterie plate and house-cured gravlax. Swing by late at night and you can nosh on baked brie and steak tartar until 4am.

★ **5 Ninth** 5 Ninth Ave between Gansevoort and Little West 12th Sts (212-929-9460). Subway: A, C, E to 14th St; L to Eighth Ave. Mon–Fri noon–11pm; Sat, Sun 11am–11pm. Average main course: $22. The Asian-inflected instincts of chef-owner Zac Pelaccio at this spare, brick-walled duplex of dining rooms are as sharp as ever, but presentation can be precious, prices high and portions model-size. Thick chips of bacon teeter atop four tiny oysters, each on a spoonful of vivid-green sweet-pea puree; it's a lovely balance of sweet, savory and salty, but the plate is clean in four bites. Poached lobster in a ginger beurre blanc is also too small (and too good) to share, though the kobe rib eye in chunky coconut chutney is more generously portioned. In the summer, sip a cocktail on the peaceful back deck.

Gilt 455 Madison Ave between 50th and 51st Sts (212-891-8100). Subway: E, V to Fifth Ave–53rd St. Tue–Thu 5:30–10pm; Fri, Sat 5:30–10:30pm.. Three-course prix fixe: $78. Gilt offers popular yet experimental fare in a dining room whose floor is covered with orange rubber overlays, while the bar exudes the quirky ambience of a lunar landscape thanks to the placement of a giant plastic honeycomb sculpture. Billed as a three-course prix fixe on the menu, the meal includes at least a half-dozen extra courses—which helps justify the $78 price. The ride starts with a series of amuse-bouches; hibiscus-covered marshmallows melt on the tongue, and beet-flavored tuiles taste like candy. One terrific appetizer wraps a crabmeat-and-gingerbread filling in a transparent fish gelée, bracketed sandwich-style with dried-seaweed crackers. The only drawback is that wine choices lean on too many big-ticket French bottles.

★ **The Good Fork** 2007 Eat Out Award, Readers' Choice: Best new Brooklyn restaurant; Best new neighborhood spot. 391 Van Brunt St between Coffey

and Dikeman Sts (718-643-6636). Subway: F, G to Smith–9th Sts. Tue–Sun 5:30–10:30pm. Average main course: $16. This affordable, sophisticated Brooklyn restaurant—evocative of a first-class dining car with its glossy wood paneling—consistently packs in local crowds. Much of the credit goes to chef Sohui Kim (Blue Hill, Annisa), whose Asian-inspired menu flirts with European influences in dishes like Atlantic cod with red lentils and Chinese long bean in a lemon beurre blanc sauce. Getting there can be a tougher sell: Expect at least a ten-minute walk from the subway.

★**Gordon Ramsay at The London** The London NYC Hotel, 151 W 54th St between Sixth and Seventh Aves (212-468-8888). Subway: F to 57th St. Daily noon–2pm, 5:30–10:30pm. Three-course prix-fixe dinner: $80. Seven-course prix-fixe dinner: $110. The 12 tables that occupy the dining room of the first stateside restaurant from celebrity chef Gordon Ramsay are famously difficult to score. The menu hews close to hat of Ramsay's eponymous three-star flagship in London: French cuisine with international influences, served as either a three-course or seven-course prix fixe meal—with extra amuse-bouches and palate cleansers. The chef's take on French cuisine is always interesting: The signature dish, cannon of lamb, is like a deconstructed stew; roast leg medallions and confit share the plate with candied onions, shallots, tomatoes and exotic spices. Desserts are just as important: The exceptionally fluffy apricot soufflé requires advance ordering, and a bonbon trolley peddled toothsome cotton candy, caramel popcorn and fruit jellies. Ramsay has delivered on the promises of his perfectionist TV alter ego. **Other location** Maze,

Border patrol
Take a taste tour at E.U. (European Union).

JENNY WOODWARD

Get fresh

What's for dinner? Whatever's in season.

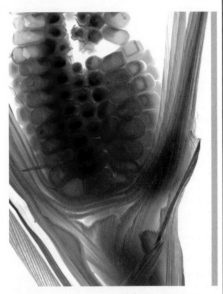

Over the past few years, local foods have become as much a part of the New York dining landscape as foie gras and designer restrooms. Selecting produce cheek-by-jowl with celebrated chefs at the Union Square farmers' market is almost de rigueur, as are the seasonally driven menus that highlight the chefs' findings.

But it isn't just the superfresh taste that diners are responding to. The growing awareness of issues like food miles—how far food travels from farm to table—and the environmental cost of buying, say, an out-of-season tomato grown in Mexico have fed restaurant-goers' desire for local ingredients.

One of the first people to champion local foods was Peter Hoffman, who opened **Savoy** in 1990 with the express idea of using ingredients sourced from local farmers. Dan Barber took up the mantle in 2000 with **Blue Hill**, whose seasonal menus now feature produce grown at **Stone Barns** in Westchester and meat raised in the Hudson Valley. You can still spot Hoffman at the Union Square market, along with other chefs including Marco Moreira of **Tocqueville**. In fact, chefs throughout the city are devoted to all things seasonal and local.

Among them are Marc Meyer, whose **Cookshop** devotes one of its walls to a lengthy list of the restaurant's local suppliers, and Bill **Telepan**, whose eponymous restaurant's menus are dictated by the seasons. In Brooklyn, such eateries as **Rose Water** and **Ici** use local producers, notably from the borough's Red Hook Community Farm, where organic fruit and vegetables are grown and harvested largely by neighborhood teenagers.

The London NYC Hotel, 151 W 54th St between Sixth and Seventh Aves (212-468-8888).

Klee Brasserie 200 Ninth Ave between 22nd and 23rd Sts (212-633-8033). Subway: C, E to 23rd St. Daily 6–11pm. Average main course: $24. The bar in front of chef Daniel Angerer's place screams Chelsea with its designer lighting, while the dining area evokes a ski chalet thanks to white-wood paneling. In addition to affordable bar snacks, including hot almonds and mini lobster rolls, the fare shows equal parts imagination and appreciation of fine ingredients. The nicely marbled *kurobuta* pork *tonnato* is fantastic, as are entreés like slow-roasted duck with plums and honey, and Rhode Island swordfish—thick as filet mignon. Hints of Angerer's native Austria come through in the desserts: apple strudel and Sacher torte *mit schlag*.

Knife + Fork 2007 Eat Out Award, Readers' Choice: Best new prix fixe 108 E 4th St between First and Second Aves (212-228-4885). Subway: F, V to Lower East Side–Second Ave; 6 to Astor Pl. Tue–Sat 5:30–11pm; Sun 5:30–10pm. Average main course: $26. Chef Damien Brassel (Sapa, Bolo) mans the kitchen all alone in his tiny East Village restaurant, which combines haute cuisine with familial intimacy. Dishes skew Pan-European and change weekly based on what's fresh. Order the six-course tasting menu, a bargain at $45, and you get to try nearly half the menu. Lots of classic delicacies pop up: cured salmon with a wasabi crème fraîche, goat cheese and polenta, quail, foie gras. But operating solo means there are no checks and balances, so don't expect perfection.

★ ▲**Landmarc at the Time Warner Center** 10 Columbus Circle at Broadway, third floor (212-823-6123). Subway: A, C, B, D, 1 to 59th St–Columbus Circle. Daily 7am–2am. Average main course: $26. It's fitting that chef Marc Murphy opened a second version of his Tribeca classic in the world's greatest food court. The long hours, ample seating, no-reservations policy (except for parties of six or more) and sophisticated meat-and-potatoes fare make this the most democratic eatery in the mall. Steak and mussels remain the house emphases, but the biggest draw is the wine list—the razor-thin markups and 50 half bottles make for maximum sampling. **Other location** Landmarc Tribeca, 179 West Broadway between Leonard and Worth Sts (212-343-3883).

Maze The London NYC Hotel, 151 W 54th St between Sixth and Seventh Aves (212-468-8888). Subway: F to 57th St. Daily noon–2pm, 5:30–10:30pm. Average small plate: $16; four-course prix fixe $55; six-course prix-fixe $75. Waiters at Gordon Ramsay's glimmering modern space at the London Hotel, with leather banquettes the shade of faded denim and an inviting chrome-accented bar, might recommend ordering four small plates from the menu, but three serve well, tantalizing your palate and only slightly sparing your wallet. A beet-and-ricotta dish is a stunning quartet of wafer-thin beet slices crowned with clouds of soft cheese. Another visually arresting plate contrasts the pinkness of nearly raw salmon with bright yellow scrambled eggs and black caviar. In a hat's-off to the host country, dessert brings forth a PB & J with a satiny peanut butter *semifreddo*, cherry jam and cherry sorbet. The biggest surprise of all: Chef Ramsay is occasionally in the house. **Other location** Gordon Ramsay at The London, The London NYC Hotel, 151 W 54th St between Sixth and Seventh Aves (212-468-8888).

Mo Pitkin's House of Satisfaction 34 Ave A between 2nd and 3rd Sts (212-777-5660). Subway: F, V to *Lower East Side–Second Ave. Daily 5–11pm. Average main course: $11.* The quirky menu here is a mishmash of Jewish comfort food and American-diner classics, with some Latin-inspired hits (the Cuban Reuben with pulled pork and corned beef) tossed in for good measure. Potato latkes are soft and warm in the center and hot and crisp on the outside. And when you're in a big booth sipping an Orange Julius before dinner, you'll feel like a kid again, only better: The version here is spiked with vanilla vodka.

Monkey Town *58 North 3rd St between Kent and Wythe Aves, Williamsburg, Brooklyn (718-384-1369). Subway: L to Bedford Ave. Daily 6pm–1am. Average small plate $8, average main course: $19.* Even in a neighborhood where you can dine among suspended rowboat fountains, inside a tree house or on floors covered with sand, Monkey Town stands out. The dining room has an industrial-romantic vibe: Smooth cement floors are dotted with candles, low tables and futonlike couches. In the back is a 48-seat screening room with four floor-to-ceiling screens. Chef Ryan Jaronik (Masa Boston) recently took over the kitchen and has created a daring menu of primarily small plates. Such inventive fare includes espresso-rubbed venison with ancho squash flan, and cherry-braised cabbage with coffee sauce.

★ **Public** *210 Elizabeth St between Prince and Spring Sts (212-343-7011). Subway: N, R, W to Prince St; 6 to Spring St. Mon–Thu 6–11:30pm; Fri 6pm–12:30am; Sat 11am–3:30pm, 6pm–12:30am; Sun 11am–3:30pm, 6pm–12:30am. Average main course: $22.* This sceney designer restaurant inside a former bakery brings a touch of the Meatpacking District to Nolita. Moodily lit and industrially chic, its two conjoined spaces showcase a sleek mix of concrete, exposed brick and wood paneling. The mastermind behind Public's globally inspired cuisine is British-trained Brad Farmerie, whose travels have left a cosmopolitan mark on his culinary concoctions. Reflecting Pan-Pacific, Middle Eastern and Southeast Asian influences, the clipboard menu offers creative dishes like grilled kangaroo on a coriander falafel; snail and oxtail ravioli; and pan-seared Tasmanian sea trout, all poetically presented and paired with unique wines.

★ ▲◐**Rice** *81 Washington St between Front and York Sts, Dumbo, Brooklyn (718-222-9880). Subway: A, C to High St; F to York St. Daily noon–11pm. Average main course: $10.* Not a restaurant for the indecisive, Rice offers an array of savory toppings (grilled shrimp satay bathed in almond-peanut sauce, ratatouille, vegetarian meatballs). Mix and match them with your choice of ten different rices, including Bhutanese red rice, Thai black rice steamed in coconut milk, and straightforward brown and basmati. Park benches double as seating in the warehouselike space, or you can grab a table on the pretty, flower-filled patio. **Other locations** *292 Elizabeth Street between Bleecker and Houston Sts (212-226-5775)* ● *115 Lexington Ave at 28th St (212-686-5400)* ● *Rice: Fort Greene, 166 DeKalb Ave at Cumberland St, Fort Greene, Brooklyn (718-858-2700).*

◐**SavorNY** *63 Clinton St between Rivington and Stanton Sts (212-358-7125). Subway: F to Delancey St; J, M, Z to Delancey–Essex Sts. Mon, Tue 5–11pm; Wed–Sat 5pm–midnight; Sun 5–11pm. Average small plate: $10.* This pretty sliver of a place is almost hidden among the frenetic bars and superhip eateries of Clinton Street. The simple design—gold walls, dark-wood seats—affords a haven for laidback locals who want affordable, interesting vino and serious small-plate action. Dishes are labeled "finger" or "fork," depending on pickupability. Standouts

Sight seeing
Choose your eats from a cheeky '50s-style Automat at Bamn!

include sweet and saucy BBQ duck (forget the fork and lick your fingers) and meltingly lovely Wagyu beef encrusted in salty-spicy chimichurri.

★ **The Spotted Pig** *314 W 11th St at Greenwich St (212-620-0393). Subway: A, C, E to 14th St; L to Eighth Ave. Mon–Fri noon–2am; Sat, Sun 11am–2am. Average main course: $15.* Yes, this West Village spot on a quiet, charming little block is still hopping—and even after opening more seating upstairs, a wait is always expected. Some might credit the big names involved (Mario Batali consults and co-owner April Bloomfield, of London's River Café, is in the kitchen). The burger is a must-order: a top-secret blend of ground beef grilled rare (unless otherwise specified) and covered with gobs of pungent Roquefort. It arrives plated with a tower of crispy shoestring fries tossed with rosemary. But the kitchen saves the best treat for dessert: a delectable slice of moist, spiced ginger cake with a dollop of crème fraîche.

The Stanton Social *99 Stanton St at Ludlow St (212-995-0099). Subway: F, V to Lower East Side–Second Ave. Mon–Wed 5pm–2am; Thu, Fri 5pm–3am; Sat 11:30am–3am; Sun 11:30am–2am. Average small plate: $11.* Plenty of trendy spots have opened on the Lower East Side, but none with as much eye candy as this. Gorgeous chandeliers, lizard-skin banquettes and retro rounded booths only hint at the 1940s-inspired elegance of the three-level restaurant. Not that the decor steals the show. Chris Santos (Suba, Wyanoka) has created 45 sharable, international plates—light dishes followed by heavier ones—all of which receive special treatment. French onion soup comes in dumpling form, and red-snapper tacos are covered with an irresistibly fiery mango-and-avocado salsa.

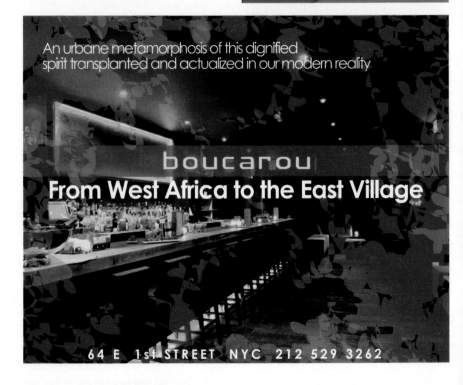

French

See also: *American Creative, Eclectic, Mediterranean*

Bon goût
Bar Tabac's "bistro bites" are a cheap ticket to France.

$15 and under

Bacchus *409 Atlantic Ave at Bond St, Boerum Hill, Brooklyn (718-852-1572). Subway: A, C to Hoyt–Schermerhorn; F, G to Bergen St. Daily noon–midnight. Average main course: $15.* As the name suggests, the emphasis here is on vino (20 selections by the glass, 200 by the bottle). The mellow locals aren't necessarily wine buffs, so the staff's dead-on recommendations are much appreciated. Head to the low-lit dining room or tree-lined garden for a pleasant sit-down meal. Entrées like *moules* Bacchus (mussels cooked in red wine, bacon, onions and herbs) and *confit de canard* (roasted duck leg) are always satisfying. Service is friendly, if *laissez-faire*.

Bar 6 *502 Sixth Ave between 12th and 13th Sts (212-691-1363). Subway: F, V to 14th St; L to Sixth Ave. Mon–Fri 11am–1am; Sat, Sun 10:30am–1am. Average main course: $15. Prix fixe: $19.50.* Settle in under the expansive skylight and ceiling fans at this breezy French afternoon of a place and watch the staff make it all look easy. The frisée salad balances the bitter crunch of frisée with the sweet saltiness of *lardons*, while the steak frites au poivre offers absolutely faultless frites. And a pitch-perfect croque-madame, made with Canadian ham, Gruyère and two fried eggs, promises pure embarrassment for other grilled cheese concoctions. The easiness of the place is infectious, so just embrace your champagne and relax.

Bar Tabac *128 Smith St at Dean St, Boerum Hill, Brooklyn (718-923-0918). Subway: F, G to Bergen St. Mon, Tue 10am–1am; Wed–Sat 10am–2am; Sun 10am–1am. Average main course: $15.* Bar Tabac has become the anchor of Smith Street's thriving French expat scene. On Bastille Day, the café hosts a *pétanque* tournament; every day, it aims to re-create the bonhomie of those Parisian hangouts that sell cigarettes and lottery tickets. A foosball table near the entrance and the small pot of Dijon mustard on each table are nice touches, but the food is what counts. At $5 apiece, the "bistro bites" (skewered scallops, merguez, snails, etc.) are a good way to start. Perfectly salted frites are crisp outside and moist inside, and you can even get a nicely grilled shell steak on the side.

▲**Belleville** *330 Fifth Ave at 5th St, Park Slope, Brooklyn (718-832-9777). Subway: M, R to Fourth Ave–9th St. Daily noon–midnight. Average main course: $15.* Every table is usually full at this convivial crowd magnet, so hungry would-be diners must nurse glasses of vin rouge at the two zinc-topped bars. Chef Joe Elorriaga has lightened the typical bistro menu, cutting down on cream and butter and adding some contemporary touches. A salad of baby spinach and feta, piled on top of carpaccio-style beets, makes it easy to eat your vegetables. Filet mignon with green peppercorns is tender and juicy, if a bit small. Among the usual desserts is a snappy ringer: bracing grapefruit sorbet with charred ruby-red grapefruit segments in caramel sauce.

Bouchon Bakery *Time Warner Center, 10 Columbus Circle at Broadway, third floor (212-823-9366). Subway: A, C, B, D, 1 to 59th St–Columbus Circle. Mon–Sat 11:30am–9pm; Sun 11:30–7pm. Average main course: $13.* The appeal is obvious: Sample Thomas Keller's food for far less than it costs at Per Se, where the tasting menu is now a whopping $250 per person. The

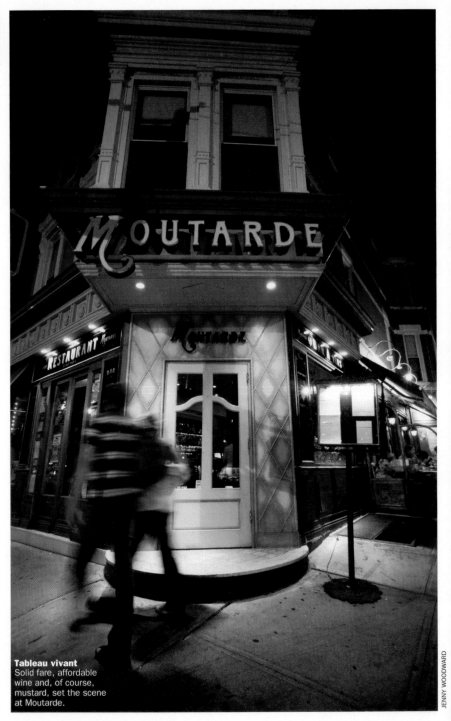

Tableau vivant
Solid fare, affordable
wine and, of course,
mustard, set the scene
at Moutarde.

JENNY WOODWARD

reality is that you will have to eat in an open café setting in the middle of a mall, under a giant Samsung sign, and choose from a limited selection of sandwiches, salads, quiches and spreadable entrées (pâté, foie gras and so on). That said, this is a great place for lunch. The servers are friendly and can describe every ingredient on every plate. The sandwiches (around $13 a pop) are impeccably plated—though portions can be small. Wine is available by the bottle or carafe. Impatient types can buy everything on the menu at the storefront across the way.

Café Lafayette 99 South Portland Ave at Fulton St, Fort Greene, Brooklyn (718-858-6821). Subway: C to Lafayette Ave, G to Fulton St. Mon–Thu 10am–11pm; Fri, Sat 10am–midnight; Sun 10am–11pm. Average main course: $15. With fewer than 30 seats, this café is a kind of secret locals like to keep to themselves—in order to have a better chance of scoring one of the red booths. Appetizers such as escargots share menu space with (decidedly less French) onion rings and shrimp fritters; the fabulous salad of warm spinach, bacon chunks, feta and caramelized walnuts is a meal in itself. Excellent mushroom risotto can be ordered as an appetizer or an entrée. The coq au vin can be a bit tough, but is redeemed by a side of the best potato gratin west of Lyon, followed by an exquisite apple tart.

⊙Chez Brigitte 77 Greenwich Ave between Bank and W 11th Sts (212-929-6736). Subway: A, C, E, 1, 2, 3 to 14th St; L to Eighth Ave. Daily 11am–10pm. Average main course: $8. Tiny Chez Brigitte's lunch is one of the best deals in the West Village: your choice of veal stew, chicken fricassee, chicken cutlets and more—accompanied by roasted potatoes, yellow rice, peas and salad, all for $6. The restaurant-size can of peas on the counter belies any suggestion that they're from the garden, but everything else certainly tastes fresh. Any way you order you're bound to find a bargain.

Epicerie 168–170 Orchard St at Stanton St (212-420-7520). Subway: F, V to Lower East Side–Second Ave. Mon–Thu 5pm–midnight; Fri 5pm–1am; Sat 11am–1am; Sun 11am–midnight. Average main course: $15. Open the door to Epicerie and you'll find yourself in a re-creation of a small Parisian grocery store with shelves filled with French knickknacks and cans of choucroute and petits pois. The unpretentious bistro classics are just as appealing. Steak tartare is a well-seasoned pile-up of tender fillet, tomatoes and capers. Hungry patrons huddle on Mondays for all-you-can-eat mussels, which come in a buttery broth of white wine and shallots, accompanied by crisp frites. After dinner, retreat to the adjoining Café Charbon for Belgian tap beer.

▲Fada 530 Driggs Ave at North 8th St, Williamsburg, Brooklyn (718-388-6607). Subway: L to Bedford Ave. Mon–Thu 10am–midnight; Fri 10am–1am; Sat 10am–1am; Sun 10am–midnight. Average main course: $15. Like any bistro worth its sea salt, Fada is built for people-watching. Long mirrors line the walls, French doors are flung open to the street and, when weather permits, café tables dot the sidewalk, where the proximity to the L train provides a steady stream of eye candy. Service can be slow, but the pace gives you more time to scan the crowds—and savor the food. Camembert and figs wrapped in puff pastry are a rich start. The aioli traditionale is a grand platter of steamed codfish, boiled eggs and assorted vegetables, all ready to be drizzled with garlicky aioli sauce.

Fanny 425 Graham Ave between Frost and Withers St, Williamsburg, Brooklyn (718-389-2060). Subway: L to Graham Ave. Mon–Thu 11am–10pm; Fri, Sat 11am–11pm; Sun 11am–10pm. Average main course: $14. Fanny is filled with antique-looking exposed-filament bulbs (replicas of the first model invented by Con Edison); wood, slate and concrete walls; and cherry-maple wood tables. The owners, both French expats, have stocked the menu with bistro classics: An appetizer of steamed mussels is served in a terra-cotta crock with an addictive buttery and garlicky white-wine-and-shallot sauce. Among the entrées, the roasted chicken with mushrooms fricassee and spinach is most notable for its delightfully tender and juicy meat and for the way the chef—a French-trained Japanese man named Hiro Kiriyama—cooks the skin to a perfect crisp. Kiriyama prepares the desserts, too, and his gooey, raisin-and-pine-nut-studded apple strudel with fig ice cream arrives warm and tasted freshly bakes.

Flea Market Cafe 131 Ave A between St. Marks Pl and 9th St (212-358-9280). Subway: L to First Ave. Mon–Fri 10am–11pm; Sat, Sun 9am–midnight. Average main course: $15. Gilles Ray's unassuming ode to the art of the (secondhand) deal is always boisterous and bustling, and the menu is as classic as a vintage Citroën. Soupe à l'oignon is capped with Gruyère, while steak au poivre is charred, juicy and accompanied by crisp fries. Goat cheese and caramelized onions overflow from a savory variation on tarte Tatin; a pretty pink slab of salmon is drizzled with herbed olive oil and a scattering of chunky green pistachios. Servers can be a little harried, which means orders can lag (or get mixed up), but a glass from the reasonably priced wine list will take the edge off.

★ Florent 69 Gansevoort St between Greenwich and Washington Sts (212-989-5779). Subway: A, C, E to 14th S; L to Eighth Ave. Daily 24hrs. Average main course: $15. When Florent Morellet opened this French-inflected diner opened in the '80s, it was an instant success with both adventurous downtowners who dared to venture off the beaten path and the neighborhood's rough trade (trannie hookers and the Johns who loved them) that ruled the area. Thirty years and stunning gentrification have done nothing to diminish Florent's appeal. Settle in for garlicky escargots, French onion soup or classic steak and eggs. Unfortunately, illicit activity in the washroom is no longer acceptable.

Gribouille 2 Hope St at Roebling St, Williamsburg, Brooklyn (718-384-3100). Subway: L, G to Metropolitan Ave–Lorimer St. Tue–Sun 8am–7pm. Average main course: $14. Authenticity reigns at this Williamsburg Gallic cafe: Mushrooms are flown in from France for the tarte flambées; a framed record by '60s singer Jacques Dutronc hangs in a corner of the simply appointed space; the doting waitstaff hails from Paris. Former Gramercy Tavern sous pastry chef Jeanne Nievert whips up savory dishes such as European-sized (think: smaller portions than most NYC restaurants) croque-madames and poached salmon, as well as sweet items, notably the textbook-perfect croissants and tarts.

Grand 275 275 Grand Ave between Clifton Pl and Lafayette Ave, Clinton Hill, Brooklyn (718-398-4402). Subway: C, G to Clinton–Washington Aves. Tue–Thu 8am–11pm; Fri 8am–2am; Sat 11am–2am; Sun 11am–11pm. Average main course: $7. Who knew a tiny café-cum-DJ-hut could wield such influence? Mark Chung and Carmen Grau's Grand 275 has gone a long way toward

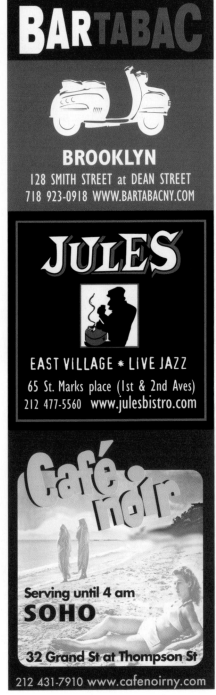

transforming a formerly sketchy block. Chung and Grau (previously of Mesa Grill and the Odeon, respectively) have been welcomed in turn by a neighborhood hungry for stylish grub. A community garden donates fresh mint for mojitos, and Pratt students swarm in for the $11 mimosa weekend brunch. The Grand's 2am closing time never fails to disappoint late-night partyers. The good news is, they can always get some shut-eye and come back at 11am, when the doors open for breakfast.

Jean Claude *137 Sullivan St between Houston and Prince Sts (212-475-9232). Subway: C, E to Spring St. Mon–Thu 6–11pm; Fri, Sat 6–11:30pm; Sun 6–11pm. Average main course: $15.* For the last decade, Jean-Claude Iacovelli's eponymous bistro has found a following by delivering Paris to Soho with barely a nudge in price. The restaurant remains a solid bet when you're craving rustic French fare without pretense or planning (though they take reservations, you won't often need one). Count on big flavors and generous portions. Seared foie gras on a sweet-potato bed is charred on the outside and creamy within. Meaty bordelaise-sauced hanger steak comes with decadent gratin potatoes. Save room for the exceptional tarte Tatin.

★ **Jules** *65 St Marks Pl between First and Second Aves (212-477-5560). Subway: L to First Ave, 6 to Astor Pl. Mon–Fri 11am–4pm, 5:30pm–12:30am, Sat 10am–4:30pm, 5:30pm–1am; Sun10am–4:30pm, 5:30–12:30am. Average main course: $15.* Habitués of this chic enclave may have scored high-paying jobs uptown, but they still prefer to play downtown style. Candles flicker, tables are separated by groovy beaded partitions, and the music has a swinging, loungey feel (lively groups like to be near the bar; quieter diners head for the narrow back room). There's nothing nouveau about the food, though. Jules's offerings are unapologetically hearty—beef stew simmered in red wine or spiced lamb shanks with figs. Dover sole is just flown in from France, according to the affable waiter, and the filet mignon special must be ordered medium-rare.

▲**Lucky Strike** *59 Grand St between West Broadway and Wooster St (212-941-0772). Subway: A, C, E to Canal St. Mon–Thu; Fri, Sat noon–4am; Sun noon–2am. Average main course: $15.* Less glittering boîte than rakish hang, this 18-year-old workhorse has a look dating all the way back to the last bistro craze—distressed mirrors, a copper-topped bar and dull wooden floors round out the worn-in decor. Tourists and Soho habitués chill

Foodie call Open until 2am, the Pink Pony satisfies late-night yens.

French $15 and under

over tasty standards like warm lentil salad, steak frites and croque-monsieur, all haphazardly flopped on plates with nary a garnish in sight. The prices are reasonable and the flavors familiar, which is how the regulars like it. A decent selection of wines by the glass, inventive cocktails and the kitchen's long hours make this a good stop after a day (or night) of knocking around Soho.

★ ▲**Moutarde** *239 Fifth Ave at Carroll St, Park Slope, Brooklyn (718-623-3600). Subway: M, R to Union St. Mon–Thu 11am–midnight; Fri 11am–2am; Sat 10:30am–2am; Sun 10am–midnight. Average main course: $14.* Mustard is taken very seriously at Moutarde; instead of the usual bread and butter, diners get a ceramic palette daubed with various mustards and presented with bits of toasted bread, carrots and celery. The waitstaff is charming, the prices affordable, and the bistro-solid appetizers include duck confit on greens, pan-seared foie gras with candied sweet potatoes and leeks, and steamed mussels with chorizo. Seafood entrées are particularly strong: potato-crusted skate with sautéed spinach, cod with celery-root puree and apple-fennel salad, and grilled salmon with honey-mustard sauce. It's likely that you'll meet a match for your meal on the reasonably priced wine list.

Patois *255 Smith St between DeGraw and Douglass Sts, Carroll Gardens, Brooklyn (718-855-1535). Subway: F, G to Carroll St. Tue–Thu 6–10:30pm; Fri, Sat 6–11:30pm; Sun 11am–3pm, 5–10pm. Average main course: $14.* Even though cafés are as common as baby strollers along this half-mile stretch of Smith Street, the neighborhood's neoprepsters still come back to the place that started the whole Gallic craze. Everyone dives for the oysters and wolfs down heaping helpings of tender steak

Read 'em & eat

aioli: a garlic mayonnaise

béarnaise: a sauce made from a reduction of vinegar, tarragon, shallots, egg yolks and butter

béchamel: a white sauce made by stirring milk into a butter-flour *roux*

brochette: a meat or vegetable speared on a skewer and then grilled

crêpes suzette: sweet crêpes sautéed in butter and set ablaze (often tableside) with an orange liqueur

JENNY WOODWARD

with crisp golden fries or the garlicky escargot suffused with spinach and topped with puff pastry. Tables in the rustic outdoor garden remain in high demand.

▲Pink Pony *176 Ludlow St between Houston and Stanton Sts (212-253-1922). Subway: F, V to Lower East Side–Second Ave. Daily 10am–2am. Average main course: $14.* High ceilings, romantic messages written on the walls ("Please hold me the forgotten way"), slow but congenial service and good lighting all add to the charm of this boho haunt. Owner Lucien Bahaj, who also runs the nearby French bistro Lucien, offers dependably tasty café fare until 2am. Choose from sweet options—a toasted honey, peanut butter and banana sandwich—or savory ones like salmon with risotto and parsley sauce. Miles of secondhand books are piled on shelves, an old-fashioned jukebox plays Nina Simone and John Coltrane, and poetry readings round out the artsiness of it all.

Resto Léon *351 E 12th St between First and Second Aves (212-375-8483). Subway: L to First Ave. Mon–Thu 11:30am–midnight; Fri, Sat 11:30am–1am; Sun 11:30am–midnight. Average main course: $15.* Resto Léon's enjoyable meals are heightened by a staff that takes pleasure in preparing and serving your feast. Start with a poached egg dropped in the center of a rich, fragrant broth of red wine, shallots and mushrooms. Move on to standards like tender hanger steak au poivre and an overflowing bowl of mussels in creamy white-wine broth. Stick around for some late-night high jinks: The impulsive, fun-loving French staff can turn the whole place into a party at the drop of a *chapeau*.

Robin des Bois *195 Smith St between Baltic and Warren Sts, Carroll Gardens, Brooklyn (718-596-1609). Subway: F, G to Bergen St. Mon–Thu 4pm–midnight; Fri noon–1am; Sat 11am–1am; Sun 11am–midnight. Average main course: $14.* The busy decor—halfway between a '70s ski lodge and an overstocked secondhand shop—is part of the charm at this Brooklyn hangout. Feel free to ignore the menu staples that could be found at any French bistro (beet salad, steak au poivre, croque-monsieur). Investigate the more oddball offerings: spicy merguez sausage on creamy-smooth lentils or the *rillettes* made with duck, instead of the usual pork. Desserts include solid versions of classics (chocolate cake), as well as more ambitious confections like *clafoutis* (a dense, fruity flan). The fine selection of digestifs ends dinner on a high note, especially if you're lounging in the garden.

★ ▲718 Restaurant *35-01 Ditmars Blvd at 35th St, Astoria, Queens (718-204-5553). Subway: N, W to Astoria–Ditmars Blvd. Mon–Thu 5:30–10:30pm; Fri 5:30pm–1am; Sat noon–5pm, 5:30pm–1am; Sun noon–4pm, 5:30–10:30pm. Average main course: $15.*

Read 'em & eat

croque-monsieur: a ham-and-cheese sandwich dipped in egg batter then sautéed in butter or grilled in a press

langoustine: prawn

timbale d'escargots: snail casserole served in garlic butter

Diners at 718 have a slightly stunned look—they can't believe how exceptional and economical the place is. Its high standards have made it one of the most talked about restaurants in Queens. The stylish Parisian decor—half-moon banquettes, spangly chandeliers—is a fitting backdrop to inspired, modern takes on tuna (sesame-kissed, sushi-grade and grilled), duck (fruit-brightened terrine, velvety grilled breast) and crème brûlée (in three flavors). Brunch and late-night tapas are equally enticing.

Sorrel *605 Carlton Ave at St. Marks Ave, Prospect Heights, Brooklyn (718-622-1190). Subway: B, Q to Seventh Ave; 2, 3 to Bergen St. Tue, Wed 5:30–10:30pm; Thu–Sat 5:30–11:30pm; Sun 5:30–10:30pm. Average main course: $15. Three-course prix fixe: $25.* Sorrel is a former corner bodega turned minimalist, brick-walled restaurant in Prospect Heights. But the food coming out of Russian-born chef Alexandre Tchistov's kitchen makes this more than just a gift to the locals. Tchistov's ridiculously inexpensive but delicious prix fixe—a nightly $25 three-course market menu—has been know to include a terrific smoked-mackerel-and-watermelon salad and oven-roasted skate wing over a puree of Yukon Gold potatoes. Stray into the à la carte menu and you get to sample spicy hanger-steak tartare with charred *ciabatta* (from a local bakery) brushed with olive oil; a half-dozen seared scallops piled on a plate with sweet corn, red peppers and a sublime ginger–beurre blanc sauce; or a silky orange-yogurt panna cotta that's like some grown-up version of a Creamsicle.

★ Tartine *253 W 11th St at 4th St (212-229-2611). Subway: 1 to Christopher St–Sheridan Sq. Daily 9am–10:30pm. Average main course: $15.* The nook that Brittany-born Thierry Rochard opened in 1990 still cleaves to its stand-in-line policy and classic bistro heritage. The inevitable wait and tight space would be well worth it for the frites alone, and the BYOB policy with no corkage fee adds to the allure. Saucy, spicy chicken smothered in garlic and white wine—and served with a scoop of guacamole—is the only dish that deviates from French flavors. But with choices like *bouchée à la reine* (translation: really good chicken potpie), why stray from the français?

Tournesol *50-12 Vernon Blvd between 50th and 51st Aves, Long Island City, Queens (718-472-4355). Subway: 7 to Vernon Blvd–Jackson Ave. Tue–Fri 11:30am–3pm, 5:30–11:30pm; Sat 11:30am–3:30pm, 5:30–11:30pm; Sun 11:30am–3:30pm, 5–10pm. Average main course: $15.* Locals predominate at this terrific (and affordable) bistro. Garlicky escargots, tender steak frites and flavorful grilled chicken are definitive versions of familiar dishes, and the nonfroufrou desserts are first-rate. The wine list, full of lesser-known regional choices, may require some navigational assistance, so ask the trio of Gascons who run Tournesol. They know, and they've got time to tell you.

Zucco: Le French Diner *188 Orchard St between Houston and Stanton Sts (212-677-5200). Subway: F, V to Lower East Side–Second Ave. Daily noon–midnight. Average main course: $15.* The name Zucco refers both to this tiny candlelit restaurant and to the charismatic proprietor, who acts as server, bartender, host and busboy. The menu is modeled after truck stops in France—making it a cheap and simple meat-and-potatoes place. Only here, the potatoes arrive as Gruyère-topped gratin. If you want meat, the Angus shell steak, crowned with creamy peppercorn sauce, is remarkably tender. Order a bottle of wine and you'll find that the itsy-bitsy Parisian wineglasses are—like everything else here—endearing.

Say fromage
Artisanal carries 250 cheese varieties and a menu that goes beyond the block.

$16 to $24

A.O.C. *314 Bleecker St at Grove St (212-675-9463). Subway: 1 to Christopher St. Daily 8am–midnight. Average main course: $17.* Yes, it has a killer wine list, but the restaurant's initials don't stand for *appellation d'origine contrôlée*. The moniker derives instead from the title of a popular French gastro-film, *L'Aile ou la Cuisse* ("the wing or the thigh"). You'll find an extensive menu, from breakfast and lunch (pastries, croque-monsieur) to dinner standards (duck confit, *moules frites*). Salmon tartare is a comfort food of sorts, served with homemade potato chips and cocktail sauce, while hanger steak is lightened by a sauce of wine, shallots and port.

▲**Alouette** *2588 Broadway between 97th and 98th Sts (212-222-6808). Subway: 1, 2, 3 to 96th St. Mon–Thu 5:30–11pm; Fri, Sat 5:30–11:30pm; Sun 5:30–10pm. Average main course: $18.* Chantal and Kenneth Gin's two-level restaurant, draped in romantic red velvet, relies upon bistro basics and occasionally incorporates culinary elements from the owners' Eurasian background. The menu includes standards such as goat cheese tart and duck confit, and more ambitious pairings like monkfish and lemongrass, and salmon and bok choy. The three-course $22 prix fixe, offered daily from 5:30 to 6:30pm, is a great deal.

★ **Artisanal** *2 Park Ave at 32nd St (212-725-8585). Subway: 6 to 33rd St. Mon–Thu 11:45am–11pm; Fri 11:45am–midnight; Sat 11am–midnight; Sun 11am–10pm. Average main course: $22.* In the handsome Deco room, Artisanal carries on the *grand café* tradition. Great

acoustics muffle the roar of the crowd enjoying Terrance Brennan's quality bistro fare—like fantastic warm *gougères*, flavorful steak frites, charcuterie and Provençal fish soup. The oft-ordered fondue reflects the restaurant's cheese focus: More than 250 different varieties are on offer to taste and take home. Adding to Artisanal's considerable appeal: prix-fixe meals, late-night bites, daily specials, brunch and a bar menu geared toward solo diners.

★ **Balthazar** *80 Spring St between Broadway and Crosby St (212-965-1414). Subway: N, R, W to Prince St; 6 to Spring St. Mon–Thu 7:30–11:30am, noon–5pm, 5:45pm–12:30am; Fri 7:30–11:30am, noon–5pm, 5:45pm–1:30am; Sat 8am–3:45pm, 5:45pm–1:30am; Sun 8am–3:45pm, 5:45pm–12:30am. Average main course: $23.* Not only is the iconic Balthazar still trendy, but the kitchen rarely makes a false step. At dinner, the place is perennially packed with rail-thin lookers dressed to the nines. But the bread is great, the food is good, and the service is surprisingly friendly. The $99 three-tiered seafood platter casts the most impressive shadow of any dish in town. The frisée *aux lardons* is exemplary. Roasted chicken on mashed potatoes for two, *délicieux*. Skate with brown butter and capers, yum.

Bandol Bistro *181 E 78th St between Lexington and Third Aves (212-744-1800). Subway: 6 to 77th St. Mon–Wed 5–10pm; Thu, Fri 5–1am; Sat noon–3:30, 5–1am; Sun noon–3:30, 5–10pm. Average main course: $19.* The wine list at this diminutive Provençal restaurant is the star attraction—150 wines by the bottle and 40 by the glass—but why don't you have some food with that vintage? Begin with the refreshing tartare *de*

Side dish

Restaurant style

Get goods to go for a DIY meal.

Hankering for that perfect cut of meat, some deliciously stinky cheese or a signature fruit napolean, but don't want to wait for a reservation? Some restaurants will sell you the ingredients and let you do the cooking at home.

For Gallic specialties, **Les Halles** (*411 Park Ave South at 29th St, 212-679-4111*) is the city's go-to spot, featuring a meat case filled with *entrecôte*, filet *de boeuf* and *côte d'agneau*. At the unpretentious bistro **Epicerie** (*168–170 Orchard St at Stanton St, 212-420-7520*), you'll find a re-creation of a small Parisian grocery store, with shelves stocking French knickknacks and cans of *choucroute* and *petits pois*. For dessert, pick up a cake, pastry or tart from **Payard Pâtisserie & Bistro** (*1032 Lexington Ave between 73rd and 74th Sts, 212-717-5252*), where signature works of edible art include the Louvre, a glossy orb of chocolate and hazelnut mousse.

Its funky-kitsch decor notwithstanding, the **Bright Food Shop's Kitchen Market** (*216 Eighth Ave at 21st St, 888-HOT-4433*) is a serious supplier of Asian and Mexican ingredients for the home cook, with more than 30 varieties of dried chilies, herbs and spices, and hard-to-find bottled hot sauces. At **Artisanal Fromagerie, Bistro and Wine Bar** (*2 Park Ave at 32nd St, 212-725-8585*), more than 250 different cheeses are waiting to be taken home, including the restaurant's signature fondue blend, a Provençal cheese wrapped in brandy-steeped chestnut leaves, or a four-year-old Gouda. If the sights and scents overwhelm, defer to one of the several white-clad cheese experts; you'll be forgiven—this isn't Boar's Head after all.

When the crowds at the hundred-year-old **Barney Greengrass, The Sturgeon King** (*541 Amsterdam Ave between 86th and 87th Sts, 212-724-4707*) get to be too much, don't bother sitting down. In addition to the boasted delicacy, the in-house store offers beluga, osetra and sevruga caviars, kippered salmon and whitefish salads, and yep, chopped liver.

Finally, you don't have to be Jewish to appreciate the butcher shop at kosher steakhouse **Le Marais** (*150 W 46th St between Sixth and Seventh Aves, 212-869-0900*). Prime-aged beef, bison, duck, pate and some of the city's tastiest beef jerky can be picked up or delivered Monday through Thursday.

saumon. If bouillabaisse is available, order it; Bandol's light, tangy rendition is crammed with monkfish, snapper, mussels and skate. The heady sautéed duck breast with dried cherries and wild rice is luscious. And, oh, the warm chocolate soufflé! Pliant outer layers reveal a sinful richness within.

▲**Bistro du Nord** *1312 Madison Ave at 93rd St (212-289-0997). Subway: 6 to 96th St. Mon–Fri 11:30am–3pm, 5–10pm; Sat, Sun 11am–3pm, 5–10pm. Average main course: $22.* Black-jacketed waiters buzz between the two floors decorated with red leather benches and a huge multitiered chandelier. Jazz and chatter keep the Moulin Rouge mood light, but the food is serious. Slices of duck *magret* fanned across the plate are drenched in a cassis sauce with caramelized shallots. Organic roasted chicken breast is crisp and juicy, served on a bed of spinach and basmati rice and dressed with tomato, white wine and wild-mushroom sauce. Vegetarian selections include a house-made leek-and-tomato tartlet.

Bistro les Amis *180 Spring St at Thompson St (212-226-8645). Subway: C, E to Spring St. Mon–Thu, ; Fri, Sat 11:30am–1am; Sun 11:30am–midnight. Average main course: $20.* The black-and-white Doisneau prints, the white lace curtains, the pressed tin ceiling: Everything about this beloved Soho bistro seems untouched by time. Spring Street locals linger over steak frites with herb butter or sip Bordeaux at the worn oak bar. There are standards (delightfully meaty crab cakes in creamy lobster sauce) along with such surprises as escargot ravioli with spinach, basil and wild mushroom, and an oven-roasted monkfish that gets its kick from a boldly flavored wasabi sauce. Your first time here? The courtly owner just might offer you a glass of port and a red rose to take home.

Bouillabaisse 126 *126 Union St at Columbia St, Carroll Gardens, Brooklyn (718-855-4405). Subway: F, G to Carroll St. Mon, Tue, Thu 5–10pm; Fri, Sat 5–11:30pm; Sun 5–10pm. Average main course: $18.* Chef Neil Ganic moved his former beloved Brooklyn Heights bistro, La Bouillabaisse, further into Brooklyn, where diners are now met with rustic bistro decor, a friendly waitstaff and a large, movable chalkboard that reveals the day's offerings: roasted-red-pepper and goat cheese salad, maybe, or peppery cod with crisp green beans. The restaurant offers several takes on the signature dish (oddly, they're not the best items on the menu) and a reasonably priced wine list.

▲**Brasserie Julien** *1422 Third Ave between 80th and 81st Sts (212-744-6327). Subway: 4, 5 to 86th St; 6 to 77th St. Mon–Wed 3:30–10:30pm; Thu 3:30pm–midnight; Fri 3:30pm–2am; Sat 11:30am–2am; Sun 11:30am–10:30pm. Average main course: $22.* This sexy French eatery remains one of the best restaurants in the neighborhood. The menu is a mix of brasserie classics (mussels, pâté, cheese plates, steak frites, fondue) and chef-owner Philippe Feret's pricier creations, such as a fried soft-shell crab atop a lovely mix of balsamic-touched green beans. Even the burger here is a marvel, piled literally six inches high with cheese, bacon and wispy fried onions. A jazz combo works the room Thursday through Saturday, and those pinching their euros can load up on a cash-only, three-course meal for $25.

Café Cluny *284 W 12th St at 4th St (212-255-6900). Subway: A, C, E to 14th St; L to Eighth Ave. Mon 8am–11pm; Tue–Fri 8am–midnight; Sat*

9am–midnight, Sun 9am–11pm. Average main course: $24. It took only a few word-of-mouth whispers to draw fashionable hordes to this new bistro from Odeon owner Lynn Wagenknecht. The cuisine is urban bistro, but the decor is all country: A corner bar separates two artfully cluttered mushroom-gray rooms festooned with antlers, taxidermy and framed vegetable prints. The short menu, overseen by Odeon chef Vincent Nargi, tends toward the rich and heavy. There's a fine falling-off-the-bone duck confit with mustard-kissed brussels sprouts, and an intriguing swordfish au poivre featuring earthy elf mushrooms and succulent swordfish covered in a classic peppercorn sauce.

★ **Cafe Loup** *105 W 13th St between Sixth and Seventh Aves (212-255-4746). Subway: F, V, 1, 2, 3 to 14th St; L to Sixth Ave. Mon noon–3pm, 5:30–11:30pm; Tue–Fri noon–3pm, 5:30pm–midnight; Sat 5:30pm–midnight; Sun noon–3:30pm, 5:30–11:30pm. Average main course: $20.* Since 1990, chef-owner Lloyd Feit has been rewarding loyal guests with brawny, Asian-accented bistro fare. His standards are solid: supergarlicky escargots, *tournedos de boef* (petite filet minons with a reduction of cognac, cream and green peppercorns). And the less traditional dishes, such as marinated grilled tuna with two mustards, set on bok choy, are lighter yet equally tasty choices. The *chaussons aux poires* (phyllo pastry with carmelized anjou pear and Tahitian vanilla ice cream) is alone worth a visit.

▲**CamaJe** *85 MacDougal St between Bleecker and Houston Sts (212-673-8184). Subway: A, C, E, B, D, F, V to W 4th St; 1 to Houston St. Daily noon–midnight. Average main course: $21.* Adorned with works by local artists, this casual, intimate neighborhood bistro offers standard French fare like an excellent charcuterie plate and a hearty lamb stew, as well as a number of American-influenced dishes (chipotle-barbecued baby back ribs or Arctic char on a bed of lentils with smoked bacon). The dessert menu is highlighted by the housemade *Banoffee* (banana, caramel and chocolate) Pie, while an affordable wine list and attentive waitstaff enhance the appeal. In addition to cooking classes, Camaje offers "Dark Dining" for the truly intrepid—diners are blindfolded and left to enjoy special menus guided only by their remaining senses.

Cercle Rouge *241 West Broadway between Beach and White Sts (212-226-6252). Subway: A, C, E to Canal St; 1 to Franklin St. Mon–Fri noon–midnight; Sat, Sun 11am–midnight. Average main course: $23.* This by-the-book bistro—aged mirrors, French movie posters and laissez-faire waiters—does a roaring trade in red wine and steak frites, particularly come dusk when Wall Streeters in loosened ties swarm the bar. The chef, who hails from Toulouse, turns out classics that would make his compatriotes proud—beef tripe stew steaming in a clay pot, foie gras resting on a caramelized bed of honeydew marmalade—while also accommodating the American palate, with buffalo chicken wings dunked into a crème fraîche–whipped blue cheese sauce.

Chat Noir *22 E 66th St between Fifth and Madison Aves (212-794-2428). Subway: F to Lexington Ave–63rd St. Daily noon–11pm. Average main course: $23.* Opening yet another French bistro on the Upper East Side—around the corner from La Goulue, no less—might seem ill-advised, unless you happen to own the competition. Chat Noir, the spot from La Goulue's Suzanne Latapie, is an intimate adjunct to its scene-heavy sibling. Warm light

Color code
At Bistro du Nord, green accents the leek-and-tomato tartlet, and red enlivens the dining room.

French $16 to $24

Size matters
Space is small, but
flavors are big at
Le Petit Marché.

CINZIA REALE-CASTELLO

fills the dining room, despite its location in a brownstone basement. The menu pushes familiar Francophile fare: tuna tartare with diced carrots and apples is a lighter alternative to standard pâté, and the steak frites comes with a béarnaise sauce so delicious, you'll want to eat it with a spoon.

★ **Félix** *340 West Broadway at Grand St (212-431-0021). Subway: A, C, E, 1 to Canal St. Daily noon–midnight. Average main course: $21.* Antique ads, large glass doors that open onto the sidewalk and a pressed-tin ceiling afford a timeless backdrop to a scene you'll recognize from numerous films. Unlike most long-standing restaurants, the food has actually improved over Félix's 16-year tenure. You come here to eat steak frites—or at least that's what you'll see on almost every table. Choose among peppercorn, béarnaise or Roquefort sauces to dress a remarkably tender piece of meat, and locals will attest that the accompanying golden frites are among the best in town. Félix is most frenzied during weekend brunch, when patrons spill out the front door with cocktails in hand.

★ **Gavroche** *212 W 14th St between Seventh and Eighth Aves (212-647-8553). Subway: A, C, E, 1, 2, 3 to 14th St; L to Eighth Ave. Mon 5–10pm; Tue noon–4pm, 4:30–10pm; Wed–Fri noon–4pm, 4:30–11pm; Sat 4:30–11pm; Sun noon–4pm, 4:30–10pm.. Average main course: $22.* If the country-bistro feel and cheery demeanor of Gavroche's patrons don't instantly win you over, the irresistible aromas of its traditional French cooking will. Simple wooden seating with checkered tablecloths, a sweet little bar and a blackboard with one daily special announce that the real focus here is the sumptuous cuisine. The wild-mushroom ravioli with white truffle oil and Parmesan appetizer is not to be missed; braised duck in lingonberry sauce with diced potatoes and grilled dorado with fennel, carrots and chilled sweet potatoes are excellent reminders that the French do indeed know everything.

Ici *246 DeKalb Ave at Vanderbilt Ave (718-789-2778). Subway: C to Lafayette Ave, G to Clinton–Washington Aves. Tue–Thu 8am–4pm, 5–10pm; Fri, Sat 8am–4pm, 5–11pm; Sun 8am–4pm, 5–10pm. Average main course: $16.* Owned by Laurent Saillard (better known as the stern general manager on The Restaurant) and his wife, Ici has an elegant, pared-down prettiness, with white-painted brick walls and a warm-weather patio out back. French-accented waitresses deliver simple, straightforward food. The brief menu changes often, but a summer meal included cool, minty cucumber soup; juicy roasted chicken with lemon-almond couscous; and two thin, mild fillets of mackerel crisscrossed over a kimchi-and-cucumber salad.

Jacques *20 Prince St between Elizabeth and Mott Sts (212-966-8886). Subway: N, R, W to Prince St; 6 to Spring St. Mon 5:30–11pm; Tue–Fri noon–11pm; Sat, Sun 11:30am–midnight. Average main course: $20.* In image-conscious Nolita, being part sidewalk café, part brunch spot and part date place could create an identity crisis. But attentive service and tasty Moroccan-inflected food make Jacques a hidden gem just a block from the perpetually (and annoyingly) jammed Café Gitane. The spicy lamb meatballs, shrimp and mussels tagine and rich mushroom fricassee each possess an abundance of assertive flavors, thanks to North African spices and that dependable taste enhancer—butter. In this model-strewn neighborhood, that's a culinary move bordering on daring.

Jarnac *328 W 12th St at Greenwich St (212-924-3413). Subway: A, C, E to 14th St; L to Eighth Ave. Tue–Thu 6–10pm; Fri, Sat 6–11pm; Sun 11am–2:45pm, 6–10pm. Average main course: $24.* The West Village is littered with small French bistros, but when in doubt, Jarnac is the charming standby. Sit amid antique walls and windows open wide and you can look onto a pretty, quiet street. Throughout the night you can often spot chef Maryann Terillo meandering through the dining room. Her menu changes daily, but you can usually order the Jarnac BLT, in which the traditional fillings are replaced by more upscale heirloom tomatoes, pancetta and arugula. In a variation of steak and eggs, a juicy rib eye is topped with a layer of shaved Parmesan and a fried organic egg. Monkfish is a more subtle alternative, sitting in a delicate lobster-saffron *velouté*.

Juliette *135 North 5th St between Bedford Ave and Berry St, Williamsburg, Brooklyn (718-388-9222). Subway: L to Bedford Ave. Mon–Thu 5pm–midnight; Fri 5pm–1am; Sat 10:30am–4pm, 5pm–1am; Sun 10:30am–4pm, 5–11pm. Average main course: $16.* Bearing all the hallmarks of the nouveau bistro—rust-dappled mirrors, tiny tables, insanely good looking diners, a noise level that exceeds a racket—Juliette still manages a few pleasant surprises. The wine list is crammed with bargains (many solid bottles hit the $25 mark), and the kitchen pulls off some pretty neat tricks, too. Seared Cape Cod squid marries fruity-sweet with citrusy-tart, by way of jalapeño and watermelon; steak au poivre showcases the kick of superfresh pink, green and black peppercorns with a knockout veal reduction. But best of all, in warm weather you can dine on the pretty roof-deck.

La Petite Auberge *116 Lexington Ave between 27th and 28th Sts (212-689-5003). Subway: 6 to 28th St. Mon–Fri noon–11pm; Sat 4:30–10pm. Average main course: $19.* This Gallic charmer stands out among the area's clutch of Indian restaurants. It's a beguiling bistro with dark-wood paneling and artifacts from Brittany adorning the walls. The menu lists French staples, including buttery escargots and trout with a lemon-caper sauce, along with delectable specials like creamy scallops with mushrooms and shrimp. The signature dessert is a traditional soufflé worth every second of the 40-minute wait: It's golden on the outside, fluffy on the inside and bursting with Grand Marnier.

▲**Le Bateau Ivre** *230 E 51st St between Second and Third Aves (212-583-0579). Subway: E, V to Lexington Ave–53rd St; 6 to 51st St. Daily 8am–4am. Average main course: $20.* Forget the faux bistros you've tried—here's the real, social thing. Mirrored walls make Le Bateau Ivre's bar perfect for people-watching; close-set tables in the comfortable dining area encourage you to swap recommendations for food and wine with strangers. And there's a lot to recommend. Oysters, clams or a caviar-and-blini combo with a tasting tray of five wines for $20, make a perfect, romantic late-night snack. Grilled lamb chops, burgers and fish (like seared sea bass with string beans and mushrooms) are unsurpassed. Crowds usually thin out by 3am; any earlier than that and you should make a reservation.

Le Bilboquet *25 E 63rd St between Madison and Park Aves (212-751-3036). Subway: F to Lexington Ave–63rd St. Daily noon–11pm. Average main course: $24.* With loud, sexy beats pumping through the tiny space, Le Bilboquet seems more like a nightlife destination than a restaurant. But it's the food that keeps the place packed: Thick chunks of fresh tuna teeter between layers of lightly fried wonton skins; tender strips of steak tartare come with a tower of crisp frites. And you won't find a more piquant steak au poivre this side of the Seine—a thick cut lies in a black peppery pool. Prices are a bit high, but the regulars with slicked-back hair don't seem to mind.

Le Charlot
19 E 69th St between Madison and Park Aves (212-794-1628). Subway: 6 to 68th St–Hunter College. Daily noon–midnight. Average main course: $22. By about 8pm at this clubby haunt, quiet conversation is out, and noise, fun and food are in. Roasted goat cheese in a rich flaky pastry and silky, full-flavored foie gras terrine lead the appetizer pack. For your entrée, consider one of the mussel dishes, especially the Thai variation with ginger, lemongrass and cilantro, or go straight for the succulent steak au poivre. (Pairing your meal with a good wine shouldn't be a problem; the list is nearly 20 pages long.) Le Charlot's desserts, which include profiteroles and tarte Tatin, do the classics justice.

Le Jardin Bistro
25 Cleveland Pl between Kenmare and Spring Sts (212-343-9599). Subway: N, R, W to Prince St; 6 to Spring St. Mon–Fri noon–3pm, 6–11pm; Sat, Sun noon–3:30pm, 6–11pm. Average main course: $20. This unobtrusive restaurant has muted-yellow walls, carefully placed botanical drawings and lace curtains that shield diners from the gray landscape of Cleveland Place. The menu is short on spice and surprise, but long on hearty staples such as country pâté, bouillabaisse and steak frites. It's worth a visit—even in the months when the breathtaking back garden, a cobblestoned secret with grapevine-covered trellises, is closed.

Le Madeleine
403 W 43rd St between Ninth and Tenth Aves (212-246-2993). Subway: A, C, E to 42nd St–Port Authority. Mon, Tue, Thu noon–3pm, 5–11pm; Wed 11:30am–3pm, 5–11pm; Fri noon–3pm, 5–11:30pm; Sat noon–2:30pm, 4:30–11:30pm; Sun noon–3pm, 5–10pm. Average main course: $19. Picking a pretheater spot can paralyze the most hardened New Yorker. Relax: Le Madeleine's heart is in the right place, and the food is inventive enough to stave off any bistro ennui. Puffy, goat-cheese beignets top a salad of sliced beets, while a generous bowl of Prince Edward Island mussels in saffron-tomato broth gets some heat from bits of crumbly merguez sausage. Chef Fabian Pauta pays attention to details: Creamy polenta is almost too good to play second fiddle to the spice-crusted duck, and sautéed codfish is enlivened by earthy portobello mushrooms. Three types of prix-fixe menus are tailored to your appetite, wallet and the time of day.

Le Petit Marché
46 Henry St between Cranberry and Middagh Sts, Brooklyn Heights (718-858-9605). Subway: A, C to High St; 2, 3 to Clark St. Tue–Sat 5–11pm; Sun 11am–3pm, 5–11pm. Average main course: $24. In a city filled with Paris-on-the-Hudson bistros, this 50-seat French neighborhood eatery still manages to impress. The tight brick-walled space, with a low tin ceiling that amplifies boisterous conversations, may scare off claustrophobes. But the food from chef Robert Weiner (Le Parker Meridien), like a seared "sashimi tuna" appetizer with pickled vegetables and sweet-soy and hot-mustard sauces, and duckling with (not-too-sweet) sweet-potato puree and Asian pear chutney, should give diners many reasons to tolerate the noise.

★ Le Père Pinard
175 Ludlow St between Houston and Stanton Sts (212-777-4917). Subway: F to Delancey St; J, M, Z to Delancey–Essex Sts. Mon–Wed 5pm–midnight; Thu 5pm–1am; Fri, Sat 5pm–2am; Sun 5pm–midnight. Average main course: $17. Just walking by, you can tell that the people inside this bistro and wine bar are having more fun than you are. That's because they're mopping up heavenly garlic-butter broth from their plates of perfect mussels, spreading house-made pâtés onto fresh baguette or digging into the lusciously glazed duck à l'orange. Take advantage of the early-evening, three-course prix fixe for just $14. In warm weather, the fun spills out to the garden.

★ Le Singe Vert
160 Seventh Ave between 19th and 20th Sts (212-366-4100). Subway: 1 to 18th St. Mon noon–4pm, 5:30–11pm; Tue–Thu noon–4pm, 5:30pm–midnight; Fri noon–4pm, 5:30pm–1am; Sat 11:30am–4pm, 5:30pm–1am; Sun 11:30am–4pm, 5:30–11pm. Average main course: $16. It's a bistro, all right: You'll find tight tables, torch songs en français and charmingly accented (and occasionally inattentive) waiters. Steak frites, served with chive butter or pepper sauce, is swell, as are standbys like moules frites and the more refined skate sautéed in brown butter. You'll need all the bread you can get your hands on to clean up after the bubbling, garlicky escargots. Order from the oyster bar and you'll be rewarded with a large selection of seasonal bivalves. If you're on a budget, try the $25.95 three-course dinner prix fixe.

Le Veau d'Or
129 E 60th St between Park and Lexington Aves (212-838-8133). Subway: N, R, W to Lexington Ave–59th St; 4, 5, 6 to 59th St. Mon–Sat noon–3pm, 5:30pm–midnight. Prix fixe: $25. If this place was good enough for Truman Capote to pass out in, it's good enough for you. Classics are the order of business, and everything is just as it should be—whether it's a nicely dressed celery-root rémoulade or the chef's chunky pâté, accompanied by a crock of very spicy, direct-from-Dijon mustard. Another fine crock will appear with the choucroute garni, a straightforward plate of sauerkraut surrounded by pork products galore. The biggest hit is coq au vin—the chicken is smothered in a thick, tangy wine sauce studded with soft pearl onions and lots of crisp, smoky bacon.

Les Halles
411 Park Ave South between 28th and 29th Sts (212-679-4111). Subway: 6 to 28th St. Daily 7:30am–midnight. Average main course: $19. Though Anthony Bourdain is just the "chef-at-large" at Les Halles these days, his meat-oriented philosophy still permeates the place, from the butcher shop inside the restaurant to steak knives that appear at every place setting. With classic French fare like steak tartare and crêpes suzette prepared tableside for a largely out-of-towner crowd, it's practically a theme-park restaurant—the theme being simply that animals are delicious. Steaks, sausages and chops done over a dozen different ways are solid, but the kitchen's efforts lack a certain joie de vivre. **Other location** 15 John St between Broadway and Nassau St (212-285-8585).

Loulou
222 DeKalb Ave between Adelphi St and Clermont Ave, Fort Greene, Brooklyn (718-246-0633).

$16 to $24 **French**

Jam and bread
Métisse lures the Columbia crowd with Gallic dishes.

JENNY WOODWARD

Critics' picks

The best…

$16 to $24 French

Frisee aux lardons

❏ Artisanal
❏ Pastis
❏ Payard Bistro
❏ Le Singe Vert

Duck confit

❏ Café Cluny
❏ Patois
❏ Moutarde

Steak au poivre

❏ Raoul's
❏ Le Bilboquet
❏ Les Halles

Tarte *Tatin*

❏ Nice Matin
❏ Lucien
❏ Brasserie Julien

Subway: C to Lafayette Ave; G to Clinton–Washington Aves. Mon, Wed, Thu 5:30–10:30pm; Fri 5:30pm–11:30; Sat 11am–3pm, 5:30pm–11:30; Sun 11am–3pm, 5:30–10:30pm. Average main course: $18. A squat two-story building is home to one of Fort Greene's bistro pioneers, and the food pleases longtime locals as well as newcomers. The slender room is bathed in soft gold light and has a fireplace at the back; there's also a year-round garden. Most of the entrées are fish preparations—bouillabaisse is a concoction of fish cooked in spicy red curry with saffron aiolo; grilled salmon is served over a salad of white beans and mushrooms with a chilled mint-cucumber yogurt sauce. Bistro purists will be satisfied, too, with steak frites and roasted chicken with a thyme sauce and seasonal vegetables.

★ **Lucien** *14 First Ave between 1st and 2nd Sts (212-260-6481). Subway: F, V to Lower East Side– Second Ave. Daily 10am–2am. Average main course: $17.* This revered old splinter of Paris is always a good option. The slender room is charming: ratty wood tables are covered in white paper, and the bar features aged mirrors and dangling globe lights. Classics like grilled sardines à la St. Tropez, rabbit in Dijon mustard sauce, and cassoulet *toulousain* are uncannily re-created, with a few thoughtful touches that sometimes even improve on the originals. The kitchen's *pièce de résistance* remains the *pigeonneauróti*, a pyramid of portobello mushrooms, potatoes and broccoli rabe crowned with a roasted squab whose flavors are intensified with a basting of drippings and a bit of foie gras.

★ **Marseille** *630 Ninth Ave at 44th St (212-333-3410). Subway: A, C, E to 42nd St–Port Authority. Mon–Fri noon–3pm, 5:15–11:30pm; Sat 11am–3pm, 5:15–11:30pm; Sun 11am–3pm, 5:15–10pm. Average main course: $23.* Part of Simon Oren's *république française* (Nice Matin, French Roast and Pigalle, to name a few), Marseille puts a refined spin on the melting-pot cuisine of the famous port city, with plenty of North African influences. The bouillabaisse features haddock, skate, cod and mussels that are cooked separately, then added to a light broth with a generous dose of garlic, while Tunisian chicken is served with a ragout of eggplant, tomatoes, green olives and kumquats. Sensual desserts include an espresso parfait with marscapone sabayon. The dining room is polished and suave yet inviting—all Art Deco influences, burnt-umber walls and proscenium arches.

★ **Métisse** *239 W 105th St between Amsterdam Ave and Broadway (212-666-8825). Subway: 1 to 103rd St. Mon–Fri 5:30–11pm; Sat–Sun 10:30am–11pm. Average main course: $18.* This colorful Gallic bistro—covered in red-and-yellow walls, purple floors and gilt-framed oil paintings—has been popular with the local Columbia crowd since opening in 1994. The kitchen tackles traditional bistro fare like spot-on steak frites, silky foie gras pâté and escargots, yet isn't afraid to reinterpret the classics. Crisp Long Island duck, for example, is doused with a tangy cherry-and-raisin reduction and sits atop spinach imbued with garlic. The warm chocolate cake with vanilla ice cream is nothing new, but it'll still send diners away contented.

▲**Montparnasse** *230 E 51st St between Second and Third Aves (212-758-6633). Subway: E, V to Lexington Ave– 53rd St; 6 to 51st St. Mon noon–3pm, 5–10pm; Tue–Fri noon–3pm, 5pm–midnight; Sat 5pm–midnight; Sun noon–3pm, 5–10pm. Average main course: $22.* Both decor and menu are bistro standard, but the food is fresher, prettier and tastier than what's on offer at many cookie-cutter French joints. An elegant slice of country duck terrine makes a beautiful appetizer, as does a mound of arugula topped by a warm disk of Montrachet goat cheese. Seared hanger steak in red-wine sauce is thoroughly enjoyable. Add a skilled waitstaff, an engaging wine list and a neighborhood crowd that knows how to behave, and you've got a midtown retreat to cherish.

Nice Matin *201 W 79th St at Amsterdam Ave (212-873-6423). Subway: 1 to 79th St. Daily 7am–3:30pm, 5:30pm–midnight. Average main course: $18.* The most upscale of Simon Oren's roster of regional French bistros, Nice Matin draws mature locals seeking a nonchallenging night out. Chef Andy D'Amico's southern French fare isn't particularly inventive, but it's tasty and well executed. Tender beef short ribs are nestled in creamy celery-root puree surrounded by a rich red-wine reduction, while grilled sweetbreads are swathed in fragrant rosemary aïoli. The generous slice of caramel-drizzled tarte Tatin is properly flaky. The optical-illusion wallpaper and carousel-top columns make for date-friendly surroundings. If only the waitstaff's attention didn't wander.

★ ▲**The Odeon** *145 West Broadway between Duane and Thomas Sts (212-233-0507). Subway: A, C, 1, 2, 3 to Chambers St. Mon–Wed 11:45am–1am; Thu, Fri 11:45am–2am; Sat 9am–2am; Sun 9am–1am. Average main course: $22.* The Odeon has been part of the downtown scene for so long that it's hard to remember a time when Tribeca wasn't home to the iconic bistro. It's still a great destination for drinks, and diners can't go wrong with the tried-and-true standards: French onion soup blanketed with bubbling Gruyère, crunchy fried calamari made to be dipped in tartar and spicy chipotle sauces, and steak au poivre with fries. The final hint of 1980s-style decadence: a wonderfully nostalgic caramelized banana tart.

★ **Opia** *Habitat Hotel, 130 E 57th St between Park and Lexington Aves, second floor (212-688-3939). Subway: N, R, W to Lexington Ave–59th St; 4, 5, 6 to 59th St. Mon–Thu 11:30am–1am; Fri, Sat noon–4am; Sun 11:30am–1am. Average main course: $22.* Off the second-floor lobby of the Habitat Hotel is one of the city's better kept secrets—a luxe multiroom restaurant that serves classic bistro favorites like stellar steak

Turn the beet around
Chef Vincent Nargi
puts a spin on things
at Café Cluny.

French $16 to $24

frites with peppercorn sauce, along with other simple, tasty fare like fish & chips, and roasted chicken with mushrooms and asparagus. At lunch in warmer months, this place has another secret: One party of up to five can dine alfresco on a private balcony overlooking the bustle of 57th Street.

★ **Paradou** *8 Little West 12th St between Greenwich and Washington Sts (212-463-8345). Subway: A, C, E to 14th St; L to Eighth Ave. Mon–Wed 6pm–midnight; Thu, Fri 6pm–1am; Sat 11am–4pm, 6pm–1am; Sun 11am–4pm. Average main course: $22.* When the Meatpacking masses are bottlenecked at the door to Pastis, you can defect to this sweet little alternative—a place with no attitude, a modern Provençal menu and one of the most bucolic gardens in town. Flowering hydrangea makes a pretty backdrop for postshopping (or preclubbing) patrons lingering over glasses of wine. Entrées come plain (grilled sandwiches) or fancy (rabbit leg confit, beef cheeks). Dessert crêpes are wrapped around sexy confections like caramelized apples and calvados or dark chocolate and candied orange. And the cheese plate is truly excellent.

Parigot *155 Grand St at Lafayette St (212-274-8859). Subway: J, M, Z, N, Q, R, W, 6 to Canal St. Mon 5–11pm; Tue–Fri noon–11pm; Sat 11:30am–4pm, 5–11pm. Average main course: $18.* Located on a desolate corner in the no-man's-land where Soho meets Little Italy, this bijou French bistro shines like a warm, welcoming lantern. Named after a French term for a common Parisian, Parigot is the latest venture from chef-owner Michel Pombet (Jolie). The tiny space, with two walls of windows dressed with lace curtains, is packed

with tables—but the food is worth braving the clutter for. Crab cakes come gift-wrapped in phyllo pastry, and a lamb stew demands another basket of bread to mop up the delicious broth. The only bum note is a tilapia overrun by too-salty ginger-and-soy sauce, but all is forgiven when the fluffy chocolate mousse cake arrives. It is uncommonly good.

Pastis *9 Ninth Ave at Little West 12th St (212-929-4844). Subway: A, C, E to 14th St; L to Eighth Ave. Mon–Thu 9am–2am; Fri 9am–2:30am; Sat 9am–5pm, 6pm–2:30am; Sun 9am–5pm, 6pm–2am . Average main course: $20.* Yes, this Keith McNally production is still chic, still reliable and still crowded. The decor is quintessential Parisian bistro—aged tiles, nickel bar, distressed mirrors—and so is the food. You'll find buttery organic pan-seared salmon and thick, succulent steak with slender frites. To avoid the clamorous nighttime scene, make a reservation for weekend brunch.

▲**Pergola des Artistes** *252 W 46th St between Broadway and Eighth Ave (212-302-7500). Subway: N, Q, R, W, 42nd St S, 1, 2, 3, 7 to 42nd St–Times Sq. Tue–Sat 11am–8:30pm. Average main course: $19.* Marie and Jacques Ponsolle, who grew up in a Pyrenean village, opened Pergola in 1962 and now run it with their children, Christian and Laurent. The room is so small—and the food so good—that eavesdropping regulars like to offer advice: "Get the steak. It's excellent!" Also recommended are the bouillabaisse and the thin-crust Alsatian tart, which is topped with onions, bacon and parsley. As Marie works the room, chatting about her favorite Broadway stars, she makes sure you're not so transfixed by the mousse (with chunks of solid chocolate hidden in its rich folds) that you miss your curtain.

Provence *38 MacDougal St between Prince and Houston Sts (212-475-7500). Subway: C, E to Spring St. Mon–Sat 5:30–11:30pm; Sun 5:30–10pm. Average main course: $24.* Marc Meyer and Vicki Freeman, the husband-and-wife team behind Five Points and Cookshop, bought then reopened this beloved Soho spot, which is the very place where they got engaged roughly 15 years ago. A marble bar has replaced the wooden one in the bustling front room, leather banquettes and exposed beams now adorn the secluded rear dining area, and dated trellises have been removed from the enclosed garden. All in all, Provence is more charming than ever, even if the kitchen—helmed by Barbuto veteran Lynn McNeely—produces uneven results. Provence does impress with two key pleasures: frites, which McNeely cuts thick, doses heavily with garlic and salt, and serves with the house mayonnaise; and wine. The team behind Cookshop's excellent entirely organic list has put together a smallish all-French compendium, with lots of finds, including a bargain $32 Côtes du Ventoux. Many could happily live on these two things alone.

★ **Quercy** *242 Court St at Baltic St, Carroll Gardens, Brooklyn (718-243-2151). Subway: F, G to Bergen St. Tue–Thu noon–4pm, 5–10:30pm; Fri noon–4pm, 5–11pm. Average main course: $16.* Inspiring deep contentment rather than *amour fou*, inexplicably uncrowded Quercy, with its pretty rose-shaded walls and unobtrusive French pop-song soundtrack, is dependable in the best possible way. There's nothing terribly novel

The secret garden
You might want to keep Le Jardin Bistro's backyard to yourself.

about the food, but the well-prepared trout amandine, rack of lamb with rosemary and parsley, dry-aged Black Angus steak au poivre, or escargots and shiitakes in butter and cognac all satisfy. Quercy complements bistro favorites with a short but reasonably priced wine list that well represents the region in southwest France for which the restaurant is named.

★ ▲**Rouge** *107-02 70th Rd at Austin St, Forest Hills, Queens (718-793-5514). Subway: E, F, V, G, R to Forest Hills–71st Ave. Mon–Thu noon–3pm, 5–10pm; Fri, Sat noon–3pm, 5–11:30pm; Sun noon–3pm, 4–10pm. Average main course: $20.* Rouge's sexy red walls can shelter a romantic weeknight tête-à-tête or heat up a busy Saturday night—and the food lives up to expectations. Traditional starters such as the frisée salad are well made, and the cheese-and-charcuterie plate is deftly composed. Satisfying entrées include rich bacon-and-basil-tinged *coquilles St. Jacques* and a seared duck breast lavished with a cranberry-and-peppercorn glaze. If you don't have a reservation, the bar is an inviting place to wait for a table.

★ **Sel et Poivre** *853 Lexington Ave between 64th and 65th Sts (212-517-5780). Subway: F to Lexington Ave–63rd St; 6 to 68th St–Hunter College. Mon–Thu noon–10:30pm; Fri, Sat noon–11pm; Sun noon–10:30pm. Average main course: $18.* Sel et Poivre has the beautiful bistro vibe down. Pale-yellow walls are hung with evocative black-and-white streetscapes. Pureed red snapper and sea bass blend with a tangy tomato broth to make a full-bodied soup. The accompanying plate of homemade croutons, *rouille* and shreds of Swiss cheese come with charming instructions from the waiter: "Spread ze sauce on ze crouton, top wees *fromage*, and float in ze soup like leetle boats." The mushroom-leek risotto is rich and dense and tastes subtly of dry white wine; the sautéed skate *au beurre noir* is similarly flavorful and luxurious. The $27 prix fixe includes three courses.

▲**Seppi's** *123 W 56th St between Sixth and Seventh Aves (212-708-7444). Subway: F, N, Q, R, W to 57th St. Mon–Sat noon–2am; Sun 10:30am–2am. Average main course: $21.* The decor is spot on (black-and-white booths, pressed-tin ceilings); the hours are rare for midtown (you can order until 2am nightly); and the steak au poivre is properly peppery. The menu delivers the classics—escargots in their shells, roasted duck with honey and anise—and does so with success. Chocoholics come on Sundays to indulge in the divine $24 prix-fixe *chocolat* brunch, which starts with a chocolate mimosa and follows with a buffet of chocolate delicacies both savory (steak and eggs with cocoa beans) and sweet (white and dark chocolate dipped strawberries).

▲**Village** *62 W 9th St between Fifth and Sixth Aves (212-505-3355). Subway: A, C, E, B, D, F, V to W 4th St. Mon–Fri 6–11pm; Sat, Sun 11:30am–3pm, 6–11pm. Average main course: $21.* Village, with its scruffy walls and steel-enclosed skylights, has the lived-in air of a West Village perennial. Chef-owner Stephen Lyle, formerly of the legendary Odeon, has earned a devoted following by being all things to all people. Solo diners can savor an outstanding burger on a stool at the bar, while anyone craving comfort food can enjoy a dinnertime omelette with salad and fries or superlative frisée with Roquefort and bacon. Heartier appetites will be sated by a tasty strip steak Bernaise. The weekend jazz brunch is exceedingly popular.

JENNY WOODWARD

Sister act
La Gouloue sibling Chat
Noir is more intimate
but no less delicious.

French $16 to $24

TALIA SIMHI

$25 and over

Bistro Cassis *235 Columbus Ave between 70th and 71st Sts (212-579-3966). Subway: B, C to 72nd St; 1, 2, 3 to 72nd St. Daily noon–3pm, 5–11pm. Average main course: $25.* This Upper West Side eatery lacks the flawlessly antiqued mirrors and wicker chairs that make the city's myriad French bistros so utterly recognizable. Instead, this low-key spot pours its energy into the food. The extensive menu includes all the usuals—from niçoise salad to escargots—without forsaking quality. The memorable pistachio-crusted lamb is served with a flaky wild-mushroom tart; fresh herbs are generously strewn over salads and steak frites alike. Skip the cream puffs and go for the crêpes suzette.

★ ▲**Bouley** *120 West Broadway at Duane St (212-964-2525). Subway: A, C, 1, 2, 3 to Chambers St. Daily 11:30am–11:30pm. Average main course: $40.* David Bouley's fine-dining flagship—with discreet service and an affordable wine list—may be the least daunting spot in town for blowing a bundle on an extravagant meal, attracting a more understated crowd than its more frequently hyped chef-named competitors. Though the candlelit dining room under a vaulted red ceiling is subdued, the menu and food are more exciting than ever. The Return to Chiang Mai is a gorgeous terrine layering lobster, mango and artichoke in a serrano ham wrapper, while a baby lamb chop entrée looks photo-styled for a wedding magazine spread—the supremely tender chops perched over a bright green streak of minted zucchini puree.

Brasserie 8½ *9 W 57th St between Fifth and Sixth Aves (212-829-0812). Subway: F to 57th St; N, R, W to Fifth Ave–59th St. Mon–Sat 11:30am–midnight; Sun 11:30am–9pm. Average main course: $25.* Appearance isn't everything, but in Brasserie 8½'s case, it's up there. Survey the minimalist decor: a grand, snaking staircase and extra-deep leather banquettes. Marvel at Fernand Léger's only known stained-glass piece, which divides the open kitchen from the dining room. Chef Julian Alonzo, who studied under David Bouley, creates a suitably modern dining experience: Black-sesame-studded tuna tartare is served with fresh-grated wasabi; and a lump-crabmeat cake finds a fresh edge in its side salad of sea beans and razor-thin artichoke slices. The devil's-food Ring Ding dessert is deliciously amusing.

Brasserie Ruhlmann *45 Rockefeller Plaza between 50th and 51st Sts (212-974-2020). Subway: B, D, F, V to 47–50th Sts–Rockefeller Ctr. Mon–Fri 7am–11pm; Sat, Sun 11:30am–11pm. Average main course: $25.* Celebrity chef Laurent Tourondel (BLT Fish, BLT Steak) took over the kitchen at this French restaurant—named for a top 1920s furniture designer—after the original chef left, and the menu has subsequently been BLT-erized. The dishes lean heavily on seafood, Tourondel's specialty. His excellent tuna tartare sits high on a bed of avocado, and the oysters Rockefeller, with a layer of browned Gruyère and Parmesan, are the best we've ever had. The ebony and ivory wall insets and intricate mosaic floor are stunning, but it's hard to resist a spot at the 165-seat outdoor patio overlooking the plaza.

★ ▲**Café Boulud** *20 E 76th St between Fifth and Madison Aves (212-772-2600). Subway: 6 to 77th St. Mon–Fri 5:45–11pm; Sat 5:30–11pm; Sun 5:45–10pm. Average main course: $35.* The high prices and starchy senior clientele suggest that this "casual" alternative to chef-owner Daniel Boulud's fine-dining restaurant, Daniel, is indeed a neighborhood spot—for dwellers between Park and Fifth. Although service can be inconsistent (initial attention from the waitstaff seems to dwindle by dessert, and plates might even rest empty for 45 minutes), the food is technically excellent and refreshingly unfussy. A buttery foie gras *torchon* comes with evanescent Muscat gelée; rare slices of duck breast sport a nice salt crust; scoops of pistachio ice cream and apricot sorbet atop honeyed meringue make for a pleasantly chewy vacherin.

Café des Artistes *1 W 67th St between Central Park West and Columbus Ave (212-877-3500). Subway: 1 to 66th St–Lincoln Ctr. Mon–Fri noon–3pm, 5:30pm–midnight; Sat 11am–3pm, 5:30pm–midnight; Sun 10am–3pm, 5:30pm–midnight. Average main course: $30.* Although men are no longer required to wear jackets at this storied restaurant, women continue to flaunt baubles the size of grapes, the waiters embrace service as a career, and there's not an actor-model-whatever in sight. Howard Chandler Christy's murals of cavorting wood nymphs still anchor the room. Chef Bill Peet (formerly of Lutèce, Asia de Cuba and, more recently, 44) has ensured that the menu remains strong on seafood. And purists will evermore find such stalwarts as *pot-au-feu* and caramelized rack of lamb. The hands of your veteran waiter may shake slightly as he pours from one of 3,000 bottles, but he'd never, ever spill a drop.

▲**Café Gray** *Time Warner Center, 10 Columbus Circle at Broadway, third floor (212-823-6338). Subway: A, C, B, D, 1 to 59th St–Columbua Circle. Mon–Sat 5–11pm. Average main course: $37.* Mistakes happen—the bread can be dense and bland, and water not ordered might appear on the bill—but the prices on the Café Gray menu are no mistake at all: a $26 risotto appetizer, $37 snapper, $39 short ribs. These exorbitant fees won't buy you a seat with a view (the windows overlooking Central Park are blocked by chef Gray Kunz's open kitchen), or a romantic scene (it's a brasserie—inside a shopping mall). Or even a memorable meal. Summer corn ravioli are bogged down with a rich cream sauce; veal and sea bass entrées, though perfectly cooked, are also heavily sauced—and both arrive on a bed of wilted spinach. End on an upside with moist chocolate rum cake, but you might find your money would have been better spent downstairs at J.Crew.

▲**Café Pierre** *Pierre Hotel, 2 E 61st St at Fifth Ave (212-940-8195). Subway: N, R, W to Fifth Ave–59th St. Daily 6–10pm. Average main course: $40.* The service, decor and clientele of the venerable Pierre Hotel look as if they haven't changed since 1964. Before you sit down, you'll notice the piano bar (with a live cabaret singer), Italian marble and trompe l'oeil ceiling of a cloud-strewn sky. Only the food shows signs of modernity: Chef Jason Johnston (formerly of the Bellagio in Las Vegas), works wonders with the dishes, though he's still beholden to the classics (Dover sole is a top seller). His butternut-squash bisque is lush, velvety and swirled with cream. And the half chicken is slow-poached in duck fat and

served with a riesling sauce. It's so rich, you might as well just mainline butter..

★ **Chanterelle** *2 Harrison St at Hudson St (212-966-6960). Subway: 1 to Franklin St. Mon–Wed 5:30–11pm; Fri, Sat noon–2:30pm, 5:30–11pm; Sun 5:30–11pm. Three-course prix fixe: $95.* Unlike so many other shrines to fine dining, Chanterelle still feels like a warm, small-time operation, albeit one with big-time prices. After 28 years, owners David and Karen Waltuck continue to wow gastronomes with a handwritten menu that changes every four weeks and a serene, elegant space. Chef David Waltuck (he of the 2007 James Beard Award for best New York chef) is steeped in French tradition, but he also continually churns out new, fun dishes: An asparagus flan comes with fresh morels, while halibut is wrapped in prosciutto and paired with a roasted-corn ragout.

★ **DB Bistro Moderne** *55 W 44th St between Fifth and Sixth Aves (212-391-2400). Subway: B, D, F, V to 42nd St–Bryant Park; 7 to Fifth Ave. Mon–Sat noon–2:30pm, 5:15–11pm; Sun 5–10pm. Average main course: $30.* It's always interesting to see a master of high-end cuisine dress down: Here you can order a beer with dinner, and you don't have to use your quiet voice in either of the chic dining rooms. Servers can tell you all about the country duck pâté, but they won't try to up-sell you on a pricey bottle of wine. Daniel Boulud's original $32 DB Burger (sirloin, braised short ribs, foie gras and black truffles on a Parmesan bun), which famously launched New York's haute-burger war, has been one-upped during truffle season by the $59 DB Burger Royale (topped with one layer of freshly shaved black truffles) and again with a $120 version (two layers).

★ **Daniel** *60 E 65th St between Madison and Park Aves (212-288-0033). Subway: F to Lexington Ave–63rd St; 6 to 68th St–Hunter College. Mon–Thu 5:45–11pm; Fri, Sat 5:30–11pm. Prix fixe: $98–$155.* The revolving door off Park Avenue and the grandiose interior, with neoclassical columns and velvet seats, announce it: This is fine dining. The cuisine at Daniel Boulud's flagship, which is rooted in French technique with *au courant* flourishes like fusion elements and an emphasis on local produce, is refined without blowing you away—though it has its moments. Cooked *pluots* are a smart acidic counterpoint to seared foie gras. Vermont veal cooked three ways aptly showcases crisp sweetbreads, rare tenderloin and braised cheeks. The pastry chef's creations are as whimsical as they are delicious—a frothy vacherin is dotted with potently flavored peaks of lemon meringue and raspberry marshmallow.

★ ▲**Fleur de Sel** *5 E 20th St between Fifth Ave and Broadway (212-460-9100). Subway: N, R, W to 23rd St. Mon–Sat noon–2pm, 5:30–10:30pm; Sun noon–2pm, 5–9pm. Three-course prix fixe: $76; six-course prix fixe: $89; eight-course prix fixe: $112.* Finding a relaxed, quiet restaurant in the Flatiron District isn't easy, but chef-owner Cyril Renaud favors simplicity over splash and tradition over trend. Crisp linens, plush banquettes and warm, amber lighting create an intimate, understated setting. If dreamy paintings of Brittany (by Renaud himself) don't give away his origins, the menu will. Halibut comes with endives, bacon and a balsamic reduction. For dessert, crêpes are folded around caramelized apple slices and topped with Devonshire cream. The half-price wine special on Mondays is another draw.

Gascogne *158 Eighth Ave between 17th and 18th Sts (212-675-6564). Subway: 1 to 18th St. Mon 5:30–10:30pm; Tue–Thu noon–3pm, 5:30–10:30pm; Fri, Sat 5:30–11:30pm; Sun 5–10:30pm. Average main course: $25.* Named after a region noted for its culinary indulgences, this haute establishment is all about foie gras and other luxurious dishes—carefully prepared and presented. Time your visit right and the prices won't break you. A $27 cash-only, preheater prix-fixe menu offered nightly before 7:30pm (and all evening Mondays for $29) delivers four courses for about the price of one à la carte entrée. Carnivores will love the honey-roasted duck breast, top-notch cassoulet and rack of lamb with thyme. A verdant garden in the back offsets the richness of the dishes with some good old alfresco dining.

★ ▲**Jean Georges** *Trump International Hotel & Tower, 1 Central Park West at Columbus Circle (212-299-3900). Subway: A, C, B, D, 1 to 59th St–Columbus Circle. Mon–Thu noon–2:30pm, 5:15–11pm; Fri, Sat 5:15–11pm. Three-course prix fixe: $98; tasting menu: $148.* Unlike so many of its vaunted peers, Jean-Georges has avoided becoming a shadow of itself because the cooking still has the power to take your breath away. The foie gras terrine starter is legendary for a reason: Every bite of the velvety pâté that harbors roasted strawberries on a round of brioche (all coated in a thin brûlée shell) is worth savoring. A more ascetic dish of green asparagus with rich morels and an asparagus *jus* showcases the vegetables' essence. Inventive themed dessert quartets from pastry chef Johnny Iuzzini might include "summer," which features an uncannily ripe-tasting red plum sorbet and a saline palate cleanser of sliced nectarines, crunchy pistachios and briny goat cheese. **Other location** *Nougatine and Mistral Terrace, Trump International Hotel & Tower, 1 Central Park West at Columbus Circle (212-299-3900).*

★ **JoJo** *160 E 64th St between Lexington and Third Aves (212-223-5656). Subway: F to Lexington Ave–63rd St. Mon–Thu noon–2:30pm, 5:30–10pm; Fri, Sat noon–2:30pm, 5:30–11pm; Sun noon–2:30pm, 5:30–10pm. Average main course: $25.* If you could eat in only one man's restaurants for the rest of your life, you'd be wise to choose Jean-Georges Vongerichten. There's exotic Spice Market (Subcontinental), moderately dressy Vong (Vietnamese), hyperstylish 66 (Chinese), jacket-and-tie Jean Georges (French) and, of course, the intimate JoJo, where you feel as if you're dining in the chef's private townhouse. Dishes stay comfortably in UES-crowd-pleasing territory but have surprising little twists: A beet-and-goat-cheese combo is reconfigured into nuggets of fresh red and yellow beets paired fondue-style with a crock of melted goat cheese; a foie gras dish is served as a brûlée. The molten chocolate cake might as well have been invented here: The moist chocolate exterior can barely contain its liquid dark-chocolate insides, which spill out and mingle with a scoop of smooth vanilla ice cream. It's a divinely gloppy ending to a meal at Vongerichten's most comforting venue.

L.C.B. Brasserie Rachou *60 W 55th St between Fifth and Sixth Aves (212-688-6525). Subway: E, V to Fifth Ave–53rd St; F to 57th St. Daily noon–midnight. Average main course: $25.* This is French for the French, a classic restaurant with apricot walls, long mirrors and brass fixtures that exudes a relaxed atmosphere—with classically high prices. The wine list is extensive; the foie gras, luscious; and the cheese platter, a highly aromatic satisfaction. Despite the

level of luxury, L.C.B. is not a romantic destination: The noise level is high, and tables are so close that privacy is impossible. Concentrate on chef Jean-Jacques Rachou's food instead. You'd need to book a transatlantic flight to find a more savory cassoulet than the one served here, and the tender steak au poivre is a good example of why this dish is so beloved. With a well-informed (but not snooty) staff and a lofty soufflé that would have brought a tear to Julia Child's eye, L.C.B. shows why French cuisine is the standard against which others have been measured.

▲**L'Absinthe** *227 E 67th St between Second and Third Aves (212-794-4950). Subway: 6 to 68th St–Hunter College. Mon–Sat noon–3pm, 5:30–11pm; Sun noon–3pm, 5:30–10pm. Average main course: $30.* In this Art Nouveau dining room you can imagine artists from the turn of the century savoring the mind-altering liqueur that gives this brasserie its name. Lutèce veteran Jean-Michel Bergougnoux divides his menu into "French contemporary" dishes like *panko*-crusted sushi-grade tuna in a wasabi-gazpacho sauce, and "brasserie classics." You can dive into all things rich: The glorious *poularde truffée et ses legumes pochés* is a whole chicken poached in black-truffle broth until the bird is impossibly tender.

L'Atelier de Joël Robuchon *Four Seasons Hotel New York, 57 E 57th St between Madison and Park Aves (212-350-6658). Subway: N, R, W to Fifth Ave–59th St; 4, 5, 6 to 59th St. Daily 11:30am–2:30pm, 6pm–midnight. Average main course: $35.* Finally, Joël "Chef of the Century" Robuchon opened a restaurant in New York City, last year. The location? The plush Four Seasons Hotel, but the best spots are at the bar, where chefs work in a pristine open kitchen run by Yosuke Suga. L'Atelier has the primary Robuchon hallmark: a focus on a few luxurious ingredients, each elevated to a surprising potency. The langoustine spring roll is packed with sweet meat and fried basil leaf. The best dessert, a striking sugar sphere holding a custard yolk with rose-and-blackberry coulis, is unlike anything you'll find elsewhere in the city.

L'Ecole *462 Broadway at Grand St (212-219-3300). Subway: J, M, Z, N, Q, R, W, 6 to Canal St. Mon–Fri 12:30–2pm, 5:30–9pm; Sat 5:30–9pm. Prix fixe: $39.95.* One person's homework is another's feast. L'Ecole's staid yellow-and-crimson dining room has been the training ground for students at the French Culinary Institute since 1984. Would-be chefs, overseen by top-cooks-turned-academics, are in the kitchen; patrons get a bargain $26.50 three-course prix-fixe lunch or $40 five-course prix-fixe dinner (from 8 to 10pm). Expect Continental dishes like escargots with herb butter and panfried cod with yellow tomato coulis. Although the culinary creations may not always earn an A-plus, L'Ecole offers the thrill of sampling a future master's work, accompanied by first-class service and a worthy wine list.

La Goulue *746 Madison Ave between 64th and 65th Sts (212-988-8169). Subway: 6 to 68th St–Hunter College. Daily noon–11:30pm. Average main course: $29.* Whether or not this mahogany-paneled neighborhood bistro (named for a cancan dancer at the Moulin Rouge) strays too far from traditional Parisian cuisine, moneyed, casually chic Upper East Siders pack the place. The classic-but-clamorous atmosphere makes La Goulue one of the best hangouts around. Appetizers,

Gold standard
L'Atelier de Joël Robuchon
raises the bar with its rich
ingredients and pristine
open kitchen.

French $25 and over

CINZIA REALE-CASTELLO

Serves you right
L'Absinthe's menu
sates any palate with
both contemporary
and classic cuisine.

PATRIK RYTIKANGAS

like goat-cheese gnocchi indulgently bathed in a sweet asparagus sauce, take interesting risks, and entrées include an unbelievably juicy duck à l'orange. For dessert, a large chocolate soufflé teaming with ice cream is so indulgent, it feels immoral to leave a single bite.

▲**La Grenouille** *3 E 52nd St between Fifth and Madison Aves (212-752-1495). Subway: E, V to Fifth Ave–53rd St. Tue–Thu noon–3pm, 5:30–10:30pm; Fri noon–3pm, 5–11pm; Sat 5–11pm (bar is open Tue–Sat noon–10pm). Average main course: $47. Bar menu items: $8–$17.50.* While many old-fashioned French restaurants have closed in recent years, La Grenouille continues to carry the haute torch, though it is now possible to have a casual meal here, too. During dinner, men must wear jackets and servers don bowties. Dinner is divided into two camps: classic dishes and seasonal ones. Unsurprisingly, frog legs are the house specialty, and the Dover sole with mustard sauce is far more interesting than it sounds. Yes, it's still basically a big, fancy restaurant, the clientele is fairly buttoned-up, and the dishes all have lots of fancy sauces, but it's a great place to celebrate a special occasion. And now you can walk in wearing jeans—and not spend a fortune.

Le Bernardin *155 W 51st St between Sixth and Seventh Aves (212-489-1515). Subway: B, D, F, V to 47–50th Sts–Rockefeller Ctr; N, R, W to 49th St. Mon–Thu noon–2:30pm, 5:15–10:30pm; Fri noon–2:30pm, 5:15–11pm; Sat 5:15–11pm. Four-course prix-fixe dinner: $107. Six-course tasting menu: $180.* Although this midtown restaurant is perhaps the most celebrated seafood destination in Manhattan, the painted seascapes in the hushed, carpeted dining room feel very disconnected from this upper crusty setting. Items from Eric Ripert's menu (which includes Almost Raw, Barely Touched and Lightly Cooked sections) are good, but not great. An appetizer of paper-thin yellowfin tuna draped over a slice of toast with foie gras is delicate but bland. Calamari stuffed with wood ear mushrooms and prawns offers an interesting if unspectacular take on surf and turf. And while the fragrant ginger-and-cardamom-infused tomato broth that bathes a black bass is stunning, the fish itself can be slightly overcooked. A place with a reputation this great should have better food.

Le Cirque *One Beacon Court, 151 E 58th St between Lexington and Third Aves (212-644-0202). Subway: N, R, W to Fifth Ave–59th St; 4, 5, 6 to 59th St. Mon–Fri 11:45am–10:45pm; Sat 5:30–10:45pm. Average main course: $40.* Of the three incarnations of Sirio Maccioni's famed circus-themed restaurant, the latest is probably the easiest reservation to score. Located in the Bloomberg skyscraper, the soaring dining room is fashioned to look like a big-top tent and features the expected collection of old, rich characters. The menu is patchy, but a few dishes are reminiscent of Le Cirque's old razzle-dazzle: foie gras ravioli is perfectly cooked, Mozambique *langoustines* swim in a fiery red-curry, ginger and kafir lime sauce, and a dessert is encased in dry ice that pumps smoke across the table.

Le Refuge Inn *586 City Island Ave between Beach and Cross Sts, City Island, Bronx (718-885-2478). Travel: 6 to Pelham Park, then take the BX 29 bus to City Island Ave and Cross St. Tue–Sun noon–10pm. Prix-fixe bruch $25; prix-fixe lunch $35; prix-fixe dinner $45.* Tastefully appointed with 19th-century antiques, the three small dining rooms of this French-run Victorian bed-and-breakfast in City Island present an intimate setting for exquisite Gallic country fare. The prix fixe menus—for brunch ($25), lunch ($35) and dinner ($45)—change each month, but the attentiveness to every dish is consistent. The *timbale d'escargots* (snail casserole) appetizer is judiciously accented with garlic, while the subtle *canard à l'orange* and the couscous *de la mer* (with curried shrimp) might make you wish you'd booked a room to ensure a table the next day.

★ ▲**Mas** *39 Downing St between Bedford and Varick Sts (212-255-1790). Subway: A, C, E, B, D, F, V to W 4th St; 1 to Houston St. Mon–Sat 6pm–4am. Average main course: $32.* This fashionable spot with clean lines, chocolate tones and a warm golden glow arrived in the Village with an instant scene, courtesy of chef Galen Zamarra (formerly of Bouley Bakery). But look past the flashy diners for the real excitement: a menu that focuses on seasonal and organic ingredients. A salad of sweet Maine crab and portobello benefits from a tinge of citrus, and a black-trumpet-and-chanterelle stew is topped with a delicate lasagna noodle. Organic hen, cooked with saffron and truffle, deboned and served sliced, is deeply moist, and the bigeye tuna, which is given a delightfully meaty edge by brown butter and crisp shallots, is swoonworthy. Even strange-on-paper dessert combos, such as warm rhubarb tart with black-olive ice cream, work wonderfully.

Orsay *1057 Lexington Ave at 75th St (212-517-6400). Subway: 6 to 77th St. Mon–Sat noon–11pm; Sun 11am–10pm. Average main course: $26.* If you were trust-fund rich, Orsay would be the kind of place you'd eat at three times a week. The food is good enough to please those with refined tastes, but the laid-back brasserie atmosphere is far less stuffy than that of other eateries at these prices. The menu changes with the seasons, but expect perfectly cooked steak frites served with a choice of sauces, a top-quality raw bar, and more inventive dishes, including a flavorful stew of cod, seasoned with rosemary, bay leaves and vegetables. Desserts are surprisingly impressive, especially the classic tarte Tatin and the rich chocolate tart.

★ **Payard Pâtisserie & Bistro** *1032 Lexington Ave between 73rd and 74th Sts (212-717-5252). Subway: 6 to 77th St. Mon–Thu noon–3pm, 5:45–10:30pm; Fri, Sat noon–3pm, 5:45–11pm. Tea: Mon–Sat 3:30–5pm. Average main course: $25.* Glance past the espresso machines at this Paris-inspired bakery and restaurant, and you'll spy an elegant mahogany-paneled dining room with face-lift–friendly lighting and glittering belle epoque mirrors. Executive chef Philippe Bertineau prepares contemporary dishes like seared sea scallops with sunchokes puree and a drizzle of vanilla–sea urchin clam broth, and classics including a traditional bouillabaisse. Desserts by chef-owner François Payard include a detailed fruit Napolean made of crêpes layered with mango cream and lychee.

★ ▲**Per Se** *2007 Eat Out Award, Readers' Choice: Best splurge. Time Warner Center, 10 Columbus Circle at Broadway, fourth floor (212-823-9335). Subway: A, C, B, D, 1 to 59th St–Columbus Circle. Mon–Thu 5:30–10pm; Fri–Sun 11:30am–1:30pm, 5:30–10pm. Tasting menu: $250–$280.* Expectations are high at Per Se—and that goes both ways. You are expected to come when they'll have you—you might be put on standby for four nights, only to win a 10pm Tuesday spot—and fork over $150 a head if you cancel less than two days before. You're expected to wear the right clothes, pay

Evil genius
Being bad feels good with Mas's organic and seasonal desserts.

a nonnegotiable service charge and pretend you aren't eating in a shopping mall. The restaurant, in turn, is expected to deliver one hell of a tasting menu for $250 ($280 if you want foie gras). And it does. Dish after dish is flawless and delicious, if not altogether surprising, beginning with Thomas Keller's signature salmon tartare cone and luxe oysters-and-caviar starter. Have you tasted steak with mashed potatoes and Swiss chard, or *burrata* cheese with olive oil drizzled on top, or chocolate brownies with coffee ice cream? Possibly. Have you had them this good? Unlikely. In the end, it's all worth every penny—as long as someone else is paying.

★ **Picholine** *35 W 64th St between Central Park West and Broadway (212-724-8585). Subway: A, C, B, D, 1 to 59th St–Columbus Circle. Mon–Thu 5–11pm; Fri 5–11:45pm; Sat 11:45am–2pm, 5–11:45pm; Sun 5–9pm. Two-course prix-fixe meal: $64.* Following a renovation last year that culminated in barely perceptible design tweaks (the crystal chandeliers now sport silk lamp shades, and gray mohair replaced cotton on the banquettes), Terrance Brennan's Picholine remains a shrine to fine dining. In the dining room, the menu features two-course prix-fixe meals for $64. Dishes like featherlight sheep's-milk gnocchi with shrimp and chanterelles in parsley *pistou* exhibit the Mediterranean style of cooking that made Brennan famous. Fromager Max McCalman continues to oversee the notable cheese cellar, and a bar menu gives diners more ways to taste Brennan's handiwork for under $20.

★ **Raoul's** *180 Prince St between Sullivan and Thompson Sts (212-966-3518). Subway: C, E to Spring St. Daily 5pm–1am. Average main course: $25.* A parade of copycats has been trying to achieve what Raoul's has been doing since 1975—serving first-rate French fare in an authentic bistro setting. Raoul's didn't scour flea markets for antique furnishings for its timeworn look—it's the real deal. Dim lighting, pressed-tin ceilings and walls, black-and-white leather booths, and paintings of female nudes beckon lovers and late-night gourmands. The food is good too: A thick, charred cut of sirloin smothered in a black-peppercorn sauce is so tender you could cut it with a butter knife; and Muscovy duck breast arrives the perfect hue of pink with a grilled peach and *jus*-drenched stuffing.

Triomphe *The Iroquois, 49 W 44th St between Fifth and Sixth Aves (212-453-4233). Subway: B, D, F, V to 42nd St–Bryant Park; 7 to Fifth Ave. Mon–Fri 7–10:30am, 11:45am–2:30pm, 5:30–11pm; Sat 7–10:30am, 5:30–11pm; Sun 7–10:30am. Average main course: $30.* This gem is true to its name. Executive chef Steven Zobel's menu is full of confident balancing acts in which no ingredient is superfluous. Pumpkin wontons, a seasonal dish, make sweet, chewy counterpoints to the herbed Parmesan broth and white-truffle oil in which they are served. On the permanent menu, you'll find pan-seared sea scallops with porcino mushrooms in foie gras butter. Coriander-crusted Australian rack of lamb yields wonderful flavors and juices, which Zobel takes to another level with port-soaked, foie gras–stuffed prunes. The remarkable desserts, such as profiteroles in butterscotch sauce, are irresistible; the Pavlova, a meringue shell filled with whipped cream and fresh fruit, is as light and airy as the legendary dancer's form.

German

See also: *Austrian*

Charlie's Inn *2711 Harding Ave between Balcom and Graff Aves, Bronx (718-931-9727). Travel: 6 to Westchester Sq–East Tremont Ave, then Bx42 bus to Balcom Ave. Tue, Wed, Sun noon–9pm; Thu–Sat noon–10pm. Average main course: $16.* This is really an Irish bar attached to a German beer garden—and a spacious one at that. It's also a meat-and-potatoes eatery featuring a German-American menu for off-duty cops. The sauerbraten and Wiener and Jäger schnitzel are hardly the Rhine variety, but they're still passable (all entrées come with homemade spaetzle, those little dollops of anti-Atkins love). Desserts resemble variations on spackling compound, so indulge in the starters.

Heidelberg *1648 Second Ave between 85th and 86th Sts (212-628-2332). Subway: 4, 5, 6 to 86th St. Mon–Thu, Sun 11:30am–10:30pm; Fri, Sat 11:30am–11:30pm. Average main course: $16.* For more than 70 years, this Yorkville holdover has clung to its roots: dirndled waitresses, men in lederhosen and steins of Spaten. Schaller & Weber, the neighboring butcher, supplies much of the meat; sausage platters are weighted down with *bauernwurst, weisswurst* and bratwurst. Adventurers can explore "Old-World favorites" like pig knuckles. Most dishes come with spaetzle, sauerkraut or potato salad, but don't fill up too much—you'll want to try the homemade apple strudel or chocolate fondue for two.

Lederhosen *39 Grove St between Bedford and Bleecker Sts (212-206-7691). Subway: 1 to Christopher St–Sheridan Sq. Tues–Thu noon–11pm; Fri, Sat noon–midnight. Average main course: $15.* Germans have been guzzling masses of sheer beer for long enough to know what soaks it up best: fat, boiled knockwurst with crusty rolls and hot mustard, mountains of *kartoffelsalat* and giant slabs of Wiener schnitzel. Lord help any light eater at Lederhosen: In the goofy confines of this hyper-German restaurant, you're expected to eat and drink like you're in a real *biergarten,* and even the soup is carbo-loaded (gulasch with spaetzle). You can easily stuff yourself for $15, but lunch offers the best deals for the hungry man: wurst, potato salad or fries, cabbage sauerkraut and bread for $5.

★ ⊙Mandler's: The Original Sausage Co. *26 E 17th St between Fifth Ave and Broadway (212-255-8999). Subway: L, N, Q, R, W, 4, 5, 6 to 14th St–Union Sq. Mon–Wed 9am–10pm; Thu, Fri 9am–11pm; Sat, Sun 11am–11pm. Average main course: $6.* Mandler's is guaranteed to make any wiener-lover happy. Eleven varieties of wurst, brats and Italian-style sausage, among others, are served on one of six types of bread with a choice of toppings, such as sweet relish or sautéed onions with mushrooms. Naturally, other entrées feature sausage—pasta is tossed with sausage in sauce, and a sampler includes a half link of four. There is even a sausage fondue. A handful of beers and bottles of wine are available, but a giant sized homemade pink lemonade works just as well. **Other location** *Mandler's, 601 Eighth Ave at 39th St (212-244-4222).*

Rolf's Restaurant *281 Third Ave at 22nd St (212-473-8718). Subway: 6 to 23rd St. Mon–Fri 11:30am–10:30pm; Sat, Sun noon–10:30pm. Average main course: $20.* This bar and grill combines traditional German food and beer with a healthy serving of kitsch, notably with its annual Christmas decorations. Year-round, you can enjoy a wide range of German dishes, especially meats and sausages, while an array of faux Medieval paintings peaks out behind obsessively entwined oak branches. The portions are extremely generous; more sauerbraten than anyone really could (or perhaps should) eat. There are five different schnitzel offerings, but you can't go wrong in ordering the simple Wiener schnitzel. In the end, the zeitgeist is more Epcot Center than Bavaria, and like the theme park, it's a fun ride.

Schnitzel Haus *7319 Fifth Ave between 73rd and 74th Sts, Bay Ridge, Brooklyn (718-836-5600). Subway: R to 77th St. Mon–Thu 11am–10pm; Fri–Sun 11am–11pm. Average main course: $20.* On a strip of Bay Ridge that's home to countless hookah lounges, this German beer house easily sticks out. Inside, black-and-white photos of the *Vaterland* grace shiny wood walls, and tuba-heavy folk music plays in the background. Friendly waitresses perfectly pronounce Warsteiner beer and sauerbraten in their south Brooklyn accents, and are ready to bring you a pint or stein. While the place is cheerful, the food lacks. Sausages like venison and cherry are moist and fresh, but the veal schnitzel can be overcooked and under seasoned, which might be forgivable but for the $18 price tag.

Zum Stammtisch *69-46 Myrtle Ave between 69th Pl and 70th Sts, Glendale, Queens (718-386-3014). Subway: M to Fresh Pond Rd. Mon–Thu, Sun noon–10pm; Fri, Sat noon–11pm. Average main course: $16.* This reliable outpost has been drawing a crowd of regulars for over 40 years. They keep coming because not much has changed, not even the dirndl-wearing waitstaff. No trendy pan-anything cuisine here: the *ochsenmaulsalat* (beef tongue salad) is way better than it sounds, as is the liver dumpling soup, and the local meat provisioners, among the city's finest, supply the essentials for outstanding Jäger schnitzel and robust sauerbraten. You'll find an impressive selection of German beers on tap and an edible Black Forest cake.

Read 'em & eat

palatschinken: crêpelike pancakes either sweet or savory

sauerbraten: a marinated beef roast

wurst: sausage; *blutwurst* (blood sausage), *bratwurst* (sausage made with pork and veal), *knackwurst* (highly seasoned sausage made with pork and beef), *weisswurst* (white sausage made with veal and bacon)

ovelia
PSISTARIA | BAR

music

food

drink

day * night *

dinner
coffee bar
brunch
outside bar
raw bar
cocktails
happy hour
disc jockey

www.ovelia-ny.com

34-01 30TH AVE
ASTORIA, NY 11103
718. 721. 7217

Greek

See also: *Mediterranean, Middle Eastern*

Agnanti Meze *78-02 Fifth Ave at 78th St, Bay Ridge, Brooklyn (718-833-7033). Subway: R to 77th St. Daily noon–10:30pm. Average main course: $15.* You might want to consider a breath mint after consuming the savory offerings—most of which are expertly flavored with a combination of dill, onion, garlic and lemon—at this fantastic Greek restaurant. Its pumpkin-orange walls, beige linens and candle-lit tables ooze warmth. A mouthful in more ways than one, the *kolokythokeftedes mykonos* croquettes, made from zucchini, scallions, dill and feta cheese, were deliciously tangy. Agnanti is praised for its grilled octopus appetizer, which is liberally sprinkled with oregano, olive oil and vinegar. Service is casual and friendly; and they'll be happy to call a car if you've sampled too much of the Greek-heavy wine list.

Anthos *36 W 52nd St between Fifth and Sixth Aves (212-582-6900). Subway: B, D, F, V to 47–50th Sts–Rockefeller Ctr. Mon–Thu noon–2:45pm, 5–10:30pm; Fri noon–2:45pm, 5–11pm; Sat 5–11pm. Average main course: $35.* At this haute Greek spot from chef Michael Psilakis (Kefi, Onera), the setting is lush—big front windows, curved ceiling, cherry blossom prints (*anthos* means "blossom")—but the focus is squarely on the cuisine. A master of seafood, Psilakis shows it best in his crudo: vibrant bites of fish with Greek touches such as blood-red tuna topped with mastic oil and yellowtail paired with fennel pollen and ouzo-marinated cherries. For dessert, the kitchen continues to toy with Greek standards: Sesame ice cream is coated in a sweet-salty sesame paste that is a riff on halvah.

★ **Avra** *141 E 48th St between Lexington and Third Aves (212-759-8550). Subway: E, V to Lexington Ave–53rd St; 6 to 51st St. Mon–Fri noon–midnight; Sat 11am–midnight; Sun 11am–11pm. Average main course: $26.* Arched doorways and a limestone floor evoke an Ionian seaside village; fabric draped like sails over wooden ceiling beams adds to the breezy feel. Appetizers such as grilled whole sardines and feta-and-tomato-stuffed squid whet the appetite for the main attraction: impeccably fresh fish, priced by the pound and laid out on a bed of ice. Whole fish—a flaky royal dorado, for example—is charcoal-grilled and simply dressed with lemon juice, olive oil and oregano. For more flourish, try the clay pot–baked salmon Corfu, which comes wrapped in crisp grape leaves.

Elias Corner *24-02 31st St at 24th Ave, Astoria, Queens (718-932-1510). Subway: N, W to Astoria–Ditmars Blvd. Daily 5–11:30pm. Average main course: $17.* Beware: This no-reservations taverna gets packed on weekends. The reason? A glistening display of fresh fish that is destined to be the source of your dinner. Elias's gilled critters are exceptional even in a neighborhood throbbing with Greek restaurants—though steak and lamb dishes are also available. Those in the know order the swordfish

Greek mythology
Chef Michael Psilakis's exotically prepared seafood is part of the allure of Anthos.

kebabs (when available) and light Hellenic white wine. Dessert isn't served on weekends, but cafés proffering baklava and inky coffee are nearby.

★ **Estiatorio Milos** *125 W 55th St between Sixth and Seventh Aves (212-245-7400). Subway: F, N, Q, R, W to 57th St. Mon–Fri noon–2:45pm, 5–11:45pm; Sat 5–11:45pm; Sun 5–10:45pm. Average fish: $35 per pound.* An impressive selection fills the ice bar at this established haunt: Mediterranean fish such as *sargo*, *pageot* and *loup de mer*, along with Arctic char from Iceland, Dover sole from Holland and black sea bass from North Carolina, plus various tentacled treats. In the quasi-industrial, cafeteria-like space, customers order the Greek way—by pointing. All selections are served grilled, with olive oil, herbs, lemon and capers. Warning: As it's priced by the pound, a prize catch can lead to a hefty bill.

▲**Gus' Place** *192 Bleecker St between MacDougal St and Sixth Ave (212-777-1660). Subway: A, C, E, B, D, F, V to W 4th St. Mon–Thu noon–11pm; Fri, Sat noon–midnight; Sun noon–11pm. Average main course: $19.* The 2006 reincarnation of Gus' Place may lack the space and blue-and-white Aegean elegance of its former Waverly Place self, but the cuisine has never tasted so wonderfully, elegantly Greek. Amid the new warm country ambience inflected with homey touches like vintage black-and-white family photos from Greece, you can happily make a meal of small plates like *prasopita* (leek, fennel and feta pie), zucchini fritters, shrimp-and-cod cakes and steamed mussels. Each dish seems to trump the next—but the winning

CINZIA REALE-CASTELLO

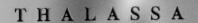

entrée is a piping-hot Greek fish stew in a saffron-and-fennel broth.

Kefi *222 W 79th St between Amsterdam Ave and Broadway (212-873-0200). Subway: 1 to 79th St. Tue–Thu 5–10pm; Fri, Sat 5–11pm; Sun 5–10pm. Average main course: $14.* Diners should expect no less from chef Michael Psilakis (Dona, Anthos) than they did at Onera, his haute Greek eatery that previously occupied this space. In its latest reimagining, the place is casually dressed down with bare wooden tables and blue-and-white fabrics billowing from the ceiling. Artful yet laid-back dishes included memorable meze, like the open-faced spinach pie—a phyllo dough cup filled with béchamel sauce, sautéed spinach and feta—and excellent entrées, like a hearty lamb shank with orzo in red-wine sauce. Reasonable prices—appetizers top out at $9.95, entrées at $15.95—make sticking around for a dessert of Greek yogurt with honey a no-brainer.

Mezzo-Mezzo *31-29 Ditmars Blvd at 33rd St, Astoria, Queens (718-278-0444). Subway: N, W to Astoria–Ditmars Blvd. Mon–Fri 11am–midnight; Sat 11am–1am; Sun 11am–midnight. Average main course: $18.* This eatery beckons with a stone-walled rustic atmosphere and service befitting much pricier joints. Belly dancers and Middle Eastern musicians add weekend bounce. Even more uplifting is the chef's instinct for Greek standards and Mediterranean classics. Lemony stuffed squid oozes with herbed feta; lamb kebabs flaunt hunks of deftly grilled meat; and garlic-tossed seafood pasta is studded with shrimp, squid, clams and salmon, all cooked to tender perfection. *Mezzo-mezzo* might mean "half and half," but this place gets the whole Hellenic taverna thing right.

★ ▲**Molyvos** *871 Seventh Ave between 55th and 56th Sts (212-582-7500). Subway: N, Q, R, W to 57th St. Mon–Thu noon–3pm, 5:30–11:30pm; Fri noon–3pm, 5:30pm–midnight; Sat noon–3pm, 5pm–midnight; Sun noon–11pm. Average main course: $25.* Molyvos remains one of Manhattan's most sophisticated Greek spots. An appetizer of crisp veal sweetbreads nests on gigante beans, and *haloumi* cheese is doused in ouzo and set aflame at the table. Alongside classic main dishes such as moussaka and rabbit stew are whole-fish specials and lamb *yuvetsi* baked in a clay pot. Supersweet desserts include *loukoumades*, fritters resembling doughnut holes served in a pool of cinnamon-thyme honey.

Ovelia *34-10 30th Ave at 34th St, Astoria, Queens (718-721-7217). Subway: N, W to 30th Ave. Mon–Thu 11:30am–11pm; Fri, Sat 11:30am–midnight; Sun 11:30am–11pm. Average main course: $28.* Rather than open another cookie-cutter souvlaki joint or Greek taverna in Astoria, the owners have gotten groovy with the decor at this restaurant and lounge. The octopus is a marvel of tentacles parboiled until tender, then grilled. Classic dips go beyond the usual *skordalia* and include spicy mashed feta served with warm, oregano-scented pita bread. The addictive meat platter combines velvety sweetbreads, rotisserie chicken, roasted pork and lamb, herb-dusted liver and orange-zest–spiked homemade *loukaniko* sausage. Try some of the better-than-expected Greek wines.

▲**Pylos** *128 E 7th St between First Ave and Ave A (212-473-0220). Subway: F, V to Lower East*

Side–Second Ave; L to First Ave. Mon–Tue 5pm–midnight; Wed, Thu noon–4pm, 5pm–midnight; Fri, Sat noon–4pm, 11:30am–1am; Sun 5pm–midnight. Average main course: $21. Named after the Greek clay pot, thousands of which are hanging from the ceiling, this upscale Greek restaurant stands out from the East Village dining scene for its beautiful decor and refined modern take on Hellenic fare. The meal starts with a gratis helping of warm, nicely chewy pita triangles served with the spread of the day (like a creamy fava-bean dip). Of the attractive appetizers, most appealing is a napoleon of thickly sliced, earthy beets layered with a minty feta mousse. A pistachio-crusted wild striped bass entrée was less successful. Despite a few minor missteps, the place is packed nightly.

★ ▲**Snack Taverna** *63 Bedford St at Morton St (212-929-3499). Subway: 1 to Houston St. Mon–Fri noon–3pm, 6–11pm; Sat noon–4pm, 6–11pm; Sun noon–4pm, 6–10pm. Average main course: $18.* When owners Elias Varkoutas and Adam Greene opened Snack, a tiny five-table Soho café, they had no plans for an upscale spin-off. But here it is—larger, bright and simple, with banquettes, exposed brick and shelves stocked with products from the homeland. Elegant French techniques are put to good use in classic Greek dishes. Meatless *moussaka*, layered with prunes, eggplant and potato, sits in a pool of deliciously light béchamel sauce. The all-Greek wine list includes many bottles under $30; dessert fans can chase semolina cake with a cup of superstrength Greek coffee.

★ ▲**Thalassa** *179 Franklin St between Hudson and Greenwich Sts (212-941-7661). Subway: 1 to Franklin St. Mon–Thu noon–3pm, 5:30–11pm; Fri noon–3pm, 5:30pm–midnight; Sat 5:30pm–midnight. Average main course: $32.* Surprisingly intimate for its large size, this Greek seafood emporium serves up unfussy yet elegant preparations of haute-Mediterranean seafood that are positively swoonworthy. Plump, pillowy scallops encased in delicate phyllo make for a standout appetizer, and a piece of fresh Dover sole needs little human intervention to improve it. Attentive service and an exhaustive wine list—including many excellent Greek bottles—cap off an impressive dining experience. Order the baklava for dessert—the conspiracy of toasted almonds, honey and flaky pastry, accompanied by a lush mango sorbet, make this a sublime example of its species.

Read 'em & eat

dolmádes: vine leaves stuffed with rice, meat and spices

galaktoboureko: a phyllo pie filled with farina-based custard

saganaki: kasseri cheese (made from sheep's or goat's milk) fried in butter or oil and sprinkled with lemon juice; usually served as an appetizer

skordaliá: a tangy garlic- and potato-based dip

tsatsiki: a dip made from cucumber, yogurt, lemon juice and garlic

"Street food from India steals the spotlight..."
Michelin 2006

"Not to be missed."
Interview/Art in America

BOMBAY TALKIE

212.242.1900 189 Ninth Avenue New York, NY 10011 Fax: 212.242.6366

DINNER Sunday–Thursday 5pm–10:30pm Friday & Saturday 5pm–11:30pm
Please visit our website bombaytalkie.com

Indian/Subcontinental

See also: *Asian*

That's entertainment Screen stars and tasty dishes now showing at Marsala Bollywood.

▲**Amma** *246 E 51st St between Second and Third Aves (212-644-8330). Subway: E, V to Lexington Ave–53rd St; 6 to 51st St. Daily noon–2:45pm, 5–10:15pm. Average main course: $28.* Amma is the Hindi word for "mother," and if you let Mom take care of you—there's a seven-course tasting menu for $50 per person—you'll thank her later. The courteous waitstaff will help you sort out the à la carte menu. You might try crisp fried okra or *bhel puri*, a lighter interpretation of the classic street food. Thick, buttery tandoor-grilled lamb chops are perfectly complemented by pear chutney. Bread and rice cost extra: Order a side of nicely charred nan to scoop up the tangy sauce of the tender chicken tikka masala. Cut the apron strings? Never.

▲**Angon on Sixth** *320 E 6th St between First and Second Aves (212-260-8229). Subway: F, V to Lower East Side–Second Ave; 6 to Astor Pl. Tue–Sun 12:30–3pm, 5–11:30pm. Average main course: $12.* Chef Helen Gomez has a setting truly worthy of her talents. The pretty dining room is decorated in muted spice colors and lit by gourd-shaped paper lanterns. The staff is attentive, gregarious and quick to apologize for the inevitably long waits between courses. *Aloo tikka* (deep-fried potato balls) are richly creamy, and samosa *chat* are covered in deliciously herby yogurt sauce. The sweet caramelized onions in the *khichuri* (a lentil-and-rice dish) are nicely balanced by the side of spicy chicken curry. But no meal is complete without an order of the spectacular *dal* fry, a house specialty of fried and baked lentils, complexly flavored with turmeric, onion, garlic, ginger and cilantro.

▲**Bombay Talkie** *189 Ninth Ave between 21st and 22nd Sts (212-242-1900). Subway: C, E to 23rd*

St. Mon–Thu 5–10:30pm; Fri, Sat 5–11:30pm; Sun 5–10:30pm. Average main course: $18. When this slick Indian eatery opened nearly two years ago, it combined two dining trends: street food and upscale Indian cuisine. The menu evolved over time, but the restaurant still churns out tasty bites. Try the luscious, lacy *dosa* filled with saucy ground lamb. But little sets apart the main courses (red snapper with a stewy tomato-and-onion sauce and chicken tikka) from the fare at humbler Indian spots. What Bombay Talkie does have is gloss: Sleek teakwood surfaces, a screen that plays Bollywood films and a fancy cocktail list. The *Umrao Jaan* is a distinctive mix of gin, lime juice and saffron syrup—certainly more upscale than street.

▲**Brick Lane Curry House** *306–308 E 6th St between First and Second Aves (212-979-2900). Subway: F, V to Lower East Side–Second Ave. Mon–Thu 1–11pm; Fri, Sat 1pm–1am; Sun 1–11pm. Average main course: $18.* Specializing in *phal*, a habañero curry that's popular along London's Brick Lane restaurant row, Curry House issues a how-hot-can-you-go challenge to every diner. The nine types of curry are ranked by burn level. Because the menu warns that *phal*, the hottest, is "more pain and sweat than flavor," nonasbestos palates should go with gentle but bouncy *jalfrazi* sauce, which is excellent over lamb.

▲◉**Chennai Garden** *129 E 27th St between Park Ave South and Lexington Ave (212-689-1999). Subway: 6 to 28th St. Tue–Fri 11:30am–3pm, 5–10pm; Sat, Sun noon–10pm. Average main course: $11.* The sparsely decorated café won't attract passersby with its looks, but it does have some of the tastiest South Indian

TALIA SIMHI

Side dish

Sub division

Indian food in New York—like Indian food in the subcontinent—is a polyglot affair.

Northern

Most familiar to New Yorkers (particularly those who frequent Sixth Street), northern Indian fare is of Moghal origin and Persian influence. It's notable for elaborate *biriyani*, or rice casseroles, chock with meat, fruit and nuts; meat braised in dairy-based *korma* sauces; and tandoori clay furnaces used for yogurt-marinated meats and flatbreads. The spicing relies on fragrant mixes of cinnamon, nutmeg and cardamom.

Pakistani

Pakistani food exhibits many northern influences with its *biriyanis*, rich butter and tomato *makhani* sauces and tandoori kebabs. The *masalas* (or mixture of spices) here use coriander and cinnamon, packing more punch than the Mughal variety. The Kabab King Diner in Jackson Heights is the place to go for its compendium of kebabs, highlighted by the spice-encrusted *bihari* kebab (beef strips) and the addictive chicken makhani.

Western

In the western Indian state of Gujarat, grains thrive in the fertile soils and vegetable varieties abound. Flours come in a dazzling array, ranging from lentils and chickpeas to rice and wheat. *Muthia*, a classic Gujarati snack of steamed lentil, rice and wheat flour with spices and vegetables, can best be sampled at Vatan, in Murray Hill, as part of its all-you-can-eat procession of 20 Gujarati dishes.

Southern

Rice, coconut and whole chilis take center stage in southern Indian cuisine. Fermented rice and lentil batter stars in *dosa* (gigantic crepes), *idli* (steamed, puck-sized cakes) and hearty vegetable and chili-laced pancakes called *uthappam*. At Saravanaas, on 26th Street, all are served with various chutneys and *sambar*, South India's ubiquitous lentil and vegetable stew.

Coastal

Seafood is an important player in coastal cuisines like that of Bangladesh, which makes extensive use of rice, fish, mango and mustard seeds. Spicy Mina in Woodside, Queens captures this style nicely with its whole fish cooked in a deliciously pungent mustard sauce and *aam dal*, lentils boiled with mango and spices.

food in Manhattan—and it's kosher and vegetarian. *Channa chat* (cold chickpeas in a yogurt and smoky-sweet tamarind sauce), and lentil *chat* (lentil flour fritters drenched in mustard-seed-and-chili yogurt), may be our new favorite comfort food. Curries from Gujarat and Punjab include *undhiyu*, an unusual combination of yam, eggplant and snow peas in a rich, mildly peppery butter sauce. The warm rice pudding is one more reason to come back.

▲**Chola** *232 E 58th St between Second and Third Aves (212-688-4619). Subway: N, R, W to Lexington Ave–59th St; 4, 5, 6 to 59th St. Mon–Sat noon–3pm, 5–11pm; Sun noon–3pm, 5–10:30pm. Average main course $16.* The usual suspects (samosas, chicken tikka masala, lamb vindaloo) are on hand at this midtown South Asian eatery, but regular customers come for less familiar regional and Indian-influenced Malaysian specialties like the Chicken Malai. Dishes like this make it worth tolerating the noisy, crowded dining room.

▲**Copper Chimney** *126 E 28th St between Park Ave South and Lexington Ave (212-213-5742). Subway: 6 to 28th St. Mon–Fri noon–3pm; Mon–Thu 5:30–10:30pm; Sat, Sun noon–11:30pm. Average main course: $14.* With its wall of candles and long banquette covered with orange pillows, this stylish space adds a glamorous touch to the neighborhood. The overly attentive staff encourages you to start with "chicken sixty-five," little red cubes of poultry that have been marinating overnight in chili powder, turmeric and lime juice. The samosas are refreshingly nongreasy, largely because they are baked in a tandoori oven. Vegetarians will be excited by the range of options, like the *navrattan kurma*, which mixes nuts, cauliflower and pineapple in a wonderfully creamy, rich onion sauce. And the mango mousse, a spongy pudding-like concoction, is a dreamy alternative to those cottage cheese balls you typically see at the end of an Indian dinner.

★ ▲**Curry Leaf** *99 Lexington Ave at 27th St (212-725-5558). Subway: 6 to 28th St. Mon–Thu 11:30am–3pm, 5–10:30pm; Fri, Sat 11:30am–3pm, 5–11pm; Sun 11:30am–3pm, 5–10:30pm. Average main course: $12.* There must be a good reason diners trek past countless other neighborhood restaurants to seek out this low-key spot. In fact, there's a whole menu's worth of good reasons, from perfectly seasoned *matar paneer* to blistering lamb vindaloo, as well as the extremely friendly, well-informed staff. Simply mention how delicious the chicken *makhani* is, and the waiter will rattle off a list of ingredients—and call nearby specialty market Kalustyan's (same owners) to ensure that every spice is in stock. You might even be lucky enough to receive an after-dinner treat of sweet cardamom rice on the house. **Other location** *151 Remsen St between Clinton and Court Sts, Brooklyn Heights, Brooklyn (718-222-3900).*

★ ▲**Dawat** *210 E 58th St between Second and Third Aves (212-355-7555). Subway: N, R, W to Lexington Ave–59th St; 4, 5, 6 to 59th St. Mon–Sat noon–3pm, 5:30–11pm; Sun 5–10:30pm. Average main course: $19.* Dawat is perfect for both power lunches and romantic dinners. Indian-food maven Madhur Jaffrey's menu is surprisingly light, and the knowledgeable waitstaff will help you craft a perfect meal. Fried appetizers such as *aloo tikkyas* (potato-and-curry-leaf patties with coriander and chili chutneys) are flavorful without being oily; entrées are seasoned perfectly. Don't neglect the seafood: Sweet, moist Parsi-style salmon is smothered with fresh coriander, steamed in a banana leaf, then unwrapped and presented like a gift.

▲⊖**Delhi Palace** *37-33 74th St between 37th Road and 37th Aves, Jackson Heights, Queens (718-507-0666). Subway: E, F, V, G, R to Jackson Hts–Roosevelt Ave; 7 to 74th St–Broadway. Mon–Thu, 11:30am–10pm; Fri, Sat 11:30am–10:45pm; Sun 11:30am–10pm. Average main course: $11.* Long a competitor of the neighboring Jackson Diner, this dependable, sunflower-hued curry emporium may have the edge these days, especially in terms of its less-nightmarish waits and friendlier staff. The fare remains feisty, with definitive *vindaloos* finessed to an uncommon riot of flavor (skewered chicken *tikka* is also a must-try). Samosas and other fried appetizers are less crispy than often experienced, allowing for more pungent pea notes.

★ ▲**Dévi** *8 E 18th St between Fifth Ave and Broadway (212-691-1300). Subway: L, Q, N, R, W, 4, 5, 6 to 14th St–Union Sq. Mon–Thu noon–2:15pm, 5:30pm–10:30pm; Fri, Sat noon–2:15pm, 5:30–11pm; Sun 5–10pm. Average main course: $24.* "Over-the-top" adequately describes Dévi's ornate bi-level space, a bordellolike mix of brightly-hued brocades where diners use gold cutlery to sample an impressive array of upscale Indian dishes prepared by chefs Suvir Saran and Hemant Mathur. The freshly baked, bubbly *nan* is a necessary accompaniment to spicy entrées, like a plate of enormous tandoori prawns. Desserts, by pastry chef Surbhi Sahni, also score points: Try the light, creamy mango cheesecake, or just sate your sweet tooth with the complimentary petits fours offered with the check.

Earthen Oven *53 W 72nd St at Columbus Ave (212-579-8888). Subway: B, C, 1, 2, 3 to 72nd St. Daily 11:30am–2:45pm, 5–11pm. Average main course: $17.* The Tiffany-style lamps, particleboard-like ceiling and leafy plants in plastic pots suggest that the owners don't expect locals to care much about ambience. It is a hard sell—especially since prices here are steeper than they are at surrounding takeout joints. But chefs Durga Prasad and Alexander Paul Xalxo (both of Tamarind) deliver a superior selection of unusual and generously portioned offerings. In addition to entrée mainstays like *vindaloo* and *tikka masala*, they prepare a wonderfully fiery fish masala, featuring an intriguing sauce seasoned with fresh curry leaves, ginger, coconut and *kokum* (a sour medicinal fruit native to western India). Among the many esoteric vegetarian offerings is a complex chickpea dish made with ginger, green chilies, pomegranate seeds and dried mango.

▲**Hampton Chutney Co.** *68 Prince St between Crosby and Lafayette Sts (212-226-9996). Subway: N, R, W to Prince St; 6 to Spring St. 11am–9pm. Average dosa: $9.* Delicate *dosas* are stuffed with traditional or Western combinations—such as spiced potatoes and curried chicken or grilled asparagus with roasted peppers and goat cheese—and paired with freshly made chutney. The vegetarian *thali* plate features a daily curry, dal, chutney and yogurt (skip the bland, leathery nan). Some folks may think the burbling chants piped into the room are soothing; if you find them annoying, just get your eats to go. And the name? Oddly enough, this upscale quickie-food joint originated in Amagansett. **Other location** *464 Amsterdam Ave between 82nd and 83rd Sts (212-362-5050).*

Meaty pursuit
Master tandoor chefs man the ovens at Yuva.

CINZIA REALE-CASTELLO

Tasty delight
Jean-Georges Vongerichten offers scrumptious bite-size savories at Spice Market.

▲**Indigo Indian Bistro** *357 E 50th St between First and Second Aves (212-421-1919). Subway: E, V to Lexington Ave–53rd St; 6 to 51st St. Daily noon–3pm, 5:30–10pm. Average main course: $18.* Take two steps down into a bright, elegant space and enjoy a refined version of *bhel puri*, a sweet-spicy mix of rice puffs, chickpea-flour noodles, chopped red onion and cilantro blended with tamarind sauce. It's just one of the many *chat*, or street snacks, that begin a meal of carefully prepared, sophisticated classics (no wonder the crowd here is a cosmopolitan group of U.N. professionals). *Malai kofta*, lightly fried cheese dumplings bathed in a gently seasoned tomato-cream sauce, is a delicious complement to a plate of lemon, tomato and tamarind rices flavored with crisp curry leaves, cloves and almonds.

▲**Jackson Diner** *37-47 74th St between Roosevelt and 37th Aves, Jackson Heights, Queens (718-672-1232). Subway: E, F, V, G, R to Jackson Hts–Roosevelt Ave; 7 to 74th St–Broadway. Mon–Thu 11:30am–10:30pm; Fri, Sat 11:30am–10:30pm; Sun 11:30am–10pm. Average main course: $13.* Harried waiters and Formica-topped tables complete the diner experience at this weekend meet-and-eat headquarters for New York's Indian expat community. Watch Hindi soaps on Zee TV while enjoying samosa *chat* topped with chickpeas, yogurt, onion, tomato, and a sweet-spicy mix of tamarind and mint chutneys. Specials like *murgh tikka makhanwala*, tender pieces of marinated chicken simmered in curry and cream, are fiery and flavorful—be sure to ask for mild if you're not immune to potent chilies.

☉**Kabab King Diner** *73-01 37th Rd at 73rd St, Jackson Heights, Queens (718-457-5857).*

Subway: E, F, V, G, R to Jackson Hts–Roosevelt Ave; 7 to 74th St–Broadway. Daily 24hrs. Average main course: $7. Put His Highness's kebabs aside for just one moment because you'd be hard-pressed to find more satisfying curries. Favorites include chicken *makhani* in a fiery lentil-based sauce, and the ever-popular yogurt-marinated chicken tikka. As for the kebabs, competitors may precook and reheat their skewers, but the King's are always grilled to order. The result is an explosion of flavor. Try the *bihari*, a skewer of tender beef so peppery it must be tempered with a spoonful of cooling *raita*. Finish with a cup of steaming *doodh patti*, a strong, milky, licorice-flavored tea that is fit for royalty. **Other locations** *Kabab King of New York 16 E 23rd St between Broadway and Madison Ave (212-475-7575).* ● *Kabab King Palace 74-16 37th Rd between 74th and 75th Sts, Jackson Hts, Queens (718-205-8800).*

★ ▲☉**The Kati Roll** *99 MacDougal St between Bleecker and W 3rd Sts (212-420-6517). Subway: A, C, E, B, D, F, V to W 4th St. Tue–Thu 12:30pm–midnight; Fri, Sat 12:30pm–5am; Sun 12:30pm–midnight. Average roll: $4.* Indian wraps are the deal here: *Paratha* bread is stuffed with your choice of ingredients, such as spicy potatoes, chicken or beef. Order the *unda* chicken roll, a grilled piece of paratha smothered with a bubbling egg and marinated chicken and topped with masala and a drizzle of cilantro chutney. The finished product is as long as a hot dog, fatter than an egg roll, and better than any to-go food in the neighborhood. There are only four tables inside, so most fans grab their rolls to go.

PHILIP FRIEDMAN

⊕Lassi *28 Greenwich Ave between Charles and 10th Sts (212-675-2688). Subway: A, C, E, B, D, F, V to W 4th St. Tue–Sun noon–10pm. Average main course: $9.* You never know what you'll find on the rotating menu of curries, vegetarian side dishes and sweets at this tiny Indian takeout shop. One day it might be a supremely tender (and aptly named) butter chicken in a mild tomato-based sauce, followed by chocolate-jasmine pudding. The next day you might spot spicy *keema mattar* (ground lamb with peas). Some constants remain: Flaky *paratha* flatbreads with slightly charred edges are available with five different fillings, including cauliflower, cheese and daikon. And of course there are *lassis*, thick yogurt drinks in a variety of flavors, including traditional mango, coffee, rose and, best of all, the wildly fragrant cardamom.

Masala Bollywood *108 Lexington Ave between 27th and 28th Sts (212-679-1284). Subway: 6 to 28th St. Mon–Thu noon–11pm; Fri, Sat noon–midnight; Sun noon–11pm. Average main course: $13.* Decorated with a flat-screen TV showing Bollywood flicks and glossy photos of India's leading ladies, Masala Bollywood isn't just a pretty new face. *Church gate aloo chat,* a hearty snack of potatoes and chickpeas, is tossed with a terrifically tangy yogurt sauce. Chicken korma tastes anything but ordinary; tender pieces of meat are smothered in a nutty sauce—an ideal match for the excellent tandoor breads. Across the board, spices highlight rather than overwhelm, but if you find yourself with a vindaloo you can't handle, order a frothy mango lassi. It's a delicious fire extinguisher.

Mint *150 E 50th St between Lexington and Third Aves (212-644-8888). Subway: E, V to Lexington Ave–53rd St; 6 to 51st St. Daily 11:30am–3pm, 5–11pm. Average main course: $19.* Mint doesn't just churn out the usual curry conventions and hope that a sitar player makes it all seem authentic. The dining room is almost spalike—a mod aqua lounge leads into a peaceful, dimly lit space lined with fuchsia and orange drum lights. Chef Gary Sikka's food puts most local takeout places to shame, as it should; a meal costs almost twice here what you pay at one of them. Chicken tikka masala, the obvious crowd-pleaser, is just that: remarkably juicy pieces of chicken in a rich, boldly spiced (but not too fiery) sauce. Layers of flavor run through every dish. The sauce on the *pakku,* a Sikkamese stewed-lamb entrée, is deep, dark and rich—with a kick that calls for at least three glasses of water.

Moksha *18 Murray St between Broadway and Church St (212-608-0707). Subway: A, C, 1, 2, 3 to Chambers St. Mon–Thu noon–3pm, 5:30–10pm; Fri, Sat 5:30–11pm; Sun noon–3pm, 5:30–10pm. Average main course: $18.* Moksha is a subdued, sophisticated restaurant wholly focused on turning out interesting Indian food. The space has a calming effect; gaze at the soaring ceilings or close your eyes and listen to the trickling waterfall wall. Here, it's the food that's aggressive. You can start with crisp, fried chickpea cakes served with a pleasantly sharp yogurt sauce, then move on to a tangle of tender calamari rings, and finally hit the high notes with lusciously fatty lamb chops and an unattractive but intensely flavorful eggplant stew. Instead of smothering the main ingredient with an overpowering sauce, chef Peter Beck (formerly of Tamarind) highlights the flavor of the eggplant by accessorizing it with spices. Beck's dishes tingle rather than burn—which simply means that he has nothing to hide.

▲⊕Pongal *110 Lexington Ave between 27th and 28th Sts (212-696-9458). Subway: 6 to 28th St. Mon–Fri noon–3pm, 5–10:30pm; Sat, Sun noon–10:30pm. Average main course: $10.* If you're used to North Indian fare, the casually elegant Pongal will fill in a few blanks with dishes from the South. Staff at this kosher vegetarian spot provide a brief culinary geography lesson and realistically assess how scorching the "hot spices" really are. Condiments are exceptional, superfresh, and ideal for dipping the *idli* (steamed rice cakes) and *medu vada* (lentil doughnuts). The *dosa* are big and finely seasoned. The truly great *tuver baingan* has refreshingly unmushy eggplant, pigeon peas and an unforgettable bite that just might bring you back for more. **Other location** *81 Lexington Ave at 26th St (212-696-9458).*

▲Raga *433 E 6th St between First Ave and Ave A (212-388-0957). Subway: F, V to Lower East Side–Second Ave; L to First Ave. Tue–Thu 6–11pm; Fri, Sat 6pm–midnight; Sun 6–11pm. Average main course: $18.* Standing apart from East 6th Street's curry hawkers, Raga offers modern dishes in a seductive setting. Brick walls, painted deep orange, are accented by lamps tucked into mosaic cubbyholes, and window seats are strewn with pillows. Instead of the usual tikka masala and beer, savor grilled spiced prawns followed by lamb chops with a tamarind glaze and coconut-scented rice. You'll be able to find a good match on the extensive wine list. Even desserts are memorable, especially the cobbler—fragrant baked fruit set off by crunchy walnuts and served with vanilla ice cream.

▲Salaam Bombay *317 Greenwich St between Duane and Reade Sts (212-226-9400). Subway: 1, 2, 3 to Chambers St. Daily 11:30am–3pm, 5:30–11pm. Average main course: $32.* The Hindu god Ganesh stands guard above the arched entryway of this brass-and-burgundy-toned curry palace, which offers a heady range of well-prepared specialties. The salmon *tikka* and *jinga bagharela*—jumbo shrimp sautéed with garlic, mustard seed and curry leaf—are among the best dishes here. Freshly chopped garlic perks up the nan, and creamy rose-petal ice cream is a fragrant finale. Linger for a while on the weekends, when a musician plucks the sitar.

▲Saravanaas *81 Lexington Ave at 26th St (212-679-0204). Subway: 6 to 28th St. Tue–Fri noon–3pm, 5–10pm; Sat, Sun 11am–10pm. Average dosa: $8.* If you've been depriving yourself of carbs and

Read 'em & eat

biryani: (also *biriani*) rice dotted with spiced meat or vegetables

chat: a savory snack made of fried dough and filled with a variety of ingredients, including yogurt, onions and myriad spices

dosa: (or *dosai*) a very thin, lightly fried pancake, usually made of rice flour and lentil flour

josh: (also *gosht* or *goshi*) meat, usually lamb

kofta: a meat or vegetable dumpling

need a place to load up, this southern Indian palace of gluten is your place. Every item on the menu is a form of starch—including rice, *dosas*, and an array of Indian breads, the best of which is a flaky, buttery *paratha*. Crisp lentil-doughnut appetizers are the right start—the medhu vada version comes with a sweet coconut chutney. Dosas, though, are the main draw. The two-foot-long thin and crisp crêpes can be made of rice and lentils, cream of wheat or Bengal gram flour and filled with all sorts of ingredients, including a wonderful not-too-spicy vegetable masala. The space has its quirks: The lighting is as bright as Duane Reade's and the walls are hung with magenta fabric dotted with plastic flowers.

★ ▲**Spice Market** *403 W 13th St at Ninth Ave (212-675-2322). Subway: A, C, E to 14th St; L to Eighth Ave. Mon–Wed noon–4pm, 5:30pm–midnight, Thu–Sat noon–4pm, 5:30pm–1am; Sun noon–4pm, 5:30pm–midnight. Average main course: $25.* Famed designer Jacques Garcia transformed a 12,000- square-foot space into this stunning Mumbai palace, with antique wall carvings and a ceremonial wedding pagoda where chef-owner Jean-Georges Vongerichten himself got married. The space is vast, but chances are you'll still have to accept a late reservation or drop in for a space at the long counter facing the immaculate open kitchen. Dishes are meant to be shared; check spiciness with your server beforehand, so you don't end up with your mouth on fire and no bread in sight. The seasoning balance can be perfect, as with star anise in a dish of shrimp and egg noodles, or a delicate herb salad atop moist halibut. Desserts include Ovaltine kulfi, which tastes like an exotic frozen Milky Way. Ultimately, you're eating pricey snack food, but it's all in good fun.

Spicy Mina *64-23 Broadway at 65th St, Woodside, Queens (718-205-2340). Subway: G, R, V to 65th St. Daily 11am–11pm. $13.* The thin floral curtain dividing this Bangladeshi eatery conceals home-schooled kitchen wizardry from a spartan 30-seat dining room. Bewitch your taste buds with *fuchka*, wheat-flour puffs packed with chickpeas, spices, fried noodles, yogurt, and tamarind chutney. Mina recasts standard Indian fare like *saag paneer* as sautéed fresh spinach delicately spiced and strewn with generous pebbles of tangy homemade cheese. Apart from a few bright paintings, the setting is mundane, but order anything the waitstaff recommends as "totally different," such as fish in mustard oil, and you'll be enchanted.

Read 'em & eat

korma: a mild, creamy yogurt-based curry, often enriched with nuts

lassi: a yogurt drink that can be sweet or sour

masala: (or *masaladar*) literally "blend of spices" in Hindi

nan: (or *naan*) a flatbread cooked in a tandoor (clay oven)

paneer: Indian cheese similar in texture to tofu

★ ▲**Tabla** *11 Madison Ave at 25th St (212-889-0667). Subway: N, R, W, 6 to 23rd St. Mon–Sat noon–2pm, Mon–Wed 5:30–10:00pm; Thu–Sat 5:30–10:30pm; Sun 5:30–10:00pm. Prix fixe: $54–$92.* It's easy to be intimidated at Tabla. Enter the packed Bread Bar before ascending a giant wooden staircase to a dome-shaped dining room where men and women in designer duds dine on upscale Indian food with a Western influence. Chef Floyd Cardoz mixes fennel seed with familiar rosemary and tarragon to create tastes that are at once unique and recognizable. Greenmarket foods like watermelon are used in curries, and foie gras may be paired with plums in the summer and apples in the fall. Expect fresh seafood spiced with Indian flavors like coconut curry all year round on Tabla's ever-changing tasting menus. **Other location** *Tabla Bread Bar 11 Madison Ave at 25th St (212-889-0667).*

★ ▲**Tamarind** *41 E 22nd St between Broadway and Park Ave South (212-674-7400). Subway: N, R, W, 6 to 23rd St. Mon–Thu 11:30am–3pm, 5:30–11:30pm; Fri, Sat 11:30am–3pm, 5:30pm–midnight; Sun 11:30am–3pm, 5:30–11:30pm. Average main course: $22.* Fusion reigns at this bright, modern Flatiron restaurant: Even traditional coconut chutney is transformed into a mayonnaise-based dip for plump cod-and-crab cakes. Tender venison chops have a spicy, fruity sauce of cranberries and chilies. The artful presentation and robust flavors offset the somewhat pretentious service. An adjacent tearoom serves sandwiches on Indian breads and 14 kinds of tea. **Other location** *Tamarind Tea Room 43 E 22nd St between Broadway and Park Ave South (212-674-7400).*

▲◐**Vatan** *409 Third Ave between 28th and 29th Sts (212-689-5666). Subway: 6 to 28th St. Tue–Thu 5:30–9pm; Fri, Sat 5:30–10:30pm; Sun 5–9pm. Prix fixe: $23.* Vatan's spacious, elegant dining room is punctuated by elevated, pillow-strewn alcoves, where patrons sit cross-legged and feel like the royalty pictured in Moghul miniature paintings. The appetizer alone consists of close to ten tasting portions of all-vegetarian Gujarati dishes like mini samosas, deep-fried hot peppers, spinach with corn and *channa masala*. The main course is even more lavish, with puri, spiced cauliflower, rice pudding and *khadhi* soup, among many other delights. The only choices you have to make are what to drink and whether or not to have a gratis second helping of whatever your heart desires—the royal treatment indeed.

Yuva *230 E 58th St between Second and Third Aves (212-339-0090). Subway: N, R, W to Lexington Ave–59th St; 4, 5, 6 to 59th St. Mon–Fri 11:30am–3pm, 5:00–11pm; Sat, Sun 11:30am–4pm, 5–11pm. Average main course: $20.* Opening a restaurant in New York City can be daunting, but husband-and-wife team Kedar Shah and Hritu Deepak had a few things working in their favor: master tandoor chef Dhandu Ram (from Khyber Grill) and pastry wiz Jehangir Mehta (Aix, Jean Georges) consulting on desserts. And they can always seek advice from Shah's father, who owns the popular Salaam Bombay. Yuva's 60-seat room has some old-world Indian touches—chocolate-brown stucco walls and nooks, canopied ceilings and rich upholstery fabrics. But the menu is more modern: In addition to the expected samosas, kebabs and *vindaloos,* you'll find honey-glazed lamb ribs, a whole section dedicated to "slow-cooked" dishes, and Mehta's sublime chocolate cakes and sundry pastries.

Indian/Subcontinental

Italian

See also: *Mediterranean*

Salad daze
Start off a hearty pasta meal at Sotto Voce with an *insalata tre colori*.

$15 and under

Acqua Santa *556 Driggs Ave at North 7th St, Williamsburg, Brooklyn (718-384-9695). Subway: L to Bedford Ave. Mon–Fri noon–11pm; Sat 11am–midnight; Sun noon–midnight. Average main course: $14.* A lovely patio, partly covered by grapevines that grow more lush as summer progresses, isn't Acqua Santa's only attraction. The friendly staff and hearty fare make for an enjoyable meal at any time of year. Start with the *spiedino*, a decadent slab of mozzarella that's lightly battered and fried, then topped with a lemony caper-studded sauce. It's the perfect size for sharing. Beet gnocchi, tossed with shrimp and asparagus, provide a rich yet surprisingly light main course. Let others line up all summer long; you can slip into this gem off-season and enjoy a wintertime treasure.

▲**Alíseo Osteria del Borgo** *665 Vanderbilt Ave between Park Pl and Prospect Pl, Prospect Heights, Brooklyn (718-783-3400). Subway: B, Q to Seventh Ave; 2, 3 to Grand Army Plaza. Tue–Thu 6–10pm; Fri, Sat 6–11pm; Sun 5–10pm. Average main course: $14.* Albano Ballerini's slow-food baby emphasizes antipasti, which encourage nibbling and swapping. A plate of *formaggi* and *salumi* includes a soft, earthy truffled cheese and hard disks of spicy salami. Behind the tiny bar, Ballerini carves one of the evening's two roasts. An incredibly soft leg of lamb sucks up plenty of flavor from its garlic-and-herb sauce. Unusual wines from the Marches region fill the list, and the excellent house vintage is only $13 for a half liter.

Assenzio *205 E 4th St between Aves A and B (212-677-9466). Subway: F, V to Lower East Side–Second Ave. Mon noon–midnight; Tue–Sun 5pm–midnight. Average main course: $15.* In the romantic candlelit confines of Assenzio, you can sample the restaurant's namesake liqueur—absinthe—as well as an extensive wine list. Don't let the spirits go to your head before you savor the food. Authentic Sardinian flavor permeates everything from the *insalate* to the *tagliere*. *Gnochetti* is an explosion of tiny croissant-shaped dumplings covered in a heavenly wild-boar *ragù*, and the suckling pig makes a juicy sidekick to roasted artichoke hearts and pecorino cheese.

Baci & Abbracci *2007 Eat Out Award, Readers' Choice: Best new pizza joint 204 Grand St between Bedford and Driggs Aves, Williamsburg (718-599-6599). Subway: L to Bedford Ave. Average pizza: $12. Average main course: $14.* Saucer-shaped light fixtures and a chrome-furniture–filled back garden lend this Italian eatery a Euro chic vibe with grandma-style rusticity. The menu includes classics like pastas and veal milanese, but the highlight is pizza from the wood-burning oven. We liked a sauceless pie topped with smoked mozzarella, strips of pancetta and sweet onions. *Torta di nonna*, a sabayon tart with chocolate-cream piping and crushed pine nuts and pecans, was named for—you guessed it—grandma.

▲**Bar Pitti** *268 Sixth Ave between Bleecker and Houston Sts (212-982-3300). Subway: A, C, E, B, D, F, V to W 4th St; 1 to Houston St. Daily noon–midnight. Average main course: $14.95.* While appetizers of creamy Burrata cheese and antipasto of cured Italian meats are tasty and refreshingly simple, less effort is put into

You're so vin
D.O.C. Wine Bar
intoxicates with
small dishes and
70 Italian wines.

entrées. Seafood could use more seasoning, and coating for the veal Milanese is little more than dry breadcrumbs. Even the special veal meatballs could use a kick. Guests relish the ambience of this comfortable, chic tangerine-colored dining room, however, and it is not uncommon to see a celebrity or two at a neighboring table. Stick to the panini and wine list and you can't go wrong.

▲**Bar Toto** *411 11th St at Sixth Ave, Park Slope, Brooklyn (718-768-4698). Subway: F to Seventh Ave. Mon–Thu 11am–midnight; Fri, Sat 11am–1am; Sun 11am–midnight. Average main course: $8.* This attractive corner restaurant consists of one large room, open in the center, with tables aligned against banquettes along two walls. The arrangement is stroller-friendly for early family dinners and supportive of the bar scene that comes later (happy hour starts at 11pm). Staples are impressive and easy on the pocket (no panino, pasta or individual pizza is more than $9), and the execution is more ambitious than the prices imply. Artfully constructed entrées, such as a tuna steak on a mound of risotto, reveal a creative eye in the kitchen. Desserts lack verve, but everything else will keep Park Slope's parents, drinkers and daters coming back for more.

▲**Basilio Inn** *6 Galesville Ct off Lily Pond Ave, by the Verrazano Bridge, Staten Island, (718-447-9292). Travel: From the Staten Island Ferry, take the S51 bus to Lily Pond Rd. Mon–Fri noon–3pm, 5–10pm; Sat 5–10pm; Sun 1–8pm. Average main course: $15.* Lose a few hours in the charming gold and brick-red dining room of this 19th-century carriage house, while Naples-born owner Maurizio Asperti regales you with tales of his father's maritime adventures. Think you don't like

anchovies? Try the *spiedini alla romana*, a soft cake of gently fried mozzarella in a lemony sauce of capers, tomato and just enough anchovy. The gigantic scampi are accented with the perfect balance of fresh garlic, lemon and wine, and the creamy Parmesan sauce of the rigatoni carbonara has a gorgeous smoky aroma from the thick slices of sautéed pancetta within. You might consider heading to the bocce court to work up an appetite for the divine house-made tiramisu.

◑**Bianca** *5 Bleecker St between Bowery and Elizabeth St (212-260-4666). Subway: B, D, F, V to Broadway–Lafayette St; 6 to Bleecker St. Mon–Thu 5–11:30pm; Fri, Sat 5pm–midnight; Sun 5–11:30pm. Average main course: $12.* Black-clad downtowners gather outside this intimate trattoria, poring over the menu while waiting for a table. Inside, their patience is rewarded by the gnocci *fritti*—puffy slabs of fried dough just begging to be torn apart and filled with smoky salami, mortadella and prosciutto. Pastas are housemade and perfectly cooked, although the tagliatelle bolognese could benefit from a more flavorful sauce. On a blustery evening, *brodetto*, a hearty fish soup from Italy's Adriatic coast, is a comforting choice. The ricotta cheesecake is a nod to Nonna's old recipe collection.

Caffè Emilia *139 First Ave between St. Marks Pl and E 9th St (212-388-1234). Subway: L to First Ave. Daily 8am–midnight. Average main course: $9.* A ho-hum interior sporting orange sponge-painted walls, a techno soundtrack and black-and-white photos of Modena, Italy, could make it easy to dismiss this sliver of a space as just another quaint-but-unremarkable East Village spot. What a pity that would be. Beyond the front counter lies a small

Home colors
Chef-owner William Mattiello brings Modena tortellini to Via Emilia.

outdoor garden, where you can enjoy straightforward light fare such as *tramezzini*, antipasti and salads typical of the Emilia-Romagna region. A delicate appetizer of beef carpaccio, paper-thin slices of artichoke and shaved Parmesan is particularly enjoyable, while a salad of cannellini beans and shrimp arrives anointed with honey-sweet balsamic vinegar and doesn't skimp on toothsome crustaceans. Finish with the crêpe cake, alternating layers of tender pastry and luscious vanilla cream, accompanied by a glass of Lambrusco sparkling red wine.

★ ▲**Celeste** *502 Amsterdam Ave between 84th and 85th Sts (212-874-4559). Subway: 1 to 86th St. Mon–Thu 5–11pm; Fri 5–11:30pm; Sat noon–3:30pm, 5–11:30pm; Sun noon–3:30pm, 5–10:30pm. Average main course: $15.* There's hardly room to breathe—let alone eat—at this popular Upper West Side spot. Celeste offers authentic fare in a country setting, and has a large fan club. A wait is to be expected, but you can call ahead to see how long it'll be. Once you're in, start with *carciofi fritti,* fried artichokes that are so light, they're evanescent. Three housemade pastas are prepared daily by chef Giancarlo Quadalti; the tagliatelle with shrimp, cabbage and pecorino stands out. Carb watchers are offered dishes like chicken cutlet with crushed almonds. Those who can manage a few more bites are advised to try the *pastiera,* a grain-and-ricotta cake flavored with candied fruit and orange-blossom water.

D.O.C. Wine Bar *83 North 7th St at Wythe Ave, Williamsburg, Brooklyn (718-963-1925). Subway: L to Bedford Ave. Mon–Thu 6pm–midnight; Fri, Sat 6pm–1am; Sun 6pm–midnight. Average small plate: $8.* Tucked on a quiet side street, this unpretentious spot charms with

brown-paper-covered tables and menus held together with wooden spoons. To satisfy any hunger that might develop while you're perusing the list of 70 Italian wines, D.O.C. serves a menu of small plates: a mouthwatering assortment of cheeses; vegetarian "carpaccio," which comes as a heaping mound of thin, perfectly rolled slices of carrot and zucchini topped with Parmesan shavings. An assortment of *pistokku*—traditional flatbread from Sardinia—is served pizza-style, warm and crisp with toppings such as *bresaola,* goat cheese and arugula. Most diners will choose to end their meal with a ricotta mousse and, of course, another glass of wine.

▲**Da Nico** *164 Mulberry St between Broome and Grand Sts (212-343-1212). Subway: J, M, Z to Bowery; 6 to Spring St. Mon–Thu noon–11pm; Fri, Sat noon–midnight; Sun noon–11pm. Average main course: $15.* If your out-of-town guests insist on visiting Little Italy, steer them past the cramped sidewalk cafés and into the serene backyard garden at Da Nico. Attentive waiters serve traditional Italian fare: coal-oven pizzas, saucy pastas, and generous main dishes like veal chops and grilled salmon. The pizza is your best bet—crisp crust, bright tomato sauce and plenty of melty mozzarella. Not stuffed yet? Try the softball-size *tartufo,* a globe of ice cream coated in crunchy chocolate with a candied cherry center. The free plate of piping-hot zeppole will send you away full and happy.

Dieci *228 E 10th St between First and Second Aves (212-387-9545). Subway: L to First Ave. Mon–Sat 6pm–midnight. Average main course: $10.* Chef Junichi Ota was born in Japan, but it's his training near Bologna that's the foundation for this Italian restaurant. The

PATRIK RYTIKANGAS

subterranean, 25-seat spot is dominated by a curved bar that sees a parade of small-plate offerings, like squid-ink risotto and lamb bolognese. For all the hearty ingredients, the food still bears a telltale Japanese delicateness, whether it's the octopus salad that blooms, thanks to raisin-sweet sun-dried tomatoes, or pillowy braised pork belly given an herbaceous pop from onion sprouts. The sizes and prices (around $10 per not-so-small plate) encourage liberal tasting without breaking the bank.

Dominick's *2335 Arthur Ave between Crescent Ave and E 186th St, Bronx (718-733-2807). Travel: B, D, 4 to Fordham Rd, then Bx12 bus to Arthur Ave. Mon, Wed, Thu, Sat noon–11pm; Fri noon–11pm; Sun 1–9pm. Average main course: $15.* Dominick's would like you to know that the real Little Italy is in the Bronx. At Charlie DiPaolo's wine-pod dining room—the most popular on Arthur Avenue—neighborhood folks, out-of-towners and tracksuited wiseguys feast at long, crowded tables on massive platters of veal parmigiana and steaming bowls of mussels marinara or linguine with white clam sauce. There's no menu, but you can trust your waiter's advice.

▲**Ferdinando's Focacceria** *151 Union St between Columbia and Hicks Sts, Cobble Hill, Brooklyn (718-855-1545). Subway: F, G to Carroll St. Mon–Thu 11am–7pm; Fri, Sat 11am–10pm. Average main course: $15.* History covers the walls in the form of black-and-white photographs of Italy. Although it's much more than a *focacceria*, the family-run Sicilian restaurant keeps that part of the name because it has been there from the beginning, 100 years ago. Francesco Buffa (Ferdinando was his father-in-law) takes a hands-on approach, canning the sardines that are used in the house specialty, pasta *con sarde*, and making both the fluffy *panelli* (deep-fried chickpea-flour pancakes) and piping-hot potato croquettes. The supple *braciole*—a tenderized veal roll stuffed with bread crumbs, Parmesan cheese, garlic and parsley—will make you glad some things don't change.

◑**Fragole** *394 Court St between Carroll St and 1st Pl, Carroll Gardens, Brooklyn (718-522-7133). Subway: F, G to Carroll St. Mon–Sat noon–11:30pm; Sun noon–10:30pm. Average main course: $12.* Generations of Italian families and neighborhood parents with stroller-ensconced tots come for modestly priced fare, whose lack of pretense is celebrated right on the menu: "No fancy sauces, no frills or nouvelle cuisine." As advertised, the carpaccio *del cuore* is dressed simply with salt, pepper and olive oil and complemented with avocado and tomato. In the fettuccine Bella Elena, house-made noodles are tossed with tomato sauce, cream, peas and a regrettably skimpy amount of sweet sausage. *Tagliata* Toscana, on the other hand, is a bountiful platter of grilled, sliced sirloin steak on a bed of crunchy greens.

★**Frank** *88 Second Ave between 5th and 6th Sts (212-420-0202). Subway: F, V to Lower East Side–Second Ave; 6 to Astor Pl. Mon–Sat 10:30am–1am; Sun 10:30am–midnight. Average main course: $12.* Convivial, clamorous and altogether lacking in intimacy, Frank feels every bit like the setting of an oversized family gathering—without the dysfunction. Keeping a watchful eye over the proceedings from the soft-hued walls are black-and-white photographs of owner Frank Prisinzano's ancestors, the inspirations for the eatery's traditional Italian cooking and Old World feel. The open kitchen dispatches excellent housemade pastas, like a weighty gnocchi in a tomato and basil sauce, and familiar entrées like a succulent roasted rosemary

chicken alongside a mound of mashed potatoes and rich gravy. Go ahead and stuff yourself—that elbow you just whacked isn't your Uncle Rick's.

Frankies Spuntino 17 Clinton Street *17 Clinton St between Houston and Stanton Sts (212-253-2303). Subway: F, V to Lower East Side–Second Ave. Mon–Thu 11am–midnight; Fri, Sat 11am–1am; Sun 11am–midnight. Average main course: $14.* The Manhattan outpost of Frankies is as beloved as the Brooklyn original: A steady crowd ambles in most evenings (no reservations here), and though there are just 24 seats, the result is cozy and cool—not cramped. Snackers can nibble on cheeses, cured meats and unusual salads, including a stellar combo of watercress, caramelized apple and Gorgonzola romano. Entrées, like the roasted prime rib eye sliced cold with tomato, red onion and pecorino romano are more filling. Drinkers can sip more than a dozen wines by the glass or try one of 70 bottles.

Frost Restaurant *193 Frost St at Humboldt St, Williamsburg, Brooklyn (718-389-3347). Subway: L to Graham Ave. Tue–Sun noon–11pm. Average main course: $15.* Intense heat isn't often associated with Italian cooking, but the whole chili peppers that come with the bread at this joint are truly tongue-numbing (don't say the waiter didn't warn you). Such spiciness whets the appetite for hearty Southern Italian cooking. Shrimp *alla* Frost is served in a garlicky cream sauce over linguine, with a generous helping of steamed broccoli; the lamb chop is perfectly tender and crowned with sautéed onions, peppers and mushrooms. Bow-tied waiters and leather banquettes transport you to the '70s—when Williamsburg was just a small town in the big city.

Giorgione 508 *508 Greenwich St at Spring St (212-219-2444). Subway: C, E to Spring St. Mon–Fri 7am–11pm; Sat 8am–11pm; Sun 8am–4pm. Average main course: $15.* Giorgione 508 is the annex of the original trattoria opened by Dean & DeLuca's Giorgio DeLuca. 508 offers breakfast, lunch and dinner, and stocks gourmet provisions—note the inviting spread of pastries, breads, dried meats and cheeses. The center of

Read 'em & eat

bolognese: a rich meat sauce for pasta; wine, milk or cream may be used

bresaola: air-dried salted strips of beef served as an appetizer

caponata: a cooked mixture of anchovies, capers, eggplant, olives, onions, pine nuts, tomatoes, vinegar and olive oil

carciofi: artichokes

fagioli: beans, usually the white kidney variety

frutti di mare: seafood

mozzarella di bufala: mozzarella cheese made from the milk of water buffalo (American mozzarella is made from cow's milk)

Spring into Elegance

The real Italian experience

San Benedetto Mineral Water: style, culture, design and quality for those with a passion for the unique taste of Italian lifestyle. **San Benedetto, the number one brand in Italy.**

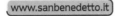

www.sanbenedetto.it

SAN BENEDETTO

the slim, faux-industrial space is the glass-topped bar. Pull up a perch and choose from a fine selection of wines by the glass to accompany pink slices of veal with robust olive-and-artichoke chutney or sweet piquillo peppers oozing warm goat cheese filling. Lusty ribbon noodles with a braised pork *ragù* make a compelling *secondo*. Even better is the knockout saffron-laced seafood stew—a real bargain—with scallops, clams, mussels and crawfish crammed into a drinking cup.

Gnocco Cucina & Tradizione
337 E 10th St between Aves A and B (212-677-1913). Subway: L to First Ave, 6 to Astor Pl. Mon–Fri 5pm–midnight; Sat, Sun noon–midnight. Average main course: $15. Owners Pierluigi Palazzo and Rossella Tedesco named their restaurant after their favorite treat (soon to be yours as well). A specialty of the area around Bologna, gnocchi *fritti* are fried, puffy pockets of dough served piping hot with a plate of thinly sliced prosciutto, salami and *capocollo*. Wrap the meat around the *gnocco*, stuff it inside, or eat it separately. Main courses include the usual assortment of pastas and *secondi*, but it's the fried gnocchi and the giant garden space that will keep you coming back.

Grotta del Mare
307 E 77th St between First and Second Aves (212-535-2866). Subway: 6 to 77th St. Daily 4pm–10:30pm. Average main course: $13. Just around the corner from the UES's fratty epicenter is this rather grown-up Italian spot with an emphasis on seafood. Aside from the cuisine, the ocean theme is nonexistent—the warm interior features blond wood paneling and cranberry-colored walls. Stick to pizza and antipasti: The 11-inch, thin-crust pie is a winner, as is the delicate carpaccio and the crostini piled with shrimp and chunky tomatoes. Skip the limited wine list, pay the bargain $9.95 corkage fee and toast your adult taste with your own bottle of vintage vino.

I Tre Merli Bistro
183 W 10th St at W 4th St (212-929-2221). Subway: 1 to Christopher St. Mon–Thu 11am–11pm; Fri, Sat 11am–midnight; Sun 11am–11pm. Average main course: $15. The casual "uptown" spin-off lacks the attitude and high prices of the original, so settle in at the long bar and enjoy a selection of *salume* and cheeses served on wooden cutting boards and matched with good wines by the glass. Diners intent on lingering at a table might begin with delicate lobster *bruschetta* or flash-fried mushrooms with truffle oil. Pastas include house-made spaghetti with fresh tomato sauce and boar ravioli with a port-wine reduction. *Secondi* are moderately priced too: $17.50 for fried calamari or steak with herbed fries. **Other location** *I Tre Merli, 463 West Broadway between Houston and Prince Sts (212-254-8699).*

★ ▲'inoteca
98 Rivington St at Ludlow St (212-614-0473). Subway: F to Delancey St; J, M, Z to Delancey–Essex Sts. Mon–Fri noon–3am; Sat, Sun 10am–3am. Average small plate: $9. Spending time in this wine-and-snacks haven is a bit like visiting a small trattoria in Italy: Friends gather together to share great food and good, well-priced wine in a room that is abuzz with life and chatter. The truffled egg toast remains the signature dish. But salads and antipasti—tender grilled calamari with *borlotti* beans and fennel, and dense, delicious meatballs—are perfect with a bottle from the small-producer Italian wine list. The tables are close—all the more reason to make friends with other diners. But if you *do* want privacy, gather six or more friends and reserve a seat in the downstairs wine cellar. **Other**

All in the family
A Dean & Deluca annex, Giorgione 508 serves three meals a day.

location *'ino, 21 Bedford St between Downing St and Sixth Ave (212-989-5769).*

▲ Joe's of Avenue U
287 Ave U between Lake St and McDonald Ave, Gravesend, Brooklyn (718-449-9285). Subway: F to Ave U. Mon–Sat 11am–8:30pm. Average main course: $12. Bountiful trays of Sicilian staples like chunky caponata, baked fennel au gratin and salt cod *alla siciliana* are proffered in Joe's cafeterialike setting. If it's a Friday or Saturday, you might choose pasta with sardines, wild fennel and pine nuts. Then try a thick fried snapper fillet, doused with the lightest of white-wine sauces. This is one of the last places outside Palermo where you can score a *vestedda* (fried spleen-and-cheese sandwich); the *panelli* (chickpea fritters) are heavenly when topped with ricotta and Parmesan and served on a roll.

John's of 12th Street
302 E 12th St between First and Second Aves (212-475-9531). Subway: L to First Ave; N, Q, R, W, 4, 5, 6 to 14th St–Union Sq. Mon–Thu 4–11pm; Fri, Sat 4–11:30pm; Sun 4–10:30pm. Average main course: $14. You can imagine some '50s beatnik taking his date to John's for a rough-around-the-edges romantic dinner. The place has been here for 100 years, and it's a fine example of its type—caramel-colored vinyl booths, Chianti bottles dripping with candle wax, and pasta with any of ten sauces (from simple garlic, oil and anchovies to rich carbonara). Comfort yourself with the usual: minestrone; mozzarella, basil and tomato; tiramisu topped with chocolate shavings. Or try one of the faultless nightly specials: a bruschetta of the celebrated garlic bread, layered with avocado and diced tomatoes, or veal ▶

The upper crust

A baker's dozen of the top pizza joints in the city.

The power of pie
Fans will wait...and wait and wait...for one of Di Fara's creations.

Denino's Pizzeria & Tavern Owned by the Denino family since 1937, this white-brick tavern is all about the crust. The pizza here has the most unusual bottom you've ever seen—in a good way. Bread crumbs are added, rather than cornmeal. A slice is just thin enough to be crunchy, yet strong enough not to flop. The company slogan: "In crust we trust." *524 Port Richmond Ave between Hooker Place and Walker St, Port Richmond, Staten Island (718-442-9401). Travel: From the Staten Island Ferry, take the S44, S59 or S94 bus to Hooker Place/Carlo Denino Way*

Di Fara Pizza Rebounding strongly from a brief health-inspection-related closure, 70-year-old artisanal piemaster Domenic DeMarco continues to roll out magnificent creations his way (though he now wears a hat). Perfectly charred, his pies are swimming in sweet tomato sauce, hand-torn mozzarella, fresh herbs and drizzles of olive oil. Waits can be obscene, but nobody does it better—still. You don't want to rush this guy. *1424 Ave J at 15th St, Midwood, Brooklyn (718-258-1367). Subway: 2 to Avenue J*

Franny's Franny's has emerged as a Brooklyn phenomenon of sorts, drawing pizza pilgrims from across bridges and tunnels—and comparisons to Di Fara and Totonno's. Franny's uses locally sourced, sustainable ingredients, such as organic eggs, combined with old-world equipment (a wood-fired oven) to create bubbly, browned pies. Individual portioned pies with clams, chilies and parsley are always a hit. *295 Flatbush Ave between Prospect Pl and St. Marks Ave, Prospect Heights, Brooklyn (718-230-0221). Subway: B, Q to Seventh Ave; 2, 3 to Bergen St.*

Grimaldi's Pizzeria This pizzeria was founded in 1990 by Patsy Grimaldi, a nephew of Patsy Lancieri (the man behind Patsy's). Some critics say the standards have dropped, but the joint is crowded, the jukebox still honors Sinatra and the pizzas remain works of virtuosity: thin crust covered with a mozzarella-to-sauce ratio that achieves the Platonistic ideal. *19 Old Fulton St between Front and Water Sts, Dumbo, Brooklyn (718-858-4300). Subway: A, C to High St; F to York St.*

Joe & Pat's For the thinnest and crunchiest of pizza, head to Joe & Pat's. A lovely black-brown sear engulfs the entire outer edge, which has nary a lip at certain points along its circumference. The warm raw-milk mozzarella is strategically placed in cubes and caramelized in spots. The sauce, made of imported Italian canned tomatoes and herbs (basil, oregano), is slightly sweet and available by the slice (for $2). And, yes, you'll want a second. *1758 Victory Blvd at Manor Rd, Staten Island (718-981-0887). Travel: from the Staten Island Ferry, take the S61, S62, or S64 bus to Victory Blvd/Manor Rd.*

ALEXANDER MILLIGAN

Joe's Most of the best old-school pizza joints sell by the pie only—no slices. Joe's is that rare exception: It's a haven for thin-crusted, crunchy slices. Owner Pino Pozzuoli prepares sauce every six hours from fresh tomatoes and will put fresh mozzarella on a slice if you want it. Folks line up to get inside the cramped space. Boozers, take note: It's open until 4am (5am on weekends). *7 Carmine St between Bleecker St and Sixth Ave., West Village (212-366-1182). Subway: A, C, E, B, D, F, V to West 4th Street.*

Lazzara's Pizza Café If your grandma made pizzas—you don't see many female pie makers even today—they might look something like the ones at this Garment District gem. The superthin crusts are rectangular and have crisp raised edges, with ample char and some nuttiness. Each slice is covered with delicious, tangy sauce and a perfect square of melted mozzarella. Those in the know order the plain pie and try to snag an extra-crunchy corner slice. *221 W 38th St between Seventh and Eighth Aves, Midtown West (212-944-7792). Subway: N, Q, R, W, 42nd St S, 1, 2, 3, 7 to 42nd St–Times Sq*

Lombardi's Supposedly, this is where it all began: Gennario Lombardi opened the shop in Soho in 1905—the first pizzeria in the U.S. It's hard to vouch for how the pizzas tasted a century ago, but there's more elbow room now after a renovation last year, if not the charm of the old-time joint. Still, Lombardi's continues to bake a hot contender for best pie in the city. *32 Spring St between Mott and Mulberry Sts., Chinatown–Little Italy (212-941-7994). Subway: 6 to Spring St.*

Naples 45 Show some respect: These pies have the (rarely granted in the States) seal of approval from the Associazione Verace Pizza Napoletana. That means the flour and tomatoes are imported from Italy, and the mozzarella is made by a Neapolitan artisanal cheese maker. The blistered disks come in individual and shareable sizes. Naples 45 caters to the midtown workaday throngs and is closed on weekends. *Met Life Building, 200 Park Ave at 45th St, entrance on 45th St, Midtown East (212-972-7001). Subway: 42nd St S, 4, 5, 6, 7 to 42nd St–Grand Central.*

Nick's Pizza Both the pizza and the place are pristine. Diners sit in green booths under a pressed-tin ceiling, surrounded by black-and-white photos of old Forest Hills. Served on a traditional silver platter, the pizzas are quaint: The cheese pie is slathered with a zesty tomato sauce and dotted with melted circles of locally sourced fresh mozzarella. Owner Nick Angel is a local hero—at least as long he continues to balance his crusts' char with its soft, light interior. *108-26 Ascan Ave between Austin and Burns Sts, Forest Hills, Queens (718-263-1126).Subway: E, F, V, G, R to Forest Hills–71st Ave.*

Otto Expectant diners at Mario Batali's upscale pizzeria are assigned a city, and then wait for it to be posted on a board imported from an Italian train station. It's a nifty idea, but waits can be as long as 40 minutes. The 700-bottle wine list favors offbeat selections available in quartino or mini carafes. Pies are cooked on flat-iron griddles, but the centerpiece here is the selection of individual-size pizzas. Toppings such as shell-on clams or lardo, thin slices of luscious pork fat, are terrific and come on a pitch-perfect crust. *1 Fifth Ave at 8th St., Greenwich Village (212-995-9559). Subway: A, C, E, B, D, F, V to W 4th St; N, R, W to 8th St–NYU.*

Sullivan Street Bakery The slices here are rectangular, don't have a shred of mozzarella and taste best lukewarm. Baker Jim Lahey makes half-pan, thin-crust pizzas, and doughier six-foot-long pizza biancas. He converts basic ingredients—durum wheat, water, sea salt and yeast—into crusts then dresses them with simple toppings. The pizza bianca looks like bread revealing an amazing depth of flavor, redolent with salt, olive oil and rosemary. It's available to-go only—and it goes fast. *533 W 47th St between Tenth and Eleventh Aves, Midtown West (212-265-5580). Subway: C train to 50th St.*

Totonno's Before opening this modest little pizzeria in 1924, Anthony "Totonno" Pero worked at the original Lombardi's—said to be the first pizzeria in America. Today, pie makers here make the stuff the same way—with fresh dough, Brooklyn-sourced mozzarella and imported Italian canned tomatoes. Spin-offs have popped up in Kips Bay, on the Upper East Side and Yonkers, but none compares to the original. *1524 Neptune Ave between W 15th and 16th Sts, Coney Island, Brooklyn (718-372-8606). Subway: F to Avenue X.*

Better with age
Lombardi's, the oldest pizza joint in the U.S., still bakes up a damn good pie.

Italian $15 and under

scaloppine *al limone* with spaghetti. It's not fancy, but everything feels just right.

L'Ulivo *184 Spring St between Sullivan and Thompson Sts (212-343-1445). Subway: C, E to Spring St. Daily 10am–midnight. Average main course: $15.* The specialty *carciofi alla giudia*, a traditional Roman-Jewish dish of artichokes fried in olive oil, is done particularly deftly at this unpretentious Soho trattoria. And the thin-crust pizza is crisp and fresh, topped with just enough cheese and a light tomato sauce enlivened by slivers of garlic and basil. Toss in a towering *tricolore* salad of julienned endive, arugula and radicchio, and you've got a satisfying meal.

▲**La Gioconda** *226 E 53rd St between Second and Third Aves (212-371-3536). Subway: E, V to Lexington Ave–53rd St; 6 to 51st St. Mon–Fri noon–3pm, 5–10:30pm; Sat, Sun 5–10:30pm. Average main course: $15.* So this is what Mona Lisa was smiling about. In La Gioconda's intimate, warm dining room, overseen by a portrait of Leonardo da Vinci, you can dig into appetizers such as refreshing arugula salad with shaved Parmesan and a lemon vinaigrette. Grilled eggplant slices rolled with goat cheese, then topped with mozzarella and chopped tomatoes, are flavorful, if a bit tough; thick bands of homemade pappardelle with a lamb *ragù* are hearty. You may leave here with a mysteriously happy look on your face.

La Locanda *432 Graham Ave between Frost and Withers Sts, Williamsburg, Brooklyn (718-349-7800). Subway: L to Graham Ave. Mon–Sat 11:30am–9pm. Average main course: $9.* If you've been in Williamsburg since before it was cool, you probably know about La Locanda. But even if you just got off the hipster boat, Cono Colombo will happily welcome you to his bright, no-nonsense restaurant. Try the shrimp *oreganate* special: fresh shrimp coated in herbs and bread crumbs, then broiled and served sizzling over linguine in olive oil and garlic. Such simple pleasures are plentiful here.

Lunetta *116 Smith St between Pacific and Dean Sts, Boerum Hill, Brooklyn (718-488-6269). Subway: F, G to Bergen St. Tue–Sun 5:30–11pm. Average small plate: $11.* If you think this Italian restaurant looks like an Asian noodle bar, you're not crazy. Chef-owner Adam Shepard (Bond St.) ran the Japanese eatery Taku in this spot and barely changed the interior before reopening as an Italian restaurant. Although the portions are tiny, you'll love the linguine and plump littleneck clams with escarole in a rosemary-seasoned white-wine broth, and the side of pan-seared mushrooms (a mix of oyster, cremini, white button and shiitake). Two staples on the dessert menu are *il labratorio gelato* and a biscotti plate from local bakery One Girl Cookies. Choose both.

☺**Mangiami** *9 Stanton St between Bowery and Chrystie St (212-477-7047). Subway: F, V to Second Ave–Lower East Side. Daily 5pm–midnight. Average main course: $12.* What's not to love about the name ("eat me" in Italian)? It's no surprise that LES locals have followed the order. Every meal begins with gratis olives and crusty bread—dig in while you ponder the well-priced wine list (glasses start at $5). Some pastas, like spaghetti carbonara, are deliciously rich, while lighter bets include the *involtino di pollo*—chicken stuffed with mozzarella and spinach in a lemony tomato sauce—and a long list of excellent pressed sandwiches. Owner Gianfranco Costa designed the space himself, hanging large fabric-wrapped

canvases on the walls and bringing in sleek zebra-wood chairs. The restaurateur gene runs in the family; his brother Michele is the man behind Pepe Rosso.

★ ▲◑**Max** *51 Ave B between 3rd and 4th Sts (212-539-0111). Subway: F, V to Lower East Side–Second Ave. Daily noon–midnight. Average main course: $10.* This homey, low-ceilinged trattoria welcomes diners with tantalizing scents emanating from the kitchen. Tucked away on the list of sides, the *melanzane al funghetto*—diced eggplant served in a tangy tomato sauce—will have you sopping up every last bit of sauce. An appetizer of prosciutto and mozzarella *di bufala* arrives with a generous serving of greens and tomatoes. Rich lasagna, baked in individual pottery dishes, is a far cry from those tired Little Italy slabs. A special of lobster ravioli packs juicy morsels of seafood in a tomato-cream sauce. But crème brûlée at an Italian restaurant? Shhh: It's that good. **Other locations** Max SoHa, *1274 Amsterdam Ave at 123rd St (212-531-2221)* ● Tribeca Max, *181 Duane St at Greenwich St (212-966-5939).*

★ ▲**Noodle Pudding** *38 Henry St between Cranberry and Middagh Sts, Brooklyn Heights (718-625-3737). Subway: A, C to High St; 2, 3 to Clark St. Tue–Thu 5:30–10:30pm; Fri, Sat 5:30–11pm; Sun 5–10pm. Average main course: $14.* This quiet street in deepest Brooklyn Heights might seem an unlikely place to find such a riotous range of Italian cooking—yet here it is. *Strozzapreti* pasta with eggplant, tomato and ricotta is a sassy blast straight from Sicily. Rabbit that's braised, then roasted with vegetables and herbs and served with polenta, tastes of Tuscany, and *schiaffoni all'amatriciana* (fat, cylindrical noodles in a sauce of tomato, pancetta and onion) is a glorious postcard from Rome.

PT *331 Bedford Ave between South 2nd and 3rd Sts, Williamsburg, Brooklyn (718-388-7438). Subway: L to Bedford Ave; J, M, Z to Marcy Ave. Mon–Thu 6–11:30pm; Fri, Sat 6pm–12:30am; Sun 6–11:30pm. Average main course: $15.* You could easily miss this subterranean spot; the glass door is marked with two small letters representing an old Italian term for "post office." The candlelit interior is romantic—though you'll probably have to share one of six communal wood tables with other couples. The garden seating out back is no less romantic, and a bit roomier. Chef Stefano Baldantoni

Read 'em & eat

osso buco: braised veal shank in a rich onion tomato sauce

panna cotta: a dessert made of cream, milk and gelatin that's molded and chilled

pesce spada: swordfish

pesto: a tangy pasta sauce derived from basil, pine nuts, garlic and oil

polenta: a finely ground side dish made from dried cornmeal

vitello tonnato: veal with tuna-anchovy sauce, served cold

The sweet hereafter
Don't miss Lunetta's
desserts—like the fig
crostada or biscotti.

KENNETH CHEN

(D.O.C. Wine Bar) offers a little bit of everything, at prices that seem high for the neighborhood. But the dishes, many of which are available in half portions, are terrific. You'll especially enjoy breaded sweet scallops atop a fennel-and-mixed-green salad, and *caramella*, a candy-wrapper–shaped pasta stuffed with venison *ragù*. The all-Italian wine list is rotated almost monthly.

Park Side *107-01 Corona Ave at 51st St, Corona, Queens (718-271-9321). Subway: 7 to 103rd St. Mon–Sat noon–11:30pm; Sun 1–10pm. Average main course: $15.* Not one but two photographs of veteran "bada-bing" comedian Pat Cooper greet your entrance at what is, hands down, the best old-fashioned southern Italian restaurant in Queens, the sort of dressed-up "red sauce joint" that fled Manhattan years ago. Cold or hot, the seafood tastes fresh and is never overwhelmed by the perfect red or white sauces; likewise, the veal and chicken are properly pounded and sauced. The homemade tiramisu is not to be missed, even if the Lemon Ice King of Corona is just across the street.

▲Patricia's *1080 Morris Park Ave between Haight and Lurting Aves, Bronx (718-409-9069). Travel: 2 to E 180th St, then take the Bx21 bus to Lurting Ave. Mon–Thu 11am–11pm; Fri–Sun 11am–midnight. Average main course: $12.* This Morris Park beacon is famous among chowhounds for its brick-oven pizza, and that's not all Patricia's does right. The hot antipasti include huge stuffed mushrooms, baked clams, luscious fried shrimp and eggplant rolled around ricotta cheese. The *linguine arrabbiata* has a spicy sauce with chunks of tender tomato. As for dessert, watch out: The chocolate-polenta cake might cause you, quite involuntarily, to turn to the next table and blurt, "What are rents like around here?" Don't forget to order espresso—it comes with a self-serve bottle of anisette. **Other location** *3764 E Tremont Ave at Randall Ave, Bronx (718-918-1800).*

Perbacco *234 E 4th St between Aves A and B (212-253-2038). Subway: F, V to Lower East Side–Second Ave. Mon–Fri 5pm–midnight; Sat, Sun noon–midnight. Average main course: $15.* This rustic restaurant holds a dizzying array of Italian wines by the glass; the bartender even visits your table to make sure the food matches the drink. Small plates dominate the menu, and a pleasant pungency lurks in much of the food here. Fried green olives are a must-order: The delicious hollow spheres are stuffed with spiced beef and pork, deep-fried and served in a paper cup. Smoked mozzarella is grilled and then laid atop violet radicchio laced with bacon. Pancetta surrounds monkfish that collapses in the mouth. Mouth-puckering pistachio ice cream makes for a nice finish.

Petrarca *34 White St at Church St (212-625-2800). Subway: A, C, E to Canal St; 1 to Franklin St. Daily 11:30am–1am. Average main course: $15.* It took a remarkable feat of architectural alchemy to transform the Baby Doll Lounge, a bawdy old-time strip club, into this inviting neighborhood restaurant. It is now a casual lower-priced offshoot of Arqua, the Tribeca veteran across the street. Breezy service and a festive crowd invite lingering and nibbling over *quartinos* of Tuscan wine, bowls of garlic-drenched mussels, and platters of meat and cheese. The menu highlights simple, homey fare: solidly executed bias-cut sausage, made with chicken and mushrooms; flattened rosemary-scented baby chicken; and rib-sticking pastas. Baby Doll fans can think of it as a great way to sate that other appetite.

★▲**Pisticci** *125 La Salle St between Broadway and Claremont Ave (212-932-3500). Subway: 1 to 125th St. Daily 11am–3:30pm, 4:30–11pm. Average main course: $14.* It's easy to miss the tiny CUCINA ITALIANA sign outside, but once you step in, Pisticci makes a lasting impression. You'll be surrounded by the colorful work of local artists and, on Sunday evenings, the sounds of live jazz. Start with a generous portion of fresh steamed mussels in white-wine sauce, and follow with well-balanced pasta combinations, such as *maltagliati* with ricotta, spinach and lamb; pappardelle bathed in a meaty *ragù*; or spaghetti tossed with expertly sautéed octopus, tomatoes, garlic oil and tarragon. Daily meat and seafood specials are usually memorable as well. In summer, opt for a sunny outdoor table.

▲➍**Risotteria** *270 Bleecker St at Morton St (212-924-6664). Subway: 1 to Christopher St–Sheridan Sq. Daily noon–11pm. Average main course: $14.* It's a bold move to build a restaurant around risotto—but then again, risotto makes the perfect canvas for just about any ingredient. Choose from three types of rice imported from the Po valley: traditional *arborio*, creamy *carnaroli* or delicate *vialone nano*. Then select what you want in the dish, from 50 combinations of exceptional ingredients. The indecisive will be torn between such offerings as lamb and spinach with lemon, or Italian sausage with portobello and oven-dried tomatoes. (Pizza, salads and panini are also available.) If you've ever struggled to make the perfect risotto at home, you'll marvel at the precision: When the bowl arrives at your table, the last drop of broth evaporates before your eyes.

Outward bound
For a breath of fresh air, opt for PT's patio.

Scopello *63 Lafayette Ave between Fulton St and South Elliott Pl, Fort Greene, Brooklyn (718-852-1100). Subway: C to Lafayette Ave, G to Fulton St. Mon–Wed 5–11pm; Thu–Sun 5pm–midnight. Average main course: $15.* Coral walls, a lengthy bar and high ceilings lend an appropriately Mediterranean feel to complement the stellar Sicilian pickings. Homemade crabmeat-stuffed ravioli and braised short ribs enliven the menu. This is island cuisine, though, so you'll want to try a fish dish, such as fresh, tender, baked sardines scented with bay leaves and lemon and dotted with raisins and pine nuts. All breads and desserts (except ice cream) are made in-house. If you're catching a show at BAM, make this your first stop.

▲**Sotto Voce** *225 Seventh Ave at 4th St, Park Slope, Brooklyn (718-369-9322). Subway: F to Seventh Ave. Mon–Thu noon–11pm; Fri, Sat noon–midnight; Sun noon–11pm. Average main course: $15.* When the weather is nice, seating along bustling Seventh Avenue is in high demand, but the exposed-brick room with tightly packed, candle-lit tables offers a more intimate setting. The gigantic, reasonably priced menu includes more than a dozen pastas, and hearty dishes like a fillet of moist salmon wrapped in thin slices of roasted potatoes and a pork loin stuffed with spinach, prosciutto and mozzarella. A long list of $12 brunch specials, with bottomless Bloody Marys and mimosas, draws a line on the weekend.

Tanti Baci Caffè *163 W 10th St between Waverly Pl and Seventh Ave South (212-647-9651, 212-647-9655). Subway: A, C, E, B, D, F, V to W 4th St; 1 to Christopher St–Sheridan Sq. Mon–Thu 11am–11pm; Fri, Sat 11am–midnight; Sun 11am–11pm. Average main course: $15.* Villagers have learned to overlook the claustrophobically low ceilings and basement locale of this slightly scruffy candlelit haunt. While there's always a mix-and-match list of fresh pastas and sauces, choose from among the handwritten specials. Overstuffed meat lasagna and fried rice balls, gooey with mozzarella and Parmesan, are so deftly prepared, it's hard to believe they were created in the minuscule corner kitchen. Drinkable reds for less than $20 a bottle help the thrift-store paintings and less-than-friendly service go down smoothly. The outdoor space is charming and subtly romantic on warm summer nights .

Teodora *141 E 57th St between Lexington and Third Aves (212-826-7101). Subway: N, R, W to Lexington Ave–59th St; 4, 5, 6 to 59th St. Daily noon–11pm. Average main course: $15.* Fans of the Boot who think Emilia-Romagna has the best food in Italy should enjoy this farmhouse-style restaurant, which favors classics from that region. Pastas, like a creamy lasagna made with béchamel, are as hearty as they are luxurious; moist sea bream is expertly prepared and matched with crisp potatoes and earthy Swiss chard. Desserts can be rote at Italian restaurants, but Teodora's gelato-filled profiteroles are enrobed in chocolate sauce, and the tiramisu is flawless.

▲☺**Tonio's Restaurant** *306 Seventh Ave between 7th and 8th Sts, Park Slope, Brooklyn (718-965-4252). Subway: F to Seventh Ave. Mon–Thu noon–10pm; Fri noon–11:30pm; Sat 1–11:30pm; Sun 1–10pm. Average main course: $15.* There's nothing too remarkable about Tonio's—and that's a good thing. Tomato sauce is hearty and sweet; tangy minestrone is loaded with vegetables. Meat dishes are expertly

Italian $15 and under

cooked and embellished with uncomplicated spices and garnishes. There's also a wide selection of appetizers for sharing (antipasti, pepperoni, clams, mussels, prosciutto) and several veal, seafood and vegetarian entrées. It all adds up to a satisfying meal.

▲**Uva** *1486 Second Ave at 77th St (212-472-4552). Subway: 6 to 77th St. Mon–Fri 4pm–2am; Sat, Sun noon–2am. Average main course: $15.* Despite a menu filled with smartly conceived Northern Italian dishes, an enviable wine list and a stylish, Sicilian drawing-room decor, the dominant feature of Uva is noise. Packed with Upper East Siders on first dates, Uva reverberates with energy—but not necessarily the kind you'd want. And that's a pity, considering that the menu—chockful of main courses such as ricotta gnocchi with black truffles, excellent pork tenderloin and sea scallops wrapped in speck—deserves the kind of attention that's virtually impossible amid the din.

▲☺**Via Emilia** *47 E 21st St between Broadway and Park Ave South (212-505-3072). Subway: 6 to 23rd St. Mon–Thu noon–3pm, 5–11pm; Fri noon–3pm, 5–11:30pm; Sat 5–11:30pm. Average main course: $15.* Chef-owner William Mattiello hails from Modena, near Bologna, the birthplace of tortellini, so his menu features the little ring-shaped pasta filled with pumpkin and served with sage-and-butter sauce, and a giant-size version stuffed with ricotta and spinach. Another regional specialty: *gnocci fritti,* a shareable appetizer that lets diners make sandwiches from hot, airy bread pillows and a large plate of cured meats. Via Emilia's interesting wine list has lots of *lambrusco,* a sweet, fizzy red that's priced cheap and goes down easy.

PATRIK RYTIKANGAS

$16 to $24

A Voce
2007 Eat Out Award, Readers' Choice: Best new restaurant of the year 41 Madison Ave, entrance on 26th St between Madison Ave and Park Ave South (212-545-8555). Subway: N, R, W, 6 to 23rd St. Mon–Fri 11:30am–3pm, 5:30–11pm; Sat, Sun 5:30–11pm. Average main course: $24. The space, located off Madison Square Park, is a big, loud glass cube decorated with stainless steel, lacquer and Eames swivel aluminum chairs. When chef Andrew Carmellini (Lespinasse, Le Cirque, Café Boulud) hits his marks, he produces some awesome dishes. The duck meatballs, a delicious starter, feature foie gras centers and a dried-cherry glaze. *Primis* include veal tortelloni Milanese with fennel, citrus and gaeta olives, while grilled tuna with rapini pasta, roasted peppers and oranges, and braised veal with polenta, gremolata and orange are among the *secondi*. Citrus reappears on the dessert menu, too, in a tiramisu with Meyer lemon *crema* and limoncello.

★ ▲al di là
248 Fifth Ave at Carroll St, Park Slope, Brooklyn (718-783-4565). Subway: M, R to Union St. Mon, Wed, Thu 6–10:30pm; Fri 6–11pm; Sat 5:30–10:30pm; Sun 5–10pm. Average main course: $17. Aspiring restaurateurs along Fifth Avenue in Park Slope should study the convivial place on the corner. Eight-year-old al di là remains unsurpassed in the neighborhood. Affable owner Emiliano Coppa orchestrates the inevitable wait (due to the no-reservations policy) with panache. Coppa's wife, co-owner and chef Anna Klinger, produces Northern Italian dishes with a Venetian slant. It would be hard to improve upon her braised rabbit with black olives atop polenta, and even simple pastas, such as the housemade tagliatelle *al ragù*, are superb. **Other location** al di là vino, 607 Carroll St at Fifth Ave, Park Slope, Brooklyn (718-783-4565).

★ ▲Arezzo
46 W 22nd St between Fifth and Sixth Aves (212-206-0555). Subway: F, V, N, R, W to 23rd St. Mon–Thu noon–10:30pm; Fri noon–11:30pm; Sat 5–10:30pm. Average main course: $24. Chef Margherita Aloi (Le Madri) grew up in Piemonte, a mountainous region known for its chestnuts, mushrooms and truffles. In keeping with the restaurant's rustic-monastic vibe, much of her menu is cooked in a wood-burning oven. The fires render beautifully charred veal chops and whole fish, as well as a masterful warm salad of roasted butternut squash, mushrooms, pearl onions, chestnuts, Parmesan and escarole. The best desserts are lovely combinations of traditional sweets and oven-fired fruits, such as chocolate panna cotta with roasted pears.

Aroma
36 E 4th St between Bowery and Lafayette St (212-375-0100). Subway: 6 to Astor Pl. Tue–Thu 6pm–midnight; Fri, Sat 6pm–2am; Sun 6pm–midnight. Average main course: $18. Owners Alexandra Degiorgio and Vito Polosa have carved a slender wine bar out of a former streetwear boutique, and the result is enchanting: Raindrop-crystal chandeliers hang from the ceiling, olives are laid out single-file in porcelain vessels, and a long brick wall displays the Italian wines (including Gragnano, a rare sparkling red). The dishes are carefully conceived: braised duck salad is loaded with a generous amount of pancetta and a poached egg; tender roast veal shoulder comes with Gorgonzola gnocchi. Stop in Monday nights for a five-course tasting menu, which runs just $30.

★ Barbuto
775 Washington St between Jane and W 12th Sts (212-924-9700). Subway: A, C, E to 14th St; L to Eighth Ave. Mon–Wed noon–11pm; Thu–Sat noon–midnight; Sun noon–10pm. Average main course: $20. Owner Fabrizio Ferri (who runs the Industria Superstudio complex) and chef Jonathan Waxman are behind this raw, cement-floored space with a season-driven kitchen that is anchored by both a brick and a wood oven. Top-notch, earthy fare includes marvelously light calamari in a lemon-garlic sauce; *chitarra all'aia* mixes pasta with crushed walnuts, garlic, olive oil and Parmesan; and fried Vermont veal, which is faultless. In the summer, the garage doors go up and the West Village crowd of beautiful people mob the corner from noon until last call.

▲Barolo
398 West Broadway between Broome and Spring Sts (212-226-1102). Subway: C, E to Spring St. Daily noon–1am. Average main course: $24. On quiet Thompson Street, you can find the party just by following the clinking of glasses and the clamor of a crowd spilling into the pretty back garden. And the food is better than it needs to be for such lush surroundings. Chopped calamari, artichokes and zucchini are formed into a patty and fried golden and crisp on the outside. Don't miss the whole-wheat linguine laced with string beans and potatoes and smothered in rich, chunky pesto. Barolo is serious about wine, and on a warm summer evening, there's no better pairing than a choice bottle and a glorious garden to sip it in.

▲Becco
355 W 46th St between Eighth and Ninth Aves (212-397-7597). Subway: A, C, E to 42nd St–Port Authority. Mon noon–3pm, 5–10pm; Tue noon–3pm, 4:30pm–midnight; Wed 11:30am–3pm, 4:30pm–midnight; Thu, Fri noon–3pm, 5pm–midnight; Sat 11:30am–2:30pm, 4pm–midnight; Sun noon–10pm. Average main course: $25. Prix-fixe dinner: $21.95. Co-owned by cookbook scribe and PBS personality Lidia Bastianich, this perpetually busy Restaurant Row dining complex—with four welcoming dining rooms decorated in different degrees of hominess—runs like a well-oiled machine, powered by a battery of energized servers. The famous $21.95 all-you-can-eat special, popular with the pre-theater crowd, offers unlimited servings of three watery, hastily prepared pastas of the day; better to stick to the pricier regular menu, which offers savory, family-style dishes in portions that are eminently well suited to sharing.

▲Bellavitae
24 Minetta Ln at Sixth Ave (212-473-5121). Subway: A, C, E, B, D, F, V to W 4th St. Mon–Fri 6pm–midnight; Sat 5:30pm–midnight; Sun 5:30pm–11pm. Average main course: $20. Many of the ingredients at this trattoria are imported from food artisans in Italy and available to diners for purchase separately, including olive oil, radicchio and pastas. But the prepared foods are the real draw. Grilled figs wrapped in pancetta are an intoxicating sweet-and-salty combo that warrants a double order. Tiny, marble-size meatballs rolled in Parmesan and bread crumbs are fried to crisp perfection. Entrées like penne with sausage and broccoli rabe and sliced steak with a light salsa *verde* are expertly prepared. And there's an extensive Italian wine list, with 125 selections by the bottle and around 20 by the *quartino*.

Biricchino
260 W 29th St at Eighth Ave (212-695-6690). Subway: 1 to 28th St. Mon noon–3pm, 5–9pm; Tue–Fri noon–3pm, 5–10pm; Sat 5–10pm. Average

Give peas a chance Pastas and steaks shine at Macelleria.

KENNETH CHEN

Marco Polo Ristorante

FIVE STAR DIAMOND AWARD WINNER

*From the region of Puglia, Italy, Executive Chef Bruno Milone creates his authentic
Mediterranean dishes, complemented with our award-winning wine list,
all to be found in the heart of Brooklyn's Carroll Gardens.*

Dine with us on all occassions (Valentine's Day, Easter, Mother's Day, etc.)

Open 7 days — All major credit cards accepted

Banquet Room Available

Your Host: Joseph Chirico

345 COURT STREET • BROOKLYN
718-852-5015 www.marcopoloristorante.com

Salute! has made a lasting impression among its patrons because of their desirable location, serene setting, and delicious authentic fare. Salute! is renowned for Executive Chef Carlo Apolloni's Ossobucco, which seasonally changes style and accompaniments. A few more favorites include the Mediterranean sea bass and the braised beef ravioli stuffed with wild mushrooms. Enhancing the total dining experience, celebrated restaurateur Gennaro Sbarro has personally hand picked an extensive assortment of the finest wines, served by bottle or glass. The wines range in aroma and flavor and are indigenous to regions around the world.

Salute! Ristorante Italiano

270 Madison Ave. (39th St. Corner) | www.salutenyc.com | 212.213.3440

Breakfast, Brunch, Lunch and Dinner

main course: $24. A flashing yellow sign on Eighth Avenue displays the name of this little eatery—Italian for "naughty boy." But inside the mirror-and-wood-paneled dining room, there's not much naughtiness. The restaurant is an offshoot of the 83-year-old Salumeria Biellese sausage plant next door, which provides charcuterie to some of the nation's best restaurants. Try the sampler of five assorted house-made sausages *alla griglia*, featuring intense flavor combinations like duck with Grand Marnier, or sample some of the city's best *bresaola* and nine-month-aged prosciutto.

Cafe 2/Terrace 5 *9 W 53rd St between Fifth and Sixth Aves (212-408-1299/408-1288). Subway: B, D, F, V to 47–50th Sts–Rockefeller Ctr; E, V to Fifth Ave–53rd St. Mon, Wed, Thu 11am–5:30pm; Fri 11am–7:30pm; Sat, Sun 11am–5:30pm. Average main course: $16.* You are never far from objects of beauty at MoMA, not even when you're eating: Danny Meyer's Cafe 2, with views of the sculpture garden, is equipped with a gorgeous vintage 1932 Berkel proscuitto slicer. Diners line up at the bar to order pizza, pasta, panini, and plates of cheese and *salumi*, all of which pair with an all-Italian list of wines by the glass, *quartino* and bottle. Upstairs at Terrace 5, former Bouley pastry chef Marc Aumont oversees a jewel box of a café, designed by museum architect Yoshio Taniguchi. Here, you'll find furniture and tableware by leading Danish designers, light snacks and lots of chocolate. In warm weather, try for a spot on the coveted 40-seat balcony overlooking the sculpture garden.

Caffé Bondi *1816 Hylan Blvd between Buel and Dongan Hills Aves, Staten Island (718-668-0100). Travel: From the Staten Island Ferry, take the Staten Island Railway to Dongan Hills. Mon–Thu, noon–10pm; Fri, Sat noon–midnight; Sun 10pm. Average main course: $21.* Chef-owner Salvatore Anzalone was concerned about the authenticity of his cuisine, so he consulted a Sicilian food historian when creating this traditional southern Italian menu. The research paid off: The pasta *con sarde*—*percatelli* al dente covered with sardines, pine nuts, fennel and currant sauce—is delicious, as is the rich carbonara studded with smoky pancetta. Thinly pounded veal cutlets are rolled around a stuffing made from mushrooms, walnuts and a smattering of bread crumbs. And although you're not likely to have a long wait for a table, the bar in the far corner of the butter-yellow dining room is a lovely spot to sip a little chianti and listen to the soaring voices of Italian tenors.

Carmine's *200 W 44th St between Seventh and Eighth Aves (212-221-3800). Subway: A, C, E to 42nd St–Port Authority; N, Q, R, W, 42nd St S, 1, 2, 3, 7 to 42nd St–Times Sq. Mon 11:30am–11pm; Tue–Sat 11:30am–midnight; Sun 11:30am–11pm. Average main course: $20.* Getting a table under the mismatched chandeliers and bygone-day photos is a pretty tough ticket, even by Theater District standards. But despite the roar of the crowd, the staff makes every table feel like the only one ordering huge family-style specialties from the kitchen. And big here doesn't equal bland. The brown marsala sauce slathered over tender chicken is delicate and sweet; eggplant parmigiana is thickly layered with tomato sauce and bubbling cheese. Desserts (like the aptly named Titanic) verge on the obscene, and the odds are high that you will sit next to a tourist group clutching *Chicago* Playbills, and that you will hear "Happy Birthday" sung more than once. **Other location** *2450 Broadway between 90th and 91st Sts (212-362-2200).*

Good taste
The design of A Voce is as enticing as the food.

▲**Cono & Sons O'Pescatore Restaurant** *301 Graham Ave at Ainslie St, Williamsburg, Brooklyn (718-388-0168). Subway: L to Graham Ave. Mon–Sat 11am–11pm; Sun noon–11pm. Average main course: $17.* Neither a sentimental re-creation nor a tired has-been, Cono & Sons is a living tribute to old-style red-sauce cooking. The kitchen has been turning out classics, with an emphasis on seafood, for 45 years (20 in the current location). You'll find familiar antipasto selections with unfamiliar freshness, including such daily specials as a whole artichoke stuffed with cheese, prosciutto and bread crumbs, or a seafood salad of mussels and squid marinated in olive oil and just the right amount of lemon. There is also an extensive choice of veal and chicken dishes and familiar pastas. It all reminds you of why you loved Italian food before you'd ever heard of Tuscany.

★ ▲**Crispo** *240 W 14th St between Seventh and Eighth Aves (212-229-1818). Subway: A, C, E, 1, 2, 3 to 14th St; L to Eighth Ave. Mon–Thu 5–11:30pm; Fri, Sat 5pm–midnight; Sun noon–10pm. Average main course: $17.* The tables at this lively little joint are packed a bit tightly, but no worries; a sip of vino and some of chef Frank Crispo's creations will soon have you feeling expansive. Inventive appetizers include warm octopus salad, doused with olive oil and coiled atop creamy boiled potatoes, and the acclaimed warm polenta, enriched with mascarpone and Parmesan, then topped with slices of smoked mozzarella, pepper, chives and a layer of see-through-thin prosciutto San Daniele. The hearty, salty pastas stick to tradition, and there are daily fish specials. Chocolate desserts are on target; try the dark-chocolate *torta*, presented in a pool of hazelnut *zabaglione* with rum-soaked raisins.

Da Tommaso *903 Eighth Ave between 53rd and 54th Sts (212-265-1890). Subway: C, E, 1 to 50th St. Mon–Sat noon–midnight; Sun 3–11pm. Average main course: $18.* Smack in the middle of the most hectic part of town, Da Tommaso offers a welcome shelter from the urban storm. Step into the peaceful dining room, slide into one of the burgundy booths and sink your fork or spoon into a plate of polenta *con funghi*, or the *paesana* salad, an abundant plate of…everything. Fusilli *alla Laura*, with spinach, prosciutto and roasted garlic, is a savory delight. The saltiness of veal *valdostana*—veal cutlets layered with spinach, prosciutto and fontina—is tempered by the bite of the greens and the creaminess of the cheese. If cannoli are your thing (they're made on the premises), prepare to pop your buttons.

★ **Falai** *2007 Eat Out Award, Critics' Pick: Best jack-of-all-trades, Iacopo Falai 68 Clinton St between Rivington and Stanton Sts (212-253-1960). Subway: F to Delancy St; J, M, Z to Delancey–Essex Sts. Tue–Thu 6–10:30pm; Fri–Sun 6–11pm. Average main course: $20.* This was the first outpost in what is beoming a mini empire for chef Iacopo Falai. And his success isn't without merit: Who can resist a sexy little Italian joint with a modern menu and beautiful crowd in a happening part of town? Although the portions are on the small side (as is the by-the-glass wine list), the prices are reasonable and the dishes inspired and well executed. The baby octopus is tender and perfectly seasoned; beef medallions are lusciously steaklike, drizzled with a raisin-brunello sauce; and the pork comes with cocoa nubs and fennel seeds. If for no other reason, come for dessert: Falai honed his pastry skills at Le Cirque 2000 and makes a killer passion-fruit soufflé and profiteroles. **Other locations** *Falai Panetteria, 79 Clinton St at Rivington St (212-777-8956)* ● *Caffe Falai, 265 Lafayette St between Prince and Spring Sts (917-338-6207).*

Fred's at Barneys *660 Madison Ave at 61st St, ninth floor (212-833-2200). Subway: N, R, W to Fifth Ave–59th St. Mon–Fri 11:30am–9pm; Sat 11am–8pm; Sun 11am–6pm. Average main course: $24.* Be sure to try on clothes before you head up to the ninth floor of Barneys, because executive chef Mark Strausman's food will leave you feeling full, happy and loath to scrutinize your stuffed self in a mirror. Among the most delectable items (in a wide range of offerings) are lobster bisque, roasted salmon and the dessert quintet, a sampler of cakes and other sweets. If you're determined to count calories, try the celebrated Mark's Madison Avenue Salad with canned Italian tuna. Fred's plays host to many a power lunch (the dinner crowd tends to be calmer), so if you're here for schmoozing, make an afternoon reservation.

Gemma *The Bowery Hotel, 335 Bowery at 3rd St (212-505-9100). Subway: B, D, F, V to Broadway–Lafayette St; 6 to Bleecker St. Mon–Wed 7am–midnight; Thu–Sat 7am–1am; Sun 7am–midnight. Average main course: $20.* The latest from Eric Goode and Sean McPherson (their first venture following the übersuccessful Waverly Inn) proves exceptionally time efficient. One trip to this aspiring hot spot saves visits to a handful of its ilk, which for some reason pack 'em in. Along with impressionable hordes of single women, gay men and sugar-daddy dates, you can suffer the unimaginative menu—*crudi* (scallops and black truffle, yellowfin tuna and citrus), antipasti (crostini with basil and acidless tomatoes, textbook fritto misto), pastas (orecchiette and broccoli rabe) and mains (a hideously sinewy veal chop)—with often-dismal execution. Atop Gemma's menu is a Latin motto that translates to "a grain of salt." Which is exactly how diners should take this latest version of Goode-McPherson fabulousness.

▲**Gennaro** *665 Amsterdam Ave between 92nd and 93rd Sts (212-665-5348). Subway: 1, 2, 3 to 96th St. Mon–Thu 5–10:30pm; Fri, Sat 5–11pm; Sun 5–10:30pm. Average main course: $12 ($20 per-person minimum).* Normally, a per-person minimum might make you bristle, but at this wildly popular neighborhood restaurant, it's just an excuse to order dessert—or wine. The antipasto platter for two is not only a meal in itself, it also happens to be the best thing on a very nice menu. Roughly double the cost of the other dishes ($22), it contains more than double the amount of food. The daily-changing starter plate is likely to include rock shrimp, caponata, prosciutto, roasted peppers, bruschetta, fresh mozzarella, portobello mushrooms, grilled eggplant and a seafood salad—which puts you in the perfect position to skip the pasta and entrée and go straight to tiramisu or flourless chocolate-hazelnut cake.

▲**Gonzo** *140 W 13th St between Sixth and Seventh Aves (212-645-4606). Subway: F, V, 1, 2, 3 to 14th St; L to Sixth Ave. Mon–Thu 5:30–10:30pm; Fri 5:30pm–midnight; Sat 5pm–midnight; Sun 5–10pm. Average main course: $20.* In Italian, *gonzo* is slang for "cool"—which is as good a word as any for chef Vincent Scotto's trattoria. Starters include *cichetti* (Italian-style tapas) and other antipasti, as well as soups, side dishes and grilled pizzas—superb, paper-thin and slightly smoky-tasting. The flavorful chicken gets its moistness from being cooked under a brick. A *gianduiotto* (chocolate-hazelnut *semifreddo*) is more authentic than the praline ice-cream sandwich, but either is a fine way to cap off a meal. A note to you cool cats: The high-ceilinged rear dining room may appear more desirable than the snug front bar, but the noise back there comes close to being a roar.

▲**Grano Trattoria** *21 Greenwich Ave at 10th St (212-645-2121). Subway: A, C, E, B, D, F, V to W 4th St; 1 to Christopher St–Sheridan Sq. Daily 11am–11:30pm. Average main course: $21.* The staffers at this sexy, sunset-hued little trattoria welcome you as if they've been expecting you all night, ushering you into a comfortable space divided by a small bar. The more intimate front section looks out onto the Jefferson Library garden, while the brighter, livelier back half lets you view the open kitchen. An *autunalle* salad is topped with goat cheese and apricots; spiral pasta, house-made by chef-owner Maurizio Crescenzo, is paired with wild-boar sausage and mushrooms. Wood-oven-roasted lamb with Parmesan potatoes and garlic sauce typifies Grano's rustic cuisine. Request two spoons for the chocolate polenta with vanilla sauce.

★ ▲**Grotto** *100 Forsyth St between Broome and Grand Sts (212-625-3444). Subway: B, D to Grand St; J, M, Z to Bowery. Mon–Wed 6–11pm; Thu–Sat 6pm–midnight. Average main course: $17.* This hidden subterranean spot (look for the red neon sign above an inconspicuous stairway), is tucked away on an obscure Lower East Side block, but it's worth seeking out. The restaurant has three equally enchanting dining areas: a slender, candlelit alcove with exposed brick and rustic farmhouse tables; another room resembling the cabin of a ship, with porthole windows and navy wainscoting;

Choked up
Fried artichokes are addictive at Gusto Ristorante e Bar Americano.

CINZIA REALE-CASTELLO

Italian $16 to $24

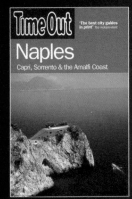

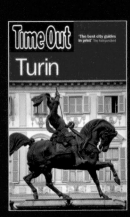
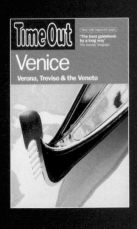

and, in the back, a garden strewn with Christmas lights, pillows and candles. Chef Mathew Knoll sends out consistently well-executed dishes. Pumpkin is stuffed into tender pockets of pasta and laid down in a light butter-sage sauce; organic Cornish hen is pan-roasted in a spicy balsamic reduction, which yields delightfully juicy meat. Instead of the traditional apple tart, Schmidt pairs apple strudel with a sampling of apple, cinnamon, raisin and vanilla ice creams—which, much like everything else about this place, provides a bounty of unexpected gifts.

▲Gusto Ristorante e Bar Americano

60 Greenwich Ave at Perry St (212-924-8000). Subway: 1, 2, 3 to 14th St. Mon–Thu noon–11:30pm; Fri, Sat noon–midnight; Sun noon–10pm. Average main course: $23. This bustling neighborhood brasserie has turned Greenwich Avenue into a dining destination. It's a restaurant running on all cylinders: The fetching decor, which includes a Viennese chandelier, white tiles and black-velvet banquettes, is modeled after old Italian movies; the service is warm and the food delicious. Thrilling opening numbers include addictively crisp fried artichokes and a foccaccia-like flatbread that gets smeared with Gorgonzola and Bosc pears before being baked golden and bubbly. The pastas are rustic and toothsome: Ribbons of pappardelle are slathered with a rich braised wild-boar *ragù*; pockets of paper-thin ravioli are stuffed with whipped butternut squash and plated in a butter sauce. For brunch, choose between six variations on the Bloody Mary, including the Genovese, made with basil-infused vodka, asparagus and sun-dried tomato.

★ ▲I Coppi

432 E 9th St between First Ave and Ave A (212-254-2263). Subway: L to First Ave; 6 to Astor Pl. Mon–Thu 5–11pm; Fri 5–11:30pm; Sat 11am–3pm, 5–11:30pm; Sun 11am–3pm, 5–10pm. Average main course: $22. The rustic, homespun atmosphere at I Coppi makes you feel as if you've wandered into a trattoria in some quiet Italian village. And indeed, everything has been imported straight from Tuscany: the olive-oil-filled *coppi* (urns) resting on the bar, and the chef-and-owner duo, sisters Maristella and Lorella Innocenti. You'll find an especially wide selection of house-made pastas; the ricotta and Swiss chard *gnudi* in a brown-butter and sage sauce is especially delicate. More substantial mains, like the stewed braised boar served with soft polenta, are hearty and flavorful. The real gem is the all-Tuscan wine list full of chiantis, brunellos and Super Tuscans. Try to grab a table in the lovely garden out back, where the exposed brick, low lights and lush plant life beckon romance.

★ Il Corso

19 W 55th St between Fifth and Sixth Aves (212-957-1500). Subway: E, V to Fifth Ave–53rd St; F to 57th St. Mon–Fri noon–3:30pm, 5–11pm; Sat 5–11pm; Sun noon–3:30pm, 5–10pm. Average main course: $22. This spectacular eatery is still first class and still small and intimate in a deal-making way, with food that stands apart from the Italian crowd. The big, beautiful rib eye lies on a bed of arugula, and veal *piccata* is paired with mushrooms and Asiago cheese. Risotto with fresh radicchio and shrimp is well worth its 20-minute preparation time. Chef Andrea Giacomoni even manages to turn a mixed-vegetable appetizer into something special, topping asparagus and zucchini with crumbled goat cheese and a drizzle of truffle oil. The incredibly creamy tiramisu, served in a wine glass, is a happy ending.

▲Ivy's Bistro

385 Greenwich St at North Moore St (212-343-1139). Subway: 1 to Franklin St. Mon–Fri

8:30am–11pm; Sat, Sun 10am–11pm. Average main course: $18. Locals have become repeat visitors, both for the service and the food, which often has extra flourishes. Goat-cheese salad is served with a sculpted mound of pear slices on a bed of mesclun drizzled with raspberry vinaigrette. Rigatoni *alla* vodka is thick homemade pasta in a light, smooth tomato-and-shiitake sauce. A red velvet bench extends across one wall to provide space for large groups; simple candles and small lights cast a warm yellow glow. The bar's after-work crowd can get a little raucous, so come early to savor your food in peace.

▲Locanda Vini & Olii

129 Gates Ave at Cambridge Pl, Clinton Hill, Brooklyn (718-622-9202). Subway: C, G to Clinton–Washington Aves. Tue–Thu 6–10:30pm; Fri, Sat 6–11:30pm; Sun 6–10pm. Average main course: $22. Owners François Louy and Catherine de Zagon Louy (Cipriani, Balthazar) have returned to their Italian roots (and their home neighborhood) to create earthy, authentic food. Seasonal entrées might include *branzino al cartoccio*, fish baked in parchment with shallots and baby spinach, or beef braised in red wine and pepper. Pastas can be as simple as gnocchi with tomato and basil or as original as a chestnut *lasagnette* with chickpeas and *luganega*, a mild sausage. A full dessert cart brings a decision-defying array; the ricotta cheesecake made with rosewater offers a not-too-sweet finish.

▲Luca

1712 First Ave between 88th and 89th Sts (212-997-9260). Subway: 4, 5, 6 to 86th St. Mon–Sat noon–3pm, 5–11pm; Sun 5–11pm. Average main course: $19. Milan-born chef-owner Luca Marcato has a pretty trattoria and a secret weapon: Luis Lozada, the shy fellow who brings your bread basket and pours your water. He is also Luca's gifted pastry chef and pasta maker. Savor his warm pear tart with Gorgonzola—flaky, light and just this side of dessert—and his homemade tagliatelle, pappardelle or bigoli, topped with perfectly seasoned duck, lamb or veal *ragù*. Don't pass up Lozada's ricotta tart. A worthy $23 prix fixe is served all night.

▲Lupa

170 Thompson St between Bleecker and Houston Sts (212-982-5089). Subway: A, C, E, B, D, F, V to W 4th St. Daily noon–midnight. Average main course: $18. This much-hyped trattorria sure packs 'em in. The frenetic pace—of the staff, the bar, and the adjacent table just off your elbow—are further aggravated by a solid layer of techno. Knowledgeable staff brings fantastic wines from a manageable list, but overall the food proves uneven. An orecchiette with greens and sausage packs a rich, spicy punch, but the ricotta gnocchi can be overcooked. A silky smooth panna cotta is worth the visit, while both the saltimbocca and pork shoulder can be heavy-handed. Is Lupa resting on its laurels a bit early?

▲Macelleria

48 Gansevoort St between Greenwich and Washington Sts (212-741-2555). Subway: A, C, E to 14th St; L to Eighth Ave. Mon–Fri 11am–11pm; Sat, Sun noon–midnight. Average main course: $22. Give Macelleria credit for beating the Meatpacking District's explosion by a year or two. *Macelleria* means "meat market" (the back room once housed carcasses), but the small menu isn't only about steaks and chops. Pastas are a specialty, and the spaghetti carbonara's eggy sauce comes alive with hunks of salty pancetta. The signature porterhouse for two won't make you forget Luger's, but it could decrease the number of trips you make to Brooklyn. As at Luger's, the vibe is no-frills: An urban-

The best...

Tiramisu

❑ Abboccato

❑ A Voce's citrus tiramisu

❑ Gennaro's classic

Carciofi alla Giudea *(artichokes fried in olive oil)*

❑ Giorgione 508

❑ Gusto Ristorante e Bar Americano

❑ Celeste

Meatballs

❑ Frankie's 17 Clinton Street Spuntino's classic with red sauce

❑ Perilla's spicy duck with raw quail egg

❑ Bellavitae's fried meatballs

❑ Caffe Falai's veal meatballs

Gnocchi

❑ Lupa's ricotta with sausage and fennel

❑ Maremma's classic with sweet-pea puree, prosciutto and pecorino cheese

❑ Barbuto's potato with sweet corn and basil (seasonal)

---

barn main dining room sits above a bat-cave wine cellar, where patrons can dine among the crates and escape the Meatpacking craziness.

Marco Polo *345 Court St at Union St, Carroll Gardens, Brooklyn (718-852-5015). Subway: F, G to Carroll St. Mon–Fri 11:30am–11pm; Sat 3pm–midnight; Sun 1–10pm. Average main course: $22.* While nearby Smith Street continues to fill up with style-conscious restaurants and lounges, Marco Polo remains firmly rooted in a 24-year Brooklyn heritage. The frosted glass accents, mural of Venice and old-world service feel a bit showy and overdone. But that is all part of the restaurant's charm. You'll find hearty Northern and Southern Italian dishes like red wine fettuccine with grated Parmesan cheese, a house pasta specialty. The risotto with pureed green and yellow asparagus is firm and flavorful, and a juicy sirloin steak is sautéed in a tangy balsamic-and-butter sauce. Desserts stick with tradition: Order the old-fashioned ricotta cheesecake or homemade gelato.

Maremma *228 W 10th St between Bleecker and Hudson Sts (212-645-0200). Subway: 1 to Christopher St–Sheridan Sq. Tue–Thu 5:30–10:30pm; Fri, Sat 5:30–11:30pm. Average main course: $20.* Maremma serves up delightfully left-of-center rustic Italian fare from the Tuscan countryside in a two-story restaurant with a quirky cowboy theme underscored (but not belabored) by folksy wood furniture, pictures of livestock, and other fun yet subtle horn and hoof references. First-timers are encouraged to order Maremma's signature "sloppy Giuseppe" appetizer (braised oxtail), but the less splashy dishes are just as rewarding. The *strozzapreti* ("priest-

choker") combines chard, ricotta and *guanciale* bacon for an appetizer almost as rich and filling as a main, and the *peposo*, a classic Tuscan beef stew with flat noodles, would be comfort food were it not for the persistent black pepper that teases the tongue.

▲**Mario's** *2342 Arthur Ave between 184th and 186th Sts, Bronx (718-584-1188). Travel: B, D, 4 to Fordham Rd, then Bx12 bus to Arthur Ave. Tue–Thu, noon–9:45pm; Fri, Sun noon–10:45pm; Sun noon–9:45pm. Average main course: $18.* A neighborhood institution since 1919, the room still looks as it did when it appeared in *The Godfather*. The Migliucci family has stayed in business by pleasing the customer; if you don't see what you want on the menu, feel free to ask for embellishments or modifications to the Neapolitan-inspired cuisine. Do as the regulars do and order the signature gnocchi, which arrive perfectly light and plump with a deliciously savory and tangy sauce. For something more hearty, try the saltimbocca *alla romana* (veal braised in Marsala wine and served over spinach sautéed with prosciutto), or the generous lobster-tail *oreganata*, accompanied by a baked clam.

Nero *46 Gansevoort St at Greenwich St (212-675-5224). Subway: A, C, E to 14th St; L to Eighth Ave. Mon noon–11pm; Tue–Thu noon–midnight; Fri, Sat noon–1am; Sun noon–11pm. Average main course: $19.* The 70-seat space, formerly Zitoune, is dark and rustic and, maybe as a concession to the Meatpacking District crowds, equipped with a DJ booth. Chef Camillo Bassani cooks Italian cuisine with international accents: carpaccio or oxtail soup to start, followed by amaretto-pumpkin stuffed *tortelli* or pan-seared monkfish with honey mustard and crispy leeks. Snag one of 25 sidewalk tables and choose from the 200-strong Italian-wine list.

Novità *102 E 22nd St at Park Ave South (212-677-2222). Subway: 6 to 23rd St. Mon–Fri noon–3pm, 5:30–11pm; Sat 5:30–11:30pm; Sun 5–10pm. Average main course: $20.* Novità serves real Italian food for grown-ups, and the pleasantly muted setting lets it shine. Chef-owner Marco Fregonese knows how to treat you right: His kitchen showers diners with little gifts, from bruschette with oven-dried tomatoes and fresh mozzarella to little biscotti at meal's end. A salad of mushrooms, baby artichokes and celery is crisp and bright in its lemon dressing, with slivers of Parmigiano-Reggiano lending a nutty edge. Tender venison is rolled with spinach and prosciutto, then served in a glossy reduction of red wine and beef broth. Finish with the cold, creamy hazelnut *semifreddo*, punctuated by crunchy bits of nougat and nuts.

The Orchard *162 Orchard St between Rivington and Stanton Sts (212-353-3570). Subway: F, V to Lower East Side–Second Ave. Mon–Sat 6–11pm. Average main course: $24.* From the looks of the place, chef-restaurateur John LaFemina seems to be as gifted in the wood shop as he is in the kitchen: He designed the restaurant and built the blond wood tables and chairs—with nifty silver pull-handles on the back—on his own. LaFemina's menu is equally impressive. He tops crisp, wafer-thin flatbreads with toothsome ingredients like steak tartare, *robiola* cheese and dried cranberries, and adds vivid textures and flavors to the olive-oil–poached halibut with crispy black-bean salad, potatoes, carrots and cilantro.

Osteria del Sole *267 W 4th St at Perry St (212-620-6840). Subway: 1 to Christopher St–Sheridan*

Joy ride
Vespa revs up
homey pastas and
seasonal plates.

Italian $16 to $24

Sq. *Mon–Thu noon–midnight; Fri, Sat noon–1am; Sun noon–midnight. Average main course: $20.* Sophisticated decor and first-rate food have made this a regular stop for young Italian expats longing for a taste of home. Chef and co-owner Raffaele Soli stands out from the West 4th Street competition by offering a Sardinian-influenced menu. The carpaccio (beef, salmon or tuna), bathed in olive oil and lemon, makes an exquisite starter. Dishes such as gnocchi in white-truffle sauce prove that *heavy* is not always a bad word. Through the floor-to-ceiling windows, you can watch the West Village masses trolling the streets for a meal as good as the one you're eating. Wish them luck.

Paola's *245 E 84th St between Second and Third Aves (212-794-1890). Subway: 4, 5, 6 to 86th St. Mon–Tue noon–10pm; Wed–Sat noon–11pm; Sun noon–10pm. Average main course: $24.* The mirrors in Paola's dining room come in handy when you're trying to catch the occasionally slow staff, but there's plenty else to stare at here. Tables are packed with chattering families and couples sharing carafes of wine and generous portions of very fresh (and surprisingly light) dishes, like calamari in a skillet and creamy pasta with asparagus and cheese, which somehow manages to avoid the usual heft of cream sauce. In warm weather, the sidewalk tables have no mirrors—but a seat on the leafy block might have the best view of all.

▲**Pó** *31 Cornelia St between Bleecker and W 4th Sts (212-645-2189). Subway: A, C, E, B, D, F, V to W 4th St. Mon, Tue 5:30–11pm; Wed–Fri 11:30am–3pm, 5:30–11pm; Fri, Sat 11:30am–2:30pm, 5:30–11:30pm; Sun 11:30am–2:30pm, 5–10pm. Average main course: $19.* Squeezing into this tiny trattoria is as rewarding as ever, even if founding chef Mario Batali is but a distant memory. Lee McGrath, the current head of the kitchen, isn't preoccupied with being a one-man industry—he's just busy making the meals. If you can't choose from among such exemplary entrées as juicy grilled guinea hen and robust porcini-crusted cod, the seasonal $50 six-course tasting menu is a good way to go. McGrath invents new dishes nightly—perhaps tortellini filled with feta and asparagus, or aioli-brushed skirt steak atop baby tomatoes. At the end of such a generous meal, getting out of the place is the biggest challenge. **Other location** *Pó, Brooklyn 276 Smith St between Sackett and DeGraw Sts (718-875-1980).*

▲**Queen** *84 Court St between Livingston and Schermerhorn Sts, Brooklyn Heights (718-596-5954). Subway: M, R to Court St; 2, 3, 4, 5 to Borough Hall. Mon–Thu 11:30am–11pm; Fri 11:30am–midnight; Sat 4pm–midnight; Sun 4–10:30pm. Average main course: $17.* Smooth, barely salty mozzarella is made in-house daily and served with an ever-changing side (perhaps garlicky roasted asparagus). A meaty mountain of thyme-seasoned osso buco needs only a fork, and the filet mignon gets an herbal boost from its rosemary-infused sauce. To cap your meal, dunk crunchy Tuscan almond cookies into *vin santo* or indulge in a dish of house-made gelato (pray for plums to be in season). The 45-year-old Queen is forced to share her block with McDonald's, but that doesn't diminish her regal aplomb.

Regional *2607 Broadway between 98th and 99th Sts (212-666-1915). Subway: 1, 2, 3 to 96th St. Mon–Wed 5–11pm; Thu, Fri 5–11:30pm; Sat 11am–3:30pm, 5–11:30pm; Sun 11am–3:30pm, 5–10:30pm. Average main course: $18.* This restaurant exposes Upper West

JENNY WOODWARD

Modern love
Lacopo Falai sexes up
Italian fare at Falai.

Siders to lesser-known culinary gems from not one but 20 different Italian regions. Whole-wheat noodles in duck *ragù*, from Veneto, is the tastiest lesson you could ever hope to consume. Regional is big on wine, too, and includes a reasonable by-the-glass selection. The room is also a winner—a thoroughly modern, open (and loud) space with high ceilings and more breathing room than most trattorias.

Roberto Passon
741 Ninth Ave at 50th St (212-582-5599). Subway: C, E to 50th St. Daily noon–11pm. Average main course: $17. Enrico Malta and Tom Bifulco didn't need another restaurant. Otherwise known as the New York City Restaurant Group, they practically own the town with Puttanesca, Arte Café, and eleven other places in the city. But Roberto Passon has a third man's name attached to it (we'll let you guess whose), and his cooking has elevated this pan-Italian spot from generic neighborhood joint to bona fide dining destination. You can make a meal out of the white asparagus cooked in brown butter, paired with a perfectly poached egg and piles of prosciutto. Or sample the succulent slow-braised rabbit flanked by pieces of grilled white polenta. It's heavy stuff, however; a steamy summer night calls for the menu's lighter side, like sautéed octopus with chives and steamed potatoes.

Roberto's
603 Crescent Ave at Hughes St, Bronx (718-733-9503). Travel: B, D, 4 to Fordham Rd, then Bx12 bus to Arthur Ave. Tue–Thu noon–2:30pm, 5–10pm; Fri noon–2:30pm, 5–11pm; Sat 5–11pm; Sun 4–10pm. Average main course: $18. Put your hungry self in the capable hands of Roberto Paciullo, a Salerno native who runs a no-frills eatery in the Bronx's venerable Italian enclave. Grab a seat at one of the wooden tables and let Paciullo create a proper four-course feast from the blackboard specials. Tasty, tentacle-heavy grilled calamari have the meaty consistency of steak; tinfoil-baked *radiatore* come bathed in a vibrant red sauce or olive oil; and short ribs shine in a rich chili-pepper-and-beer sauce. It's all blissfully simple.

Sapori D'Ischia
55-15 37th Ave between 55th and 56th Sts, Woodside, Queens (718-446-1500). Subway: G, R, V to Northern Blvd. Mon–Sat 11:30am–3:30pm, 5:30–11pm; Sun 2–10pm. Average main course: $17. The eat-in annex of an Italian-food-importing warehouse sports an old-fashioned mural of Ischia's harbor. Although the art seems to herald trattoria informality, a chef with Bouley training—William Prunty—creates elegant, modern takes on familiar dishes. Pizza is drizzled with truffle oil; artichokes morph into a rapturous pudding; tender steak, lamb, chicken, rabbit, veal and fish undergo similar alchemy. Unusual chiantis and malvasias from the in-house wine bar, a spot-on saffron panna cotta and splendid service round out your MetroCard excursion to Ischia.

Scottadito Osteria
788A Union St between Sixth and Seventh Aves, Park Slope, Brooklyn (718-636-4800). Subway: B, Q to Seventh Ave; 2, 3 to Grand Army Plaza. Daily 11am–11pm. Average main course: $18. To compete with all the old-school *salumieri* in the Slope, Scottadito Osteria butchers and cures all its own meat. This means house-made prosciutto, speck (bacon) and *guanciale* (cured from hog jowls); ricotta gnocchi with butter and sage; and a lamb chop with fried artichokes and lemon relish. The earthy cantina is the collaborative effort of Donald Minerva and Michele Di Bari. Among the

rustic Tuscan trappings are terra-cotta walls, exposed beams, an eat-in wine cellar and a sunny atrium.

Spiga
200 W 84th St at Amsterdam Ave (212-362-5506). Subway: 1 to 86th St. Mon 5:30–10:30pm; Tue–Sat 5:30–11pm; Sun 5:30–10:30pm. Average main course: $22. Chef-owner Salvatore Corea continues to up the Italian-food ante on the Upper West Side with this ambitious restaurant. The environment screams ski chalet; dark wood accents the brick walls of this little box of a space. The food is hearty—big portions, rich ingredients, heavy sauces. But some of Corea's ingredients surprise. Gelatin pops up on the list of antipasti: It accompanies a *sottocenere* cow's milk cheese that has been aged under ashes. Forgo dessert for the deliciously sweet pastas: Pumpkin ravioli with parmesan sauce tastes almost like cheesecake.

⊙Supper
156 E 2nd St between Aves A and B (212-477-7600). Subway: F, V to Lower East Side–Second Ave. Mon–Thu 11am–1am; Fri, Sat 11am–2am; Sun 11am–1am. Average main course: $17. This member of Frank Prisinzano's team of well-priced eateries (Frank, Lil' Frankie's Pizza) proves that a good dinner can be an uncomplicated affair. The decor has a grown-up feel, with rustic wooden tables, antique chandeliers and a supersleek private dining room in the basement wine vault. Yet simplicity rules the menu. An appetizer of coaster-size beet slices and silky goat-cheese pieces is a collision of exquisite flavors. Main courses allow the freshness of each ingredient to shine: linguine with butter and fresh mint; gnocchi with tomato sauce; spaghetti with lemon and Parmesan. Salmon *tagliata*, two seared hunks atop arugula, is accented by a light fava-bean puree. Food this cheap and cheerful means you won't have any problem cleaning your plate.

▲Vento
675 Hudson St between 13th and 14th St (212-699-2400). Subway: A, C, E to 14th St; L to Eighth Ave. Mon 10am–midnight; Tue–Sat 10am–1am; Sun 10am–midnight. Average main course: $19. Everybody comes to Vento—models, 'burbanites, suits, scenesters and nobodies—and they all seem to wedge in at once. The wait, even with reservations, borders on torturous, but the coolheaded staff occasionally soothes tempers with complimentary glasses of prosecco and slices of pizza. Once you're seated, more wine comes quickly. The menu is full of great distractions, too, like *crudo* of bigeye tuna dressed with olive oil, sea salt and slivers of jalapeño, or homemade *tortelli* stuffed with fresh ricotta in sage butter and a touch of balsamic. The desserts—squiggly zeppole tossed in cinnamon sugar with a citrus crème, or hazelnut *semifreddo* with an oozing chocolate center—will really make you forget the hour spent waiting.

▲Vespa
1625 Second Ave between 84th and 85th Sts (212-472-2050). Subway: 4, 5, 6 to 86th St. Mon–Wed 5pm–11pm; Thu, Fri 5pm–midnight; Sat noon–4pm, 5pm–midnight; Sun noon–4pm, 5–11pm. Average main course: $19. Vespa is a casual *enoteca* where you're just as welcome to guzzle your wine as to swirl and sniff it. A menu of seasonal dishes, like a summery gnocchi with red and yellow tomatoes, and a heartier house-made *cavatelli* with pancetta and heavy cream, successfully showcases the possibilities of plain old pasta. A squid-and-octopus salad is stocked with appealingly tender meat; steamed mussels are just as plump and briny as those you'll find in the city's best brasseries. The outdoor terrace is breezy, though not quite as much so as a ride on the namesake scooter.

$25 and over

Abboccato *136 W 55th St between Sixth and Seventh Aves (212-265-4000). Subway: F, N, Q, R, W to 57th St. Mon noon–3pm, 5:30–10pm; Tue–Fri noon–3pm, 5:30–11pm; Sat 7:30–10:30am, noon–3pm, 5–11pm; Sun 7:30–10:30am, 4–10pm. Average main course: $28.* When he sends out authentic Greek food at Molyvos, executive chef Jim Botsacos is only telling half the story: his father's. As chef-partner at Abboccato ("touch of sweetness"), he pays tribute to his Italian mother. Each dish is associated with a region of Italy, such as Umbrian-style quail and octopus with Sicilian oregano. To make his carbonara taste like the real thing, Botsacos uses richer, more flavorful duck eggs. His *vaniglia e cioccolato*, meanwhile, combines two classic dishes into one: vanilla-scented veal cheeks and wild boar stewed in red wine, spices and chocolate. It's dinner and dessert rolled into one.

Babbo *2007 Eat Out Award, Readers' Choice: Best restaurant you can't get into 110 Waverly Pl between MacDougal St and Sixth Ave (212-777-0303). Subway: A, C, E, B, D, F, V to W 4th St. Mon–Sat 5:30–11:30pm; Sun 5–11pm. Average main course: $28.* Reputedly one of the best Italian restaurants in the city, Mario Batali's Babbo is certainly among the hardest to get into. The warmly lit, white-walled townhouse is alive with reggae, rock 'n' roll and the ambient chatter of diners who enthusiastically lift pasta-laced forks and wineglasses to their mouths. Sadly, such liveliness can't be said for the food. The balsamic and brown-butter sauce that bathes the goose-liver ravioli can be overly reduced and borderline burnt. And while the grilled pork chop with artichokes and *cipolline* onions is beautifully caramelized, that's no great feat. Save for the atmosphere and affordable wines by the *quartino*, little about this restaurant merits the hype.

Beppe *45 E 22nd St between Broadway and Park Ave South (212-982-8422). Subway: N, R, W, 6 to 23rd St. Mon–Fri noon–2:30pm, 5:30–11:30pm; Sat 5:30–11:30pm. Average main course: $29.* Paying $10 for a pair of fried zucchini flowers and $18 for a plate of spaghetti is a tough sell if you're used to dining on cheap neighborhood Italian. Just do it: The splurge will buy you a seat in Beppe's charming, Tuscan-inspired dining room and a painstakingly crafted meal. Those crisp zucchini flowers go straight from the farmers' market to the fryer. And that $18 spaghetti is tossed with a rich chianti-and-tomato sauce and bits of pork. Lest you forget where you had such a meal, the staff sends you home with a muffin packed inside a Beppe-labeled box, a parting gift that further helps justify the bill.

Centovini *25 W Houston St between Greene and Mercer Sts (212-219-2113). Subway: B, D, F, V to Broadway–Lafayette St; 6 to Bleecker St. Mon–Fri noon–3pm, 5:30–11pm; Sat noon–4pm, 5:30–11pm; Sun noon–4pm, 5:30–10pm. Average main course: $29.* Are wine lovers the target clientele for this collaboration between Murray Moss (of Moss) and Nicola Marzovilla (of I Trulli)? Sure: One hundred bottles and 28 glasses of Italian rarities can be sipped at the rubber-coated tables or the long marble bar. The casual design does not suggest fine dining, and yet the price of a meal is quite high. If you're willing to splurge, order the sublime veal cheeks with cannellini puree and baby carrots. The servers are well versed in both the menu and the wine

list, can help you pick an *aglianico* and have no trouble explaining what a *sucrine* salad is.

▲'Cesca *164 W 75th St between Columbus and Amsterdam Aves (212-787-6300). Subway: B, C, 1, 2, 3 to 72nd St. Mon–Thu 5–11pm; Fri, Sat 5–11:30pm; Sun 5–9pm. Average main course: $28.* A-list patrons fill the tables at this Upper West Side hot spot, drawn to the restaurant's hearty dishes—the bigger, the meatier, the saucier, the better. *Fritto misto* is a mammoth mound of deep-fried shrimp, squid, fennel, zucchini and more. It's an endless starter and merely suggests what's to come. Just hearing the names of 'Cesca's dishes will fill you up: pancetta-wrapped calf's liver; pasta *al forno*, with meat *ragù* and *crema di* Parmigiano; *riso di* Canaroli with honey-glazed squab; enormous pork shanks and roasted vegetables. Even if you usually shun doggie bags, this place might change your mind. Everything's just too tasty to leave behind.

▲Coco Pazzo *23 E 74th St between Fifth and Madison Aves (212-794-0205). Subway: 6 to 77th St. Mon–Sat 6–11pm; Sun 5–10pm. Average main course: $30.* Snuggle up to your sweetie, order a 1997 SuperTuscan and savor your elite tax-bracket status in a flawlessly romantic nest. The hushed atmosphere and attentive staff create a reverent setting for chef Mark Strausman's Tuscan-inspired cooking. A heaping plate of fried wild mushrooms is served with mixed herbs; a special risotto is offered each evening. The *tagliata alla fiorentina*, a rib eye, is seared on the outside and has a ruby interior.

▲Da Silvano *260 Sixth Ave between Bleecker and Houston Sts (212-982-2343). Subway: A, C, E, B, D, F, V to W 4th St; 1 to Houston St. Mon–Thu noon–11:30pm; Fri, Sat noon–midnight; Sun noon–11pm. Average main course: $26.* Despite the oak tables and other country touches, you are not in a meatball joint: Bottles of wine range from $45 to $395, and specials include a 22-ounce lobster *catalana*, steamed and served on a silver platter with shallots and julienned fennel and celery. The pasta puttanesca, generous with capers and sardines, is not afraid to be fishy (in a good way). Desserts include a shake of mango and vanilla ice cream with crème de cassis. Famous models, actors and literati continue to flock here, although getting a seat has been easier since the opening of Cantinetta, a less chichi—though still pricey—brother. **Other location** *Cantinetta, 260 Sixth Ave between Bleecker and Houston Sts (212-844-0282).*

Del Posto *85 Tenth Ave between 15th and 16th Sts (212-497-8090). Subway: A, C, E to 14th St; L to Eighth Ave. Mon, Tue 5–11pm; Wed–Fri noon–2pm, 5–11pm; Sat 4:30–11pm; Sun 4:30–10pm. Average main course: $31.* With four-star ambitions and prices to match, Mario Batali's Del Posto set the bar awfully high when it opened in 2005, but the cavernous restaurant has become nothing less than the city's top destination for refined, upscale Italian cuisine. The clubby dining room, serenaded nightly by a twinkling grand piano, feels like the lobby of a very opulent grand hotel. The kitchen, under the stewardship of longtime Batali protégé Mark Ladner, challenges its French competition in butter consumption. A gorgeous mixed-mushroom appetizer drowns in the stuff, as do ethereal ricotta-filled *gnudi* and flaky thyme-flower-sprinkled turbot fillets. The most showstopping dishes, intended for sharing, include hunks of lamb and veal and pitch-perfect risotto

Stairway to heaven
Mario Batali's Del Posto
has pleased a higher
judge—New York diners.

Italian $25 and over

Showing their hand
I Trulli creates delicious
pastas from scratch.

KENNETH CHEN

for two. The all-Italian wine list is suitably encyclopedic and exorbitantly priced.

★ **Felidia** *243 E 58th St between Second and Third Aves (212-758-1479). Subway: N, R, W to Lexington Ave–59th St; 4, 5, 6 to 59th St. Mon–Thu noon–2:30pm, 5–11pm; Fri noon–2:30pm, 5–11:30pm; Sat 5–11:30pm; Sun 4–10pm. Average main course: $32.* The intimate townhouse dining room, lined with dark wood and red leather chairs, is as alluring as ever. And the kitchen, in the capable hands of executive chef Fortunato Nicotra, still turns out lovely seasonal, ingredient-driven dishes, just as Lidia Bastianich did when she opened the restaurant in 1981. The menu relies on the strength of quality raw materials—grilled octopus with *fagiolini*, cherry tomatoes and spring-onion salad virtually sings. Almost every dish, including a pile of crisp, tempura-light soft-shell crabs and a big bowl of charred, tender octopus, is drizzled with olive oil so delicious you could drink it. Settle for one of the 1,000 plus bottles of wine instead.

Fiamma Osteria *206 Spring St between Sixth Ave and Sullivan St (212-653-0100). Subway: C, E to Spring St. Mon–Thu noon–2:30pm, 5:30–11pm; Fri noon–2:30pm, 5:30pm–midnight; Sat 5:30pm– midnight; Sun 5–10pm. Average main course: $25.* The sleek tiled entryway, glass elevator and understated golden decor once served as a chic backdrop for exceptional dishes at Steve Hanson's Soho eatery. That same aesthetic now seems merely nice, and the vibe of the place is that it's best-suited for business dinners or get-togethers with the in-laws. Chef Fabio Trabocchi's menu—including such entreés as veal and spinach ravioli in brown butter sage sauce or seared tuna with toasted fennel and artichokes—is quite good, if not terribly original. And the staff is pleasant and efficient, though prone to upselling.

▲**F.illi Ponte** *39 Desbrosses St at West St (212-226-4621). Subway: A, C, E, 1 to Canal St. Mon–Fri 11:30am–3:30pm, 5:30–11pm; Sat 5:30pm–midnight. Average main course: $35.* F.illi Ponte has its priorities straight. The photos of Joe Torre et al. are hung in a back room; solidly authentic food from the old country is the main event; and the two upstairs dining rooms yield spectacular views across the Hudson through 16-foot windows. The wine is poured right to the rim (a collection of 2,000 bottles takes up the top three floors of this former longshoremen's hotel). Start with the antipasto *misto*, which includes a shrimp the size of a fist. Continue with a meaty pasta, then top it off with the huge, fork-tender osso buco or a platter of "angry lobster," cooked with hot peppers and oil. Then you can give up eating for a week.

i Trulli *122 E 27th St between Park Ave South and Lexington Ave (212-481-7372). Subway: 6 to 28th St. Mon–Thu noon–3pm, 5:30–10:30pm; Fri noon–3pm, 5:30–11pm; Sat 5:30–11pm; Sun 5:30–10pm. Average main course: $32.* The Marzovillas—founders of both this restaurant and a wine store across the street— deliver the rustic cuisine of Puglia with flair. While the prices and ambience are hardly humble (the back patio is one of the city's best outdoor dining spots), the kitchen keeps the food simple. Dora Marzovilla handmakes the pastas everyday, and new chef Patrick Nuti prepares them and makes everyong else on the menu. **Other location** *Enoteca i Trulli, 124 E 27th St between Park Ave South and Lexington Ave (212-481-7372).*

★ ▲**Il Buco** *47 Bond St between Bowery and Lafayette Sts (212-533-1932). Subway: B, D, F, V to Broadway–Lafayette St; 6 to Bleecker St. Mon 6pm–midnight; Tue–Thu noon–4pm, 6pm–midnight; Fri, Sat noon–4pm, 6pm–1am; Sun 5pm–midnight. Average main course: $28.* The old-world charm of well-worn communal tables, dangling copper cookware and flickering lamps may help explain why a 14-year-old restaurant is still tough to get into on a Saturday night. Seasonal produce and artisinal ingredients shape the menu of chef Ignacio Mattos (Chez Panisse, Spotted Pig). Dunk the warm country bread in Umbrian olive oils produced exclusively for Il Buco. *Primi* include *porchetta alla romana*, slow-roasted pig with white polenta and sautéed Tuscan black kale, or Dijon-crusted Meiller Farm lamb chop and leg with *puntarelle*. You'll have no trouble finding a wine to match; Il Buco's list is one of the city's best.

Il Cantinori *32 E 10th St between University Pl and Broadway (212-673-6044). Subway: N, R, W to 8th St–NYU. Mon–Thu noon–3pm, 5:30–11:30pm; Fri noon–3pm, 5:30–midnight; Sat 5:30pm–midnight; Sun 5:30–11:30pm. Average main course: $32.* Close your eyes and imagine an attractive Tuscan restaurant with sophisticated service and impeccable food. That's Il Cantinori. For appetizers, the *luganega con broccoletti* (grilled thin Italian sausage with sautéed broccoli rabe) is spicy and done to perfection, and the *vongole con pesto* (clams steamed in white wine, tomatoes and, yes, pesto) has an unusual but memorable flavor. If you have a taste for veal but happen to miss the special of eye-crossingly succulent, thick and juicy *carré di vitello con puree piselli* (crown roast of veal with mashed potatoes and peas), try the scaloppine *al balsamico*. Phenomenal as the dishes are, they pale in comparison with the desserts: The warm chocolate cake will satisfy the pickiest connoisseur.

▲**Il Giglio** *81 Warren St between Greenwich St and West Broadway (212-571-5555). Subway: 1, 2, 3 to Chambers St. Mon–Fri noon–3pm, 5–11pm; Sat 5–11pm. Average main course: $28.* Chef Rolando Mendez knows the secret to keeping one of the city's most celebrated kitchens in business: Turn the spotlight on the food. True, the dining room glows and the soft peach walls are adorned with the occasional frolicking-nymph tapestry. But all eyes are on the plates being handed out by the attentive staff. The headwaiter details the daily specials—an intoxicating escargot appetizer marinated in garlic and mushrooms, for instance—with as much care as he would a marriage proposal. If you don't order one of the specials, the entrée choices are a touch predictable—sautéed veal or chicken, say, prepared with a white-wine sauce. The sky-high check may cause a slight panic; perhaps the complimentary after-dinner liqueur will take the edge off.

Il Mulino *86 W 3rd St between Sullivan and Thompson Sts (212-673-3783). Subway: A, C, E, B, D, F, V to W 4th St. Mon–Fri noon–2:30pm, 5–11pm; Sat 5–11pm. Average main course: $40.* Il Mulino resembles an Upper East Side fine-dining establishment—dark, cramped and filled with formally dressed diners. Swooping down on you, gruff servers arrive bearing cheese, meat, marinated zucchini, tomatoes and three kinds of bread. They proceed to rattle off dozens of specials. The wine list starts at $45 or so, and you may be up-sold to something "better." Even so, the food is magnificent and the portions gargantuan. A ravioli

Side dish

Learn from the pros

Get your culinary chops in some of the city's top kitchens

Forget, for a moment, all the fancy decor, the waiters responding to your every request and all the other reasons you like to dine out. Your most basic desire is to be fed—preferably a fantastic meal. But for those times you'd rather stay home and whip up something yourself, some rather accomplished chefs are quite happy to pass along their expertise.

Bouley Bakery & Market (130 West Broadway at Duane St, 212-608-5829) serves many functions, not the least of which is pedagogical. At night, the upstairs restaurant's open kitchen and sushi bar serve as stages on which diners get up-close views of the chefs' wizardry. For a more formal education, sign up for a demo at **Bouley's Test Kitchen** (88 West Broadway between Chambers and Warren Sts, 212-219-1011), where visiting chefs cover techniques, ingredients and presentation on such diverse topics as making Japanese dashi to chocolate parfaits.

At **Sueños** (311 W 17th St between Eighth and Ninth Aves, 212-243-1333), acclaimed chef Sue Torres leads regional Mexican cooking classes every Saturday from noon to 2:30pm. Groups of six or more can design their own curriculum or sign up for one of the entrée-oriented offerings, like chile-rubbed pork chop or red snapper steamed in a banana leaf.

Renowned cheese experts lead evening classes on a wide range of topics at **Artisanal's Premium Cheese Center** (500 W 37th St at Tenth Ave; 877-797 1200), including cheese and bourbon whiskey pairings and how to make your own mozzarella. Cheese-lovers can also sign up for a two-day master class, where they taste and learn about more than 100 cheeses.

Charming **Camaje** (85 MacDougal St at Bleecker St, 212-673-8184) offers hands-on group classes for six people amidst the frenzy of the working kitchen, or custom-designed private classes for up to twenty people. Its most unique offering is the One Night Stand, in which chef Abby Hitchcock throws open the kitchen to a group of friends who cooks a meal to be served in the restaurant's dining room.

appetizer could pass as an entrée; the osso buco—nearly falling off the bone and surrounded by mounds of creamy risotto—is too hefty to finish. You won't have room for dessert, but the waiter will describe something (mascarpone cheesecake, perhaps), and you'll order it anyway and eat half, at best. When the bill comes, you'll really understand the meaning of big.

Il Postino *337 E 49th St between First and Second Aves (212-688-0033). Subway: E, V to Lexington Ave–53rd St; 6 to 51st St. Mon–Sat noon–3pm, 5–11:30pm; Sun 5–10:30pm. Average main course: $30.* Delicate cut flowers on every table and pale floral wallpaper create an atmosphere of serenity at this tony midtown eatery. Chef Errico Gerado clearly sees his Pan-Italian cuisine as an art form; that's why the hushed, romantic room is a haven for tycoons and their out-of-town guests. In their midst, you can savor appetizers like paper-thin tuna carpaccio with capers. Pastas, such as mushroom ravioli in a savory porcino sauce, are aggressively salty but rich in flavor. Gerado is a wizard with fresh fish and steaks, too; the veal chop is so big and juicy, it's almost cartoonlike. If none of this appeals to you, then, as the waiter will inform you, the kitchen will make whatever you want.

Insieme *Michelangelo Hotel, 777 Seventh Ave at 51st St (212-582-1310). Subway: B, D, F, V to 47–50th Sts–Rockefeller Ctr; N, R, W to 49th St. Mon–Thu 7–10am, noon–2pm, 5:30–11pm; Fri 7–10am, noon–2pm, 5:30–11:30pm; Sat 8–11am, 5:30–11:30pm; Sun 8am–11am. Average main course: $30.* Chef Marco Canora and sommelier Paul Grieco, the partners behind Hearth, polish their craft at this Italian spot inside the Michelangelo Hotel. At Insieme (Italian for "together"), white tables appear sans cloths, track lighting contributes a soft glow, and cascades of long, white strings provide privacy for a row of booths. The menu features traditional dishes in one column, and "modern" takes in the other. Traditional lasagna comes as a sandwich of spinach pasta and Parmesan sitting atop beef-and-pork *ragù*, cemented together with a thick béchamel, while a sliced roasted pork loin (a contemporary dish) is served perfectly medium-rare on a confetti of pink-and-white beans in a pool of sage-heavy *jus*.

★ ▲**L'Impero** *45 Tudor City Pl at 43rd St (212-599-5045). Subway: 42nd St S, 4, 5, 6, 7 to 42nd St–Grand Central. Mon–Thu noon–2:30pm, 5:30–10:30pm; Fri noon–2:30pm, 5–11:30pm; Sat 5–11:30pm. Average main course: $28.* It is testimony to chef Scott Conant's prowess that L'Impero can attract a crowd night after night. Located in Tudor City, the restaurant is a hideaway of sorts, where framed mirrors and candles suspended on wire rods give the clean-lined room a romantic glow. Conant's modern Italian cuisine is equally alluring. He employs a few fresh, seasonal ingredients and keeps the menu small, serving seemingly banal dishes. Who else would dare to offer house-made spaghetti with tomato and basil? The *capretto* (baby goat) is a signature dish, and Conant works wonders with fish, too: Branzino comes with baby tomatoes, capers, olives and orange. The chef has also developed a sophisticated menu of tarts, gelati and cakes, as well as a spectacular cheese plate that marries sweet flavors to each cheese, pairing ricotta *di bufala* with truffle honey, for example. Remote, pricey and deceptively simple, L'Impero is a fascinating journey to another place.

It's a brick...house
Peasant's open kitchen
is lettin' it all hang out.

PATRIK RYTIKANGAS

Morandi *211 Waverly Pl between Seventh Ave South and Charles St (212-627-7575). Subway: 1, 2, 3 to 14th St. Mon–Fri 8am–3pm, 5:30–midnight; Sat, Sun 10am–4pm, 5:30–midnight. Average main course: $25.* Creating a winning restaurant usually requires far more art than science, but the immediate success of Morandi, the Italian debut for Keith McNally, king of the pseudo-French eatery (Pastis, Balthazar), amounts to simple math: x (cram them in) times y (turn them over) equals z (money machine). Morandi is yet another old-world theme park, though little is specifically Italian besides the racks of wine in straw baskets. McNally's formula also includes reliable, straightforward food. Chef Jody Williams' lengthy menu is more authentic than the surroundings, and her eats are consistently good or better, if uninspired. Heavy carne dishes, including crusty pork-and-veal meatballs with pine nuts, raisins and tomato paste, and a huge, gorgeously pink veal chop, smothered in gooey fontina and prosciutto, are quite good. Service, though professional, is frenetic: Dishes came one on top of the other, and most tables turn over in 90 minutes or so.

★ ▲**Peasant** *194 Elizabeth St between Prince and Spring Sts (212-965-9511). Subway: J, M, Z to Bowery; 6 to Spring St. Tue–Sat 6–11pm; Sun 6–10pm. Average main course: $25.* The open kitchen at Peasant is straight out of a fairy tale—a magical little brick-on-brick workshop where chef-owner Frank DeCarlo pulls sizzling hen, shimmery sardines and T-bone steaks from a crackling fire. Most of DeCarlo's rustic dishes are masterful: spicy charred octopus, luscious skate, tender golden-skinned hen, crisp-crusted pizzas. And as soon as you place your order (whether here or in Peasant

Wine Bar, the charming spot downstairs), the holy trinity arrives: fresh ricotta and a bottle of olive oil from DiPalo's, with a basket of Sullivan Street Bakery bread.

Rainbow Room Grill *30 Rockefeller Plaza between 49th and 50th Sts, 65th floor (212-632-5100). Subway: B, D, F, V to 47–50th Sts–Rockefeller Ctr. Daily 5–11:30pm. Average main course: $35.* The explanation for Rainbow Room's staying power after more than 70 years is clear: From the 65th floor, you have the ultimate view of Manhattan. At sunset in the Grill, tourists and well-heeled midtown types collect at the sleek Deco bar as a pianist plays jazzy numbers. If you can tear yourself away from the skyline, you'll be reminded that the Grill has been part of the Cipriani empire for a decade, which means impeccable white-suited waiters and a menu of wildly pricey, old-school Northern Italian specialties that are high on quality but low on imagination. Classic ice-chilled shrimp cocktail comes with amazingly juicy-fresh jumbo shrimp. Pastas can be heavy, like the green *tagliolini* mixed with slices of ham and cream, then baked. Entrées, such as two beef medallions served in a *pepe verde* sauce, are satisfyingly straightforward. This Rainbow is touristy, but the city would certainly lose some luster if it faded away. **Other location** *Rainbow Room, 30 Rockefeller Plaza between 49th and 50th Sts, 65th floor (212-632-5100).*

★ **Remi** *145 W 53rd St between Sixth and Seventh Aves (212-581-4242). Subway: B, D, E to Seventh Ave. Mon–Thu noon–11pm; Fri, Sat noon–11:30pm; Sun noon–9:30pm. Average main course: $25. Three-course prix fixe: $27.* Deep-black risotto, colored by squid cooked in its own ink, is a typical Venetian dish, and it's

Room with a view
The Rainbow Room Grill
satisfies more than just
the sense of taste.

frequently a special here. But the lively, playful space—designed by architect Adam Tihany—is your first clue that Remi isn't too bound by tradition. Chef Giovanni Pinato's *cichetti*, presented in whimsical angular plates, include fried stuffed olives and marinated octopus. His tuna-filled ravioli is a classic, and gnocchi with baby goat is spiked with olives and artichoke hearts. *Semifreddo* and gelato grace the dessert menu.

▲**San Pietro** *18 E 54th St between Fifth and Madison Aves (212-753-9015). Subway: E, V to Fifth Ave–53rd St. Mon–Sat noon–3pm, 4–11pm. Average main course: $34.* The Bruno brothers (chef Antonio, president Gerardo and wine director Cosimo) go straight to the family farm in Campania to get top-notch ingredients for their high-end oasis in midtown. (Frette napkins and white-coated waiters signal that you'll want to put this one on the expense account.) Luscious *burrata* (an extra-creamy version of mozzarella) pairs beautifully with prosciutto and figs, and an appetizer of octopus, potatoes and green beans is perfectly dressed in a basil-and-lemon puree. Delicate house-made *scialatielli* pasta is topped with clams, asparagus and tomatoes. The massive wine list includes plenty of hard-to-find Italian vintages.

▲**Sant Ambroeus** *1000 Madison Ave at 77th St (212-570-2211). Subway: 6 to 77th St. Daily 8am–11pm. Average main course: $29.* Everyone gets a little restless around the age of 19, and Sant Ambroeus—the beloved Upper East Side café, gelateria, *paninoteca*, wine bar, patisserie and restaurant—was no exception. It left its longtime Madison Avenue home in 2001, plopped down a few years later in the West Village, and now, it's back

in its original location. Executive chef Mario Danieli also returned to prepare many of the classic Northern Italian dishes fans have grown to love, like a tender breaded veal *piccata*, a sprightly shaved-fennel and crab salad, and spaghetti topped with hearty bolognese. **Other location** *259 W 4th St at Perry St (212-604-9254).*

▲**Spigolo** *1561 Second Ave at 81st St (212-744-1100). Subway: 4, 5, 6 to 86th St. Mon 5–10pm; Tue–Sat 5–11pm; Sun 5–10pm. Average main course: $26.* In passing, you might mistake the brick-walled place for just another pasta-slinging joint. Chef Scott Fratangelo (Union Square Cafe) cooks up imaginative Italian fare like the grilled jumbo shrimp with farro, raisins and pine nuts, *garganelli* with fennel and sausage *ragu*, and a brick-roasted baby chicken with local greens and *panzanella* salad. His wife Heather, also of Union Square Cafe, handles desserts, and here's hoping you aren't too full to try them. The caramel *affogato* and *bombolini* will put your morning coffee and doughnuts to shame.

▲**Trattoria dell'Arte** *900 Seventh Ave between 56th and 57th Sts (212-245-9800). Subway: N, Q, R, W to 57th St. Mon–Sat 11:45am–11:30pm; Sun 11am–10:30pm. Average main course: $28.* At this colorful Italian eatery directly across the street from Carnegie Hall, the walls have ears—or rather, a giant sculpture of an ear, along with a huge eye and a single enormous tit. The exuberant decor is matched by a menu that runs from deeply rich fare, such as linguini carbonara with lobster, to austere pizzas with crisp, papyrus-like crusts. The Roman Ghetto–style baby artichokes are a perfect appetizer, but picky eaters are also free to assemble their own starters at the well-stocked antipasto bar.

JENNY WOODWARD

Japanese

See also: *Asian, Eclectic, Korean*

Heated debate
Hibino makes the choice between raw or cooked a tough one.

▲**Aki** *181 W 4th St between Barrow and Jones Sts (212-989-5440). Subway: A, C, E, B, D, F, V to W 4th St. Tue–Thu, Sun 6–10:45pm; Fri, Sat 6–11:45pm. Average main course price: $26.* You feel as if you're interrupting a private dinner party when you enter this stark, miniscule haven. Luckily, you won't have to worry about niceties like forcing yourself to clean your plate to please your host, since many items on the Japanese-fusion menu are quite superlative. Though odd-sounding, a starter of eel napoleon—fried tofu, *shiso*-topped fish, pumpkin puree with crunchy wonton chips—is rich in textures, while Korean chili paste and pink fish powder punch up classic *chirashi*. Elegant desserts such as green-tea tiramisu coddle you before you rejoin the West Village fray.

Amber *1406 Third Ave at 80th St (212-249-5020). Subway: 6 to 77th St. Mon–Fri noon–3pm, 5pm–midnight; Sat, Sun noon–midnight. Omakase: $45 and up.* Natural elements pervade this trendy Japanese lounge, where a waterfall trickles down a stretch of pebbles and wooden tables are supported by slender birch or oak trunks. A tropical red-wine sauce adds punch to—rather than overpowering—the superbly crispy duck. The sushi doesn't need such adornment, particularly the Snow White and the Seven Dwarves entrée—a white tuna and white asparagus roll served alongside six pieces of divine fatty tuna and a hollowed-out cucumber filled with spicy scallops. Only the TV over the bar breaks Mother Nature's spell.

★ **Bar Masa** *Time Warner Center, 10 Columbus Circle at 60th St, fourth floor (212-823-9800). Subway: A, C, B, D, 1 to 59th St–Columbus Circle. Mon–Sat* 11:30am–3pm, 6pm–midnight. *Average main course: $27.* If Masa is the sushi version of a Martha Stewart Thanksgiving banquet, then Bar Masa is the children's table. You're still eating food from the Great One (Masa Takayama), but it's just not quite the same. Plenty of admirable qualities are at play: no-reservations and a casual dress code in a stylish room (polished bubinga wood bar, oya wall tiles) suddenly make a taste from a sushi god a spontaneous possibility. The grazing menu groups food into 11 categories (such as fried, hibachi-grilled, udon or soba), but while options are artful and delicate, it ultimately takes cash and stomach resources away from the sushi. Those expecting the ethereal raw fish from next door will be disappointed—the kids' table, after all, gets the drumsticks not the breast.

Blue Ribbon Sushi *119 Sullivan St between Prince and Spring Sts (212-343-0404). Subway: C, E to Spring St. Daily noon–2am. Average sushi meal (seven pieces, one roll): $22.* Whether you settle on a $4 bowl of make-it-yourself miso soup and some California rolls, or opt for the top-of-the-line $125 chef's choice sushi platter, you'll find the service equally friendly and enthusiastic at this below-street-level Soho fave. The cooked dishes (like the miso-cured aged black cod) are worthy alternatives to the sushi, which, short of dining aboard a fishing vessel, is as fresh as it gets. Order a serving of the flawless green-tea crème brûlée to end your night on a high.
Other location *Blue Ribbon Sushi Brooklyn, 278 Fifth Ave between Garfield Pl and 1st St, Park Slope, Brooklyn, (718-840-0408).*

Bond St. *6 Bond St between Broadway and Lafayette St (212-777-2500). Subway: B, D, F, V to*

Broadway–Lafayette St; 6 to Bleecker St. Sun, Mon 6–11pm; Tue–Sat 6pm–midnight. Average roll: $10. Omakase: $40–$100. The servers are as attractive and attentive as ever, and the tri-level space still glows with urban-Zen chic. Although most patrons order the superfresh but pitifully sized sushi, chef Marc Spitzer's fusion dishes steal the show—particularly, the decadent, buttery shrimp, crab and trout risotto that's piled high with a fluffy mound of smoky bonito. Or opt for the bite-size bliss of the *omakase* tasting menu. These days, there's a new breed of loudmouth diner here, braying about how much he knows about sake; you can avoid him by requesting the private back room.

★ ▲**Cube 63** *63 Clinton St between Rivington and Stanton Sts (212-228-6751). Subway: F to Delancey St; J, M, Z to Delancey–Essex Sts. Mon–Thu 5pm–midnight; Fri, Sat 5pm–1am. Average sushi meal (eight pieces and one roll): $18.* The chic dining room is just a sliver, but the inventive flavors seem bigger than any four walls could easily contain. Jumbo-size specialty rolls crowd nearly every table: Shrimp tempura hooks up with eel, avocado, cream cheese and caviar in the Tahiti roll; the Volcano has crab and shrimp topped with a pile of spicy lobster salad, the entire dish set aflame with a blowtorch. Be sure to venture from the devilishly delicious raw fish for a bite of Tuna Nuta, miniature chunks of lightly seared tuna atop honey-mustard–glazed spears of asparagus.

▲**Donguri** *309 E 83rd St between First and Second Aves (212-737-5656). Subway: 4, 5, 6 to 86th St. Tue–Sun 5:30–9:30pm. Average main course: $25.* The slender 24-seat dining room is smaller than most studio apartments, but patrons are too busy eating dishes they've never encountered before to care. Richly marbled *kampachi* belly is snow white and served as sashimi; it's firmer than toro but just as buttery. Raw fluke rolled around a sweet red pepper looks like a firecracker but tastes like candy—until a surprise pat of wasabi explodes in your mouth. End with a glass of jellied white rice cakes and sweet red beans.

★ **EN Japanese Brasserie** *435 Hudson St at Leroy St (212-647-9196). Subway: 1 to Houston St. Mon–Thu, Sun 5:30–11pm; Fri, Sat 5:30pm–midnight. Average main course: $15.* Sibling restaurateurs Bunkei and Reika Yo give us a sense of Japanese living in this multilevel space. On the ground floor are tatami-style rooms; on the mezzanine are re-creations of a living room, dining room and library of a Japanese home from the Meiji Era. But the main dining room is where the action is: Diners sit at tables either on the periphery or around a small pond under high ceilings. Chef Koji Nakano is running with the home theme too by offering handmade miso paste, tofu and *yuba* (soy-milk skin) in dishes like Berkshire pork belly braised in *sansho* miso; foie gras and poached daikon steak with white miso vinegar; and seared *chutoro* marinated in garlic soy. The menu changes frequently with seasonal specials. Try the sake and shochu flights (or wonderful original cocktails) and you'll get an authentic Asian buzz, too.

15 East *15 E 15th St between Fifth Ave and Union Sq West (212-647-0015). Subway: L, N, Q, R, W, 4, 5, 6 to 14th St–Union Sq. Mon–Sat 6–10:30pm. Ten-piece sushi dinner: $55.* Toqueville co-owner Marco Moreira has returned to his aquatic roots—he was trained as a sushi chef—in the restaurant's former space. Architect Richard Bloch (Masa) has muted the colors and created a

distinct sushi bar and dining room, turning what felt like a country inn into a solemn temple of Japanese cuisine. Sushi is very expensive (ten pieces of nigiri for $55; à la carte still more punitive), but consistently luscious: The scallop is as smooth as chocolate mousse, and almost as sweet. For tuna aficionados, a $75 sampler with six different cuts includes an *otoro* on par with the city's best. Choose the raw offerings over the cooked (they still haven't found their sea legs).

Haku *2425 Broadway between 89th and 90th Sts (212-580-2566). Subway: 1 to 86th St. Mon–Thu, Sun 5–11pm; Fri, Sat 5pm–midnight. Average main course: $20.* Soothing blue mosaic tiles on the walls are a concession to the low-key style that neighborhood locals seem to prefer in their sushi joints, as are the more traditional sushi platters and entrées. Sushi chef Scott Lin allows the flavors of the fish to stand out; slices of bluefin toro melt in your mouth. But not everything works: An appetizer of fried shiitakes stuffed with shrimp sounds intriguing, but the mushrooms are a little rubbery and the shrimp slightly overcooked. A bonus: The selection of Hitachino Japanese ale is a mouth-watering alternative to the usual Asahi Super Dry.

▲**Hakubai** *The Kitano Hotel, 66 Park Ave at 38th St (212-885-7111). Subway: 42nd St S, 4, 5, 6, 7 to 42nd St–Grand Central. 11:45am–2:30pm, 6–10pm. Average main course: $50.* Over centuries, Japanese restaurants have refined the art of *kaiseki ryori*—a virtuoso progression of seasonal small plates. At Hakubai, the seven-course meal might start with lightly battered, fried river fish and a tiny block of sweet, dense tofu. More recognizable Japanese dishes may follow, like miso soup and a selection of sashimi. At the centerpiece of the meal are three blissfully succulent blocks of kobe beef, grilled on rocks and served with tender bamboo and asparagus. Service is exceedingly attentive, and the pace of the meal is relaxed, although the brightly lit, blond-wood setting isn't made for lounging. For that, you'll have to get a room upstairs.

▲**Hana Cafe** *235 Smith St between Butler and Douglass Sts, Carroll Gardens, Brooklyn (718-643-1963). Subway: F, G to Bergen St. Mon–Thu noon–11pm; Fri, Sat noon–11:30; Sun 1–11pm. Average sushi meal (15 pieces): $16.* You won't leave this neighborhood sushi joint and then feel hungry two hours later. It's simply too hard to resist the words *crunch* and *tempura* beckoning from all parts of the menu. The fried tofu is mesmerizing: Papery-thin bonito flakes flutter atop lightly battered, custardy bean curd. Order the specialty rolls with balance in mind: The lush lobster tempura roll with asparagus, caviar and mayo needs a light counterpoint, such as the riceless *kyuri* maki of eel, caviar

Read 'em & eat

gyoza: dumplings commonly filled with meat, then fried or steamed

negimaki: broiled meat drenched in teriyaki sauce wrapped around scallions

omakase: the chef's choice of a series of dishes

Priced to move
Le Miu delivers Nobu-like
fare for a fraction of the cost.

and crabmeat rolled in cucumber. Finish with a creamy fried banana inside a crisp batter shell or a scoop of fried green-tea ice cream in a thick, cakey crust. **Other location** *Sushi Hana, 524 86th St at Fifth Ave, Bay Ridge, Brooklyn (718-238-4513).*

▲**Hatsuhana** *17 E 48th St between Fifth and Madison Aves (212-355-3345). Subway: E, V to Fifth Ave–53rd St; 6 to 51st St. Mon–Fri 11:45am–2:45pm, 5:30–10pm; Sat 5–10pm. Average sushi meal (ten pieces, one roll): $40.* This midtown classic, popular among Metro-North travelers on shopping expeditions with their preteens, was one of the first restaurants to introduce New Yorkers to the then-mysterious delights of sushi and sashimi, nearly three decades ago. It's still worth a visit for its lovely bento-style Box of Dreams, which is divided into nine compartments, like a tic-tac-toe board. In each is a different combination of sushi or cooked fish and vegetables over rice, such as a meaty, melt-on-your-tongue *uni* with seaweed and *shiso*; cooked eel with cucumber slices; and two triangles of *tamago* (slightly sweetened egg) with cooked shrimp. It's a refreshing presentation, and a nice reminder that even an institution like Hatsuhana can remain inventive. **Other location** *237 Park Ave at 46th St (212-661-3400).*

★ **Hedeh** *57 Great Jones St at Bowery St (212-473-8458). Subway: B, D, F, V to Broadway–Lafayette St; 6 to Bleecker St. Mon–Sat 5pm–midnight. Average main course: $27.* It is always comforting to walk into a dining room, peer into a pristine open kitchen and see that the staff-to-diner ratio is about 1:1. At this spare restaurant, food comes before flash. Behind the long sushi counter, an army of cooks slice shimmery, beet-red triangles of

tuna, drape tender slivers of eel over perfectly sticky mounds of rice and assemble texturally ingenious shrimp. When raw fish isn't enough, you can fill up on richly marbled, wasabi-rubbed lamb chops and kickin' wasabi mashed potatoes.

▲**Hibino** *333 Henry St at Pacific St, Cobble Hill, Brooklyn (718-260-8052). Subway: M, R to Court St; 2, 3, 4, 5 to Borough Hall. Mon–Thu noon–2:30pm, 5:30–10pm; Fri noon–2:30pm, 5:30–10:30pm; Sat 5:30–10:30pm. Average main course: $14.* If your Japanese dining experience is limited to sushi and soba, this is a great place to broaden your Nippon palate. Dine at the sleek oak sushi bar or at small tables lit by a row of spherical hanging lights. The menu deftly covers appetizers, entrées, sushi and *obanzai*, Kyoto-style tapas. It's rotated almost daily and is reported on their quirky blog, *hibino-brooklyn.com/blog.* The sushi is excellent, but it's the cooked food that stands out: Chicken teriyaki is skin-on organic fowl with al dente asparagus and okra pods, and the soy pudding dessert is beyond creamy.

Inagiku *The Waldorf-Astoria, 111 E 49th St between Park and Lexington Aves (212-355-0440). Subway: E, V to Lexington Ave–53rd St; 6 to 51st St. Mon–Fri noon–2pm, 5:30–10pm; Sat, Sun 5:30–10pm. Average main course: $26.* A surprisingly understated find inside the Waldorf-Astoria, Inagiku serves solid sushi—notably, California rolls with real crabmeat—and a tapas-style menu of "little dishes," which can be combined to make a meal. These small plates range from delicate cold fare like homemade tofu flecked with avocado and served on a bed of crushed ice to the rustic *burikama shioyaki*, a big grilled neckbone of yellowtail

PHILIP FRIEDMAN

you eat with your hands to get at all the buttery, tender meat and crisp, salty skin.

Ise *58 W 56th St between Fifth and Sixth Aves (212-707-8702). Subway: F to 57th St. Daily 11:30am– 2:45pm, 5–10:45pm. Average sushi meal (eight pieces, one roll): $18.* The brightly lit, narrow space feels like a bona fide *izakaya* (local pub) in Tokyo. At the short bar up front, drinks are served. Outside the *shoji* doors of private tatami rooms are orderly rows of shoes belonging to the groups of boisterous Japanese businesspeople within. Ise has two menus: one of Japanese bar snacks like *yakitori* and *gyoza*, another with appetizers and entrées like sushi combination platters. There's also a well-prepared, seasonally changing "complete dinner" that feeds two and includes sashimi, sushi, tempura, salad, miso soup, steak in a sweet soy-sauce marinade with mushrooms, grilled vegetables and dessert, all for $40. No wonder this place feels like home to its many ex-pat regulars. **Other locations** *56 Pine St between Pearl and William Sts (212-785-1600)* ● *151 E 49th St between Lexington and Third Aves (212-319-6876).*

Izakaya Ten *207 Tenth Ave between 22nd and 23rd Sts (212-627-7777). Subway: C, E to 23rd St. Mon–Sat 5pm–midnight. Average small plate: $6.* Lannie Ahn, the owner of this slim Japanese pub—which recently replaced D'or Ahn (and, briefly, Anzu)—enlisted the help of designer Moto Ichijo, who covered the formerly gray exterior with an eye-popping mural and added squat wooden tables to complete the makeover. Small Japanese pub-grub dishes include tender sliced pork belly served in a cast-iron skillet, made zippy with ginger. Tempura options go beyond the usual: Plump shrimp wrapped in *shiso* leaves is one winning variation. Note: You will need five or six dishes to make a meal for two. And those overflowing sake glasses? They're filled that way purposely, to signify good luck.'

Japonais *111 E 18th St between Park Ave South and Irving Pl (212-260-2020). Subway: L, N, Q, R, W, 4, 5, 6 to 14th St–Union Sq. Mon–Thu 5pm–11pm; Fri, Sat 5–11:30pm; Sun 5–10pm. Average main course: $25.* The latest Asian megarestaurant, an 11,350-square-foot offshoot of a Chicago hot spot, appears to be Gramercy's answer to Morimoto and Buddakan. The striking Jeffrey Beers design features French doors and a balcony lounge (the Red Room) that overlooks the main dining area. The sushi is better than average, but updated Chinese dishes take star billing. Giant steamed buns are stuffed with sweet pork marinated in sake, mirin and soy sauce, and "Le Quack Japonais," a fancy version of Peking duck, is proffered in thick, juicy slices. Too bad the staff is surly.

Jewel Bako *239 E 5th St between Second and Third Aves (212-979-1012). Subway: 6 to Astor Pl; F, V to Lower East Side–Second Ave. Mon–Sat 6:30–11pm. Omakase: $50, $85.* The East Village's first real destination sushi bar remains one of the top spots in the neighborhood for pristine raw fish—and, with tables lined up under a blond wood cocoon, among the coziest. Over the years portions have grown, but the food remains as gorgeous as ever. A trio of tartares comes topped with three different caviars; a flaky wild salmon filet steamed in paper in sea urchin sauce is unveiled at the table. The budget-minded will gravitate toward the oversize maki filled with intriguing combinations like seared red snapper, cucumber and *shiso*. The best deal on a sushi

splurge is still the *omakase*, an ultragenerous platter of whatever's freshest that day.

Kai *822 Madison Ave between 68th and 69th Sts (212-988-7277). Subway: 6 to 68th St–Hunter College. Mon–Sat noon–3pm, 5:30–9:30pm. Omakase: $75–$200.* If your rendezvous is an intimate one, Kai (Japanese for gathering) is indeed a good place to have it. The minimal, bamboo-accented design in this second-floor space above high-end teashop Ito En makes the tight quarters bearable; a hushed atmosphere allows for quiet conversation and concentration on the food. Served on slate slabs, tidy portions of Japanese fare—as in *sakizuke*, an elegant arrangement of unusual one-bite morsels (the mountain-peach jelly, a bright-pink orb within a translucent cube, is especially intriguing)— resemble modern art more than comestibles. They will titillate your palette but only fill your stomach if you're willing to splurge on several courses.

Ki Sushi *122 Smith St between Dean and Pacific Sts, Boerum Hill, Brooklyn (718-935-0575). Subway: F, G to Bergen St. Mon–Thu, Sun noon–3pm, 5–11pm; Fri, Sat 5pm–midnight. Average roll: $6.* Brooklyn's greatest deal for sushi lovers may very well be the $25 *omakase* meal at this Smith Street restaurant. Add $3 and get the "supreme" version, which features seafood air-shipped from Tokyo's Tsukiji market, in portions that can be enormous. There are also 20 or so classic rolls—spicy tuna, California—plus 15 specialty rolls. Despite kitschy names like Foxy Lady and Spicy Girl, these are often delicious and beautifully architectural. Dark wood banquettes, brick walls and flickering candles add casually elegant ambience, and the waiters are swift and attentive, describing dishes both before you order and once the plate arrives.

Koi *Bryant Park Hotel, 40 W 40th St between Fifth and Sixth Aves (212-642-2100). Subway: B, D, F, V to 42nd St–Bryant Park; 7 to Fifth Ave. Mon–Wed 5:30– 11pm; Thu–Sat 5:30–midnight. Average main course: $23.* Unlike the first-name-worthy Nobu and Masa, Los Angeles's Koi has never been about the chef; it's about the scene, as listers from A to D work the tables. The dining room is more sedate than the lounge, despite the plastic Erector Set–style sculpture hugging the ceiling. There's a real koi pond in the floor of the dining area, where bamboo shoots line the perimeter, and the space has been carved into three levels. The cold dishes are positioned as de facto appetizers, the hot dishes serve as entrées, and the sushi falls in between as a wild card. How you order doesn't much matter: Everything comes out whenever it's ready, and everything is served as a share plate. Sushi purists, take note: Koi is at its weakest with standard maki and cut rolls, and hits high notes only when the chef riffs with the raw fish.

Le Miu *107 Ave A between 6th and 7th Sts (212-473-3100). Subway: F, V to Lower East Side–Second Ave; 6 to Astor Pl. Tue, Wed, Sun 5:30pm–midnight; Thu–Sat 5:30pm–2am. Average roll: $10.* A coterie of chefs from places like Nobu and Megu teamed up to open this 70-seat East Village sushi parlor decked out with well-spaced tables, a bright bar up front and a sushi bar in back. The menu has a familiar feel, but there's a confident sass to the food; the miso soup, for example, carries a kick, thanks to *yuzu* pepper flakes. The sushi is good, but the most interesting options come from the land: artistic piles of lotus root, broccoli rabe and other vegetarian options enliven fish-free rolls. Of the hot

Japanese

Drink up
Sake 101

Just as sushi is now considered about as exotic as mac and cheese, sake is the preferred beverage when eating Japanese, and has even earned a place on some non-Asian drink menus. Not only does sake's subtle yet complex flavor perfectly complement sushi, it also offers a fast and sweet buzz: Higher in alcohol content than wine (14 to 18 percent, compared with wine's 10 to 12 percent), it also leaves a practically inconsequential hangover. But like its grape-based Western counterpart, not all sake is created equal, requiring some knowledge to appreciate the Japanese rice wine.

Sake comes in three categories, according to its production. Sake made from rice that is least polished is called *junmai*. These are often fuller, richer-bodied sakes—those you'd pair with heavier sauces and stronger flavors—and they have above-average acidity. An easy-to-find junmai sake is the Nishida Denshu, a smooth, aromatic drink with hints of vanilla and an easy finish.

The next level up is *ginjo*. These are, on average, more delicate and complex; the rice grains are polished to 60 percent of their original size. The result is intensely fragrant and complex in flavor; beginners should try side-by-side taste comparisons with junmai to notice the differences. For a first taste, look for a ginjo called Narutotai Genshu, a rich brew with tart but balanced citrus notes that pairs well with oysters.

Top-of-the-line sakes are called *daiginjos*. These, with grains polished 50 percent, are extremely fragrant and cost about twice as much as junmai sakes by the glass. One to try is Masumi Yumedono, an exceptional daiginjo with lively fruit aromas like strawberry and melon.

In addition to Japanese restaurants, sake bars like **Decibel** (240 E 9th St between Second and Third Aves, 212-979-2733) and **Sakagura** (211 E 43rd St between Second and Third Aves, 212-953-7253) are terrific places to further your education. You will generally find bartenders happy to sate your thirst as well as your curiosity.

entrées, the Angus sirloin, served sliced and medium-rare with a thick sesame paste, is fantastic. The five-course tasting explores most of the menu for just $45, which is less than half the price of the cheapest Nobu *omakase*.

★ ▲**Megu** *62 Thomas St between Church St and West Broadway (212-964-7777). Subway: A, C, 1, 2, 3 to Chambers St. Mon–Wed 11:30am–2:30pm, 5:30–10:30pm; Thu–Fri 11:30am–2:30pm, 5:30–11:30pm; Sat 5:30–11:30pm; Sun 5:30–10:30pm. Average main course: $30.* Since the day this awe-inspiring temple of Japanese cuisine opened in 2004, diners have been criticizing its overblown prices and unwieldy, complicated menu. But critics forget to mention that this is one of the most thrilling meals you'll find in New York. Spring for one of the tasting menus, which begins with a brainteaser of a dish: a spoon holding a raw "egg," which actually combines pineapple juice, coconut milk and a chemically induced yolklike membrane. What follows is a parade of ingenious little bites and surprising presentations. Scrumptiously fatty toro comes with a plastic syringe of creamy tuna marrow. Immaculate slices of chilled raw kobe beef look like marble slabs on the plate but melt in the mouth. Megu is equally serious about sushi. Three simple, glistening pieces delivered at the end of the meal are as breathtaking and pleasurable as any you've had.

▲**Miyagi** *220 W 13th St between Seventh and Greenwich Aves (212-620-3830). Subway: A, C, E, 1, 2, 3 to 14th St; L to Eighth Ave. Mon–Fri noon–11pm; Sat 5:30–11:30pm; Sun 5:30–10:30pm. Average sushi meal (eight pieces, one roll): $20.* Skip the sushi and explore the vast menu of well-executed cooked standards and interesting offbeat choices at this subdued little spot. Start with the Fried Alaska (ground salmon, asparagus and mint wrapped in a soy sheet and lightly fried) and *yuba-ae* (broccoli rabe tossed with delicate tofu skin in a tangy-sweet miso dressing). Entrées include well-prepared *donburi*, teriyaki, soba and udon dishes. Ask for *shichimi togarashi* (pepper-and-sesame seasoning) to sprinkle on top. For dessert, try tempura ice cream—fried vanilla Tofutti drizzled with chocolate sauce and garnished with whipped cream, roasted almonds, fresh strawberries and chocolate-covered Pocky sticks.

★ **Momofuku Noodle Bar** *163 First Ave between 10th and 11th Sts (212-475-7899). Subway: L to First Ave; N, Q, R, W, 4, 5, 6 to 14th St–Union Sq. Mon–Thu, Sun noon–4pm; 5:30–11pm; Fri, Sat noon–4pm; 5:30pm–midnight. Average main course: $15.* This popular East Village noodle shrine has just 30 seats, and pilgrims are often forced to wait outside. If you can, sit at the bar a few feet from the minuscule open kitchen, where chefs busily fry, chop and sauté. The menu here changes seasonally, but vegetarians beware—almost every dish contains heirloom Berkshire pork and/or soft-boiled eggs. In the Momofuku ramen, for example, a gigantic bowl of flavorful broth filled with pieces of pork, scallions, peas and bamboo shoots, an egg lies atop a tangle of noodles.

Momoya *85 Seventh Ave at 21st St (212-989-4466). Subway: 1 to 23rd St. Daily noon–3pm, 5:30–11pm. Average main course: $18.* Momoya could sail by on looks alone, but the food is terrific, too. Impeccably fresh fish, like silky toro, practically melts on the tongue. Standard *shumai* is gussied up with strawlike noodles that wrap around each dumpling like rubber bands. The specialty rolls are, well, special: Spicy tuna is topped

PHILIP FRIEDMAN

with flamed yellowtail and almonds; another roll marries jalapeño, salmon, tuna, cucumber and scallop tartare.

★ **Morimoto** *2007 Eat Out Award, Readers' Choice: Best new out-of-town restaurateur, Stephen Starr* 88 Tenth Ave between 15th and 16th Sts (212-989-8883). Subway: A, C, E to 14th St; L to Eighth Ave. Mon–Wed noon–2:30pm, 5:30pm–10:45pm; Thu, Fri noon–2:30pm, 5:30–11:45pm; Sat 5:30–11:45pm; Sun 5–10:45pm. Average main course: $36. Masaharu Morimoto, best known as the god of all things Japanese on *Iron Chef America*, cemented his reputation at Nobu, and comparisons are inevitable. But while Nobu's magic starts when the food hits the tongue, there's a determined effort here to elicit a wow before it's consumed; even the green-tea palate cleanser comes with a stylish prop (a shaving-style brush for stirring). Morimoto cures yellowtail like pastrami, encrusting the outside with peppery spices, and places buffalo mozzarella alongside sashimi. He also offers braised black cod in ginger soy, which is a clear descendant of the black cod in miso made famous at Nobu. Sushi and sashimi don't appear until late in the meal—you get five stellar nigiri pieces as a last entrée if you order the $120 tasting menu—and he wisely lays off the razzle-dazzle here. The fish is first-rate—soft, clean, brimming with flavor. Only the expense makes you think twice, but it is in line with what upper-echelon Japanese restaurants now charge. And if you score good seats, you can think of it as dinner and a show.

★▲**Mottsu** 285 Mott St between Houston and Prince Sts (212-343-8017). Subway: N, R, W to Prince St; 6 to Spring St. Mon–Thu noon–3pm, 5–11pm; Fri, Sat noon–3pm, 5–11:30pm; Sun 5–10pm. Average main course: $20. Average sushi meal (ten pieces, one roll): $20. Reasonable prices, unpretentious service and interesting combinations that change with the seasons—of course locals enjoy Mottsu. Japanese businessmen, far from their usual midtown haunts, also frequent the curved sushi bar, chatting with the sushi chef to the thrum of Cuban music. Fresh sushi, sashimi and rolls (the Cholesterol includes king crab, avocado, egg and tempura flakes) are available, as are cooked dishes, such as teriyaki chicken or salmon and sautéed tilefish finished with a clam-anchovy sauce. There are plenty of roll options for vegetarians; budget-watchers will like the $15 twilight meal offered from 5 to 7pm.

▲**Nippon** 155 E 52nd St between Lexington and Third Aves (212-758-0226). Subway: E, V to Lexington Ave–53rd St; 6 to 51st St. Mon–Thu noon–2:30pm, 5:30–10pm; Fri noon–2:30pm, 5:30–10:30pm; Sat 5:30–10:30pm. Average sushi meal (seven pieces, one roll): $21. Nippon sticks with tradition: Since 1963, the gliding waitresses have worn kimonos, and private tatami rooms are available. The menu, too, offers classic fare such as sashimi, tempura, *sukiyaki, shabu-shabu* and *yakitori*, each solidly presented. And to offer traditional putterfish, owner Nobuyoshi Kuraoka was instrumental in persuading the FDA to allow the import of the species, which has toxic organs and must be prepared by specially trained chefs. Nippon's real specialty is a seven-course *fugu* meal, available from November to February for $210.

★**Nobu** 105 Hudson St at Franklin St (212-219-0500). Subway: 1 to Franklin St. Mon–Fri 11:45am–2:15pm, 5:45–10:15pm; Sat, Sun 5:45–10:15pm. Average sushi dinner: $32; omakase *tasting menu: $100 and up.* Since opening in 1994, the original Nobu

High times
MEGU delivers a thrilling dining experience.

Japanese

has promised impeccable fish and serious stargazing—and it still delivers both: luscious fluke sashimi with crunchy, salty bits of dried miso at your table, Martha Stewart at the next. While chef Nobu Matsuhisa and his partners have taken Nobu worldwide, they've left this Tribeca mainstay in its slightly weathered but beloved form. Even regulars struggle to choose from the more than 40 cold and hot dishes before the umpteen sushi and tempura options. Many composed dishes, like yellowtail tartare and the ever-popular miso cod, are surefire winners; others, like extratangy salmon skin salad, aren't. Pick a few, then design your dream sushi platter—or just order the *omakase*. **Other locations** *Nobu 57, 40 W 57th St between Fifth and Sixth Aves (212-757-3000)* ● *Next Door Nobu, 105 Hudson St at Franklin St (212-334-4445).*

▲**Omen** *113 Thompson St between Prince and Spring Sts (212-925-8923). Subway: N, R, W to Prince St; 6 at Spring St; C, E to Spring St. Daily 6pm–midnight. Average main course: five-course prix fixe: $60.* Don't expect ramen and rolls. Master chef Norio Shinohara turns Japanese cuisine on its head at this low-profile spot with high-art eats. Raw quail eggs quiver on tuna tartare; watermelon sorbet crowns shrimp and asparagus; salmon arrives in the shape of a swollen rose; and black codfish, its bone-white flesh marinated in miso, rests on a bright-green bamboo leaf. The brick-walled dining room is spare but for the exquisite MoMA-worthy lamps wrapped in billowing white paper, and you'll frequently spot Omen fan Yoko Ono sitting under their glow at one of the wooden tables. As for imbibing, the choice is clear: sake. Each is helpfully listed by its alleged "properties"—try the smooth "Seduction," then find someone to test it out on.

▲◑**Oms/b** *156 E 45th St between Lexington and Third Aves (212-922-9768). Subway: 42nd St S, 4, 5, 6, 7 to 42nd St–Grand Central. Mon–Fri 8am–7:30pm; Sat 11:30am–5pm. Average main course: $8.* The name is pronounced "omusubi," and it refers to the Japanese stuffed rice ball that serves the same purpose as a sandwich: It's a starchy, satisfying, portable meal. The 14-seat restaurant's nori-wrapped, palm-size triangles of rice are packed with tasty fillings (pickles, bonito flakes, pastrami). Grab a few of these and you'll have a healthful, original lunch for less than five bucks. Or order a deal of three rice balls, a small appetizer and a cup of miso soup for about the same price as a fast-food combo.

Pearl on the Sushi *695 Ninth Ave at 48th St (212-977-8809). Subway: C, E to 50th St. Mon–Thu, Sun noon–11:30pm; Fri, Sat noon–midnight. Average sushi roll (six pieces): $7.* Pearl has a fan base of locals and off-the-clock chefs, and while there's not much to speak of for decor (a collection of sand dollars, starfish and other seashells is stuck on the wall), the food is remarkable. Special rolls, like one with strawberry cream cheese and roe wrapped with salmon, are built with explosive textures and flavors. The lobster roll looks nothing like the Maine variety: The salad is laced with wasabi and spicy mayo, bundled in rice and cut into 12 thick slabs. The Sunshine Roll—the winner of the bunch—is inside out, with a salmon center and a shell of avocado and fresh mango. Thick milk shakes and smoothies in flavors like honeydew or green tea make a fine dessert.

Quickly Shabu Shabu *237B Grand St between Bowery and Chrystie St (212-431-0998). Subway: B, D to Grand St; J, M, Z to Bowery. Daily*

10am–11pm. Average main course: $13. This Chinatown shop's unassuming Grand Street facade gives way to unexpected futurism: soft orange booths and hanging globes. The shabu-shabu consumed underneath is an adventure in experimentation, and among the city's best. Patrons cook their meals in a hot pot at their table, using top-notch ingredients such as mini fillets of pork and chicken. The attentive waitstaff will prepare a dipping sauce if you look helpless enough. Best of all is the wide range of designer bubble teas, free with the meal.

Restaurant Ichimura *1026 Second Ave between 54th and 55th Sts (212-355-3557). Subway: E, V to Lexington Ave–53rd St; 6 to 51st St. Mon–Fri 6pm–1am; Sat 5–11pm. Average sushi meal (eight pieces, one roll): $28.* A long sushi bar dominates the sleek white-walled room, and on most nights regulars have reserved their seats (one doctor comes so often a table bears a silver reservation card with his name on it). You'll hear more Japanese spoken than English. While there's an extensive list of à la carte sushi, the specialty is the *omakase*, or chef's choice ($75 to $120), a series of numerous fine-tuned minicourses all determined by chef Eiji Ichimura. The meal is exclusively fish, such as bright-orange disks of creamy monkfish liver, buttery-soft fatty-tuna sushi or fried tilefish and grilled salmon. Premium sakes served in pretty frosted glasses help take the edge off the pricey tab.

Rosanjin *141 Duane St between Church St and West Broadway (212-346-0664). Subway: A, C, 1, 2, 3 to Chambers St. Mon 5:30–10pm; Tue–Sat 11:30am–2pm, 5:30–10pm; Sun 11:30am–2pm. Omakase: $150 per person.* An intimate, swank dining room awaits those who come to indulge in the ultimate form of Kyoto-style *kaiseki:* a two-and-a-half-hour, eight-course dining experience. Unfortunately, an illuminated chiseled-rock wall and luxe seating arrangements (there are but seven tables) do nothing to mitigate the $150 per person price tag; that is the responsibility of the elaborate meal itself, and it comes up short. The tiny courses are hit-and-miss: A dollop of sea urchin in the opener can be both too cold and oddly flavorless, but an artful tower of sashimi several plates later is flawless. A dessert of vanilla ice cream and fruit is too plain for inclusion in what ought to be a medley of delightful surprises.

Sachiko's on Clinton *25 Clinton St between Houston and Stanton Sts (212-253-2900). Subway: F to Delancey St; J, M, Z to Delancey–Essex Sts. Daily 6pm–1am. Average main course: $20.* It's no longer enough to simply open a Japanese restaurant and serve great sushi. New Yorkers expect something more, and Sachiko's delivers. This petite downtown eatery woos beverage snobs with rare sake imported from the 850-year-old Japanese producer Sudo Honke. Design-savvy locals appreciate its bright-orange walls, minimalist concrete-and-bamboo garden and sliding wood screens for private dining areas. And food lovers dig the first-rate fresh fish at the sushi bar, soba dishes and *kushiage* skewers of deep-fried fish and vegetables.

Sakura Café *388 Fifth Ave between 6th and 7th Sts , Park Slope, Brooklyn (718-832-2970). Subway: F, M, R to Fourth Ave–9th St. Mon–Sat 5–11pm; Sun 5–10pm. Average main course: $12.* Everything at this traditional Japanese restaurant is light, delicate and gentle—the decor, the food, even the service. Owner Fumiko Akiyama has outfitted the place with a cherrywood bar, green bamboo floors and handmade

Show men
Austere little Aki focuses
on Japanese fusion.

pendant lights. And although Tokyo-trained chef Shinji Nishikawa doesn't take many risks, he balances flavors every step of the way. A salad of cool crab and cucumber, for example, is a play of sweet and salty flavors, brought to life with a soy-spiked mayonnaise; grilled black cod gets a *yuzu*-soy glaze; and the sushi, flown in from Japan, features creative rolls like the Sakura, a tight wrap of smoked salmon, avocado and—surprise—mango. A three-glass sake sampler should get you through at least half the meal.

Sasabune NY *401 E 73rd St at First Ave (212-249-8583). Subway: 6 to 77th St. Mon–Fri noon–2pm, 5:30–10:30pm; Sat 5:30–10:30pm. Average omakase: $75.* The only menu is for drinks, as the sushi prepared at the tiny sister of a popular Los Angeles sushi spot is governed entirely by the whim of the chef's *omakase.* Nothing to fear (except maybe the wasabi—note that they use the much spicier real stuff). Sasabune's *omakase* is a party of fresh seafood chef Kenji Takahashi finds each morning at the New Fulton Fish Market. He and his team dole out raw numbers, from favorites like salmon or yellowtail to more obscure sea creatures including bonito in a spicy-sweet homemade sweet soy sauce and black cod in an eel sauce you'll want to mop up with your fingers.

▲**Shabu-Tatsu** *216 E 10th St between First and Second Aves (212-477-2972). Subway: L to First Ave. Mon–Thu, Sun 5–11:30pm; Fri, Sat 5pm–1:45am. Average main course: $20.* Join the neighborhood regulars—and demonstrate your chef skills—at this tiny barbecue spot. Gathering around bubbling hot pots and grills built into smooth wooden booths is as much a social event as a meal. Simmer your dinner shabu-shabu-

style in salty seaweed broth. (Sesame sauce and lemon soy sauce add a welcome zing to what could otherwise be bland boiled beef and vegetables.) For a spicier experience, use the grill *yakiniku*-style for meat flavored in spicy bean paste or mustard sauce. All dinners come with a salad, rice, tea and ice cream.

▲♥**Snacky** *187 Grand St between Bedford and Driggs Aves, Williamsburg, Brooklyn (718-486-4848). Subway: L to Bedford Ave. Mon–Thu 6pm–1am; Fri, Sat 6pm–4am; Sun 6pm–midnight. Average small plate: $4.* In the tiny sake bar–dining room, a postpunk soundtrack plays while chefs behind the scenes assemble tasty small plates. Entrées in miniature are nothing new, but rarely are they so perfectly complete: Salty-sweet sesame noodles, quesadillalike-crabmeat wontons and cold silken tofu form a sizable yet delicate meal. Grilled eel is so tender that the lightly seasoned meat easily separates from its fatty skin. If you don't take your sake straight up, an ice-cold Coconutzu Freeze (a sake-based piña colada) provides a high-voltage brain freeze.

▲**SobaKoh** *309 E 5th St between First and Second Aves (212-254-2244). Subway: F, V to Lower East Side–Second Ave. Tue–Fri 5:30–10:45pm; Sat, Sun noon–3pm, 5–10:45pm. Average main course: $14.* New York's prized noodle joints have taught us to be picky about what we slurp, and one more has arrived to do the same. At Soba Koh, chef-owner Hiromitsu Takahashi makes soba noodles fresh daily from organic buckwheat. They are served hot, in a rich broth, or cold, either with a dipping sauce or in fusiony creations like soba "risotto" with crab, shiitake and ginkgo nuts. But it's not all soba here: You'll also find steamed egg custard with

Tailspin
Izakaya Ten reels 'em in
with Japanese pub grub.

TALIA SIMHI

sea urchin and *shiso*-marinated grilled quail. The stark, bright dining room is open only for dinner, but you can watch the noodle-making process between noon and 3pm every day but Monday.

★▲**Soto** *357 Sixth Ave between Washington Pl and W 4th St (212-414-3088). Subway: A, C, E, B, D, F, V to W 4th St. Mon–Sat 5:45–11:45pm. Average main course: $18.* Sushi master Sotohiro Kosugi has been quietly working wonders behind an unmarked white facade on a congested stretch of lower Sixth Avenue. The hidden blond-wood dining room is an appropriately reverential setting for some of the most inspired—and visually stunning—raw fish in town. However, the restaurant's real *raison d'être* is its daily-changing menu of cooked and raw shareable plates. Lush toro tartare, topped with avocado coulis and a caviar *quenelle*, warrants a pilgrimage, as does a tower layering cool lobster meat and sea urchin mousse within a wall of lotus root slices. Petals of raw Long Island fluke, brushed with a bracing yuzu-lime dressing, are sliced so thin they're translucent. Even simple fried fish is raised here to the level of art.

▲⊖**Soy** *102 Suffolk St between Delancey and Rivington Sts (212-253-1158). Subway: F to Delancey St; J, M, Z to Delancey–Essex Sts. Mon–Fri noon–10:30pm; Sat 5–11pm. Average main course: $8.* Etsko Kizawa has a passion: to educate New Yorkers on the virtues of Japanese home cooking, in all its soyful glory. Try her miso soup full of vegetables, or a plate of *nikujaga*, a beef-and-potato stew. Specialties include a deep-fried tofu Treasure Sack stuffed with vegetables, and a seaweed salad with carrots and shiitake mushrooms. Chocolate-red-bean- or green-tea-tofu pudding goes down smooth as silk. If you can't score a table in the sparely decorated storefront, get a fresh-fruit soy smoothie to go.

▲**Sugiyama** *251 W 55th St between Broadway and Eighth Ave (212-956-0670). Subway: A, C, B, D, 1 to 59th St–Columbus Circle. Tue–Sat 5:30–11:45pm. Kaiseki dinner: $45–150.* First-timers expecting a hushed temple of *kaiseki* may be surprised to find Nao Sugiyama's casual café, where expense-account businessmen cluster in booths and "I just flew in from Aspen on my jet" types perch at the food bar. If you're ready to splurge, order Chef Nao's Choices (an eight-course modern kaiseki for $100). Sugiyama shows his genius in endless combinations, and gleefully answers questions about the tiny *sawagani* crab sitting on your plate or the cocktail of uni and mountain-yam foam in mirin-spiked dashi. Switching from raw to cooked and light to heavy to light again, dinner runs from a creamy sea-urchin-and-tofu "pâté" to an intensely grapefruity "wine jelly" finish. Call ahead for vegetarian *kaiseki*.

Sui *54 Spring St between Lafayette and Mulberry Sts (212-965-9838). Subway: B, D, F, V to Broadway–Lafayette St; 6 to Bleecker St. Mon–Thu noon–3pm, 5–11:30pm; Fri noon–3pm, 5pm–1:30am; Sat 5pm–1:30am; Sun 5–11:00pm. Average main course: $20.* Eel and cheese sounds like a freaky combination but…it's delicious. The Eeler owes its success to the cheese: The fresh mozzarella is warm and milky, and makes a lovely match for the succulent eel. The entire menu (which has French flourishes) is an exercise in creative combinations: toro tartare with truffle oil, salmon rolls with dill and apple, *panko*-crusted tuna in coconut-curry sauce, and more eel…with goat cheese. Service is leisurely—good if you're happy to linger in the serene, minimalist space,

but bad if you prefer your entrée piping hot. Unlike many too-cool fusion spots, Sui's portions are huge, so you can actually get full here. Try to remember that you must squeeze in the sweet apple spring rolls and a pot of one of the beautifully described teas.

★▲**Sumile Sushi** *154 W 13th St between Sixth and Seventh Aves (212-989-7699). Subway: F, V, 1, 2, 3 to 14th St; L to Sixth Ave. Tue–Thu 5:30–10:30pm; Fri, Sat 5:30–11pm. Ten-piece sushi dinner: $35.* Japanese-French eatery Sumile has gone the sushi route. Chef Josh DeChellis still heads the kitchen, but the new bill of fare will be largely unrecognized by fans of the once-imaginative restaurant (thankfully, the egg custard with duck confit has not been plucked from the menu). The raw fish is all right by neighborhood standards, and the ten-piece sushi dinner, if not stellar, is priced competitively. The former drinking area has been converted into a sushi bar, but the modern, chapel-like dining room remains fundamentally the same.

▲**Sushi of Gari** *402 E 78th St between First and York Aves (212-517-5340). Subway: 6 to 77th St. Tue–Sat 5–10:45pm; Sun 5–9:45pm. Average main course: $28.* While many neighborhood Japanese joints serve sushi rolls with wacky names, Sushi of Gari chef Masatoshi Sugio prefers to play with unusual ingredients and oddball combinations. Adventurous eaters brave long lines to cram into his small place and order a sushi tasting menu (Gari's Choice) that runs between $70 and $80. Sugio has been known to pair seared foie gras with daikon radish; salmon with tomato and onion; and spicy tuna with mayo, Tabasco and sesame oil. Less adventurous souls can order regular sushi and sashimi—which are supremely fresh, if not especially memorable—or hot dishes like *negimaki*, teriyaki, tempura, udon, soba and dumplings. If you want sashimi, pay the extra $13 for the "special" version, which swaps in exotic fishes for the usual tuna and yellowtail. **Other location** *Sushi of Gari 46, 347 W 46th St between Eighth and Ninth Aves (212-957-0046).*

▲**Sushi Samba** *245 Park Ave South between 19th and 20th Sts (212-475-9377). Subway: 6 to 23rd St. Mon–Wed noon–1am; Thu–Sat noon–2am; Sun 1pm–midnight. Average main course: $21. Average sushi meal (seven pieces, one roll): $24.* It's rare to retain New York cred after half a decade, but Sushi Samba continues to pack 'em in, thanks to top-notch cocktails and an innovative menu fusing Japanese, Brazilian and Peruvian cuisines. Traditional sushi and sashimi are available, as are South American–style meats, but the real fun is where the cultures cross. Ceviche consists of bites of sashimi splashed with citrus juices. Chilean sea bass is marinated in miso, and sushi rolls come with ingredients such as mango and a wild concoction called "barbecue mayonnaise." Live DJs and a rooftop garden at the downtown branch draw a younger crowd than the Park Avenue location, but the lively music and '60s-mambo-craze–inspired design at both spots ensure a scene no matter where you are. **Other location** *Sushi Samba 7, 87 Seventh Ave South at Barrow St (212-691-7885).*

▲**Sushi Seki** *1143 First Ave between 62nd and 63rd Sts (212-371-0238). Subway: F to Lexington Ave–63rd St. Mon–Sat 5:30pm–2:30am. Average omakase: $50.* At this respected Japanese restaurant, the service is as valued as the food. The knowledgeable staff can describe each item on the unconventional *omakase* menu: Fresh yellowtail is spiked with tiny slices of jalapeño and the tender sautéed scallops are drizzled with a spicy, creamy fish-roe mayonnaise. Cooked dishes, such as a moist Chilean sea bass with a light, spicy black-bean sauce, also suggest a deft touch. Thirty different sakes and a kitchen open until 2:30am make this a popular spot for late-night gourmands and off-the-clock chefs in the know.

Sushi Yasuda *204 E 43rd St between Second and Third Aves (212-972-1001). Subway: 42nd St S, 4, 5, 6, 7 to 42nd St–Grand Central. Mon–Fri noon–2:15pm, 6–10:15pm; Sat 6–10:pm. Average sushi meal (eight pieces, half roll): $20.* The culinary equivalent of observing Buddhist monks at prayer, this all-bamboo space seems to absorb the day's stresses. Be sure to make a reservation to sit with the master chef, who happily chatters with guests while surprising them with an array of market-fresh fish. This is a heaven for lovers of the raw stuff; flavors of the seafood aren't masked by baser Americanized combos (no California rolls here). Start with the lovely and light fishbone-stock miso soup and four different types of eel. Be sure to try a piece of the dessert-sweet egg-custard sushi——a surefire palate tickler.

☺**Tebaya** *144 W 19th St between Sixth and Seventh Aves (212-924-3335). Subway: 1 to 18th St; F, V to 23rd St. Daily 11:30am–11pm. Average main course: $5.* You won't find any blue-cheese dressing in this house of chicken wings. This specialty shop does wings Japanese-style: sesame-sprinkled and delicately fried. Owner Hoi Bang, who has worked in sushi restaurants around the city, inherited a passion for poultry from his family; they run a chicken wing shop in Nagoya, Japan. If wings aren't your thing, a chicken *katsu* sandwich might hit the spot. Any order can—and should—be bulked up with potemochi: creamy-centered discs of crisp potatoes topped with a dollop of butter and house-made miso sauce.

★**Tomoe Sushi** *172 Thompson St between Bleecker and Houston Sts (212-777-9346). Subway: 1 to Houston St. Mon 5–11pm; Wed–Sat 1–3pm, 5–11pm. Average sushi meal (8 pieces, half roll): $22.* Why the inevitable line outside for a cramped table in Tomoe's small dining room in the sushi-saturated Village? The consistent freshness of the sushi and the range of the à la carte menu (boasting five different types of roe among its school of 31 fish) has earned Tomoe an unimpeachable reputation, but it's appetizer specials like the sumptuous fried soft shell crab in *ponzu* sauce or the banana tempura—all announced on sheets of paper taped to the

---

Read 'em & eat

ponzu: (*ponju* or *ponsu*) a tart dipping sauce of lemon juice, soy sauce, mirin and dried bonito flakes

tataki: a dish of thinly sliced beef or tuna seared very rare in hot oil

udon: soft, thick wheat noodles, typically served in a soup

yakitori: a dish of chicken marinated in soy sauce, sugar and sake, placed on skewers and broiled or grilled

---

white walls—that lure in-the-know diners. Be sure to pass the word on to the line as you leave.

Toraya *300 E 52nd St between First and Second Aves (212-838-4351). Subway: E, V to Lexington Ave–53rd St; 6 to 51st St. Mon–Sat 6–10:30pm. Omakase: $45–$50.* Chef Isamu Soumi's menu is a winning combination of traditional fare from the Niigata prefecture, north of Tokyo, and his own flights of fancy. The prix-fixe dinner changes roughly every two weeks. You might poke your chopsticks into a bowl of *oshitashi* (steamed spinach), then nibble on fried sardines wrapped around smooth tofu and paired with sweet pickled-plum sauce. Fish preparations, such as steamed tilefish topped with creamy wasabi, are phenomenal. Tiny as it is (only nine people can sit at the downstairs counter, and another handful at two tables in the upstairs tatami room), Toraya draws a steady clientele of Japanese professionals.

Ushi Wakamaru *136 W Houston St between MacDougal and Sullivan Sts (212-228-4181). Subway: A, C, E, B, D, F, V to W 4th St. Mon–Sat 6pm–midnight. Average main course: $15.* It's no surprise that Japan-philes flock to this austere sliver of a restaurant: Those new to the cuisine might not know what to make of the tiny cube of green-tea tofu that's served as an *amuse-bouche*, or might blanch at the shrimp heads in the miso soup. Entrées feature classic maki (no Elvis roll here), sushi and sashimi, and little else. Put yourself in the hands of chef-owner Hideo Kuribara and you'll be richly rewarded. A special might include sushi pieces topped with burstingly fresh salmon roe, the choicest slice of fatty tuna or a generous mound of shredded, fresh crab. Kuribara's attention to quality and detail is ferocious: The wasabi is real (a rare luxury), and the intensely flavored, almost bitter, green-tea ice cream is house-made.

☺**Yakitori Totto** *251 W 55th St between Broadway and Eighth Ave (212-245-4555). Subway: A, C, B, D, 1 to 59th St–Columbus Circle.. Mon–Thu 5:30pm–1am; Fri 5:30pm–2am; Sat 5:30pm–2am; Sun 5:30pm–midnight. Average small plate: $3.* Come dinnertime, there's often a wait for a table or a seat at the L-shaped bar, which wraps around the open kitchen where a bandana-clad chef grills skewers treats over charcoal. Though there are veggie options, meat is big here. A dedicated Japanese after-work crowd scarfs down the juicy kobe beef tongue, delicious chicken hearts and other innards. Japanese standards, like *onigiri* (balls of rice stuffed with salmon, pickled plum or cod roe) and juicy gyoza (pork dumplings with crisp skins) are fine choices as well. If you're in the mood for something raw, try the *takowasa*, a tiny bowl of slippery octopus infused with wasabi.

Yamato *168 Seventh Ave between Garfield Pl and 1st St, Park Slope, Brooklyn (718-840-0099). Subway: F to Seventh Ave. Mon–Thu noon–3pm, 5–11pm; Fri noon–3pm, 5pm–midnight; Sat 1pm– midnight; Sun 1–11pm. Average main course: $18.* A little slice of East Village cool transplanted to Park Slope, Yamato offers appealing menu of straightforward sushi and fusion maki, served in a sleek dining room with chartreuse walls and slate floors. Mozzarella meets salmon in the Topo roll; the Yamato contains crisp fried eel, avocado and mango. An appetizer of pan-seared scallops with black-truffle oil and jalapeño vinaigrette is tender and tantalizing, but on the whole, the raw is better than the cooked.

Korean

See also: *Asian, Japanese*

Counter culture
Try the scallion pancakes and short-rib *kalbi* at Kori.

Bann *350 W 50th St at Ninth Ave (212-582-4446). Subway: C, E to 50th St. Mon–Fri 11:30am–2:30pm, 5:30–10pm; Sat, Sun noon–10:30pm. Average main course: $22.* For those who love to watch meat sizzle, Bann (from Woo Lae Oak owner Young Choi) is a boon to the midtown restaurant scene. The Korean barbecue features a hefty plate of thinly sliced chicken, fish, beef or pork ready for grilling in the center of the table, with accompanying kimchi for another dimension of flavor. The prepared dishes are invariably prettier: oyster tempura, for example, is served on a giant starfish. The "Tropical Snow" dessert is a tower of coconut ice cream surrounded by sweet beans and fruit jellies topped with raspberry coulis, crème anglaise and purple yams and set upon shaved coconut ice in a bowl made of ice.'

Bonbon Chicken *98 Chambers St between Broadway and Church St (212-227-2375). Subway: A, C, 1, 2, 3 to Chambers St. Mon–Sat 11am–10pm; Sun noon–9pm. Small chicken: $7.* Think Asian-style KFC at this downtown Korean fried-chicken spot. Choose from small, medium or large portions of wings, drumsticks or tiny boneless breast strips, and one of two sauces (tangy soy-garlic or a not-so-spicy spicy). In a concealed kitchen, the chicken is dredged in a light coating of flour, and deep-fried not once, but twice to order. When your bird is ready, a metal door swings open and out slides a cute bag that contains your hot meat, some middling Asian slaw and a sweet—but cold—buttered roll. Chow at one of four communal tables, take it to go, or have it delivered.

Bori Gogae *40-10 Union St between 41st and Roosevelt Aves (718-888-1644). Subway: Subway: 7 to Flushing–Main St. Mon–Sat 7am–9pm. Average main*

course: $5. Jewish mothers might panic at learning there's a new chicken soup in town, ladled out with a smile and very nearly as nourishing as their own. This tiny Korean takeout spot of barely a couple of tables specializes in *juk*, the thickened rice porridge that works like a salve for many a homesick Asian. The several varieties include chicken, pine nut and, our favorite, lima bean. None are especially zesty (drop a few slices of pungent daikon pickle slices on top) but they're certainly smooth and comforting. And that's all this place is about.

▲**Choga** *145 Bleecker St between La Guardia Pl and Thompson St, second floor (212-598-5946). Subway: A, C, E, B, D, F, V to W 4th St. Mon–Thu, Sun 11am–midnight; Fri, Sat 11am–3am. Average main course: $17.* Korean and Japanese food are prepared equally well at this hip little spot (and the kitchen stays open late). Enjoy fresh raw octopus and cucumber splashed with a tangy ponzu sauce; hot, crisp panfried dumplings are perfect for dunking in nutty soy-sesame dip. Cocktails include Asian flavors as well, like the choga-ginseng (ginseng wine, plum wine and peppermint sprigs) and the choga-politan, made with soju , Midori, Cointreau and fresh lime. The sweet back room is perfect for small private parties.

★▲**Do Hwa** *55 Carmine St at Bedford St (212-414-2815). Subway: 1 to Houston St. Mon–Thu noon–11pm; Fri noon–midnight; Sat 5pm–midnight; Sun 5–10pm. Average main course: $19.* It's no surprise to find homestyle fare with Pan-Asian flair here—one co-owner is executive chef Myung Ja Kwak, who, with design-guru daughter Jenny, opened Dok Suni's and helped ignite a nouveau-Korean trend. In fact, Jenny's

IMOGEN BROWN

Korean

Side dish

Get cookin'

Half the allure of eating Korean is in grilling it yourself.

There are few things more nerve-racking than not knowing what you're doing when there's fire involved. But cooking *bulgogi*, thinly sliced, marinated and boneless rib eye; *kalbi*, or short ribs; and other Korean protein-packed dishes at your table can be a simple, fun affair, sure to win over the pickiest of carnivores. Just follow these steps to ensure that your meal—not to mention you—won't get burned. If you can't handle the heat of DIY barbecue, you can always ask your server to have the kitchen do the work.

•**It's better to share** One order of barbecue should be enough for two people, particularly when preceded by appetizers such *pajun* (scallion pancakes) and *mandoo* (dumplings).

•**Fire in the hole** Most Seoul-food spots feature gas grills built into the tables and ceiling vents, which will spirit smoke. Your waiter or waitress will light the grill, adjust the heat (don't attempt this yourself) and usually place your meat and vegetables on the sizzling surface. Though servers at places such as Kum Gang San or Korea Palace will tend your barbecue throughout the entire process and even serve you, it's not considered rude to take matters into your own hands. But folks manning the grill should be ready to dole out cooked items immediately—cuts tend to be razor-thin and not as delicious when covered in carbon.

•**Bundle up** To properly enjoy Korean barbecue, make a small parcel—not a Chipotle-sized burrito—of protein, rice and sauce in a lettuce leaf (served with the meal), which you can devour in one bite. Rip a piece of lettuce in half widthwise with your hands. Next, using your chopsticks, add a scoop of rice, meat and other traditional accompaniments such as fermented bean paste, shredded scallion, sliced jalapeños and kimchi. Some dishes arrive with raw garlic cloves, which you can roast on the grill. *Banchan*, the side dishes that accompany every Korean meal, should be enjoyed separately from your barbecue.

sister Moon Sun is Do Hwa's pastry chef. Classic dishes continue to please, whether or not you've cooked them yourself (some tables have built-in barbecues). Newer items include *duk boki*, sticky-rice cakes sautéed with vegetables in a red-pepper sauce. The movie-poster covers on the menus are a shout-out to the other co-owner, Quentin Tarantino.

▲**Dok Suni's** *119 First Ave between St. Marks Pl and E 7th St (212-477-9506). Subway: L to First Ave; 6 to Astor Pl. Mon 4:30pm–11pm; Tue–Fri 4:30–midnight; Sat noon–midnight; Sun noon–11pm.. Average main course: $14.* Vintage Korean newspapers plastered on the walls, a hip downtown crowd and Asian-inflected cocktails make this venerable East Village kimchi palace a more stylish cousin to 32nd Street and Flushing's Seoul-food joints. Though Dok Suni's tables lack grills, the menu's barbecued offerings are excellent and spare you from reeking of charred meat: A sweet chili-pepper sauce enlivens broiled chicken and juicy, garlicky pork ribs rival any Texan-style rack. If you need time to digest your feast, polite servers let you linger as long as you like over free glasses of postmeal persimmon tea.

Han Bat *53 W 35th St between Fifth and Sixth Aves (212-629-5588). Subway: B, D, F, V, N, Q, R, W to 34th St–Herald Sq. Daily 24hrs. Average main course: $14.* If you like Korean but aren't into grilling your own, 24-hour Han Bat is your spot: There's no grilling at the table: Your work is on the front end, figuring out what to order. The menu isn't logically divided into courses, so the descriptions are indispensable—and often intriguing. You'll just have to order dishes like *Sam Gye Tang*: "The Body Cavity of a Small Chicken Is Stuffed with Glutinous Rice, Young Ginseng Shoots and Jujubes."

▲**Korea Palace** *127 E 54th St between Park and Lexington Aves (212-832-2350). Subway: E, V to Lexington Ave–53rd St; 6 to 51st St. Mon–Fri 11:30am–10:30pm; Sat 4:30–10:30pm. Average main course: $20.* To the strains of a pianist whose repertoire includes both Chopin's Nocturne in D flat and Journey's "Open Arms," Korea Palace serves seafood stews and grilled-at-table meats, as well as the imposing Royal Table d'Hôte, a 12- to 15-course tasting menu ($60 to $70; one-day advance notice required). The mild broth of *duk mandoo gook* brims with meat dumplings and slivers of rice cake; for something racier, try *doenjang chigae*, a spicy squid soup. At the end, you'll be glad you didn't let the snarling stone tigers by the entrance scare you away.

▲**Kori** *253 Church St between Franklin and Leonard Sts (212-334-0908). Subway: 1 to Franklin St. Mon–Fri noon–3pm, 5:30–11pm; Sat 5:30–11:30pm. Average main course: $16.* Chef-owner Kori Kim serves dressed-up but unfussy fare in a cool space: high ceilings, orange walls warmed by candlelight and grooving world beats. The traditional *pajun* (scallion pancake) is hot, crisp, and filled with tender squid and shrimp—a fine complement to Kim's duck-and-cabbage salad. Short-rib *kalbi* are marinated in a citrusy Asian-pear-and-soy puree, then grilled to smoky tenderness. For dessert, try *goguma*, delicate fried Korean sweet potato drizzled with ginseng syrup.

Kum Gang San *138-28 Northern Blvd at Union St, Flushing, Queens (718-461-0909). Subway: 7 to Flushing–Main St. Daily 24 hours. Average main course price: $20.* There's no white piano perched atop

Korean

a fake waterfall here, but what this sprawling Flushing BBQ outpost loses in tacky grandeur compared with its Manhattan cousin, it gains with service and consistency. The marinated meat, grilled at your table, remains a justifiable draw (particularly the house-special *kalbi*, heavy on garlic), but the big surprise is a supple, tangy octopus, stir-fried with onions, noodles and pepper sauce. As to be expected, the after–after-party crowd can be boisterous; bring a loud group of your own. **Other location** *49 W 32nd St at Broadway (212-967-0909).*

★**Momofuku Ssäm Bar** *2007 Eat Out Award, Critics' Pick: Most hypeworthy 207 Second Ave at 13th St (212-254-3500). Subway: L to First, Third Aves; Daily 11am–2am. Average main course: $16.* Momofuku Ssäm Bar Chef David Chang's latest feels like two restaurants fused into one: a Korean Chipotle, and a self-aware joint serving designer ham and pricey platters. Waiters hustle to noisy rock music in this 50-seat space, which feels like Megu compared with its predecessor's crowded counter dining. Chefs create concoctions priced to sample, including the wonderfully fatty pork-belly steamed bun with hoisin sauce and cucumbers, and the house *ssäm* (Korean for "wrap"), which might be the finest burrito in the city. Chang flirts with watch-your-wallet territory: $115 for a 32-ounce rib eye and $180 for a hog butt feeding six to eight, served with a dozen oysters.

New York Kom Tang Soot Bul Kalbi

32 W 32nd St between Fifth Ave and Broadway (212-947-8482). Subway: B, D, F, V, N, Q, R, W to 34th St–Herald Sq. Mon–Sat 24hrs. Average main course: $15. Tender *kalbi* (barbecued short ribs) are indeed the stars here; their signature smoky flavor comes from being cooked over *soot bul* (wood chips). The city's oldest Korean restaurant also makes crisp, seafood-laden *haemool pajun* (pancakes); sweet, juicy *yuk hwe* (raw beef salad); and garlicky *bulgogi*. *Kom tang*, or "bear soup," is a milky beef broth that's deep and soothing.

Seoul Soondae *158-15 Northern Blvd at 158th Street, Flushing, Queens (718-321-3231). Subway: 7 to Flushing–Main St. Daily 10:30am–2am. Average main course price: $8.95.* While there is a full menu of other dishes—including an exceptional version of *jaeyuk boekum* (spicy sautéed pork loin)—*soondae*, the house specialty at this spacious and attractive Flushing spot, is the main draw. Described on the menu as "nourishing Korean sausage," the dense black sausage, fashioned

Read 'em & eat

bibimbap: rice topped with a variety of vegetables

bulgogi: boneless, grilled, marinated beef

kalbi: spare ribs, marinated and barbecued

kimchi: (also *kimchee*) various pickled vegetable and chilies

pajun: a scallion pancake

soju: (also *shoju*) a strong Korean vodka

from pig's blood and potato vermicelli, may strike the uninitiated as oddly bland but the restaurant's almost entirely Korean clientele loves them. Virtually every diner here orders soondae, simply grilled or sautéed at the table with pig's intestine and a heap of shredded vegetables.

⊙▲**Shin Po** *146-13 Northern Blvd at 146th St, Flushing, Queens (718-939-8400). Subway: 7 to Main Street–Flushing. Mon–Thu, Sun 10:30–2am; Fri, Sat 10:30am–3am. Average main course price: $10.* While this bright and cheerful Korean diner's most popular dishes are pictured in life-sized photos plastered on the walls, it's soon apparent that dumplings are Shin Po's main draw. The pork-filled specimens that emerge from the kitchen—available steamed as a starter or deep-fried and dropped into an entrée noodle soup— are exceptionally juicy and plump. Vegetarians will find respite in the meatless selection of cold noodle dishes, among them a fine plate of thin buckwheat noodles with hot chili paste and a whole garden's worth of raw shredded veggies.

Won Jo *23 W 32nd St between Fifth Ave and Broadway (212-695-5815). Subway: B, D, F, V, N, Q, R, W to 34th St–Herald Sq. Daily 24hrs. Average main course: $19.* The appeal of this huge K-town joint is simple: The food is first-class. What reads on the menu like a basic sautéed fish is actually a plateful of meaty morsels of mackerel in a peppery soy sauce. Intensely spicy *yuk gae jang* is laden with thin slices of tender beef, seaweed and cellophane noodles. Other standards are solid, such as *pajun* (savory pancakes), *kalbi* (braised short ribs) and *mandoo* (dumplings). Explore the daunting zillion-page menu and you'll likely find more treasures.

▲**Woo Chon** *8–10 W 36th St between Fifth and Sixth Aves (212-695-0676). Subway: B, D, F, V, N, Q, R, W to 34th St–Herald Sq. Mon–Sat 10:30am–2:30am; Sun 10:30am–1am. Average main course: $20.* Though it lacks the glitz and bustle of similar spots located on Koreatown's main drag, this humble haunt offers equally authentic fare in a bi-level space adorned with faded scrolls and dark-wood tables. Come hungry: Free rice cakes stewed in chili sauce and edamame are followed by a flotilla of fresh *banchan*—the small side dishes which accompany Korean meals. Skip the sushi page of its extensive menu for a Seoul-style feast of homey fried beef-and-pork dumplings, thinly sliced brisket that you cook on a tabletop grill and a gratis dessert of fresh fruit.

▲**Woo Lae Oak** *148 Mercer St between Houston and Prince Sts (212-925-8200). Subway: B, D, F, V to Broadway–Lafayette St; R, W to Prince St., 6 to Bleecker St. Mon–Thu, Sun noon–10:30pm; Fri, Sat noon–11:30pm. Average main course: $22.* At the East Coast branch of a popular L.A. restaurant, the exposed brick seems Soho, but the styling (and the size) is pure West Coast: Gauzy fabrics hang above picture-perfect flower arrangements. While the able chefs turn out a mean plate of sashimi (or, more accurately, *sang sun hwe*), the fastest movers are the colorful side dishes of spiced, pickled vegetables that begin each meal. The in-table gas grill provides surprisingly romantic date entertainment, and helps retain the communal spirit of a Korean dinner. Whether your meal is traditional (lively, filling bibimbap), nouveau (flaming giant clam) or somewhere in between (barbecued ostrich), it all goes equally well with *soju*, the national distilled liquor.

Kosher

See also: *American, Indian, Middle Eastern, Steakhouses, Vegetarian/Organic*

Singular sensation
Retreat to Solo, watched
over by in-house rabbis.

Le Marais *150 West 46th St between Sixth and Seventh Aves (212-869-0900). N, Q, R, W, S, 1, 2, 3, 7 to 42nd Street–Times Square. Sun–Thu noon–midnight; Fri noon–3pm. $29.* Relinquish what prejudices you might have against Times Square eateries to uncover this gem of a kosher French bistro/butcher's that does most things well (skip dessert) and some things superbly. Best bets are the *assiette de charcutailles*, featuring some of New York's tastiest (and expensive) beef jerky, followed by dry rubbed beef short ribs, a hunk of meat that nails the balance between melt and flavor, or a piquant steak au poivre. And while the house frites are *pas mal*, the cassoulet of seasonal vegetables will have even Gentiles observing the Sabbath.

Salut *63-42 108th St at 63rd Dr, Rego Park, Queens (718-275-6860). Subway: G, R, V to 63rd Dr–Rego Park. Mon–Thu, Sun 11am–11pm; Fri 11am–5pm; Sat 9pm–11pm. Average main course: $14.* Dinner at knifepoint is the specialty of this Uzbeki kosher kebab house, where platters piled high with cumin-tinged, skewered-and-grilled

meats constantly emerge from the bustling kitchen. Start with hot-pocket *cheburekes, mantus* (meat dumplings) and *samsas* (like samosas), or a hearty soup—and make sure to sop it up with the airy, crisp "national bread." It's easy to spot Salut's "Regostan" regulars: They're the ones sitting around irradiated-size bottles of vodka watching Russian soaps on the overhead satellite TV screen.

Solo *550 Madison Ave between 55th and 56th Sts (212-833-7800). Subway: E, V to Fifth Ave–53rd St; 6 to 51st St. Mon–Thu noon–3pm, 5–11pm; Fri noon–3pm; Sat one hour after sundown–midnight; Sun 10am–2pm, 4–10pm. Average main course: $36.* Hidden away in the the Sony Atrium is this haute cuisine kitchen, watched over by in-house rabbis. Every combination in chef Hok Chin's Asian and Mediterranean repertoire sounds beautiful and tastes equally fine. The luscious breast of duck arrives as a naked cut and inside a puff pastry, on a bed of sautéed pea shoots. Chilean sea bass comes perfectly prepared and complemented by an earthy drizzle of truffle oil. After dinner, the warm chocolate cake with chocolate sauce will leave you speechless.

☉**Taam Tov** *41 W 47th St between Fifth and Sixth Aves, second floor (212-768-8001). Subway: B, D, F, V to 47–50th Sts–Rockefeller Ctr. Mon–Thu 10am–5pm; Fri 10am–2 hours before shabbos. Average main course: $10.* Located on the second floor in a Diamond District building, Taam Tov (Hebrew for "good taste") may not be the easiest place to find, but the bustling, absurdly inexpensive Uzbek spot is well worth the search. Soups are nearly meals unto themselves: cilantro-spiked beef borscht, noodle-rich *lagman* (a beef broth with pasta and vegetables). Plates of kebabs with heaps of french fries are popular, but there are plenty of lesser-known regional specialties too, including *manti* (meat dumplings) and rice-based dishes like *plov*.

Talia's Steakhouse & Bar *668 Amsterdam Ave between 92nd and 93rd Sts (212-580-3770). Subway: 1, 2, 3 to 96th St. Mon–Thu 4:30pm–midnight; Fri noon–5pm; Sat 7pm–2am; Sun 10am–midnight. Average main course: $23.* Talia's success springs from its modesty. The menu is varied yet simple, and the food, though not cheap, is consistently good. Remember that this is a steakhouse; the grilled meats should certainly be sampled. Dim lighting, bistro decor and live music on Mondays and Saturdays make Talia's intimate enough for a date yet dignified enough for a business meeting.

☉**Zhemchuzhina Restaurant** *64-47 108th St between 64th Rd and 65th Ave, Forest Hills, Queens (718-275-2220). Subway: G, R, V to 63rd Dr–Rego Park. Sun–Thu 11am–10:30pm; Fri 11am–sundown; Sat 8pm–midnight. Average samsa: $2.* At this shoebox-size eatery, a red neon sign declares hot *samsa*. Consider this a command to order one. The dish is a benchmark of Bukharan cuisine—Central Asian Jewish food—and it's a stomach stuffer: a flaky, baseball-shaped pastry crammed with sautéed onions and minced lamb. Equally irresistible is the mashed-potato–filled *chebureki*. It's like a fried pierogi, and costs just $1.50.

Read 'em & eat

kishka: (also called *stuffed derma*) beef intestine stuffed with matzo meal, chicken fat and spices

kreplach: meat-filled dumplings served in soup

plov: rice dish with lamb, carrots and onions

KENNETH CHEN

Latin American

See also: *American Regional, Argentine, Brazilian, Caribbean, Mexican, Peruvian*

Clean lines
Savor the lively taste
of shellfish *asopado*
at organics-focused
Palo Santo.

CINZIA REALE-CASTELLO

Aces *32-07 36th Ave at 32nd St, Astoria, Queens (347-495-6991). Subway: G, R, V to 36th St; N, W to 36th Ave. Mon–Thu 5–11pm; Fri, Sat 5pm–2am; Sun 11am–4pm, 5–11pm. Average main course: $16.* To complement the pilgrimage of rent refugees to Astoria, chef-driven bistros have moved in alongside the celebrated ethnic dives. Aces is an exemplar of this new genre with a minimalist but sexy glittering red bar and shadowy dining room. Co-owner Miguel Aranda (Country, Town) concocts his own syrups and infusions for creative cocktails like cinnamon mojitos, while partner Daniel Huerta (Town, Josie's, Josephina) enlivens market-savvy cuisine with Latin American sauces (peppery mole on melting short ribs, sweet corn on luscious pan-seared scallops) and South of the Border sides (plantains, *huitlacoche*).

Boca Chica *13 First Ave at 1st St (212-473-0108). Subway: F, V to Lower East Side–Second Ave. Mon–Thu, Sun 5:30–11pm; Fri, Sat 5:30–midnight. Average main course: $13.* Latin, lively and loud, Boca Chica fits right in at the clamorous, cab-bleating crossroads at First and 1st. The zesty, garlicky *comida Latina* arrives by way of the Caribbean: crisp plantain chips with thick black bean dip; tongue-tingling shrimp ceviche; and panfried skirt steak heaped with chimichurri. The fiesta-friendly spot (witness the boisterous bachelorette and birthday parties) has leopard-print banquettes, battered, blond-wood floors and Day of the Dead wall hangings of dancing skeletons. Wet your lips with tropical tipples like mint-infused mojitos and caipirinhas to the sassy tunes of voluble (read: conversation-killing) salsa music.

Bogotá Bistro *141 Fifth Ave between Douglass and DeGraw Sts, Park Slope, Brooklyn (718-230-3805). Subway: M, R to Union St; 2, 3 to Bergen St. Mon, Wed–Thu, Sun 5–11pm; Fri, Sat 5pm–1am. Average main course: $15.* Although the place is named after a city in Colombia, the menu reaches all over South and Central America: quesadillas, arepas, empanadas, ceviche, fish tacos and skirt steak. Yes, it's a greatest-hits package, but it works: The arroz con pollo is a delicious haystack of shredded chicken with carrots, red peppers, scallions, lots of cooling cilantro and sliced avocado. There are exotic dishes, too, like smoky pork empanadas with *aji* (a hot, vinegar-spiked Colombian salsa). Think of the generous portions as Latin comfort food—all served by a cheery staff in a big, bright space with a pretty garden.

Centrico *211 West Broadway at Franklin St (212-431-0700). Subway: 1 to Franklin St. Mon–Sat 5–11pm. Average main course: $19.* Aarón Sanchez, cohost of the Food Network's *Melting Pot*, brings a deft hand to a long and inviting selection of Latin dishes. The fare is complex, such as sweet corn tarts that combine roasted tomato with a creamy-fiery blend of tomatillo and avocado. The plantains, filled with mashed smoky black beans, are lighter than you might expect plantains could be. It would be easy to order only small plates—frog legs, oysters, ceviche. But then you'd miss Centrico's great entreés, which ooze flavor, often thanks to chipotle, garlic and lime.

☉El Sitio *68-28 Roosevelt Ave at 69th St, Woodside, Queens (718-424-2369). Subway: 7 to 69th St. Daily 10am–midnight. Average main course:*

Table for one
Pasita is a perfect spot to sample bite-sized Venezuelan *pasapalos*.

Latin American

Guadalupe *597 W 207th St at Broadway (212-304-1083). Subway: A to 207th St–Washington Heights. Daily 11am–midnight. Average main course: $15.* The lofty space at this polished newcomer has a superlong bar—perfect for cultivating fans of tropical cocktails. Fresh and icy, the pulpy raspberry mojito and cloudy tamarind margarita could double as desserts. The Pan-Latin cuisine is highlighted by fish tacos with salsa verde; the tortillas are wrapped around lightly battered, deep-fried red snapper fillets. Less expensive Latino soul food is available nearby, but you won't be eating the stuff inside a fuchsia room bedecked with paintings of Christian icons and vast picture windows.

⊖**Honduras Maya** *587 Fifth Ave between Prospect Ave and 16th St, Park Slope, Brooklyn (718-965-8028). Subway: M, R to Prospect Ave. Mon–Thu, Sun 10am–9pm; Fri, Sat 10am–11pm. Average main course $8.* Crustacean lovers will have a hard time locating a better, cheaper *sopa de jaiba* (crab soup). A couple of beasties are quartered and dunked into a bowl of coconut-milk broth, and you pay only $8 for the thrill of extricating the meat from the shell and claws with your bare hands. You can warm up for your meal with *baleadas* ($3 for two), thick pancakelike tortillas folded over refried black beans, crumbled cheese and a dollop of cream. They're not on the menu, but the staff will be happy to make them for you.

★**Ideya** *349 West Broadway between Broome and Grand Sts (212-625-1441). Subway: A, C, E to Canal St. Mon–Wed 12:30–11pm; Thu, Fri 12:30pm–midnight; Sat 11:30am–midnight; Sun 11:30am–11pm. Average main course: $18.* The breezy good nature of any eatery is something to celebrate, but pair it with an exceptionally fresh and well-thought-out menu and you've got the makings of a neighborhood—in this case, Soho—oasis. Whitewashed walls and an open door in summer complement the bistro's vibrant Latin sounds, as do an array of tropical drinks, a gratis offering of salty plantain chips and house-made salsa, and appetizers such as the ensalada tropical, a pile of soft baby spinach alongside sliced avocado, tomatoes and papaya. Entrées like the luscious *dorado a la veracruzana* —mahi-mahi pan-roasted with caramelized onion, capers and black olives—and not to-be-missed desserts (secret-recipe flan, tres leches cake) only up the spot's Latino cred.

Luz *177 Vanderbilt Ave between Myrtle and Willoughby Aves, Clinton Hill, Brooklyn (718-246-4000). Subway: C to Clinton–Washington Aves. Mon–Wed 5–11pm; Thu 5–11:30pm; Fri 5pm–midnight; Sat 3pm–midnight; Sun 11am–11pm. Average main course: $14.* Fort Greene's restaurant renaissance continues with this Nuevo Latino joint with a minimal South Beach decor and hip-shaking (though low-volume) Latino soundtrack. The menu reaches out to more countries than a backpacking Aussie. Peruvian ceviches mingle with tender Colombian arepas. There's even a Mexican take on the overplayed, soupy-centered, warm chocolate cake, amped up here with spicy chocolate, warm bananas and pineapple ice cream. The prices here are reasonable, making this a neighborhood spot where you might actually meet your neighbors.

★**Mamajuana Cafe** *247 Dyckman St at Seaman Ave (212-304-0140). Subway: 1 to Dyckman St. Daily 6pm–midnight. Average main course $20;*

$11. This '60s-era, Formica-countered luncheonette serves tasty Hispanic soul food to a Pan-Latin clientele. Go straight for rice-based concoctions like paella and arroz con pollo—or try a platter of tender stewed meat and a quartet of starchy sides (rice, plantains, fries, and red and black beans). Cool your palate with a mango *batido* (shake), and on your way out, grab an expertly pressed *cubano* sandwich for tomorrow's lunch.

▲⊖**Empanada Mama** *793 Ninth Ave at 51st St (212-698-9008). Subway: C, E to 50th St. Daily 9am–midnight. Average empanada: $2.50.* Javier Garcia has opened a Hell's Kitchen location of his empanada shop, following three in Queens. He and his partners serve 40 varieties of the main attraction, with fillings that range from basic chicken and beef to creative choices like cheese steak and pepperoni pizza. After you pop a couple of savory versions, go for a sweet ending: The Elvis is made with peanut butter and banana.

Esperanto *145 Ave C at 9th St (212-505-6559). Subway: L to First Ave, 6 to Astor Pl. Mon–Thu, Sun 6pm–midnight; Fri, Sat 6pm–1am. Average main course: $15.* Live music serenades booths of flirty diners at this low-lit spot, a justified scene. The tapas are consistently tasty, with a zingy tuna ceviche leading the way. Tuck into chayote salad with lime dressing, Brazilian pork stew or grilled seafood on greens. Service runs hot and cold, but great attention is paid to preparing entrées. The cocktails are fruity and well-mixed—and perhaps the real reason to come.

TALIA SIMHI

average small plate $10. Part lounge, part restaurant, part outdoor party, Mamajuana Cafe is the unofficial meeting ground for Inwood's glitterati. Tapas-style appetizers, like tender beef skewers accompanied by Cabrales fondue or a sweet plantain stuffed with delicious salt cod, and desserts, such as a mousselike coconut flan, fare better than hit-or-miss entrées (a perfectly cooked "brick-pressed" Cornish hen over yuca mash has just the right balance of sweet and savory, while plantain-crusted salmon on a bed of artichoke hearts has no crust and little heart), but the generous portions won't leave you hungry. Cocktails include the (reputedly) aphrodisiac Mamajuana shot (a Taino concoction of herbs, spices and roots mixed with rum, wine and honey).

▲**Paladar** *161 Ludlow St between Houston and Stanton Sts (212-473-3535). Subway: F, V to Lower East Side–Second Ave. Mon–Thu 5–11pm; Fri 5pm–1am; Sat noon–4pm, 5:30pm–1am; Sun noon–4pm, 5:30–11pm. Average main course: $15.* The food is so affordable, it's hard to believe it comes from Food Network regular and celebrity chef Aarón Sanchez, who has worked at the city's most touted Nuevo Latino eateries (including the now-defunct Patria and Chicama). Sample his bold flavors in empanadas stuffed with chicken *picadillo* and topped with smoky tomato salsa, or pan-roasted halibut served over creamy coconut rice with an orange vinaigrette. On warm days, the back garden is filled with boozers; at night they migrate to the bustling front bar.

★**Palo Santo** *652 Union St between Fourth and Fifth Aves, Park Slope, Brooklyn (718-636-6311). Subway: M, R to Union St. Mon–Thu 6–10pm; Fri 6–11pm; Sat 11am–3pm, 5–11pm; Sun 11am–3pm, 5–10pm. Average main course: $19.* Heavy wooden chairs and tables inlaid with wood and glass baubles lend a fairytale feeling to this romantic nook. Though the menu changes often, the focus is always on organic, fair-trade ingredients—and flavor, of course. In addition to light fare such as sandwiches and empanadas, a full dinner menu includes paella Valencia, guava-glazed roasted free-range chicken. The waitstaff is smart and can recommend a silken coffee crème brûlée and a peppy Gewürztraminer-like white wine. You'll leave feeling like a pampered princess.

▲⊙**Pan Latin Café** *400 Chambers St at River Terr (212-571-3860). Subway: 1, 2, 3 to Chambers St. Daily 8am–9pm. Average main course: $9.* You can catch glimpses of sailboats passing the Hudson River Park while you're waiting for your breakfast or lunch. Inside, colorful paintings cheer up the small space. Try the *pernil* Cuban sandwich, pressed pork leg in garlic-guava sauce. Other daily offerings include baked breads, gazpacho, tamales, empanadas and plátanos maduros. If you're in the mood for something sweet, go for the smooth caramel flan. Or grab a Mexican guava soda and *pan dulce*, amble to the water's edge and sail away.

Pipa *ABC Carpet & Home, 38 E 19th St between Broadway and Park Ave South (212-677-2233). Subway: N, R, W, 6 to 23rd St. Mon–Thu noon–11pm; Fri, Sat noon–midnight; Sun 11am–10pm. Average main course: $22.* Flickering chandeliers, wood beams and huge mirrors bestow a goth vibe on this dim tapas spot inside ABC Carpet & Home. Surrounded by overflowing shopping bags, the well-groomed patrons recuperate from

trekking through six floors of housewares with plates such as sweet peppers stuffed with crabmeat and shrimp in a creamy, smoky sauce. Dishes that are more promising on paper than on the tongue, like the potato *buñuelos*, may make you grateful for diminutive portions.

★**Raices** *25-39 Steinway St between 25th and 28th Aves, Astoria, Queens (718-204-7711). Subway: G, R, V to Steinway St. Mon–Thu, Sun noon–11pm; Fri, Sat noon–midnight. Average main course: $14.* Bold navy doors also open into the small, brightly decorated dining room at Raices. Appetizers such as ceviche and *jalea* make way for less traditional entrées such as *tallarines saltados*, beef or chicken sautéed in ginger and soy sauce and served over linguine. A refreshing *lúcuma* (a fruit imported from Peru) ice cream beats tiresome flan—if you haven't already satisfied your sweet tooth with one of the seven types of mojitos.

Samba *9604 Third Ave between 96th and 97th Sts, Bay Ridge, Brooklyn (718-439-0475). Subway: R to Bay Ridge–95th St. Tue, Wed, Sun 5–11pm; Thu–Sat 5pm–1am. Average main course: $.* It's owned by an Italian and situated in Bay Ridge, but this sleek bar-restaurant is Latin to the core. The tropical exoticism extends from the leopard-print ceiling and creative dishes to the Shakira look-alikes who line the backlit bar for live music on Saturday nights. Baked oysters are topped with spinach, chorizo and *queso blanco*; salmon is plantain-crusted; Chilean sea bass comes in a zesty saffron-and-orange sauce. Surrender to yet another pineapple martini or one of the affordable Argentine or Chilean wines. Whether you drink or don't, you'll leave Samba with a buzz.

Terra Cafe *7 Henshaw St between Dyckman Ave and Riverside Dr (212-567-6500). Subway: A, C, 1 to Dyckman Ave. Wed–Fri 4–11pm; Sat, Sun noon–11pm. Average main course: $12.* Nestled in a tiny street just north of Fort Tryon Park, this small, intimate spot boasts a thoughtful Latin-inflected menu and a pulsating Afro-Cuban soundtrack. Have a glass of the zesty house sangria and savor a Brazilian *churrasco* skirt steak served on a bed of crisp eggplant slices, or sample the modest assortment of tapas. Fresh salads and sandwiches are

Read 'em & eat

arepa: corn pancake filled with cheese, meat or beans, then grilled, baked or fried

chuletas: pork chops

maduros: sweet plantains, similar to banana but thicker and starchier

picadillo: ground meat (often shredded beef or chicken) used as filling for tacos or as a stew

pupusa: stuffed cornmeal tortilla

tres leches: a light cake made from three types of milk and often topped with whipped cream or meringue

Side dish

Fish tale

Ceviche takes center stage in many South American cuisines.

Although the neuvo Latino craze that peaked in the 1990s with such restaurants as Patria and Bolivar (both now defunct) passed like so many other trends into the recesses of New York's culinary memory, it did popularize several dishes, sauces and ingredients that still titillate the city's collective palate. *Chimichurri* now rolls off the urbane diner's tongue as easily as *au poivre*, while caipirinhas and mojitos lubricate pre-dinner conversations in even the most upscale joints. Yet despite rumors of its aphrodisiacal powers, few could have foreseen the popularity of ceviche.

Raw fish or shellfish marinated in citrus juices, ceviche (pronounced *seh-VEE-cheh*) is a centuries-old South American concoction claimed with equal fervor by both Ecuadorians and Peruvians as their national dish, and believed by some to derive from the Incas. The marinade serves to flavor the fish and to "cook" it without heat, for the acidic juice of the citrus denatures the proteins in the fish and makes its flesh firm. Served at room temperature, it tastes much more like a cooked dish than the raw seafood of sushi or sashimi.

Instead of wasabi, chili peppers (from the fruity *ají amarillo* to the fiery serrano) can be added to the marinade—but ceviche is not necessarily a spicy dish. Its array of garnishes reflects the diversity of Latin American cooking. Peruvians like to serve ceviche with sweet potato slices; Ecuadorians often dress it in a tomato-based sauce; the Mexican version sometimes nests on toasted tortillas. In New York, ceviche can pop up at an überhip fusion spot as an elegant appetizer wedged into a martini glass with an edible swizzle stick, or it can serve as the center of a hearty main course at a Latin American eatery.

Sadly, we cannot substantiate ceviche's success as an aphrodisiac. Restaurants don't actually serve love, you need to bring your own.

also available, making this a terrific spot to assemble a picnic before a visit to the nearby Cloisters.

Yuca Bar *111 Ave A at 7th St (212-982-9533). Subway: L to First Ave, 6 to Astor Pl. Mon–Thu 11am–11pm; Fri–Sun 11am–1am. Average main course: $17.* A slew of mojitos, margaritas and sangrias draw students, artists and old-timers, who tumble through the breezy space's veranda doors and onto the narrow outside patio. But it's the flavorful Latin food that distinguishes Yuca Bar from run-of-the-mill cantinas. Nibblers can choose from an extensive assortment of tapas, including tuna ceviche served in a coconut shell or a trio of tantalizing empanadas. Those with heartier appetites can have their pick of more-substantial dishes like *churrasco* skirt steak or guava-barbecued short ribs—or, better yet, sample a variety of meats with a colossal *carnitas* platter.

Bolivian

▲☻**Mi Bolivia** *44-10 48th Ave between 44th and 45th St , Woodside, Queens (718-784-5111). Subway: 7 to 46th St. Mon–Fri 12:30–10pm; Sat, Sun 11:30am–midnight. Average main course: $9.* A world of language confusion, kitschy '80s decor and a menu that includes a pork-head sandwich, sauced beef tongue and scrambled beef with egg sauce await you at this lively Bolivian restaurant. Warm up for the event with the house special, peanut soup (it sells out quickly), then prepare to fill up. Entrées come with a plateful of sides: Roasted pork shares space with sweet potatoes, plantains, corn and salad. The charcoal beef stew—hearty enough on its own—comes with potato, rice and egg. Vegetarians and light eaters might be better off with saner-size *salteñas*: buttery pastries with assorted savory fillings.

☻**Nostalgias** *85-09 Northern Blvd between 85th and 86th Sts, Jackson Heights, Queens (718-533-9120, 718-429-8113). Subway: 7 to 82nd St–Jackson Hts. Tue–Thu 11am–10pm; Fri 11am–4am; Sat 10am–4am; Sun 10am–10pm. Average main course: $9.* Eating at a discotheque is not normally recommended, but you might want to bust a move to this spot, where you'll find home-style dishes like *charquicán* (a delicious, hearty heap of shredded beef and chickpeas) and *humitas* (corn husks filled with baked sweet corn and white cheese). Ignore the fish offerings (Bolivia is landlocked, after all) and try the *sajta de pollo* (grilled chicken in a red-chili sauce). Time it right, and you'll digest before the music starts pumping.

Chilean

★**Pomaire** *371 W 46th St between Eighth and Ninth Aves (212-956-3055, 212-956-3056). Subway: A, C, E to 42nd St–Port Authority. Sun–Thu noon–11pm; Fri, Sat noon–midnight. Average main course: $15.* Pomaire bills itself as New York's only Chilean restaurant, but the country's food is so good you'll wish there were others. Decorated like a rustic *estancia*, the eatery is an appealing introduction to a comforting, restrained cuisine. Fried beef empanadas are classically prepared, with hard-boiled egg, olives, raisins and onion. *Cazuela*, a brothy stew with chicken, corn, squash, potato and rice, could have

Warm welcome
Centrico's menu is
as inviting as it's
dining room.

emerged from a Santiago kitchen. The selection of
seafood is imported daily from Chile.

Colombian

Chibcha *79-05 Roosevelt Ave at 79th St, Jackson
Heights, Queens (718-429-9033). Subway: E, F, V, G,
R to Jackson Hts–Roosevelt Ave; 7 to 82nd St–Jackson
Hts. Daily 4pm–4am. Average main course: $14.* Let
the colorful murals, blaring Latin music videos and
Spanish-speaking waitstaff be your guides—though it
might be hard to imagine putting away the *bandeja típica
antioqueña*: an overflowing plate of beef and rice topped
with bacon, beans, plantains, an arepa and a fried egg.
But go ahead—you can work off the calories dancing to
the merengue band in the next room. Whole fried porgy
with fried *tostones* and yuca is another worth-the-weight-
gain specialty.

Tierras Colombianas *33-01 Broadway at
33rd St, Astoria, Queens (718-956-3012). Subway: G,
R, V to Steinway St; N, W to Broadway. Mon–Thu,
Sun noon–11pm; Fri, Sat noon–midnight. Average
main course: $12.* Sophia Antonakos, the owner, is
as Greek as many of the neighboring restaurateurs in
Astoria, but the food at her bright corner storefront
is purely Colombian—and purely hearty. Enormous
platters of grilled steak and crisp, chewy *chicharrón*
(fried pork cracklings) are piled with rice, plantains,
beans, avocados and fluffy arepas; the fisherman's
platter is a mound of garlic-sauced shrimp, squid,
calamari and fish. A rotating lineup of soups includes
oxtail and beef tripe.

Ecuadoran

Braulio's & Familia *39-08 63rd St between
Roosevelt and 39th Aves, Woodside, Queens (718-
899-3267). Subway: 7 to 61st St–Woodside. Daily
10am–11pm. Average main course: $10.* The ceviche
at this small Ecuadorian spot is twice the size and half
the price of its martini-glassed Manhattan kin. In fact, a
serving of ceviche, plus a bowl of Braulio's comforting
"ball soup" with meat, makes an exceptional order. The
other main enticement is Braulio himself, the host-chef
who makes every diner feel like one of the *familia*.

El Patio *100-14 Northern Blvd at 100th St,
Corona, Queens (718-446-4622). 7 to 103rd St–Corona
Plaza. Mon–Thu, Sun 9am–1am; Fri, Sat 9am–4am.
Average main course price: $11.* This shotgun shack
does duty as everything from breakfast nook to backyard
hideaway to sports bar. Two giant flat-panel TVs
reflected by mirrored walls make Spanish-language
programming a constant companion (the jukebox may
occasionally join in), but the gutsy Ecuadoran cuisine
can stand up to the cacophony. Order stewed goat that's
tender and properly gamy, a seafood rice casserole
that's smoky, fishy, salty, greasy—and addictive—and
a *chicharrón*-capped peak of roast pork perched atop a
white hominy mountain sprinkled with salted corn nuts.

⊖El Tesoro Ecuatoriano *4015 Fifth Ave
between 40th and 41st Sts, Sunset Park, Brooklyn (718-
972-3756). Subway: R to 45th St. Mon–Thu 9am–11pm;
Fri–Sun 9am–3am. Average main course: $10.* Make
sure you go to this Ecuadoran joint on a weekend, when

caldo de bola is on offer. The centerpiece of this $7 soup is a softball of mashed plantains, ground beef, peas, raisins and chunks of hard-boiled egg. The spongy orb sits in a cilantro-accented broth surrounded by carrots, potatoes and corn on the cob—and it's a perfect opener for El Tesoro's other specialty: seafood. Of the nearly 20 ceviches, you'll be particularly seduced by the one overflowing with shrimp ($8). The accompanying giant kernels of roasted corn will have you grabbing for something to cut the starch, like a supersweet tropical apple soda.

El Salvadoran

▲⊖**Bahia** *690 Grand St between Graham and Manhattan Aves, Williamsburg, Brooklyn (718-218-9592). Subway: L to Grand St. Mon–Thu 11:30am–10pm; Fri 11:30am–11pm; Sat 9am–11pm; Sun 9am–10pm. Average main course: $10.* The near-nautical theme and vague aroma of cleaning products might bring a motel restaurant to mind, but if you make the right choices from the huge menu, your meal will be far from bland. *Pupusas*, stuffed cornmeal tortillas that are a matter of national pride in El Salvador, are top-shelf. Order one of each snack-size treat (chicken, pork, zucchini, bean and cheese) and call it dinner. Or feast on the grilled tilapia fillet. Plantains come in several forms, most notably a creamy, cinnamony empanada *de leche* that you'll go bananas over.

⊖**Izalco** *64-05 Roosevelt Ave between 64th and 65th Sts, Woodside, Queens (718-533-8373). Subway: 7 to 69th St. Mon, Tue, Thu, Sun noon–9pm; Fri, Sat noon–11pm. Average main course price: $14.* The thundering 7 train occasionally muffles the blaring Latin music videos and the kitchen symphony of sizzling and chopping, but the Salvadoran fare in this welcoming Queens canteen has diners singing hosannas. Fluffy *elote* tamales crammed with chicken, chickpeas, potatoes and peppers lure your attention away from bizarre decor that includes a fake bird being attacked by a plastic scorpion. The Latino clientele gobble up *salpicon*, a refreshing cold beef salad laced with radish, mint, onion and cilantro, and *carne asada*, grilled to delicious nuttiness and plated with caramelized plantains which stick delightfully in your teeth.

⊖**La Cabaña Salvadoreña** *4384 Broadway between 187th and 188th Sts (212-928-7872). Subway: A to 190th St, 1 to 191st St. Daily 11am–10pm. Average main course: $5.* The cuisine of El Salvador hasn't exactly taken New York by storm, but after a meal here, you might wonder why. Start with a *pupusa*, a chewy corn cake filled with pork and cheese and grilled golden brown, for a paltry $2. Then treat yourself to a $13 entrée of ceviche—shrimp, crab, tomatoes and green peppers in a lively citrus marinade—and a Regia Cerveza, the local brew, available in chubby quart bottles for just $6.50.

Uruguayan

El Chivito d'Oro *84-02 37th Ave at 84th St, Jackson Heights, Queens (718-424-0600). Subway: 7 to 82nd St–Jackson Hts. Mon–Thu, Sun 11am–1am; Fri, Sat 11am–2am. Average main course: $13.* Try not to faint as the server delivers the *parrillada*, a tray piled high with grilled skirt steak, short ribs, sweetbreads, regular and blood sausages, veal loin and more—you'll

lose track after falling into a protein coma. Some of the cuts are a bit fatty and on the well-done side, but the overall quality is surprisingly high for the price: A single serving costs $19 and feeds three normal eaters; a double ($27) would feed a family of five. Remarkably, vegetarian dishes aren't afterthoughts: enormous pasta plates, tortilla *española* of potatoes and eggs, and a huge portion of spinach pie stuffed with hard-boiled eggs for just $3.

Venezuelan

▲⊖**Caracas Arepa Bar** *91 E 7th St between First Ave and Ave A (212-228-5062). Subway: F, V to Lower East Side–Second Ave; 6 to Astor Pl. Tue–Sat noon–11pm; Sun noon–10pm. Average arepa: $4.* Surely, there's no more cultured a substitute than a grilled cheese sanwich than a piping-hot arepa filled with *juayanes* cheese. This endearing spot, with flower-patterned, vinyl-covered tables, zaps you straight to Caracas. The secret is in the arepas themselves: Each patty is made from scratch daily. The pitalike pockets are stuffed with a choice of 20 fillings, like chicken and avocado. Top off your snack with a *cocada*, a thick and creamy milk shake made with freshly grated coconut and cinnamon.

★⊖**El Cocotero** *228 W 18th St between Seventh and Eighth Aves (212-206-8930). Subway: 1 to 18th St. Daily 11am–11pm; June–Aug closed Mon. Average main course: $15.* A *mañana, mañana* mood infuses this languid spot, with plantains hanging in the front window, lazily spinning ceiling fans and dewy palms. Venezolanos love their arepas, best sampled here on the *degustación* platter, which arrives with a variety of fillings, including *pabellón*, liberally spiced (if a bit tough) flank steak. The savory *hallaca* tamale, bulging with chicken, pork and fat raisins, is swaddled in a banana leaf. Heat up the evening (and your throat) with *guarapita*, a potent mix of passion fruit and *aguardiente*, or "firewater."

★ ▲**Flor's Kitchen** *170 Waverly Pl between Sixth and Seventh Aves (212-229-9926). Subway: 1 to Christopher St. Sun–Thu 11am–11pm; Fri, Sat 11am–midnight. Average main course: $15. Average arepa: $5.* While lingering is a sin in Flor's mobbed East Village location, this West Village outpost is ideal for it: There are two spacious rooms and pillow-lined window seats at a prime people-watching intersection. Take your time over a plate of arepas with a dozen delicious stuffings, including stewy *carne mechada* (shredded beef) and breakfast-style *perico* (scrambled eggs, tomatoes and onions). *Pabellón*, shredded braised meat with chunks of sweet plantain, requires some belt-loosening. And you may need to wait a while to work up an appetite for the traditional Venezuelan desserts, like flan or the tasty *tres leches* cake.

Pasita *47 Eighth Ave between 12th and 13th Sts (212-255-3900). Subway: A, C, E to 14th St; L to Eighth Ave. Tue, Wed, Sun 5–11pm; Thu–Sat 5pm–midnight. Average main course: $13.* At this cozy West Village spot with exposed brick, flickering candles and rickety wood tables, the shareable Venezuelan snacks known as *pasapalos* are mini versions of Latin American classics. The best of these are *arepitas*, tiny crisp arepas served with chunky avocado *guasacaca*. Pasita also serves thin-crust pizzas: The *champiñon* (a pie topped with roasted mushrooms, artichoke hearts, caramelized onion, mozzarella and ricotta) might not be particularly Latin, but it sure is good.

Mediterranean

See also: *French, Greek, Italian, Middle Eastern, Moroccan*

Dressed to the nines
Pera Mediterranean
Brasserie's *meze* platter
has a stellar mix.

▲**Antique Garage** *41 Mercer St between Broome and Grand Sts (212-219-1019). Subway: J, M, Z, N, Q, R, W, 6 to Canal St. Noon–4pm, 5pm–midnight. Average small plate: $12.* Formerly an auto-repair shop, the Antique Garage has good acoustics and ample carpeting to control the volume of its garrulous crowd, which comes for the live music as well as the food. Other assets: faded paintings and time-worn mirrors on the walls, heirloom plates and flickering candles on the tables. The kitchen manages to live up to the good first impression with decent portions of *borek* (feta-stuffed phyllo), sardines wrapped in grape leaves, and tuna steaks swimming in red-pepper puree, all of which are included in the selection of salads and small dishes. The informal presentation matches the laid-back service.

Barbounia *250 Park Ave South at 20th St (212-995-0242). Subway: 6 to 23rd St. Mon 11:30am–4pm, 5:30–11pm; Tue–Sat 11:30am–4pm, 5:30–midnight; Sun 11:30am–4pm, 5:30–11pm. Average main course: $24.* Barbounia is superfabulous in a supercomfortable way. Pillows line the banquettes, and a feathers-and-glitter chandelier lords over a series of arches and columns. Chef Michael Cressotti (Sushi Samba), leans heavily on Greek and Turkish cuisine, with lots of upscale takes on souvlaki, kebabs and the like. Order the namesake Barbounia (red mullet) for a starter, which yields a crisp-skinned tiny fish with a hint of licorice, or the *saganaki*, a thrilling combination of sizzling hot kasseri cheese, small slices of cherry-and-walnut bread and a truffle-scented fig marmalade. There's lots of grilled fish and meats, but more interesting are the composed entrées like pan-seared

veal medallions with mascarpone polenta. For dessert, the Turkish Delight is a sweet interpretation of three Turkish flavors—candied apricots, spice cake and a terrific, dark pungent coffee custard.

Branzini *299 Madison Ave at 41st St (212-557-3340). Subway: 42nd St S, 4, 5, 6, 7 to 42nd St–Grand Central. Mon–Sat 11:30am–11:30pm. Average main course: $17.* At swell little Branzini, opened by chef Rick Moonen beneath the Library Hotel, the menu doesn't lie. Small-plate starters really are small; too bad, because they're habit-forming, such as four fat lobster ravioli in tomato-basil broth, or a meaty crab cake over salad. The second course compensates in size, whether it's a simple roasted chicken or the restaurant's namesake fish, with lemon and olive oil. The true large plates, however, come as dessert. The warm banana tart is enormous and wonderful, and caramel seeps through the fruit.

★ ▲**Convivium Osteria** *68 Fifth Ave between Bergen St and St. Marks Pl, Park Slope, Brooklyn (718-857-1833). Subway: B, Q, 2, 3, 4, 5 to Atlantic Ave; 2, 3 to Bergen St.. Mon–Sat 6–11:30pm; Sun 5:30–11pm. Average main course: $20.* At this tiny favorite on Park Slope's restaurant row, the music is Portuguese fado, the decor (copper pots, rough-hewn communal tables) is faux farmhouse, and the food is fantastic. The wide-ranging menu includes hearty comfort food from Portugal, Spain and Italy. Several appetizers and main courses described as "for two"—like the massive rib-eye steak carved at your table—would satisfy an even larger group. A thick port sauce adds further earthiness to chunky pine-nut–crusted lamb. The only drawback is a lack of reasonably priced wines on the extensive list.

TALIA SIMHI

Tune in.

Time Out New York's
weekly video blogs.
timeoutnewyork.com/vlog

Just the thing to satisfy your hunger for restaurant and bar news

Gabriella Gershenson
Eat Out

Get out.

Dani *333 Hudson St at Charlton St (212-633-9333). Subway: 1 to Houston St. Mon–Thu noon–10pm; Fri noon–10:30pm; Sat 5:30–10:30pm. Average main course: $23.* After winning over fans at the Tribeca Grill, chef Don Pintabona spent a few years running a Florida restaurant and penning a cookbook. Dani, his return to lower Manhattan, owes much to its forefather a few blocks south. Both restaurants are spare, loftlike and industrial; spacious windows and booming acoustics make Dani feel larger than it is. For his solo venture, the chef looked to his Sicilian roots for culinary inspiration and added North African influences that rarely pop up on local Italian menus. Pintabona adds couscous to fish, a touch of *harissa* to shrimp, and saffron and cumin to miniature mussels in a bread-sopping broth. Portions are modest enough to leave room—not just for dessert, but for a middle-of-the-meal pasta course

★ **Django** *480 Lexington Ave at 46th St (212-871-6600). Subway: 42nd St S, 4, 5, 6, 7 to 42nd St–Grand Central. Mon–Fri 11:30am–2:30pm, 5:30–10pm. Average main course: $26.* Despite its ambitious French-Mediterranean menu, this bi-level spot thrives on cocktails and snacks. To reach the dining room, you'll need to fight your way through the after-work crowd to the upstairs sanctuary, under a billowing tent. Here, you'll find playful, expense-account food such as smoky octopus anointed with a lively caper-berry-and-pickled-onion relish and shelled lobster on a heaping buttery tangle of tagliatelle. The downstairs party makes an appearance in an outrageous shareable dessert—a headache on a plank featuring shot glasses filled with spirit-infused sorbet cocktails.

★ **Epices du Traiteur** *103 W 70th St between Columbus Ave and Broadway (212-579-5904). Subway: B, C, 1, 2, 3 to 72nd St. Mon–Thu, Sun 5:30–10:30pm; Fri, Sat 5:30pm–midnight. Average main course: $20.* The fried Tunisian pastry known as *brik,* filled with tuna and a poached egg, is the signature appetizer at this low-key North African bistro. The menu moves to Morocco for entrées, offering tagines brimming with tender chunks of lamb. If you prefer poultry, *b'steeya* is a deep pastry filled with aromatic shredded chicken and sprinkled with cinnamon and sugar. The charming little place is not undiscovered: Make reservations if you're catching a Lincoln Center curtain.

Extra Virgin *259 W 4th St between Charles and Perry Sts (212–691–9359). Subway: 1 to Christopher St–Sheridan Sq. Tue–Fri noon–3:30pm, 5:30pm–midnight; Sat, Sun 11am–4pm, 5:30pm–midnight. Average main course: $19.* The saucy moniker suits this sexy bar, but it officially refers to the premium olive oils liberally poured over chef Joseph Fortunato's dishes. Share an order of crisp, slender fries and a bowl of rich Gorgonzola fondue, then move on to the roasted artichoke with poached egg or mushroom-crusted Virgin chicken with sweet-pea risotto. For dessert, just order another glass of wine and watch the beautiful people parading past you on the sidewalk.

Isabella's *359 Columbus Ave at 77th St (212-724-2100). Subway: B, C to 81st St–Museum of Natural History; 1 to 79th St. Mon–Fri 11am–4:30pm, 5–11:30pm; Sat 11am–4pm, 5pm–12:30am; Sun 10am–4pm. Average main course: $24.* Perky waiters with sunglasses perched on their heads scurry between buzzing dinner tables at this unfussily elegant indoor-outdoor spot. Let the servers crack their good-natured jokes as they bring you masterfully poured cocktails: They are probably vying for their big breaks. Your waitress's attention isn't the only

thing to smile about here—this spot is part of the city's first restaurant group to be certified green. Consider a delicate crab cake with an inspired apple-and-jicama cole slaw and a capellini generously served with light and sweet shrimp and lobster as your reward for eating eco-friendly.

Kashkaval *856 Ninth Ave between 55th & 56th Sts (212-581-8282). Subway: C, E to 50th St. Daily noon–midnight. Average main course price: $12.* Kashkaval, with its warm woods and soft lighting evoking a turn-of-the-century general store, strikes an unlikely balance between a sleepy wine bar and a bustling gourmet emporium. The restaurant, tucked behind the retail shop, suffers serious pacing issues (entrées can arrive 20 minutes apart, orders botched beyond recognition), but all is forgiven when tangy artichoke dip or hot pink, beet *skordalia* flashes across the tongue. Resist the urge to make a meal of Kashkaval's impressive roster of charcuterie; entrées—like heaping plates of savory elephant beans piled over orzo, and deep pots of fondue ripe for the dipping—are not to be missed.

The Little Owl *90 Bedford St at Grove St (212-741-4695). Subway: 1 to Christopher St–Sheridan Sq. Mon–Wed 5–11pm; Thu, Fri 5pm–midnight; Sat 11am–2pm, 5pm–midnight; Sun 11am–2pm, 5–10pm. Average main course: $20.* This small, wood-paneled venue stays steadily packed, thanks to generous portions of Italian classics—everything but pizza and pasta—elevated by signature twists. What is essentially a meatball hoagie has been transformed into a slider starter featuring three pecorino-spiked orbs of meat on miniature brioche buns. More complex flavors mingle in a salad that matches tender pink duck-breast slices with almonds, arugula, Parmesan and a hint of black truffle. If you can't get a table, consider eating at the bar—all five seats of it.

Olea *171 Lafayette Ave at Adelphi St, Fort Greene, Brooklyn (718-643-7003). Subway: C to Lafayette Ave, G to Clinton–Washington Aves. Mon–Thu, Sun 10am–4:30pm, 5–11pm; Fri, Sat 10am–4:30pm, 5pm–midnight. Average main course: $16.* Terra-cotta floors and antique mirrors give the dining room its taverna personality, backed by a transporting Mediterranean menu of falafel-crusted artichoke hearts; salty *haloumi* cheese panfried with *harissa* oil; and mushroom risotto with pistachio oil. The presentation is rough and ready, but service is pleasingly snappy. The caramel *affogato*—ice cream served with a pot of steaming espresso poured over the top—should be considered absolutely non-negotiable.

★ **Olives New York** *W Union Square Hotel, 201 Park Ave South at 17th St (212-353-8345). Subway: L, N, Q, R, W, 4, 5, 6 to 14th St–Union Sq. Mon–Thu 7–10:30am, noon–2:30pm, 6–10:30pm; Fri 7–10:30am, noon–2:30pm, 6–11pm; Sat 6–11pm; Sun 5:30–10pm. Average main course: $30.* Almost every seat in this posh Todd English nook in the downtown W Hotel is a prime position for people-watching: Giant, mostly uncovered windows nicely frame the stream of Greenmarket revelers and skatepunks alike—perfect for the longish wait between courses. A wonderful warm escargot-and–goat cheese flatbread will keep your stomach from grumbling before the arrival of a juicy, tender brick oven–roasted chicken in a foamy garlic glaze. The desserts can be fairly vanilla—both figuratively and, in the case of a soufflé with Tahitian vanilla ice cream, literally—but a delicious, supersweet butterscotch tiramisu will disappear quick if you don't pay more attention to your dining partner's fork than the crowd outside.

▲**Pangea** *178 Second Ave between 11th and 12th Sts (212-995-0900). Subway: L to Third Ave; N, Q, R, W, 4, 5, 6 to 14th St–Union Sq. Mon–Thu, Sun noon–midnight; Fri, Sat noon–1am. Average main course: $15.* Crowds from the nearby Village East Cinemas have decamped to Pangea for postmovie bites since the '80s, but the restaurant's age is finally starting to show. Try to sit near the windows or outside—it's noisy inside thanks to low ceilings. The menu, which touches on Middle Eastern, Italian and Asian cuisine, is wildly inconsistent. Tuscan shrimp rolled in fresh herbs over white beans are refreshing and hearty, but the Moroccan chicken with preserved lemon is cloyingly sweet. Hedge your bets with never-fail options like fried calamari or burgers to best enjoy this little standby.

Pera Mediterranean Brasserie *303 Madison Ave between 41st and 42nd Sts (212-878-6301). Subway: 42nd St S; 4, 5, 6, 7 to 42nd St–Grand Central. Mon–Sat 11:30am–10:30pm. Average main course: $27.* The open kitchen is the focal point at this Turkish and Greek spot, which is as well suited for a power lunch as it is for a midshopping snack. Pera's stock-in-trade is fire and spice, and men in chef's whites hover over open flames firing up treats such as the "mini shish trio"—grilled lamb, beef sausage and *harissa*-rubbed shrimp skewers. On the lighter side, spongy, tiny, stone-oven-baked pizzas (called *pidettes*) are only $3, and the meze platters offer a variety of refreshing salads and dips, like a stellar roasted eggplant puree. Greek and Israeli wines are a welcome touch, as is a dessert of shredded phyllo dough, soft cheese, simple syrup and *kaymak* (water-buffalo cream).

The Place *310 W 4th St between Bank and W 12th Sts (212-924-2711). Subway: A, C, E, L to 14th St; 1 to Christopher St–Sheridan Sq. Mon–Thu 6pm–10:30pm, Fri 6pm–11pm, Sat 5pm–11pm, Sun 5:30pm–10:00pm. Average main course: $19.* On a summer evening, a table on the sidewalk terrace of this endearing little West Village restaurant is a perfect place to be. A tiny bar up front lures locals and neighborhood strollers for a glass of wine and small plates like char-grilled calamari and tiger shrimp with fresh mango salsa. Couples gravitate toward the candlelit back room with low wooden beams and stone walls for more serious dining, which can include delicately pan roasted cod with jersey corn, asparagus, and sugar-snap peas in a saffron beurre blanc, or fresh pappardelle with braised duck and baby artichokes. No one minds if you linger over the flaky apple tart topped with cool cinnamon ice cream.

Read 'em & eat

branzini: Mediterranean sea bass

brik: a thin Tunisian triangular pastry, often filled with an egg, tuna and onion

haloumi: a Cypriot cheese made from a mixture of sheep's and goat's milk

harissa: Tunisian chili paste used as a meat rub, or when mixed with oil or water, as a condiment

---

★ **Rose Water** *787 Union St between Fifth and Sixth Aves, Park Slope, Brooklyn (718-783-3800). Subway: B, Q to Seventh Ave; M, R to Union St; 2, 3 to Bergen St. Mon, Tue 5:30–10pm; Wed, Thu 5:30–10:30pm; Fri 5:30–11pm; Sat 10am–3pm, 5:30–11pm; Sun 10am–3pm, 5:30–10pm. Average main course: $18.* Owner John Tucker and chef Ethan Koftvar were using organic, sustainably raised ingredients, preferably from local producers, long before it became fashionable. That's why they've earned a loyal following of locals who settle in the muted, earth-toned room to peruse a menu that changes frequently but is reliably stacked with bold flavors. Appetizers might be asparagus soup with pickled asparagus, pearl onions and Parmesan, or artichoke hearts with broiled crab mousseline, rhubarb chutney and basil puree. Main courses may include grilled striped bass with fiddleheads, bacon, shiitake mushrooms and almond milk, or tender braised beef short ribs with braised red cabbage, mustard spaetzle and horseradish-dill cream.

◉**Sultana** *160-2 North 4th St between Bedford and Driggs Aves, Williamsburg, Brooklyn (718-218-8545). Subway: L to Bedford Ave. Mon–Thu, Sun 3pm–2am; Fri, Sat, 3pm–4am. Average main course price: $10.* Girls who like girls—and those who enjoy smoking *shisha*—get along merrily at this Williamsburg hookah lounge and Mediterranean restaurant, formerly Banbalotto. The LGBT-friendly orange and teal-colored hangout, outfitted with artfully draped veils and a pillow-strewn seating area, creates the ideal setting for languorous smoking—26 varieties of flavored *shisha* are available—as well as the slow savoring of lamb kebabs, lemony hummus and silky babaganoush, all served in generous portions meant for sharing. Diners may find the weekdays fairly deserted, but the energy picks up on weekends—Friday nights feature a belly dancer, DJ and plenty of ladies looking for love.

▲**Superfine** *126 Front St at Pearl St, Dumbo, Brooklyn (718-243-9005). Subway: F to York St. Tue–Fri 11:30am–3pm, 6–11pm; Sat 6–11pm; Sun 11am–3pm, 6–10pm. Average main course: $16.* Of the people, by the people: All three owners are long-term locals, and many residents were enthusiastic helpers during the lengthy construction process. The seating plan at Dumbo's unofficial HQ is a little funky, as is the mix of china, glass and plastic water tumblers on the tables. But no one quibbles with the organic food or the friendly service. Chef Laura Taylor changes the menu daily: Specials might include tender Australian steak or seared tuna, and there's always something for vegetarians. Sunday's bluegrass brunch is a huge hit with everyone.

★ **Tempo Restaurant & Wine Bar** *256 Fifth Ave between Carroll St and Garfield Pl, Park Slope, Brooklyn (718-636-2020). Subway: B, Q, 2, 3, 4, 5, to Atlantic Ave; D, M, N, R to Pacific St; 2, 3 to Bergen St. Mon–Thu, Sun 5:30–10:30pm; Fri, Sat 5:30–11:30pm. Average main course: $24.* It's hard to decide what to love best about this fine Park Slope eatery. The waitstaff is congenial and particularly knowledgeable about the extensive wine list; the dining area is appointed in soothing earth tones and flattering golden light; and the food—a mélange of Spanish, Italian, Moroccan and French—is reliably tasty. Signature dishes like chickpea fries in green-olive aioli and the surprisingly creamy mushroom polenta inspire flashbacks and repeat visits, while the sticky date-and-toffee pudding is transcendent. **Other location** *Tempo Presto, 254 Fifth Ave at Garfield Pl, Park Slope, Brooklyn (718-636-8899).*

Mexican

See also: *Latin American, Spanish*

Liquid lunch
Start off with a colorful margarita at Maracas Mexican Bar & Grill.

★ **Alma** *187 Columbia St at DeGraw St, Cobble Hill, Brooklyn (718-643-5400). Subway: F, G to Bergen St. Mon–Thu 5:30–10pm; Fri 5:30–11pm; Sat 10am–2:30pm, 5:30–11pm; Sun 10am–2:30pm, 5:30–10pm. Average main course: $16.* A popular destination on Columbia Street's restaurant row, three-story Alma serves fancy regional Mexican food in a giddy, casual atmosphere. Although the ground floor bar and midlevel dining room are pleasant, diners clamor for a seat on the rooftop patio (open year-round) for inspiring views of the Manhattan skyline and the glittering, accidental beauty of cargo-loaders below. The food ranges from old standards (fresh, cilantro-heavy salsa, and creamily addictive guac) to sophisticated dishes like *huachinango a la naranja*, a red snapper with orange sauce, that are as airy and light as the view.

★ ▲☉**Bonita** *338 Bedford Ave between South 2nd and South 3rd Sts, Williamsburg, Brooklyn (718-384-9500). Subway: L to Bedford Ave. Mon–Thu, Sun 11am–11:30pm; Fri, Sat 11am–midnight. Average main course: $10.* Chef Juventino Avila's dishes are both pretty and ample, arriving with huge mounds of greens, tomatoes and corn cut straight from the cob. First-rate guacamole is accompanied by fried-to-order chips; fish tacos and *carne asado* are additional standouts. So committed is the pair to locally grown organic produce, they plan to grow their own. **Other location** *243 DeKalb Ave between Clermont and Vanderbilt Aves, Fort Greene, Brooklyn (718-622-5300).*

★ ▲☉**Café el Portal** *174 Elizabeth St between Kenmare and Spring Sts (212-226-4642). Subway: J, M, Z to Bowery; 6 to Spring St. Mon–Sat noon–midnight. Average main course: $10.* Some of chic Elizabeth Street's best food comes from this teeny alcove run by Ignacio Carballido, whose hardworking mother rules the kitchen. One smoky special includes chiles rellenos (roasted poblano chilies stuffed with cheese in a light cream sauce). Other delights are a juicy chicken thigh and drumstick swimming in rich mole, and moist chunks of fish filling two soft corn tortillas. Mexican beers are available, as is the authentic Michelada—Corona in a glass with salt, lime and hot sauce. This is also one of the few places in town that serves fresh cucumber water, a traditional blend of cukes, sugar, water and lime juice.

☉**Chavella's** *732 Classon Ave between Park and Prospect Pls, Prospect Heights, Brooklyn (718-622-3100). Subway: C to Franklin Ave; 2, 3 to Eastern Pkwy–Brooklyn Museum. Tue–Thu 11am–10pm; Fri, Sat 11am–11pm; Sun 11am–9pm. Average main course: $9.* Chavella's doesn't offer much by way of decor—the kitchen is hidden behind green blinds, the floor tiles are a basic tan, and patrons sit at simple wooden tables. But this reasonably priced spot shouldn't be overlooked as a place to eat out. The trio of salsas (spicy salsa verde, smoky chipotle and chunky pico de gallo) is served with freshly fried, multicolored chips, replenished free of charge. Order the *bistec* taco and you'll receive two soft corn tortillas cradling tender marinated flank steak, fresh cilantro and pico de gallo for just $2.50. Addictive grilled ears of corn are buttered, then topped with dollops of creamy chipotle mayo and a sprinkling of *cotija* cheese. A tip: Make a pit stop at the deli on the corner, since the place is cash only and BYOB.

TALIA SIMHI

AUTHENTIC MEXICO CITY-STYLE AND REGIONAL HOME COOKING

LA PALAPA EAST VILLAGE
77 SAINT MARK'S PLACE
BTWN 1st and 2nd AVENUES
212.777.2537

LA PALAPA WEST VILLAGE
359 SIXTH AVENUE
BTWN W. 4th ST and WASHINGTON PL
212.243.6870

Enjoy our Fresh Fruit Margaritas, Sangrias and Extensive Tequila Selection

Serving Lunch, Brunch and Dinner 7 days a week!

¡Nuevo! La Palapa's "Bento Boxes" served Monday-Friday 5-7
Great to Share!! Bento de Bocadillos, Bento Vegetariano, Bento de Mariscos, Bento de Carne

La Palapa's ~Zihuatanejo~ Playa La Ropa Weekend Brunch Special! 3 Courses 12.95
Enjoy such house specialties as our Huevos Rancheros Verde and our Pan Frances Estilo Torrejas!

WWW.LAPALAPA.COM

26th and 27th Sts (212-294-1000) ● 825 Third Ave at 50th St (212-336-5400).

★ ▲**Fiesta Mexicana** 75-02 Roosevelt Ave at 75th St, Jackson Heights, Queens (718-505-9090). Subway: E, F, V, G, R to Jackson Hts–Roosevelt Ave; 7 to 74th St–Broadway. Daily 10am–10pm. Average main course: $14. Fiesta Mexicana does the job—breakfast, lunch or dinner—with flair. Instead of rice-and-bean platters, expect a more complex cuisine, focusing on the smoky spices and fruit-sweetened sauces of central Mexico. Camarones *enchipotlados* presents shrimp bathed in an incredible chipotle puree; *cochinita pibil* offers savory marinated pork; and enchiladas de mole are delicious. Habanero salsa (by request only) ratchets up the heat; tame the fire with silky caramel crêpes.

★ ▲**Itzocan Café** 438 E 9th St between First Ave and Ave A (212-677-5856). Subway: L to First Ave; N, R, W to 8th St–NYU; 6 to Astor Pl. Daily noon–11pm. Average main course: $12. Amid Aztec geometric bas-reliefs, diners at the 14-seat Itzocan Café explore an ambitious fusion of Mexican and French cuisines. Try the sweet corn soufflé, imbued with an earthy *huitlacoche*, a traditional Mexican truffle, or the *queso fundido*, a rich fondue of molten Brie and Monterey Jack, chockfull of garlic-laden chorizo and poblano peppers. The pan-roasted chicken breast, stuffed with tangy goat cheese, is slathered in a red mole sauce, an ethereal mélange of chocolate, chili peppers, nuts and bananas. Note that the kitchen opens right onto the dining room. **Other location** *Itzocan Bistro, 1575 Lexington Ave at 101st St (212-423-0255).*

La Esquina 106 Kenmare St at Cleveland Pl (646-613-7100). Subway: 6 to Spring St. Taqueria daily 8am–5am; café daily noon–midnight; restaurant daily 6pm–2am. Average main course: $18. This cabbie-pit-stop-turned-taco-stand has a hidden passageway to an elaborate underground grotto and restaurant. There are three distinct dining and drinking areas: first, a street-level dinerlike chrome taquería, serving a short-order menu of fish tacos and Mexican *tortas*. Around the corner is a 30-seat café, with rough-cut wood walls and shelves stocked with books and old vinyl. Last, and most spectacularly, there's a dungeonesque restaurant and lounge accessible through a back door of the taquería (to enter you have to confirm that you have a reservation). It's worth the hassle: a world of fine tequilas, Mexican tiled murals, *huitlacoche* quesadillas and lump blue-crab tostadas awaits you.

La Hacienda 219 E 116 St between Second and Third Aves (212-987-1617). Subway: 6 to 116th St. Pass beneath the red-clay-shingled canopy and down a few steps into a bright room with a low ceiling decorated with black-and-whites photos of the Mexican hinterland. A deer's head and colorful masks await you, but that's not why you're here. It's the mammoth portions that draw locals and downtowners alike. Most notable are the thick, gooey quesadillas that come with fillings like tasty zucchini flowers and a juicy roasted half-chicken comes coated with spicy and sweet brown mole poblano sauce. In a 'hood filled with south-of-the-border spots, La Hacienda sticks out for food and decor.

⊖**Los Amigos Mexican Restaurant** 22-73 31st St between Ditmars Blvd and 23rd Ave, Astoria, Queens (718-726-8708). Subway: N, W to Astoria–Ditmars Blvd. Daily 11:30am–2am. Average

More than meets the eye
Seek out La Esquina's underground grotto and restaurant.

Crema 111 W 17th St between Sixth and Seventh Aves (212-691-4477). Subway: A, C, E to 14th St; L to Eighth Ave. Tue, Wed, Sun noon–11pm; Thu–Sat noon–midnight. Average main course: $22. Julieta Ballesteros, of Mexicana Mama, gives upscale Mexican a whirl at this colorful Chelsea eatery. The menu is mercifully short, and you won't see the words *burrito* or *enchilada* anywhere on it. Instead, you get dishes like tostadas *en call de hacha*, two minicorn tortillas topped with scallops, avocado, mango salsa and a spicy chipotle aioli. Ballesteros is adept at mixing sweet and savory: The superb Chilean sea bass is served on a starchy plantain puree with a pineapple escabeche. Sweet cocktails, some made with rum or beer instead of tequila, can function as alternatives to dessert.

★ ▲**Dos Caminos Soho** 475 West Broadway at Houston St (212-277-4300). Subway: B, D, F, V to Broadway–Lafayette St; C, E to Spring St. Sun–Thu 11am–midnight; Fri, Sat 11am–midnight. Average main course: $124. Steve Hanson's empire spans the cuisine globe (Asian, Italian, etc.), but Mexican food seems best suited to his way of making a fiesta out of a meal. DC Soho, like the Park Avenue original, cranks out freshly mashed guacamole, gets everyone lubed up on strong margaritas, then teases appetites with spicy little shredded-pork tacos on warm tortillas. But good luck crashing the festivities. The bar is too small for all the pretty young things who yearn to crowd around it; and the prized patio seats are well nigh impossible to snag during prime time. You can lament the mishaps—eternal waits, entrées before appetizers—but these are inevitable glitches for such a popular place. **Other location** *Dos Caminos, 373 Park Ave South between*

main course: $9. Cheap Mexican cuisine has always been a starving-artist staple, and boho Astorians flock here well into the night. Inside the unprepossessing storefront—owned by folks from Puebla—is a menu of carefully made, nongreasy chow. The nachos could be the best you've ever chased with an icy Corona. They're piled high with savory toppings like cinnamon-spiced chorizo, marinated beef, chicken, beans, Monterey Jack and top-notch guacamole. The tacos and burritos are excellent, especially the sublime chorizo versions. For dessert, a fruit *batido* is as thick and satisfying as an ice-cream shake.

Maracas Mexican Bar & Grill 33

Greenwich Ave between Sixth and Seventh Aves (212-593-6600). Subway: A, C, E, B, D, F, V to W 4th St; 1 to Christopher St–Sheridan Sq. Sun–Thu noon–midnight; Fri, Sat noon–2am. Average main course: $13. At Maracas, a wonderfully kitschy, casual eatery, the anything-goes approach carries over to the encyclopedic menu, which features every Mexican appetizer and entrée you've ever heard of—and a bunch of Nuevo Latino options. You can even order wings, burgers and a chicken melt with bacon. The menu isn't the only thing that's large; the portions are enormous, too. You might have to doggie-bag the burrito after eating too many appetizers—great guac served with still-hot fried tortilla chips and perfectly gooey *chilaquiles*. Fortunately, the servers are adept at wrapping up leftovers.

⊖Matamoros Puebla Grocery 193 Bedford

Ave between North 6th and North 7th Sts, Williamsburg, Brooklyn (718-782-5044). Subway: L to Bedford Ave. Mon, Wed–Sun 10am–10pm; Tue 10am–8pm. Average taco: $2. In the spotless kitchen, hair-netted women from Matamoros, Puebla, fold corn tortillas and turn out some of the city's best tostadas, tacos and soups. The modest menu covers such street-food basics as *tortas* (sandwiches) and tamales. The women scribble orders on pink Post-its and plop tacos covered in salsa verde or rojo onto paper plates, finishing orders with a radish garnish. Ask for a vegetarian taco (*sin carne*), which is not on the menu; it comes with two slabs of avocado. All orders are available *para llevar* (to go)—you'll be glad of that at peak times.

Maya 1191 First Ave between 64th and 65th Sts

(212-585-1818). Subway: F to Lexington Ave–63rd St. Sun, Mon 5–10pm; Tue–Thu 5–10:30pm; Fri, Sat 5–11pm. Average main course: $24. Richard Sandoval reinvents Mexican cuisine at this romantic Upper East Sider, the first in his string of upscale international restaurants (he recently opened Maya Dubai). The steak tacos, served with cilantro- and jalapeño-flavored corn tortillas, and the seared scallops with grilled watermelon are but a few of the standouts on the eclectic menu. Heavier main courses are enlivened with inventive sides like chile poblano–potato gratin; desserts like the "tres leches" bread pudding have similarly creative Mexican accents. An extensive selection of wine, cocktails (notably the signature Margarita Maya) and 100 different kinds of tequila foster a thriving bar scene. **Other location** *Pampano, 209 E 49th St at 3rd Ave (212-751-4545).*

▲Mercadito 179 Ave B between 11th and

12th Sts (212-529-6493). Subway: L to First Ave. Mon–Thu noon–4pm, 5pm–midnight; Fri noon–4pm, 5pm–1am; Sat 11am–4pm, 5pm–1am; Sun 11am–4pm, 5–11pm. Average main course: $13. This slim, urban beach shack shrouded in bamboo thatch serves some of the city's most consistently satisfying Mexican food. Instead of finding happy-hour throngs checking beepers for tables, you'll see a chef-owner inside the open kitchen. At Mercadito, whose name means "little market," the portions are designed to be small: Instead of huge platters filled out with rice and beans, you'll find miniature tacos and tostados bursting with original flavors. Start with guacamole enlivened by mango or pineapple, or gooey *queso fundido*, a cheese fondue made of smoked Gouda, Chihuahua and Manchego cheeses. The tacos, served in foursomes, are consistently excellent; the skirt steak's a standout. For dessert, order the warm plantains Foster with a cold mound of vanilla ice cream. **Other location** *Mercadito Grove, 100 Seventh Ave South at Grove St (212-647-0830).*

▲Mexicana Mama 525 Hudson St between

Charles and W 10th Sts (212-924-4119). Subway: 1 to Christopher St–Sheridan Sq. Tue–Sun noon–11pm. Average main course: $14. Julieta Ballesteros has left the nest—and Mama suffers for her departure. While the daily roster of homemade salsas served with a brown paper bag of crisp tortilla chips remain, gone are the subtleties and inventiveness that made this tiny spot a welcome addition to the regional Mexican dining scene. Serrano salsa is overly emulsified, and the Mexican benchmark pastel *tres leches* is so soaked it's hard to make out the cake. Fortunately, a crispy-tender corn on the cob bathed in a sharpish *queso* and a tender red snapper *en chile morita* still express some of the kitchen's former deftness. You'll have less of a wait for a table to try them. **Other location** *47 E 12th St between Broadway and University Pl (212-253-7594).*

★ Mi Cocina 57 Jane St at Hudson St (212-627-

8273). Subway: A, C, E to 14th St; L to Eighth Ave. Mon–Thu 4:30–10:45pm; Fri 4:30–11:45pm; Sat 11:30am–2:30pm, 4:30–11:45pm; Sun 11:30am–2:30pm, 4:30–10:15pm. Average main course: $20. "Mi Cocina" is a mighty plain-Jane name for such a sophisticated, pleasurable place. From the casual polish of the dining room to the impressive tequila list, chef-partner Jose Hurtado-Prud'homme aims to please with complex flavor combinations. *Camarones en pipián,* shrimp in a pumpkin–seed–and–cilantro sauce and spiced with serrano chili, has a piquant kick. *Caldo largo de alvarado,* filled with chunks of red snapper and fat shrimp, is among the tastiest fish soups of all time.

Read 'em & eat

caldo largo de alvarado: chili-spiced fish soup

chimichanga: a deep-fried burrito whose tortillas are folded and filled with meat, beans, or cheese

cochinita pibil: Yucatán slow-cooked pork marinated with *achiote* fruit or oranges

huitlacoche: a soft and creamy black mushroom that grows on corn and can be pureed for *mole*

Side dish

Border patrol

Looking past Taco Bell for real Mexican cuisine.

Meat, cheese, beans and chilies bundled in a tortilla forms most Americans' idea of Mexican cuisine. While that unchallenging amalgam may be true of the fast-food chains that pawn themselves off as "Mexican," the real thing is a far more intriguing blend of indigenous and European influences that varies considerably throughout our southern neighbor's regions.

Unsurprisingly for an area well known for cattle breeding, the cuisine of **northeastern Mexico** is all about beef. Generally, the meat is grilled and served with wheat-flour tortillas (most Mexican cuisines favor corn tortillas) but the area's nomadic heritage has also given rise to an array of dried, salted and shredded beef dishes.

In the **Yucatán Peninsula**, a marriage of Mayan, Spanish and Caribbean influences creates a cuisine in which fruit-based (rather than chili-based) sauces dominate. The most well known of these is the sweet and succulent *pibil*, in which chicken or pork is marinated in achiote paste, oranges, pepper, garlic and cumin before being baked in a banana leaf.

Unsurprisingly, seafood figures prominently in the cuisines of the **Gulf and Pacific Coasts**. In Veracruz, Gulf shrimp, red snapper, sea bass and octopus are often topped with a sauce made of tomatoes, olives, capers and chilies. The coasts are

also home to a variant of ceviche, whose white-fleshed fish fillets are marinated in lime, cilantro, onion and oil. **Puebla** cooking reflects its Aztec, Spanish, Arabic and Asian heritages. Mole poblano, a kitchen-sink invention of spices, chilies,

nuts and chocolate, and chiles en nogada (chiles stuffed with meat, almonds and raisins and topped with pomegranate seeds and walnut sauce) are the region's most famous exports. Puebla is also renowned for its sweet-tooth fixes, such as *camote*, a sweet-potato dessert, and rompope, Mexican eggnog.

The cuisine of **Oaxaca** reflects a mix of culinary cultures, as is evidenced by its nickname, "Land of Seven Moles." It is further famous for fried grasshoppers (*chapulines*), string cheese (*quesillo*), fruit-stuffed pork and beef tongue with sweet-and-sour tomato juice. Oaxacan mole is sweetened by the addition of bananas, and its coffee is laced with cinnamon and sugar.

★ **Pampano** *209 E 49th St between Second and Third Aves (212-751-4545). Subway: E, V to Lexington Ave–53rd St; 6 to 51st St. Sun, Mon 5–10pm; Tue–Thu 5–10:30pm; Fri, Sat 5–11pm. Average main course: $23.* Maya's Richard Sandoval is one of the city's most creative Mexican chefs, and this classy seafood outpost is a midtown favorite. Mini lobster tacos taste as if the tender meat and fresh tortillas had been grilled beachside; striped bass is carefully steamed in a banana leaf, with plantain and bell pepper. Sandoval's taco stand, at Third Avenue and 49th Street, isn't your typical street meat; the offerings come from Pampano's kitchen. **Other location** *Pampano Taqueria, 805 Third Ave between 49th and 50th Sts (212-751-5257).*

▲**Rosa Mexicano** *9 E 18th St between Broadway and Fifth Ave (212-533-3350). Subway: L, N, Q, R, W, 4, 5, 6 to 14th St–Union Sq. Mon–Sat 11:30am–11:30pm; Sun 4–11pm. Average main course: $24.* Rosa Mexicano was once a lone paragon of fine Mexican dining. But with three restaurants in Manhattan, one in Washington, DC, and two more on the way (in Atlanta and Miami), it has become an upscale chain. Rosa Mexicano's guacamole, prepared tableside to your specifications, launched a pestle craze in New York; the stuff is still the chunky, spicy standard by which others are judged. The rest of the food, however, has lost some of its flair. Boneless short ribs can be stringy and overpowered by a stewed heap of tomatoes and peppers. And yet, despite the middling food and high prices, crowds still can't get enough of the place—must be the addictive pomegranate margaritas. **Other locations** *1063 First Ave at 58th St (212-753-7407)* ● *61 Columbus Ave at 62nd St (212-977-7700).*

★ **Sueños** *311 W 17th St between Eighth and Ninth Aves (212-243-1333). Subway: A, C, E to 14th St; L to Eighth Ave. Mon–Wed, Sun 5–11pm; Thu–Sat 5pm–midnight. Average main course: $20.* Familiar dishes, prepared with a twist: That's the signature of chef-owner Sue Torres, who cut her teeth at Rocking Horse Cafe. At her colorful underground restaurant, you're likely to find unlikely specialties such as lobster-and-corn fritters or pressed-to-order fresh tortillas. There's also a terrific Sunday brunch menu that caters to the hungover and the hungry. The bar offers dozens of tequilas and six types of margaritas at prices from $10 to $69—higher than you'd expect at a Mexican restaurant.

Zarela *953 Second Ave between 50th and 51st Sts (212-644-6740). Subway: E, V to Lexington Ave–53rd St; 6 to 51st St. Mon–Thu noon– 3pm, 5–11pm; Fri, noon–3pm, 5– 11:30pm; Sat 5–11:30pm; Sun 5–10pm. Average main course: $18, $42 prix fixe.* As Mexican cuisine gets more and more haute, it's refreshing to find Zarela as warm, friendly and delicious as it was when it introduced New Yorkers to "real Mexican food" over twenty years ago. Folk-art decor, tissue-paper cutouts and a knowledgeable, attentive staff create a festive yet relaxed vibe that complements such dishes as chile relleno stuffed with "poor man's *picadillo*"—an expert combo of flavor and punch; sweetly sticky plantains served with Oaxacan mole; or one of the city's best *cochinito pibil*, Yucatán slow-cooked pork marinated with *achiote* and oranges. Daily specials, like a meaty grilled octopus spiked with jalapeño and garlic, point to an assured hand in the kitchen; thank goodness some things never change.

Apple dumpling
Manzana con miel is
served seasonally at
Mexicana Mama.

Mexican

CINZIA HEALE-CASTELLO

Drink up

Tequila 101

Alcohol connoisseurs who dismiss tequila as wormwater consumed as a shot off another person's navel should consider the following: Mexico's national drink was born when Spanish *conquistadores* brought the distilling process to the New World in the sixteenth century. Natives of the town of Tequila in the western Mexican state of Jalisco were quick to apply the process to the blue agave plant, whose sugars they'd long been fermenting. Liquor made from any of the other 399 agave varieties is called *mezcal*. The notions that tequila and mezcal are made from a cactus, or that the latter contains the hallucinogen mescaline, belong to the realm of myth.

Not all tequilas are made entirely of tequila. Mexico permits distillers to fill as much as 49% of the bottle with additives like molasses or cane sugar and still label it tequila such as **Jose Cuervo** and **Sauza**. Note that truly 100 percent tequila distinguishes itself as "100% agave tequila" (like **Don Fulano Imperial** or **El Tesora de Don Felipe Paradiso**).

Within the pure agave tequilas, there are three styles. Blanco is unaged and clear (think vodka); reposado is light redwood-barrel-aged (think rum); and anejo is produced by heavy bourbon-barrel aging (think whiskey). Pure tequila makes a huge difference in taste: When drinking it straight you get none of the bite that keeps the lime industry thriving. On the other hand, when it comes to margaritas, the tequila actually makes very little difference—with all that ice, it's so cold you can't taste it.

And as for the worm, it's put in some mezcal bottles as a sales gimmick—not that the venerable drink needs much help selling.

Get fresh
Bonita uses local, organically-grown produce.

Zócalo *174 E 82nd St between Lexington and Third Aves (212-717-7772). Subway: 4, 5, 6 to 86th St. Mon 11:30am–9pm; Tue–Fri 11:30am–9:30pm; Sat 11:30am–9pm; Sun 11:30am–6:30pm . Average main course: $25.* Far more ambitious than the typical margarita-slinging joints that dominate this neighborhood, the lively, colorful Zócalo updates regional dishes. Chef David Espinoza offers combinations such as spicy pork ribs cooked in a banana leaf, and a tender chili-rubbed hanger steak served with a goat-cheese enchilada. The guacamole appetizer comprises three varieties of the avocado classic that will please any palate. Despite that inventiveness, Zócalo may seem a tad overpriced. **Other location** *Grand Central Terminal, Lower Concourse, 42nd St at Park Ave (212-687-5666).*

★ **Zona Rosa** *40 W 56th St between Fifth and Sixth Aves (212-247-2800). Subway: F, N, Q, R, W to 57th St. Mon–Fri 11:30am–3pm, 5–10:30pm; Sat 5–10:30pm. Average main course: $23.* Zona Rosa features a bar and an upstairs dining room for the happy-hour hordes, and a mellower, brown-hued room downstairs for the low-key pretheater crowd. Guests are greeted with a newspaper cone of chili-powdered jicama, cucumber and orange slices—a great lead-in for starters such as shrimp ceviche with a ruby-red sauce that tastes as bright as it looks, or an earthy *huitlacoche* and wild-mushroom empanada. Chef Adrian Leon's expert saucing gives entrées depth, such as a kicky *pasilla* chili sauce on the grilled, marinated chicken breast. Sweet finishes like roasted pineapple crepes round out a satisfying menu.

Middle Eastern

See also: *Afghan, Kosher, Moroccan, Turkish*

Quite a looker
Taboon is a lusty oasis
in west midtown

★ ▲**Al Bustan** *827 Third Ave between 50th and 51st Sts (212-759-5933). Subway: E, V to Lexington Ave–53rd St; 6 to 51st St. Noon–3pm, 5:30–10pm. Average main course: $21.* You'll feel as though you've stepped into a friend's dining room here—and that friend also happens to be a very good cook whose dishes are stunningly presented. Parsley-heavy tabouli is neatly balanced with lemon juice and olive oil; hummus is smooth and nutty; laban bi khiar has a garlicky tang that contrasts nicely with the cool mint and yogurt. Entrées, such as delicious grilled chicken skewers or luscious lamb stew with okra and tomatoes, are just as good.

★ ▲◑**Alfanoose** *8 Maiden Lane between Broadway and Nassau Sts (212-528-4669). A, C, J, M, Z to Fulton St–Broadway/Nassau. Mon–Sat 11:30am–9:30pm. Average falafel: $5.* Owner Mouhamad Shami found the city's falafel too oily, so he introduced his own at this cafeteria-style spot, which also serves fine shawarma, kebabs, baba ghanoush and other Middle Eastern standards. The crunchy chickpea fritters are also worth a try: The tasty patties are lighter than most and subtly spiced with cumin and coriander. The fare here is healthier than most takeout, but that doesn't mean it isn't cheap, or fast. Still, Alfanoose wisely dims the lights in the evening, encouraging some diners to linger and enjoy their meal in-house.

▲◑**Black Betty** *366 Metropolitan Ave at Havemeyer St, Williamsburg, Brooklyn (718-599-0243). Subway: L to Lorimer St; G to Metropolitan Ave. Mon–Fri 6:30pm–midnight; Sat, Sun 11am–4pm, 6:30pm–midnight. Average main course: $10.* Seven years after Billyburg pioneers Bud Schmeling and Sandy Glover transformed the forlorn Highway Lounge into a

rockin' neighborhood bar, its fierce lineup of live music continues to draw a hot young crowd. But Black Betty is also a restaurant, serving good Middle Eastern eats, like flaky Turkish pastries stuffed with spicy lamb or spinach and feta. The falafel platter is more than enough food for two, and there are first-rate vegetarian offerings as well as couscous with spicy merguez, beef or chicken. After dinner, cool your palate with a pint of Stella and stake out a good place to catch the show.

▲◑**Bread & Olive** *24 W 45th St between Fifth and Sixth Aves (212-764-1588). Subway: B, D, F, V to 42nd St; 7 to Fifth Ave–Bryant Park.. Mon–Fri 10am–9pm; Sat 10am–6pm. Average main course: $10.* Diners descend in hordes for Bread & Olive's falafel and citrus-marinated shawarma, which are rolled with tomatoes, pickles and tahini sauce into pita bread that's baked in the restaurant's brick oven. Dinner, like lunch, is a modest affair. Sides such as *loubieh bi zayt* (string beans sautéed with tomato and onion) come in foil trays. Although primarily a take-out spot, the small rear dining room is inviting enough for a sit-down: The walls are painted in raucous Day-Glo, the staff is enthusiastic, and the sound system thumps Arabic beats.

Byblos *200 E 39th St at Third Ave (212-687-0808). Subway: 42nd St S, 4, 5, 6, 7 to 42nd St–Grand Central. Mon–Thurs, Sun 11:30am–11pm; Fri, Sat 11:30am–1am. Average main course: $20.* White tablecloths, mauve walls and abstract paintings amount to a clean but generic setting with no obvious Middle Eastern motif. This is quickly overlooked in the wake of warm, attentive service and perfect, homemade humus and baba ghannouj. Other appetizers include *ful medames* (slow-simmered fava

PATRIK RYTIKANGAS

beans with lemon and garlic) and citrusy roasted quail. Among the diverse entrées are a fresh, grilled fillet of sole and juicy chicken shish kebab, which is well seasoned and accompanied by a heaping portion of marinated vegetables. A full bar offers Almaza, a Lebanese brew, and on Friday and Saturday nights, a belly dancer shakes things up.

★ ▲**Casa la Femme North** *1076 First Ave between 58th and 59th Sts (212-505-0005). Subway: N, R, W to Lexington Ave–59th St; 4, 5, 6 to 59th St. Mon–Wed, Sun 5pm–midnight; Thu 5pm–1am; Fri, Sat 5pm–3am. Average main course: $21.* The relocation of Soho's long-standing seduction spot—along with its flashy belly dancers and fabric-partitioned, cushion-strewn tents—has not diminished its charm. The multicourse prix fixe ($55) begins with thick, peppery hummus and progresses to crabmeat kofta, which, for all intents and purposes, is an Arabian crab cake. Smokers will want to give the ornate hookah a shot: The bubbling draw of mild, apple-cured tobacco is exotic enough to make dinner under the Queensboro Bridge feel like an adventure at the oasis.

Falafel Chula *436 Union Ave at Metropolitan St, Williamsburg, Brooklyn (718-387-0303). Subway: L to Lorimer St; G to Metropolitan Ave. Mon–Sat noon–midnight. Average main course: $7.* Your dollar goes far at this tiny Middle Eastern joint from the Egyptian immigrant family that brought you Taco Chula. Start with a plate of homemade pickles or the creamy baba ghanoush and move on to a heaping mixed grill of tender spice-inflected chicken, shish kebab and kofta. The restaurant's namesake is a family recipe made the Egyptian way—with fava beans rather than chickpeas; one of the three available varieties is the flavor-laced Parisien, which is stuffed with French fries, fried eggplant, cucumber and sauerkraut. Seating is limited, but in warmer months the tiny dining room leads to a cozy outdoor eating area, where you can bring your own booze.

▲**Fountain Cafe** *183 Atlantic Ave between Clinton and Court Sts, Brooklyn Heights, Brooklyn (718-624-6764). Subway: F, G to Bergen St; M, R to Court St. Daily 10:30am–10:30pm. Average main course: $13.* You could feed a caravan from a dinner platter at this Syrian spot along Brooklyn's Arab Alley. Smoky *kibbeh*, tender stuffed grape leaves and mildly spicy chicken-kefta kebabs spiked with parsley and onions arrive on plates piled high with salad, rice or fries, and hummus or baba ghanoush. Since you'll already be stuffed, go all out and try the *halawat al-jeben*, a luscious mixture of sweet cheese and semolina cooked on a griddle, topped with ricotta, then rolled up and doused with rose water and honey.

★ ◉**Hummus Place** *109 St Marks between First Ave and Avenue A (212-529-9198). Subway: 6 to Astor Pl; L to First Ave. Mon–Fri, Sun 11am–midnight; Sat 11am–2am. Average hummus plate: $5.* If you want to know how good hummus should taste, check out this slender East Village restaurant (there are two more locations, one in the West Village and one on the Upper West Side). We're particularly fond of the supersmooth traditional hummus. It's rich enough to be called "vegetarian chopped liver" and comes with a smart selection of condiments including pickles, olives, raw onion and chewy, bubbly pita for scooping. **Other locations** *99 MacDougal St between Bleecker St and Minetta Ln (212-533-3089).* ● *305 Amsterdam Ave at W 74th St (212-799-3335).*

★ ▲**Kabab Café** *25-12 Steinway St at 25th Ave, Astoria, Queens (718-728-9858). Subway: N, W to Astoria Blvd.. Tue–Sun noon–11pm. Average main course: $12.* Cheerful proprietor Ali el-Sayed wants you to be happy at the pint-size Kabab Café, where the food is delectable. Start with velvety baba ghanoush (studded with apples for a sweet twist) and *eggeh*, a golden-brown egg fritter. Logs of ground lamb and beef kofta are well-spiced, and the classic *moussaka* is a hearty vegetarian option.

★ ■**Mamlouk** *211 E 4th St between Aves A and B (212-529-3477). Subway: F, V to Lower East Side–Second Ave. Tues–Sun 7pm–midnight. Prix fixe: $40.* Meze of hummus, falafel and *za'atar*—flatbread topped with dried sesame seeds and olive oil—begin a six-course tasting menu that segues into a salad rich with black olives, tomatoes and avocado. Next up are thick vegetable stew or luscious moussaka. Two meat dishes provide the main course: chicken, either accompanied by walnuts and tart pomegranate juice or, on some nights, served kebob style over a bed of creamy lentil puree; and lamb, sometimes braised in a rich, tomato sauce. The pillow-strewn settees are particularly handy on weekends, when stuffed patrons sit back between courses to puff on hookahs and enjoy entertainment from belly dancers.

▲**Miriam** *79 5th Ave at Prospect Place, Park Slope, Brooklyn (718-622-2250). Subway: 2,3 to Bergen St. Mon–Thu, Sun 5–11pm; Fri, Sat 5pm–midnight; Sun 10am–4pm. Average main course $17.* Middle Eastern cuisine goes far beyond the same old falafel at this innovative bistro. Miriam's lantern-lit interior is perfect for a date—and the list of creative dishes helps drive dinner conversation. Herbs, spices and fresh combinations dominate an inspired Israeli-fusion menu featuring abundant salads and diverse entrées. Marjoram-crusted striped bass is served with cauliflower purée, sautéed garlic, green beans and an herb salad, and a tilapia cake is enriched with carrots, shallots, fennel, parsley and scallions. The true bargain is the $7.95 brunch, featuring eggs, granola, burgers and Israeli dishes. It is, predictably, crowded. **Other location** *229 Court St between Baltic and Warren Sts, Cobble Hill, Brooklyn (718-522-2220).*

Mombar *25-22 Steinway St between 25th and 28th Aves, Astoria, Queens (718-726-2356). Subway: N, W to 30th Ave.. Tue–Sun 5–11pm. Average main course: $15.* Look for the gorgeous mosaic eye marking the door of this relaxing eatery. Chef-owner Moustafa el-Sayed also designed the twinkling mosaics that adorn the walls and tables. Sink back into the pillows and savor nouveau Egyptian creations like sesame phyllo bread, spiced stuffed sausage, garlic-kissed quail and molasses-glazed duck. Indecisive? Put yourself in the hands of the chef with the $30 tasting menu and a bottle of light Algerian wine.

★ ▲◉**Moustache** *90 Bedford St between Barrow and Grove Sts (212-229-2220). Subway: 1 to Christopher St–Sheridan Sq. Daily noon–midnight. Average main course: $9.* Located on a leafy, brownstone-lined West Village street, this beloved cheap-eats haven serves some of the city's best Middle Eastern food. The small, exposed-brick dining room packs in a neighborhood crowd nightly—it's not unlikely to see a line outside this no-reservations spot. But it's worth the wait. The freshly baked pitas, still puffed up with hot air when served, are perfect for scooping up what is arguably the best hummus in the city, rich with olive oil, zesty lemon and whole chickpeas. More elaborate offerings include *ouzi*: rice, chicken, vegetables and raisins cooked in phyllo and a lamb *pitza*, a light, savory-spicy affair. **Other location** *265 E 10th St between First Ave and Ave A (212-228-2022).*

Persepolis *1407 Second Ave between 73rd and 74th Sts (212-535-1100). Subway: 6 to 77th St. Mon–Thu, Sun noon–11pm; Fri, Sat noon–midnight. Average main course: $18.* Such a simple, unassuming restaurant is an appropriate setting for uncomplicated, hearty and delicious food. *Gaimah bada joon,* a vegetable stew, has a rich, savory broth, and the Caspian (boneless chicken and chopped steak over rice) has a lively marinade. Fans of more Mediterranean-oriented Middle Eastern cooking should be prepared for authentically Persian variations: The "khumus" and tabouli, for example, are drier and prepared differently than familiar versions; the yogurt and cucumber is…yogurt and cucumber.

▲☺**Pyramida** *401 E 78th St at First Ave (212-472-5855). Subway: 6 to 77th St. Mon–Thu, Sat, Sun 11am–11pm; Fri 2–11pm. Average main course: $9.* At this little four-table storefront, you can get hard-to-find *koshari,* the humble rice dish flecked with lentils, macaroni, fried onions and spicy tomato sauce. You can also order a damn fine meal of "falafel and more" (the "more" means a mountain of hummus or baba ganoush). Giant *kibbeh* torpedoes are served on a bed of rice tossed with raisins, toasted almonds and cinnamon. Despite the alluring savories, Pyramida's reputation is staked on its freshly squeezed, frothy lemonade. Proprietor Ahmed Reda won't give away his secret, but it has something to do with lemon zest.

▲**Rectangles** *1431 First Ave between 74th and 75th Sts (212-744-7470). Subway: 6 to 77th St. Mon–Thu, Sun 11:30am–midnight; Fri, Sat 11:30am–1am. Average main course: $15.* After losing its East Village lease, this Yemenite-Israeli standby relocated to the Upper East Side. Walnut paneling and floors, colorful tapestries and antique wooden chairs make the 60-seat café feel as if it's been around for years. Regulars will find many of their old favorites like baba ghanoush with warm pita, and all manner of kebab. Chef Tzipi Said grills beef, turkey, lamb, fish and baby chicken seasoned with her proprietary blend of freshly ground pepper, cumin, cloves and cardamom. There's also a 16-seat outdoor café.

★▲**Taboon** *773 Tenth Ave at 52nd St (212-713-0271). Subway: C, E to 50th St. Mon–Fri 5–11pm; Sat 5:30–11:30pm; Sun noon–3pm, 5–10pm. Average main course: $24.* One of the city's hipper Middle Eastern restaurants, this lusty space is a welcome oasis on the western fringes of midtown. Flickering candles, a tiled open kitchen and a working stone oven offer a nice backdrop to the piquant, Pan–Middle Eastern cuisine. Standards like tsatsiki and hummus are well executed, but more inventive dishes, like the savory pastry cigars filled with sweetbreads, oyster mushrooms, parsley, preserved lemon and harissa, are more interesting.

☺**Taïm** *222 Waverly Pl at W 11th St and Seventh Ave (212-691-1287). Subway: 1 to Christopher St–Sheridan Sq. Daily noon–10pm. Average falafel: $4.50.* Falafel doesn't usually come in different flavors—unless it's made by an Israel-born chef who's worked under Bobby Flay. At her new falafel and smoothie bar, Taïm, Ludo chef Einat Admony seasons chickpea batter three ways: traditional (with parsley and cilantro), sweet (with roasted red pepper) and spicy (with Tunisian spices and garlic). She pairs the terrific falafel with tasty salads like marinated beets, spicy Moroccan carrot salad or baba ghanoush, and three dipping sauces. The smoothies are exotic too—date-lime-banana, pineapple–coconut milk and a refreshing cantaloupe-ginger—and can be made with whole, skim or soy milk.

▲☺**Tanoreen** *7704 Third Ave between 77th and 78th Sts, Bay Ridge, Brooklyn (718-748-5600). Subway: R to 77th St. Tue–Sun 10:30am–10:30pm. Average main course: $11.* On the weekends, Tanoreen is packed with locals in love with the lamb-heavy cuisine of charming chef-owner Rawia Bishara. Break open a golden, football-shaped ball of *kibbeh* and be seduced by the savory aroma of ground lamb, onions and pine nuts. Bishara whips up ever-changing specials; if you're lucky, you'll drop by when she's serving sublimely soft lamb-stuffed baby eggplant. Rose-water rice pudding is perfectly pleasant, but it's just fluff compared to the must-have cheese *knafeh.* Served piping hot, pizza-style, this mammoth pie has a crust of shredded phyllo and a sweet-savory filling of oozing Arabic cheeses. Don't even think about getting out of here in a hurry: There's only one waiter.

▲☺**Tripoli** *156 Atlantic Ave at Clinton St, Brooklyn Heights, Brooklyn (718-596-5800). Subway: M, R to Court St; 2, 3, 4, 5 to Borough Hall. Mon, Wed, Thu, Sun noon–10:30pm; Fri, Sat noon–11:30pm. Average main course: $11.* Eating at Tripoli on a Friday night, you might be one of only two groups in the place. But the staff of this family-run Lebanese eatery don't seem bothered: They've been serving their native cuisine in this Brooklyn Heights spot since the early '70s, and they aren't going anywhere. The restaurant turns out traditionally hearty staples like baba ghanoush and spinach pie, followed by meaty entrées, including charcoal-broiled leg of lamb and tahini-walnut-and-almond-crusted fish fillets. If you show up on a slow night, it feels as though they're cooking just for you.

▲☺**Waterfalls Cafe** *144 Atlantic Ave between Clinton and Henry Sts, Brooklyn Heights, Brooklyn (718-488-8886). Subway: F, G to Bergen St; M, R to Court St. Noon–10:30pm. Average main course: $10.* You'll find this family-run, ten-table spot amid the cluster of Middle Eastern shops at the west end of Atlantic Avenue, but the diners represent all facets of the Brooklyn prism—a scruffy white boy and his Asian date, a gaggle of teen prepsters from Brooklyn Heights, groups of Arabic speakers in spirited after-dessert conversation. Dive, don't dip, into the pita-perfect *mouhammara,* a flavorful Syrian spread of walnut and sweet red peppers, followed by a perfectly seasoned plate of lamb-stuffed cabbage. Skip the baklava (a bit of a tough chew) and the gritty, unsweetened apricot pudding (clearly an acquired taste).

Read 'em & eat

shawarma: marinated meat (usually lamb or chicken) grilled on a spit and served kebab style

shish tawook: (also *shish taok*) chargrilled chicken that has been marinated in garlic, lemon juice and olive oil

tabouli: a salad of chopped parsley, tomatoes, onions, lemon juice and olive oil

za'atar: a tart, flavorful spice blend that varies across the Middle East, but commonly includes thyme, sesame seeds, suma and marjoram

Moroccan

See also: *African, French, Mediterranean, Middle Eastern*

★ **Barbes** *21 E 36th St between Fifth and Madison Aves (212-684-0215). Subway: 6 to 33rd St. Mon–Thu 11:30am–midnight; Fri, Sat 11am–1am; Sun 11:30am–midnight. Average main course: $24.* Traditional Moroccan fare mixes with a bit of France at Barbes, named for the North African neighborhood in Paris and decorated with hanging Moroccan fixtures and an oversized palm tree. Kebabs of cumin- and saffron-spiced lamb or marinated chicken and shrimp jump-start a meal that might continue with bistro fare like duck confit and steak frites, or Moroccan choices like rack of lamb or tagines of chicken or fish. The hummus is particularly fluffy and flavorful.

★ ▲**Café Mogador** *101 St. Marks Pl between First Ave and Ave A (212-677-2226). Subway: L to First Ave; 6 to Astor Pl. Mon–Thu, Sun 9am–1am; Fri, Sat 9am–2am. Average main course: $15.* If you think "too much garlic" is a reasonable criticism, head elsewhere. And that's fine with the rest of us, who'll gladly take your table and unwind at this warmly lit, white-walled garden-level café, frequented by a chill, international East Village crowd. Here, you'll eat simple, filling Moroccan food with smooth touches, like fresh shallots in the broth for mussels (a frequent special) and extremely tasty olive oil drizzled atop hummus and baba ghanoush; the mixed platter comes with both, as well as exceptional tabouli.

☺**Kemia Bar** *630 Ninth Ave at 44th St (212-582-3200). Subway: A, C, E to 42nd St–Port Authority. Tue–Fri 6pm–2am; Sat 8pm–3am. Average tapa: $6.* The simple Moroccan tapas at this basement speakeasy-like lounge would taste good anywhere, but they're even better here, in one of Hell's Kitchen's most stunning rooms: Moody lighting, red-leather banquettes and damask wallpaper transport you to a sultan's private lair. Marseille chef Andy D'Amico keeps things familiar but adds small twists: Creamy hummus gets nutty seven-grain toast points, and couscous-crusted shrimp comes with a dipping sauce of cooked red pepper and tomato salsa. Entrées like chicken tagine and lamb *kefta* are sturdy enough to stand up to the strong cocktails.

La Maison du Couscous *484 77th St between Fourth and Fifth Aves, Bay Ridge, Brooklyn (718-921-2400). Subway: R to 77th St. Daily noon–11:30pm. Average main course: $13.* This dive is low on pretense and high enough on flavor to draw Manhattan adventurers. *Briwats*, bite-size phyllo pastries stuffed with lamb, chicken or seafood, are sweet or savory marvels. Tagines, like lamb with prunes and almonds or chicken with lemon and carrots, would please a Casablancan. The namesake dish comes in many permutations, including lamb with vegetables, chicken with onions and raisins and, of course, couscous royale.

▲**Le Souk** *47 Ave B between 3rd and 4th Sts (212-777-5454). Subway: F, V to Lower East Side–Second Ave. Mon–Thu, Sun 6pm–2am; Fri, Sat 6pm–3am. Average main course: $19.* This mild-mannered hangout turns raucous on weekends, with belly dancers and Mid-Eastern grooves. During the week, the scene is mellower, when the crowd lounges on wall-to-wall couches with overstuffed pillows (though the dancers still make an appearance). Start with herb-infused flatbread and lemony olive tapenade, followed by stuffed squid or *ajja* merguez (poached, cumin-seasoned lamb sausage). Note: Groups of five or more are held to the prix-fixe menu.

Park Terrace Bistro *4959 Broadway at 207th St (212-567-2828). A to 207th St. Mon–Thu 5–10pm; Fri, Sat noon–3pm, 5–10:30pm; Sun noon–3pm, 5–8:30pm. Average main course: $19.* Behind a façade that, despite best efforts, evokes a hotel bar, lies this charming neighborhood restaurant decorated with colored-glass lanterns and moody paintings of Moroccan street scenes. While regulars gather at the bar, tables fill up with first-daters and families who dine on pillowy pita accompanied by creamy hummus, eggplant and roasted peppers; Fifteenth-Century Couscous studded with shrimp, scallops, almonds and apricots; or a beautifully prepared tagine, such as flaky sea bass on a bed of olives, lemon and caramelized carrots. If you simply can't eat another bite, opt for the house tea, a refreshing blend of mint and rosewater poured dramatically into a small, jeweled glass.

Tagine Dining Gallery *537 Ninth Ave between 39th and 40th Sts (212-564-7292). Subway: A, C, E to 42nd St–Port Authority. Daily 4:30pm–4am. Average main course: $15.* A grubby stretch of Hell's Kitchen is brightened by Tagine's imaginative North African decor and exceptional, reasonably priced food. Roasted, marinated eggplant stars in the tangy *zalouk*, and vegetable *borek* features vividly spiced vegetables in flaky dough. Chicken Meisel—braised with herbs, preserved lemon, saffron and white wine—is positively succulent. End the meal with the *basbousa*, semolina cake with pine nuts and honey. You'll also find an impressive nightly lineup of live world music and belly dancing, plus a three-hour Moroccan cooking class the last Sunday of every month.

Read 'em & eat

b'steeya: (also called *pastilla*) sweet and savory meat pie with flaky pastry crust

merguez: a spicy lamb sausage

tagine: (*tajin* or *tajine*) slow-cooked stew of meat, vegetables and spices, often served with couscous; also refers to the vessel used to cook it in, which has an inverted cone lid

zalouk: a spicy dip made of eggplant, tomato and garlic

Peruvian

See also: *Argentine, Brazilian, Latin American*

Chimu *482 Union Ave between Conselyea St and Meeker Ave, Williamsburg, Brooklyn (718-349-1208). Subway: L to Lorimer St, G to Metropolitan Ave. Mon–Thu noon–11pm; Fri, Sat noon–1am; Sun 10am–11pm. Average main course: $14.* Hot chili peppers have found a home under the BQE. A helping of crunchy, salty *choclo* (spicy corn kernels) warms up your taste buds for cool ceviche, zesty mussels, *aji de gallina* (steamed white rice with shredded chicken in a creamy yellow sauce), or *tamale criollo* (corn pie stuffed with chicken, eggs and olives, and covered in Creole sauce). Warm apple crêpes drenched in raspberry sauce aren't particular to Peru, but the added scoop of *lucumi* ice cream gives the dish authentic flair.

Coco Roco *392 Fifth Ave between 6th and 7th Sts, Park Slope, Brooklyn (718-965-3376). Subway: F, M, R to Fourth Ave–9th St. Sun–Thu 11:30am–10:30pm; Fri, Sat 11:30am–11:30pm. Average main course: $13.* Start by ordering a pitcher of potent, fruit-stocked sangria—you'll need it to take the edge off the spicy food to follow. Right when you sit down, bowls of fried plantain chips and roasted corn are placed on your table, with a creamy green-pepper sauce for dunking. They pair well with the loud salsa music and will prime you for the more-filling sustenance to come. Top-quality ingredients flown in from Peru ramp up the authenticity of the appealing ceviches and tangy favorites like *pulpo al olivo* (rosemary-seasoned octopus with an olive sauce) and *jalea* (mixed seafood battered in purple cornmeal and lightly fried). **Other location** *139 Smith St between Bergen and Dean Sts (718-254-9933).*

Inti Raymi *86-14 37th Ave between 86th and 87th Sts, Jackson Heights, Queens (718-424-1938). Subway: 7 to 90th St–Elmhurst Ave.. Mon–Thu noon–11pm; Fri noon–midnight; Sat 10am–midnight; Sun 10am–11pm. Average main course: $15.* The killer ceviche, excellent chicken-and-pork tamales and addictive *papas rellenas* are all filling enough that you need never leave the *entradas* section of the menu. Main dishes like *tacu tacu*, a rice-and-bean dish topped with beef, lamb stew or breaded steak, can tilt the scale from hearty to downright heavy. Instead, go crazy with the tasty appetizers and then move straight on to dessert: The humitas, a warm

Big bird
Pio Pio's Matador combo includes a whole rotisserie chicken.

raisin-dotted corn tamale, is just sweet enough, and the *lucumi* ice cream is cooler than a tropical breeze.

Pardo's *92 Seventh Ave South between Bleecker and Grove Sts (212-488-3900). 1 to Christopher St–Sheridan Sq. Mon–Thu, Sun noon–11pm; Fri, Sat noon–midnight.. Average main course price: $10.* Capitalizing on the long-standing success that local Peruvians (Pio Pio, Coco Roco) have found with their version of crispy chicken, this South American chain opened its first city location in 2006, featuring wood-paneled walls and trendy Latin music. The main attraction is rubbed with 14 spices, ranging from spicy to sweet, and left to marinate for several hours before a 40-minute spin on the spit. The result is moist meat with a salty-spicy crisp crust.

Pio Pio *1746 First Ave between 90th and 91st Sts (212-426-5800). Subway: 4, 5, 6 to 86th St. 11am–11pm. Average main course: $14.* The white tablecloths, colorfully chic interior and attentive waitstaff may make you hesitate to eat with your hands. It would be a real shame to miss a single scrap of the excellent rotisserie chicken, so if you're too shy to gnaw a drumstick in public, get your overflowing, affordable platter to go. You must order chicken (the restaurant's name is Spanish for the "cheep cheep" sound of baby chicks); the only question is which preparation you want. The most popular plate, the Matador combo, is a whole roasted chicken plus rice, beans, avocado salad and fried plantains, with a creamy jalapeño dipping sauce on the side—more than enough for a family of four. **Other locations** *84-13 Northern Blvd between 84th and 85th Sts, Jackson Hts, Queens (718-426-1010)* ● *62-30 Woodhaven Blvd between Dry Harbor and 62nd Rds, Rego Park, Queens (718-458-0606).*

Read 'em & eat

jalea: a deep-fried mix of seafood, sometimes served with cassava

papas rellenas: deep-fried mashed potatoes stuffed with beef

peruano tamales: cornmeal stuffed with meat, seafood or vegetables, and steamed in banana leaves

TALIA SIMHI

Portuguese

See also: *Brazilian, Mediterranean, Spanish*

Open and shut case
Tintol excels at exquisite
small plates.

Alfama *551 Hudson St at Perry St (212-645-2500). Subway: 1 to Christopher St–Sheridan Sq. Mon–Thur 6pm–11pm; Fri 6pm–midnight; Sat noon–3pm, 6–midnight; Sun noon–3pm, 5–11pm. Average main course: $25.* When Alfama lost its original chef, it found a new lease on life by infusing modern flair to what used to be an entirely classic menu. Among the better standard dishes is a succulent salt-cod fillet perched on a buttery mountain of mashed potatoes. The pricey "new-wave" additions include an octopus dish, an inspired arrangement of meaty hunks paired with potatoes; crisp, paper-thin peppers; shredded egg and cilantro coulis; and Mozambique prawns, charred to perfection and topped with hot-chili chutney. And you'll still find cheeses and a fine selection of ports and wines, many available by the glass.

Read 'em & eat

bacalhau: salt cod (a staple)

caldeirada de peixe: a fish or shellfish stew

chouriço: pork sausage, often used in stew

piri-piri: a sauce made from small hot chilies, red peppers and herbs; usually served with meat or fish dishes

sardinhas assadas: roasted or char-grilled sardines

Luzia's *429 Amsterdam Ave between 80th and 81st Sts (212-595-2000). Subway: 1 to 79th St. Mon–Fri noon–11pm; Sat, Sun 10am–midnight. Average main course: $22.* Flaneurs restaurant-hopping on Amsterdam Avenue will find a pleasant perch at Luzia's. The Portuguese menu is eclectic: Shrimp is stuffed in samosa-like Goan turnovers, or served swimming in garlic-suffused olive oil. Entrées range from meaty (velvety duck breast, tender osso buco) to quintessentially Iberian (a clam, potato and *chouriço* stew or seafood paella).

Pão *322 Spring St at Greenwich St (212-334-5464). Subway: C, E to Spring St; 1 to Houston St. Mon–Thu noon–2:30pm, 6–11pm; Fri noon–2:30pm, 6–11:30pm; Sat 6–11:30pm; Sun 1–11pm. Average main course: $19.* The name—which means "bread" in Portuguese—hints at the simple pleasures of this tiny wood-paneled resto. Classic tapas include cod cakes and garlicky baked octopus, which are fun to pair with one of 60 reasonably priced Portuguese wines. For those desiring more than small bites, the traditional *cataplana* pork and clams in a smooth red-pepper sauce suits greater appetites. Come early to grab a spot in Pão's sidewalk seating area.

Tintol *155 W 46th St between Sixth and Seventh Aves (212-354-3838). Subway: B, D, F, V to 47–50th Sts–Rockefeller Ctr. Daily noon–midnight. Average small plate: $8.* Tintol is an oasis in a sea of ugly eateries; a brick wall extends the length of the restaurant, and high ceilings give it a regal air. The menu lists dozens of dishes under various headings—hot and cold tapas, salads, sides, fried foods—and everything works, whether it is a $4 bowl of mixed olives or a $9 octopus salad. Don't overlook the wine: 30 of the 150 bottles are available by the glass.

CINZIIA REALE-CASTELLO

Russian

See also: *Eastern European*

Anyway Cafe *34 E 2nd St at Second Ave (212-473-5021, 212-533-3412). Subway: F, V to Lower East Side–Second Ave. Sun–Thu noon–midnight; Fri, Sat noon–4am. Average main course: $13.* The relaxed crowd is less giddy than you might expect for a place serving vodka in such tempting flavors as wasabi and ginger. Start with a mild smoked-trout roulade with horseradish cream and salmon caviar, or the *brynza* (a spiced, spreadable cheese) with sliced tomatoes. End with a humble but fine dessert—crêpes with raspberry coulis and rich chocolate fondue are highly recommended. The main course, you ask? Stick to simple items—crêpes and *pelmeni.* Jazz and folk musicians play nightly. **Other locations** *1602 Gravesend Neck Rd at East 16th St, Sheepshead Bay, Brooklyn (718-934-5988)* ● *111 Oriental Blvd at West End Ave, Brighton Beach, Brooklyn (718-648-3906).*

Cafe Glechik *3159 Coney Island Ave, Brighton Beach, Brooklyn (718-616-0494). Subway: B, Q to Brighton Beach. Daily 9am–10pm. Average main course: $12.* In the midst of all the vodka-lubricated supper clubs of Brighton Beach, this Ukrainian-Russian neighborhood joint, adorned with folk costumes, babushkas and random tchotchke, churns out tasty peasant fare to satisfy most carnivorous cravings. Potatoes or buckwheat kasha and a salad accompany all the hefty entrées—from chicken gizzards stew to kebabs and beef Stroganoff, but what really leads the pack on the bilingual menu are the *pelmeni* and *vareniki,* small steamed dumplings stuffed with anything from veal and sour cherries to farmer cheese and pork-beef combo.

Caviar Russe *538 Madison Ave between 54th and 55th Sts (212-980-5908). Subway: E, V to Fifth Ave–53rd St; 6 to 51st St. Mon–Sat noon–10pm. Average main course: $29.* The imported stuff is offered by the mother-of-pearl spoonful (sevruga $6; golden osetra $18; beluga $35) or in portions of 25 to 500 grams (priced from $50 to $250), with traditional blini, toast or potatoes. The noncaviar part of the menu reveals strong French influences; witness such delicious, balanced entrées as crisp-skinned duck confit with moist meat atop foie gras; and seared red snapper in a light sauce over delicate Maine crabmeat, sprinkled with a generous portion of thinly sliced morels. Lunch, a $20 prix fixe, is a relative bargain, even if you add the splendid Jewel of Russia vodka—clean, bracing, and served almost frozen in an icy glass ($11).

FireBird Russian *365 W 46th St between Eighth and Ninth Aves (212-586-0244). Subway: A, C, E to 42nd St–Port Authority. Tue, Thu, Fri 5:15–11:15pm; Wed, Sat 11:15am–2:30pm, 5:15–11:15pm; Sun 5:15–8pm. Average main course: $34. Three-course prix fixe: $50.* Named for Michel Fokine's 1910 ballet, this opulent restaurant transports you to prerevolutionary Russia. The walls are a collage of Ballet Russe costumes and Léon Bakst reproductions, and golden eggs dangle from a gilded tree. Start with delicate beluga caviar folded with sour cream and bits of egg into a buttery blini. A czar-quality feast follows: Full-bodied Ukrainian borscht teems with slivers of smoked duck, braised pork and beef brisket; meaty disks of sturgeon are coated in a risottolike blend of rice and onion, then wrapped in puff pastry. Desserts yield, as did the Russian aristocracy, to French influence.

⊖**Gina's Cafe** *409 Brighton Beach Ave between 4th and 5th Sts, Brighton Beach, Brooklyn (718-646-6297). Subway: B, Q to Brighton Beach. Mon–Thu, Sun 11am–11pm; Fri, Sat 11am–midnight. Average main course: $10.* Cheap diners have to love Brighton Beach: Even the most modern of its Russian cafés is priced as if it were in Soviet Moscow. Sprightly caviar and all manner of *vareniki* cost less than five bucks. With the restaurant's contemporary decor come a few contemporary dishes, like Asian duck salad, most of which are to be avoided. But not Gina's Salad, a fresh take on the Caesar: lightly dressed greens with generous strips of lox and first-rate salmon caviar. Sour cream stars in the traditional cold borscht, and with tender beef in a rendering of Russia's most recognizable dish—Count Stroganoff would be proud.

★ **Petrossian** *182 W 58th St at Seventh Ave (212-245-2214). Subway: N, Q, R, W to 57th St. Mon–Sat 11:30am–3pm, 5:30–11:30pm; Sun 11:30am–3pm, 5:30–10:30pm. Average main course: $33.* Inside the gorgeous rococo Alwyn Court, with fire-breathing salamanders encrusting its facade, you can sit on elegant, ergonomic black leather stools at a granite bar, under etched Erté mirrors, and order whatever your wallet will bear of fine-grained sevruga, slightly nutty osetra or pearly, pop-in-your-mouth beluga, all washed down with a glass of bubbly. Or you could sit in the dining room and try to find satisfaction in the rest of the menu. Why bother? Though the fare is good, little is worth a detour from the caviar. **Other location** *Petrossian Boutique & Café, 911 Seventh Ave between 57th and 58th Sts (212-245-2217).*

★ **Pravda** *281 Lafayette St between Houston and Prince Sts (212-226-4944). Subway: B, D, F, V to*

Read 'em & eat

beef Stroganoff: slices of beef in a rich sour cream and mushroom sauce

beluga: the most prized and expensive of caviars (osetra is the second and sevruga third)

pelmeni: Siberian ravioli dumplings

zakuski: an assortment of appetizers pickles, smoked fish, marinated vegetables and caviar

Broadway–Lafayette St; N, R to Prince St; 6 to Spring St. Mon–Wed 5pm–1am; Thu 5pm–2am; Fri, Sat 5pm–3am; Sun 6pm–1am. Average main course: $17. The staircase opens into a cavernous subterranean brasserie that almost resembles a Cold War–era movie set, from the cement ceiling to the stainless-steel toilet seats. Stylish couples and the Soho working class sit in curved red banquettes and leather armchairs, sipping from colorful martinis and sampling snacky Soviet fare like spinach and cheese piroshki and blini with a choice of fish. Smoked sturgeon scattered with dill and accompanied by a dollop of crème fraîche is a toothsome choice. Caviar is, of course, found in various guises, including an unorthodox application atop smoked-salmon pizza. The bracingly bourgeois molten chocolate cake is hard to say *nyet* to.

Primorski *282 Brighton Beach Ave between Brighton 2nd St and 3rd Sts, Brighton Beach, Brooklyn (718-891-3111). Subway: B, Q to Brighton Beach. Mon–Thu 11am–midnight; Fri 11am–2am; Sat 11am–3am; Sun 11am–1am. Average main course: $14.* An exercise in timeless kitsch, this dark-red, windowless Russian stalwart has been holding strong since the early eighties. On a quiet weeknight, you may wonder what the hoopla is all about, but weekends draw groups of Russian revelers feasting on vodka and flavorful fare to the sound of live music under the reflections of a disco-ball. The Georgian chef cranks out recipes from the motherland—delicious *lavash* bread, hearty cheese-filled *khachapuri* patties and *solyanka* lamb stew—as well as international favorites like filet mignon, chicken Kiev and a smoked fish platter. No need to be shy about requesting a doggy bag—the waitstaff practically insists.

The Russian Tea Room *2007 Eat Out Award, Readers' Choice: Best reopening. 150 W 57th St between Sixth and Seventh Aves (212-581-7100). Subway: F, N, Q, R, W to 57th St. Mon–Fri 11:30am–2pm, 5–11pm; Sat 11am–2:30pm, 5–11pm, Sun 11am–2:30pm, 5–10pm. Average main course: $40.* The recently reborn socialite center has never looked—or tasted—better. Nostalgia buffs will be happy to hear that nothing's happened to the gilded-bird friezes or the famously tacky crystal-bear aquarium. The food, thankfully, has not been frozen in time. Chef Gary Robins modernizes the menu, looking to former Soviet republics for inspiration. He makes the best borscht in the city, and gets more exotic with entrées like lamb chop with purple basil crust, eggplant caviar and ratatouille. Die-hard fans of the classics can dig into Chicken Kiev and beef Stroganoff. But the pleasure doesn't come cheap. Main courses run toward $40, and the portions are dainty.

Russian Vodka Room *265 W 52nd St between Broadway and Eighth Ave (212-307-5835). Subway: C, E, 1 to 50th St. Mon, Sun 4pm–1am; Tue–Thu 4pm–2am; Fri, Sat 4pm–3am. Average main course: $16.* This frenetic hangout is no Moscow memory lane; it lives for today. Glossy black marble, wall-to-wall carpet and sturdy green banquettes decorate the room. The vast horseshoe-shaped bar is always packed with a mix of young Russian and American rowdies with roving eyes. In the bright dining room, inebriated patrons feast on gravlax with potato pancakes and cabbage pie. Entrées like chicken *tabaka* (a split Cornish game hen broiled under a press) are unabashed greasy goodness. And while there's much debate about the authenticity of certain flavors of "Russian infused vodka," the horseradish shot packs a punch that goes well with the food and the flirting.

Back in the USSR
The Russian Tea Room's menu is inspired by former Soviet republics.

CINZIA REALE-CASTELLO

Seafood

See also: *Asian, Chinese, Greek, Japanese, Mediterranean, Steakhouses*

Mussel in Black Pearl's lure is its shellfish and chic cocktails.

▲⊙**AQ Café** *Scandinavia House, 58 Park Ave between 37th and 38th Sts (212-879-9779). Subway: 42nd St S, 4, 5, 6, 7 to 42nd St–Grand Central. Mon–Sat 10am–5pm. Average main course: $10.* On the ground floor of Scandinavia House, the city's temple of way–northern European culture, is a seafood-oriented self-serve eatery with upscale Ikea-style decor. Straight-up Swedish food, overseen by Marcus Samuelsson of Aquavit, includes superb gravlax, pickled herring and shrimp-salad sandwiches. Tomato soup (served hot or cold) is really a bouillabaisse of salt-cured cod and crayfish. For landlubbers, the meatballs are outstanding—and you don't have to buy a coffee table to get them.

★ ▲**Aquagrill** *210 Spring St at Sixth Ave (212-274-0505). Subway: C, E to Spring St. Mon–Thu 6–10:30pm; Fri, Sat 6–11:30pm; Sat noon–3:30pm, 6–11:30pm; Sun 6–10:30pm. Average main course: $24.* This shrine to the brine boasts an impressive display of all things piscatory. Don't worry if your expertise is limited to tuna on rye; the staff knows everything there is to know about chef-owner Jeremy Marshall's menu. They'll tell you all about the 25 varieties of fresh oysters, or wax rhapsodic about the charms of sea urchin in citrus-soy dressing, cod with wild-mushroom fondue and Maine lobster salad. The dining room is bland and a little old-fashioned, but that just gives the food its rightful place in the limelight.

BLT Fish *21 W 17th St between Fifth and Sixth Aves (212-691-8888). Subway: F, V to 14th St; L to Sixth Ave. Mon–Thu 5:30–11pm; Fri, Sat 5:30–11:30pm; Sun 5–10pm (upstairs closed Sun). Average main course: $18 (downstairs); $34 (upstairs).* The formula at BLT Fish seems to be a sure thing: Marry Laurent Tourondel's proven fishmonger skills combined with BLT Steak's smart approach (quality ingredients, myriad sauces, à la carte sides) and a hot downtown address, and you've got a successful restaurant. Of course, the X factor is always the execution, but Tourondel misses nary a beat. While the first-floor menu will leave you sufficiently stuffed on heaps of fried calamari and big buckets of mussels, the upper half of the restaurant offers the superlative seafood experience. Tourondel serves almost exclusively standard catches like tuna, snapper and *loup de mer,* yet the food is anything but standard. Every entrée comes with one or two obvious, suggested pairings, and any diner who chooses to override a lemon caper brown-butter sauce on Dover sole with, say, veal *jus* deserves what he or she gets.

Black Pearl *37 W 26th St between Broadway and Sixth Ave (212-532-9900). Subway: F, V, N, R, W to 23rd St. Mon–Wed 11:30am–3pm, 5pm–11pm; Thu, Fri 11:30am–3pm, 5pm–midnight; Sat 5pm–midnight; Sun 5pm–11pm. Average main course: $18.* This Maine-style seafood joint's second coming represents a dark-horse darling turned corporate. The new spot has a bar and cavernous dining room painted a tomato red and embellished with a theme-parky shingled roof. But the Pearl hasn't completely sold its soul: Its famed lobster sandwich—a grilled white bun loaded with mayoless, butter-laced hunks of sweet meat—remains a purist's dream. For dessert, a very '90s blueberry cocktail from the extensive martini list beats the soggy blueberry crisp.

★ **Blue Fin** *W Times Square Hotel, 1567 Broadway at 47th St (212-918-1400). Subway: N, R, W to 49th St. Mon, Sun 7–11am, 11:30am–4pm, 5pm–midnight;*

CINZIA REALE-CASTELLO

School cafeteria
At Wild Salmon, Jeffrey Chodorow shows off what he's learned about seafood and successful restaurants.

Seafood

TALIA SIMHI

Tue–Thu 7–11am, 11:30am–4pm, 5pm–12:30am; Fri, Sat 7–11am, 11:30am–4pm, 5pm–1am. Average main course: $26. This noisy, singles-friendly, packed-to-the-gills bar, just steps from the TKTS booth, has probably been the scene of more than a few hookups. A school of fish is suspended overhead, and a staircase floats up to the dining area, decorated with backlit faux-tortoiseshell panels and mod white chairs. Chef Eric Woods cranks out crowd-pleasers such as sesame-crusted bigeye tuna with ginger-soy vinaigrette and pan-seared halibut with green and white asparagus in a vanilla-flavored brown butter. The crab-cake appetizer, with an accompanying mixed-green salad, is the perfect way to start reeling in your own catch of the night.

▲**Blue Water Grill** *31 Union Sq West at 16th St (212-675-9500). Subway: L, N, Q, R, W, 4, 5, 6 to 14th St–Union Sq. Mon, Tue 11:30am–midnight; Wed, Thu 11:30am–12:30am; Fri, Sat 11:30am–1am; Sun 10:30am–midnight. Average main course: $26.* Another Steve Hanson success story, Blue Water has several distinct personalities, owing to its separate dining areas: The front bar area is filled with young business types; couples and boisterous larger groups take to the back room. Downstairs, live, mellow jazz plays in the dining room. One daily special, red snapper, comes with not one, but two vinaigrettes. Fortunately, the fussiness doesn't extend to the raw oysters or to fish served "simply grilled." Desserts come from the B.R. Guest organization's commissary recipe file—so if you liked the caramelized-banana ice-cream tower you had at Ocean Grill, you'll be glad to find that it's here as well.

☉**Bobby's Fish and Seafood Restaurant** *3842 Ninth Ave at 206th St (212-304-9440). Subway: 1 to 207th St. Daily 24hrs. Average main course: $10.* Need *mariscos, papas fritas* and jukebox merengue at 3am? Bring your friends, your appetite and your Spanish skills to this all-night, cafeteria-style seafood shack in Inwood. At $20, the grilled *langosta* combo is one of the cheaper lobster dinners in town: Two one-and-a-half-pound, butter-doused crawlers are fired on the grill until the shell turns crisp and crackable; the meat inside stays sweet, and it's all served in a throwaway foil pan.

Bongo *299 Tenth Ave between 27th and 28th Sts (212-947-3654). Subway: C, E to 23rd St; 1 to 28th St. Mon, Tue 5pm–2am; Wed 5pm–1am; Thu–Sat 5:30pm–3am. Average main course: $16.* Decorated entirely with vintage furniture—Eames chairs, couches that date from mid-century—Bongo has a ramshackle charm that few bar-lounges along this desolate stretch of Tenth Avenue can match. The short menu consists almost entirely of winning seafood choices, though the gooey mac-and-cheese side is a crowd-pleaser. The oyster list is surprisingly extensive for such a tiny place, and Bongo's lobster rolls and teriyaki-glazed tuna burgers (made with freshly ground, sushi-quality fish) could go fin-to-fin with offerings from more well-known, expensive joints. Still, Bongo is a bar at heart, and if it's a quiet, relaxing meal you're looking for, you'd best not eat at a place named after a drum.

Brooklyn Fish Camp *162 Fifth Ave between DeGraw and Douglass Sts , Park Slope, Brooklyn (718-783-3264). Subway: 2, 3 to Bergen St. Mon–Sat noon–3pm, 6–11pm. Average main course: $21.* We've been reminded by recent cinema gaffes like *Bewitched* and The *Honeymooners* that remakes of beloved originals rarely

live up to expectations. Mind you, Brooklyn Fish Camp is no flop: Menu holdovers from the seminal Mary's Fish Camp—the cultish lobster roll, rosemary-stuffed whole fish and succulent lobster knuckles—are as fresh and delicious as the spin-off as they are on Charles Street. And new additions like baby squid salad with Thai pesto are equally satisfying. But the thrill of scoring a precious seat at the tiny West Village original simply doesn't carry over to the Brooklyn location, which is too spacious and lacking in character to feel special. You'll eat well at least, and while the weather's nice you can eat outside, too: There's a lovely deck in back.

★ **Central Park Boathouse Restaurant** *Central Park Lake, park entrance on Fifth Ave at 72nd St (212-517-2233). Subway: 6 to 68th St–Hunter College. Mon–Fri noon–4pm, 5:30–9:30pm; Sat, Sun 9:30am–4pm, 6–9:30pm. Average main course: $28.* Get a fresh perspective on your own city. The setting is serene enough to offset the somewhat stiff service and hefty prices. The Boathouse salad is a gorgeous sculpture of tomatoes, cucumbers, red onion, olives and large, rectangular chunks of feta cheese. Crab cakes, more crab than cake, are worth every penny. Fish and fowl are fresh and beautifully presented, if a bit bland. Allow yourself to linger over lavender panna cotta before taking the restaurant's trolley back to civilization. Paying for location is par for the course in New York; here, it's well worth it.

Clemente's Maryland Crabhouse *Venice Marina, 3939 Emmons Ave at Knapp St, Sheepshead Bay, Brooklyn (718-646-7373). Travel: B, Q to Sheepshead Bay, then B4 bus to Knapp St. Daily noon–midnight. All-you-can-eat crab: $30.* During warm weather, you can sit on the deck of the bay and enjoy the all-you-can-eat blue-crab special. You may end up with more meat on you than in you, but the tasty critters—coated with Old Bay or steeped in garlic and butter—are worth the mess. When blue-crab season ends in the fall, owner Jimmy Muir ships in the stone variety from Florida. Clemente's serves chowder, fried calamari and other seafood dishes to wimps who can't rise to the shellfish challenge. If you're going for the record, plan to stay awhile; a Marylander once downed more than 11 dozen crabs in an afternoon.

★ ▲**Cru** *24 Fifth Ave at 9th St (212-529-1700). Subway: A, C, E, F, V, Grand St S to W 4th St. Tue–Sat 5:30–11pm. Average main course: $23.* If you can pony up for the $78 prix fixe, sit in the main dining room, where the courteous waitstaff will help you select vino from the extensive list contained in two thick leather-bound volumes. The menu is seafood-heavy (tender seared scallops, flaky Atlantic halibut), but meatier dishes, like pasta with a luscious rabbit-sausage sauce, also excite. Those without deep pockets can dine in the more casual front lounge.

Ditch Plains *2007 Eat Out Award, Critics' Pick: Best kids' food for grown-ups 29 Bedford St at Downing St (212-633-0202). Subway: A, C, E, B, D, F, V to W 4th St; 1 to Houston St. Daily 9am–2am. Average main course: $12.* This New England–style fish shack, named for chef-owner Marc Murphy's favorite surfing spot, is in fact sophisticated and sleek—no seaside knickknacks here. They don't take reservations, but the kitchen keeps dinerlike hours (7am to 2am every day), and the menu is packed with classics like mac and cheese, hot dogs and hamburgers. The restaurant doesn't outdo nearby Pearl's or Mary's on the shellfish front, but Murphy (Landmarc) holds his own with the $23 lobster roll, a mound of chopped, luscious meat with scallions, tarragon and aioli on a soft roll with a side of sweet-potato chips.

Docks Oyster Bar & Seafood Grill

633 Third Ave at 40th St (212-986-8080). Subway: 42nd St S, 4, 5, 6, 7 to 42nd St–Grand Central. Daily 11:30am–11pm. Average main course: $25. The cacophonous, multilevel space almost feels like a glorified chain restaurant (it is, sort of—there's an uptown location). But Docks is a notch above places that serve bottomless baskets of popcorn shrimp. This is a candlelit, white-tablecloth affair—with a buzzing bar scene. Oysters are from Maine and British Columbia. Fried scallops and fish are surprisingly light (the accompanying shoestring fries, however, can be overdone). The creamy, tart key lime pie is ideal for cleansing a breaded and battered palate. **Other location:** *2427 Broadway at 89th St (212-724-5588).*

Ed's Lobster Bar *222 Lafayette St between*
Kenmare and Spring Sts (212-343-3236). Subway: B, D, F, V to Broadway–Lafayette St. Tue, Wed noon–3pm, 5–11pm; Thu, Fri noon–3pm, 5pm–midnight; Sat noon–midnight; Sun noon–8pm. Average main course: $19. Chef Ed McFarland (Pearl Oyster Bar) takes on the city's shellfish-shack formula—pioneered at his old stomping ground—at this tiny new Soho spot. If you secure a place at the 30-seat marble bar or one of the few tables in the whitewashed eatery, expect superlative raw-bar eats, delicately fried clams and lobster served every which way: steamed, grilled, broiled, chilled, stuffed into a pie and the crowd favorite, the lobster roll. Here, it's a buttered bun stuffed with premium chunks of meat with just a light coating of mayo.

Francisco's Centro Vasco *159 W 23rd*
St between Sixth and Seventh Aves (212-645-6224). Subway: F, V, 1 to 23rd St. Mon–Fri noon–midnight; Sat, Sun noon–1am. Average main course: $19. Vasco is Spanish for the seafaring Basque people, but dinner is usually a Maine event—fresh lobster, reasonably priced. Scribbled on the waiter's notepad is the latest by-the-pound list of available lobsters, unknowingly living out their last moments in the kitchen; Francisco's Favorite is stuffed with crabmeat and sprinkled with Swiss cheese. Desserts are ordinary—splurge instead on bigger shellfish. The simple formula appears to be working: So many people line up to get into the so-uncool-it's-cool room (a neon outline of a lobster hangs in the window), the maître d' occasionally resorts to using a velvet rope.

▲Fresh *105 Reade St at West Broadway (212-406-*
1900). Subway: A, C, E, 1, 2, 3 to Chambers St. Mon–Fri 11:30am–2:30pm, 5–10:30pm; Sat 5–11pm, Sun 4–9pm. Average main course: $27. Fresh's blue-hued, nautical themed space is a natural draw for anyone who can pay top dollar for quality seafood. The room is elegant but not stiff, and the waitstaff is professional without being overbearing. Proving that you get what you pay for, the $17 appetizer of fried clams far surpass the rubbery strands that most of us settle for. The "kobe" tuna—a thin, buttery cut of pink, barely seared fish served over a yellow pepper stuffed with sticky garlic rice—lives up to its lofty name. A simpler choice, the $19 fish and chips, might be the one dish that doesn't warrant its higher-than-usual price.

Grand Central Oyster Bar & Restaurant *Grand Central Terminal, Lower*
Concourse, 42nd St at Park Ave (212-490-6650).

Subway: 42nd St S, 4, 5, 6, 7 to 42nd St–Grand Central. Mon–Fri 11:30am–9:30pm; Sat noon–9:30pm. Average main course: $24. New York City was once a world-renowned oyster town, and this beloved 90-year-old landmark, nestled in Grand Central's lower level, reminds diners of that former glory. Two large rooms flank a white-topped counter where eaters can choose from 30 or so varieties of bivalves, including hard-to-find types like Chincoteagues from Virginia. They're all served with good old mignonette sauce. Since these little delicacies aren't terribly filling, O-Bar compensates with its famously gargantuan desserts: The apple pie bursts with so many razor-thin slices of fruit that it deserves landmark status all by itself.

★ **Jack's Luxury Oyster Bar** *101 Second Ave at 6th St (212-253-7848). Subway: F, V to Lower East Side–Second Ave; 6 to Astor Pl. Mon–Sun 6pm–midnight. Average tasting plate: $12.* The move from its original townhouse home to a smaller space around the corner hasn't hurt Jack and Grace Lamb's quirky little restaurant. They've kept it stylish, using the same red-and-white checkered wallpaper and offbeat accents (e.g., bird figurines) as before. The result is a great East Village date spot with a bicoastal selection of oysters that rotates daily, lobster every which way and serious wines ($40 to $2,000 a bottle). The small plates are delicious: lobster-knuckle chowder full of meat and sweet corn; plump clams and rounds of chorizo in garlicky broth; sea bass perfectly steamed in parchment; and tender butter-poached lobster.

⊖**Johnny's Reef Restaurant** *2 City Island Ave at the south end of City Island, Bronx (718-885-2086). Travel: 6 to Pelham Bay Park, then Bx29 bus to City Island. Mon–Thu, Sun 11am–1am; Fri, Sat 11am–1:30am. Average main course: $10.* The decor at this 45-year-old City Island institution is reminiscent of a school cafeteria—including the long lines. The attraction here is inexpensive seafood and shameless deep-fat-frying: filet of sole, red snapper, whiting, smelts, mini–lobster tails, shrimp, scallops, soft-shell crabs, clams, oysters and squid. Any of these come freshly breaded and mercilessly fried for about $10. The Clam Bar, meanwhile, offers shucked-before-your-eyes littlenecks and cherrystones for $10 a dozen. On a nice day, grab your grub and drink, head out to the picnic tables and enjoy the view of Long Island Sound.

★ ▲**Lure Fishbar** *142 Mercer St at Prince St (212-431-7676). Subway: N, R, W to Prince St. Mon–Thu 11:30am–11pm; Fri 11:30am–midnight; Sat 5pm–midnight; Sun 4:30–10pm. Average main course: $25.* This sexy subterranean restaurant is decked out in a retro-luxe yacht decor. Hit the sushi bar to compare the flavors and textures of different tunas and salmons (there are also two types of eel). Perhaps the restaurant's greatest achievement is its treatment of the classics. Dishes that have become rote at so many upscale eateries—seared yellowtail tuna, dry-aged sirloin steak—are executed here with the dazzling skill usually reserved for trendier plates.

★ **Mary's Fish Camp** *64 Charles St at W 4th St (646-486-2185). Subway: 1 to Christopher St–Sheridan Sq. Mon–Sat noon–3pm, 6–11pm. Average main course: $20.* Named after owner (and former Pearl Oyster Bar partner) Mary Redding, this tiny space has the fun, low-key feel of an informal coastal Florida seafood house, only without shrimp peelings on the floor. Whole fish,

The life aquatic
Lure Fishbar reels in
fresh tuna, salmon
and eel, and rolls it all
up with style.

PHILIP HIELDMAN

Tackle box
Ed's Lobster Bar hooks regulars with—what else?–its buttery lobster rolls.

such as red snapper, *daurade* and tilapia, are simply prepared: Stuffed with fresh herbs, they're cooked quickly at high heat to keep the flesh flavorful and moist. Lobster comes either grilled or in a roll. Join the crowd and have a tall, gooey hot-fudge sundae for dessert.

McCormick & Schmick's *1285 Sixth Ave at 52nd St (212-459-1222). Subway: B, D, F, V to 47th–50th Sts. Mon–Sat 11:30am–11pm; Sun 4–10pm. Average main course: $25.* In an atypically vast space in Manhattan, this newer outpost of a popular Western seafood chain hawks "100 items of more than 30 varieties of seafood" shipped in daily from around the world. The menu is printed twice a day to keep up with the latest catch. That means you get to choose between perfectly seared local jumbo sea scallops or grilled arctic char flown in from Iceland. Reserve a spot on your table for the crab cake: Because of its high ratio of fresh lump crabmeat to bread crumbs and a delicate, flash-fried crust, it'll pass taste-testing by any transplanted Baltimorean. Service is friendly, too.

★ **The Mermaid Inn** *96 Second Ave between 5th and 6th Sts (212-674-5870). Subway: F, V to Lower East Side–Second Ave. Mon–Thu 5:30pm–11:00pm; Fri, Sat 5:30pm–midnight; Sun 5pm–10pm. Average main course: $20.* The third restaurant from Danny Abrams (the Harrison), the Mermaid Inn has fulfilled its promise as a great neighborhood seafood restaurant. The decor is oceanographic chic, but the seasonal menu's best items are the simple ones. Yes, there is the overstuffed lobster roll and spicy seafood spaghetti, but they pale in comparison to the raw bar or fish such as grilled mahi-mahi with a bright-green chive mash and truffled onions.

And for dessert: It's chef's choice, which is always chocolate pudding.

★ **Neptune Room Restaurant & Bait Bar** *511 Amsterdam Ave at 84th St (212-496-4100). Subway: B, C, 1, 2, 3 to 86th St. Mon–Thu 5:30–11pm; Fri 5:30–11:30pm; Sat 11am–4pm, 5:30–11:30pm; Sun 11am–4pm, 5:30–10pm. Average main course: $25.* The owners of downtown's Jane offer inventive seafood amid appealing yachtlike decor. Belly up to a raw bar or the "bait bar," which serves imaginative $7 *crudo* plates: tender yellowtail drizzled with honey; whole dill-and-Dijon-laced wild salmon with blueberries. Blue-crab panna cotta is an ultrarich cake of crab-flecked cream sprinkled with toasted almonds and smoked paprika. A main-course *cioppino* features lobster-size langoustines in a punchy, garlicky tomato broth. Cool off with an ice-cream float, made with local soda and vanilla gelato.

★ **Oceana** *55 E 54th St between Madison and Park Aves (212-759-5941). Subway: E, V to Fifth Ave–53rd St. Mon–Fri noon–2:30pm, 5:30–10:30pm; Sat 5–10:30pm. Three-course prix fixe: $78.* Power brokers and 25th-anniversary celebrants are united in their abiding enthusiasm for Oceana, a midtown institution that thrills patrons with its brief, balanced menu culling the best of seafood preparations from around the globe. This is a fine-tuned, reliable operation, with assured service and a serious wine list. Portions are small and exquisite: A Louisiana-style appetizer of shrimp and gnocchi, embellished with chanterelles, arugula and pecorino romano, achieves the perfect balance of rich and delicate flavors. An entrée of pompano, trussed up in coconut cilantro curry over baby bok choy, is dizzyingly tasty. For dessert, a plate of sorbets in a gallery of colors softens the shock of the bill.

★ Pearl Oyster Bar
18 Cornelia St between Bleecker and W 4th Sts (212-691-8211). Subway: A, C, E, B, D, F, V to W 4th St. Mon–Fri noon–2:30pm, 6–11pm; Sat 6–11pm. Average main course: $24.
There's a good reason this convivial, no-reservations, New England-style fish joint always has a line—the food is outstanding. The lemon-scented lobster roll, sweet meat laced with mayonnaise on a butter-enriched bun, is better than you could have imagined. More sophisticated dishes fare equally well: A bouillabaisse is a briny lobster broth packed with mussels, cod, scallops and clams, with an aioli-smothered crouton balanced on top—a great value at $18. The supremacy of a bittersweet chocolate mousse topped by an enormous quenelle of barely sweetened whipped cream is a surprise at a spot better known for its sundaes. Finally, a restaurant worthy of its hype.

Petite Crevette
144 Union St at Hicks St, Cobble Hill, Brooklyn (718-855-2632). Subway: F, G to Carroll St. Mon–Sat noon–3pm, 5–11pm; Sun 5–10pm. Average main course: $16.
Whoever came up with the name for this spot certainly has a sense of humor. "Little shrimp" may sound redundant, but it makes perfect sense once you set foot inside this odd 18-seat shoe box. Brightly painted tropical fish are tacked onto teal walls, and the banquettes—upholstered with tawny velour—resemble church pews. If the food weren't so great, the decor would just seem creepy. But chef Neil Ganic (Bouillabaisse 126) has gained a cult following for his seafood. He makes fresh fish stock daily, which enhances the corn-and-crab chowder and the crackling red-snapper fillet steeped in a coconut-milk–tinged saffron broth. If you like intimate experiences, show up early—the place doesn't take reservations and it gets packed.

Shaffer City Oyster Bar & Grill
5 W 21st St between Fifth and Sixth Aves (212-255-9827). Subway: F, V, N, R, W to 23rd St. Mon–Fri noon–11pm; Sat 5–11:30pm. Average main course: $23.
Sorry, you can't pick your fish from the enormous tank at the lovely wooden bar. But you can order from the excellent oyster menu, which has dozens of selections, accompanied by texture and taste descriptions. Or start with grilled shrimp served on a crunchy risotto cake with sweet-and-sour chipotle glaze. Follow with tender red snapper fillet atop crisp haricots verts and aromatic jasmine rice. The wine list is ample and smart; the menu even suggests the right port to go with the molten-chocolate soufflé.

Tides
102 Norfolk St at Delancey St (212-254-8855). Subway: F to Delancey St; J, M, Z to Delancey–Essex Sts. Tue–Thu noon–3pm, 5:30–11pm; Fri, Sat 5:30–11:30pm; Sun 5:30–10pm. Average main course: $22.
In this minuscule Lower East Side spot, 120,000 bamboo sticks hang from the ceiling, forming a dramatic canopy. Two angular wooden booths consume almost half the dining room; the rest is outfitted with a banquette, where tea lights shine from recessed nooks in the tables. Chef Judy Seto knows how to make a lobster roll: Her version is chock-full of buttery lobster meat, slathered with just enough punchy mayo and piled onto a not-too-bready hot dog bun. Grilled baby octopus skewers are cooked just right. Soft-shell crabs can be a bit greasy coming out of the kitchen, but Seto definitely has the chops to keep neighbors coming back for more.

The Water Club
500 E 30th St at FDR Dr (212-683-3333). Subway: 6 to 28th St. Mon–Sat noon–3pm, 5–11pm; Sun 11am–3pm, 5–11pm. Average main course: $35.
Think of it as Tavern on the Water. A barge has been permanently moored on the East River and its two levels converted into a bar and dining rooms. The view is brilliant, the dress code leans toward Brooks Brothers, the service ranges from leisurely to flat-out slow, and the food is usually worth the wait. Oysters might include bluepoints, Malpeques and Hood Canals. Arctic char on a bed of beans is paired with leeks. Lobsters are cracked tableside and can be steamed, grilled or stuffed—with crabmeat. You'll start on a surprisingly delightful note: The still-warm bread basket holds freshly baked cornbread rolls, scones and olive-speckled slices of bread.

Waterfront Crabhouse
2-03 Borden Ave at 2nd St, Long Island City, Queens (718-729-4862). Subway: 7 to Vernon Blvd–Jackson Ave. Mon, Tue noon–10pm; Wed, Thu noon–11pm; Fri, Sat noon–midnight; Sun 3–10pm. Average main course: $17.
For what you might pay for an appetizer at one of midtown's plush piscine palaces, you can get mammoth portions of ultrafresh surf and turf at this old-school LIC restaurant and bar. The brick building and boxing-memento-laden bar date from the 1880s, when riverfront rowdies swarmed the ferry dock just yards away. Cajun-style spicy shrimp and meltingly tender calamari segue to savory seafood stew, brawny bouillabaisse and tempting apple crisp. The dining room is decorated with Victorian carousel ponies, and the service is extra-friendly.

Wild Salmon
622 Third Ave at 40th St (212-404-1700). Subway: 42nd St S, 4, 5, 6, 7 to 42nd St–Grand Central. Mon–Wed 11:30am–2pm, 5:30–10pm; Thu, Fri 11:30am–2pm, 5:30–11pm; Sat 5:30–11pm; Sun 11:30am–5pm. Average main course: $30.
It seems restaurant impresario Jeffrey Chodorow has finally gotten it right in this unlucky space. The onetime home to Tuscan Steak, Tuscan and English Is Italian is now a homage to the Pacific Northwest. Along with hanging a school of 250 metallic fish from the 30-foot-high ceiling, Wild Salmon has imported chef Charles Ramseyer (Ray's Boathouse in Seattle). Salmon is not all that's on the menu: It also features roasted scallops wrapped in lamb prosciutto and a classic seafood cioppino. But if salmon is what you came for, try the popular king salmon cooked on a cedar plank.

Read 'em & eat

John Dory: a delicately flavored fish with a flat body and spiny head found in European waters

sablefish: a mild-tasting, white-fleshed fish from the Pacific Northwest

sea bream: (known as *orata* in Italian and *daurade* in French) a firm, low-fat fish

skate: a kite-shaped fish (also called *ray*) whose fins yield mild sweet flesh

skookum: a plump oyster from the Skookum Inlet or Puget Sound that has a smoky-sweet taste

Spanish

See also: *Caribbean, Latin American, Mexican, Portuguese*

Balancing act
Seared Guinea
Hen atop yellow
waxed beans is a
Mercat staple.

★ **A.O.C. Bedford** *14 Bedford St between Sixth Ave and Downing St (212-414-4764). Subway: 1 to Houston St. Mon–Thu, Sun 5:30–11pm; Fri, Sat 5:30–11:30pm. Average main course: $26.* Exposed brick, flickering candlelight and plush fabrics—good dinner dates are made of these.To add to the romance, no-nonsense dishes from France and Spain are all constructed from top-quality ingredients. Paper-thin slices of *jamón serrano* are served with a garlicky tomato confit; juicy suckling pig nestles into vanilla-scented mashed potatoes. At the end of the meal, impress your flame with the crêpes suzette, which are flambéed tableside.

Bar Carrera *175 Second Ave between 11th and 12th Sts (212-375-1555). Subway: 6 to Astor Pl. Daily 5pm–2am. Average small plate: $3.50.* Food plays a significantly bigger role here than it does next door at Frederick Twomey's wine bar, Bar Veloce. The Basque menu lists tasty bites such as serrano-ham sandwiches on mini brioches and slices of pork belly with juniper-accented chickpea puree, priced at $3.50 apiece. In keeping with the theme, the wine list highlights obscure favorites from the Iberian Peninsula.

★ **Boqueria** *2007 Eat Out Award, Critics' Pick: Best raiding of the hen house 53 W 19th St between Fifth and Sixth Aves (212-255-4160). Subway: Subway: F, V, N, R, W to 23rd St. Mon–Thu, Sun noon–2am. Average small plate: $6; main course $20.* Given that Boqueria is named for Barcelona's centuries-old food market, you might expect chef Seamus Mullen to prepare classic tapas and drinks. Not quite. Mullen's *bacalao* (dried, salted cod), a standard tapas ingredient, is served as an extraordinarily airy and crisp beignet; fried quail egg is paired with chorizo; and the most successful sangria is

a refreshing, unorthodox beer version that mixes lager, pear puree, lemon juice and triple sec. The small Chelsea space somehow fits ten tables in the bar area and a 16-seat communal table, and exposed-filament lightbulbs lend the room a fashionably austere atmosphere.

★ ▲**Casa Mono/Bar Jamón** *Casa Mono, 52 Irving Pl at 17th St; Bar Jamón, 125 E 17th St at Irving Pl (212-253-2773). Subway: L to Third Ave; N, Q, R, W, 4, 5, 6 to 14th St–Union Sq. Daily noon–midnight. Average small plate: $14.* Mario Batali and chef Andrew Nusser have successfully ventured into Spanish territory with their tapas-style restaurant that seems to specialize in making dreaded foods irresistible: Sweetbreads in a nutty batter are fried and served atop fennel softened in *anis del mono*, and brussels sprouts are surprisingly winsome and smoky. The most inspired dish is oxtail-stuffed piquillo peppers. Stop by Bar Jamón next door for an aperitif or after-dinner drink.

★**Degustation** *2007 Eat Out Award, Critics' Pick: Best place to stalk the chef 239 E 5th St between Second and Third Aves (212-979-1012). Subway: F, V to Lower East Side–Second Ave; 6 to Astor Pl. Mon–Sat 6–11pm. Average small plate: $12. Tasting menu: $50.* This wine-and-tapas joint is the third eatery in this spot from restaurateurs Jack and Grace Lamb. Gargantuan head-on shrimp are so good you ought to suck the savory juices out of the head, and a modern take on the roast-beef sandwich—a tower of meat and microgreens on a toasted rye round with onion marmalade and foie gras mayo—delights.

El Quijote *226 W 23rd St between Seventh and Eighth Aves (212-929-1855). Subway: C, E, 1 to 23rd St. Sun–Thu noon–midnight; Fri, Sat noon–1am. Average*

Open for business
Gather at Bar Carrera for
obscure Spanish wines
and tapas.

main course: $25. Nestled in the Chelsea Hotel and serving since 1930, El Quijote appears untouched by time. While seafood remains the most popular choice on the massive menu, they know their steak here, too. Try the tapa of filet mignon tips, sizzling in a frying pan, or the special appetizer combo for two. Lobster in green sauce, like everything else, is *gigante*. (Be sure to spoon the extra-garlicky salsa over everything in sight.) Paella, available four different ways, is also a good choice for the table.

★ ▲**1492 Food** *60 Clinton St between Rivington and Stanton Sts (646-654-1114). Subway: F to Delancey St; J, M, Z to Delancey–Essex Sts. Mon–Thu, Sun 6–11:30pm; Fri, Sat 6pm–1am. Average small plate: $11.* Spanish tapas are the real deal at 1492: crisp and creamy croquetas filled with ham, mussels or porcini; ham on tomato-rubbed fresh bread; and the signature salty-sweet, bacon-wrapped, almond-stuffed dates. You'll want to share the larger dishes too: plates of *churrasco* with perfectly seasoned fries are big enough for two or three. Sit in the dining room or take a seat at the long wooden bar and linger over a bold Spanish red and a cheese plate. .

Kaña Tapas Bar *324 Spring St between Greenwich and Washington Sts (212-343-8180). Subway: C, E to Spring St; 1 to Houston St. Tue–Thu, Sun 6–11:30pm; Fri, Sat 6pm–4am (kitchen closes at 11:30pm). Average tapa: $6.* Come for the olive oil–doused baby bites from Spain and stay for the sultry salsa tunes that rouse diners to groove on the battered wooden floors of this narrow, candlelit space. Hot, moist croquettes stuffed with diced ham pair well with the earthy red wine. Try the fresh *frutos de mar*, like plump, pink-veined shrimp flecked with garlic, and piquant octopus smothered in tomato sauce.

▲**La Paella** *214 E 9th St between Second and Third Aves (212-598-4321). Subway: 6 to Astor Pl. Mon 5–10:30pm; Tue–Thu, Sun noon–10:30pm; Fri, Sat noon–midnight. Average paella: $17. Average tapa: $9.* Patrons sit on wooden benches at intimate, wobbly tables; dried roses line the ceiling and Spanish tunes set the mood. (There's an even cozier downstairs room.) On a date? Order the sangria with the *platos mixtos*, a tapas sampler that includes a potato omelette and cold octopus salad tossed with olive oil, tomatoes and parsley. *Gambas al ajillo* (garlic shrimp) are succulent, swimming in a broth begging to be soaked up by some dense bread. Traditional paella is also meant for sharing. Ignore the American entries on the dessert menu; go for the sweet, creamy flan.

▲**Las Ramblas** *170 W 4th St between Jones and Cornelia Sts (646-415-7924). Subway: A, C, E, B, D, F, V to W 4th St. Mon–Thu, Sun 4pm–midnight; Fri, Sat 4pm–1am. Average small plate: $7.* Soft incandescent lighting, exposed-brick walls, tall wood-slab two-tops and a flat, wall-mounted fountain would make Las Ramblas sexy and intimate in any neighborhood, but as luck would have it, this tapas bar alighted in the Village. Rustic traditional fare such as *gambas Saint Martin* (plumpy shrimp slathered in garlic, lemon and white wine) and *setas al jerez con almendras* (wild mushrooms with almonds in sherry) arrive sizzling in clay crocks with an intensity of flavor to match their heat.

Matador *57 Greenwich Ave at Perry St (212-691-0057). Subway: A, C, E, B, D, F, V to W 4th St. Mon–Thu 5pm–midnight; Fri 5pm–midnight; Sat noon–midnight; Sun noon–10pm. Average main course: $18.* A cheery red-and-yellow awning flutters over sidewalk tables, giving way to a sedate, dusky-toned dining room. Inside, the priorities are clear: At the dark-wood bar sit four-gallon glass jugs of sangria (try the Brazilian, spiked with rum), which fuel the nightly happy hour. The decent, though hardly memorable, Spanish menu reveals hints of Cuba, like crisp yuca fries, along with *pintxos de pollo*, juicy chicken threaded onto skewers; chorizo sausage heaped with slithery fried onions; and a respectable rendition of Spain's comfort food, a dense wedge of egg-and-potato omelet with a piquant squiggle of aioli.

Mercat *45 Bond St between Bowery and Lafayette St (212-529-8600). Subway: B, D, F, V to Broadway–Lafayette St; 6 to Bleecker St. Mon–Sat 6pm–midnight. Average small plate: $13.* The chefs behind this lively Catalonian tapas spot logged cooking time in Spain, and it shows. Munch on tapas essentials like blistered *padrón* peppers and fantastic *patatas bravas*—fried potatoes with a searing garlic-and-smoked-paprika aioli—at the marble bar or in the dimly lit dining room. More-involved dishes, like aged hanger steak with ratatouille and horseradish sauce, are just as rewarding.

⊖**Ñ** *33 Crosby St between Broome and Grand Sts (212-219-8856). Subway: 6 to Spring St. Sun–Thu 5pm–2am; Fri, Sat 5pm–4am. Average tapa: $5.* You'll just be able to squeeze up to the bar at this tiny, packed, tapas bar. After a plate of the aceitunas caseras, a heaping assortment of house-marinated, spiced Spanish olives (only $2.75), or *pulpo a la gallega*, octopus with potatoes and paprika, you may have a hard time squeezing out. If it's Wednesday—when flamenco bands play and the place gets *really* crowded—abandon all hope of exiting.

★ ▲**Oliva** *161 E Houston St at Allen St (212-228-4143). Subway: F, V to Lower East Side–Second Ave. Mon–Thu, Sun 5:30pm–midnight; Fri, Sat 5:30pm–1am. Average main course: $16. Average tapas: $8.* This lively Spanish spot takes its cues from tapas bars in the Basque region. A bright red *toro* is stenciled on each table, and the daily selections of *pintxos* are inscribed on a mirror over the bar. Serrano ham croquettes and phyllo-wrapped mushrooms are tasty interludes before heartier dishes, such as heavy-on-the-seafood, light-on-the-rice paella. Sunday through Thursday, a Latin band livens up the joint—all the more reason to order another pitcher of sangria.

▲**Pintxos** *510 Greenwich St between Canal and Spring St (212-343-9923). Subway: C, E to Spring St. Mon 5–10pm; Tue–Thu 11am–10pm; Fri 11am–11pm; Sat 11am–11pm. Average main course: $20. Average tapas: $6.* You'll have to keep your party small at this tiny, blue-tiled gem—the dining room has only 13 tables. It's a small concession for the chance to try excellent Basque specialties such as addictively crisp and salty croquettes (peppers stuffed with creamy codfish). Main courses revolve around beef, such as filet mignon with peppers from Navarra, and they beg for a big, bold wine from the affordable wine list.

Solera *216 E 53rd St between Second and Third Aves (212-644-1166). Subway: E, V to Lexington Ave–53rd St; 6 to 51st St. Mon–Fri noon–11pm; Sat 5:30–11pm. Average main course: $33. Average tapa: $8.* Tables draped in white linen announce serious dining, as do some of the noteworthy selections from a substantial tapas menu, like zesty piquillo peppers stuffed with goat cheese and wrapped in *serrano* ham. Wondering what to pair them with? The menu matches liqueur with select appetizers and desserts. A *cuarteto* (quartet) of desserts

includes the *crema catalana* (a dead ringer for crème brûlée), the *delicia de flan* (frozen flan wrapped in pastry dough and deep fried), Adriá-esque cinnamon foam with walnuts, and caramel ice cream.

⊖**Tapeo 29** *29 Clinton St at Stanton St (212-979-0002). Subway: F to Delancey St; J, M, Z to Delancey–Essex Sts. Tue–Sun 6pm–midnight. Average small plate: $6.* Keeping tabs on tapas is never easy. One minute you're splitting a bowl of olives and the next you're throwing down $80 for a few bites of duck and your share of the wine. Not so at this Clinton Street wine bar. In authentic tapas style, the menu is built for late-night snacking, not overpriced share-plate feasting: Small bites include toasted bread topped with freshly chopped tomatoes or a little heap of fresh-from-the-fryer calamari. Each item is portioned to keep you moving to the next, but you should double your order of sautéed shrimp. The tender things arrive sizzling in a pool of garlicky olive oil that continues boiling long after it hits the table—and stays hot until you soak up the last drop with crusty bread.

★ ▲**Tia Pol** *205 Tenth Ave between 22nd and 23rd Sts (212-675-8805). Subway: C, E to 23rd St. Mon 5:30pm–11:00pm; Tue–Thu 11am–3pm, 5:30–11pm; Fri 11am–3pm, 5:30pm–midnight; Sat 11am–3pm, 6pm–midnight; Sun 11am–3pm, 6–10pm. Average small plate: $7.* Size matters in West Chelsea—a megaclub opens in the neighborhood every other week. Nevertheless, we appreciate tiny Tia Pol, with its small plates menu and dining room of just nine tables. Simplicity is the theme. Owners Mani Dawes, Heather Belz and Alexandra Raij concentrate on an all-Spanish wine list, and the kitchen turns out mainly traditional tapas, flaunting fresh seafood in dishes like sautéed cockles and razor clams. Other dishes showcase unlikely combinations: tomato-covered bread with lima-bean puree and chorizo and chocolate on bread rounds from Tom Cat bakery.

⊖**Xicala Wine & Tapas Bar** *151B Elizabeth St between Broome and Kenmare Sts (212-219-0599). Subway: J, M, Z to Bowery. Noon–2am. Average tapa: $7.* The habit-forming dishes served at the tiny Mexican restaurant Café el Portal were drawing so many customers that the owners opened Xicala, a small wine bar a block away, to serve as a waiting room. But the tapas at Xicala make the place a destination in itself. The bartender-waiter can match your wine choice with appropriate tapas, such as *papas con chorizo*, diced potatoes with a sausage hash; a warm dish of codfish sautéed with peppers; or a weekend special of shrimp, cod and octopus ceviche served with crackers. After tasting them, you'll be glad Café el Portal had a line.

Read 'em & eat

al ajillo: with olives and garlic

albondigas: meatballs

jamón serrano: a ham similar to prosciutto

patatas bravas: a tapa of fried potatoes usually served in spicy tomato sauce

pintxos: tapas in Basque

Spanish

Little feat

The appeal of tapas and other small-plates menus grows.

Eye candy
Savor P*ong's shrimp ceviche with mango puree.

It's hard to imagine a time when dining at a tapas restaurant wasn't an established New York tradition. Though small-plates dining is common in many countries, the whole idea of making a meal out of diminutive portions was popularized stateside in the last decade by the Spanish, whose custom of snacking while drinking has translated well to the city. Given that a few appetizer-sized portions generally cost more than one entrée, you can see why restaurateurs are keen to jump on the tapas bandwagon.

True tapas are one or two bites, quick noshes priced at two or three bucks a pop. But as the small-plates trend has grown in popularity, dishes of varying size and price have been labeled "tapas," and few today adhere to the authentic definition.

You can find meze, the Greek and Turkish small plates, all over the city at restaurants such as **Pera Mediterranean Brasserie**, **Turkuaz** or at chef Michael Psilakis' upscale **Anthos** and low-key **Kefi**. **Pasita**, a romantic Venezuelan eatery in the West Village, serves *pasapalos*, mini versions of Latin American classics such as *arepitas* and empanaditas. Casually sceney **'inoteca** on the Lower East Side specializes in petite Italian noshes, with a variety of tramezzini and antipasti. David Chang's much-hyped Korean-influenced **Momofuku Ssam Bar** offers, aside from the burrito-like creations known as ssam, an arresting assortment of appetizer-sized plates

such as grilled sweetbreads, artisanal ham and sea urchin topped with whipped tofu. Pastry chef Pichet Ong's dessert restaurant **P*ong** serves both sweet and savory bits. And at **Maze**, Gordon Ramsay's recently rechristened casual eatery inside the London Hotel (formerly called The London Bar), diners are advised to order four courses—though three of the luxurious French offerings will really be enough.

However tapas is Spanish, and the reigning spot in the New York tapas scene is arguably **Casa Mono**, Mario Batali and Joe Bastianich's Gramercy eatery, one of the hardest reservations to make during the last few years. Chef Andrew Nusser prepares traditional snacks as well as a host of exotic dishes, many with organ meats. Casa Mono proved so popular that Batali and Bastianich opened another tapas spot, the more casual **Bar Jamón**, right next door.

There are far too many Spanish tapas restaurants in the city to list, but a few more of note are worth mentioning here: Chelsea's three-year-old **Tia Pol**, a sliver of a space filled with six rough-hewn wooden tables, is always hopping. Its menu trots 'round Spain, with excellent Andalucían, Basque and Catalonian dishes that can be paired with vino from the all-Spanish list. The Flatiron District got it's own tapas hotspot last year, when chef Seamus Mullen and restaurateur Yann de Rochefort (of Lower East Side small-plates spot Suba) opened the sleek, white-tiled **Boqueria**. Here, diners aren't confined to tapas: they can order mid-sized dishes and full entrées as well. Recently opened East Village bar-snack spot **Mercat** shines thanks to a roster of traditional Catalonian fare (favoring salt cod and noodle dishes) as well as innovative dishes that give evidence to the French training of chefs David Seigal (Bouley) and Ryan Lowder (Jean Georges).

Other great tapas spots include the West Village's **Las Ramblas**, winner of a 2006 *TONY* Eat Out Award for best new Spanish restaurant that actually serves Spanish food, and **Bar Carrera**, the skinny East Village spot from Frederick Twomey, which offers a delicious assortment of inexpensive pintxos (a Basque version of tapas), such as pork belly with juniper-flavored chickpea puree.

Though the market's seemingly saturated with tapas spots, the trend has got legs—more and more grazing-friendly eateries open every month. New Yorkers are eating it up, as these establishments allow you to completely customize your meal, picking and choosing your way through menus like never before. And unlike dining in a more formal, standard setting, if you don't like one dish, all is not lost—just move on.

Food for thought
Mini skewers with
quail eggs are an
intriguing start at
Las Ramblas.

Steakhouses

See also: *American, Argentine*

Beefy guy
Chef Michael Lomonaco prepares select cuts at Porter House New York.

Angelo and Maxie's *233 Park Ave South at 19th St (212-220-9200). Subway: 6 to 23rd St. Mon, Tue 11:30am–3pm, 5–11pm; Wed–Fri 11:30am–3pm, 5pm–midnight; Sat 5pm–midnight; Sun 5–10pm. Average main course: $25.* At Angelo and Maxie's, steak is served with a smile and a refreshing lack of seriousness. The Roquefort-topped filet mignon could please (and feed) Fred Flintstone *and* Nigella Lawson; it's nearly as buttery-soft as the accompanying vat of creamed spinach. The waiter assembles a fine steak tartare, and the shrimp in the shrimp cocktail are juicy and firm. Although dessert seems foolhardy after this caloric wallow, the belt-busting black-and-white cheesecake and two-story sundae will leave you blissfully comatose. As New York steakhouse bills go, the damage here is minimal.

★ **BLT Steak** *106 E 57th St between Park and Lexington Aves (212-752-7470). Subway: N, R, W to Lexington Ave–59th St; 4, 5, 6 to 59th St. Mon–Thu 11:45am–2:15pm, 5:30–11pm; Fri 11:45am–2:15pm, 5:30–11:30pm; Sat 5:30–11:30pm. Average main course: $32.* Just one in an arsenal of restaurants that bear his initials, this is Laurent Tourondel's interpretation of an American steakhouse, in an elegant room with ebony tables and walnut floors. Traditionalists can get a Caesar salad, or try beef carpaccio with lemon and arugula. Meat lovers might be disappointed by the modest cuts—only the 40-ounce porterhouse for two was truly brontosaurus-size—but there are sides and sauces aplenty. The foie gras BLT with apple-smoked bacon is so good, he named it after himself.

Ben & Jack's Steakhouse *219 E 44th St between Second and Third Aves (212-682-5678).*

Subway: 42nd St S, 4, 5, 6, 7 to 42nd St–Grand Central. Mon–Fri 11:30am–10:30pm; Sat, Sun 5–10:30pm. Average main course: $38. Former Peter Luger headwaiter Wolfgang Zwiener scored big by opening his own steakhouse. Soon after, three other Luger servers—brothers Jack and Russ Sinanaj, along with cousin Ben—opened their own place. But Ben & Jack's distinguishes itself with retro touches and a half-dozen private, clubby dining rooms. Once the meal starts, the formula returns to the mother ship: Chef Burim Bajrami (another Luger veteran) prepares jumbo black-tiger shrimp and, of course, a "house" red horseradish sauce spiked with molasses, eschalots and anchovies. For the main event, B&J's porterhouse takes the Luger style—pre-sliced, with a terrific charred exterior—and runs with it. Soft and tender, the pieces peel off like high-grade sushi. The short but smart wine list is led by top California producers such as Kistler and Ridge.

Ben Benson's Steakhouse *123 W 52nd St between Sixth and Seventh Aves (212-581-8888). Subway: B, D, F, V to 47–50th Sts–Rockefeller Ctr; 1 to 50th St. Mon–Thu 11:45am–11pm; Fri 11:45am–midnight; Sat 5pm–midnight; Sun 5–10pm. Average main course: $34.* Ben Benson's echoes with laughter and clinking glasses. That joyous spirit might explain the number of regulars who've consumed tons of 16-ounce filets mignons (and who have been commemorated with wall-mounted brass plates). Start with palate-cleansing bluepoints if they're available. When choosing a cut of beef, you really can't go wrong. Try a T-bone or a tenderloin; you'll have some left over to bring home. Creamed spinach is a bit of a cliché with steak, but we haven't found many batches this good.

TALIA SIMHI

Drink up

Port 101

Port may be the most misunderstood drink in the city. People have a sense of what it is—a fortified wine (brandy is added during fermentation)—but many would dismiss it as just some sweet, expensive booze for old guys. They'd be wrong to do so. For the misinformed, a guide to decanting some of the myths:

Myth 1: It's too sweet Sure, some are sweet—gloriously so. But there are lighter, drier varieties. Tawny ports are considered the easiest to drink, many are dry and nutty.

Myth 2: It's only for after dinner Actually, white port and tonic works well when you want something refreshing—consider subbing your next after-work G&T for a P&T. Extra-dry white port can be sipped neat, on the rocks, or with a twist.

Myth 3: It's pricey Well, you can find vintage ports for hundreds of dollars a bottle, but a single glass of ruby or tawny can cost less than ten bucks—cheaper than many wines.

Myth 4: It's for seasoned drinkers (read, geezers) Ports are around 20% alcohol by volume, making them thoroughly approachable when compared to digestifs at 40% ABV or more. Since they won't rip your throat as they go down, even the novice tippler can consume comfortably.

Most confusion arises from the word vintage. Note that, if the label says vintage character, it is a blend of young ports designed to taste like a vintage port. If it says late bottled vintage, it has been made from the grapes of a single vineyard (unlike rubys and tawnys). Only about two percent of bottles are no-kidding-around vintage ports.

★ **Bull & Bear** *Waldorf-Astoria, 570 Lexington Ave at 49th St (212-872-4900). Subway: E, V to Lexington Ave–53rd St; 6 to 51st St. Mon–Fri noon–11:15pm; Sat, Sun 5–11:15pm. Average main course: $35.* Back in the day, a few high-rolling regulars spent so much time in the Waldorf-Astoria's steakhouse that their mail was delivered to the bar. Such customer loyalty is no surprise: The captain greets you with a wide smile and the porterhouse for one weighs a whopping 24 delicious ounces. In addition to dry-aged certified prime angus beef, chef Eric Kaplan puts great care into his side dishes, like garlic-whipped potatoes, Yorkshire pudding and crisp buttermilk onion rings. The digital stock ticker, running on the wall near the bar, informs diners whether or not they've cleaned up—so they can order accordingly.

Butcher Bros. Steakhouse *29-33 Newtown Ave between 29th and 30th Sts, Astoria, Queens (718-267-2771). Subway: N, W to 30th Ave. Mon–Thu, Sun 5–10:30pm; Fri, Sat 5pm–midnight. Average main course: $25.* Cleaver is as cleaver does: The "brothers" are Dino and Johnny Redzic, whose butchering pedigree goes back four generations. Their experience shows in tender, air-cured steaks and other staples of the genre, including oysters, shrimp cocktail and Caesar salad. Dino claims his place has the largest wine list in the neighborhood. Just take his word for it—you don't want to challenge a man with his knife skills.

★ **Craftsteak** *2007 Eat Out Award, Readers' Choice: Best new steakhouse 85 Tenth Ave between 15th and 16th Sts (212-400-6699). Subway: A, C, E to 14th St; L to Eighth Ave. Sun–Thu 5:30–10pm; Fr, Sat 5:30–11pm. Average main course: $45.* There were plentiful hiccups at launch and the prices run steep even by steakhouse standards, but Tom Colicchio has methodically honed the grand, modern Craftsteak into one of the better steakhouses in New York. His pro-choice formula from the original Craft takes a beefy turn in preparation style (corn vs. grass-fed, Wagyu vs. 42-day-aging) and in sides (no fewer than 30 options, including seven types of mushroom). Most of the dozens of starters are unusual (think raw tuna slices with watermelon and basil), as is Colicchio's preferred steak-cooking method: roasted, rather than grilled, which helps accentuate beautifully marbled Wagyu, but can make pedestrian cuts taste like pricey pot roast. Regardless, pleasant culinary and aesthetic distractions abound.

Dylan Prime *62 Laight St between Greenwich and Hudson Sts (212-334-4783). Subway: A, C, E, 1 to Canal St. Mon–Wed noon–2:30pm, 5:30–11pm; Thu, Fri noon–2:30pm, 5:30pm–midnight; Sat 5:30pm–midnight; Sun 5:30–10:30pm. Average main course: $27.* On weeknights, the candlelit dining area hosts the usual alpha pack. On weekends, however, it works its magic on couples sharing cozy banquettes near the room's centerpiece, a see-through wine cellar. Starters are made for swapping bites: The house-made *garganelli* is loaded with lobster chunks, rock shrimp and smoked bacon. For a lighter touch, order the mustard-studded salmon tartare. Move on to any of the five cuts of dry-aged steaks; you can mix and match crusts and sauces (try Maker's Mark bourbon sauce with your rib eye). There's no reason to go sober into that good night: Finish with an espresso martini or one of the Pie-Tinis—drinks that taste like their dessert counterparts.

Embers *9519 Third Ave at 95th St, Bay Ridge, Brooklyn (718-745-3700). Subway: R to Bay*

Ridge–95th St. Mon–Sat 5–11pm; Sun 2–10pm. Average main course: $20. You'll see some substantial slabs of beef, and we're not talking about the hefty fellas in active wear and gold chains. (They celebrate special occasions in this modest dining room, along with neighborhood moms and kids.) Enormous steaks, such as a 36-ounce T-bone—for one—are fresh from sibling Vinnie's Meat Market next door. Sides include soft, garlicky green beans and a crusty, twice-baked prosciutto-and-mozzarella-filled house specialty called potato potpie. Lamb, veal, fish, pork chops and lobster tails are broiled simply or prepared Embers-style, in hollandaise sauce. Given the quality and quantity, it's a wonder that you pay so little—and no wonder that the regulars are so big.

Frank's Restaurant
410 W 16th St between Ninth and Tenth Aves (212-243-1349). Subway: A, C, E to 14th St; L to Eighth Ave. Mon–Sat 11am–11pm; Sun noon–10pm. Average main course: $32. Talk about staying power: This nearly century-old restaurant delivers a better meal than many of its trendy neighbors. It's a meat-eater's mainstay, serving beefy fare since 1912, long before the area became a dining destination. In addition to offal offerings such as calf's liver and sautéed sweetbreads, the menu has handpicked, dry-aged cuts for every taste, whether you like it robust and chewy (shell), supple and juicy (skirt), or just plain huge (T-bone). The spare, masculine surroundings have a drab feel, but all negative thoughts evaporate when you dig into a surprisingly silky slice of cheesecake—a fitting end to a classic steakhouse dinner.

Harry's Steak & Cafe
1 Hanover Sq at Pearl St (212-785-9200). Subway: 4, 5 to Bowling Green. Mon–Fri 11:15am–11pm; Sat 4–11pm. Average main course: $28. Underground nooks make the new and improved rendition of Harry's of Hanover perhaps the city's most intimate steakhouse. Tucked away in a Financial District basement, this quasisecret spot has a wine-cellar table situated in a cozy corner; male-bonders will appreciate the 12-seat banquet table flanked by murals of monks and wenches. The prime aged porterhouse for two is tender and nicely encrusted, the service semitheatrical (waiters offer freshly cracked pepper from yard-long mills), and the wine list is filled with New World bargains for when the plastic's your own.

★ Keens Steakhouse
72 W 36th St between Fifth and Sixth Aves (212-947-3636). Subway: B, D, F, V, N, Q, R, W to 34th St–Herald Sq. Mon–Fri 11:45am–10:30pm; Sat 5–10:30pm; Sun 5–9pm. Average main course: $32. The ceiling and walls are hung with pipes, some from such long-ago Keens regulars as Babe Ruth, J.P. Morgan and Teddy Roosevelt. Even in these nonsmoking days, you can catch a whiff of the restaurant's 120 years of history. Beveled-glass doors, a working fireplace and a forest's worth of dark wood suggest a time when "Diamond Jim" Brady piled his table with bushels of oysters, slabs of seared beef and troughs of ale. The menu still lists a three-inch-thick mutton chop (imagine a saddle of lamb but with more punch) and desserts such as trifle. Sirloin and porterhouse (for two) hold their own against any steak in the city.

Kobe Club
68 W 58th St between Fifth and Sixth Aves (212-644-5623). Subway: F to 57th St; N, R, W to Fifth Ave–59th St. Mon–Wed 5:30pm–midnight; Thu–Sat 5:30pm–2am. Average main course: $35. Jeffrey Chodorow (China Grill, Asia de Cuba, Ono) replaced Alain Ducasse's Mix in New York with this clubby steakhouse, which feels more like Lotus than Luger. Designer Dodd Mitchell framed the dark, S&M-inspired bar area with a wall of leather strings; 2,000 samurai swords hang from the dining room ceiling. Up-selling is virtually nonstop: There are three varieties of raw shellfish (the most expensive costs $160), $150 vodka punch bowls and truffles in ten menu items. A Wagyu sampler—including real-deal kobe from Japan—can be ordered either à la carte or in a tasting platter for $190. Sure, the food is great—but can you afford it?

Maloney & Porcelli
37 E 50th St between Madison and Park Aves (212-750-2233). Subway: E, V to Lexington Ave–53rd St; 6 to 51st St. 11:45am–11pm. Average main course: $30. It's really loud in here: Be prepared to holler. On the upside, there's plenty to shout about, like the 30-ounce rib steak that erupts with definitive flavor. (There's also a comparatively bite-sized 16-ounce filet mignon.) And fear not the Angry Lobster, a halved five-pound Maine crustacean spiked with chili powder, cayenne pepper and rich lobster oil. Chef Patrick Vaccariello's velvety au gratin is made with French cream, Gruyère and Parmesan and served straight from the skillet. Surprises extend to desserts: no cheesecake here. If you're in the mood for the two-ton experience, choose baked Alaska, bananas Foster or, best of all, Drunken Doughnuts—a half dozen house-made circles that are sugar-dusted tableside and paired with a trio of liqueur-laced jams. Who needs after-dinner drinks?

Old Homestead Steak House
56 Ninth Ave between 14th and 15th Sts (212-242-9040). Subway: A, C, E to 14th St; L to Eighth Ave. Mon–Thu noon–10:30pm; Fri noon–11:30pm; Sat 1pm–11:30pm; Sun 1pm–9:30pm. Average main course: $33. Opened in 1868 as a dockworkers' chophouse, this clubby establishment in the now-cool Meatpacking District draws a New York cross section that includes pretty much everyone except its own neighborhood's hard-core fashion crowd. But even those finicky eaters

Read 'em & eat

hanger steak: a chewy cut from the muscles behind the ribs

flanken: a long, thin strip of beef taken from the chuck end of the short ribs. A Jewish dish, usually boiled and served with horseradish, is named after this cut.

porterhouse: a cut from the large end of the tenderloin, including meat from the top loin muscle and a T-shaped portion of the backbone (T-bone)

prime rib: a common misnomer for the rib roast, which is the large section of meat along the rib cage

rib eye: the most tender cut, from the center of the rib roast

will be impressed by starters like the jumbo crab cake and seared yellowfin, which is as tender as sashimi. Still, folks come here for the beef. Spring for the flavorful New York sirloin (strip steak), or a juicy, well-seasoned prime rib that will rock your concept of roast beef. Any way you carve it, the Old Homestead stands the test of time—and bucks trends.

★**Peter Luger** *178 Broadway at Driggs Ave, Williamsburg, Brooklyn (718-387-7400). Subway: J, M, Z to Marcy Ave. Mon–Thu 11:45am–10pm; Fri, Sat 11:45am–11pm; Sun 12:45–10pm. Steak for two: $81.* A segment of this classic restaurant is undergoing renovations, but that hasn't stopped customers from flocking to Gotham's most famous steakhouse. Although a slew of Luger copycats have prospered in the last several years, none have captured the elusive charm of this stucco-walled, beer-hall-style eatery, with well-worn wooden floors and tables, and waiters in waistcoats and bow ties. Excess is the thing, be it the reasonably health- conscious tomato salad (thick slices of tomato and onion with an odd addition of steak sauce), the famous porterhouse for two, 44 ounces of sliced prime beef, or the decent apple strudel, which comes with a bowl full of *schlag*. Go for it all—it's a singular New York experience that's worth succumbing to.

Porter House New York *Time Warner Center, 10 Columbus Circle at 60th St, fourth floor (212-823-9500). Subway: A, C, B, D, 1 to 59th St–Columbus Circle. Mon–Thu noon–4:30pm, 5–10:30pm; Fri noon–4:30pm, 5–11pm; Sat 5–11pm; Sun 5–10pm. Average main course: $30.* The latest restaurant from chef Michael Lomonaco (Windows on the World) joins the all-star lineup at the Time Warner Center and takes over the former V Steakhouse space. Designer Jeffrey Beers replaced V's baroque extravagance with a sexy brown-and-tan interior. Portions are large and prices are fair, all things considered: The seared-scallops starter ($18) is so big it could be an entrée. The steaks get a glorious char, though it can overpower the flavor of the meat. The wine list doesn't offer much on the lower end of the price spectrum, but there are plenty of half bottles.

Post House *Lowell Hotel, 28 E 63rd St between Madison and Park Aves (212-935-2888). Subway: F to Lexington Ave–63rd St. Mon–Fri noon–10:30pm; Sat, Sun 5:30–10:30pm. Average main course: $40.* This place swings for the fences. Plaques mark DiMaggio's and Mantle's regular tables. The mostly male staff is outfitted properly with white coats and a gruff attitude. Appetizers focus on classics such as calamari and crab cakes, which are delicious, and small enough to remind you that you've come for the beef. So bring it on: Prime rib, filet mignon tips, beef Wellington with Madeira sauce—each cut has been dry-aged for four weeks. Add pillows of mashed potatoes and creamy spinach. Even basic desserts like chocolate cake and banana cream pie are outstanding.

★**Quality Meats** *57 W 58th St between Fifth and Sixth Aves (212-371-7777). Subway: F to 57th St; N, R, W to Fifth Ave–59th St. Mon–Wed 11:30am–3pm, 5–10:30pm; Thu–Sat 11:30am–3pm, 5–11:30pm; Sun 5–10pm. Average main course: $35.* Michael Stillman—son of Smith & Wollensky founder Alan Stillman—presents this highly stylized industrial theme park, complete with meat-hook light fixtures, wooden butcher blocks, white tiles and exposed brick.

Lespinasse-trained chef Craig Koketsu nails the steaks, from the tender filet mignon to the $110 double-rib steak, and breathes new life into traditional side dishes. Puddinglike corn crème brûlée and the airy "gnocchi & cheese," a clever take on macaroni and cheese, are remarkable. High-concept desserts are best exemplified by the outstanding coffee ice cream, crammed with doughnut chunks and crowned with a miniature doughnut.

★ **Robert's Steakhouse** *603 W 45th St at Eleventh Ave (212-245-0002). Subway: A, C, E to 42nd St–Port Authority. Mon–Fri 5:30pm–12:30am; Sat 7pm–1am. Average main course: $48.* Surely there's a catchier name for this dazzling steakhouse in the Penthouse Executive Club. Booty and the Beef? The Loin King? Chef Adam Perry Lang (formerly of Daniel and Le Cirque) wisely plays it straight, serving serious food in a silly setting—the mezzanine of Bob Guccione's 10,000-square-foot salute to pulchritude. Lang's dishes are every bit as seductive as the tawny ladies pole-dancing below. Steaks are marvelous, whether a thick-as-your-fist, 28-ounce dry-aged New York strip, or kobe beef served with buckwheat soba and shiitake mushrooms. Dessert might bring molten chocolate cake with rich pistachio ice cream. Or you could wait for one of the G-string divas offering lap dances to come to your table. Whatever you choose, your waiter will merely smile and ask, ever so politely, "Shall I remove this dish, or are you still working on it?"

Rothmann's Steakhouse & Grill *3 E 54th St between Fifth and Madison Aves (212-319-5500). Subway: E, V to Fifth Ave–53rd St; 6 to 51st St. Mon–Fri 11:30am–11pm; Sat 4–11pm; Sun 5–10pm. Average main course: $28.* The original chef was a blood relative of Peter Luger himself, so you can forgive some copycatting. Both houses broil their aged beef under high heat, which makes the steaks juicy inside and nicely charred outside. Both serve a giant porterhouse for two, conveniently sliced, and prop up the plate with a small saucer so the juices pool on one end. But this is how Rothmann's differs: It serves cuts other than the big P; its clientele consists mainly of Brooks Brothers types; and the decor is actually decorous. It also has one of the city's most extensive wine lists: Some 850 bottles represent every price range. You'll drink to that.

STK *26 Little W 12th St between Ninth Ave and Washington St (646-624-2444). Subway: A, C, E to 14th St; L to Eighth Ave. Daily 5:30pm–2am. Average main course: $35.* You won't find any kobe or grass-fed beef at this sexy and enormous Meatpacking District steakhouse from the folks who run One lounge around the corner. You will see a lot of attractive people and a menu that plays up the nonsteak options. The goal, it seems, is to draw fish and veggie lovers as much as carnivores. Of the half-dozen salads, the roasted beets were the most colorful and delicious. The steaks were consistent crowd-pleasers, and have been wisely organized into three categories—small, medium and large. That said, the 34-ounce "cowboy rib steak," served on the bone, isn't as daunting as it sounds.

Shula's *270 W 43rd St at Eighth Ave (212-201-2776). Subway: N, Q, R, W, 42nd St S, 1, 2, 3, 7 to 42nd St–Times Sq. 6:30am–11pm. Average main course: $32.* Owned by the onetime Miami Dolphins coach, Shula's has its share of big-league sports kitsch:

High stakes
Dine under a dazzling
sword display at the
Kobe Club.

TALIA SIMHI

The menu is written on a football, and trophies and other memorabilia fill the low-lit rooms. Kick off with the cold lobster cocktail—a small tail, a large claw and the midsection, served with mustard sauce. The porterhouse, even the 24-ounce peewee-league version, is so flavorful that even salt and pepper seem superfluous. Exemplary hash browns are seasoned with a hint of nutmeg. The warm chocolate soufflé is a winning touchdown.

★ **Smith & Wollensky** *797 Third Ave at 49th St (212-753-1530). Subway: E, V to Lexington Ave–53rd St; 6 to 51st St. Mon–Fri 11:45am–11pm; Sat, Sun 5–11pm. Average main course: $36.* This temple of turf is firmly entrenched in the appealing middle ground between old-time religion steakhouses and cheeky *arrivistes* like Dylan Prime and Strip House. Just order a cut of meat you like, then prepare to be transported: Porterhouse, filet and rib eye are dry-aged on site, crisply charred, and fork-tender. Even the seafood, such as the appetizer of chilled lobster, crabmeat and shrimp (for two), can be surprisingly good. You pay dearly for worshiping here, but every once in a while, you deserve to be treated this well. **Other location** *Wollensky's Grill, 201 E 49th St at Third Ave (212-753-0444).*

★ **Sparks** *210 E 46th St between Second and Third Aves (212-687-4855). Subway: 42nd St S, 4, 5, 6, 7 to 42nd St–Grand Central. Mon–Thu noon–11pm; Fri noon–11:30pm; Sat 5–11:30pm. Average main course: $32.* Sparks used to be a mob hangout. Now it's just mobbed. Even with a reservation, you may twist your pinky ring for an hour at the cramped bar. It's worth the wait—especially when a starter of plump broiled shrimp with garlicky lemon butter reaches your table. The signature sirloin is a lean, mean 16-ounce hunk of prime with heft, chew and a salty, lightly charred exterior. Beef scaloppine and steak *fromage* (filet mignon topped with Roquefort) are also outstanding. When your fork slides through a velvety wedge of chocolate mousse cake, you'll feel sorry for Gambino crime boss Paul Castellano, who was famously whacked as he approached the entrance one night in 1985: He died before enjoying his last good meal.

Staghorn Steakhouse *315 W 36th St between Eighth and Ninth Aves (212-239-0923). Subway: A, C, E to 34th St–Penn Station. Mon–Fri noon–11pm; Sat 5–11pm. Average main course: $34.* This little steakhouse in the no-man's-land between upper Chelsea and Hell's Kitchen has carved out a niche as an underdog favorite—if only because it's not affiliated with Peter Luger in any way and doesn't offer grass-fed beef. Staghorn sticks to the basics: formal service, straightforward steaks, lots of wine. Nearly every dish follows tried-and-true formulas and while the porterhouse for two—a good gauge of what a steakhouse can do—is small compared with some of the mastodon-size portions in the city, it's plenty juicy and charred just right. The wine list goes way beyond the usual California cabernets and starts in the relatively low $30 range. The scene dies early, so plan on being done by 10pm.

★ **Strip House** *13 E 12th St between Fifth Ave and University Pl (212-328-0000). Subway: L, N, Q, R, W, 4, 5, 6 to 14th St–Union Sq. Mon–Sat 5pm–11:30pm; Sun 5pm–11pm. Average main course: $36.* Strip House cultivates a retro-sexy vibe with its suggestive name, red furnishings and

vintage pinups. But it's still a modern meat shrine flaunting French influences. Executive chef David Walzog makes sure his New York strips arrive at your table sizzling, seasoned with sea salt and peppercorns, and showing no sign of extraneous fat. Order the New York strip and you'll experience the sublime combination of a perfectly charred outside with a luscious rare-red inside. Purists will start with a standard like jumbo shrimp or steamed clams; health nuts can sample a salad (Bibb lettuce or mixed baby greens); and the adventurous will veer toward the ultrarich lobster bisque or foie gras *torchon*. Everyone will enjoy the black-truffle creamed spinach, one of several gourmet takes on classic steak sides. In keeping with the macho theme, the desserts include slices of cheesecake and chocolate cake so gargantuan that they'll prompt laughs or gasps, depending on how much room you have left.

Wolfgang's Steakhouse *409 Greenwich St between Beach and Hubert Sts (212-925-0350). Subway: 1, 2, 3 to Chambers St. Mon–Thu noon–10:15pm; Fri noon–11:15pm; Sat 5–11:15pm; Sun 5–10:15pm. Average main course: $37.* It was a gamble for Wolfgang Zwiener, the former Peter Luger waiter, to open his own steakhouse in midtown in 2004, and riskier still for him to attempt an offshoot of his offshoot. But this is one of the best (albeit priciest) restaurants of its ilk. While the space doesn't have the Guastavino ceiling tiles that make the Park Avenue location so attractive, it is bigger and roomier, and has its own sleek, dark-wood elegance. The kitchen pumps out all the classics—shrimp or crabmeat cocktail, mozzarella and beefsteak-tomato salad, creamed spinach, sautéed or steamed broccoli—but also offers some tasty alternatives; the German potatoes (baked to a crisp with fried onions) are a nice change of pace if you're considering onions rings and/or baked potatoes. Most important, the steaks kick ass: They're thick, juicy and charred enough to be flavorful without tasting like carbon. Big groups can order porterhouses for two, three or four; solo diners can dig into a filet mignon, rib eye or sirloin and not feel like they're getting the second-best item on the menu. Oenophiles will appreciate the hefty bottle selection, but there is no printed list of wines by the glass—a minor flaw.

Read 'em & eat

shell steak: a cut of the short loin with the tenderloin cut off

sirloin: a cut that lies between the short loin and the round, and includes part of the backbone, hip bone and tenderloin

skirt steak: the boneless top-loin muscle, also known as *New York strip steak*

T-bone: a T-shaped portion of the backbone cut from the center of the short loin

tenderloin: the most tender boneless cut from the short loin (filet mignon is cut from the tenderloin)

Thai

See also: *Asian*

Steak holder
The spicy beef salad is a good starter at Open the Sesame.

JEFF GURWIN

▲☉**Amarin Cafe** *617 Manhattan Ave between Driggs and Nassau Aves, Greenpoint, Brooklyn (718-349-2788). Subway: G to Nassau Ave. Sun–Thu 11am–10:30pm; Fri, Sat 11am–11pm. Average main course: $7.* If you're seeking refuge from the wave of glammy Thai spots to hit Williamsburg in recent years, head north to where the only frills are the local artwork on otherwise bare blue walls. All the brilliance here goes into the food: A pair of golden, crisp crab cakes are first good, then great when dunked in rich, coconutty peanut sauce. Basil chicken, ordered medium-spiced, is quite hot; shrimp with asparagus is given added zing when scattered with crunchy cashews.

▲☉**Arunee Thai Cuisine** *37-68 79th St between Roosevelt and 37th Aves, Jackson Heights, Queens (718-205-5559). Subway: E, F, V, G, R to Jackson Hts–Roosevelt Ave; 7 to 82nd St–Jackson Hts. Mon–Fri 11am–10:30pm; Sat, Sun noon–10:30pm. Average main course: $8.* Veterans of highly seasoned food can handle Arunee's "medium Thai spicy." Choose anything hotter and you'd better have some serious chili training. Stuffed chicken wings are partially deboned and filled with minced vegetables, onion and glass noodles. Tasty salads include *yum nuea,* succulent pieces of beef tossed with lime, onion, chili and toasted rice powder, and *yum pla murk,* tender tubes of squid mixed with Chinese celery, lemongrass, lime, onion and chili peppers. Tender tongues should opt for the mild panang chicken-and-vegetable curry.

▲**Bann Thai** *69-12 Austin St between 69th Ave and Yellowstone Blvd, Forest Hills, Queens (718-544-9999). Subway: E, F, V, G, R to Forest Hills–71st Ave. Daily 11:30am–11pm. Average main course: $14.* Colorful

walls adorned by folkloric batiks and sculptures (with and without running water) lend a soothing aura to Bann Thai, an exceptionally fine spot on Forest Hills' semi-tony "high street." The mixed seafood dishes (*pong pang* for hot, *pla jean* for mild) and the Massaman curries are particularly rich, and the traditional salads, such as *nam sod* (minced pork) and *larb* (minced chicken) are seasoned with originality. This bi-level beauty is rather upscale, yet as cramped and rushed as most Thai places.

Beet *344 Seventh Ave between 9th and 10th Sts, Park Slope, Brooklyn (718-832-2338). Subway: F to Seventh Ave. Mon–Thu noon–11pm; Fri, Sat noon–midnight; Sun 12:30pm–10:30pm. Average main course: $10.* "Beet" is a small word for a Park Slope restaurant with a big concept. Pat Rodsomarng, who owns nearby Mango, operates this modern Thai eatery and is cooking both traditional dishes and his own French-inspired inventions. Every meal includes your choice of salads, soups, noodles, dumplings, curries, and boozy innovations like cognac-ginger beef or red snapper with champagne-vanilla butter sauce. The 40-seat room is beet-colored, too. The only thing missing is the liquor license. Until it arrives, diners can order alcohol off a menu from a store next door.

Breeze *661 Ninth Ave between 45th and 46th Sts (212-262-7777). Subway: A, C, E to 42nd St–Port Authority. Mon–Thu, Sun 11:30am–11:30pm; Fri–Sat noon–midnight. Average main course: $16.* With a progressive look—tangerine walls, triangular mirrors and menus printed on CDs—and a refined menu, Breeze sails past the other Hell's Kitchen contenders, combining French techniques and Thai cuisine to spellbinding effect. Addictive fried dumplings filled with wild mushrooms and

caramelized onions are topped with a delectable soy–black truffle foam. Nearly as tasty is the grilled salmon, which comes glazed in a zesty fire-roasted chili-orange sauce.

★ ▲**The Elephant** *58 E 1st St between First and Second Aves (212-505-7739). Subway: F, V to Lower East Side–Second Ave. Mon–Thu 11:30am–11:30pm; Fri, Sat 11:30am–1am; Sun 5:30–11:30pm. Average main course: $17.* Creamy lemongrass-lime soup and salmon tartare are just two of the dishes that make it worth charging through the thicket of young drinkers who cluster around the entrance. Thai standards, such as green curry with chicken and seared duck breast (marinated in five spices and brushed with a cinnamon glaze), are exceedingly good. And don't worry if you start seeing Pink Elephants—just grab a cocktail menu and order one for yourself.

●**Em Thai** *278 Smith St between Sackett and DeGraw Sts, Carroll Gardens, Brooklyn (718-834-0505). Subway: F, G to Carroll St. Mon–Thu, Sun noon–11pm; Fri, Sat noon–11:30pm. Average main course: $10.* While the modernist design touches—vinelike wall sculptures, Lucite lamps and resin chairs—are cool, they're also cold. Ambience aside, the prodigiously portioned and surprisingly light dishes win you over. Savor the citrus kick in the green papaya salad and the flakiness of the spring rolls, which are stuffed with vermicelli, cabbage and taro root. Big bowls of fragrant coconut-milk–based *Massaman* curry topped with fried onions and cashews are sharable, as is a dish called Two Best Friends—a belly-filling portion of tender shrimp and squid with onion, bell pepper and scallions in a hot chili sauce.

▲●**Fake Orchid** *440 E 9th St between First Ave and Ave A (646-654-1991). Subway: L to First Ave, 6 to Astor Pl. Mon, Wed–Sun 5–11pm. Average main course: $11.* Don't complain about your own tiny kitchen until you've seen the one at this pint-size Thai home-cooking joint—that looks like a studio apartment converted into a restaurant. A divider between the stove and a half-dozen tables, plus a few kitschy decorations, is all that separates the cook from the diners. Fantastic *tom kha* soup, wickedly delicious curries and tender grilled pulled pork compensate for the informality. You'll feel as if you've been invited over for dinner, and at these prices, it's almost as good a deal.

▲**Holy Basil** *149 Second Ave between 9th and 10th Sts, second floor (212-460-5557). Subway: L to First Ave; 6 to Astor Pl. Mon–Thu 5–11:30pm; Fri 5pm–midnight; Sat 4pm–midnight; Sun 4–11pm. Average main course: $14.* If you prefer a mild melding of the four "Thai tastes"—sweet, salty, sour and spicy—nirvana, in this pleasant, bi-level space, lies in the artfully heaped curry with tofu and vegetables. *Pet kaprow* is a tower of crisp duck threaded with white onion, green peppers and brittle leaves of the sweet spice for which the place is named. Desserts are not a strength: Instead, finish your meal with a smooth, rich Thai iced tea—a sublime concoction of strong orange tea, rich cream and spoonfuls of sugar.

▲●**Jeeb** *154 Orchard St between Stanton and Rivington Sts (212-677-4101). Subway: F, V to Lower East Side–Second Ave. Mon–Thu, Sun 11am–11pm; Fri, Sat 11am–midnight. Average small plate: $5.* You could easily miss this tiny restaurant, set a few steps below ground level with a roomy brick-walled garden—one of the best dining spots in the summer. Not a tapas dish is a disappointment. Golden curry puffs are slightly sweet pastries filled with curried potatoes; salmon dumplings are plump and meaty. And larger dishes, like a seafood-

studded red curry and rice noodles with basil, have just the right amount of bite.

▲●**Joya** *215 Court St between Warren and Wyckoff Sts, Cobble Hill, Brooklyn (718-222-3484). Subway: F, G to Bergen St. Tue–Thu noon–11pm; Fri, Sat noon–midnight; Sun 1pm–midnight. Average main course: $8.* You've had it bland and you've had it spicy: Now, welcome to *loud* Thai. On Saturday nights, post-collegiate twentysomethings, drinks in hand, groove to a DJ spinning music. You half-expect someone to bust a move—until the fragrant aroma of *tom yum* soup hits you. Take a seat in the dimly lit, industrial-looking dining room, and start with greaseless fried calamari with an addictive sweet-and-spicy chili sauce, or the nicely zesty beef salad. Stick with a curry as your main. Like it fiery? Ask your server to turn up the heat a few notches. If he can hear you.

▲●**Kai Kai Thai Bistro** *131 Ave A between St. Marks Pl and E 9th St (212-420-5909). Subway: 6 to Astor Pl. Daily noon–11pm. Average main course: $6.* Popular and tiny (only five tables), Kai Kai now has a third outpost, on Carmine Street. The menu is unsurprising, but the kitchen has a way with spices, giving each dish a distinct flavor. Ginger vinaigrette accents green Thai dumplings, and coconut-*galangal* soup is pungent and fiery with lemongrass and chili. Flavorful, nongreasy pad thai is available with chicken, shrimp, crabmeat, lobster, vegetables or tofu. *Massaman* and *panang* curries with shrimp are made fresh and quickly, and daily specials like sea-clam curry are worth marking on your calendar. Kai Kai is so nice, they had to name it twice and repeat it thrice.
Other locations *Kai Kai, 78 E 1st St between First Ave and Ave A (212-777-2552)* ● *Kai Kai, 35 Carmine St between Bedford and Bleecker Sts (212-627-7745).*

★ **Kin Khao** *171 Spring St between Thompson St and West Broadway (212-966-3939). Subway: C, E to Spring St. Mon–Thu 5:30–11pm; Fri 5:30pm–midnight; Sat 5:30pm–midnight; Sun noon–5pm, 5:30–11pm. Average main course: $17.* After more than a decade, this trendy Thai bistro is still going strong. The Far-East standards are solidly executed: shiitake-mushroom-and-shrimp spring rolls with chili dipping sauce; wok-fired salmon with red curry and kafir lime leaves; whole fried sea bass with sweet and sour sauce. While you wait for your table (hey, it's Soho), sip a ginger kamikaze and flip through one of the glossy fashion rags at the bar.

★ **Kittichai** *60 Thompson Hotel, 60 Thompson St between Broome and Spring Sts (212-219-2000). Subway: C, E to Spring St. Mon–Wed 7am–11am, 12pm–2:30pm, 5:30pm–11pm; Thu–Sat 7am–11am, 12pm–2:30pm, 5:30pm–midnight; Sun 11:30am–3:30pm, 5:30–11pm. Average main course: $24.* If varieties of orchids in dramatic bottles don't capture your attention, the beautiful people sipping cocktails made with coconut milk or fresh juices will. The mood is set by orange-hued lighting that bounces off fabric dividers and candles floating in a pool at the center of the room. Chef Ian Chalermkittichai (Four Seasons Bangkok) cooks haute Thai with a sweet accent: Chicken lollipops come with a pungent, sweet-spicy dipping sauce and tender short ribs are braised in an excellent green curry with sweet basil. In warm weather, grab a seat on the small leafy patio out front.

Ma-Ya *234 E 4th St between Aves A and B (646-313-1987). Subway: F, V to Lower East Side–Second Ave. Tue–Thu 5–11pm; Fri, Sat 5pm–midnight. Average main course: $14.* Chef Taweewat Hurapan (Rain and Rain

Decisions decisions
Thai and French-inspired
dishes compete for
your attention at Beet.

East) is cooking up mouthwatering dishes from his native Thailand. In the tiny, meandering two-story space, diners shimmy into little nooks to savor subtly sweet mounds of coconut sticky rice, ungreasy platefuls of sautéed Japanese eggplant, and—best of all—crisp, whole deep-fried fish that collapse into a pool of rich, garlicky sauce. It's a whole lot of flavor for your buck, with a reasonably priced wine list to match.

☺**Open the Sesame** *198A Orchard St between Houston and Stanton Sts (212-777-7009). Subway: F, V to Lower East Side–Second Ave. Tue–Thu, Sun noon–11pm; Fri, Sat noon–11:30pm. Average main course: $10.* Thai spots are all over this 'hood, but this cutely named eatery stands out by pushing the charm factor. The narrow space is outfitted with the chef's original artwork, while the menu features standard Thai fare peppered with some unusual fusion additions. The spicy beef salad—strips of sirloin and pieces of romaine in a chili-lime dressing—is a good place to start, and broad noodles stir-fried with chicken, scrambled egg, string beans, red pepper and carrots was among the best rice pasta dishes we've ever had. But the biggest draw here are the sandwiches—lemongrass chicken, garlic pork chop, grilled vegetables—on Italian bread, each for less than $4.95. A meal for under $5 on the Lower East Side? Now that's cute.

▲**Planet Thailand** *133 North 7th St between Bedford Ave and Berry St, Williamsburg, Brooklyn (718-599-5758). Subway: L to Bedford Ave. Mon–Thu, Sun 11:30am–1am; Fri, Sat 11:30am–2am. Average main course: $12.* Cinder-block walls and polished concrete floors add to the industrial-chic decor at this well-loved Billyburg standby; there's even room for installation art,

like a suspended rowboat fountain. Sushi chefs and a Japanese hibachi operation have materialized to add a little Pan-Asian pizzazz: The Williamsburg Bridge combo is a colorful, show-stopping platter loaded with hand rolls, sushi and sashimi. Still, nothing takes away from the freshness and low prices that made this spot popular in the first place. **Other location** *Thai Cafe, 429 Manhattan Ave at Kent St, Greenpoint, Brooklyn (718-383-3562).*

▲☺**Pukk** *71 First Ave between 4th and 5th Sts (212-253-2741). Subway: F, V to Lower East Side–Second Ave. Sun–Thu 11:30am–11pm; Fri, Sat 11:30am–midnight. Average main course: $7.* This is not exactly a traditional Thai restaurant—the chicken and duck are made out of soy, and the tiny 30-seat dining room is fashioned to look like the inside of a swimming pool, covered floor to ceiling in circular white tiles and basking in a lime-green glow. The flavors, however, are as bright and intense as the real thing: tender eggplant in a spicy basil sauce; papaya salad nipped with a chili-lime vinaigrette; rich noodles swimming in green, red and yellow curries. It's all good, cheap and meat-free. Just beware the desserts: They're vegan, and they taste like it.

★ ▲☺**SEA Thai Restaurant and Bar** *114 North 6th St at Berry St, Williamsburg, Brooklyn (718-384-8850). Subway: L to Bedford Ave. Mon–Thu 11:30am–12:30am; Fri, Sat 11:30am–1:30am. Average main course: $12.* The DJ's beats are thumping, the central pool is presided over by a giant Buddha and the Billyburg crowd is decked out in the latest Bedford Avenue threads. For a place that's so stylin', the prices are shockingly cheap and the food is remarkably good. Jade seafood dumplings are stuffed with shrimp and crab and come with a nutty

Massaman sauce. "Rama the King," a blend of creamy Massaman and red curries topped with crunchy Terra Chips, is a reliable entrée. Another winning combination is a half-chicken grilled with lemongrass and panang curry. Service can be scattered, but pomegranate mojitos will help you keep your cool. **Other location** *SEA, 75 Second Ave between 4th and 5th Sts (212-228-5505).*

Siam Square *564 Kappock St at Netherland Ave, Bronx (718-432-8200). Subway: 1 to 225th St. Tue–Thu 5–10pm; Fri, Sat 5–10:30pm. Average main course: $13.* In an intimate dining room just off the Henry Hudson Parkway, Siam Square serves liberal portions of inspired Thai food. Straw crafts, mounted pottery and musical instruments grace the walls, while Buddha statues regard diners savoring such traditional appetizers as chicken satay or the more unusual Siam Square "crêpes"—thin, triangular crispy pancakes filled with seafood. The range of entrées is impressive, and their piquancy can be modulated by requesting medium spicy, rather spicy, spicy, very spicy and (ominously) "for those who dare."

★ ▲☺**Sripraphai** *64-13 39th Ave between 64th and 65th Sts, Woodside, Queens (718-899-9599). Subway: 7 to 61st St–Woodside. Mon, Tue, Thu–Sun 11:30am–10pm. Average main course: $10.* It's not hard to find Thai food in New York these days. It's just hard to find Thai food like this. Every dish is distinctively spiced and traditional. Catfish salad offers fluffy, deep-fried minced fish with mint, cilantro, chopped cashew and lemon juice. Green curry with beef is a thick, spicy broth filled with roasted Thai eggplant and spices. Although there are dining rooms on two levels and a garden (open during the warm months), there is usually a short wait. Transplanted Manhattanites and Thai wise guys with gold pinkie rings sit side by side eyeing each other's plates, mentally filing away what to order the next time.

☺**Sticky Rice Thai Barbecue** *2007 Eat Out Award, Critics' Pick: Best place for a carnivore and a vegetarian to break bread 85 Orchard St between Broome and Grand Sts (212-274-8208). Subway: F to Delancey St; J, M, Z to Delancey–Essex Sts. Mon–Wed, Sun 11am–11pm; Thu–Sat 11am–midnight. Average main course: $11.* Contrary to what the name implies, the menu at this BYOB eatery from Diane Wongprasert (Pad Thai) offers curries, barbecue, soups and salads—with rice mostly as a side dish. Though the mismatched decor falters (red-leather booths sit under an exposed-brick ceiling, while the mod bar area is pure early-'90s minimalist), the food succeeds. Firecrackers—shredded chicken, curry paste and basil wrapped in tofu skin—stand out as a starter, while vegetarian options like a grilled satay of portobello mushroom and tofu are refreshingly diverse.

★ ▲**Thai on Clinton** *6 Clinton St between Houston and Stanton Sts (212-228-9388). Subway: F to Delancey St; J, M, Z to Delancey–Essex Sts. Mon–Fri 5–10:30pm; Sat, Sun noon–10:30pm. Average main course: $12.* The all-white design of the small, spare room signals that you're in for a heavenly experience. TOC offers a full menu of classics—gorgeously presented, inexpensive and devastatingly good. Duck salad is loaded with finger-licking skin-on pieces; the Massaman curry is silky and filling. Spicy whole red snapper is butterflied, crisp on the outside and steamy inside. Pad thai—a great way to tell if a place is worth its tamarind—arrives al dente with an even balance of salt, sugar and lime. Top it all off with fried ice cream, served flambéed. The friendly staff can be slightly forgetful, but you'll easily forgive.

▲☺**Ubol's Kitchen** *24-42 Steinway St at Astoria Blvd, Astoria, Queens (718-545-2874). Subway: N, W to Astoria Blvd. Mon–Thu noon–11pm; Fri–Sun noon–midnight. Average main course: $10.* Good news for curry lovers: Though former owner Ubol has left the building, the chili-powered kitchen's still got it goin' on. "Pork in the Garden" has a lovely tang from the combination of chili, sugar and lime juice; deep-fried duck in creamy red-curry sauce is surprisingly crisp. The coconut juice, served with fleshy bits of sweet, tender coconut, is a must. Desserts are tropical: Banana, mango and the like are paired with sweetened coconut rice.

Vong *200 E 54th St at Third Ave (212-486-9592). Subway: E, V to Lexington Ave–53rd St; 6 to 51st St. Mon–Fri noon–3pm, 5:30–11pm; Sat 5:30–11pm. Average main course: $27.* When Vong opened in 1992, it was an edgy hotspot for pan-Asian cuisine. Now, at 8:30 on a Saturday night, the dining room can be half-empty with a big family belting out the "Happy Birthday" song. The restaurant, one of Jean-Georges Vongerichten's firsts, has seen better days, and the food isn't up to the chef's usual standards. Appetizers like shrimp satay and crab spring rolls with assorted dipping sauces are tasty but generic. A cod fillet comes with woody chunks of artichoke and bitter, beefy-tasting sauce; duck breast is perfectly cooked but paired with its own over-reduced sauce and yet another spring roll. Vong's primary strength might be the reason it's still around: It's conveniently located for a midtown business lunch.

▲☺**Zabb Queens** *71-28 Roosevelt Ave between 71st and 72nd Sts, Woodside, Queens (718-426-7992). Subway: E, F, V, G, R to Jackson Heights–Roosevelt Ave; 7 to 69th St. 5pm–2am. Average main course: $8.* In Jackson Heights, under the rumbling train tracks of the elevated 7 line, dwells New York's first restaurant devoted to the modest and fiery cuisine of Isaan, the northeastern region of Thailand. The menu also lists plenty of standard dishes, such as pad thai and coconut curries, which are less sweet than most versions, thanks to the use of a house-made curry paste. Unique to Isaan are some unusual salads, including one of ground catfish in which bits of dried chilies fleck the salty fish. Exhilarating but uncomplicated *tom yum* features exceptionally plump shrimp and enough murky, delicious hot-and-sour broth to feed three.

Thai

Read 'em & eat

khao: (also *kow* or *khow*) rice

massaman curry: (also known as *Muslim curry*) a rich sauce, made from coconut, potatoes and peanuts

pad: stir-fry

panang: a dry, aromatic curry made with chilies, coriander, shrimp paste, lime, lemongrass, cilantro, ginger and shallots

prik: chili; *prik* pon is red-chili powder

tom yum: a hot and sour soup that may feature prawns (*tom yum goong*), chicken (*tom yum gai*) or fish (*tom yum pla*)

Turkish

See also: *Afghan, Middle Eastern*

Home plate
Dig into Turkish comfort food at Pasha.

★ ▲**Ali Baba** *212 E 34th St between Second and Third Aves (212-683-9206). Subway: 6 to 33rd St. Daily 11:30am–10:30pm. Average main course: $14.* The highlight at this midtown stalwart are the divine *yogurtlu* kebabs, juicy lamb served with a tangy tomato, garlic and yogurt sauce. Kebabs are accompanied by rice, pickled cabbage, spiced red onion and a fiery, charred fresh chili. Cool it by downing a glass of *salgam*, a tart red carrot juice not often found outside Turkey. Warm homemade *pide* (flatbread with black and white sesame seeds) partners perfectly with *lebni* (a thick yogurt dip of walnuts, garlic and dill) or with *piyaz* (white beans and onion dressed in a zippy lemon vinaigrette).

▲**Pasha** *70 W 71st St between Central Park West and Columbus Ave (212-579-8751). Subway: B, C to 72nd St. Mon–Sat 5–11pm; Sun 4–10pm. Average main course: $18.* Turkish comfort food is the specialty at this Upper West Side favorite. Try the manti (tender, steamed lamb-and-mint dumplings covered with garlicky yogurt) or a traditional meze sampler. The *hunkar begendi*, a tomato-based lamb stew served over pureed charcoal-grilled eggplant, is worth ordering for the name alone. Even the myriad kebabs are tricked out, with extras like eggplant wraps and house-made yogurt. The regal, plush interior creates an air of nonstuffy elegance.

▲**Peri Ela** *1361 Lexington Ave between 90th and 91st Sts (212-410-4300). Subway: 4, 5, 6 to 86th St. Daily noon–11pm. Average main course: $20.* The dark wood walls, pressed-tin ceiling and Pop Art tableaux picturing the sort of scantily clad women you might find on the beach in Bodrum would make this Carnegie Hill Turkish restaurant feel at home in Istanbul's most

fashionable precincts. Homesick Turks share big meze spreads and Turkish wine from a well-priced menu that covers the usual *meyhane* (taverna) staples like a rich, creamy *cacik*, a classic garlic-laced yogurt dip, and a winning combo plate of ground lamb *kofta*, a lamb chop, and cubes of chicken and lamb kebabs. In keeping with its Euro vibe, instead of thick Turkish coffee, espresso—what hip, young Turks drink—is listed with the sweet, sticky baklava and rolled custard *kazandibi*.

★ ▲**Turkish Kitchen** *386 Third Ave between 27th and 28th Sts (212-679-1810). Subway: 6 to 28th St. Mon–Thu noon–3pm, 5–110:30pm; Fri noon–3pm, 5:30–11pm; Sat 5:30–11pm; Sun 11am–3pm, 5–10pm. Average main course: $16.* There's a hint of the bordello—blood-red walls, Anatolian brass trinkets—in this tastefully shagadelic setting for regional meze and mains. (The lovestruck can request a secluded balcony table.) Try the *patlican salatasi*, a satiny-smooth smoked-eggplant dip, before digging into the tender lamb kebabs and *tavuk pirzola*, chicken stuffed with green peppers, tomatoes and creamy Turkish cheese. *Kadayif*, honey-drizzled shredded phyllo sprinkled with pistachios, makes for a sweet ending.

★ ▲**Turkuaz** *2637 Broadway at 100th St (212-665-9541). Subway: 1 to 103rd St; 1, 2, 3 to 96th St. Sun–Thu 11:30am–11pm; Fri–Sat 11:30am–midnight. Average main course: $19.* The beige curtains draped along the walls and looming across the ceiling of Turkuaz's spacious dining room create the effect of a tent, but there's nothing rustic about the presentation or quality of the food here. The combination cold appetizer plate assembles six spreads, highlighted by a sumptuous *tarama*, an invigorating *cacik* (blending yogurt, cucumber and garlic) and a tangy eggplant stuffed with currants and pine nuts. Continue the sampling with the mixed grill or opt for one of several tender yogurt kebab entrées. Try holding it all in when the belly dancing starts at 10pm on weekends.

Read 'em & eat

baklava: a sweet pastry made of ground nuts and layered in phyllo leaves

cacik: yogurt-cucumber spread with garlic and dill

dolma: stuffed grape leaves (often filled with a spiced lamb-and-rice mixture)

kofta: beef or lamb meatballs ground with onions and spices

meze: hors d'oeuvres; also the time preceding a meal during which they are served

KENNETH CHEN

Vegetarian/Organic

See also: *Asian, Cafés, Indian*

Green zone
Go for DIY fixin's
at Maoz.

CINZIA REALE-CASTELLO

★ ▲☻**Angelica Kitchen** *300 E 12th St between First and Second Aves (212-228-2909). Subway: L to First Ave; N, Q, R, W, 4, 5, 6 to 14th St–Union Sq. 11:30am–10:30pm. Average main course: $10.* Organic-minded, kid-toting parents and vegan East Villagers commune over the tofu at this enduring health-food hot spot. Share the Pantry Plate (rich walnut-lentil pâté, mellow hummus and ruby sauerkraut), but snag the velvety, sesame-sauced Soba Sensation for yourself. Massive, superpopular Dragon Bowls (rice, beans, tofu, steamed veggies) get their kick from dressings like creamy carrot or eggless Sea Caesar. Don't know your kombu from your kudzu? The helpful menu glossary gets you ready for the macrobiotic big-leagues in no time flat.

▲☻**Bliss** *191 Bedford Ave between North 6th and 7th Sts, Williamsburg, Brooklyn (718-599-2547). Subway: L to Bedford Ave. Tue–Sat 5:30–10:30pm; Sun 5–10pm. Average main course: $17. Three-course prix fixe: $20.* The name, which refers to the nearby Bliss Street subway stop, is apt: This is a joyfully low-priced, palate-wowing bistro in Williamsburg. The market-driven American cuisine is as flavorful as the fare on more celebrated menus across the East River. The mushroom ravioli has a terrific earthiness, and tangy house-cured salmon melts in your mouth. A handful of simple entrées cover land and sea: Shell and hanger steaks are deftly grilled. Seafood comes in a variety of forms: pan-seared, filleted or set on pasta.

▲**Blossom Vegetarian Restaurant** *187 Ninth Ave between 21st and 22nd Sts (212-627-1144). Subway: C, E to 23rd St. Mon–Thu 5–10pm; Fri–Sun noon–3pm, 5–10pm. Average main course: $18.* For cautious carnivores, Blossom offers one big surprise:

All the eggless pastas and mock meats actually taste pretty good. For vegans, it's a candlelit godsend. Guiltily dreaming of veal scaloppine? Try the pan-seared seitan cutlets, tender wheat gluten served with basil mashed potatoes, Swiss chard, a white-wine caper sauce and artichokes. With fake-meat entrées averaging $18, carnivores may feel compelled to eat the real thing elsewhere, but vegetarians have indeed found a great new date place.

▲☻**Bonobo's Vegetarian** *18 E 23rd St between Broadway and Park Ave South (212-505-1200). Subway: N, R, W, 6 to 23rd St. Average main course: $8.* A knowledgeable counter staff at this airy, plant-strewn restaurant hands out liberal samples that should help you choose from the lengthy organic and raw-food menu. A spicy tomato-basil stew is vibrant and acidic, while a silky bell pepper–coconut soup is sweet and fragrant. Artfully arranged salads are bright platforms for tangy dressings like agave-mustard and lemon-garlic tahini.

▲**Candle Café** *1307 Third Ave at 75th St (212-472-0970). Subway: 6 to 77th St. Mon–Sat 11:30am–10:30pm; Sun 11:30am–9:30pm. $14.* This light and airy café has a groovy yet sophisticated vibe and meals to match: vegan, skillful, elegant and flavorful. Candle Café is a neighborhood favorite where everyone is treated like regulars by the friendly, patient staff—used to dealing with hardcore vegans, celiacs and allergy-prone eaters (there's even a gluten-free menu, just like at the eatery's more upscale sister spot, Candle 79). Summer rolls with tofu sing with freshness, the paradise casserole (a layered hunk of sweet potato, black beans and millet) is

Lite 'n' lively
Colors and flavors are as bountiful as a greenmarket at Blossom.

a heavenly—though not heavy—concoction, and chipotle tofu is a perfectly spiced treat.

▲**Candle 79** *154 E 79th St at Lexington Ave (212-537-7179). Subway: 6 to 77th St. Mon–Sat noon–3:30pm, 5:30–10:30pm; Sun noon–4pm, 5–10pm. Average main course: $17.* Tucked away on an unromantic Upper East Side block, this surprisingly atmospheric spot is a find for anyone who loves food and animals—live ones, that is. The intimate, bi-level townhouse setting is infused with an ambience gourmet-minded vegetarians crave but rarely encounter. Best is the food itself—fresh, creative and inclusive (a separate gluten-free menu keeps celiacs sated), with delectable dishes including the seitan *piccata*, its crisp paillards bathed in a light bath of lemon butter and capers, and the saffron-flavored paella, studded with seitan sausage and seasonal veggies. Service is knowledgeable and attentive, the desserts impossibly rich.

▲**Caravan of Dreams** *405 E 6th St between First Ave and Ave A (212-254-1613). Subway: F, V to Lower East Side–Second Ave; 6 to Astor Pl. Mon–Fri, Sun 11am–11pm; Sat 11am–midnight. Average main course: $15.* Vegetarians, vegans and raw-foodists unite! This longtime East Village hangout offers both regular meat-free dishes—grilled seitan nachos, black-bean chili, stir-fries—and "live foods," made from uncooked fruits, vegetables, nuts and seeds. Live "hummus" (whipped from cold-processed tahini and raw almonds instead of the usual chickpeas) can be scooped up with pressed flaxseed "chips"; the live Love Boat pairs almond–Brazil nut "meatballs" with mango chutney and cool marinara sauce on a napa cabbage leaf. Naturally, there are loads

of salads and some macrobiotically balanced rice-and-seaweed combos.

★ ▲**Counter** *105 First Ave between 6th and 7th Sts (212-982-5870). Subway: F, V to Lower East Side–Second Ave. Mon–Thu 5pm–midnight, Fri 5pm–1am; Sat noon–4pm, 5–1am; Sun noon–4pm. Average main course: $13.* Belly up to this counter and don't give a second thought about the quality of food you're about to consume: All items are prepared with organic ingredients whenever possible, and the wine list is strictly organic. Even purists are catered to at Counter, with raw dishes on the menu, alongside healthy cooked fare such as barbecue seitan po'boys and shepherd's pie.

▲◯**Foodswings** *295 Grand St between Havemeyer and Roebling Sts, Williamsburg, Brooklyn (718-388-1919). Subway: L to Bedford Ave. Tue–Thu 5pm–midnight; Fri, 5pm–2am; Sat noon–2pm, 5pm–2am; Sun 2–11pm. Average main course: $7.* Foodswings' owner, the fabulously named Freedom Porio-Tripodi, is a dedicated, political, life-loving vegan who just happens to crave every American's birthright: diner food. Instead of marinated tofu and bean sprouts, the menu is full of animal-free, road-trip-worthy pleasures like faux fish sticks; soy-cheese nachos; antipasto salad filled with veggie ham, soy mozzarella, artichoke hearts and red peppers; and sandwiches like a mock-turkey club, a tempeh Rubenesque and a "tuno" melt. Billyburg clubbers can stop in from 11pm to 2am on Fridays and Saturdays for the Midnight Munchie menu.

★ ▲**Gobo** *401 Sixth Ave between Waverly Pl and W 8th St (212-255-3242). Subway: A, C, E, B, D, F,*

V to W 4th St. Daily 11:30am–11pm. Average main course: $18. Beechwood tables and mood lighting create a clean, minimalist and sophisticated decor at this crowded restaurant, where waits can be up to an hour without reservations. Attentive and charming service enhances the appeal, as will the large range of faux meat plates like the soy fillet with coconut curry rice, or green-tea noodles with vegan Bolognese sauce, flavorful enough to entice even seitan skeptics. Health-conscious diners beware; much of the flavor comes from thick sweet-and-sour marinades, gooey ginger glazes and deep-frying. **Other location** *1426 Third Ave at 81st St (212-288-4686). Subway: 4, 5, 6 to 86th St. 11:30am–11pm. Average main course: $13.*

▲⊙**The Green Table** *75 Ninth Ave at 15th St (212-741-6623). Subway: A, C, E to 14th St; L to Eighth Ave. Mon–Sat noon–9pm; Sun noon–6pm. Average main course: $8.* The food is based on sustainability—seasonal and local products that don't drain natural resources—and the menu of soups, salads and entrees changes accordingly. You'll find such dishes as tasty chicken potpie or a meze sampler of smooth duck pâté on a tiny toast round and caviar and sour cream on a small potato, depending on the season. The list of organic and biodynamically grown wines, beers and hard ciders is more extensive than the food menu. If you indulge in a baked-to-order oatmeal cookie or a rich chocolate-rosemary *pot de crème*, you'll still feel that you're doing good—for the planet. Or drop by to pick up a snack, like the addictive organic popcorn with ancho-orange salt.

▲**Heartbeat** *W New York, 149 E 49th St between Lexington and Third Aves (212-407-2900). Subway: E, V to Lexington Ave–53rd St; 6 to 51st St. Mon–Fri 7–11am, noon–2:30pm, 6–10pm; Sat, Sun 8am–noon;. Average main course: $28.* Although both Michel Nischan—poster boy for all foods seasonal, local and organic—and his replacement, John Mooney, have moved on, Drew Nieporent's Heartbeat remains committed to mostly heart-healthy seasonal dishes. Many of the meats, some of the wines, and all of the fruits and vegetables served in the golden-hued dining room are organic, and the ingredients are as impeccable as ever. Luckily, steak and chocolate cake are always in season.

▲**Josie's** *300 Amsterdam Ave at 74th St (212-769-1212). 1, 2, 3 to 72nd St. Mon–Thu noon–11pm; Fri noon–midnight; Sat 11am–midnight; Sun 10:30am–10:30pm. Average main course: $17.* The bright and whimsical decor—the front door handle is a giant red chili pepper—lends a playful vibe to the seriously health-conscious menu, which expounds Josie's philosophy of using organic, seasonal cuisine and limited dairy ingredients. The food is inconsistent, though, as some tasty dishes—black bean dumplings and angel hair pomodoro, potato and broccoli dumplings—are as heavy as diner grub, while others like the luscious salad topped with creamy grilled tofu or macadamia-encrusted chicken are fresh and delightful. A loud spot filled with locals and their kids, Josie's is festive and convenient for pre- or post–Beacon Theater din-din. **Other location** *565 Third Ave at 37th St (212-490-1558).*

▲⊙**Kate's Brooklyn Joint** *295 Berry St between South 2nd and 3rd Sts, Williamsburg, Brooklyn (718-218-7167). Subway: L to Bedford Ave. Mon–Fri 4–11pm; Sat, Sun 10:30am–11pm. Average main course: $11.* Whoever thinks vegetarian food has to be boring and healthy never visited Kate's Joint. Buffalo UnChicken

wings—batter-fried tofu slathered in a spicy sauce—go as well with a cold beer (BYOB) as anything from KFC. And the McKate—a greasy, politically correct version of the Big Mac—piles together thin soy patties, lettuce, tomato, pickles, onions and special sauce on a whole-wheat bun. While no amount of meat-free options can make up for the couldn't-be-bothered decor—industrial black chairs, dull terra-cotta tiles, canary-yellow walls—their version of the dirty-water dog, a smoky soy frankfurter in a focaccia roll with juicy sauerkraut, made us particularly happy that Kate has moved to Brooklyn. **Other location** *Kate's Joint, 58 Ave B at 4th St (212-777-7059).*

▲**Mana** *646 Amsterdam Ave between 91st and 92nd Sts (212-787-1110). Subway: 1, 2, 3 to 96th St. Mon–Thu 11:30am–10:30pm; Fri, Sat 11am–11pm; Sun 11am–10pm. Average main course: $16.* Join the clutch of regulars who flock to this mellow, uptown oasis of clean living, whose casual dining room opens onto the street on warm evenings. Some menu items are microbiotic inspired—like the Simple Palate, a plate of seasonal greens, beans, rice and tofu—while others are hearty, like the Vegetable Gomai, a creamy miso stew of chunky root vegetables, seitan and tofu. Salads are extremely fresh and light, as are the broiled-fish options and the pastas. The vegan chocolate cake is so rich you won't miss the dairy.

▲⊙**Maoz Vegetarian** *38 Union Sq East between 16th and 17th Sts (212-260-1988). Subway: L, N, Q, R, W, 4, 5, 6 to 14th St–Union Sq. Mon–Thu 11am–1am; Fri, Sat 11am–3am; Sun 11am–11pm. $4.50 sandwich, $7.75 combo meal.* A great concept undone by a chaotic, way-too-small location, this DIY-fixins falafel joint lets you top your chickpea patties with the goodies of your choice—if you can fight your way to the salad bar. Dill cucumbers, carrot medallions, couscous, tomato-and-onion salad, shredded cabbage—the combinations are seemingly limitless (even if your lunchtime patience might not be). Experiment with four different sauces, including a mild traditional tahini or a worth-the-wait garlic sauce. The same garlic sauce does soggy pomme frites a world of good.

▲⊙**The Organic Grill** *123 First Ave between St. Marks Pl and E 7th St (212-477-7177). Subway: F, V to Lower East Side–Second Ave; 6 to Astor Pl. Mon–Thu noon–10pm; Fri noon–11pm; Sat 10am–11pm; Sun 10am–10pm. Average main course: $10.* This casual, cozy, friendly vegetarian café (with a couple of fish options on its menu) rounds up the usual suspects of herbivore cuisine: vegetables steamed or sautéed; salads; grilled-tofu sandwiches and simple macro plates. Stick to these most basic entrées—paired with one of the organic wines, beers or teas from an impressive chalkboard list—and you'll be fine. More complex fare, such as the layered tempeh-vegetable napoleon, tend toward excessive oiliness. And beware: The blaring staccato rock music here is often a jarring intrusion on your meal.

★ ▲**Pure Food and Wine** *54 Irving Pl between 17th and 18th Sts (212-477-1010). Subway: L, N, Q, R, W, 4, 5, 6 to 14th St–Union Sq. Mon 5:30pm–10pm; Sat 5:30pm–11pm; Sun 5:30pm–10pm. Average main course: $23.* The dishes delivered to your table—whether out in the leafy patio or inside the ambient dining room—are minor miracles, not only because they look gorgeous and taste terrific, but because they come from a kitchen that lacks a stove. Everything at Pure is raw and vegan—from the spicy Thai lettuce wraps appetizer to the lasagna, a rich stack of zucchini, pesto and creamy "cheese" made from cashews. Wines, most organic, are top-notch, as are the desserts, especially the confoundingly fudgy chocolate layer cake.

★ ▲**Quintessence** *263 E 10th St between First Ave and Ave A (646-654-1823). Subway: L to First Ave, 6 to Astor Pl. Daily 11:30am–11pm. Average main course: $13.* Get your sprouted seeds and nuts at a serene, little raw-food joint, and join celebs like Alicia Silverstone and Liv Tyler (and models picking up their takeout). The menu skips around the globe, from Mediterranean nachos with spicy hummus and guacamole to Indian *malai kofta*, balls of sprouted chickpeas in creamy almond-curry sauce. There's even a "Big Mac": an . Desserts continue the live-food vibe, but they can be a little too virtuous.

★▲**Red Bamboo Brooklyn Vegeterian Soul Lounge** *2007 Eat Out Award, Readers' Choice: Best vegetarian 271 Adelphi St at DeKalb Ave, Fort Greene, Brooklyn (718-643-4325). Subway: C to Lafayette Ave; G to Clinton–Washington Aves. Mon–Thu 11am–11pm; Fri 11am–1am; Sat noon–1am; Sun: noon–11pm.. Average sandwich: $9.* Sprouts, shoots, leaves—we're all for healthy vegetarian eating. But sometimes the best way to judge a flesh-free joint is by how convincing its mock meat is. Red Bamboo Brooklyn, a vegan and vegetarian Caribbean home cookery, owns this category. Slip into the intimate brick-walled space and start with an appetizer combo: a trio of soul chicken (in a light *panko* coating), Cajun fried shrimp (with a convincing sea-salt aftertaste) and kicky buffalo barbecue wings (a stick takes the place of the bone). The Willy Bobo sandwich, which layers soy ham, pickles and vegan Swiss cheese on grilled coco bread, is better known to carnivores as a classic *Cubano*—herbivores know it as a craveworthy alternative to duller veg fare.

▲**'sNice** *45 Eighth Ave at 4th St (212-645-0310). Subway: A, C, E to 14th St; L to Eighth Ave. Mon–Fri 7:30am–10pm; Sat, Sun 8am–10pm. Average sandwich: $8.* 'Snice *is* nice—if what you're looking for is a cozy neighborhood joint where you can read a paper, do a little laptopping, and enjoy cheap, simple and satisfying veggie fare. Far roomier than it appears from its corner windows, the exposed-brick café has what may well be the largest blackboard menu in the city, covered with carefully wrought descriptions of each burrito, sandwich and salad's ingredients (all $7.50 apiece at the counter). Standouts include the quinoa salad with mixed greens and avocado dressing, and the brie, pear and arugula baguette dressed with raspberry mustard.

▲**Soy Luck Club** *115 Greenwich Ave at Jane St (212-229-9191). Subway: A, C, E to 14th St; L to Eighth Ave. Mon–Fri 8am–10:30pm; Sat, Sun 9:30am–10pm. Average sandwich: $8.* The sleek interior may look retro (note the Herman Miller and Knoll furnishings and polka-dot plates), but this West Village spot is as 21st-century as they come: The place offers free Web connections (through Wi-Fi and DSL) and a wide array of soy-infused drinks and snacks. Sandwiches have a gourmet-deli appeal and include mouthwatering combos like chicken, asparagus, truffle oil and fontina, and fresh turkey stacked with Brie and green-apple slices. Spelt crêpes are stuffed with ingredients sweet or savory, such as goat cheese, pesto and egg, or soy-nut butter and jelly (a grown-up rendition of PB&J).

▲☺**Tiengarden** *170 Allen St between Rivington and Stanton Sts (212-388-1364). Subway: F, V to Lower East Side–Second Ave. Mon–Sat noon–10pm. Average main course: $9.* This is the closest to truly personal treatment that you're ever likely to find in a restaurant. The diminutive vegan café seats about as many people as a Manhattan studio apartment might, and each dish is prepared with great care. Try the seaweed rolls—tofu wrapped in *nori* and sheets of bean curd, panfried with lemon—and herbed home fries.

▲☺**Vegetarian Dim Sum House** *24 Pell St between Bowery and Mott St (212-577-7176). Subway: J, M, Z, N, Q, R, W, 6 to Canal St. Daily 10:30am–10:30pm. Average dim sum: $3.* After passing Chinatown shops displaying glistening ducks and flopping fish, vegetarians will be relieved to step into this meat-free haven. The menu offers excellent mock dishes, including "shrimp" dumplings (made with rice flour, yams and tofu), sesame "chicken" (deep-fried bean-curd skin) and Peking "spareribs" (make that "spareyams"). Don't miss the fresh fruit shakes.

▲☺**Village Natural** *46 Greenwich Ave between Sixth and Seventh Aves (212-727-0968). Subway: A, C, E, B, D, F, V to W 4th St; 1 to Christopher St–Sheridan Sq. Mon–Fri 11am–11pm; Sat 10am–11pm; Sun 10am–10pm. Average main course: $11.* Cosmopolitan seems like the right word for such diverse treats as spicy Moroccan-style couscous, burritos wrapped in whole-wheat tortillas, and Chinese cabbage stuffed with cashews and steamed vegetables. Tofu and steamed vegetables are tossed with garlic sauce and piled on brown rice or buckwheat soba noodles. But weekend brunch brings you back home, with a choice of whole-grain, blue-corn, oat-bran, sweet-potato or buckwheat pancakes, topped with organic fruit or organic Vermont maple syrup.

▲☺**Wild Ginger Pan-Asian Vegan Café** *212 Bedford Ave between North 5th and 6th Sts, Williamsburg, Brooklyn (718-218-8828). Subway: L to Bedford Ave. Mon–Thu, Sun 11am–11:30pm; Fri, Sat noon–11:30pm. Average main course: $11.* Vegan dining feels more like a hip lifestyle choice than a restricted diet at the Williamsburg outpost of this Manhattan eatery. Sparse decor and flickering candlelight lull diners into a blissful state, though the lengthy menu of mock-meat interpretations of Thai, Chinese and Japanese dishes helps too. Lightly battered salt-and-pepper king-oyster mushrooms approximate the shape and texture of a great fried calamari, while General Tso's soy protein—chunks of breaded faux chicken, red chilies and broccoli—is spared the sweet treatment and doused with a spicy brown sauce instead. **Other location** *380 Broome St between Mott and Mulberry Sts (212-966-1883).*

▲**Zen Palate** *34 Union Sq East at 16th St (212-614-9291). Subway: L, N, Q, R, W, 4, 5, 6 to 14th St–Union Sq. Mon–Sat 11am–11pm; Sun midnight–10:30pm. Average main course: $14.* Just call it Zen Palette—these artful dishes are arranged as much for beauty as for taste. Jicama, mushrooms and bok choy are wrapped in golden, mini moo-shu pancakes, neatly tied with scallion ribbons, then bathed in a flavorful sauce. A painted sky above the sunny yellow walls cheers up the dining room in winter, but come summer, most diners head for the outdoor seating. Artwork, after all, is best viewed in natural light. **Other locations** *663 Ninth Ave at 46th St (212-582-1276, 212-582-1669) ● 104 John St at Cliff St (212 962 4208).*

Vietnamese

See also: *Asian, French*

★ ▲**Bao 111** *111 Ave C between 7th and 8th Sts (212-254-7773). Subway: L to First Ave. Mon—Sat 6pm–2am. Average main course: $19.* Copious candles, plump pillows and potent cocktails make this modern Vietnamese spot ideal for a tryst. A stylish crowd regularly mobs its bar, waiting for their shot at a tiny dark-wood table, where they can nibble starters like lollipop fried chicken with thick-cut yuca fries and an extremely incendiary habanero-laced hot sauce. More substantial fare includes entrées like Iron Pot chicken (chunks of gingery onions, tender meat and creamy quail eggs) and grilled pork tenderloin. The blood-red back dining room makes an ideal setting in which to let luscious chocolate torte and black sesame ice cream seduce you if your date fails to. **Other location** *Bao Noodles, 391 Second Ave between 22nd and 23rd Sts (212-725-7770).*

▲**Boi** *246 E 44th St between Second and Third Aves (212-681-6541). Subway: 42nd St S, 4, 5, 6, 7 to 42nd St–Grand Central. Mon–Wed noon–3pm, 5:30–10pm; Thu, Fri noon–3pm, 5:30–10:30pm; Sat 5:30–10:30pm; Sun 5–9pm. Average main course: $18.* At this chic, boxy little bôite, the menu is stocked with small and large flavor-punched samplings. Start with a potent *rambutan* martini and a scattering of delicate rice-paper rolls, spicy crusted tofu and beef salad with quail eggs. Or go straight for the entrées—red snapper seasoned with turmeric, or sizzling Saigon crêpes stuffed with nearly everything (plus meatballs). Bill Yosses, the talented pastry chef from Josephs, is trying Asian-themed desserts; a recent visit revealed hits (rich, sticky jackfruit-toffee pudding) and misses (tapioca that tasted like stale basil-flavored gummy bears).

★ ▲☺**Doyers Vietnamese Restaurant**
11 Doyers St between Bowery and Pell St (212-513-1521). Subway: J, M, Z, N, Q, R, W, 6 to Canal St. Mon–Thu, Sun 11am–10pm; Fri, Sat 11am–11pm. Average main course: $8. Hidden in a basement on a zigzagging Chinatown alley, this bare-bones joint features a menu that requires (and rewards) exploration. The long appetizer list includes sweet-and-smoky sugarcane wrapped with grilled shrimp, and a delicious Vietnamese crêpe crammed with shrimp and pork. In the winter, hot-pot soups (served on a tabletop stove) feature the same exceptional broth base and come packed with vegetables,no matter the add-in.

★ ▲**Indochine** *430 Lafayette St between Astor Pl and E 4th St (212-505-5111). Subway: B, D, F, Q to Broadway-Lafayette St; R, W to 8th St; 6 to Astor Place. Tue–Sat 5:30pm–midnight; Sun,Mon 5:30–11:30pm. Average main course: $22.* For over two decades, celebs and yuppies have been rubbing elbows inside this elegantly tropical spot, where banquette seating, wallpaper with palm fronds and dim lighting attempt to recreate colonial Hanoi. So does the menu, starring French-Vietnamese specialties like pho and filet mignon carpaccio; a rich Vietnamese bouillabaisse brings the two worlds together. The *pièce de résistance* is the sumptuous *amok Cambodgien*, coconut-flavored fillet of sole wrapped in a banana leaf. Rice comes separately—order the house

Fishing expedition
A prawn in curry broth is a likely find at Mai House.

version with shrimp—while the strikingly presented Asian pear wontons make the best finale. Even with a reservation, however, be prepared to wait.

▲☺**Lan Café** *342 E 6th St between First and Second Aves (212-228-8325). Subway: F, V to Lower East Side–Second Ave. Mon–Thu noon–11pm; Fri, Sat noon–midnight. Average main course: $8. Cash only.* The decor at this vegan Vietnamese spot is nearly nonexsistent—ten tables fill the petite white-walled space—and the service is harried. But the food is so good and cheap, you may give up your meat habit. The menu lists many familiar dishes—like pho, pad thai and *banh mi* sandwiches —made with seitan (wheat gluten) and tofu. The pad thai was light and full of soft tofu, peanuts, crunchy string beans, snow peas, bean sprouts and sprigs of cilantro—with none of the sticky, gooey sauces that coat inferior versions elsewhere. Like other spots on the block, Lan is BYOB.

▲**Le Colonial** *149 E 57th St between Lexington and Third Aves (212-752-0808). Subway: N, R, W to Lexington Ave–59th St; 4, 5, 6 to 59th St. Mon noon–2:30pm, 5:30–11pm; Tue–Fri noon–2:30pm, 5:30–11:30pm; Sat, Sun 5:30–11:30pm. Average main course: $22.* After more than a decade, this elegant wood-bedecked space is still midtown's answer to downtown's enduringly fashionable Indochine. Ladies who lunch get their protein from the grilled lemongrass chicken breast, placed atop cold noodles with a peanut dressing. For the men who adorn them, there's grilled loin of pork, with mango-and-jicama salad in a passion-wasabi sauce. And they share, shamelessly, the plump grilled shrimp, served on an impressive stump of sugarcane. At night, the blue

CINZIA HEALE-CASTELLO

neon sign serves as a homing beacon for seekers of the rattan-laden second-floor bar, easily one of the sexiest in the neighborhood.

Mai House *186 Franklin St between Greenwich and Hudson Sts (212-431-0606). Subway: 1 to Franklin St. Mon–Sat 5:45pm–midnight. Average main course: $25.* The latest eatery from restaurateurs Drew Nieporent (Nobu, Tribeca Grill) and Michael Huynh (Bao 111, Bao Noodles) yields some nice, if pricey, gourmet adaptations of Asian staples. One kind of spring roll is made with shiitake, chanterelle and hen-of-the-woods mushrooms. Battered-and-fried cuttlefish replaces the usual salt-and-pepper shrimp, and beef-lovers will appreciate the tasty Wagyu cheeks stew. The main space is bright and casual, but the bar area, separated from the kitchen by a wall of ornately carved wood, is visually more impressive.

★ ▲◎**Nha Trang** *148 Centre St between Walker and White Sts (212-941-9292). Subway: J, M, Z, N, Q, R, W, 6 to Canal St. Daily 10:30am–10pm. Average main course: $8.* The few framed tourist shots of Vietnam are not much to look at, but the packed house of diners is quite happy to trade in ambience. The long menu includes traditional dishes like sticky barbecued beef and pho noodle soup with generous additions like fish balls. And for the more adventurous, frog legs in a curry sauce is a bold dish. Vietnamese drinks are a sweet treat, most made with condensed milk, like the *sinh to* with jackfruit, or a creamier soda made with milk and egg yolks. **Other location** *87 Baxter St between Walker and White Sts (212-233-5948).*

◎**Nicky's Vietnamese Sandwiches** *150 E 2nd St between Aves A and B (212-388-1088). Subway: F, V to Lower East Side–Second Avenue. Mon–Sat noon–9pm; Sun noon–7pm. Average sandwich: $4.* Good *banh mi* is a marvel of contrasting flavors and textures, brilliant ingredients combined into a simple sandwich: salty pork pâté, sweet pickled carrots, thick cuts of cool cucumber, and cilantro on a mayo-slathered, toasted baguette. Ninh Van Dang made exceptional *banh mi* at An Dong in Sunset Park, and his fans are thrilled that the restaurant has been reincarnated (albeit in slightly altered form) here. The family has expanded the sandwich lineup, adding chicken, pork chops, and portobello to the original roster of pork pâté and sardine. Ultimately, though, there's no reason to order anything but the classic. **Other location** *311 Atlantic Ave between Hoyt and Smith Sts, Boerum Hill, Brooklyn, Boerum Hill, Brooklyn (718-855-8838).*

▲◎**Pho Viet Huong** *73 Mulberry St between Bayard and Canal Sts (212-233-8988). Subway: J, M, Z, N, Q, R, W, 6 to Canal St. Daily 10:30am–10:30pm.*

Read 'em & eat

bun: rice vermicelli served in soup or stir-fries

goi: a salad often containing raw vegetables and accompanied by chicken or prawns

nuoc nam: fermented fish sauce often used in dips

pho: a soup of rice noodles and chicken or beef in an aromatic broth

Average main course: $8. Don't let the address fool you. This unassuming Mulberry Street Vietnamese spot is on the right side of Canal—a block south of the Italian tourist traps. The space is cafeteria-like, the menu filled with simple, satisfying classics: rice plates, pho and lemongrass-flavored everything (chicken, beef, fish, frog legs). The pork and beef vermicelli (*bun nem nuong* and *bun bo nuong*) are killer deals at $5 a pop. Feeling more adventurous? Experiment with the tripe dishes, perhaps best attempted after trying all three Vietnamese beers.

Safran *88 Seventh Ave between 15th and 16th Sts (212-929-1778). Subway: F, V, 1, 2, 3 to 14th St; L to Sixth Ave. Mon–Thu 11:30am–11:30pm; Fri 11:30am–midnight; Sat noon–midnight; Sun noon–11:30pm. Average main course: $24.* Behind the plain storefront at this Franco-Vietnamese eatery is a bi-level space with tasteful modern decor—orange-and-pistachio walls, a beaded metal curtain—and excellent food. The nuanced Vietnamese dishes of chef Laura Lam (Monsoon) include prawn-and-grapefruit salad with crustaceans grilled to smoky crispness, and a pan-seared fillet of sole, so sweet and tender it's practically a confection. For dessert, the hot banana cake riffs on Asian eateries' ubiquitous banana fritters.

Sapa *43 W 24th St between Fifth and Sixth Aves (212-929-1800). Subway: N, R, W, 6 to 23rd St. Mon–Wed 11:30am–2:30pm, 5:30–11:30pm; Thu, Fri 11:30am–2:30pm, 5:30–1:30pm; Sat 5:30–1:30pm; Sun 11:30am–3:30pm, 5:30–10:30pmpm. Average main course: $27.* The savvy AvroKo design team came up with a gorgeous minimalist dining room for this French-Vietnamese spot. Sapa's "roll bar" features variations on spring and summer rolls, including ones with raw wild salmon and cucumber, or foie gras and duck. Among the adventurous main dishes are cider-braised monkfish with salsify and sugarcane-marinated scallops. Inventive cocktails are available to match, and, of course, you can drink as much as you can handle.

◎**Silent H** *79 Berry St at North 9th St, Williamsburg, Brooklyn (718-218-7063). Subway: L to Bedford Ave. Tue–Sun noon–4pm, 6–11pm. Average main course: $13.* This hip, airy eatery is filled with quirky design touches, like high wooden stools that line a grass-green counter, and ceiling fans with leaf-shaped blades. If you arrive expecting the classics, you will be disappointed. Chef-owner Vinh Nguyen doesn't serve pho, but he does offer other recognizable dishes, such as *banh mi*, the now-famous Southeast Asian hoagie. The very good "Classic" incorporates pâté, salami, pickled shredded carrot, daikon, cilantro and mayo, while the nouveau "Greenpoint" throws kielbasa into the mix. Come dinnertime, the kitchen reaches higher, with a short list of Vietnamese "tapas," including a green-papaya salad topped with plump sautéed shrimp and slices of seared pork belly that melt in your mouth.

▲**Viet Café** *345 Greenwich St between Harrison and Jay Sts (212-431-5888). Subway: 1 to Franklin St. Mon–Wed 11:30am–10pm; Thu, Fri 11:30am–11pm; Sat 5–11pm. Average main course: $16.* Though it's in the middle of Greenwich Street's restaurant row, Viet Café is rarely full—surprising, considering its attractive, contemporary decor and tasty fare. Have a seat at one of the maple stools or benches and you can sample the menu of traditional appetizers—like spring rolls with shrimp, jicama, carrots and mushrooms—or light, fragrant entrées such as the steamed catch of the day with scallions and ginger, or the roasted lacquered duck.

100 Top Bars & Lounges

Tribeca & south

Bin No. 220 *2007 Eat Out Award, Readers' Choice: Best new wine bar 220 Front St between Beekman St and Peck Slip (212-374-9463). Subway: A, C to Broadway–Nassau St; J, M, Z, 2, 3, 4, 5 to Fulton St. Daily noon–midnight. Average drink: $11.* This oenophile's paradise radiates understated downtown style, with cement floors, brick walls and blood-red lighting. The tightly curated list (80 bottles, all Italian), are refreshingly described in layman's terms ("blackberry nuances"), so you don't have to be a sommelier to drink like one.

Bubble Lounge *228 West Broadway between Franklin and White Sts (212-431-3433). Subway: 1 to Franklin St. Mon–Thu 5pm–2am; Fri, Sat 5pm–4am. Average drink: $12.* With its San Francisco twin, Bubble Lounge claims to be the largest purveyor of champagne on the planet, serving 100,000 bottles of bubbly a year. Most on the list of 300 land north of $75, and if you show up early, you'll have all of them to yourself: The L-shaped spot, lighted by paper lamps and filled with couches, doesn't get jammed until late.

Jeremy's Ale House *228 Front St between Beekman St and Peck Slip (212-964-3537). Subway: A, C to Broadway–Nassau St; J, M, Z, 2, 3, 4, 5 to Fulton St. Mon–Sat 8am–midnight; Sun noon–10pm. Average drink: $6.* Need liquid assets to fortify yourself for a day of trading? Stop by this converted garage in the shadow of the Brooklyn Bridge for the 8 to 10am "eye-opener"—you'll find Wall Street types at the bar, where 32-ounce Styrofoam buckets of Coors go for $5. After work, beer and fried clams are cheap and plentiful, the regulars are in, and the game is on.

Knitting Factory *74 Leonard St between Broadway and Church St (212-219-3006). Subway: 1 to Franklin St. Daily 5:30pm–2am. Average drink: $6.* Serving an eclectic menu of experimental jazz, klezmer, indie rock—even hip-hop karaoke—this Tribeca institution has been drawing lounge lizards, industry sharks and uptown gawkers for more than two decades. The Main Space showcases big-name acts, best viewed from the balcony, while the Tap Bar, a floor down, promises spoken-word performances and eighteen draught beers. Venture even further below for the Old Office, which features a modest selection of wines.

M1-5 *52 Walker St between Broadway & Church St (212–965–1701). Subway: 6; J, M, Z; N, Q, R, W at Canal St. Mon–Fri 4pm–4am; Sat, Sun 7pm–4am. Average drink: $7.* The action at this heavily red-accented, high-ceilinged spot revolves around the pool table, where suited brokers and youthful indie screenwriters vie for games, while a cinema-sized projection screen shows sports. There's no velvet rope here, no fancy cocktails, just a well-stocked, centrally placed bar with a nice array of choice bottled suds—and a general feeling that the party's just about to start.

Tribeca Tavern *247 West Broadway between Walker and White Sts (212-941-7671). Subway: A, C, E to Canal St; 1 to Franklin St. Daily 11am–4am. Average drink: $5.* While the decor verges on the decrepit (TriBeCa Tavern may be a contender for Manhattan's Worst Restroom), it's actually quite homey: Ample tables provide plenty of seating, but the real prize is up front, where a cozy enclave provides patrons with a view of bustling West Broadway. Draft beer served by the pitcher is the best way to go.

Chinatown & Little Italy

Double Happiness *173 Mott St between Broome and Grand Sts (212-941-1282). Subway: B, D to Grand St; J, M, Z to Bowery. Sun–Wed 6pm–2am; Thu 6pm–3am; Fri, Sat 6pm–4am. Average drink: $7.* Through the door at the bottom of the steep stairs, you'll encounter the first happiness: This stone-walled subterranean haunt is made for trysts. Other joys include clubby music (deejayed rock, funk and soul), lots of eye candy (best viewed Thursday through Saturday), and an Asian-themed cocktail list that one-ups the usual cloyingly sweet choices (try a soothing green-tea martini).

Super tonic
Sample 23 kinds of gin at the swank Pegu Club.

Always Worth It.

Keep the good times going with the refreshingly smooth taste of Bud Light.

RESPONSIBILITY MATTERS

Sweet & Vicious *5 Spring St between Bowery and Elizabeth St (212-334-7915). Subway: J, M, Z to Bowery; 6 to Spring St. Daily 4pm–4am. Average drink: $8.* Two pistols found during the bar's construction are menacingly displayed in a frame by the doorway. But the subtle spot is way more sweet than vicious. Dark wooden benches line the back wall; standing room is generous. A mellow twenty- and thirty-something crowd appreciates the jukebox's reggae rotation (and Bob Marley's portrait behind the bar). Outdoor garden tables are another reason to drink and talk the night away.

Vig Bar *12 Spring St at Elizabeth St (212-625-0011). Subway: J, M, Z to Bowery; 6 to Spring St. Daily 5pm–4am. Average drink: $8.* This charming candlelit enclave has no pretension, just reasonable prices, friendly staffers and a mellow clientele. The cocktail menu is split equally between classics and creative offerings, like the summery French 06, an effervescent pear-and-champagne concoction. Go early with a date to cozy up on the sexy blue leather banquettes. Later in the evenings, a DJ packs 'em in with retro tunes, and it gets mighty tight.

Lower East Side

Arlene's Grocery *95 Stanton St between Ludlow and Orchard Sts (212-358-1633). Subway: F to Lower East Side–Second Ave. Mon–Thu 6pm–4am; Fri–Sun noon–4am. Cover: free–$10. Average drink: $5.* One of the earliest rock-music venues south of East Houston, Arlene's Grocery remains a hallowed hall—or hallowed hole—of head-banging. Downstairs from the main bar is the room where bands rock out all week long; you'll need liberal definitions of "loud" and "personal space" down there. Monthly events range from All-Ages Afternoon to Triple 666 Sunday, which is billed as "a night of debauchery."

Back Room *102 Norfolk St between Delancey and Rivington Sts (212-228-5098). Subway: F, V, J, M, Z to Delancey–Essex Sts. Daily 8pm–4am. Average drink: $9.* Look for a sign affixed to a streetside metal gate that reads the LOWER EAST SIDE TOY COMPANY. Pass through the gate and walk the length of a subterranean alleyway, then up a set of stairs to enter the Back Room. Once inside, you'll see a dimly lit den fitted with paisley fabric wall panels and a gleaming wood bar. Cocktails are served Prohibition-style in teacups, and bottled beer is brown-bagged by the barkeeps before being served.

Happy Ending *302 Broome St between Eldridge and Forsyth Sts (212-334-9676). Subway: B, D to Grand St; J, M, Z to Bowery; F to Delancey. Tue 10pm–4am; Wed–Sat 7pm–4am. Average drink: $7.* Once upon a time, this two-story space was a massage parlor that went all the way. But despite the shower-knobs poking out from the walls, the only lubricants passed around these days are cocktails, such as the Crimson Peach, a ripe blend of triple sec, Absolut Peach and fresh lemon, lime and orange juices; and Mr. Ginger—ginger ale and house-infused ginger vodka. The former sauna's underground nooks are drenched in seductive red light—still perfect for a late-night hookup.

Milk & Honey *134 Eldridge St between Broome and Delancey Sts (unlisted phone). Subway: J, M, Z to Bowery. Daily 9pm–4am. Average drink: $10.* The only clue to the entryway is an ALTERATIONS sign in the window (the space was formerly a tailor's shop). Even if you do find the graffitied door, you're supposed to call ahead to reserve. Oh, and the phone number's unlisted. This stealth speakeasy will transport you to the 1940s: Sinatra croons on the sound system, couples chat in semicircular booths, and candles offer the only light. If you're lucky enough to find the phone number, mind your manners when you arrive; house rules include "Gentlemen will not introduce themselves to ladies."

Nurse Bettie *106 Norfolk St between Delancey and Rivington Sts (917-434-9072). Subway: F to Delancey St; J, M, Z to Delancey–Essex Sts. Tue, Wed, Sun 6pm–2am; Thu–Sat 6pm–4am. Average drink: $7.* Lusty buxom '50s pinups—not doctors—rule at this coffeeshop-turned-bar named after Bettie Page. Inside, swivel stools and slouchworthy couches are commandeered by jeans-sporting Lower East Siders sipping frosty brews and sweet bubblegum martinis. The attentive bartenders' modern iPod playlists never crush conversations, and the weekend hordes mercifully leave Bettie to the locals.

Revolver *210 Rivington St between Pitt and Ridge Sts (212-505-7625). Subway: F to Delancey St; J, M, Z to Delancey–Essex Sts. Tue–Sun 9pm–4am. Average drink: $6.* Fiery jalapeño-infused tequilas are the weapons of choice at this shady rocker dive. Warhol's gun-toting Elvis Presley montage overlooks a bevy of onyx couches (the bar is stool-free), apple-red candles and primo speakers dispensing the DJ's fist-pumping rock anthems. Feisty young pleasure-seekers shimmy on the shiny black floor (or around the stripper pole), before cooling down with three-buck mugs of the lounge's light (read: generic) namesake beer.

Schiller's Liquor Bar *131 Rivington St at Norfolk St (212-260-4555). Subway: F to Delancey St; J, M, Z to Delancey–Essex Sts. Mon, Tue 9am–1:30am; Wed–Fri 9am–2:30am; Sat 10am–2:30am; Sun 10am–1:30am. Average drink: $9.* The drink menu famously hawks a down-to-earth hierarchy of wines: Good, Decent, Cheap. Not one of them will run you more than seven bucks a glass. Folks pack in for the scene, triple-parking at the bar and sipping elaborate cocktails. Views are star-studded; Sightings may include Gandolfini and Wintour. Whether you're downing white sangria or scarfing steak frites, you can't help thinking that Keith McNally's finger is still on the downtown pulse.

Soho

Ear Inn *326 Spring St between Greenwich and Washington Sts (212-226-9060). Subway: C, E to Spring St; 1 to Houston St. Sun–Thu 11:30am–4am; Fri, Sat noon–4am. Average drink: $5.* Since 1817, the historic Ear—so named because half the "B" in the neon "Bar" sign was chipped—has been popular with colorful characters haunting the docks of the Hudson. The decor is basic (dark wood bar, rickety tables and chairs) and the mood relaxed. Cheap drinks and free snacks (fried chicken, mussels or sausages) are served Monday through Friday from 4 to 7pm.

Fanelli's Café *94 Prince St at Mercer St (212-226-9412). Subway: N, R, W to Prince St. Sun–Thu 10am–1:30am; Fri, Sat 10am–4am. Average drink: $6.* In the getting-and-spending theme park that Soho has become, unpretentious Fanelli's—an 1847 neighborhood landmark—is a beloved throwback. The long, weathered bar, the prints of boxing legends and one of the city's best burgers add to the easy feel. And just like in the old days, you can actually hear the banter of locals and the merry clinking of pint glasses.

Milady's *160 Prince St at Thompson St (212-226-9340). Subway: C, E to Spring St. Daily 11am–4am. Average drink: $5.* Pretty quickly, you get it: The area has changed, but one little corner dive hasn't. Drinks are outer-borough cheap, and it's common to see pints and bottles chasing whiskey shots. Patrons spanning ages and careers combine to make this the most diverse dive of all. The lone pool table in back sees more action than the star quarterback at the senior prom, and the rock-ruled jukebox deserves props as well.

NV *289 Spring St between Hudson and Varick Sts (212-929-6868). Subway: C, E to Spring St. Wed, Fri–Sun 10pm–4am. Cover: $10–$20. Average drink: $8.* This posh club chainlet (with outposts in East Hampton and Palm Beach) comes with all the requisites: swank decor, VIP rooms, steep cover and drink prices, and a pumping dance-party beat (hip-hop on Wednesday and Sunday nights, Latin on Fridays). If that spells F-U-N to you, then you'll find NV to be way better than OK.

Pegu Club *77 W Houston St at West Broadway (212-473-7348). Subway: N, R to Prince St; B, D, F, V to Broadway–Lafayette. Sun–Wed 5pm–2am; Thu–Sat 5pm–4am. Average drink: $12.* Named after a British officers' club in Rangoon in the 1900s, Pegu Club's menu covers 23 brands of gin and classic cocktails culled from references like Charles H. Baker's 1939 book *The Gentleman's Companion: Around the World with Jigger, Beaker and Glass.* Just don't dare ask for Stoli Vanil and Coke: There isn't a soda gun or a flavored vodka in the house.

East Village

Bar Veloce *175 Second Ave between 11th and 12th Sts (212-966-7334). Subway: L to Third Ave; 6 to Astor Pl. Daily 5pm–3am. Average drink: $3.* La Dolce Vita meets the East Village at this sleek wine bar, whose name means *speed* in Italian. Yet there's no need to rush, and you'll be happy to linger among the elegantly transient *amici* in this halogen-lit, beige-wood-accented spot, sampling the menu of rustic Italian sandwiches that complements the fine, reasonably priced selection of wines.

Croxley Ales *28 Ave B between 2nd and 3rd Sts (212-253-6140). Subway: F, V to Lower East Side–Second Ave. Mon–Fri 5pm–4am; Sat, Sun noon–4am. Average drink: $6.* The 3,000-square-foot garden attached to this bar provides much more room to drink outside than in, and is large enough to be divided into three levels. The middle area is covered with an awning, and boasts a six-foot projection screen. The extensive beer menu offers 30 exceptional drafts, such as the Belgian ale De Koninck. Or skip the suds and order a Frojito ($8), a frozen mojito that'll knock the heat right out of you, wherever you drink it.

Death & Co. *433 E 6th St between Ave A and First Ave (212-388-0882). Subway: F, V to Lower East Side–Second Ave; 6 to Astor Pl. Mon–Thu, Sun 6pm–1am; Fri, Sat 6pm–2am. Average drink: $12.* The nattily attired mixologists are deadly serious about drinks at this pseudospeakeasy (find the imposing wooden door) with a Gothic flair. Black walls and cushy booths combine with chandeliers to set the somberly luxurious mood, favored by daters and downtowners bored by shot-and-beer bars.

Patrons nip at inventive cocktails, including a fiery Fresa Brava (strawberries and jalapeño-infused tequila) and the daiquiri-like St. Matilda, before grazing on prosciutto-wrapped pears and fresh-fruit spring rolls.

Decibel *240 E 9th St between Second and Third Aves (212-979-2733). Subway: L to Third Ave; 6 to Astor Pl. Mon–Sat 8pm–3am; Sun 8pm–1am. Average drink: $10.* On weekends you're almost guaranteed a wait for a seat at the small, dank basement bar. Decibel is Japanese through and through, and it's got a helluva sake bar. Most of the staff speaks little to no English, so be prepared to be lost in translation occasionally, especially when it comes to the snacks—which can be as mundane as rice crackers or as outré as shark fins and jellyfish. Drinks are a bit more straightforward: Sex on the Beach in Japanese is the same as it is in English.

Esperanto *145 Ave C at 9th St (212-505-6559). Subway: L to First Ave. Mon–Thu 5:30pm–midnight; Fri 5:30pm–1am; Sat 11am–1am; Sun 11am–midnight. Average drink: $6.* What's in a kiwi roska—and why should you drink it? Let the good folks at Esperanto enlighten you about the fresh kiwi and vodka mixture. There's a raffish, multiculti charm to the whirring overhead fans and chili-pepper garlands festooning the ceiling. The house's libations are listed on a wall near the bar, but you'll get caught in a moshpit of mojito drinkers before you can squeeze your way to it.

KGB Bar *85 E 4th St between Bowery and Second Ave (212-505-3360). Subway: F, V to Lower East Side–Second Ave; 6 to Astor Pl. Daily 7pm–4am. Average drink: $6.* Lit chicks way outnumber apparatchiks in this former Ukrainian social club. Sandwiched between two theaters on the second floor of a walk-up, the dim parlor-room bar has vintage Cold War decor, low-priced Baltika beer and free readings—all of which lure New York's literary underground, including stars like A.M. Homes and Kathryn Harrison.

Lakeside Lounge *162 Ave B between 10th and 11th Sts (212-529-8463). Subway: L to First Ave; 6 to Astor Pl. Daily 4pm–4am. Average drink: $5.* Do the math: Eight brews on tap (including Guinness and Stella) plus ten by the bottle (two in the can) and music seven nights a week, all multiplied by the past eight years, equals an Alphabet City fixture. Add a killer juke with more than 100 choice albums, and you can figure out the bottom line: The more the neighborhood changes, the more the joint stays the same.

McSorley's Old Ale House *15 E 7th St between Second and Third Aves (212-473-9148). Subway: F, V to Lower East Side–Second Ave. Daily 11am–1am. Average drink: $2.* In traditional Irish-pub fashion, McSorley's floor has been thoroughly scattered with sawdust to take care of the spills and other messes that often accompany large quantities of cheap beer. Established in 1854, McSorley's became an institution by remaining steadfastly authentic and providing only two choices to its customers—McSorley's Dark Ale and McSorley's Light Ale. Both beverages have a lot more character than PBR, though at these prices, it won't be long before you stop noticing.

Nublu *62 Ave C between 4th and 5th Sts (212-979-9925). Subway: F, V to Lower East Side–Second Ave. Daily 8pm–4am. Average drink: $7.* Newcomers to this Alphabet City outpost will have to ask the smokers outside

It's a deal
If the crowd gets too
thick at Azza, steal off to
a private game room.

TALIA SIMHI

You won't have to wait on line at
NEW YORK'S
LARGEST IRISH PUB
right across from The Garden
133 WEST 33RD STREET

THREE LEVELS

OVER 150 BEERS

35 LARGE SCREEN TV'S

DJ'S & LIVE MUSIC

KITCHEN OPEN LATE

PRIVATE PARTY ROOMS

DART ALLEY • PRIVATE POOL ROOMS • CELLAR BAR

212.629.6191
WWW.STOUTNYC.COM
OPEN SEVEN DAYS A WEEK TIL 4AM

if they've come to the right place: Only a blue light marks the spot. Inside, a European crowd settles in for the equally Euro beer selection and for the offbeat jazz and avant-garde acts. Excellent live Brazilian music and dancing are the draw on Wednesday nights. In summer, an exceedingly pleasant backyard garden eases the pressure on the small space.

Village Pourhouse
2007 Eat Out Award, Readers' Choice: Best new beer bar 64 Third Ave at 11th St (212-279-2337). Subway: F, V to Lower East Side–Second Ave; L to First Ave. Mon–Thu 5pm–1am; Fri 4pm–4am; Sat 1pm–4am; Sun 1pm–1am. Average drink: $6. The Pourhouse is the great unifier between persnickety microbrew and import adherents, and indiscriminate Bud guzzlers. Aficianados will find 24 drafts and 50-plus globe-spanning bottles. Quantity-over-quality barflies will appreciate happy hour's one-buck Bud and Bud Light drafts. All enjoy the flat screen TVs in the multiroom space.

Zum Schneider
107–109 Ave C at 7th St (212-598-1098). Subway: F, V to Lower East Side–Second Ave; L to First Ave. Mon–Thu 5pm–1am; Fri 4pm–4am; Sat 1pm–4am; Sun 1pm–1am. Average drink: $6. You might ask à la South Park, "What the fuck is a Bavarian beer garden doing in Alphabet City?" Upon entering, you'd have your answer: It's schvimming mit kustomers. In addition to the trees and checkered tablecloths, there's a guy in a ski suit doing the chicken dance near the bar. A dozen German brews are on tap, four in the bottle. After knocking back a few, you too will be shaking a tail feather.

I bow to you
Servers defer to drinkers' desires at Mobar in the Time Warner Center.

West Village

Blind Tiger Ale House
281 Bleecker St at Jones St (212-462-4682). Subway: 1 to Christopher St–Sheridan Sq; A, C, E, B, D, F, V to W 4th St. Daily 11:30am–4am. Average drink: $6. Beer geeks are in hops heaven now that this microbrew headquarters has finally secured its liquor license. Boutique brews and 28 hard-to-find drafts (like Dale's Pale Ale and Allagash's Belgian-style Double) are savored in a chummy, wood-heavy room. Late afternoons and early evenings are for serious beer sippers and after-workers enjoying plates of Murray's Cheese, while the after-dark set veers dangerously close to Phi Kappa territory.

Chumley's
86 Bedford St between Barrow and Grove Sts (212-675-4449). Subway: 1 to Christopher St–Sheridan Sq. Mon–Thu 4pm–midnight; Fri 4pm–2am; Sat 11am–2am; Sun 11am–midnight. Average drink: $6. The only thing wrong with Chumley's is that it's known the world over as a legendary New York watering hole, so out-of-towners and NYU students overcrowd the place at night and on weekends. The bar still offers an impressive selection of beer in bottles and on tap, but these days, the closest you'll get to former habitués like Fitzgerald or Burroughs is an underclassman toasting his B on the Am Lit exam.

Marie's Crisis
59 Grove St between Seventh Ave South and Bleecker St (212-243-9323). Subway: 1 to Christopher St–Sheridan Sq. Daily 4pm–4am. Average drink: $5. If you like the way people in musicals go from normal conversation to singing their hearts out, then here's the bar for you. One minute, the barmaid is pulling your pint; the next, she's belting out "Me and Bobby McGee." The mainstay of this big basement joint, once frequented

by Sondheim, is the piano, around which the show-tune lovers gather nightly. Nathan Lane or Jennifer Tilly may occasionally walk in, but the usual crowd is a mix of tourists and students "looking for something freaky," says the barman.

The Other Room
143 Perry St between Greenwich and Washington Sts (212-645-9758). Subway: 1 to Christopher St–Sheridan Sq. Sun, Mon 5pm–2am; Tue–Sat 5pm–4am. Average drink: $5. Doubling as an art gallery for up-and-coming photographers, the Other Room is sleek and civilized. You won't find any hard liquor (keeps out the louts) but the selection of fine beer and wine is varied and vast. The cool minimalist design allows patrons to focus on conversation. And the people who come here—gay, straight, fashionistas and 9-to-5 execs—are likely to have something interesting to say.

Vol de Nuit Bar a.k.a. Belgian Beer Lounge
148 W 4th St between MacDougal St and Sixth Ave (212-979-2616). Subway: A, C, E, B, D, F, V to W 4th St. Daily 5pm–2am. Average drink: $6. This small concrete courtyard fills with clusters of European grad students knocking back glasses of Hoegaarden and Stella Artois under a square of dusky sky. Dozens of Belgian beers—and only Belgian beers—are available on draft or by the bottle, along with tall cones of frites and pots of steamed mussels. There are tables inside the dark, red-walled bar, but on a sultry evening, choose the canopy of stars for a no-frills urban picnic.

Von Bar
3 Bleecker St between Bowery and Elizabeth St (212-473-3039). Subway: B, D, F, V to Broadway–Lafayette St; 6 to Bleecker St. Sun–Wed 5pm–2am; Thu–

FOOD
TILL 1:00AM
EVERYNIGHT

BURGER AU POIVRE

STRAWBERRY
SHORTCAKE

HOURS

SUNDAY - THURSDAY
12:00 NOON - 1:30 A.M.

FRIDAY - SATURDAY
12:00 NOON - 2:30 A.M.

FOOD UNTIL 1:00 A.M.
EVERYNIGHT.

BAR 89
89 MERCER STREET
BETWEEN SPRING AND BROOME
SOHO, NY
212-274-0989
WWW.BAR89.COM

Sat 5pm–4am. Average drink: $7. No kitsch, no trash, no pretense. This low-key two-room lair, all candlelit dark wood and exposed brick, is favored by those engaged in quiet conversation. It's a perfect first-date spot, and Von's barkeeps know their wine, even if you don't. Pick a full-bodied red, like the Vacqueyras, take your friend by the hand, and head for one of the benches in the back room.

Meatpacking District

APT *419 W 13th St between Ninth Ave and Washington St (212-414-4245). Subway: A, C, E to 14th St; L to Eighth Ave. Downstairs 10pm–4am. Upstairs 7pm–4am (reservation only). Average drink: $11* Kicking back in APT's formerly exclusive upstairs space is like being at an impromptu party in some trust-fund baby's Upper East Side townhouse. But it all can be yours if you call to reserve a table. Downstairs, people looking for the perfect beat gather in a minimalist, fake-wood-paneled rectangular room. On Mondays, hip-hop veteran DJ Bobbito attracts actors, rock stars and music-industry types; Thursdays through Sundays showcase other noteworthy talents.

G Spa & Lounge *18 Ninth Ave at W 13th St (212-206-6700). Subway: A, C, E to 14th St; L to Eighth Ave. Tue–Sat 8pm–3:30am. Average drink: $14.* Th Hotel Gansevoort is home to this kinda kooky spa-and-bar hybrid. Located in the basement, the red-toned space has treatment rooms that, come nighttime, serve double duty as VIP lounges. Owners Scott Sartiano and Richie Akiva (both of Butter) maintain a tight velvet rope.

Gaslight *400 W 14th St at Ninth Ave (212-807-8444). Subway: A, C, E to 14th St; L to Eighth Ave. Sun–Fri 1pm–4am; Sat 5pm–4am. Average drink: $7.* While other area hot spots have gone stratospherically upscale, one pioneer soldiers on with its vintage furniture, creaky wooden floors and affordable drinks. A selection of 15 bottled beers keeps the borderline-fratty crowd happy, placing this among the least pretentious hangs in an otherwise glitzy corner of the island.

Highline *835 Washington St at Little West 12th St (212-243-3339). Subway: A, C, E to 14th St . Mon–Thu, Sun 11:30am–1am; Fri, Sat 11:30am–2am. Average drink: $10.* This three-level restaurant, bar and cocktail-lounge–cum–cruise-ship offers an "onboard" wining-and-dining experience. Decorations are full of travel references and include pink-and-purple fabric patterned after the Thai Airways logo. The Bed Lounge evokes cabin service: You can lie back with a drink served on a tray next to your recliner. Munch appetizers like pad thai–stuffed spring rolls on the "upper deck."

Chelsea

Barracuda *275 W 22nd St between Seventh and Eighth Aves (212-645-8613). Subway: C, E, 1 to 23rd St. Daily 4pm–4am. Average drink: $6.* While the recent makeover gets high style points, this is still just a friendly little neighborhood place to have a beer and watch some drag. A pleasant mix of queeny types and chill lads converges around the small stand-up tables up front or in the back room, which is full of inviting, get-comfy couches. Drinks are always stiff (bit o' trivia: *Queer Eye*'s Kyan was once a bartender), the crowd is good-looking, and DJs keep the place pumping. The divine drag shows go down Sunday through Thursday.

Foodbar *149 Eighth Ave between 17th and 18th Sts (212-243-2020). Subway: A, C, E to 14th St; L to Eighth Ave; 1 to 18th St. Daily 11am–midnight. Average drink: $7.* Food may be the first word here, but drinks flow freely at the streamlined modern bar. That is a good thing, because you may need the tropical-fruit-infused cocktails to numb the feelings of inadequacy inspired by hot waiters and lots of muscle in business suits. Toss back a Tranny Kool-Aid or the more subdued watermelon margarita, and shed your inhibitions. You'll be vying for the attention of the Chelsea-boy regulars before you know it.

Honey *243 W 14th St between Seventh and Eighth Aves (212-620-0077). Subway: A, C, E, 1, 2, 3 to 14th St; L to Eighth Ave. Daily 5pm–4am. Average drink: $9.* Head downstairs to get the sweet lowdown on this 3,000-square-foot drinkery, safely insulated from MePa mayhem. Sip signature libations such as the Picasso Honey (honey liquor, gin and Cointreau, and a honey stick garnish) and devour cocktail-influenced eats including a "shrimp daiquiri" inside the cavernlike, mahogany-and-brick room.

Half King *505 W 23rd St between Tenth and Eleventh Aves (212-462-4300). Subway: C, E to 23rd St. Daily 9am–4am. Average drink: $7.* The writer and artist types hanging at the bar (note the stylish eyeglasses) are probably hoping that some of part-owner Sebastian Junger's literary fortunes will rub off on them. That may be wishful thinking, but what's certain is that the author of *A Perfect Storm* and his partners have created a welcoming pub with free-flowing Guinness, honest food like fish-and-chips, and regular literary readings.

View Bar *232 Eighth Ave between 21st and 22nd Sts (212-929-2243). Subway: C, E to 23rd St. Mon–Fri 4pm–4am; Sat, Sun 2pm–4am. Average drink: $6.* Ah, life's simple pleasures—dusty disco balls, video monitors interspersing endless images of abs and penises with promotions for upcoming parties, and cheap, strong drinks. The View offers a few lounge areas where you can savor these unpretentious joys with your dear friends. Oh, and the DJs play club remixes of old Chicago tunes.

Gramercy & the Flatiron District

Flatiron Lounge *37 W 19th St between Fifth and Sixth Aves (212-727-7741). Subway: F, V, N, R, W to 23rd St. Sun–Wed 5pm–2am; Thu–Sat 5pm–4am. Average drink: $10.* To get to the 30-foot mahogany bar, built in 1927, follow the arched hallway, warmed by the soft glow of candles. You'll find an Art Deco space with red leather booths, round glass tables, flying-saucer-shaped lamps and an imaginative cocktail menu: The Persephone is a subtle pomegranate martini named for the queen of Hades. Near the glistening wall of cobalt tiles, attractive patrons drink contentedly, like gods and goddesses of their own private underworld.

Lucy Latin Kitchen *ABC Carpet & Home, 35 E 18th St between Broadway and Park Ave South (212-475-5829). Subway: L, N, Q, R, W, 4, 5, 6 to 14th St–Union Sq. Mon–Tue noon–3:30pm, 5:30–11pm; Fri noon–3:30pm, 5:30pm–1am; Sat 5:30pm–1am; Sun 5:30–11pm. Average drink: $10.* When ABC shoppers require tequila assistance, they come to this white-walled

Heat seeking
Discover nascent talent at the laidback Nublu.

restaurant and lounge. After work, a good-looking young singles crowd also streams in to sample $6 Mexican beers and $11 margaritas (top-shelf tequilas, fresh strawberries and mint). The room is softened by huge, rustic wooden doors, glowing colored lights and plush oversize couches.

Old Town Bar & Restaurant *45 E 18th St between Broadway and Park Ave South (212-529-6732). Subway: L, N, Q, R, W, 4, 5, 6 to 14th St–Union Sq. Mon, Tue noon–11:30pm; Wed–Sat noon–1:30am; Sun noon–8pm. Average drink: $5.* Come here when you want beer instead of fancy cocktails, and old New York instead of high style. The tin ceiling, long wooden bar and well-worn booths make the Old Town (founded in 1892) a comfortable spot for some suds and one of the city's best burgers. You won't be disappointed.

Revival *129 E 15th St between Irving Pl and Third Ave (212-253-8061). Subway: L to Third Ave; N, Q, R, W, 4, 5, 6 to 14th St–Union Sq. Daily 4pm–4am. Average drink: $5.* This two-story townhouse bar has become a favorite hangout for suits as well as scenesters. Downstairs is the long main bar (ten beers on tap), decorated with cartoon murals of beatniks; three TVs devote equal time to sports and *The Simpsons*. The upstairs lounge has pillowy couches and a small bar. The weekend meet market and after-work happy hour can be packed with fun—or with frat hats.

3Steps *322 Second Ave between 18th and 19th Sts (212-533-5336). Subway: L to First or Third Ave. Daily 5pm–4am. Average drink: $8.* At this subterranean Gramercy groggery (once an apartment), young professionals and first-daters gather at the butcher-block

bar to nip fruity and herbed cocktails, like the citrus-mint martini and mellow cucumber Cosmo, which black-clad bartenders muddle to order. The cut-rate happy hour (weekdays, 5–9pm) finds drinks discounted to $4, fostering a loquacious, toasting crowd.

Midtown East

Azza *137 E 55th St at Lexington Ave (212-755-7055). Subway: 4, 5, 6 to 51st St–Lexington Ave. Mon–Fri 5:30pm–4am; Sat 10pm–4am. Average drink: $12.* Morocco meets Manhattan at this mazelike underground lounge. Plush couches, Persian rugs and sultrily dimmed lanterns enable make-out sessions in velvet-curtained VIP rooms. On the dance floor, clubhopping Euros bop to world beats and splurge on top-notch tonics before noshing on meze like minifalafel. If booze and boogying bore you, puff a fruity hookah and vamoose to the private game room for gentlemanly pursuits such as pool, chess, poker—and PlayStation 3.

The Campbell Apartment *Grand Central Terminal, off the West Balcony, 15 Vanderbilt Ave at 43rd St (212-953-0409). Subway: 42nd St S, 4, 5, 6, 7 to 42nd St–Grand Central. Mon–Sat 3pm–1am; Sun 3–11pm. Average drink: $12.* The sumptuous interior of the converted salon of '30s railroad tycoon John W. Campbell is authentically old-timey to your eyes, if not your wallet. Commuters in smart suits, sipping single malt Scotch and fancy champagne, are transported to an era when outsized opulence meant 25-foot ceilings, walls painted with ornate Renaissance-inspired designs, and dark wood detailing in every corner.

JONATHAN PERUGIA

Sakagura *211 E 43rd St between Second and Third Aves (212-953-7253). Subway: 42nd St S, 4, 5, 6, 7 to 42nd St–Grand Central. Mon–Thu noon–2:30pm, 6– 11:45pm; Fri noon–2:30pm, 6pm–12:45am; Sat 6pm– 12:45am; Sun 6–10:45pm. Average drink: $9.* To find this Midtown sake den, first go through the unmarked lobby of an office building, down some stairs and along a basement corridor. Finally, enter a quiet room done up in understated bamboo and blond wood, where 200 types of sake, categorized by region, await. If you can't choose one, try a Sakagura Tasting Set, which teams an appetizer, entrée and dessert with three corresponding sakes served in delicate, handblown glass vessels.

Tao *42 E 58th St between Madison and Park Aves (212-888-2288). Subway: N, R, W to Fifth Ave–59th St; 4, 5, 6 to 59th St. Daily 11am–2am. Average drink: $10.* The masses (and celebs like Ice-T) flood this sprawling tri-level space for the sheer spectacle of it all. A German-born furniture designer dreamed up the palatial interior, in which the now-famous 16-foot stone Buddha presides over a carp pond. The downstairs lounge is packed to the gills; try your luck in the mezzanine bar, which is less spacious but quieter.

Top of the Tower *Beekman Tower, 3 Mitchell Pl at First Ave (212-980-4796). Subway: E, V to Lexington Ave–53rd St; 6 to 51st St. Sun–Thu 5pm–1am; Fri, Sat 5pm–2am. Average drink: $12.* Sweeping views of midtown and the East River are not the only draws at Top of the Tower, a swank lounge with two small outdoor terraces, perched on the 26th floor of the Art Deco landmark Beekman Tower hotel. There's also live jazz piano (Thursday through Saturday) and signature cocktails like the chocolaty Gotham Martini.

Midtown West

Hudson Bar *The Hudson, 356 W 58th St between Eighth and Ninth Aves (212-554-6343). Subway: A, C, B, D, 1 to 59th St–Columbus Circle. Mon–Sat 4pm–2am; Sun 4pm–1am. Library noon–2am. Average drink: $12.* Philippe Starck's outlandish bar, with its up-lit glass floor, is Manhattan as seen on TV. A place where music- and fashion-industry honchos yak on their cells, and manicured honeys in cashmere caps toy seductively with Strawbellinis made by perfectly formed barmen with artfully mussed hair. A place where you might see somebody besides the Brits over on shopping trips; somebody like the White Stripes, or hey—isn't that Katie Couric?

Maru *11 W 32nd St between Broadway and Fifth Ave (212-273-3413). Subway: A, C, E to 34th St–Penn Station. Mon–Wed, Sun 6pm–2am; Thu 6pm–3am; Fri, Sat 6pm– 4am. Average drink: $9.* Nearly impossible to find, this chic Koreatown lounge has a discreet sign outside; patrons take a freight elevator to the bar's third-floor location, where they're greeted by a spectacular bi-level space, with white walls and soft lighting complementing soaring ceilings and wraparound banquettes. Bartenders serve upscale drinks like lychee martinis and mojitos made with vodka. Private soundproof karaoke rooms equipped with flat-screen TVs can be rented for $250.

Russian Samovar *265 W 52nd St between Broadway and Eighth Ave (212-307-5835). Subway: C, E, 1 to 50th St. Daily 4pm–4am. Average drink: $8.* At this Ruski haven, house-infused vodkas are all the rage. For $15, choose three of more than 20 seasonal varieties, which can include raspberry, apple-cinnamon or ginger. If you don't want to drink on an empty stomach, try a bowl of borscht or the beef Stroganoff.

Therapy *348 W 52nd St between Eighth and Ninth Aves (212-397-1700). Subway: C, E to 50th St. Sun–Wed 5pm–2am; Thu–Sat 5pm–4am. Average drink: $7.* The Freudian Sip (Ketel One, fresh ginger and lemonade) is served in a nice big tumbler, but that's not what draws young actors and well-heeled uptowners. The space is the star: Two levels of slate floors and blond-beamed walls are connected by a dramatic staircase and topped with a massive skylight. Mellow house and techno allow conversation and grooving; the two areas with low tables let you order tasty snacks along with your drinks.

Upper East Side

American Trash *1471 First Ave between 76th and 77th St (212-988-9008). Subway: 6 to 77th St. Daily noon–4am. Average drink: $5.* From the bikes out front to the motorcycle memorabilia inside, a Harley theme prevails here. Televisions spewing sports add to the testosterone-heavy vibe, and, predictably, beer is the drink of choice—the six on tap and 20 by the bottle include Guinness and Brooklyn Lager. A bar menu prides itself on offering "nothing fried"—just wraps, pizzas and burgers.

Bemelmans Bar *The Carlyle, 35 E 76th St at Madison Ave (212-744-1600). Subway: 6 to 77th St. Mon–Sat 11am–1am; Sun noon–midnight. Cover (after 9:30pm): $20–$35. Average drink: $13.* Choice acts keep New York's most la-di-da nightspot on the map, while the cover charge, white-jacketed service and pricey drinks keep the riffraff out. But Ludwig Bemelmans's whimsical murals exude the same magic as his *Madeline* books, and the spiffy cocktails by mixologist Audrey Saunders preserve the bar's singular character. Try the Old Cuban (champagne, aged rum, bitters and fresh mint).

Metropolitan Museum of Art Balcony Bar *1000 Fifth Ave at 82nd St (212-535-7710). Subway: 4, 5, 6 to 86th St. Tue–Thu, Sun 9:30am–5:30pm; Fri, Sat 9:30am–9pm. Average drink: $9.* The installations change each season at this rooftop bar—good reason to come back year after year. But many find the real object of beauty the southern vista of the midtown skyline. The drinks (mojitos, strawberry daiquiris and beer, all from $8 to $9.75) are standard but good, though the green of Central Park is what's most intoxicating.

Mustang Grill *1633 Second Ave at 85th St (212-744-9194). Subway: 4, 5, 6 to 86th St. Mon–Wed 11:30am–1am; Thu, Fri 11am–3am; Sat 10am–3am; Sun 10am–1am. Average drink: $7.* You'll think you landed in a Tijuana garage sale: The room is cluttered with masks, lassos, piñatas, jalapeño lights and giant pineapple-pickling jars. Although most of the clientele is probably perfectly happy with a bottle of Corona and a shot of Cuervo, Mustang peddles an impressive collection of more than 150 tequilas—dedicated samplers should check out the half-off happy hour.

Stir *1363 First Ave between 73rd and 74th Sts (212-744-7190). Subway: 6 to 68th St. Mon–Wed 5pm–2am; Thu, Fri 5pm–4am; Sat 3pm–4am. Average drink: $9.* The space is painted pale green, dimly lit with flickering votives and lined with dark chenille-covered couches.

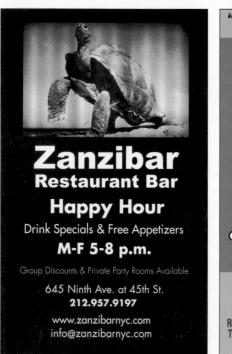

House cocktails include Tranquility (iced tea with Bacardi Limón) and specialty cocktails come with a treat around the rim, such as crushed lemon drops, Pop Rocks or hot wasabi peas. To further warn off frat boys, no baseball or trucker caps are allowed.

Subway Inn *143 E 60th St between Lexington and Third Aves (212-223-8929). Subway: N, R, W to Lexington Ave–59th St; 4, 5, 6 to 59th St. Daily 11am–4am. Average drink: $3.* It's not just getting older, it's getting better…if you're a fan of extra-dingy dives. Established in 1934, this bar has seen only one interior alteration: The grimy booths were reupholstered during the '50s (though the incrustation of dirt miraculously survived). Hard-drinking regulars agreeably make room at the bar for newcomers.

Upper West Side

All State Café *250 W 72nd St between Broadway and West End Ave (212-874-1883). Subway: 1, 2, 3 to 72nd St. Daily 11:30am–3am. Average drink: $5.* Many locals don't know this nook exists, but a quick peek reveals that plenty of other people have discovered its divey charms. There's more space among the tables farther in the back, where regulars eat pub standards and carve their names into the wooden tabletops. Charm quotient? The fireplace is lit in colder months.

The Ding Dong Lounge *929 Columbus Ave between 105th and 106th Sts (212-663-2600). Subway: B, C to 103rd St. Daily 4pm–4am. Average drink: $5.* Goth chandeliers and kick-ass music mark this dark dive as punk—with broadened horizons. Case in point: The tap pulls are sawed-off guitar necks, but those drafts include Stella Artois, Guinness and Bass. DJs spin punk and mix in some straight guitar rock, and the walls are covered with vintage concert posters (Bad Brains and the Damned). The affable local clientele and mood-lit conversation crannies disqualify the place for the truly hard-core. Swell.

Evelyn Lounge *380 Columbus Ave at 78th St (212-724-5145). Subway: B, C to 81st St–Museum of Natural History; 1 to 79th St. Daily 5pm–4am. Cover (Sat after 10pm): $5. Average drink: $8.* Because it's one of the best-looking nightspots in the area, Evelyn can get away with a dress code: no sneakers, hats or baggy pants. Velvet curtains, antique sofas and fireplaces supply an atavistic élan to all three bar areas, but you'll want the basement—settle in with one of 15 martinis (each $10) and snack on a pizza, salad or quesadilla. Thursday, Friday and Saturday nights, a DJ plays.

MObar *Time Warner Center, 80 Columbus Circle at Eighth Ave, 35th floor (212-805-8800; ext 8226). Subway: A, C, B, D, 1 to 59th St–Columbus Circle. Daily 4pm–2am. Average drink: $15.* Although MObar is on the 35th floor of the Time Warner Center, it has, unhappily, largely ceded city views to neighboring restaurant Asiate. Never mind—its interior is plenty easy on the eyes. Expect to compete with postfraternity, pre–Forbes' list types for the plush leather chairs or the large booth tucked away in the back. Staffers are dressed in modified kimonos befitting the bar's Asian theme, and they bow to patrons before taking drink orders.

North West *392 Columbus Ave at 79th St (212-799-4530). Subway: B, C to 81st St–Museum of Natural*

Czech, mate
You'll drink to the convivial atmosphere of the Bohemian Hall and Beer Garden.

History; 1 to 79th St. Mon–Thu 11:30am–1am; Fri, Sat 11:30am–4am; Sun 10:30am–midnight. Average drink: $8. Despite a noteworthy dinner menu and an extensive selection of wines and liquors, the main attraction at this neighborhood fixture remains the second-floor smoking lounge, with its ashtrays and leather love seats and banquettes scattered all around. Cigar aficionados light their Ashtons and sip Rob Roys; the striking black-and-white photos of tobacco fields give them an anthropological context.

Tap a Keg *2731 Broadway between 104th and 105th Sts (212-749-1734). Subway: 1 to 103rd St. Mon–Fri 2pm–4am; Sat, Sun noon–4am. Average drink: $5.* Co-owner John Grippo opened this unapologetic beer bar in 1993 as a resurrection of his father and uncle's Columbus Avenue joint, and what a classic dive that was. And is! To say this place has decor or appointments is just way too elegant-sounding; sonny boy just hauled the old man's decrepit equipment north, although, remarkably, the old-timey manual-key cash registers are original to this location.

Above 116th

The Den *2150 Fifth Ave between 131st and 132nd Sts (212-234-3045). Subway: 2, 3 to 135th St. Sun 11am–4pm, 6pm–1am; Mon–Thu 6pm–1am; Fri, Sat 6pm–4am. Average drink: $9.* An intimate, red-accented boîte on the ground floor of a brownstone draws Harlemites and downtowners with a variety of DJ sets. But the virtuosity on display here owes more to mixology than music. The innovative cocktail menu titillates with names like Sex in the Inner City, Uncle Tom Collins (accompanied by an Oreo cookie) and Jungle Fever (equal parts Bushmills Irish Cream and Kahlúa).

Lenox Lounge *288 Malcolm X Blvd (Lenox Ave) between 124th and 125th Sts (212-427-0253). Subway: 2, 3 to 125th St. Daily noon–4am. Average drink: $6.* The lure of Lenox Lounge rests on the laurels of its rich history. The Zebra Room in back still hosts live jazz and blues (Houston Person, Ray Schinnery), which caters to those interested in carring the old-school torch. At the main bar out front, the regulars are sipping High Lifes and Remy and working their game to the sound of P-Funk.

Monkey Room *589 Fort Washington Ave at 187th St (212-543-9888). Subway: A to 190th St. Daily 3pm–4am. Average drink: $7.* This star of the Washington Heights drinking scene aims to please all tastes, hosting DJs Fridays and Saturdays at 10pm and displaying televised sports showdowns. The extensive list of beers on tap includes Blue Moon and cherry-wheat Sam Adams, and everything's a dollar cheaper before 8pm.

St Nick's Pub *773 St. Nicholas Ave at 149th St; 212-283-7132). Subway: A, B, C, D to 145th St.* St. Nick's Pub has barely changed since the '40s, when Duke Ellington first urged taking the A train up to Sugar Hill. The whitewashed walls, low ceiling and narrow passageway along the bar toward the stage reinforce the basement feel, but St. Nick's is warmed by its neighborhood vibe, cheap drinks and random free eats. Fridays and Mondays, when the joint is enveloped by jam sessions, you'll be glad you heeded the Duke's advice.

Good vibrations
Wrap your head around the idea of a great space and good drinks at Therapy.

Uptown Jazz Lounge at Minton's Playhouse
210 W 118th St between St. Nicholas Ave and Adam Clayton Powell Jr. Blvd [Seventh Ave]; 212-864-8346). Subway: B, C to 116th St–Frederick Douglass Blvd. During the '40s, when Thelonious Monk was the resident pianist, late-night jams brought such luminaries as Dizzy Gillespie and Charlie Parker, giving birth to bebop. The long wooden bar offers a good vantage point for the nightly shows, or you can grab a table closer to the action (but be careful not to disturb the rapt German and Japanese jazz pilgrims).

Brooklyn

The Abbey *536 Driggs Ave between North 7th and North 8th Sts, Williamsburg (718-599-4400). Subway: L to Bedford Ave. Daily 3pm–4am. Average drink: $5.* The flock congregates nightly at the Abbey, which calls out equally to hipsters, punk rockers and problem drinkers. Old-fashioned pub decor is bathed in red light, the jukebox is solid, and the entertainment is no-frills: Ms. Pac-Man, MegaTouch, two TVs and a pool table. At the wooden bar, or in a church-pew booth in the back room, the faithful focus on drinking and meeting someone not of their own faith.

Barbes *376 9th St at Sixth Ave, Park Slope (718-965-9177). Subway: F to Seventh Ave. Sun–Thu 5pm–2am; Fri, Sat 5pm–4am. Average drink: $5.* Music-snob bartenders play lounge and soul while serving French wines and flaming Absente (a perfectly legal substitute for absinthe). Events fill the comfy Beat-ish back room—jazz, folk and world music performances; readings by local authors; and silent movies accompanied by live bands. Intentionally more "French" than French, Barbès manages to be fun without being ironic.

Bar Sepia *234 Underhill Ave between Eastern Pkwy and Lincoln Pl, Prospect Hts (718-399-6680). Subway: 2, 3 to Eastern Pkwy–Brooklyn Museum. Mon–Wed 5pm–2am; Thu–Sat 5pm–4am; Sun noon–midnight. Average drink: $6.* Cheerful bartender Marlon crafts the perfect summer drink: His spin on the mojito, aptly christened the Marlito, calls for Malibu rum, lemon instead of lime and chunks of pineapple (along with fresh mint leaves, of course). Sip yours on the smoker-friendly patio festooned with thrift-store treasures and surrounded by a chain-link fence draped in white Christmas lights.

Brooklyn Brewery *79 North 11th St between Berry St and Wythe Ave, Williamsburg (718-486-7422). Subway: L to Bedford Ave. Fri 6–10pm; Sat noon–5pm. Average drink: $3.* For five bucks, you get two wooden chips, each good for a glass of the brewed-on-site suds of your choice. Settle at one of the picnic tables and sip a smooth Brooklyn Pilsner or seasonal Black Stout Chocolate. The more you drink, the more you support a clean environment: The brewery is now 100 percent wind-powered.

The Brooklyn Inn *148 Hoyt St at Bergen St, Boerum Hill (718-625-9741). Subway: F, G to Bergen St. Daily 3pm–4am. Average drink: $4.* The immense dark-wood bar, bare-bones pool room and old-school jukebox attract an unpretentious crowd that's more interested in drinking than in flirting. There are plenty of choice beers on tap, including Old Speckled Hen, Dentergens Wheat and local Six Point Brown Ale—all for a reasonable $5-or-so a pint. The Inn dates back to the 19th century; tie on a few and you may even see the ghost of Walt Whitman.

MICHAEL SCOTT KENNEY

Quite a production
The famous and the merely fabulous gather at Schiller's Liquor Bar.

Fourth Avenue Pub *76 Fourth Ave between Bergen St and St. Marks Pl, Park Slope (718-643-2273). Subway: M, R to Union St; 2, 3 to Bergen St. Daily 4pm–4am. Average drink: $5.* Beer lovers belly up to the bar to munch on piping-hot popcorn and sample coast-to-coast suds at this former nail salon. Twenty-four draft beers are poured alongside nearly three-dozen bottled beers and vintage Scotches and bourbons. Chitchatty locals sit at low tables to tipple during the daily 4 to 8pm happy hour, when the drinks are two-for-one.

Galapagos *70 North 6th St between Kent and Wythe Aves, Williamsburg (718-384-4586). Subway: L to Bedford Ave. Sun–Thu 6pm–2am; Fri, Sat 6pm–4am. Cover: free–$10. Average drink: $5.* It may be a great place to have a drink while gazing at the reflecting pool off the main room, but the artsy events make Galapagos more than just another pretty face in the nabe's hipster parade. Film screenings, trapeze acts, singers, musicians, burlesque dancers, avant-garde theater and comedy light up the stage night after night; most shows are free or less than $20.

Moe's *80 Lafayette Ave at South Portland Ave, Fort Greene (718-797-9536). Subway: C to Lafayette Ave; G to Fulton St. Sun–Thu 4:30pm–3:30am, Fri–Sat 4:30pm–4am. Average drink: $6.* This isn't Homer Simpson's Moe's. The furnishings are a patchwork of the greatest retro hits—'60s mod vinyl couches, an '80s table-style video game—and there are plenty of corners for conversation. Best of all, happy hour is generous, and the bar is well stocked with pretzels. Homer would approve.

Pete's Candy Store *709 Lorimer St between Frost and Richardson Sts, Williamsburg (718-302-3770). Subway: L to Lorimer St; G to Metropolitan Ave. Sun–Wed 5pm–2am; Thu–Sat 5pm–4am. Average drink: $5.* It may be pocket-size, but that pocket is full of goodies. On Bingo Tuesday, blue-haired ladies battle yuppies for 99-cent prizes, and Wednesday's Quizz-Off draws top-drawer TP mavens; Scrabble is on Saturday. After the games, there's free music in the Pullman-car-shaped performance space, with acts on the cusp of wider recognition appearing nightly. When the weather warms, the backyard opens to stargazers.

reBar *2007 Eat Out Award, Readers' Choice: Best new bar 147 Front St between Jay and Pearl Sts, DUMBO (718-797-2322). Subway: F to York St. Mon–Wed, Sun 1pm–2am; Thu–Sat 1pm–4am. Average drink: $6.* Dumbo's beer nuts rejoiced with the arrival of this upstairs annex to the Coffee Box café. Beyond the handwrought iron gate and stained-glass windows, tattooed artists and condo owners savor the 15 taps dispensing delectable American microbrews (Ommegang Rare Vos, Weyerbacher Blithering Idiot Barley-Wine) and heady Belgian quaffs. The brew-averse will be content with organic wines and Spanish-inflected tapas.

Sheep Station *149 Fourth Ave at Douglass S, Park Slope (718-857-4337). Subway: M, R to Union St. Daily 4pm–4am. Average drink: $7.* Herd mentality? Hardly. This sleekly rustic Australian pub stands out. Its lacquered wooden floors and tin-can lights welcome chatty Park Slopers, who gobble Aussie eats like meat pies, crunchy chips and burgers topped with beets, pineapples and fried eggs. But the real lure is the local microbrews and European Hefeweizens dispensed in small, medium and reality-obliterating large sizes.

Spuyten Duyvil
359 Metropolitan Ave at Havemayer St, Williamsburg (718-963-4140). Subway: L to Bedford Ave; G to Metropolitan Ave. Sun–Thu 5pm–2am; Fri, Sat 5pm–4am. Average drink: $6. Don't arrive thirsty; it takes at least ten minutes to decide on a beer. That's because the Dutch-named outpost offers roughly 150 quaffs, largely middle-European regionals, and bartenders are eager to explain the differences between them. The cozy interior is filled with flea-market finds, most of which are for sale, and there's a bar menu of smoked meats and pâtés, cheeses and terrines.

Tini Wine Bar & Café
414 Van Brunt St between Coffey and Van Dyke Sts, Red Hook (718-855-4206). Travel: F, G to Smith–9th Sts, then take the B77 bus. Tue–Fri 4pm–midnight; Sat 11am–midnight; Sun 11am–11pm. Average drink: $7. Book-lugging locals, canoodling couples and paint-splattered artists relax on a spotless white couch and sit on square chairs at this itsy-bitsy, female-run lounge near Red Hook's waterfront. The beers and vinos are artisanal, organic and biodynamic. Teetotalers can slurp old-fashioned egg creams; snackers can munch on savory panini stuffed with locally grown produce.

Union Hall
702 Union St between Fifth and Sixth Aves, Williamsburg (718-638-4400). Subway: B, Q to Seventh Ave; M, R to Union St; 2, 3 to Bergen St. Mon–Fri 4pm–4am; Sat, Sun noon–4am. Average drink: $5. Upstairs in this bi-level bar, couples chomp miniburgers and nip at microbrews in the gentlemen's-club anteroom (decorated with Soviet-era globes, paintings of fez-capped men, fireplaces)—before battling it out on the clay bocce courts. Downstairs, in the taxidermy-filled basement, the stage is packed with blaring bands, comedians and a monthly, Mr. Wizard–ish science night. Outside, cigarette puffers convene on the patio.

Queens

Bohemian Hall and Beer Garden
29-19 24th Ave between 29th and 30th Sts, Astoria (718-274-0043). Subway: N, W to Astoria Blvd . Mon–Thu 5pm–2am; Fri 5pm–4am; Sat, Sun noon–4am. Average drink: $4. The vibe at the 1910 beer hall manages to combine the ambience of that era with the youthful spirit of junior year in Prague. Go for the cheap, robust platters of Czech sausage, $4 Stolis, Spaten Oktoberfests and the rockin' juke. From roughly Memorial Day to October, the hall's large tree-canopied, picnic-tabled beer garden beckons with thrilling unpretentiousness.

5 Burro Café
72-05 Austin St between 72nd Ave and 72nd Rd, Forest Hills (718-544-2984). Subway: E, F, V, G, R to Forest Hills–71st Ave. Daily noon–4am. Average drink: $8. The hangout has everything you love about clichéd Mexican bars—cactus murals, papier-mâché parrots, red chili-pepper lights, even a slushie machine pumping out frozen margaritas. These are served in mason-jar mugs, and there are 14 kinds of bottled beer, 5 of them Mexican. The mini Wurlitzer holds the Stranglers, the Streets and Radiohead; an X-Files pinball machine rounds out the suburban South-of-the-Border shtick.

Hell Gate Social
12-21 Astoria Blvd between 12th and 14th Sts, Astoria (718-204-8313). Subway: N, W to Astoria Blvd. Mon–Wed, Sun 7pm–2am; Thu–Sat 7pm–4am. Average drink: $5. Look for the discreet red light or you might miss this sleek, minimalist bar, which offers patrons innovative drinks—such as the Upside Down Pineapple Cake and the rosemary-infused blueberry vodka martini—at decent prices. Hell Gate Social maintains a spacious backyard with benches, and screens classic B movies on Sundays. Hells yeah.

Jade Eatery & Lounge
1 Station Sq at Continental Ave, Forest Hills (718-793-2203). Subway: E, F, G, R, V to Forest Hills–71st Ave. Tue, Wed, Sun 4:30–11:30pm; Thu–Sat 4:30pm–2am. Average drink: $10. Pickin's are rather slim for moody boîtes in central Queens, and a diverse clientele straight from central casting has embraced Jade Eatery & Lounge's twin bars. Conversation-minded drinkers head for the copper-barred main taproom, while the higher-decibel Moroccan Lounge hosts a mix of dressed-for-clubbing partyers and private-event guests. Both bars serve Asian appetizers and not-too-sweet, amply poured cocktails.

Les Amis
31-17 Ditmars Blvd between 32nd and 33rd Sts, Astoria (718-728-9191). N, W to Ditmars Blvd. Daily 8pm–4am. Average drink: $5. Despite its French name, this dimly lit Astoria neighborhood bar, which caters to an older crowd, is thoroughly Greek. The live music is slightly cheesy, but the foot-stomping, cigar-smoking locals love it—and so will you after some ouzo, or any number of the Greek wines on offer.

LIC
45-48 Vernon Blvd between 45th Rd and 46th Ave, Long Island City (718-786-5400). Subway: 7 to Vernon Blvd–Jackson Ave. Mon–Fri 3pm–4am; Sat, Sun 1pm–4am. Average drink: $4. The new owners inherited the previous bar's brick, wood and tin-ceiling fixtures, then brought in a laid-back attitude all their own—and a much more extensive drink selection. They also added an outdoor patio where you can smoke, tie up the dog and even order delivery from nearby restaurants. LIC is a convenient keep-the-party-going pit stop for music fans, who migrate down the block after P.S. 1's Warm Up evenings.

Lounge 47
47-10 Vernon Blvd between 47th Ave and 47th Rd, Long Island City (718-937-2044). Subway: 7 to Vernon Blvd–Jackson Ave. Mon–Thu noon–1am; Fri noon–3am; Sat 5pm–2am. Average drink: $7. First-time bar owners Lloyd Canning, Min Chen and Seamus McEntire built a concrete bar and furnished the space, just one subway stop into Queens, with '60s and '70s furniture and mirrors and vintage wallpaper from Holland. The pebbled garden in the back seals the deal. Reasonably priced cocktails and a menu of snacks, salads and gourmet sandwiches pull in folks from the neighborhood, Silvercup Studios and P.S. 1.

Sidetracks
45-08 Queens Blvd between 45th and 46th Sts, Sunnyside (718-786-3570). Subway: 7 to 46th St. Daily 10am–4am. Average drink: $5.50. This train-themed Sunnyside spot offers features three bars with 14 beers on tap, darts, off-track betting and probably enough TV screens to give a small child seizures. On weekend evenings, local Jackson Heights' homeboyz and gals gather en masse, though a calmer mood prevails at Sunday's Jazz Brunch.

Subject Index

Pointed statement
Aussie spot Wombat
gives new meaning to
Southern cooking.

JEFF GURWIN

Subject Index

Behind door No. 1
Entry to the Waverly Inn is tough to secure.

Good for large groups

Subject Index

Late-night or 24-hours

Subject Index

Love, American style
P.J. Clarkes' burgers are
a New York treasure.

Subject Index

Triple threat
Mussels, frites, beer: Belgian B. Café does 'em all right.

Sidewalk tables

Subject Index

Looks the part
Heidelberg is a charming throwback to yesteryear's Germantown.

PATRIK RYTIKANGAS

Neighborhood Index

Africa oyé
Take a trip to Senegal via Le Baobab.

PATRIK RYTIKANGAS

Sexy beast
Dig into the 34-ounce "cowboy rib steak" at the sleek STK.

JENNY WOODWARD

Neighborhood Index

Neighborhood Index

Soul kitchen
You'll get succulent,
home-style fixin's
at Birdies.

JEFF GURWIN

Neighborhood Index

Borough hallmark
The raw bar is one of
Blue Ribbon Brooklyn's
many attractions.

Neighborhood Index

Meal maker
Chef Meng Cheong turns
noodles into meals at—
where else?—Noodle.

Neighborhood Index

Alphabetical Index

To market, to market
Eat, shop, learn, drink—all at Bouley Bakery and Market.

PATRIK RYTIKANGAS

Alphabetical Index

Asiakan 63
710 Amsterdam Ave between
94th and 95th Sts (212-280-8878).
Subway: 1, 2, 3 to 96th St.

Asiate 63
Mandarin Oriental Hotel in the
Time Warner Center, 80 Columbus
Circle at 60th St (212-805-8881).
Subway: A, C, B, D, 1 to 59th
St–Columbus Circle.

Aspen 47
30 W 22nd St between Fifth
and Sixth Aves (212-645-5040).
Subway: F, V, N, R, W to 23rd St.

Assenzio 143
205 E 4th St between Aves A
and B (212-677-9466). Subway:
F, V to Lower East Side–
Second Ave.

Atlantic Chip Shop 78
129 Atlantic Ave between
Henry and Clinton Sts,
Cobble Hill, Brooklyn (718-
855-7775). Subway: 2, 3, 4, 5 to
Borough Hall.

August 102
359 Bleecker St between Charles
and W 10th Sts (212-929-4774).
Subway: 1 to Christopher
St–Sheridan Sq.

Aureole 48
34 E 61st St between Madison
and Park Aves (212-319-1660).
Subway: F to Lexington Ave–
63rd St; N, R, W to Lexington
Ave–59th St; 4, 5, 6 to 59th St.

Avra 133
141 E 48th St between Lexington
and Third Aves (212-759-8550).
Subway: E, V to Lexington
Ave–53rd St; 6 to 51st St.

Awash 18
338 E 6th St between First
and Second Aves (212-982-
9589). Subway: F, V to
Lower East Side–Second Ave;
6 to Astor Pl.

Awash 18
947 Amsterdam Ave between
106th and 107th Sts (212-961-
1416). Subway: 1 to Cathedral
Pkwy–110th St.

Azul Bistro 61
152 Stanton St at Suffolk St
(646-602-2004). Subway: F
to Delancey St; J, M, Z to
Delancey–Essex Sts.

B

B. Café 75
240 E 75th St between Second
and Third Aves (212-249-3300).
Subway: 6 to 77th St.

Babbo 170
110 Waverly Pl between
MacDougal St and Sixth Ave
(212-777-0303). Subway: A, C,
E, B, D, F, V to W 4th St.

Bacchus 107
409 Atlantic Ave at Bond
St, Boerum Hill, Brooklyn
(718-852-1572). Subway: A, C
to Hoyt–Schermerhorn; F, G to
Bergen St.

Baci & Abbracci 143
204 Grand St between Bedford
and Driggs Aves, Williamsburg,
Brooklyn (718-599-6599). Subway:
L to Bedford Ave.

Bahia 198
690 Grand St between
Graham and Manhattan Aves,
Williamsburg, Brooklyn (718-
218-9592). Subway: L to
Grand St.

Balthazar 113
80 Spring St between Broadway
and Crosby St (212-965-1414).
Subway: N, R, W to Prince St; 6
to Spring St.

Bamboo 52 65
344 W 52nd St between Eighth
and Ninth Aves (212-315-2777).
Subway: C, E to 50th St.

Bamiyan 17
358 Third Ave at 26th St (212-
481-3232). Subway: 6 to 28th St.

Bamn! 102
37 St. Marks Pl at Second Ave
(888-400-2266). Subway: 6 to
Astor Pl.

Bandol Bistro 113
181 E 78th St between Lexington
and Third Aves (212-744-1800).
Subway: 6 to 77th St.

Bann 189
350 W 50th St at Ninth Ave (212-
582-4446). Subway: C, E to 50th St.

Bann Thai 241
69-12 Austin St at Yellowstone
Blvd, Forest Hills, Queens (718-
544-9999). E, F, V, G, R to Forest
Hills–71St Ave.

Bao 111 251
111 Ave C between 7th and 8th
Sts (212-254-7773). Subway: L to
First Ave.

Bao Noodles 251
391 Second Ave between 22nd
and 23rd Sts (212-725-7770).
Subway: 6 to 23rd St.

Bar Americain 57
152 W 52nd St between Sixth
and Seventh Aves (212-265-9700).
Subway: 1 to 50th St; N, R W to
49th St.

Bar BQ 73
689 Sixth Ave at 20th St, Park
Slope, Brooklyn (718-499-4872).
Subway: M, R to Prospect Ave; F
to Seventh Ave.

Bar Carrera 227
175 Second Ave between 11th
and 12th Sts (212-375-1555).
Subway: 6 to Astor Pl.

Bar Masa 177
Time Warner Center, 10 Columbus
Circle at 60th St, fourth floor
(212-823-9800). Subway: A, C, B, D,
1 to 59th St–Columbus Circle.

Bar Pitti 143
268 Sixth Ave between Bleecker
and Houston Sts (212-982-3300).
Subway: A, C, E, B, D, F, V to W
4th St; 1 to Houston St.

Bar Room at 52
the Modern
9 W 53rd St between Fifth and
Sixth Aves (212-333-1220).
Subway: E, V to Fifth Ave–
53rd St.

Bar 6 107
502 Sixth Ave between 12th
and 13th Sts (212-691-1363).
Subway: F, V to 14th St; L to
Sixth Ave.

Bar Tabac 107
128 Smith St at Dean St, Boerum
Hill, Brooklyn (718-923-0918).
Subway: F, G to Bergen St.

Bar Toto 145
411 11th St at Sixth Ave, Park
Slope, Brooklyn (718-768-4698).
Subway: F to Seventh Ave.

Barbes 214
21 E 36th St between Fifth and
Madison Aves (212-684-0215).
Subway: 6 to 33rd St.

Barbounia 199
250 Park Ave South at 20th St
(212-995-0242). Subway: 6 to
23rd St.

Barbuto 158
775 Washington St between Jane
and W 12th Sts (212-924-9700).
Subway: A, C, E to 14th St; L to
Eighth Ave.

barmarché 21
14 Spring St at Elizabeth St
(212-219-9542). Subway: N, R,
W to Prince St; 6 to Spring St.

Barney Greengrass 21
541 Amsterdam Ave between
86th and 87th Sts (212-724-4707).
Subway: B, C, 1 to 86th St.

Barolo 158
398 West Broadway between
Broome and Spring Sts (212-
226-1102). Subway: C, E to
Spring St.

Basilio Inn 145
6 Galesville Ct at Lily Pond Rd,
Staten Island (718-447-9292).
Travel: From the Staten Island
Ferry, take the S51 bus to Lily
Pond Rd.

Beacon 41
25 W 56th St between Fifth
and Sixth Aves (212-332-0500).
Subway: F to 57th St.

Becco 158
355 W 46th St between Eighth
and Ninth Aves (212-397-7597).
Subway: A, C, E to 42nd St–Port
Authority.

Beet 241
344 Seventh Ave between 9th
and 10th Sts, Park Slope, Brooklyn
(718-832-2338). Subway: F to
Seventh Ave.

Bellavitae 158
24 Minetta Ln at Sixth Ave
(212-473-5121). Subway: A, C,
E, B, D, F, V to W 4th St.

Belleville 107
330–332 Fifth Ave at 5th St,
Park Slope, Brooklyn (718-832-
9777). Subway: M, R to Fourth
Ave–9th St.

Ben & Jack's 233
Steakhouse
219 E 44th St between Second
and Third Aves (212-682-5678).
Subway: 42nd St S, 4, 5, 6, 7 to
42nd St–Grand Central.

Ben Benson's 233
Steakhouse
123 W 52nd St between Sixth
and Seventh Aves (212-581-
8888). Subway: B, D, F, V to
47–50th Sts–Rockefeller Ctr;
1 to 50th St.

Beppe 170
45 E 22nd St between Broadway
and Park Ave South (212-982-
8422). Subway: N, R, W, 6 to
23rd St.

Bianca 145
5 Bleecker St between Bowery
and Elizabeth St (212-260-4666).
Subway: B, D, F, V to Broadway–
Lafayette St; 6 to Bleecker St.

Big Booty Bread Co 79
216 W 23rd St between Seventh
and Eighth Aves (212-414-3056).
Subway: C, E, 1 to 23rd St.

Big Daddy's Diner 79
239 Park Ave South between
19th and 20th Sts (212-477-1500).
Subway: 6 to 23rd St.

Birdies 57
149 First Ave between 9th
and 10th Sts (212-529-2512).
Subway: L to First Ave; 6
to Astor Pl.

Biricchino 158
260 W 29th St at Eighth Ave
(212-695-6690). Subway: 1
to 28th St.

Bistro Cassis 124
235 Columbus Ave between
70th and 71st Sts (212-579-3966).
Subway: B, C to 72nd St; 1, 2, 3
to 72nd St.

Bistro du Nord 114
1312 Madison Ave at 93rd St (212-
289-0997). Subway: 6 to 96th St.

Bistro les Amis 114
180 Spring St at Thompson St
(212-226-8645). Subway: C, E to
Spring St.

Bistro Ten 18 31
1018 Amsterdam Ave at 110th St
(212-662-7600). Subway: 1 to 110th
St–Cathedral Pkwy.

Black Betty 211
366 Metropolitan Ave at
Havemeyer St, Williamsburg,
Brooklyn (718-599-0243).
Subway: L to Lorimer St; G to
Metropolitan Ave.

Black Pearl 219
37 W 26th St between Broadway
and Sixth Ave (212-532-9900).
Subway: F, V, N, R, W to 23rd St.

Blaue Gans 72
139 Duane St between Church St
and West Broadway (212-571-
8880). Subway: A, C, 1, 2, 3 to
Chambers St.

Bliss 247
191 Bedford Ave between
North 6th and North 7th Sts,
Williamsburg, Brooklyn (718-599-
2547). Subway: L to Bedford Ave.

Blossom Vegetarian 247
Restaurant
187 Ninth Ave between 21st and
22nd Sts (212-627-1144). Subway:
C, E to 23rd St.

BLT Fish 219
21 W 17th St between Fifth
and Sixth Aves (212-691-8888).
Subway: F, V to 14th St; L to
Sixth Ave.

BLT Steak 233
106 E 57th St between Park
and Lexington Aves (212-752-
7470). Subway: N, R, W to
Lexington Ave–59th St; 4, 5, 6
to 59th St.

Blue Fin 219
W Times Square Hotel, 1567
Broadway at 47th St (212-918-
1400). Subway: N, R, W to 49th St.

Blue Hill 41
75 Washington Pl between
Washington Sq West and Sixth
Ave (212-539-1776). Subway: A, C,
E, B, D, F, V to W 4th St.

The Blue Mahoe 87
243 E 14th St between Second
and Third Aves (212-358-
0012). Subway: L to Third
Ave; N, Q, R, W, 4, 5, 6 to 14th
St–Union Sq.

Blue Ribbon 48
97 Sullivan St between Prince and
Spring Sts (212-274-0404). Subway:
C, E to Spring St.

Blue Ribbon Bakery 102
33 Downing St at Bedford St
(212-337-0404). Subway: A, C,
E, B, D, F, V to W 4th St; 1 to
Houston St.

Blue Ribbon Brooklyn 48
280 Fifth Ave between Garfield Pl
and 1st St, Park Slope, Brooklyn
(718-840-0404). Subway: M, R to
Union St.

Blue Ribbon Downing 48
Street Bar
34 Downing St between Bedford
and Varick Sts (212-691-0404).
Subway: A, C, E, B, D, F, V to W
4th St; 1 to Houston St.

Down home
Experience Jean-Georges
Vongerichten's version of a
neighborhood place at Perry St.

Alphabetical Index

Dylan Prime 234
62 Laight St between Greenwich and Hudson Sts (212-334-4783). Subway: A, C, E, 1 to Canal St.

E

Earthen Oven 139
53 W 72nd St at Columbus Ave (212-579-8888). Subway: B, C, 1, 2, 3 to 72nd St.

Ebe Ye Yie 20
2364 Jerome Ave between North and 184th Sts, Bronx (718-220-1300). Subway: 4 to 183rd St.

Ed's Lobster Bar 222
222 Lafayette St between Broome and Spring Sts (212-343-3236). Subway: B, D, F, V to Broadway–Lafayette St.

Egg 82
135A North 5th St at Bedford St, Williamsburg, Brooklyn (718-302-5151). Subway: L to Bedford Ave.

Eight Mile Creek 71
240 Mulberry St between Prince and Spring Sts (212-431-4635). Subway: N, R, W to Prince St; 6 to Spring St.

809 Sangria Bar and Grill
112 Dyckman St between Nagle and Sherman Aves (212-304-3800). Subway: 1 to Dyckman St.

El Castillo de Jagua 90
113 Rivington St between Essex and Ludlow Sts (212-982-6412). Subway: F to Delancey St; J, M, Z to Delancey–Essex Sts.

El Chivito d'Oro 198
84-02 37th Ave at 84th St, Jackson Hts, Queens (718-424-0600). Subway: 7 to 82nd St–Jackson Hts.

El Cocotero 198
228 W 18th St between Seventh and Eighth Aves (212-206-8930). Subway: 1 to 18th St.

El Patio 197
100-14 Northern Boulevard, Corona, Queens (718-446-4622). 7 to Junction Blvd; 7 to 103rd St-Corona Plaza.

El Quijote 227
226 W 23rd St between Seventh and Eighth Aves (212-929-1855). Subway: C, E, 1 to 23rd St.

El Sitio 193
68-28 Roosevelt Ave at 69th St, Woodside, Queens (718-424-2369). Subway: 7 to 69th St.

El Tesoro Ecuatoriano 197
4015 Fifth Ave between 40th and 41st Sts, Sunset Park, Brooklyn (718-972-3756). Subway: R to 45th St.

The Elephant 243
58 E 1st St between First and Second Aves (212-505-7739). Subway: F, V to Lower East Side–Second Ave.

Eleven Madison Park 49
11 Madison Ave at 24th St (212-889-0905). Subway: N, R, W, 6 to 23rd St.

Elias Corner 133
24-02 31st St at 24th Ave, Astoria, Queens (718-932-1510). Subway: N, W to Astoria–Blvd.

Embers 234
9519 Third Ave at 95th St, Bay Ridge, Bay Ridge, Brooklyn (718-745-3700). Subway: R to Bay Ridge–95th St.

Empanada Mama 194
763 Ninth Ave at 51st St (212-698-9008). Subway: C, E to 50th St.

Empire Diner 82
210 Tenth Ave at 22nd St (212-243-2736). Subway: C, E to 23rd St.

Employees Only 103
510 Hudson St between Christopher and W 10th Sts (212-242-3021). Subway: 1 to Christopher St–Sheridan Sq.

Em Thai 243
278 Smith St between Sackett and DeGraw Sts, Carroll Gardens, Brooklyn (718-834-0505). Subway: F, G to Carroll St.

EN Japanese Brasserie 179
435 Hudson St at Leroy St (212-647-9196). Subway: 1 to Houston St.

Enoteca i Trulli 173
124 E 27th St between Park Ave and Lexington Ave (212-481-7372). Subway: 6 to 28th St.

Epicerie 109
168–170 Orchard St at Stanton St (212-420-7520). Subway: F, V to Lower East Side–Second Ave.

Epices du Traiteur 201
103 W 70th St between Columbus Ave and Broadway (212-579-5904). Subway: B, C, 1, 2, 3 to 72nd St.

Esperanto 194
145 Ave C at 9th St (212-505-6559). Subway: L to First Ave; 6 to Astor Pl.

Estancia 460 62
460 Greenwich St between Desbrosses and Watts Sts (212-431-5093). Subway: A, C, E, 1 to Canal St.

Estiatorio Milos 133
125 W 55th St between Sixth and Seventh Aves (212-245-7400). Subway: F, N, Q, R, W to 57th St.

E.U. (European Union) 103
235 E 4th St between Aves A and B (212-254-2900). Subway: F, V to Lower East Side–Second Ave.

Excellent Pork Chop House 95
3 Doyers St off Bowery at Chatham Sq (212-791-7007). Subway: B, D to Grand St; J, M, Z, N, Q, R, W, 6 to Canal St.

Extra Virgin 201
259 W 4th St between Charles and Perry Sts (212–691–9359). Subway: 1 to Christopher St–Sheridan Sq.

F

F&B 75
269 W 23rd St between Seventh and Eighth Aves (646-486-4441). Subway: C, E to 23rd St.

F&B 75
150 E 52nd St between Lexington and Third Aves (212-421-8600). Subway: 6 to 51st St; E, V to Lexington Ave–53rd St.

Fabio Piccolo Fiore 173
39 Desbrosses St at West St (212-226-4621). Subway: A to Canal St.

Fada 109
530 Driggs Ave at North 8th St, Williamsburg, Brooklyn (718-388-6607). Subway: L to Bedford Ave.

Fake Orchid 243
440 E 9th St between First Ave and Ave A (646-654-1991). Subway: 6 to Astor Pl.

Falafel Chula 212
436 Union Ave at Metropolitan St, Williamsburg, Brooklyn (718-387-0303). Subway: L to Lorimer St; G to Metropolitan Ave.

Falai 162
68 Clinton St between Rivington and Stanton Sts (212-253-1960). Subway: F, J, M, Z to Delancey–Essex Sts.

Falai Panetteria 162
79 Clinton St at Rivington St (212-777-8956). 79 Clinton St at Rivington St.

Fanny 109
425 Graham Ave between Frost and Withers Sts, Williamsburg, Brooklyn (718-389-2060). Subway: L to Graham Ave.

The Farm on Adderley 23
1108 Cortelyou Rd between Stratford and Westminster Rds, Ditmas Park, Brooklyn (718-287-3101). Subway: Q to Cortelyou Rd.

Fatty Crab 65
643 Hudson St between Gansevoort and Horatio St (212-352-3590). Subway: A, C, E to 14th St; L to Eighth Ave.

Felidia 173
243 E 58th St between Second and Third Aves (212-758-1479). Subway: N, R, W to Lexington Ave–59th St; 4, 5, 6 to 59th St.

Félix 117
340 West Broadway at Grand St (212-431-0021). Subway: A, C, E, 1 to Canal St.

Ferdinando's Focacceria 147
151 Union St between Columbia and Hicks Sts, Cobble Hill, Brooklyn (718-855-1545). Subway: F, G to Carroll St.

Fette Sau 73
354 Metropolitan Ave between Havemeyer and Roebling Sts, Williamsburg, Brooklyn (718-963-3404). Subway: L to Lorimer St; G to Metropolitan Ave.

Fiamma Osteria 173
206 Spring St between Sixth Ave and Sullivan St (212-653-0100). Subway: C, E to Spring St.

Fiesta Mexicana 205
75-02 Roosevelt Ave at 75th St, Jackson Hts, Queens (718-505-9090). Subway: E, F, V, G, R to Jackson Hts–Roosevelt Ave; 7 to 74th St–Broadway.

15 East 179
15 E 15th St between Fifth Ave and Union Sq West (212-647-0015). Subway: L, N, Q, R, W, 4, 5, 6 to 14th St–Union Sq.

Financier Patisserie 83
62 Stone St between Hanover Sq and Mill Lane, (212-344-5600). 2, 3 to Wall Street.

Financier Patisserie 83
35 Cedar St at William St (212-952-3838). Subway: 2, 3 to Wall Street.

Financier Patisserie 83
3-4 World Financial Center (212-786-3220). Subway: E to World Trade Center.

FireBird Russian 217
365 W 46th St between Eighth and Ninth Aves (212-586-0244). Subway: A, C, E to 42nd St–Port Authority.

Five Front 33
5 Front St between Dock and Old Fulton Sts, Dumbo, Brooklyn (718-625-5559). Subway: A, C to High St; F to York St.

5 Ninth 103
5 Ninth Ave between Gansevoort and Little West 12th Sts (212-929-9460). Subway: A, C, E to 14th St; L to Eighth Ave.

Five Points 33
31 Great Jones St between Lafayette St and Bowery (212-253-5700). Subway B, D, F, V to Broadway–Lafayette St; 6 to Bleecker St.

Flea Market Cafe 109
131 Ave A between St. Marks Pl and 9th St (212-358-9280). Subway: L to First Ave.

Fleur de Sel 125
5 E 20th St between Fifth Ave and Broadway (212-460-9100). Subway: N, R, W to 23rd St.

Flor's Kitchen 198
170 Waverly Pl between Sixth and Seventh Aves (212-229-9926). Subway: 1 to Christopher St.

Florence's Restaurant 20
2099 Frederick Douglass Blvd (Seventh Ave) between 113th and 114th Sts (212-531-0387). B, C to 116th–Frederick Douglass Blvd.

Florent 109
69 Gansevoort St between Greenwich and Washington Sts (212-989-5779). Subway: A, C, E to 14th St; L to Eighth Ave.

Foodswings 248
295 Grand St between Havemeyer and Roebling Sts, Williamsburg, Brooklyn (718-388-1919). Subway: L to Bedford Ave.

Forbidden City 65
212 Ave A between 13th and 14th Sts (212-598-0500). Subway: L to First Ave; N, Q, R, W, 4, 5, 6 to 14th St–Union Sq.

Fountain Cafe 212
183 Atlantic Ave between Clinton and Court Sts, Brooklyn Hts, Brooklyn (718-624-6764). Subway: F, G to Bergen St; M, R to Court St.

The Four Seasons Restaurant 49
99 E 52nd St between Park and Lexington Aves (212-754-9494). Subway: E, V to Lexington Ave–53rd St; 6 to 51st St.

1492 Food 228
60 Clinton St between Rivington and Stanton Sts (646-654-1114). Subway: F to Delancey St; J, M, Z to Delancey–Essex Sts.

Fragole 147
394 Court St between Carroll St and 1st Pl, Carroll Gardens, Brooklyn (718-522-7133). Subway: F, G to Carroll St.

Francisco's Centro Vasco 222
159 W 23rd St between Sixth and Seventh Aves (212-645-6224). Subway: F, V, 1 to 23rd St.

Frank 147
88 Second Ave between 5th and 6th Sts (212-420-0202). Subway: F, V to Lower East Side–Second Ave.

Frank's Restaurant 235
410 W 16th St between Ninth and Tenth Aves (212-243-1349). Subway: A, C, E to 14th St; L to Eighth Ave.

Frankies Spuntino 17 Clinton Street 147
17 Clinton St between Houston and Stanton Sts (212-253-2303). Subway: F, V to Lower East Side–Second Ave.

Franny's 150
295 Flatbush Ave between Prospect Pl and St. Marks Ave, Prospect Heights, Brooklyn (718-230-0221). Subway: B, Q to Seventh Ave; 2, 3 to Bergen St.

Alphabetical Index

Fred's at Barneys　162
660 Madison Ave at 61st St,
ninth floor (212-833-2200).
Subway: N, R, W to Fifth
Ave–59th St.

Freemans　34
2 Freeman Alley off Rivington St
between Bowery and Chrystie Sts
(212-420-0012). Subway: F, V to
Lower East Side–Second Ave.

Fresh　222
105 Reade St at West Broadway
(212-406-1900). Subway: A, C, E, 1,
2, 3 to Chambers St.

Friend of a Farmer　34
77 Irving Pl between 18th and
19th Sts (212-477-2188). Subway:
L, N, Q, R, W, 4, 5, 6 to 14th
St–Union Sq.

Frost Restaurant　147
193 Frost St at Humboldt St,
Williamsburg, Brooklyn (718-389-
3347). Subway: L to Graham Ave.

Fuleen Seafood　95
11 Division St between Confucius
Pl and East Broadway (212-
941-6888). Subway: F to East
Broadway.

Fusia　66
972 Second Ave between 51st and
52nd Sts (212-421-2294). Subway:
E, V to Lexington Ave–53rd St;
6 to 51 St.

G

Gala Manor　95
37-02 Main St at 37th Ave,
Flushing, Queens (718-888-9293).
7 to Flushing–Main St.

The Gallery　39
SoHo Grand Hotel, 310 West
Broadway between Canal and
Grand Sts (212-965-3000). Subway:
A, C, E, 1, 9 to Canal St.

Gascogne　126
158 Eighth Ave between 17th and
18th Sts (212-675-6564). Subway:
1 to 18th St.

Gavroche　117
212 W 14th St between Seventh
and Eighth Aves (212-647-8553).
Subway: A, C, E, 1, 2, 3 to 14th St;
L to Eighth Ave.

Geisha　66
33 E 61st St between Madison
and Park Aves (212-813-1112).
Subway: N, R, W to Fifth
Ave–59th St; 4, 5, 6 to 59th St.

Gemma　162
The Bowery Hotel, 335 Bowery
at 3rd St (212-505-9100). Subway:
B, D, F, V to Broadway–Lafayette
St; 6 to Bleecker St.

Gennaro　162
665 Amsterdam Ave between
92nd and 93rd Sts (212-665-5348).
Subway: 1, 2, 3 to 96th St.

Georgia's Eastside BBQ　73
192 Orchard St between Houston
and Stanton Sts (212-253-6280).
Subway: F, V to Lower East
Side–Second Ave.

Gilt　103
455 Madison Ave between 50th
and 51st Sts (212-891-8100).
Subway: E, V to Fifth Ave–53rd St.

Gin Lane 42
355 W 14th St at Ninth Ave (212-
691-0555). Subway: A, C, E to 14th
St; L to Eighth Ave.

Gina's Cafe　217
409 Brighton Beach Ave between
4th and 5th Sts, Brighton Beach,
Brooklyn (718-646-6297). Subway:
B, Q to Brighton Beach.

Ginger　95
1400 Fifth Ave at 116th St
(212-423-1111). Subway: 2, 3,to
116th St—Lenox Ave; 6 to 116th
St—Lexington Ave.

Giorgione 508　147
508 Greenwich St at Spring St
(212-219-2444). Subway: C, E to
Spring St.

Giorgio's of Gramercy　34
27 E 21st St between Broadway
and Park Ave South (212-477-
0007). Subway: N, R, W to 23rd St.

Gnocco Cucina　149
& Tradizione
337 E 10th St between Aves A and
B (212-677-1913). Subway: L to
First Ave; 6 to Astor Pl.

Goblin Market　51
199 Prince St at Sullivan St (212-
375-8275). Subway: C, E to Spring
St; N, R to Prince St.

Gobo　248
401 Sixth Ave between Waverly
Pl and W 8th St (212-255-3242).
Subway: A, C, E, B, D, F, V to
W 4th St.

Gold St　83
2 Gold St between Maiden Ln and
Platt St (212-747-0797). Subway:
A, C to Broadway–Nassau; 4, 5 to
Fulton St.

Golden Unicorn　95
18 East Broadway between
Catherine and Market Sts (212-
941-0911). Subway: F to East
Broadway.

Gonzo　162
140 W 13th St between Sixth and
Seventh Aves (212-645-4606).
Subway: F, V, 1, 2, 3 to 14th St; L
to Sixth Ave.

Good　34
89 Greenwich Ave between Bank
and W 12th Sts (212-691-8080).
Subway: A, C, E, 1, 2, 3 to 14th St.

The Good Fork　103
391 Van Brunt St between Coffey
and Dikeman Sts, Red Hook,
Brooklyn (718-643-6636). Subway:
F, G to Smith–9th Sts.

Gordon Ramsay at　103
The London
The London NYC Hotel, 151 W
54th St between Sixth and Seventh
Aves (212-468-8888, 212-468-8889).
Subway: F to 57th St.

Gotham Bar and Grill　51
12 E 12th St between Fifth Ave
and University Pl (212-620-4020).
Subway: L, N, Q, R, W, 4, 5, 6 to
14th St–Union Sq.

Gramercy Tavern　51
42 E 20th St between Broadway
and Park Ave South (212-477-
0777). Subway: N, R, W, 6 to
23rd St.

Grand Central　222
Oyster Bar & Restaurant
Grand Central Terminal, Lower
Concourse, 42nd St at Park Ave
(212-490-6650). Subway: 42nd St S,
4, 5, 6, 7 to 42nd St–Grand Central.

Grand Sichuan　95
125 Canal St between Bowery
and Chrystie St (212-625-9212).
Subway: B, D to Grand St.

Grand 275　109
275 Grand Ave between Clifton Pl
and Lafayette Ave, Clinton Hill,
Brooklyn (718-398-4402). Subway:
C, G to Clinton–Washington Aves.

Grano Trattoria　162
21 Greenwich Ave at 10th St (212-
645-2121). Subway: A, C, E, B, D,
F, V to W 4th St; 1 to Christopher
St–Sheridan Sq.

Great Jones Café　58
54 Great Jones St between
Lafayette St and Bowery (212-
674-9304). Subway: B, D, F, V to
Broadway–Lafayette St.

Green Field Churrascaria　77
108-01 Northern Blvd at 108th St,
Corona, Queens (718-672-5202).
Subway: 7 to 111th St.

The Green Table　249
75 Ninth Ave at 15th St (212-741-
6623). Subway: A, C, E to 14th St;
L to Eighth Ave.

Gribouille　109
2 Hope St at Roebling St,
Williamsburg, Brooklyn
(718-384-3100). Subway: L, G to
Metropolitan Ave–Lorimer St.

Grimaldi's Pizzeria　150
19 Old Fulton St between Front
and Water Sts, Dumbo, Brooklyn
(718-858-4300). Subway: A, C to
High St; F to York St.

The Grocery　34
288 Smith St between Sackett
and Union Sts, Carroll Gardens,
Brooklyn (718-596-3335). Subway:
F, G to Carroll St.

Grotta del Mare　149
307 E 77th St between First and
Second Aves (212-535-2866).
Subway: 6 to 77th St.

Grotto　162
100 Forsyth St between Broome
and Grand Sts (212-625-3444).
Subway: B, D to Grand St; J, M, Z
to Bowery.

Guadalupe　194
597 W 207th St at Broadway (212-
304-1083). Subway: A to 207th
St–Washington Heights.

Gus' Place　133
192 Bleecker St between
MacDougal St and Sixth Ave
(212-777-1660). Subway: A, C, E, B,
D, F, V to W 4th St.

Gusto Ristorante e　165
Bar Americano
60 Greenwich Ave at Perry St
(212-924-8000). Subway: 1, 2, 3
to 14th St.

H

Hacienda de Argentina　62
339 E 75th St between First and
Second Aves (212-472-5300).
Subway: 6 to 77th St.

Haku　179
2425 Broadway between 89th and
90th Sts (212-580-2566). Subway:
1 to 86th St.

Hakubai　179
The Kitano Hotel, 66 Park Ave at
38th St (212-885-7111). Subway:
42nd St S, 4, 5, 6, 7 to 42nd
St–Grand Central.

Hampton Chutney Co.　139
68 Prince St between Crosby
and Lafayette Sts (212-226-9996).
Subway: N, R, W to Prince St.

Hampton Chutney Co.　139
464 Amsterdam Ave between
82nd and 83rd Sts (212-362-5050).
Subway: 1 to 79th St; B, C to 81st
St–Museum of Natural History.

Hana Cafe　179
235 Smith St between Butler and
Douglass Sts, Carroll Gardens,
Brooklyn (718-643-1963). Subway:
F, G to Bergen St.

Han Bat　190
53 W 35th St between Fifth
and Sixth Aves (212-629-5588).
Subway: B, D, F, V, N, Q, R, W to
34th St–Herald Sq; R, W to 28th St.

The Harrison　34
355 Greenwich St at Harrison
St (212-274-9310). Subway: 1 to
Franklin St.

Harry's Steak & Cafe　235
1 Hanover Square at Pearl St
(212-785-9200). Subway: 4, 5 to
Bowling Green.

Hatsuhana　180
17 E 48th St between Fifth and
Madison Aves (212-355-3345).
Subway: E, V to Fifth Ave–53rd
St; 6 to 51st St.

Hatsuhana　180
237 Park Ave at 46th St (212-661-
3400). Subway: 42nd St S, 4, 5, 6, 7
to 42nd St–Grand Central.

Havana New York　89
27 W 38th St between Fifth
and Sixth Aves (212-944-0990).
Subway: B, D, F, V, N, Q, R, W to
34th St–Herald Sq.

Heartbeat　249
W New York, 149 E 49th St
between Lexington and Third
Aves (212-407-2900). Subway: E,
V to Lexington Ave–53rd St; 6
to 51st St.

Hearth　42
403 E 12th St at First Ave
(646-602-1300). Subway: L to
First Ave.

Hedeh　180
57 Great Jones Street at Bowery St
(212-473-8458). Subway: B, D, F,
V to Broadway–Lafayette St; 6
to Bleecker St.

Heidelberg　131
1648 Second Ave between 85th
and 86th Sts (212-628-2332).
Subway: 4, 5, 6 to 86th St.

Henry's End Restaurant　35
44 Henry St between Cranberry
and Middagh Sts, Brooklyn Hts,
Brooklyn (718-834-1776). Subway:
A, C to High St; 2, 3 to Clark St.

Henry Street　23
Ale House
62 Henry St between Cranberry
and Orange Sts, Brooklyn Hts,
Brooklyn (718-522-4801). Subway:
A, C to High St; 2, 3 to Clark St.

Hibino　180
333 Henry St at Pacific St, Cobble
Hill, Brooklyn (718-260-8052).
Subway: M, R to Court St; 2, 3, 4,
5 to Borough Hall.

Hill Country　74
30 W 26th St between Broadway
and Sixth Ave (212-255-4544).
Subway: N, R, W to 28th St.

Hinsch's Confectionery　83
8518 Fifth Ave between 85th and
86th Sts, Bay Ridge, Brooklyn
(718-748-2854). Subway: R to
86th St.

Hispaniola　87
839 W 181st St at Cabrini Blvd
(212-740-5222). Subway: A to
181st St.

Holy Basil　243
149 Second Ave between 9th and
10th Sts, second floor (212-460-
5557). Subway: 6 to Astor Pl.

Home　35
20 Cornelia St between Bleecker
and W 4th Sts (212-243-9579).
Subway: A, C, E, B, D, to W 4th St.

Honduras Maya　194
587 Fifth Ave between Prospect
Ave and 16th St, Park Slope,
Brooklyn (718-965-8028). Subway:
M, R to Prospect Ave.

Hope & Anchor　24
347 Van Brunt St at Wolcott St,
Red Hook, Brooklyn (718-237-
0276). Subway: F to Smith–9th Sts.

HQ 34
90 Thompson St between Prince and Spring Sts (212-966-2755). Subway: C, E to Spring St.

★ **Hummus Place** 212
109 St Marks between First Ave and Avenue A (212-529-9198). Subway: 6 to Astor Pl; L to First Ave.

Hummus Place 212
99 MacDougal St between Bleecker St and Minetta Ln (212-533-3089). Subway: A, C, E, B, D, F, V to W 4th St.

Hummus Place 212
305 Amsterdam Ave at W 74th St (212-799-3335). Subway: 1, 2, 3 to 72nd St.

I

I Coppi 165
432 E 9th St between First Ave and Ave A (212-254-2263). Subway: 6 to Astor Pl.

i-Shebeen Madiba 20
195 DeKalb Ave between Adelphi St and Carlton Ave, Fort Greene, Brooklyn (718-855-9190). Subway: C to Lafayette Ave; G to Clinton–Washington Aves.

I Tre Merli 149
463 West Broadway between Houston and Prince Sts (212-254-8699). Subway: N, R, W to Prince St.

I Tre Merli Bistro 149
183 W 10th St at W 4th St (212-929-2221). Subway: 1 to Christopher St.

i Trulli 173
122 E 27th St between Park Ave South and Lexington Ave (212-481-7372). Subway: 6 to 28th St.

Ici 117
246 DeKalb Ave at Vanderbilt Ave (718-789-2778). Subway: C to Lafayette Ave, G to Clinton–Washington Aves.

Icon 42
W Court Hotel, 130 E 39th St between Park and Lexington Aves (212-592-8888). Subway: 42nd St S, 4, 5, 6, 7 to 42nd St–Grand Central.

Ideya 194
349 West Broadway between Broome and Grand Sts (212-625-1441). Subway: A, C, E to Canal St.

Il Buco 173
47 Bond St between Lafayette St and Bowery (212-533-1932). Subway: B, D, F, V to Broadway–Lafayette St; 6 to Bleecker St.

Il Cantinori 173
32 E 10th St between University Pl and Broadway (212-673-6044). Subway: N, R, W to 8th St–NYU.

Il Corso 165
19 W 55th St between Fifth and Sixth Aves (212-957-1500). Subway: E, V to Fifth Ave–53rd St.

Il Giglio 173
81 Warren St between Greenwich St and West Broadway (212-571-5555). Subway: 1, 2, 3 to Chambers St.

Il Mulino 173
86 W 3rd St between Sullivan and Thompson Sts (212-673-3783). Subway: A, C, E, B, D, F, V to W 4th St.

Il Postino 174
337 E 49th St between First and Second Aves (212-688-0033). Subway: E, V to Lexington Ave–53rd St; 6 to 51st St.

Inagiku 180
The Waldorf-Astoria, 111 E 49th St between Park and Lexington Aves (212-355-0440). Subway: E, V to Lexington Ave–53rd St; 6 to 51st St.

Indigo Indian Bistro 140
357 E 50th St between First and Second Aves (212-421-1919). Subway: E, V to Lexington Ave–53rd St; 6 to 51st St.

Indochine 251
430 Lafayette St between Astor Pl and E 4th St (212-505-5111). Subway: B, D, F, Q to Broadway-Lafayette St; R, W to 8th St.

Industria Argentina 62
329 Greenwich St between Duane and Jay Sts (212-965-8560). Subway: 1 to Franklin St.

'ino 149
21 Bedford St between Sixth Ave and Downing St (212-989-5769). Subway: 1 to Houston St.

'inoteca 149
98 Rivington St at Ludlow St (212-614-0473). Subway: F to Delancey St; J, M, Z to Delancey–Essex Sts.

Insieme 174
Michelangelo Hotel, 777 Seventh Ave at 51st St (212-582-1310). Subway: B, D, F, V to 47–50th Sts–Rockefeller Ctr; N, R, W to 49th St.

Inti Raymi 215
86-14 37th Ave between 86th and 87th Sts, Jackson Hts, Queens (718-424-1938). Subway: 7 to 90th St–Elmhurst Ave.

Isabella's 201
359 Columbus Ave at 77th St (212-724-2100). Subway: B, C to 81st St–Museum of Natural History; 1 to 79th St.

Ise 181
58 W 56th St between Fifth and Sixth Aves (212-707-8702). Subway: F to 57th St.

Ise 181
56 Pine St between Pearl and William Sts (212-785-1600). Subway: 2, 3 to Wall St.

Ise 181
151 E 49th St between Lexington and Third Aves (212-319-6876). Subway: E, V to Lexington Ave–53rd St; 6 to 51st St.

Istria Sport Club 100
28-09 Astoria Blvd between 28th and 29th Sts, Astoria, Queens (718-728-3181). Subway: N, W to Astoria Blvd.

It's a Dominican Thing 90
144 W 19th St between Sixth and Seventh Aves (212-924-3344). Subway 1 to 18th St.

Itzocan Bistro 205
1575 Lexington Ave at 101st St (212-423-0255). Subway: 6 to 103rd St.

Itzocan Café 205
438 E 9th St between First Ave and Ave A (212-677-5856). Subway: L to First Ave; N, R, W to 8th St.

Ivy's Bistro 165
385 Greenwich St at North Moore St (212-343-1139). Subway: 1 to Franklin St.

Izakaya Ten 181
207 Tenth Ave between 22nd and 23rd Sts (212-627-7777). Subway: C, E to 23rd St.

Izalco 198
64-05 Roosevelt Ave between 64th and 65th Sts, Woodside, Queens (718-533-8373). Subway: 7 to 69th St.

J

J.G. Melon 38
1291 Third Ave at 74th St (212-650-1310, 212-744-0585). Subway: 6 to 77th St.

Jack's Luxury 222
Oyster Bar
101 Second Ave at 6th St (212-253-7848). Subway: F, V to Lower East Side–Second Ave, 6 to Astor Pl.

Jackson Diner 140
37-47 74th St between Roosevelt and 37th Aves, Jackson Hts, Queens (718-672-1232). Subway: E, F, V, G, R to Jackson Hts–Roosevelt Ave; 7 to 74th St–Broadway.

Jacques 117
20 Prince St between Elizabeth and Mott Sts (212-966-8886). Subway: N, R, W to Prince St; 6 to Spring St.

Jacques-Imo's 59
366 Columbus Ave at 77th St (212-799-0150). Subway: 1 to 79th St.

Jacques Torres 83
66 Water St at Main St, Dumbo, Brooklyn (718-875-9772). Subway: F to York St.

Jane 35
100 W Houston St between La Guardia Pl and Thompson St (212-254-7000). Subway: C, E to Spring St; 1 to Houston St.

Japonais 181
111 E 18th St between Park Avenue South and Irving Pl (212-260-2020). Subway: L, N, Q, R, W, 4, 5, 6 to 14th St–Union Sq.

Jarnac 117
328 W 12th St at Greenwich St (212-924-3413). Subway: A, C, E to 14th St; L to Eighth Ave.

Java 70
455 Seventh Ave at 16th St, Park Slope, Brooklyn (718-832-4583). Subway: F to 15th St–Prospect Park.

Jean Claude 111
137 Sullivan St between Houston and Prince Sts (212-475-9232). Subway: C, E to Spring St.

Jean Georges 126
Trump International Hotel & Tower, 1 Central Park West at Columbus Circle (212-299-3900). Subway: A, C, B, D, 1 to 59th St–Columbus Circle.

Je'Bon Noodle House 66
15 St. Mark's Pl between Second and Third Aves (212-388-1313). Subway: R, W to 8th St–NYU.

Jeeb 243
154 Orchard St between Stanton and Rivington Sts (212-677-4101). Subway: F, V to Lower East Side–Second Ave.

Jewel Bako 181
239 E 5th St between Second and Third Aves (212-979-1012). Subway: F, V to Lower East Side–Second Ave.

Jimmy's No. 43 51
43 E 7 St between Second and Third Aves (212-982-3006). Subway: F, V to Lower East Side–Second Ave; 6 to Astor Pl.

Jing Fong 96
20 Elizabeth St between Bayard and Canal St (212-964-5256). Subway: J, M, Z, N, Q, R, W, 6 to Canal St.

Joe and Pat's 150
1758 Victory Blvd at Manor Rd, Staten Island (718-981-0887). Travel: from the Staten Island Ferry, take the S61, S62, or S64 bus to Victory Blvd/Manor Rd.

Joe's 151
7 Carmine St between Bleecker St and Sixth Ave., West Village (212-366-1182). Subway: A, C, E, B, D, F, V to West 4th Street.

Joe's of Avenue U 149
287 Ave U between Lake St and McDonald Ave, Gravesend, Brooklyn (718-449-9285). Subway: F to Ave U.

John's of 12th Street 149
302 E 12th St between First and Second Aves Subway: L to First Ave; N, Q, R, W, 4, 5, 6 to 14th St–Union Sq.

Johnny's 222
Reef Restaurant
2 City Island Ave at the south end of City Island, Bronx (718-885-2086). Travel: 6 to Pelham Bay Park, then Bx29 bus to City Island.

JoJo 126
160 E 64th St between Lexington and Third Aves (212-223-5656). Subway: F to Lexington Ave–63rd St.

Josephina 35
1900 Broadway between 63rd and 64th Sts (212-799-1000). Subway: 1 to 66th St. Lincoln Ctr.

Josie's 249
300 Amsterdam Ave at 74th St (212-769-1212). 1, 2, 3 to 72nd St.

Josie's 249
555 Third Ave at 37th St (212-490-1558). 6 to 33rd St.

Joya 243
215 Court St between Warren and Wyckoff Sts, Cobble Hill, Brooklyn (718-222-3484). Subway: F, G to Bergen St.

Jules 111
65 St Marks Pl between First and Second Aves (212-477-5560). Subway: L to First Ave; 6 to Astor Pl.

Juliette 117
135 North 5th St between Bedford Ave and Berry St, Williamsburg, Brooklyn (718-388-9222). Subway: L to Bedford Ave.

Junior's Restaurant 83
386 Flatbush Ave at DeKalb Ave, Downtown, Brooklyn (718-852-5257). Subway: M, N, Q, R to DeKalb Ave.

Junior's Restaurant/ 83
Bakery
Grand Central Terminal, Lower Concourse and near track 36, 42nd St at Park Ave (212-692-9800; 212-983-5257). Subway: S, 4, 5, 6, 7 to 42nd St–Grand Central.

K

Kabab Café 212
25-12 Steinway St at 25th Ave, Astoria, Queens (718-728-9858). Subway: N, W to Astoria Blvd.

Kabab King Diner 140
73-01 37th Rd at 73rd St, Jackson Hts, Queens (718-457-5857). Subway: E, F, V, G, R to Jackson Hts–Roosevelt Ave; 7 to 74th St–Broadway.

Alphabetical Index

Surf's her turf
Chef Laura Lam nails the nuanced prawn-and-grapefruit salad at Safran.

Alphabetical Index

Luscious Food 24
59 Fifth Ave between Bergen St and St. Marks Ave, Park Slope, Brooklyn (718-398-5800). Subway: B, Q, 4, 5 to Atlantic Ave.

Luz 194
177 Vanderbilt Ave between Myrtle and Willoughby Aves, Clinton Hill, Brooklyn (718-246-4000). Subway: C to Clinton–Washington Aves.

Luzia's 216
429 Amsterdam Ave between 80th and 81st Sts (212-595-2000). Subway: 1 to 79th St.

M

Ma-Ya 243
234 E 4th St between Aves A and B (646-313-1987). F, V to Lower East Side–Second Ave.

Macelleria 165
48 Gansevoort St between Greenwich and Washington Sts (212-741-2555). Subway: A, C, E to 14th St; L to Eighth Ave.

Mai House 252
186 Franklin St between Greenwich and Hudson Sts (212-431-0606). Subway: 1 to Franklin St.

Malagueta 77
25-35 36th Ave at 28th St, Astoria, Queens (718-937-4821). Subway: N, W to 36th Ave.

Maloney & Porcelli 235
37 E 50th St between Madison and Park Aves (212-750-2233). Subway: E, V to Lexington Ave–53rd St; 6 to 51st St.

Mama's Food Shop 59
200 E 3rd St between Aves A and B (212-777-4425). Subway: F, V to Lower East Side–Second Ave.

Mamajuana Cafe 194
247 Dyckman St at Seaman Ave (212-304-0140). Subway: 1 to Dyckman St.

Mamlouk 212
211 E 4th St between Aves A and B (212-529-3477). Subway: F, V to Lower East Side–Second Ave.

Mana 249
646 Amsterdam Ave between 91st and 92nd Sts (212-787-1110). Subway: 1, 2, 3 to 96th St.

Mandler's: The Original Sausage Co. 131
26 E 17th St between Fifth Ave and Broadway (212-255-8999). Subway: L, N, Q, R, W, 4, 5, 6 to 14th St–Union Sq.

Mandler's 131
601 Eighth Ave between 39th and 40th Sts (212-244-4222). Subway: A, C, E to 42nd St–Port Authority.

Mangiami 153
9 Stanton St between Bowery and Chrystie St (212-477-7047). Subway: F, V to Second Ave–Lower East Side.

Maoz Vegetarian 249
38 Union Sq East between 16th and 17th Sts (212-260-1988). Subway: L, N, Q, R, W, 4, 5, 6 to 14th St–Union Sq.

Mara's Homemade 59
342 E 6th St between First and Second Aves (212-598-1110). Subway: F, V to Lower East Side–Second Ave; L to First Ave; 6 to Astor Pl.

Maracas Mexican Bar & Grill 207
33 Greenwich Ave between Sixth and Seventh Aves (212-593-6600). Subway: A, C, E, B, D, F, V to W 4th St; 1 to Christopher St–Sheridan Sq.

Marco Polo 166
345 Court St at Union St, Carroll Gardens, Brooklyn (718-852-5015). Subway: F, G to Carroll St.

Maremma 166
228 W 10th St between Bleecker and Hudson Sts (212-645-0200). Subway: 1 to Christopher St–Sheridan Sq.

Margie's Red Rose 59
275 W 144th St between Adam Clayton Powell Jr. Blvd (Seventh Ave) and Frederick Douglass Blvd (Eighth Ave) (212-491-3665). Subway: A, C, B, D to 145th St.

Mario's 166
2342 Arthur Ave between 184th and 186th Sts, Bronx (718-584-1188). Travel: B, D, 4 to Fordham Rd, then Bx12 bus to Arthur Ave.

Marion's Continental Restaurant & Lounge 24
354 Bowery between Great Jones and E 4th Sts (212-475-7621). Subway: B, D, F, V to Broadway–Lafayette St; 6 to Bleecker St.

Markt 75
676 Sixth Ave at 21st St (212-727-3314). Subway: C, E to 23st St.

Maroons 90
244 W 16th St between Seventh and Eighth Aves (212-206-8640). Subway: A, C, E, 1, 2, 3 to 14th St; L to Eighth Ave.

Marquet Pâtisserie 85
15 E 12th St between Fifth Ave and University Pl (212-229-9313). Subway: L, N, Q, R, W, 4, 5, 6 to 14th St–Union Sq.

Marseille 120
630 Ninth Ave at 44th St (212-333-3410). Subway: A, C, E to 42nd St–Port Authority.

Mary's Fish Camp 222
64 Charles St at W 4th St (646-486-2185). Subway: 1 to Christopher St–Sheridan Sq.

Mas 129
39 Downing St between Bedford and Varick Sts (212-255-1790). Subway: A, C, E, B, D, F, V to W 4th St; 1 to Houston St.

Masala Bollywood 141
108 Lexington Ave between 27th and 28th Sts (212-679-1284). Subway: 6 to 28th St.

Massawa 19
1239 Amsterdam Ave at 121st St (212-663-0505). 1 to 116th St.

Matador 228
57 Greenwich Ave at Perry St (212-691-0057). Subway: A, C, E, B, D, F, V to W 4th St.

Matamoros Puebla Grocery 207
193 Bedford Ave between North 6th and North 7th Sts, Williamsburg, Brooklyn (718-782-5044). Subway: L to Bedford Ave.

Max 153
51 Ave B between 3rd and 4th Sts (212-539-0111). Subway: F, V to Lower East Side–Second Ave.

Max SoHa 153
1274 Amsterdam Ave at 123rd St (212-531-2221). Subway: A, C, B, D, 1, 9 to 125th St.

Maya 207
1191 First Ave between 64th and 65th Sts (212-585-1818). Subway: F to Lexington Ave–63rd St.

Mayrose 24
920 Broadway at 21st St (212-533-3663). Subway:R, W to 23rd St—Broadway.

Maze 104
The London NYC Hotel, 151 W 54th St between Sixth and Seventh Aves (212-468-8888, 212-468-8889). Subway: F to 57th St.

McCormick & Schmick's 224
1285 Sixth Ave at 51st St (212-459-1222). Subway: B, D, F, V to 47th–50th Sts.

Megu 182
62 Thomas St between Church St and West Broadway (212-964-7777). Subway: A, C, 1, 2, 3 to Chambers St.

Melba's 59
300 W 114th St at Frederick Douglass Blvd (Eighth Ave) (212-864-7777). Subway: B, C to 116th St.

Mercadito 207
179 Ave B between 11th and 12th Sts (212-529-6493). Subway: L to First Ave.

Mercadito Grove 207
100 Seventh Ave South at Grove St (212-647-0830). Subway: 1 to Christopher St–Sheridan Sq.

Mercat 229
45 Bond St between Bowery and Lafayette St (212-529-8600). Subway: B, D, F, V to Broadway–Lafayette St; 6 to Bleecker St.

The Mercer Kitchen 52
The Mercer, 99 Prince St at Mercer St (212-966-5454). Subway: R, W to Prince St.

The Mermaid Inn 224
96 Second Ave between 5th and 6th Sts (212-674-5870). Subway: F, V to Lower East Side–Second Ave.

Mesa Grill 59
102 Fifth Ave between 15th and 16th Sts (212-807-7400). Subway: L, N, Q, R, W, 4, 5, 6 to 14th St–Union Sq.

Meskel 19
199 E 3rd St between Ave A & B (212-254-2411).

Métisse 120
239 W 105th St between Amsterdam Ave and Broadway (212-666-8825). Subway: 1 to 103rd St.

Mexicana Mama 207
525 Hudson St between Charles and W 10th Sts (212-924-4119). Subway: 1 to Christopher St–Sheridan Sq.

Mexicana Mama 207
47 E 12th St between Broadway and University Pl (212-253-7594). Subway: L, N, Q, R, W, 4, 5, 6 to 14th St–Union Sq.

Mezzo-Mezzo 135
31-29 Ditmars Blvd at 33rd St, Astoria, Queens (718-278-0444). Subway: N, W to Astoria–Ditmars Blvd.

Mi Bolivia 196
44-10 48th Ave between 44th and 45th Sts, Woodside, Queens (718-784-5111). Subway: 7 to 46th St.

Mi Cocina 207
57 Jane St at Hudson St (212-627-8273). Subway: A, C, E to 14th St; L to Eighth Ave.

Mingala Burmese 68
1393B Second Ave between 72nd and 73rd Sts (212-744-8008). Subway: 6 to 68th St–Hunter College.

Mint 141
150 E 50th St between Lexington and Third Aves (212-644-8888). Subway: E, V to Lexington Ave–53rd St; 6 to 51st St.

Miriam 212
79 5th Ave at Prospect Place, Park Slope, Brooklyn (718-622-2250). Subway: 2,3 to Bergen St.

Miriam 212
229 Court St between Baltic and Warren Sts, Cobble Hill, Brooklyn (718-522-2220). Subway: F, G to Bergen St.

Miss Maude's Spoonbread Too 60
547 Malcolm X Blvd (Lenox Ave) between 137th and 138th Sts (212-690-3100). Subway: 2, 3 to 135th St.

Miss Mamie's Spoonbread Too 60
366 W 110th St between Manhattan and Columbus Aves (212-865-6744). Subway: B, C, 1, 9 to 110th St–Cathedral Pkwy.

Miyagi 182
220 W 13th St between Seventh and Greenwich Aves (212-620-3830). Subway: A, C, E, 1, 2, 3 to 14th St.

Mo-Bay 92
17 W 125th St between Fifth Ave and Malcolm X Blvd (Lenox Ave) (212-876-9300). Subway: 2, 3 to 125th St.

Mo Pitkin's House of Satisfaction 104
34 Ave A between Second and Third Sts (212-777-5660). Subway: F, V to Lower East Side–Second Ave.

The Modern 52
9 W 53rd St between Fifth and Sixth Aves (212-333-1220). Subway: E, V to Fifth Ave–53rd St.

Moksha 141
18 Murray St between Broadway and Church St (212-608-0707). Subway: A, C, 1, 2, 3 to Chambers St.

Molyvos 135
871 Seventh Ave between 55th and 56th Sts (212-582-7500). Subway: N, Q, R, W to 57th St.

Mombar 212
25-22 Steinway St between 25th and 28th Aves, Astoria, Queens (718-726-2356). Subway: N, W to 30th Ave.

Momofuku Noodle Bar 182
163 First Ave between 10th and 11th Sts (212-475-7899). Subway: L to First Ave; N, Q, R, W, 4, 5, 6 to 14th St–Union Sq.

Momofuku Ssäm Bar 191
207 Second Ave at 13th St (212-254-3500). Subway: L to First, Third Aves; N, Q, R, W, 4, 5, 6 to 14th St–Union Sq.

Momoya 182
85 Seventh Ave at 21st St (212-989-4466). Subway: 1 to 23rd St.

Monkey Town 105
58 North 3rd St between Kent and Wythe Aves, Williamsburg, Brooklyn (718-384-1369). Subway: L to Bedford Ave.

Montparnasse 120
230 E 51st St between Second and Third Aves (212-758-6633). Subway: E, V to Lexington Ave–53rd St; 6 to 51st St.

No tricks, just treats
William Greenberg Jr.
Desserts has been selling
tasty kosher sweets for
more than 50 years.

Alphabetical Index

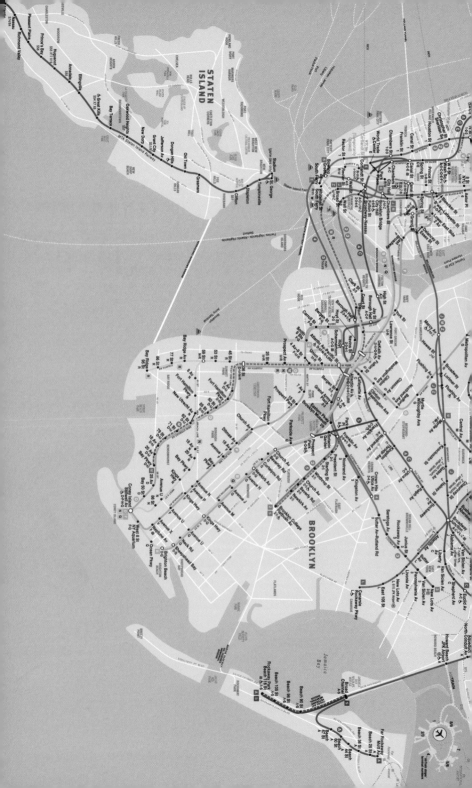

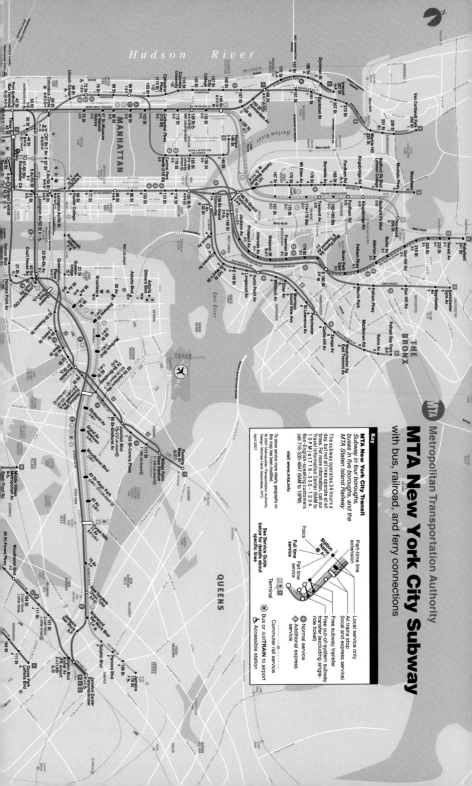

MTA New York City Subway

Metropolitan Transportation Authority

with bus, railroad, and ferry connections

Hudson River

MANHATTAN

THE BRONX

QUEENS

Key

MTA New York City Transit
Subway in four boroughs, and
buses in five boroughs, and the
MTA Staten Island Railway

The subway operates 24 hours a
day, but not all lines operate at all
times. For more information, call our
Travel Information Center (6AM to
10 PM) at 718-330-1234, or
Non-English-speaking customers
call 718-330-4847 (6AM to 10PM).

visit www.mta.info

To show service more clearly, geography on
this map has been modified.
Design: Michael Hertz Associates, NYC

April 2007

- Part-time line
  extension
- Local service only
- All trains stop
  (local and express service)
- Part-time stop
- Full time service
- Part-time service
- Terminal
- Station
- Police
- Free out-of-system subway
  transfer (excluding single-
  ride ticket)
- Free subway transfer
- Normal service
- Additional express
  service
- Commuter rail service
- Bus or AirTRAIN to airport
- Accessible station

See Service Guide
below for details about
specific lines

Manhattan

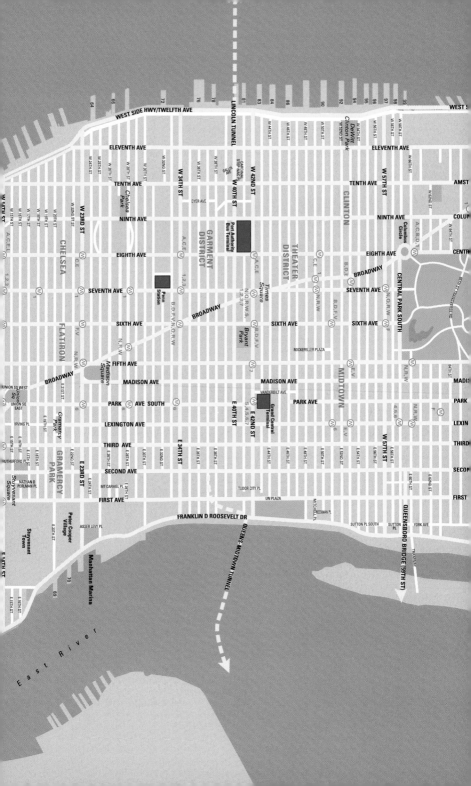

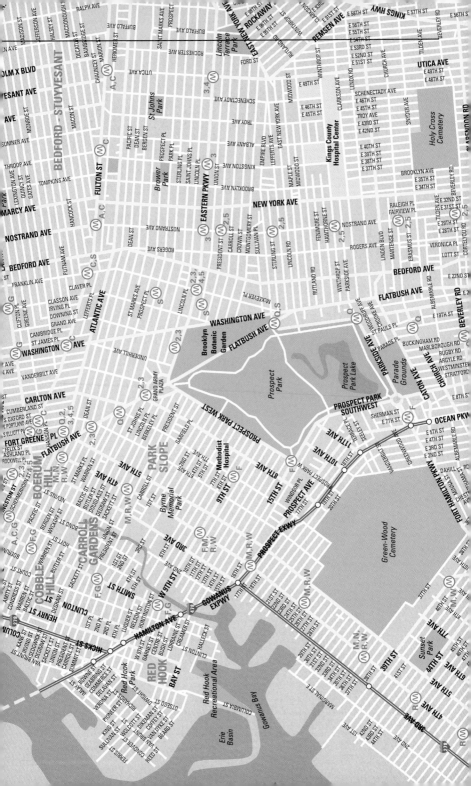